# CUSTOMS MODERNIZATION HANDBOOK

# CUSTOMS MODERNIZATION HANDBOOK

Editors

Luc De Wulf and José B. Sokol

**THE WORLD BANK**
Washington, D.C.

**Photo credits** (clockwise): Australian Customs (upper right), Douane Francaise / M. Bonodot © (lower right), Chilean Customs Administration (lower left), Société Générale de Surveillance (upper left and background photo of people), Luc De Wulf (background photo of customs files).

*Library of Congress Cataloging-in-Publication Data*

Customs modernization handbook / edited by Luc de Wulf, José B. Sokol.
    p. cm.—(Trade and development series)
  Includes bibliographic references and index.
  ISBN-0-8213-5751-4 (pbk.)
    1. Customs administration—Developing countries.   I. Wulf, Luc de, 1942-
II. Sokol, José B.   III. Series.

HJ7390.C86 2004
352.4'48'091724—dc22                                        2004059856

# CONTENTS

v

### LIST OF BOXES, FIGURES, AND TABLES

#### BOXES

**FIGURES**

**TABLES**

# FOREWORD

The experiences of recent decades have shown that the countries that have most successfully integrated into the world economy also have tended to record the highest growth rates. This result should not come as a surprise. Integration brings with it improved allocation of resources, intensified competition, and pressures to raise productivity, as well as exposure to new technologies, designs, and products. With world trade growth expanding more than twice as rapidly as world gross domestic product (GDP) over the past decade, the potential rewards from participating in world trade are considerable. Increased trade openness, through lower levels of protection in developed and developing countries, has contributed to this outcome. Nevertheless, it is widely acknowledged that an open trade regime will only foster trade integration when a range of complementary policies is in place.

One of the most important complementary policies is to put in place a well functioning customs administration that provides traders with transparent, predictable, and speedy clearance of goods. Indeed, a poorly functioning customs administration can effectively negate the improvements that have been made in other trade-related areas.

For many countries, achieving efficiency and transparency in customs operations remains a formidable challenge. In 2002, over US$6.3 trillion of goods crossed international borders. Each one of those shipments passed through customs controls at least twice—at entry and at exit. Customs services have often had to cope with these growing trade volumes without any commensurate increase in staff or resources. In addition, customs administrations continue to face changes to their operating environment, which emphasize the need to adjust and modernize their processes. These include:

- more sophisticated and demanding clients, for example, traders who have invested significantly in modern logistics, inventory control, manufacturing, and information systems

- greater policy and procedural requirements associated with international commitments
- proliferation of regional and bilateral trade agreements, which significantly increase the complexity of administering border formalities and controls
- heightened security concerns and demands to respond to the threats posed by international terrorism and transnational organized crime
- widespread revenue fraud.

Many customs administrations are struggling to meet the continually increasing demands and priorities placed on them.

During the last decade many countries devoted substantial resources to reforming and modernizing their customs administrations, often with financial and technical support from international financial institutions and bilateral donors. The World Bank, the World Customs Organization, the International Monetary Fund, the United Nations Conference on Trade and Development (the ASYCUDA program especially), and the Regional Development Banks have, for a long time, been providing such support. As a result, a number of customs administrations have improved their capacities. Yet, far too many still operate inefficiently and, to some extent, fail to fulfill their assigned objectives. Modernization of customs is therefore likely to remain on the development agenda of many governments, and the donor community will be called upon to continue its support for customs modernization.

In recognition of this, the Trade Department of the World Bank prepared this *Customs Modernization Handbook* to provide guidance to the many organizations and individuals involved in the preparation and implementation of customs modernization projects. The Handbook draws on the lessons learned from past successes and failures, both by the Bank itself and a range of other organizations. It also draws on the collective experience of a wide range of individuals with extensive practical experience in the field. The Handbook is complemented by a 2004 World Bank publication of eight case studies of customs modernization in developing countries—*Customs Modernization Initiatives.* These works, in conjunction with the recent IMF publication *Changing Customs,* which focuses on the revenue mobilization function of customs administrations, provide the necessary tools for initiating and undertaking the process of customs reform.

The guidelines contained in the Handbook are aimed at several audiences. First, they are aimed at policymakers and national managers who are called upon to take the lead in providing advice and guidance on the direction of reform efforts and securing the necessary political support for such initiatives. Second, they are aimed at project managers, national as well as from the donor community, who are required to design and implement customs modernization projects. Third, they are aimed at students of trade facilitation, who will find in the Handbook the context and operational modalities

of an organization that plays a crucial role in the overall trade logistics chain.

This Handbook is not intended to be encyclopedic. It is deliberately selective. It avoids many technical issues that are well covered in the many manuals and guidelines provided by organizations such as the World Customs Organization. Rather, it focuses on the critical issues that need to be addressed when designing and implementing effective and sustainable modernization projects and related initiatives.

We at the World Bank hope that the *Customs Modernization Handbook* will help in the achievement of the objective of helping policymakers to implement the needed reform and overall modernization that will enable customs to fulfill its role in the 21st century.

Danny M. Leipziger
Vice President and Head of the Poverty
Reduction and Economic Management Network

# ACKNOWLEDGMENTS

This project would not have been possible without the patience, understanding, and generous support and contributions provided by many colleagues and customs experts from national customs organizations, international organizations, and in the private consultancy business.

Larry Hinkle, Lead Specialist in the Bank's Africa Region, encouraged the initiation of this project, and the Africa Region provided financial support at its initiation. Ataman Aksoy and Yvonne Tsikata were instrumental in getting this project launched.

Uri Dadush, Director of the Trade Department, gave this project priority status throughout its development and provided his wisdom and guidance at the most critical stages. John Panzer, our Manager in the Trade Department, provided the team with his unfailingly enthusiastic support and leadership and ensured the timely completion of the project.

The staff of the World Customs Organization, and especially its Deputy Secretary General, Mr. Kunio Mikuriya, who also acted as Peer Reviewer, generously shared their operational experience and their time with the editors and contributed to several chapters. The staff of the Inter-American Development Bank and of the International Monetary Fund also supported the project and provided advice and comments at various times during the preparation of the book. Our special appreciation goes to François Corfmat from the IMF who was a Peer Reviewer and who made significant contributions to several chapters. All generously shared their insights and expertise during the process of defining the scope of the project and provided guidance in its preparation.

The authors of the thirteen chapters contributed their expertise and showed great patience with the many demands placed on them by the editors. Our dear late colleague Jit Gill contributed with his advice and comments with characteristic professionalism and personal warmth. Special thanks are also due to the following colleagues and friends who contributed to making this book possible: Amparo Ballivián (WB), Ed Campos (WB), Patricio Castro (IMF), Lee Deegan (Australian Customs, previously at the WCO), Antoni Estevadeordal (IDB), Bruno Favaro (UNCTAD), Odd Fjeldstad (Michelsen Institute), Alan Hall (consultant), Moshe Hirsch (Hebrew University Law School), Bernard Hoekman (WB), John Holl (consultant), Irene Hors (OECD), Darryn Jenkins (consultant), Peter Kalil (IDB), Holm Kappler (previously at the WCO), Joe Kelly (HM Customs and Excise), David Kloeden (IMF), Michael Lane (consultant), Patricia Laverly (OED), Bob Mall (WCO), Nick Manning (WB), Fabrice Millet (UNCTAD), Tony Mort (consultant), Mark Pearson (COMESA), John Raven (ICC), Will Robinson (WCO), Gonzalo Salinas (WB), Edward Siaw (consultant), Graham Smith (WB), Frederick Z. Stapenhurst (WB), Kati Suominen (IDB), Victor Thurony (IMF), Mashiho Yuasa (University of Michigan Law School), and Gianni Zanini (WB).

Our colleagues in the Trade Department of the World Bank strengthened our team and made significant contributions. Special thanks to Michel Zarnowiecki who, in addition to being Peer Reviewer, shared his technical expertise during the whole process and significantly improved several sections of the handbook. We also extend this appreciation to Mr. Gerard McLinden (at the WCO until early 2004) who not only wrote several chapters but also contributed greatly to finalizing the manuscript. Finally, the project also benefited from the patient, professional, and extremely competent support provided by Melanie Faltas and Zeba Jetha. Special acknowledgment goes to Lili Tabada, who undertook an enormous set of responsibilities, including preparing the desktop version, working with the publisher, and helping the team with her superb editing skills. She excelled in all these tasks and this project could not have been done without her competent participation.

# ABBREVIATIONS AND ACRONYMS

| | |
|---|---|
| ACI | Advanced Cargo Information |
| ACI | Airports Council International |
| ACP | Africa, the Caribbean and the Pacific |
| ACP | Autoridad del Canal de Panamá |
| ACV | Agreement on Customs Valuation |
| ADCS | Automated Data Collection System |
| AfDB | African Development Bank |
| AFTA | Asian Free Trade Association |
| AGOA | African Growth and Opportunity Act |
| ANZCERTA | Australia New Zealand Closer Economic Relations Trade Agreement |
| ANZSCEP | Agreement between New Zealand and Singapore on a Closer Economic Partnership |
| APEC | Asia-Pacific Economic Cooperation |
| ARA | Autonomous Revenue Authority |
| ARO | Agreement on Rules of Origin |
| ASAC | Aviation Security Advisory Committee |
| ASEAN | Association of Southeast Asian Nations |
| ASEZA | Aqaba Special Economic Zone Authority |
| ASYCUDA | Automated System for Customs Data |
| ATA | Air Transport Association |
| BDV | Brussels Definition of Value |
| BGMEA | Bangladesh Garments Manufacturing and Export Association |
| BIR | Bureau of Internal Revenue |
| BIVAC | Bureau of Inspection Valuation Assessment and Control |
| BOC | Bureau of Customs |
| BOT | Build-Operate-Transfer |
| BOT | Bureau of Trade |
| BOO | Build, Operate, and Own |
| CA | Crown Agents |
| CACM | Central American Common Market |
| CAM | Customs Assistance Mission |

| | |
|---|---|
| CARICOM | Caribbean Community |
| CAS | Country Assistance Strategy |
| CBI | Cross-Border Initiative |
| CBP | US Bureau of Customs and Border Protection |
| CCC | Customs Cooperation Council |
| CCO | Central Customs Office |
| CCP | Central Control Point |
| CEFACT | United Nations Centre for Trade Facilitation and Electronic Business |
| CEPS | Customs Excise and Preventive Services |
| CIF | Cost, Insurance, and Freight |
| COMESA | Common Market for Eastern and Southern Africa |
| CRO | Committee on Rules of Origin |
| CSD | Container Security Device |
| CSI | Container Security Initiative |
| CSTF | Cargo Security Task Force |
| C-TPAT | Customs–Trade Partnership Against Terrorism |
| DF | Diagnostic Framework |
| DFID | Department for International Development |
| DSS | Duty Suspension Scheme |
| DTI | Direct Trader Input |
| EAC | East African Cooperation |
| EBA | Everything but Arms |
| EC | European Community |
| ECA | Europe and Central Asia |
| ECAC | European Civil Aviation Conference |
| ECO | Economic Cooperation Organization |
| ECOWAS | Economic Community of West African States |
| EDCS | Electronic Data Collection System |
| EDI | Electronic Data Interchange |
| EEC | European Economic Community |
| EFT | Electronic Funds Transfer |
| EFTA | European Fair Trade Association |
| EPZ | Export Processing Zone |
| EU | European Union |
| FAK | Freight of all Kinds |

| | | | |
|---|---|---|---|
| FDI | Foreign Direct Investment | ILO | International Labor Organization |
| FOB | Free on Board | IMF | International Monetary Fund |
| FTA | Free Trade Agreement | IMO | International Maritime Organization |
| FTZ | Free Trade Zone | | |
| GAO | General Accounting Office | IOC | Indian Ocean Commission |
| GATT | General Agreement on Tariffs and Trade | IRU | International Road Transport Union |
| GCMS | Ghana Customs Management System | ISPS | International Ship and Port Facility Security |
| GCNet | Ghana Community Network | IT | Information Technology |
| GDP | Gross Domestic Product | ITF | International Transport Workers Federation |
| GEP | *Global Economic Prospects* | | |
| GMS | Greater Mekong Subregion | LDC | Least Developed Country |
| GOIEC | General Organization for Import and Export Control | MDCS | Mobile Data Collection System |
| | | MFN | Most Favored Nation |
| GOM | Government of Mozambique | MODAAC | ASYCUDA++ Accounting Module |
| GSP | General System of Preferences | MODTRS | ASYCUDA++ National Transit Module |
| GST | General Sales Tax | | |
| GVC | GATT Valuation Code | MOF | Ministers of Finance |
| HQ | Headquarters | MOF | Ministry of Finance |
| HRO | Harmonized Nonpreferential Rules of Origin | MPF | Ministry of Planning and Finance |
| | | MTSA | Maritime Transport Security Act |
| HS | Harmonized Commodity Description and Coding System | MUB | Manufacturing Under Bond |
| | | NAFTA | North American Free Trade Agreement |
| HWP | Harmonization Work Program | | |
| IACA | International Air Carriers Association | NCTS | New Computerized Customs Transit System |
| IATA | International Air Transport Association | NGO | Nongovernmental Organization |
| | | NPR | Nepalese Rupees |
| ICAC | Independent Commission Against Corruption | NTB | Nontariff Barriers |
| | | NVOCC | Nonvessel Operating Common Carriers |
| ICAO | International Civil Aviation Organization | | |
| | | OECD | Organisation for Economic Co-operation and Development |
| ICC | International Chamber of Commerce | OED | Operations Evaluation Department |
| ICMP | International Customs Modernization Process | | |
| | | OP | Operational Policy |
| ICR | Implementation Completion Report | OSC | Operation Safe Commerce |
| | | PAD | Project Appraisal Document |
| ICS | Inspection and Control Services | PIN | Personal Identification Number |
| ICT | Information and Communications Technologies | PRA | Port Risk Assessment |
| | | PRSP | Poverty Reduction Strategy Paper |
| IDB | Inter-American Development Bank | PSI | Preshipment Inspection |
| IDI | Institutional Development Impact | PSR | Project Status Report |
| IFALPA | International Federation of Airline Pilots Associations | PTA | Preferential Trade Agreement |
| | | RCDP | Russian Customs Development Project |
| IFIA | International Federation of Inspection Agencies | | |
| | | RFID | Radio Frequency Identification |
| IGAD | Intergovernmental Authority on Development | RIFF | Regional Integration Facilitation Forum |

| | | | |
|---|---|---|---|
| RMG | Ready Made Garments | TCCV | Technical Committee on Customs Valuation |
| RSC | Regional Steering Committee | | |
| RSO | Recognized Security Organization | TCRO | Technical Committee on Rules of Origin |
| RTCD | Road Transit Customs Declaration | | |
| SAARC | South Asian Association for Regional Cooperation | THA | Tanzania Harbors Authority |
| | | TI | Transparency International |
| SACU | Southern African Customs Union | TIMS | Trade Information Management System |
| SAD | Single Administrative Document | | |
| SADC | Southern African Development Community | TIR | Transport International Routier |
| SADOC | Système de l'Administration des Douanes et de l'Office des Changes; Computerized Support for Customs Clearance | TRA | Tanzania Revenue Authority |
| | | TRACECA | Transport Corridor Europe Caucasus Asia |
| | | TRIE | Transit Routier Inter-États |
| SAL | Structural Adjustment Loans and Credits | TRIPS | Trade-Related Aspects of Intellectual Property Rights |
| SAR | Staff Appraisal Report | TSA | Transportation Security Administration |
| SAT | Satisfactory | | |
| SBW | Special Bonded Warehouse | TTCA | Transit Transport Coordination Authority |
| SCC | State Customs Committee | | |
| SDT | Special and Differential Treatment | TTFSE | Trade and Transport Facilitation in Southeast Europe |
| SECI | South East Cooperation Initiative | | |
| SGS | Societé Générale de Surveillance | UCR | Unique Consignment Reference |
| SITPRO | Simplifying International Trade | | |
| SOLAS | International Convention for the Safety of Life at Sea | UD | Utilization Declaration |
| | | UDEAC | Union Douanière des Etats de l'Afrique Centrale |
| SPARTECA | South Pacific Regional Trade and Economic Co-operation Agreement | UNCTAD | United Nations Conference on Trade and Development |
| SSP | Sector Strategy Paper | UNECE | United Nations Economic Commission for Europe |
| SSP | Shipper Security Plan | | |
| SUNAT | Superintendencia Nacional de Administracion Tributaria; Internal Revenue Service | UNSAT | Unsatisfactory |
| | | URA | Uganda Revenue Authority |
| | | US | United States |
| TA | Technical Assistance | UTRA | Technical Unit for Restructuring Customs |
| TAEPD | Trade Assistance Evaluation Project Database | | |
| | | VAT | Value Added Tax |
| TAL | Technical Assistance Loan | WBCG | Walvis Bay Corridor Group |
| TAP | Temporary Admission for Inward Processing | WCO | World Customs Organization |
| | | WEF | World Economic Forum |
| TARIC | Tarif Integré de la Communauté; The Integrated Tariff of the Community | WTO | World Trade Organization |
| | | ZRA | Zambian Revenue Authority |

# OVERVIEW

This handbook aims to make a positive contribution to the efforts that many countries are undertaking to modernize their customs administrations. The handbook views a competent and well-organized customs service as one that successfully balances its various responsibilities to ensure a high level of compliance with revenue objectives and regulatory requirements while at the same time intervening as little as possible in the legitimate movement of goods and people across borders.

The handbook recognizes that conditions differ greatly across countries, so that each customs administration will need to tailor its modernization efforts to national objectives, implementation capacities, and resource availability. Nevertheless, meeting the modernization objectives will most likely require the adoption of the core principles discussed in this handbook: adequate use of intelligence and reliance on risk management; optimal use of information and communications technology (ICT); effective partnership with the private sector, including programs to improve compliance; increased cooperation with other border control agencies; and transparency through information on laws, regulations, and administrative guidelines.

Success in customs modernization is, as importantly, tied to the overall trade policy environment. Simple, transparent, and harmonized trade policies reduce administrative complexities, facilitate transparency, and reduce the incentives and opportunities for rent-seeking and corruption. Customs modernization, therefore, also needs to be examined from the broader and complementary perspective of trade policy reform.

## Improving Customs Processes Is Part of the Trade Facilitation Agenda

Trade facilitation measures need to complement trade liberalization if countries are to increase their external competitiveness and become better integrated into the world economy. When the European Community, introduced a common exter-

nal tariff in 1968 it quickly realized that to fully benefit from its common market, it needed to streamline customs processes. In the same vein, the World Trade Organization (WTO) in 1996—as part of the Singapore agenda—added trade facilitation to its negotiation agenda realizing that nontariff barriers, to which excessive customs costs belong, are at times more important trade barriers than tariffs and prevent the achievement of trade liberalization objectives.

Trade involves goods crossing borders. This requires that a number of procedures foreseen in the national legislation be followed. Some of these procedures pertain to issues of security and standards, while others deal with customs. Customs procedures are governed by the national legislation and implemented by customs staff that operate mostly under the Ministry of Finance. Conforming to these procedures is not costless, but these costs are often excessive. It is not the intention of the handbook to elaborate on inefficiencies nor to detail all the dysfunctionalities of customs organizations and customs operations, even though some of these are described in individual chapters, as introduction on how best to remedy them. Yet, it is their persistent recurrence and their impact on a country's competitiveness that prompted traders and political leaders to seek out ways to make their customs organizations more effective and efficient. This handbook aims at assisting them in this ambition. It must suffice, therefore, to briefly note the main inefficiencies that these reforms aim to address. First, outdated legislation may not clearly establish the authority of customs, may be out of tune with international commitment, may provide for inadequate transparency and predictability, and may require complex procedures while preventing full use of information technology and risk analysis. Second, customs staff may lack the competence to interface with traders that operate in a constantly changing and challenging business. Often their compensation packages, including career management and training, are inadequate, so that motivating and retaining qualified staff is a major challenge. Third, operational procedures are often excessively and unnecessarily complex and open to discretionary decisions while exporters have poor access to duty-free inputs. Fourth, customs all too often makes insufficient use of available communications and information technology, and thus is out of tune with modern business practices that rely on advanced notification, direct trader input, and tracking devices. This increases costs to traders, opens the door to discretionary decisions, and undermines oversight and audit activities. Fifth, high levels of corruption characterize many a customs agency, as is testified to in investors' surveys and corruption indexes. Sixth, smuggling activities undermine revenue generation and impart unfair advantages to unscrupulous traders, and undermine the intended protection policies embedded in the tariff structure. In sum, customs procedures are often excessively time consuming, unpredictable, and weak in their revenue generation function.

### Good Diagnostics Are the Key Starting Point

Customs operations consist of sets of interlocking processes. To be efficient and effective they need to be adapted to changing trade practices and modern management approaches as well as reflect the various objectives of the country. Yet, customs practices in quite a few countries are not well attuned to these criteria. Rooted in long-standing traditions, they tend to delay the clearance of cargo and conduct operations in a nontransparent manner. Experience shows that effective customs modernization processes generally start with good initial diagnostic work to identify the shortcomings of the existing system, to define a strategy for reform, and to mobilize stakeholder support. Successful modernization also requires a comprehensive approach, that is, an approach that encompasses all aspects of customs administration to address the issues identified, as well as an adequate sequencing of actions. Strategies need to be realistic and should consider the country's capacity to implement, the time that is required, and the level of stakeholder and political support that is needed.

These reform efforts also need to be consistent with the trade policies pursued and should have the capacity to adapt to changing circumstances. For example, the emphasis on issues such as trade facilitation and national security are now more prevalent than in the past.

### Human Resources Policies Need to Be at the Center of Customs Reforms

The task of customs has become increasingly difficult because of the growing complexities of trade policy due to the proliferation of regional and international trade agreements, the greater sophistication of traders, and the multiple and shifting objectives imposed on customs. Security is now a new important challenge. Uniformity of customs operations across the territory and across cargo categories is important, and speedy release of goods is crucial to supporting the competitiveness of traders. There is also a need to adhere to international standards on value and classification, as well as regional standards on rules of origin.

Good human resources management is the linchpin to effective and efficient customs administration. This is too often neglected. The management of human resources is multifaceted. It includes recruitment, training, staff compensation and promotion, as well as enforcement. None of these tasks is easy, and often must be implemented in a constrained environment. These difficulties should not discourage the investigation of possible new initiatives and alternative approaches. However, case studies do suggest that within these constraints still much more attention should be given to human resources issues.

To address the constraints imposed on human resources reforms by rigid and often outdated civil service administration policies, many countries have pursued drastic organizational changes. For example, Autonomous Revenue Agencies (ARAs) have been established to avoid rigid civil service rules, as well as to provide more financial autonomy and greater flexibility in operational matters. However, experience has shown that creating an ARA is no guarantee for success because they have too often been focused on providing better staff compensation without sufficient attention to the other elements of customs operations that enhance effectiveness and efficiency. Also, quite a few ARAs failed to maintain, over the longer term, the flexibility and the autonomy with which they were originally established.

Another mechanism to implement reforms has been the pursuit of management contracts with the private sector. Management contracts can indeed improve aspects of customs operations if they are well designed and monitored. So far, these management contracts have largely been tested in unique circumstances in countries emerging from severe conflicts (Mozambique and Angola, for example) and where institutional capacity was exceedingly weak. Engaging private service operators in those countries had the advantage of substantially improving revenue performance in the short run and under difficult circumstances. The track record for transferring management capabilities to nationals, however, is still being tested. Initial reports suggest that this has proven more difficult than originally imagined.

Changes in the organizational structure of customs can at times be instrumental to improving performance, as change can lift important operational constraints. Evidence suggests, however, that such changes will only have lasting effects if they contribute to good human resources management and better customs clearance practices.

### An Adequate Legal Framework Is Important

The modernization of customs laws and regulations and their supporting legal environment is an essential component of the reform effort. In this area, countries can refer to (or adopt) the Revised Kyoto Convention, which provides both the legal framework and a range of agreed on standards to improve customs operations with a view toward standardizing and harmonizing customs policies and procedures worldwide. Countries that are signatories of the Convention can still tailor their policies and procedures in specific ways to meet their unique legal, political, cultural, and economic requirements.

In many countries the Customs Code needs to be modernized, especially to exclude noncore customs elements, seek harmonization and compliance with agreed on international commitments, and ensure transparency and predictability by providing basic information on matters such as rules, decisions, consultation mechanisms, and adequate appeals processes. A revised Code can also help trade facilitation by supporting the use of risk management practices and by eliminating complex or redundant customs formalities that delay clearance and create opportunities for unnecessary discretionary interventions. Finally, the Code should also grant adequate authority for customs to achieve its enforcement and compliance goals.

### Improved Integrity Is Key to Promoting Investment and Growth

Customs is frequently perceived as being corrupt. To the extent that this is true, this image negatively affects the overall investment climate of the country and the processing of international trade transactions. Corruption undermines the country's external competitiveness and its attractiveness to domestic and foreign investment. If left unchecked, this image of corruption undermines the growth potential of the country.

Customs is vulnerable to corruption because the nature of its work grants its officials substantial authority and responsibility to make decisions that affect the duty and tax liability of traders or the admissibility of goods. High tariffs and complex regulations enhance opportunities and incentives. That many customs staff members are poorly paid adds to the problem.

The adoption of procedures that provide little discretion to customs staff and that have built-in accountability mechanisms reduces both the opportunity and incentive for corruption. In conjunction with improved trade policies, the first line of defense against corruption consists of implementing modern procedures that reduce face-to-face contact between traders and customs officials and that reduce the discretionary powers of customs officials. In addition, providing adequate staff compensation, enhancing the risk of detection, and strengthening the capacity to investigate and prosecute breaches of integrity would go a long way toward promoting integrity in customs. Most customs managers are of the opinion that corruption is such a prevalent phenomenon today that countermeasures would require the implementation of specially designed policy efforts. This is the approach that is promoted by the World Customs Organization and is incorporated into the Revised Arusha Declaration on Integrity in Customs.

In looking to implement the key elements of the Revised Arusha Declaration, experience suggests that a good starting point is to conduct a comprehensive assessment of the situation to identify the shortcomings that present opportunities for corruption and to establish realistic priorities, as well as practical objectives and activities, all leading to an integrity plan that should be a part of all comprehensive customs reform efforts.

### Risk Management Underpins Much of Modern Customs Practices

In an effort to achieve an appropriate balance between trade facilitation and regulatory control, customs administrations are generally abandoning their traditional, routine "gateway" checks and are now applying the principles of risk management with varying degrees of sophistication and success.

*Organizational risk* refers to the possible events and activities that may prevent an organization from achieving its objectives. Risks facing customs include the potential for noncompliance with customs laws as well as the potential failure to facilitate international trade. Customs, like any other organization, needs to manage its risks and do so while interfering as little as possible with the flow of legitimate trade. There clearly is a trade-off between control and trade facilitation. Too much of one makes it difficult to achieve the other. Customs therefore needs to apply a set of management procedures that takes this into account. These procedures include the identification, analysis, evaluation, and mitigation of the risks that may affect the achievement of these objectives.

Basic risk management has always been fundamental to customs operations, and has guided the formulation of antismuggling policies, the functioning of border controls to verify the movements of goods and passengers, and the establishment of documentary controls and physical inspection procedures. However, in recent times the increasing complexity, speed, and volume of international trade, fueled by technological advances that have revolutionized global trading practices, have significantly affected the way in which customs authorities implement risk management. This has led many customs administrations to adopt a more disciplined and structured approach to managing risk.

Customs needs to evaluate the risks that are presented by the nature of its operations. This includes the need for customs to review its operational procedures and assess where breaches of procedures are likely to jeopardize the attainment of stated objectives. Such assessment could be included in the above-mentioned overall diagnostic exercise. In other words, customs needs to provide a risk map that identifies the potential vulnerabilities of its processes and determine how its procedures may need to be geared toward ensuring better realiza-tion of its objectives. On the basis of the risk assessment, a risk containment strategy should be defined. This implies that priorities would be set, operational details would be geared toward these priorities, and resources would be effectively and efficiently deployed. If smuggling turns out to be a major problem, the strategy should reflect this, and border posts and mobile inspection teams may need to be strengthened. If undervaluation is a major problem, there may be a case for strengthening the valuation unit and for increasing the number of traders subject to post-clearance audit. If the risk is that goods tend to be misclassified to attract a lower tariff rate or are declared with lower unit counts or weights, there may be a need to physically inspect the cargo. In any event, risk management should ease the controls on the less risky aspects of trade and should focus on the part that represents the greatest risk. This would reflect a balanced approach between control and trade facilitation.

### Customs Valuation Is a Core Customs Function

Customs valuation practices are subject to the WTO Agreement on Customs Valuation (ACV), which mandates that the customs value of imported goods, to the greatest extent possible, should be the transaction value, that is, the price paid or payable for the goods. However, valuation fraud is frequently reported as a major problem in developing countries, and many of them still find that implementing the ACV presents one of the most challenging aspects of customs work. Valuation work is particularly difficult in some countries in which the reliability of commercial invoices tends to be poor, and where trade undertaken by the informal sector and in second-hand goods is significant. Also, many countries are still ill equipped to undertake post-clearance audit.

Substantial efforts have so far been made to explain the intricacies of the ACV to customs officials of developing countries. Yet, most observers realize that valuation reform, in the absence of comprehensive customs modernization programs, is likely to disappoint. A narrow focus on valuation work will fail if reform takes place within an administratively and technically ill-equipped customs. The reform elements that will benefit valuation work must include the streamlining of operational procedures, the introduction of a modern customs compliance improvement strategy based on a formalized risk management strategy, the use of post-clearance audits, the development of a commercial intelligence capacity, and the adoption of appropriate incentives and disincentives designed to progressively increase the level of voluntary compliance.

Direct technical assistance for improved valuation work might be more productive if such assistance were concentrated on the development of valuation databases, risk management systems, and post-release review and audit. A valuation database should be established and constantly updated to provide customs with a practical tool for research and risk management purposes. The valuation function in Customs could be strengthened by setting up an appropriate legal framework; establishing valuation control procedures based on selective checking, risk analysis and management, and post-release audit; establishing central and regional valuation offices; and providing specialized training.

The hiring of preshipment inspection (PSI) companies may be useful in assisting customs with valuation work during its initial reform stages, where capacity is being enhanced to carry out the valuation function. However, if PSI services are used, care needs to be exercised to maximize their utility and to ensure maximum consistency with the WTO valuation principles. This handbook spells out a number of conditions that should be investigated when considering the adoption of PSI services or when evaluating their contribution.

### Rules of Origin Should Be Simplified

Determining the country of origin, or the "nationality," of imported products is necessary for the application of basic trade policy measures such as tariffs, quantitative restrictions, antidumping and countervailing duties, and safeguard measures, as well as for requirements relating to origin marking and public procurement, and for statistical purposes. Such objectives are met through the application of basic or nonpreferential rules of origin. Countries that offer zero or reduced duty access to imports from certain trade partners apply preferential rules of origin. These differ most frequently from the nonpreferential ones. Preferential rules are designed to ensure that only goods originating from participating countries enjoy preferences.

However, rules of origin can be designed to restrict trade and, therefore, can and have been used as trade policy instruments. The proliferation of free trade agreements with accompanying preferential rules of origin is increasing the burden on customs in many countries because the clearing of preferential trade is more complex than nonpreferential trade. This suggests that the trend toward more preferential free trade agreements may conflict with trade facilitation.

The determination of the country of origin of products has, in the last few decades, become more difficult as technological change, declining transport costs, and the process of globalization have led to the splitting up of production chains and the distribution of different elements in the production of a good to different locations. The issue becomes, which one or more of these stages of production define the country of origin of the good?

WTO members have so far failed to reach an agreement on the definition of rules of origin, despite efforts undertaken in the World Customs Organization (WCO) since 1995. Having harmonized rules of origin for nonpreferential purposes would save time and costs to traders and customs officers and provide for greater certainty and predictability of trade. Harmonized rules would also help avoid trade disputes that arise from uncertainties in the determination of the country of origin with regard to antidumping and countervailing duties, safeguard measures, and government procurement decisions. In general, clear, straightforward, transparent, and predictable rules of origin, which require little or no administrative discretion, will add less of a burden to customs than complex rules.

### Good Duty Relief and Exemption Control Systems Are Important

Customs may provide duty relief for some imports. This practice is mainly used for the importation of inputs used for the manufacture of export products. The justification for doing so is simple. Any duty paid on these inputs would increase the cost of the exports and make these exports less competitive. In fact, following the widely accepted destination principle of taxation, only goods destined for domestic consumption should bear a tax burden. Duty relief for inputs that are directed toward the production of exports can be granted in two ways: either a suspense regime is applied and no duties for imported inputs are paid at the point of import; or duties are paid and later refunded, when the products into which the inputs are incorporated are exported. The WCO Revised Kyoto Convention provides guidelines on how this should be done and these can be reflected in the Customs Code and translated in operational guidelines for importers and customs staff. However, experience shows that many developing countries have difficulty in properly administering and monitoring duty relief and exemption regimes, resulting in abuse, fraud, and revenue leakage. In the absence of smoothly operating duty relief mechanisms, export manufacturers have to produce at higher cost than would be the case if they had full and easy access to production inputs at world prices.

Export manufacturers have a preference for temporary admission systems, bonded warehouses, and export processing zones over duty drawback, especially when tariffs are high, when inflation erodes the duty refunds, and when interest rates for working capital are high. The prepayment of import duties on inputs increases the production costs of the exporter. The drawbacks have all too often been disbursed late, thus substantially eroding real value when inflation and financing costs are high. However, governments in most developing countries require customs to focus on revenue collection rather than trade facilitation and, therefore, tend to prefer drawback to temporary admission systems.

Managing duty relief schemes in a secure and cost effective way requires well-defined processes and controls. It requires that special mechanisms be put in place to ensure that claims for duty relief are legitimate and correctly executed, and that goods admitted under duty suspense regimes are effectively incorporated in exports and not diverted for home consumption.

The scope of duty exemptions should be limited as much as possible as exemptions can be abused, thus leading to unfair competition and revenue losses. Moreover, there are good economic and administrative reasons for maintaining duty exemptions only as required by international conventions and for noncommercial goods. Until the redundant exemptions are eliminated, customs should devote adequate technological and man-power resources to the control and monitoring of such exemptions.

### Customs Procedures Should Facilitate Transit

Poor transit procedures are a major obstacle to trade and penalize many landlocked developing countries. A transit system aims to facilitate the transport of goods through a customs territory, without levying duties and taxes in the countries of departure and transit, in accordance with the destination principle of taxation that states that indirect taxes should only be levied in the country of consumption. The Customs Code should provide transit-related legislation, failing which, transit should be regulated by a binding agreement between customs and the different parties affected by the transit operation.

The core provisions of a good transit system include that the shipments be sealed at the point of departure, that guarantees can be made available to ensure the payments of duties and taxes if traders do not provide proof that the goods have left the country, and that customs has an information system that informs it when the goods have left the country so that the guarantee can be released. In many countries these core elements are either lacking or weak and should be the focus of any transit modernization initiative.

Trade policies should recognize that customs transit is only one part of a wider range of policy issues that affect transit. These other issues pertain to many other participants and procedures, including cross-border vehicle regulations, visas for truck drivers, insurance, police controls, and the quality of infrastructure. Even if customs transit procedures are made effective and efficient, full trade facilitation will require that these issues be addressed. The TIR (Transit Routier International—the international road transit procedures) and its network of national guaranteeing associations offer the best current reference system.

Effective and efficient transit facilitation institutions such as corridor agreements can promote active cooperation between and among transit and landlocked countries. Transit agreements are important in forming and shaping such cooperation, either at the bilateral, subregional, or regional level. Transit operations will benefit from good public–private cooperation that can identify deficiencies in border-crossing procedures.

### Security Has Become an Integral Customs Objective

The emergence of international terrorism has caused security to become a major issue for many governments, and customs administrations are increasingly called upon to contribute to national security objectives. In the past, many customs administrations performed most of their preventive operations as goods arrived at seaports, airports, and land borders, based upon an entry declaration made at the time of importation. To provide the level of security that is required, governments will increasingly depend on information and risk assessments that are undertaken in advance of the arrival of the cargo in the country of destination. International conventions that apply to sea and air transport provide for agreed upon mechanisms to enhance the security of these modes of transportation—vehicles, cargo, and personnel—as well as how these transport modes are operated. Several national governments, particularly that of the United States of America, have issued regulations and have promoted private–public sector agreements to enhance security. These, again, are largely based on the advance submission of information and certification that the particular companies adhere to a range of security standards. Such regulations are constantly being refined and implemented. Customs' skill in assessing the information through analytical processes, deployment of resources, effective communication and decision-making, therefore, has become even more important than in the past.

Protecting society involves protection of the entire international trade supply chain from the moment the cargo leaves the export country to the moment of arrival at the destination country. This changing environment requires an "all of government" approach. In this way, governments can use customs as a key resource in border security, using its experience of managing risks and knowledge of international trade as an important element of national security. Thus, customs can usefully complement the contributions made by other competent agencies, such as immigration, intelligence agencies, and those involved in policing maritime, aviation, and land operations.

While security is of great importance to governments and traders, customs has an equal responsibility to facilitate legitimate trade. If applied correctly, security can enhance facilitation by building business confidence, increasing predictability, and, as a consequence, facilitating inward investment. However, the international community will need to monitor how specific security initiatives and advance notice requirements will affect weaker trading partners, particularly those that use ports that are not receiving technical assistance to strengthen their security to the satisfaction of the ports of destination. These traders may have difficulties in fully complying with the advance notice requirements.

While it is not possible at this time to predict the trade-related consequences of the heightened security agenda, it seems probable that the countries that feel vulnerable to terrorist attack will regard consignments from certain countries as representing a higher risk. In this regard, the level of integration of the world economy is such that even countries that are not directly involved in a conflict or subject to terrorist attack suffer losses in trade and welfare as a result of increased security concerns and higher frictional costs of trade. For those countries with a high degree of reliance on trade (ratio of trade to GDP), including many developing countries, the need for concerted action in the security area becomes a key priority in the development agenda.

### Information and Communications Technology Promotes Customs Modernization

An effective customs administration that leverages technology can benefit from improved transparency, greater efficiency, and enhanced security. However, the benefits that could be derived from greater reliance on ICT has at times been undermined by the failure to streamline customs procedures, thus creating a process where outdated manual practices continue alongside computerized practices. Although ICT for customs administration is not a panacea or an end in itself, it can powerfully contribute to effective customs administration and operations when integrated into a broader modernization effort.

To meet its mission, a customs administration must effectively integrate modern practices and processes with ICT-driven customs management systems. In doing so, customs should identify realistic and practical targets and objectives that are tailored to its own specific circumstances. Desirable ICT solutions are not necessarily the very latest and most sophisticated ones available, but rather, the ones that are most appropriate for the country's operating environment, resource base, telecommunications infrastructure, and realistic development ambitions. In any event, the ICT solution chosen must assist customs in all its core business functions and must provide a platform that enables achievement of its long-term vision.

In its choice of computer solutions, customs has the option of either developing a national system that is adapted to national needs, or acquiring an off-the-shelf system. National solutions have the attraction of perfectly matching the specific requirements of a given country, of developing national computer skills, and of facilitating the system's maintenance and development. Yet, such national solutions tend to be expensive, and it has at times proven difficult for customs officials to convey to the ICT technicians the complex transactions that need to be programmed. Off-the-shelf solutions benefit from the fact that the various modules have been tested and avoid the need to "reinvent the wheel." Where these solutions do not fully satisfy national needs, or where national customs desires a variant of the solution offered, there is the possibility of customizing the solution or of adding on separate modules that interface with the off-the-shelf solution. On balance, the handbook advocates that policymakers take a hard look at off-the-shelf solutions before they consider designing a national solution.

ITC solutions tend to be expensive, even if they enhance efficiency. Experience suggests that much is to be gained from a well-balanced financing plan for the initial installation, maintenance, and upgrading, as well as financing plans to include external and domestic resources. Also, procurement procedures should be transparent and should ensure value for money by carefully weighing both the technical and financial proposals.

### Structure of the Handbook

This volume has three parts. The chapters in Part I cover cross-cutting issues that provide insights to the key elements of a successful customs modernization strategy. The chapters discuss key organizational issues that any customs service needs to deal with and focus on the legal framework of customs and the issues of integrity and risk management. The chapters in Part II provide lessons from a select set of customs reform initiatives as well as from the World Bank's own experience with its support for customs reform. The chapters in Part III successively discuss and provide guidelines on a number of issues that affect customs operation and trade facilitation. These are customs valuation, rules of origin, duty relief and duty exemption regimes, transit, security, and the use of ICT.

Each of the 13 chapters begins with a short introduction or background section that is intended as a reader's guide to the issues. This is followed by an analysis and discussion of the issues, then by the chapter's main operational conclusions and recommendations. Some chapters include an annex with a checklist of issues that need to be addressed in the areas covered. Sections on further reading and references follow. The boxes included in the chapters illustrate specific points or describe specific cases. Case studies are used to illustrate points made in the chapters; the situation on the ground may have since changed. Their usefulness rests in illustrating that theory and guidelines can be implemented. Many of these case studies and boxes were prepared by the editors of the handbook, drawing on papers prepared for this project and on the literature.

A companion volume titled Customs Modernization Initiatives: Case Studies, edited by Luc De Wulf and José B. Sokol, describes in some detail the experiences and lessons learned from eight case studies in customs modernization. It complements this handbook as it shows how in real life some of the issues described here were addressed.

# PART I

# CROSS-CUTTING ISSUES

# STRATEGY FOR CUSTOMS MODERNIZATION

*Luc De Wulf*

Research undertaken in recent years by the World Bank and others shows that participation in world trade tends to boost growth, and that countries that have integrated rapidly into the world economy also tended to record the highest growth rates.[1] This outcome should not come as a surprise. Integration brings with it exposure to new technologies, designs, and products. It also enhances competition. With world trade growth expanding more than twice as rapidly as growth of world gross domestic product (GDP) over the past decade, the potential rewards from participating in world trade are evident. Such participation is predicated on the availability of good quality products offered at competitive prices. In this regard, a trade regime that tenders low protection to domestic producers contributes to the enhancement

---

1. Rapidly integrating countries experienced annual GDP growth three percentage points higher than slow integrators. Integration refers to trade integration as well as openness to foreign direct investment (World Bank 1996).

of an economy's competitiveness because it forces domestic producers to align their costs with those in the rest of the world. Nevertheless, an open trade regime will only foster competitiveness when other accompanying policies are in place.

Over the past 20 years, average tariffs have been cut by half in developing countries and nontariff import barriers have been sharply reduced (World Bank 1996). Yet, for many developing countries, this has not necessarily led to substantial trade integration. Worse still, the poorest countries in the world, particularly those of Sub-Saharan Africa, lost market share during the 1990s. Such events were in part brought about by the failure of developing countries to produce the types of goods that would generate the most rapid export growth. Another impediment was the maintenance by other countries of a range of import barriers to products that Sub-Saharan African countries produce, including agricultural and textile goods. Import barriers include export subsidies, high tariffs, and stringent rules of origin (see chapter 9). The issues of the cotton export subsidy granted by the United States and other agricultural export subsidies of the European Union (EU) and United States were a significant reason for the disappointing results of the World Trade Organization (WTO) Ministerial Conference in Cancun in 2003. A poorly functioning trade logistics environment, as well as the combination of factors that make up the transaction costs—the cost of clearing customs, transport costs, noncustoms trade documentation requirements, and unenforceability of legal trade documents (World Bank 2003)—also contributed to the failure of many developing countries to integrate successfully into the world economy. High transaction costs, of which customs clearance costs are often an important element, may thus nullify the cost-reducing impact of trade liberalization. Few customs services have managed to provide exporters with the duty-free inputs needed to keep export prices competitive.[2]

The realization that customs services could be improved has prompted many governments to devote substantial energy and resources to modernization. They have also mobilized external assistance in this endeavor. In response, bilateral and multilateral development agencies have supported many customs reform initiatives. International donors or financial institutions such as the European Union (EU), the International Monetary Fund (IMF), the Inter-American Development Bank (IDB), the African Development Bank (AfDB), the Asian Development Bank (AsDB), the United Nations Conference on Trade and Development (UNCTAD), and the World Bank (WB), have all been engaged in customs strengthening operations. Bilateral donors, such as France, the United Kingdom, Japan, and the United States have also been active in providing such support. In addition, the World Customs Organization (WCO) has made technical assistance (TA) available. A number of customs administrations have improved their operations by taking advantage of this support. Yet, too many still operate inefficiently, adding considerable costs to trading activities while, at the same time, undermining the growth potential of their economies.

This chapter outlines the main features of a customs reform strategy and provides operational guidelines that are likely to contribute to the success of such initiatives. It has been inspired by the knowledge of good practices; the World Bank's own TA and project experiences (summarized in chapter 8); the approaches presented in a number of TA reports that have been produced by diverse customs experts and institutions, many of which remain inaccessible to the general public; lessons learned from several customs modernization initiatives (chapter 7); and consultations with many customs officials and consultants who have assisted in customs modernization initiatives. The first section reviews the key objectives of customs modernization initiatives. The second section spells out a number of contextual factors that need to be adequately addressed at the outset of a reform process to enhance its chances for success. The third section defines the key steps in preparing a customs modernization strategy. The next section elaborates on implementing key issues of the strategy. The final section provides some operational conclusions.

---

2. A recent study of trade liberalization for a sample of countries in Africa concluded "It is in the area of providing exporters with access to low tariffs and tax-free inputs that the progress of the sample countries has been the most disappointing. The sample countries had made little progress in implementing timely reimbursements to exporters of either import duties or value added tax (VAT) on inputs." (Hinkle, Herrou-Aragon, and Kubota 2003, pp. 82–83.)

## Objectives of Customs Operations

Customs administrations are expected to raise substantial revenue, provide domestic producers with protection, provide supply chain security, prevent the importation of prohibited or unsafe imports (for example, illegal weapons or out-of-date medicines), and combat the trade of narcotics through the implementation of laws and regulations that are in line with WTO commitments. Customs administrations are expected to accomplish these objectives both effectively (by achieving them) and efficiently (at the lowest possible cost to the budget and to the trading community) without compromising trade facilitation.

### Evolution of Customs Role

The responsibilities of customs continue to evolve. Customs administrations are now increasingly regarded as "the key border agencies" responsible for all transactions related to issues arising from the border crossings of goods and people. Some of these functions are undertaken in close cooperation with other national agencies.[3] The operational guidelines of customs cannot give equal weight to all functions constantly; choices and priorities are inevitable in light of changing circumstances:

- Raising revenue has traditionally been high on the agenda of governments, represented by the Ministry of Finance (MOF), because of the critical importance of import duties as a source of budget revenue for many developing countries. Revenues from import duties for a sample of African countries accounted for just under 30 percent of total tax revenue, on average. In comparison, this share averaged 22 percent for countries in the Middle East, 13 percent for Latin American countries, and 15 percent for Asian countries (see annex 1.A). While import tariffs are widely recognized as more distortionary sources of revenue than general sales and income taxes, they remain important for historic reasons, and because they are relatively easy to collect. Collection of VAT on imports constitutes another major source of budget revenue. Therefore, a control mentality that ensures that all duties are assessed and paid has permeated customs, irrespective of whether this causes delays in the release of imports. With tariff rates declining over time, customs revenues as a share of the total budget revenues have also tended to decline in most countries; but customs revenues are still a major concern of MOF officials. This priority has been reflected in many past customs reforms and TA initiatives.

- Import tariffs are meant to protect domestic producers, who expect customs administrations to ensure that all importers pay the official import taxes to ensure a level playing field. On average, customs duties amount to 17 percent of the total import value in a sample of African countries, 12 percent in the Middle East, 10 percent in Asia and the Pacific, and 7 percent in the Western Hemisphere (see annex 1.B).[4] Increasingly, import tariffs are being seen as an instrument of protection rather than of raising budget revenue. This is clearly so in developed countries where tariffs provide only a tiny share of total revenue and on average represent less than 1 percent of overall import value. Import tariffs in developing countries are high, however, thus hampering trade among developing countries as well as the competitiveness of the countries' economies (Ebril, Stotsky, and Gropp 1999).

- Trade facilitation has attracted increasing interest in recent years as evidenced by the WTO Cancún Agenda and the WCO Revised Kyoto Convention. This interest has been brought about by an increasing commitment of governments to pursue a private sector–oriented growth strategy, combined with increased private sector assertiveness and demands for better government services. Cost reductions to the trader, derived from easier customs procedures, stem largely from the possibility of reducing

---

3. See, for example, the International Convention on the Harmonization of Frontier Control of Goods (UNECE 1982) available at http://www.unece.org/trans/conventn/harmone.pdf.

4. The IMF estimated these collection rates for a slightly different sample of countries for 1995. It appears that the rates fell slightly for the sample countries in Asia and the Pacific, but stagnated and even rose slightly in Sub-Saharan Africa and Middle Eastern countries included in the sample (Ebril, Stotsky, and Gropp 1999).

inventories and the amount of operations capital, as well as the possibility for traders to satisfy increasingly stringent "just in time" requirements.

- Civil society is demanding better governance and has identified customs services as particularly prone to harboring corrupt practices. Targeting customs for improvements fully recognizes the fact that the integrity situation reflects the integrity of the greater society to which the administration belongs.
- Over the years, customs administrations have received a mandate to protect society. This has been included in the mandate of the WCO, to reflect the notion that most customs administrations are responsible for preventing the cross-border movement of dangerous and unsafe goods. However, the security concern was elevated to new heights after the events of September 11, 2001. The focus shifted from just imports to the entire supply chain, including exports. New procedures are being introduced and additional safety measures are being prepared and implemented.

### Customs Role and Priorities in the 21st Century

It is difficult to predict the future role of any institution, and there is no one correct or universally applicable response to anticipated trends in customs, as each country will respond in ways that are best suited to its needs, operating environment, national priorities, and cultural heritage. However, some general issues or themes are emerging that suggest the future role and priorities of customs.

First, in spite of declining tariff rates brought about by successive rounds of trade liberalization, the revenue mobilization and control functions of customs are likely to remain substantial, for several reasons: (a) the fiscal dependency on customs revenues is likely to linger for some time, in light of the difficulty many developing countries encounter in broadening their tax bases; (b) imports will probably constitute a major tax base for levying VAT, and customs is well positioned to control the goods at the time of importation; (c) customs will remain the responsible agency to ensure that goods that were imported for other than home consumption are not diverted to such consumption; and (d) assessing VAT refunds on exported goods will continue to require a high level of control over exported goods.

Second, in all countries, customs will continue to collect trade data for statistical and regulatory purposes.

Third, customs will continue to be responsible for effective and efficient border management to facilitate trade, a major contributor to the international competitiveness of nations. This will occur regardless of whether trade facilitation is formally incorporated into multilateral trade negotiations. As such, harmonizing, simplifying, and effectively coordinating all national border management requirements and commitments will remain priority responsibilities of customs.

Fourth, based on a heightened awareness of the threat posed by international terrorism and transnational organized crime, governments will require that customs administrations take on a larger role in ensuring national security and law enforcement. To that effect, customs administrations are likely to institute a range of changes to systems, procedures, and even administrative responsibilities to increase confidence in the level of control exercised over both imports and exports. Security checks will increasingly take place at the point of export in addition to the point of entry.

For customs administrations to effectively manage these sometimes apparently contradictory objectives, a wide range of new approaches, systems, procedures, and operating methodologies will have to be developed and implemented. Some of these are already beginning to emerge and are likely to underpin the future shape and role of customs:

- The primary focus of customs' attention will shift from physical control over consignments at the time of importation to post-release verification using audit-based controls. This will require customs to adopt comprehensive compliance improvement strategies designed to progressively increase confidence in the information provided by traders and in the accounting systems and processes they maintain. All regulatory information is likely to be exchanged electronically, and decisions on treatment of imports and exports will be made on a risk assessment basis. The compliance record of individual traders will be a key consideration as will the exchange of information and intelligence.

Such an approach will facilitate the re-engineering of core border management processes and regulatory requirements. It will also involve a new and more coherent relationship with traders, as well as increased cooperation at the national, regional, and international levels.

- Countries will increasingly rely on a single agency to take responsibility for the entire border management process. This will involve the merger of a number of different border management functions under one administrative and policy umbrella. In some cases this will be achieved administratively, and in others virtually, through increased cooperation at the policy and operational level and through the adoption of information and communications technology (ICT) infrastructure that will allow traders to discharge all their regulatory responsibilities through one single window to the government.
- Moves to ensure more effective coordination between the various government agencies charged with regulating cross-border trade and achieving meaningful rationalization of regulatory requirements will require attention at the national, regional, and international levels. While many different players are involved, it seems likely that customs is the only agency with the national and international infrastructure in place to achieve this.
- Customs will increasingly rely on the intensive use of modern information technology to provide for seamless transmission of data to all interested members of the trading community. In the future, most customs administrations will rely on electronic submission of manifests before cargo arrival, on direct trader input of import and export declarations, and on electronic payment of duties and taxes. Initiatives that have shown good results so far and that aim at electronically connecting all members of the trading community, as in Singapore, are likely to spread. This will speed up the granting of regulatory permissions and enable the collection of statistics.
- Many countries are already members of regional groups, a trend that might accelerate in coming years. Such regional groups might promote harmonization and simplification of customs procedures in accordance with international best practice standards. On the other hand, they create the need for new preferential trade regimes that impose burdens both on customs and on trade, and are prone to abuse.

## Contextual Factors Necessary for a Successful Customs Reform

Customs reform involves more than the introduction of a set of new techniques for processing cargo and passengers. Customs reform calls for a new awareness of the developments in trade, requires political commitment to push through sometime difficult measures, and must start with a good diagnosis of the present situation.

### Awareness That Customs Operates in an Increasingly Globalized Environment

The increases in world trade of recent decades have placed increasing demands upon customs.[5] In 2002, over US$10 trillion worth of goods crossed international borders. Every shipment passed through customs control at least twice, once on export and once on import, making customs a key factor in the international supply chain and in the global economy. Customs needs to adjust to new ports of entry and additional hours of service, and their job is made more complex by a plethora of regional and bilateral trade agreements. Frequently, there is no commensurate increase in customs staffing and resources to keep pace with the increased workload and more complex environment. Often, customs is not provided with the technological resources to facilitate and secure international supply chains, to keep pace with the billions of dollars spent by industry.

Faced with these challenges, many customs administrations struggle to meet all of these demands and priorities. Often, they focus on revenue collection and ad hoc priorities that are championed by the most vocal and influential interest groups. Some, however, strive to meet these challenges head on, and revisit how their administrations are designed and how they function.

In view of customs' unique position at a country's borders, its management must satisfy both domestic and international constituencies. On the international front travelers, businesses, and international air, sea, and land carriers expect services

---

5. This section relies heavily on Lane (1998).

that are uniform, predictable, easy to use, and consistent with international standards and conventions. Organizations such as the WCO, the WTO, UN Economic Commission for Europe (UNECE), UN Centre for Trade Facilitation and Electronic Business (CEFACT), and UNCTAD have set standards for the most critical customs functions. The most important ones are the following:

- The Revised Kyoto Convention (International Convention on the Simplification and Harmonization of Customs Procedures) provides the framework for processing goods in international commerce (chapter 3).
- The International Convention on the Harmonized Commodity Description and Coding System (referred to as the Harmonized System or HS), which was developed and maintained by the WCO, provides the framework for classifying all merchandise in international trade.
- The Agreement on Customs Valuation (ACV), developed by the WTO, provides the framework for determining the customs value of goods in international trade (chapter 8).
- The Agreement on Rules of Origin is the WTO initiative to develop a system for standardizing the rules of origin of internationally traded goods (chapter 9).

The skills of classifying goods, determining value and country of origin, and applying proper procedures for processing merchandise are needed by customs to comply with international conventions, meet the expectations of the international trade community, and achieve the organization's mission at the nation's borders. If customs strays, it violates international agreements. Such noncompliance may result in additional costs and time delays to importers, exporters, carriers, domestic industries, and consumers. Clearance of goods is affected by factors such as the quality of port facilities and the multitude of organizations and handoffs involved in each international trade transaction. Typically, customs is seen as responsible for all delays and wrongdoing at the border, although other agencies are involved. The international trade community may, ultimately, sanction such failures by transferring foreign direct investment (FDI) to other countries where the import–export environment complies with international standards.

Implementation of these standards and conventions is not a simple task, as illustrated by the arguments and debates at the WCO regarding valuation and rules of origin issues. These issues are discussed in some detail in chapters 8 and 9. Also, the complexity of the HS may give rise to disputes between importers and customs, due to the fact that the payment of duties depends on the classification in the HS-based customs' tariff.

As international trade increases and becomes a more important factor in the economy, the importance of customs increases and it becomes imperative for customs to administer these complex agreements uniformly, professionally, fairly, and transparently. In performing these functions, customs will be dealing with well-trained and well-compensated professionals possessing international experience who are experts in the areas of logistics, trade, transport, and law. Multinational companies have invested billions of dollars in recent years to streamline and secure their international supply chains. These modern, sophisticated logistics systems provide companies with the capability to track, trace, and monitor shipments from the factory door to the retail store. However, the physical and information flows can be severed by customs at international borders at the point of import or export. A slow, inept, or poorly trained and equipped customs increases transaction costs, thereby increasing the costs of exported goods to the industry and consumers, thus making the country less competitive. Customs must organize itself to be a trade facilitator in a rapidly changing world, as well as an efficient provider of budget revenues. This represents a major administrative challenge.

### Political Support at the Highest Level

Most customs administrations have operational responsibilities under the government policy set by their supervisors, including the MOF, and any change will require strong government support. Demand for reform is unlikely to come from inside the organization as it may require that drastic changes be introduced (Holl 2002). That customs staff are recruited young and often trained in paramilitary fashion—a tradition that finds its roots in the fact that many customs officials have law enforcement responsibilities—also generates an environment that discourages challenging existing procedures. Proposed changes may require reductions in personnel along with the introduction of information technology (IT) or, in extreme cases, the removal of the top management of customs or of customs officials deemed corrupt or inefficient. Management contracts or contracting with preshipment service providers may also be proposed.

The focus of the MOFs has always been on raising more budget revenue. This has often led to the stringent control of trade movements, adding costs to both honest and potentially dishonest traders. While reducing corruption and facilitating trade were always objectives of MOF-led reforms, these goals were rarely translated into program details and were often set aside in the process of raising revenues. These internally driven reforms frequently became stale and failed to instill new ways of dealing with the old problems. Few have become sustainable. Hence, outside support for reforms is crucial.

The trading community and civil society often lobby for the improvement of services. The trading community wants to reduce its trading costs and increase the transparency of its operations while civil society wants to eradicate the debilitating effects of corruption on social values and economic performance. As the case studies profiled in chapter 6 indicate, private sector pressure groups have frequently been crucial to fostering customs reforms and monitoring their progress. Politicians and government officials are more likely to respond with a firm policy program to local pressure groups than to administrative initiatives that are often suspected of being self-serving, that easily get lost in bureaucratic posturing, and that often lead to only marginal or cosmetic changes.[6]

The reforms will create winners and losers, and political commitment will be needed to realize the project. Traders that were accommodated under the older rules, as well as customs officials that obtained additional income in "facilitating" trade transactions or in manipulating import and export declarations to the advantage of the trader, are likely to object to reform programs that will make these practices riskier or impossible. Those that

"lose" in a successful reform may be well connected as either part of the customs administration management or sufficiently close to it to slow down the reform momentum or to influence the design and implementation of the reform. If not countered, the influence of these individuals will make the reform partial, fragmentary, and ineffective. Traditionalism and lethargy are other factors against change. Only a reform that benefits from full political support at the highest level of government will deliver its expected outcomes.

### Adequate Diagnostic Work

Customs reform is not a case of "one size fits all." The particular objectives of customs administrations and the maturity of their organizations differ among countries. Reforms must be tailored to the situation at hand. Hence, to fully account for this diversity, it is important that any customs modernization project start with a careful and complete diagnosis of the existing situation. The absence of good diagnostic work was identified as a major shortcoming in the tax and customs administration projects managed by the World Bank (Barbone, De Wulf, Das-Gupta, and Hanson 2001), and has been confirmed in more recent work, as illustrated in chapter 7. Yet, undertaking a diagnostic exercise in customs is not an exact science and a flexible approach may have to be adopted, with the diagnostic tailored to the objective of the exercise. There are a number of approaches, tools, and instruments that can be used.

**Enhancing Revenue Mobilization** Enhancing revenue mobilization has frequently been the focus of customs reforms. Diagnostic work has mainly focused on measuring revenue leakages. Both the World Bank and the IMF frequently use this approach.[7] The core indicators used to identify the slack in revenue generation include: (a) collected taxes over imports compared with potential revenue collections to identify the "gap"; (b) share of total imports exempted from taxes[8]; and (c) fraud

6. The late King Hassan II (1961–99) of Morocco championed trade and customs reform in response to presentations made by the professional associations that had most to gain from these reforms.

7. For a collection of excellent articles focusing on the mobilization of revenues see Keen (2003).

8. These were reported at 18 percent of total imports in a sample of African countries (Hinkle, Herrou-Aragon, and Kubota 2003).

in recording valuation, weight, or rules of origin. Less quantifiable indicators of revenue leakage pertain to the possibility of misclassification of imports as goods that attract lower tariff rates, as well as vagueness in the Customs Code and regulations that allow customs officials and traders to make mutually agreeable arrangements. The methodology of these diagnostic exercises is neither standard nor publicly available, but has centered on a pragmatic analysis of customs processes to identify possible improvements. The main participants in such diagnostic exercises have been MOF officials, including customs. Private sector operators have been consulted, but their viewpoint, which is not maximizing revenue mobilization, is often missing in official reports and reform programs.

**Using the World Bank Trade Facilitation Toolkit**
In 2001 the World Bank issued a toolkit for the audit of trade and transport services (Raven 2001).[9] This toolkit reflects the practical experience gained in a series of Bank missions as well as inquiries conducted in a number of developing countries, and draws on a previous publication. It provides guidelines on how to carry out an audit and analyze and interpret its findings, and identify remedial actions. The audit consists largely of a series of structured questions presented to all participants in the trade transaction, including customs officials. The responses are to be systematically reviewed under such headings as integrity, port management, regulatory framework, automation, agents' functions and attitudes, and so forth. The responses can be drawn upon to prepare a remedial action plan that is intended for all participants in the trade chain, including customs, and establishes the conditions for success. Clearly, the aim of this toolkit is to review all operations that can help or hamper trade processes, and this goes beyond customs operations. A full-fledged diagnosis of the various operations of customs will need to draw on other diagnostic tools. The issues pertaining to the administrative environment in revenue mobilization agencies in general are well treated in "A Diagnostic Framework For Revenue Administration," which was designed for domestic revenue administrations (Gill 2000).[10]

This framework guided the Bank's diagnostic work for the Russian Federation Customs Modernization Project in 2002.

**International Customs Guidelines Prepared by the International Chamber of Commerce**  The focus of the guidelines of the International Chamber of Commerce is clearly on customs (International Chamber of Commerce 2002). They present, in a summary format, the key procedures that constitute customs best practices, and assist the analyst in preparing a systematic comparison between the present state of a given customs administration and its future operations using these best practices. The explanatory notes are useful in providing the background for evaluating the present system. These guidelines constitute a good starting point for any diagnostic study.

**Covering the Fundamentals**  Lane's *Customs Modernization and the International Trade Superhighway* (2002) provides another analytical framework for the diagnostic work. The proposed approach also consists of a set of structured questions organized around a logical framework that covers fundamentals such as the environment of customs operation, including its expertise and integrity; enablers such as managing processes, automation, and the ability to analyze data; and advanced processes such as enforcement, compliance and industry partnership, audit and account management, and risk management. Lane proposed a system that would analyze the replies to these questions and provide guidance on how to formulate an implementation program that would ensure total compliance and fast release of goods, as well as reduce the cost of customs operations. This methodology focuses on revenue generation, trade facilitation, and efficiency of the customs services. The questions are formulated through a self-assessment approach, but could also be used by outside advisers working in close cooperation with customs officials.

**Pulling Together Key Elements: The WCO Capacity Building Toolkit**  The WCO's Customs Capacity Building Diagnostic Framework is being

---

9. More recently, The International Chamber of Commerce elaborated Customs Guidelines that are consistent with the toolkit of the World Bank (see www.iccwbo.org).

10. This diagnostic tool also inspired the forthcoming WCO Capacity Building Tool.

prepared in response to requests from WCO members for a sound methodology that could lead to sustainable improvements in customs administrations, particularly those in the developing world. It aims at bringing together, into one document, the key elements and foundations deemed necessary to establish an efficient and effective customs administration. It will be based on the internationally agreed conventions (Kyoto Convention, Arusha Declaration, the ACV, and the HS) as well as on the instruments and best-practice approaches for modern customs administrations. It will advocate full adherence to these conventions as a guide to the proposed modernization. The framework will include a readiness assessment guide for each of the core components of a comprehensive capacity building program, and a practical guide on how to conduct diagnostic assessments. It advocates that the assessment be undertaken by outside advisers with the active participation of stakeholders, including local customs officials. It should lead to the formulation of a prioritized action plan.

**Customs Blueprints** The European Commission has developed a set of 13 blueprints for assessing the state of customs administrations in accession countries. While intended essentially for future member states, these blueprints can be used to carry out a gap analysis in other countries.

### Desire to Reduce Trading Costs

Customs reform and modernization initiatives, together with improvements in ports and trade-related institutions, will lead to significant benefits in reducing trading costs and thus enhancing the competitiveness of a country, particularly if these initiatives focus on policy reform, technical assistance, and modernization of infrastructure. In this regard, the World Bank's Global Economic Prospects 2004 Report (GEP) estimates that if the countries that are currently below the world average in trade facilitation capacity could be raised half way to the average, trade among 75 countries would increase by US$377 billion annually (World Bank 2003). A recent study estimated that reducing the cost of international trade transactions by just 5 percent by 2006 could add US$154 billion or 0.9 percent to the Asia Pacific Economic Coopera-

tion region's GDP each year (APEC Economic Committee 2002). The same report concluded that customs reforms in Singapore, Thailand, and the Philippines are estimated to yield a US$3.9 billion increase in real annual income.

In addition to the above estimates, there are a number of other benefits related to the economic impact of customs reform and modernization initiatives. In the case of the Trade and Transport Facilitation in Southeast Europe program (TTFSE), for example, there has been a significant overall cost savings for trucks waiting at border crossing points or inland pilot terminals monitored through the TTFSE since the beginning of the project in 2000 (World Bank 2004). At inland pilot terminals, clearance times have, in all the six original members of the TTFSE, declined substantially. In Bulgaria and Bosnia they fell by 60 percent as a result of procedural improvements, preselection of declarations by a specialized unit, and advance processing of documents that are submitted by fax prior to the arrival of goods. The cost savings to transporters can thus be calculated based on the reduction in labor costs related to the lower waiting time and on greater efficiency in using the trucks. The GEP also estimates that every day spent in customs adds nearly 1 percent to the cost of goods. In developing countries transit costs are routinely two to four times higher than in rich ones. Hence, any program that makes transit operations more efficient and reduces clearance times is bound to enhance the country's competitiveness.

However, increased security arrangements in the wake of September 11 and worldwide worries about terrorism have sharply increased the costs of trade transactions. GEP estimates of the trade effects of September 11 show that world welfare declined by US$75 billion per year for each 1 percent increase in costs to trade from programs aimed at tightening border security.

A number of in-country practices tend to lower the benefits that could be brought about through customs modernization. These include resistance in implementing selectivity, lack of cooperation between border crossing agencies, excessive turnover of staff in customs, and minimal progress in addressing corruption. Customs modernization initiatives would do well to factor these possible negative reactions into the design of the reform program.

## Development of a Customs Modernization Strategy

A systematic approach to the design of the modernization strategy will enhance its chances of success. Proper attention to its content—partial or comprehensive, good sequencing, use of performance indicators, support of stakeholders, availability of adequate financial resources for implementation, and improved performance of other border agencies—will substantially benefit the customs reform process.

### Modernization Program: Comprehensive or Partial?

Most diagnoses of customs services will indicate gaps between the present state of affairs and the targeted state of affairs. The next step is to address the problems identified. There are various options for proceeding. Should a comprehensive process be designed and implemented or should partial or area-specific measures be taken depending on where successes can be achieved and on the readiness of the service? No easy answers can be found that could fit every circumstance. Yet some guidelines may be useful.

In practice, many customs reforms have been attempted using a pragmatic and area-specific approach. The general objective appears to have been to fix some urgent problems without modifying the overall functioning of customs operations. These reform initiatives have absorbed substantial domestic and external resources and have been mostly directed at strengthening budget revenue. Examples of such reforms are those that have introduced advanced IT, brought in a valuation system in accordance with the ACV, altered the management for special import regimes to support export processes, and reorganized the management structures.

Some of the partial reform initiatives have been successful. However, most observers agree that these initiatives have a poor record in terms of sustainable improvements to the overall efficiency and effectiveness of customs operations. Where the reforms were not well integrated into the overall customs operations, they had difficulties generating a substantial difference in the area where the original reform was targeted. A comprehensive reform, for instance, is necessary in implementing any customs-related WTO agreement, including the ACV. Also, automation initiatives not placed within the context of a comprehensive customs reform left an excessively complex and dysfunctional system. Some reforms failed to mobilize the necessary support of top customs officials, politicians, or the private sector—the essential element for sustainable modernization. On balance, isolated initiatives without comprehensive planning tend to be piecemeal and appear to be costly and unproductive, even if they pay for themselves in the short term. The experience with Bank-supported customs reforms fully supports this observation (see chapter 7).

The alternative approach to customs reform is to prepare a comprehensive reform program, with detailed, coherent, and well-sequenced steps, and a well-designed financing plan. Such reforms have a better chance of benefiting from the contextual factors mentioned above. The international donor community, frequently called upon to support the reforms, often favors such a comprehensive approach and stands ready to assist in phasing in the various reform components. Such comprehensive reform and modernization programs support staff training in the new procedures, and allow for adequate time to prepare the legal and regulatory environment, simplify customs processes before introducing an IT program, and call on outside advisers and service providers when necessary. All these actions can be dovetailed, thus enhancing the probability of arriving at a mutually supportive system that achieves the objectives and is sustainable over time. The case studies presented in chapters 6 and 7 seem to support this comprehensive approach.

Recent World Bank projects show that a holistic approach to reform can yield substantial results. Such projects are mainly results oriented, take a very pragmatic approach, and tackle the constraints and issues when and where they are encountered. For example, for a road project that involves border crossings, it is important that the various issues that would affect these crossings be tackled. This requires the involvement of other agencies in addition to customs. This approach can rapidly mobilize support outside the administration, and can include other ministries that have the capacity to support—or stall—the customs modernization process.

*Proper Sequencing and Pacing of Reforms*

Based on the diagnosis, reformers need to identify project components and prepare a timetable for their phased introduction. The logical framework to detail such a work program is likely to involve the following steps that can be managed by an appropriate computer software program: identify the objectives; detail the actions needed to reach each objective, ensure good sequencing, and identify the time path; establish performance criteria; identify the personnel and budgetary resources required; identify the individuals to be held accountable for implementing these actions; and set up a clear monitoring mechanism for people, instruments, and performance criteria.

Sequencing the reform measures and defining their timeframe are critical. These measures need to be carefully aligned unless delays emerge. For instance, when the diagnostic review indicates that customs processes are complex, involve multiple permissions and signatures, are costly, and delay the clearance of goods, a total revamping of the processes is called for. New processes will need to be designed. Implementing them may require that the import clearance organization be revamped, responsibilities be redesigned, staff be reassigned, and new staff trained. It may also require that offices be redesigned to accommodate the IT equipment and reduce the face-to-face contact between traders and their representatives, and the customs staff.

Only when the new procedures are agreed upon will it be possible to introduce modern IT support for processing trade transactions. A major failure of IT-driven reforms has been that the sequencing suggested above has often not been respected. Manual and computer-driven processes continue to exist side by side, negating IT's potential contribution to streamlining customs procedures. However, the introduction of IT takes time as software and hardware choices need to be made, and equipment needs to be procured and installed. In addition, staff needs to be trained in the use of the new technology to exploit the data that will become available for policy and enforcement purposes. All this requires careful phasing (chapter 13).

Another example that illustrates the importance of sequencing is one that determines the process steps required for successful implementation of risk assessment procedures. When the diagnosis indicates that customs clearing times are protracted, due in part to the practice of physically inspecting all containers, risk-based inspection processes become part of the answer. However, 100 percent inspection of imports are at times included in the Customs Code and probably stem from the view that all importers are equally likely to commit fraud, and that protecting budget revenues requires that all cargo be subjected to the same inspection process. This practice also maximizes face-to-face contact between importers and customs officials, something that modern customs practices try to avoid. The replacement of the 100 percent inspection practice with risk-based practices is one of the key provisions of the Revised Kyoto Convention and one that should be incorporated in customs modernization initiatives. This will require the refinement of risk management techniques and adjustment of operational procedures (chapter 5).

Program sequencing will need to be geared to the readiness of customs management and staff. It is argued that sufficient time must be allowed to train staff and prepare the ground for the measures proposed. This view supports a slow and gradual approach to bringing the staff on board. However, slow implementation may erode the momentum of the reform and allow forces that favor the status quo to mobilize. A middle-of-the-road approach is probably the best; not too slow so as to not lose momentum, and not too fast so as not to result in reform measures that cannot be implemented or sustained. Local preparedness for the reform as reflected in the diagnostic study, together with political commitment and assertiveness will largely determine the desired pace of the reform in any given country.

The reform program needs to take into account which measures may be outside the control of customs or the MOF. Compensation policies are often beyond their reach. At times the diagnostic study will show that low salaries in customs constitute a major obstacle to staff commitment and good performance. Customs reform cannot possibly alter the overall compensation policy of the civil service. Customs then is left with a limited set of choices: either do nothing on the compensation package or hope that noncompensation measures can be introduced to motivate staff. One measure may be to adjust bonus pay, for which some customs authorities have considerable latitude. A more drastic approach is one that provides for a salary scale in customs that is more generous than that being offered in the rest of the civil service. Reality, however, suggests that the effectiveness of customs services, and integrity issues, are unlikely to be satisfactorily addressed as long as low levels of staff compensation prevail (chapter 2).

The approach of the Moroccan customs service with respect to phasing reforms is interesting. It had available a comprehensive and detailed customs reform program that was prepared in the late 1990s with the assistance of outside consultants and the IMF. This program was used flexibly, mainly to provide a systematic sense of direction, and served as a general guide for policy reform measures that could be implemented. The year-by-year or even the month-by-month reform program, however, was based on an ongoing assessment of what was feasible in light of staff readiness and progress achieved. This approach was supported by a deliberate effort to explain the reforms to the staff, to gain the staff's broad adherence to the reform measures, and to give them credit for the successes achieved.

### Clear Performance Indicators

Performance indicators spell out what the reform program aims to achieve and provide a monitoring mechanism. The indicators should be designed with care and attention. The indicators force the reform designers to clarify and quantify the precise nature of the objectives they want to achieve. Effectiveness criteria aim to measure whether the objective has been fulfilled; efficiency indicators track the cost of obtaining the results. The diagnostic study should provide baseline data for both sets of indicators. Comparing the actual observations with the baseline data permits an assessment of the progress achieved and allows managers to evaluate whether the program is on track or needs to be adjusted. Stakeholders, government decisionmakers, and private sector users of customs services should have access to the evolution of these indicators while the reform program is being initiated, as well as after. In Morocco, for example, the time-release data is on the Internet and monthly updates are available for each point of

entry. Such transparency benefits the program and contributes to its continued support. Obviously, for indicators to remain relevant, they will need to keep pace with a sometimes rapidly changing environment.

Indicators are best used to assess progress over time. They can also be constructed for a single country or for a set of countries and compared across countries to stimulate the ones lagging behind.[11] In some cases, performance targets are included as project covenants. To generate these indicators, the reform program must strive to develop the statistical capacity to collect the necessary data and promptly transfer them to customs headquarters for analysis. The next sections describe effectiveness and efficiency indicators that have proven useful in designing customs reform programs.

**Effectiveness Indicators** *Revenue generation.* Many reforms are designed to improve the revenue generation performance at customs. Even if improving revenue performance were not the reform's key objective, the reform's impact in raising budget revenue would be closely monitored by MOF. Examples of such indicators include the following:

- Collected taxes as a share of overall imports or as a share of imports that do not benefit from special tax concessions for one reason or another. This statistic needs to be carefully adjusted for tariff changes during the observation period. Where possible, this share should be compared with the tax revenues that would have been collected using the statutory tariff rates to measure the gap between the actual and potential revenue.
- Share of total imports exempted from tariffs and duties, or monitoring of special duty regimes identified in the diagnostic as prone to fraud and lax treatment.
- Violations detected and revenues received by the Treasury as a result of adjusting the customs duty liability.
- Volume of contested or overdue import taxes.

---

11. The World Bank–funded TTFSE supports trade facilitation initiatives to Balkan countries. Indicators are constructed for each country.

*Trade facilitation.* Examples of trade facilitation indicators include the following:

- The cargo release-time indicator measures time spent processing documentation and releasing goods to the importer (see annex 1.C).[12] Correct measurement of time spent processing goods permits importers to place the blame for slow release on the institution responsible—customs, port authority, or government agencies in charge of enforcing agricultural, commercial, or safety standards. The TTFSE uses this indicator in combination with the waiting cost for trucks at the border and estimates the savings that result from reducing release time. For instance, a project in Bacau, Romania, reduced clearance time by 50 percent for an estimated annual savings of US$106 thousand.[13] The TTFSE also provides clear targets for each pilot border crossing for this purpose. According to UNCTAD studies of Zaire in the 1990s, the inventory costs to the consignee due to immobilization were estimated at 24 percent of total transit cost, adding to 6 percent, 3 percent, and 1 percent attributable to banking charges, government controls, and informal facilitating payments, respectively. Not all were due to ineffective customs services, but these estimates give an idea of the costs involved because of delays in cargo clearance. See OECD 2003.
- High rates of physical inspection of cargo delay the clearance of goods, and are also cumbersome, expensive, and provide temptation to engage in corrupt practices. Modern container stuffing methods are so efficient in economizing space that once the containers are opened and the items are extracted for inspection, customs or port and transport staff are often unable to replace all the contents. This forces the operator to find alternative means of onward transportation for part of the cargo, in addition to leaving the cargo vulnerable to damage and theft. In Morocco, the inspection rate fell from 100 percent in 1996 to 10 percent in 2003; the target is to reduce it further, to 5 percent. Reducing the rate of physical inspection cannot be isolated from other indicators and should be viewed in the context of risk management. (See annex 1.D for a further discussion of this issue.) One way of doing so is to combine the rate of detection of irregularity with the rate of inspection. If both are well done, the detection rate should go up as a percentage of inspection, implying both improved trade facilitation and more effective control.
- The time invested to produce reliable statistical import and export data is useful for the purposes of analyzing trade developments, and for the marketing purposes of the private sector.
- The number of import declarations that are managed through fast-track procedures for "authorized" importers with good compliance records might reflect a selective approach to physical inspection.
- Public perception of customs operations (trade facilitation and integrity) as reflected in customer satisfaction surveys can suggest either worsening of or improvement in cargo processing.[14]

*Security and Compliance.* The criteria can consist of the number and volume of drug seizures; the number of persons arrested, both incoming and outgoing (including illegal immigrants); and the rate of examination compared to rate of detection.

**Efficiency Criteria** Efficiency criteria indicators aim to measure the cost of delivering the service and are more difficult to quantify and interpret. Yet they are worth compiling because they focus on the good use of budgetary resources. At the margin, efficiency measures may indicate that improving

---

12. WCO (2002) provides a methodology to identify the bottlenecks of clearance procedures with concrete figures and to measure the effects of the introduction of new measures. The World Bank is supporting an initiative to design time-release software. Automated Systems for Customs Data (ASYCUDA) and other country-designed software provide time-release data. In Morocco, such data are provided for each port of entry and for normal and special regimes; data are released monthly on the Internet. In Bolivia, time-release statistics derived from the ASYCUDA software are prepared for the "Green," "Yellow," and "Red" channels and provided for four different phases of the customs clearance process. These results have pointed to the need for further process simplification and have also highlighted the lack of staff adherence to new processes (Mendoza and Gutierrez 2003). The TTFSE collates data on time release for the pilot sites of several countries and has ensured comparability of methodology.

13. See www.seerecon.org/ttfse.

14. The TTFSE program includes an annual user survey of importers and truck drivers that measures the public perception of corruption and impediments to trade.

effectiveness criteria further may be too expensive to pursue. These criteria should pertain as much to the internal costs of customs as to the costs of traders to adhere to customs procedures. The use of criteria to measure the cost for private traders to adhere to trade procedures, including customs procedures, is at its beginning stage. A U.K. organization, Simplifying International Trade (SITPRO), is extensively testing a methodology to do this.[15] Despite a promising start, the initiative is still too young for its practicality to be judged. Results are also not yet publicly available.

The TTFSE has gone farther than any other customs and trade facilitation program in identifying efficiency indicators. The indicators include revenue collected by customs staff; total revenue cost over revenue collected; salaries over revenue collected; trade volume per number of staff; customs declarations per number of staff; and cost per declaration. The results for each country, adjusted for extraneous factors that affect the absolute values of these indicators, are good meters for the direction of the efficient use of resources. Comparisons across countries may indicate the scope of possible improvement, but must be done carefully as many variables do affect the absolute value of these indicators in each country, which are often beyond the control of the customs services. For instance, the economic cost per declaration[16] in Albania in 2002 was US$24 compared to US$8 in Bulgaria. This obviously deserves further analysis before concluding that Albania's customs services are three times less efficient than Bulgaria's. More significant as an indicator of progress made is that these costs were substantially higher in 2001: US$33 in Albania and US$11 in Bulgaria. Similarly, the cost of collection in 2002 was estimated at 0.85 percent in Croatia compared to 2.6 percent in Serbia, down from 1.6 percent and 4.8 percent in 2001, respectively. A further example of how efficiency criteria can be compared across countries is shown in figure 1.1, which shows the number of declarations per staff per year for 10 Southeastern European countries.

### FIGURE 1.1   Number of Declarations per Staff per year in Southeast Europe, 2002

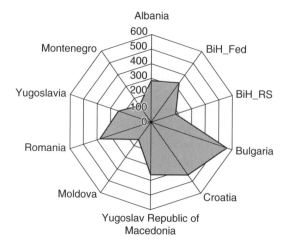

*Source:* Trade and Transport Facilitation in Southeast Europe, Regional Steering Committee.

### *The Role of Strategic Partners*

Customs processes affect the interests of a variety of stakeholders—customs staff responsible for financing government expenditure, other government agencies responsible for enforcing regulations pertaining to safety and phytosanitary standards, security personnel responsible for keeping out weapons, and traders who want to have fast and cheap access to their goods. The adherence of each of these stakeholders to the customs reform will determine its success. Any strategy should carefully manage relations with each of these stakeholders, bring them on board, and solicit their support.

**Customs Administrations Staff**   The success of the reform will stand or fall depending on the cooperation of the staff members or their implicit or explicit rejection of the reforms. They should "own" the reform. Customs staffs are responsible for the daily tasks of managing the trade processes. They receive the import declaration, verify the data provided, decide whether to physically inspect the goods, decide on many of the details that determine the access that exporters have to duty-free importer inputs, and determine the speed with which these operations are undertaken, just to name a few.

---

15. SITPRO is a U.K. nondepartmental public body for which the Department of Trade and Industry has responsibility. It receives grant-in-aid from the Department of Trade and Industry. SITPRO is dedicated to encouraging and helping business trade more effectively and to simplifying the international trading process. Its focus is on the procedures and documentation associated with international trade.

16. Total cost of the customs service divided by the number of declarations.

> ### BOX 1.1   Morocco Customs Gets Its Staff on Board for the Reform Program
>
> The staff compensation issue provides a good illustration of Morocco's efforts to bring its staff on board.
>
> - Management involved staff in the design of the reform initiatives instead of relying on outside service providers, and consulted staff on overall customs policy orientations.
> - A new Intranet was created to inform staff of the details of the reform initiatives and how this would affect them. The Intranet also assisted them in previously complex transactions such as vacation scheduling.
> - A staff attitude survey was launched and measures are being taken to improve areas of staff concern.
>
> - Staff members were reclassified according to their qualifications and the backlog of promotions was absorbed.
> - The bonus system was streamlined and attempts are underway to gear them more closely to staff performance.
> - Staff training was revamped and a detailed manual of procedures was provided online to all frontline staff. A standard schedule of fines and guidelines that give staff greater assurance in their discussions with private sector traders was also posted online.
>
> *Source:* Steenlandt and De Wulf 2004.

Because they are the frontline implementers of the reforms, with manifold contact with traders or their representatives, they impart an image of the customs administration. (See box 1.1.)

Customs clearance activities are the responsibility of customs officers who largely determine how these activities are undertaken. New procedures can be provided, automation installed, and integrity proclamations made. However, in the final analysis, the services will only be as good as the staff that provides them. For instance, when staffs reject a new IT system, they can boycott or even sabotage its introduction.[17] Staffs will tend to buy in to the objectives of the reform if they understand in detail what this means for customs generally and for themselves as individuals. Resistance to change frequently stems from mistrust and uncertainties; thus, staffs need to be brought on board. For example, when introducing risk-based inspections and strengthening post-release audits, it will be crucial to show staffs what this will mean in terms of work processes, training, and so forth. However, one should not expect good information to stop all opposition to reforms, as there will be winners and losers in any reform process.

Improving overall compensation is critical. When salaries do not cover basic family expenses it is not surprising that staff members might enhance their incomes by other, at times illegitimate, means. Recognizing this, several customs reforms have substantially enhanced salary levels (chapter 2).

One further example of associating staff closely to the sometimes controversial aspects of customs reform is the issue of how to make use of the services of a preshipment inspection (PSI) company without creating the hostile or demoralizing environment that such cooperation often brings. Peru and Mauritania are good examples of PSI operations being broadly accepted by customs staff. Such contracts function better if they are negotiated and undertaken by customs administrations rather than if they are imposed on customs by the MOF on behalf of the national government (chapter 2).

**Ministry of Finance**   The MOF is an important stakeholder because of its interest in revenue mobilization. Reform must give the ministry confidence that customs' revenue generation potential will not be undermined but enhanced. In particular, computerization brings better control over the documentary processing system, and ensures that all transactions are recorded, thus improving the rate of collection. Customs automation is expensive in terms of new software and hardware, improved communications equipment, and staff training. The MOF would be favorably impressed if presented with evidence that automation would accelerate

17. This has occasionally happened with the introduction of customs information systems—communications cables disappeared overnight and power cuts affected computerized data capture at border locations (Central Europe), computer equipment was destroyed (Bangladesh in early 1990s), databases and computers were stolen (Africa); at one location the roof of the computer room was broken to let rain ruin the IT equipment.

customs clearance and thus portray a good image to the outside world and attract FDI. However, what will convince the MOF to free up adequate budgetary resources will be the assurance that revenue performance will be enhanced. One example is provided by the Philippines, which freed budgetary resources in 2003 because of the expectations that the reforms would lead to substantially higher revenues (Bernardo 2003). Also, the MOF will subscribe to selective physical inspection of cargo only if it is convinced that the post-clearance audit functions are carefully designed and carried out. The same argument applies to the strict implementation of the ACV.

**Private Sector Stakeholders**    Traders are the most likely supporters of customs reforms. They are the first to benefit from more transparent and speedier processes and are also the first to complain about ineffective and costly services. Engaging them during the reform design and implementation and keeping them informed of its progress is crucial. Professional associations have considerable political clout that not only can be mustered to ensure that the budget provides the necessary support, but also can be used to pressure other government agencies to align their performances to that of improved customs performances. The private sector can also monitor progress and direct its focus to trade facilitation objectives. It may assist financially in the implementation of the reforms because it is among the first beneficiaries, as was the case in the Philippines and Turkey. In return for this support, the private sector can be formally consulted on reform initiatives that would be of particular interest. In Southeast Europe, "PRO-Committees" were established in every country, under the South East Cooperation Initiative (SECI) and Stability Pact umbrellas.[18] They regularly review facilitation issues, make recommendations for changes, and lobby the appropriate government agencies.

In the Philippines, under the World Economic Forum (WEF) initiative, private sector contacts were formalized with the creation of a Local Stakeholders Steering Committee that works closely with the Bureau of Customs (BOC) on behalf of civil society. The committee has an oversight responsibility over the implementation phase of the reforms. A first outcome was the donation by the semiconductor and electronics industry of the hardware, telecommunications link to the BOC systems, and front-end computers for its Automatic Export Documentation Systems. In Ghana, the creation of the Ghana TradeNet (GCNet) benefited from close private sector participation. In Turkey, the private sector built a number of border posts and operated them under the Build, Operate, and Transfer model.

However, not all private sector operators will fully support reforms. Clearly some derive advantages from the opacity within which customs operations take place. Through bribery, private sector operators are at times able to reduce their import tax burden, thus diminishing the benefits they expect to derive from a more transparent and faster release system. In this connection, Pakistani textile and garment exporters did not support the introduction of transparent methods to calculate drawback refunds, as this would eliminate subsidies embedded in the old refund system (OECD 2003).

### External Advice

There is much expertise worldwide in managing good customs services. Donors are eager to offer advice because improving customs services has a high priority in their assistance programs. Multilateral and bilateral institutions, as well as private consulting firms, are active in this area. Often, the coordination of such advice is inadequate. Customs advisers, coming from a variety of organizations, are frequently unaware of earlier advice given on the same subjects that they are called upon to consider. At times their advice is repetitive or, worse still, contradictory or inconsistent, thus ensuring that it will either be ignored or poorly applied. Obviously, a country may wish to ask for advice on the same topic from various sources as part of a deliberate strategy, but would often gain if it were to coordinate such assistance more carefully. Moreover, rather than being demand driven, these capacity building activities are often driven by the donor's own agenda for geopolitical reasons or for the sake of spending a budget to secure next year's allocation. Such support should be mobilized and, more importantly, coordinated by customs.

---

18. PRO-Committees consist of representatives of the private sector and the administrations involved in the cross-border movements of goods.

Often, TA is provided under projects aimed at the broader trade or transport development agenda. World Bank support has been framed in the context of civil service reform (Bolivia), export promotion (Bangladesh), revenue mobilization (Lebanon), or trade and transport facilitation (TTFSE in the Balkans). However, other support operations focused single-mindedly on customs reform (support for Russia customs, chapter 7). While the Bank is organized to lend to individual countries, there have been initiatives where a series of country projects were combined under a regional program (the TTFSE program, for example). This has resulted in economies of scale, closer regional integration, use of peer pressure to promote reforms, and sharing of best practice models. It has also proven to be a cost-effective way of channeling technical assistance.

The IMF has a long tradition of supporting customs reforms (Keen 2003). The IMF makes diagnostic assessments available, and assists governments in the preparation and implementation of reform strategies by providing long-term resident technical assistants. The WCO has placed at the disposal of member countries an arsenal of capacity-building initiatives, while the WTO provides support for introduction of the ACV. Bilateral agencies have also been active with advice and by stationing customs experts in developing countries for extended periods of time.

Providing TA is expensive, not only for the development agencies involved, but also for the recipient countries that often have to contribute to these assignments and allocate staff in support of the TA. There are indications that some of this assistance has not been sustainable, in part because of a failure to effectively transfer knowledge, or because what was transferred became inapplicable because customs was not receptive to the changes proposed.[19] Developing countries and development agencies owe it to themselves to periodically conduct critical reviews of the impact of their TA, particularly in terms of sustainability.

### Financing Plan

A full-fledged customs reform that includes automation upgrades and communications infra-structure is expensive. World Bank projects have often moved into the tens of millions of dollars and even to more than a hundred million. Reform expenditures should ultimately be self-financing through the improvement of revenue mobilization. However, some expenses are exceptionally heavy at the outset of the reform, particularly those related to the IT component of a project. Foreign financing frequently covers these.

Maintaining and upgrading IT equipment is expensive, particularly in light of the short and shortening IT cycle. When financing to maintain and upgrade IT equipment is not adequately included in future budgets, it undermines the efficiency of the initial investments. In the Philippines, hardly any maintenance expenses were applied after the installation of the IT equipment. The frequent outages experienced led to severe service disruptions and revenue loss, equivalent to several million dollars. The envisaged overhaul will be more expensive and disruptive of operations than periodic maintenance and upgrading would have been. Similar situations have occurred in other countries. The key lesson from the experiences of a number of countries is to build relations with the international institutions that can contribute to financing the large up-front costs, and to prepare the budget authorities for the significant annual budget allocations required for the upkeep of the IT infrastructure.

### Collaboration with Other Government Agencies

Trade relies on the services of a large number of agencies and service providers, who are all participants in the trade logistics chain. Hence, a reform limited only to customs will be substantially less effective than if other agencies and service providers were to enhance their performance too. At times, several agencies responsible for quality standards undertake separate inspections and take samples to ensure that imports conform to local quality standards. This can add substantially to the cost of imports. A study found that, at least until recently, import verification and standards inspection (applied to 50 percent of all imports) in Egypt could add 5 to 90 percent to the cost of imports. These costs could have been drastically reduced if, among other reforms, the Egyptian standards agency General Organization for Import and

---

19. For instance, seminars on WTO valuation requirements are not effective if the customs organizations the participants come from are not equipped for the required changes.

Export Control would have accepted quality certifications delivered by accredited certification companies and if local quality standards were aligned to internationally recognized ones. (See Nathan Associates 1998 and 1996.) The agency in charge of nuclear safety is also frequently involved, as are the security forces, which at times insist on participating in each and every physical inspection of cargo. In some cases, border police officials insist on either selecting the consignments for inspection by customs on the basis of criteria unrelated to customs risk management, or re-inspecting every shipment on the grounds of "fighting corruption in customs" (which should be dealt with in another manner anyway), or "combating smuggling" (which is not their mandate). Transport agencies, ports, and airports often also represent weak links in the logistics chain.

In theory, there is no reason why these different agencies, each with their own legitimate concerns, could not join forces with customs in applying advanced risk profiling methodologies to reduce intrusive inspections. The methodology would involve selecting a limited number of shipments for inspection, focusing on those that present risks, and releasing the others rapidly. In the process, the methodology would institute an effective post-release audit control. (See chapter 5.) In developing countries there are no examples of such cooperation yet, but the approach is gaining ground in several transition countries (Serbia for example). There is also evidence that discussions between customs and these other agencies are often stalled by jurisdictional rivalry.

Efficient customs operations also depend on a good legal environment and on the way judgments are rendered and enforced, on a banking system that can provide guarantees and ensure timely payments, and on port and warehouse services that operate efficiently if the improvements in time-release that result from customs reforms are not swamped by inefficiency on their part. In addition, a good communications system is needed to interconnect the various customs offices, and to permit the gradual integration of the various participants into the trade transaction through the implementation of the "single window" concept. The advances made by Singapore and Mauritius in effecting such integration under the TRADENET initiative (also being rolled out in Ghana and planned for intro-

duction in Cameroon and Tunisia) clearly illustrate the efficiency gains to be obtained by connecting all participants in one tight system.

Probably the best way to involve these other agencies in customs reforms is to cast the reform within the broader context of trade and competitiveness reforms. Customs rarely takes charge of such reforms, but constitutes a core agency and can play an active role in outreach to other agencies. In any event, with many agencies involved, the reform program should be a genuine government program, rather than a customs or MOF program. It should be one that attracts attention and active leadership from influential members of political and civil society. In the absence of such leadership, the benefits of a customs reform will be more limited than the economy deserves.

## Implementation of a Customs Modernization Strategy

Implementing a customs modernization strategy requires authority, dedication, progress monitoring, and adjustments to the strategy to take account of progress achieved as well as lessons learned. These elements are not different from those that form part of the implementation process of any other reform. A few brief suggestions may be in order.

### Leadership

Dedicated leadership will help to ensure that the reform remains on the agenda of the various policymakers inside and outside customs. With the substantial workload and diverse emergencies that customs managers often have to deal with, it may be best to assign the management of the reform program to a dedicated customs official, assisted by a small team of experts. However, it is always the Director General of Customs who should take the lead, with strong support from the government. Foreign technical staff could become part of this reform management team, but should not take a leadership role except in special circumstances. Their role should be to transfer knowledge, not to implement change. The practical shape of the direct leadership position needs to adapt to local circumstances. Those given this assignment should be recognized inside and outside of customs for

---

**BOX 1.2    An Example of Regional Leadership: The TTFSE Regional Steering Committee**

All the countries that borrowed from the Bank to support their trade and transport facilitation projects aimed, under a memorandum of understanding signed in Skopje in 2002, to establish a Regional Steering Committee (RSC). The objectives of the RSC are to:

- exchange information on border-crossing operations
- review and consider obstacles to trade
- provide a forum for sharing results
- monitor pilot site operations and promote the establishment of local cross-border customs and border agency committees
- cooperate with national and regional trade professional committees (the "PRO-Committees")
- consider policies and measures to implement international standards in relation to customs personnel (that is, the WCO's Arusha declaration)

- exchange information on national strategies, including action plans, and review progress
- consider new applications for access to the TTFSE.

The RSC now meets twice a year. Each country is represented by a National Coordinator, who can be either the Minister of Finance, or the Director General of Customs. When the National Coordinator is the Director General of Customs, he or she is mandated by the government to speak on behalf of all other border agencies.

The RSC can also establish specialized working groups (for example, IT exchanges of data), and can organize regional actions (like the joint U.S. Customs—WCO workshop on risk management in September 2003, or a self-assessment on integrity, based on the WCO methodology, in the fall of 2003).

*Source:* Michel Zarnowiecki, The World Bank.

---

their integrity and expert knowledge of customs operations, should benefit from the backing of top customs management, and should have direct access to management. They should also ensure outreach to the other stakeholders (box 1.2).

*Flexible Implementation*

The implementation plan is the key tool for monitoring the reform process. It will have a detailed timeline for implementation of the proposed actions and will identify individuals to be held accountable for keeping to this timeline. Keeping the program on track requires the various steps to be monitored, implementation problems to be detected early on, and corrective actions taken as necessary. Progress should be regularly communicated to the head of customs, to the MOF, and to the Cabinet. Flexibility will be required, because plans never work as scheduled and the unforeseen must be dealt with swiftly. The management team will need to be given sufficient flexibility to reallocate resources or to have rapid access to managers that have the authority to do so. Effectiveness indicators and efficiency criteria play a crucial role in

this course of action because they focus on achievements rather than processes.

*Involvement of Stakeholders*

Much is to be gained by keeping in close communication with all stakeholders to ensure that the reforms respond to their initial objectives and do not become part of the routine work of customs. Periodic and well-prepared assessment meetings that are open to all stakeholders should take place to inform stakeholders of progress made, problems encountered, and measures proposed to address slippages and changed circumstances. A periodic stakeholder survey should be conducted to assess stakeholders' satisfaction with the results of the reforms. This is the approach utilized by Morocco, which annually undertakes a survey, publishes its results, and reports on the measures that customs management promises to undertake to address issues. In Southeast Europe, there is an annual user survey designed to measure user satisfaction, evaluate the level of corruption, and, in conjunction with the border performance indicators, validate and compute average costs and delays along the major transport corridors.

## Operational Conclusions

Customs reform has absorbed large amounts of domestic resources from reforming countries as well as TA and financial assistance from the international donor community. A number of observers do, however, agree that in many developing countries customs administrations are in need of further modernization and reform to deliver effective and efficient services. Countries need to achieve adequate customs service standards if they are to contribute to the competitiveness of the economy, expand exportation activities, and attract FDI. The main messages of this chapter can be summarized in the following points:

- Good customs operations consist of coherent and interlocking sets of processes. Partial reforms can improve some aspects of the services, but sustainable progress will only be achieved when the reform positively affects the various key elements of the customs processes. Coherence of the reform will be undermined if crucial parts of the customs processes continue to operate under the older, dysfunctional systems. For instance, implementing the ACV, without at the same time having a good post-clearance audit system in place, will not work as intended. Reform projects that overly stress the implementation of advanced IT without prior streamlining of the trade processes themselves will likely fail, too. (Annex 1.E provides a checklist of issues that deserve attention in preparing a reform strategy.)
- Good diagnostic work is essential in identifying the shortcomings of the existing system, in defining the main strategies of the proposed reform, and in mobilizing support.
- The reforms should be "owned" by customs, whose responsibility it is to ensure the coherence of donor support; such support must be seen as temporary and must be delivered in such a way as to contribute to the sustainability of the reform.

- The reforms must be realistic. They must conform to implementation capacities and to the support they receive at the political level. Many experts know how a good customs service should be run. The art is in drawing on this expertise and preparing an ambitious but pragmatic reform program that will enhance the effectiveness and efficiency of customs operations.
- Customs reforms need the leadership of customs' top management, as well as the support of customs staff and other stakeholders. While an ownership approach by customs officials is critically important, it is equally critical to bring all stakeholders on board at the planning stage as well as at the implementation stage of the reforms. Stakeholders' voices need to be heard and the program needs to address their concerns. Both the MOF, with its concern for revenue mobilization, and the private sector, with its concern for trade facilitation, should be integral partners in the customs reform process. Efforts to make them outspoken supporters of the modernization efforts are likely to prove beneficial.
- Political support for customs is essential for the reform's success. Reforming trade processes will challenge the status quo, where benefits are provided to some, inside and outside of customs. Opposition to the reform program is to be expected. In some cases opposition will take the political route, in others the boycott route. Only support at the highest level will enable customs management to overcome anticipated obstacles. Customs managers will need the explicit support of the political leadership as well as access to top leadership.
- Using clear performance indicators to monitor the progress of the reform is essential, not only to evaluating progress, but also to adjusting the reform measures to changing circumstances, without losing sight of the big picture.

**Annex 1.A.1 Customs Revenue as a Share of Tax Revenue in Selected Countries, 2001 (percent of total tax revenue)**

| Region or Country | | Region or Country | |
|---|---|---|---|
| **Africa** | 28.7 | **Middle East** | 22.3 |
| Botswana | 37.2 | Bahrain | 41.4 |
| Burundi | 18.4 | Egypt | 20.0 |
| Cameroon | 31.6 | Iran, Islamic Rep. of | 18.4 |
| Côte d'Ivoire | 27.6 | Israel | 0.9 |
| Ethiopia | 29.3 | Jordan | 20.4 |
| Gambia, The | 44.5 | Kuwait | 71.5 |
| Kenya | 16.8 | Morocco | 20.1 |
| Lesotho | 22.8 | Oman | 10.4 |
| Mauritius | 32.8 | Pakistan | 15.4 |
| Rwanda | 30.3 | Syrian Arab Rep. | 11.7 |
| Sierra Leone | 49.8 | Tunisia | 15.4 |
| South Africa | 3.0 | | |
| | | **Western Hemisphere** | 13.3 |
| **Asia and Pacific** | 14.9 | Argentina | 8.0 |
| Fiji | 22.7 | Bahamas, The | 50.1 |
| India | 24.1 | Bolivia | 6.9 |
| Indonesia | 4.7 | Brazil | 5.8 |
| Myanmar | 7.2 | Colombia | 8.5 |
| Papua New Guinea | 24.2 | Costa Rica | 6.6 |
| Philippines | 19.6 | Ecuador | 11.8 |
| Sri Lanka | 12.7 | El Salvador | 10.0 |
| Thailand | 3.9 | Guatemala | 12.4 |
| | | Nicaragua | 10.5 |
| | | Panama | 20.2 |
| | | Paraguay | 17.5 |
| | | Peru | 12.8 |
| | | Uruguay | 4.1 |
| | | Venezuela, R. B. de | 12.9 |

*Note:* For some countries, data are from an earlier year. Regional data are unweighted averages of countries in the sample.
*Source:* World Bank estimates, IMF Government Finance Statistics.

## Annex 1.B.1 Collected Tariff Rates for Selected Countries by World Region, 2001 (percent)

| Region or Country | CTR | Region or Country | CTR | Region or Country | CTR |
|---|---|---|---|---|---|
| *All countries* | 9.5 | | | | |
| **OECD countries**[a] | 1.1 | **Non-OECD** | 11.78 | **Middle East** | 12.5 |
| Australia | 3.5 | Africa | 16.8 | Bahrain | 3.6 |
| Austria | 0.4 | Botswana | 15.6 | Egypt | 18.9 |
| Belgium | 0.7 | Burundi | 16.6 | Iran, Islamic Rep. of | 28.1 |
| Canada | 0.9 | Cameroon | 26.9 | Israel | 0.8 |
| Denmark | 0.7 | Cote d'Ivoire | 18.4 | Jordan | 7.1 |
| Finland | 0.4 | Ethiopia | 15.7 | Kuwait | 3.2 |
| France | 0.5 | Gambia, The | 14.0 | Morocco | 16.7 |
| Germany | 0.7 | Kenya | 12.4 | Oman | 2.6 |
| Greece | 0.7 | Lesotho | 26.3 | Pakistan | 10.3 |
| Iceland | 1.2 | Mauritius | 10.5 | Syrian Arab Rep. | 38.9 |
| Ireland | 0.4 | Rwanda | 18.4 | Tunisia | 7.4 |
| Italy | 0.6 | Sierra Leone | 26.6 | | |
| Japan | 3.6 | South Africa | 3.2 | **Western Hemisphere** | 7.3 |
| Mexico | 1.9 | Zimbabwe | 13.1 | Argentina | 7.4 |
| Netherlands | 0.9 | | | Bahamas, The | 21.7 |
| New Zealand | 2.0 | **Asia and Pacific** | 10.5 | Bolivia | 4.1 |
| Norway | 0.9 | Fiji | 10.4 | Brazil | 9.4 |
| Spain | 0.2 | India | 23.3 | Colombia | 7.3 |
| Sweden | 0.6 | Indonesia | 2.2 | Costa Rica | 2.1 |
| Switzerland | 0.8 | Korea, Rep. of[b] | 4.0 | Ecuador | 7.5 |
| Turkey | 1.4 | Malaysia | 3.2 | El Salvador | 4.9 |
| United Kingdom | 0.9 | Myanmar | 35.6 | Guatemala | 4.5 |
| United States | 1.7 | Nepal | 10.9 | Nicaragua | 3.1 |
| | | Papua New Guinea | 14.6 | Panama | 8.1 |
| | | Philippines | 6.0 | Paraguay | 6.1 |
| | | Singapore | 0.2 | Peru | 9.3 |
| | | Sri Lanka | 4.9 | Uruguay | 4.3 |
| | | Thailand | 10.0 | Venezuela, R.B. de | 10.4 |

CTR = collected tariff rates. Regional averages are unweighted averages of countries in the sample.

*Notes:* For some countries, data are from an earlier year. For Mexico, free-on-board (FOB) imports were used instead of cost, insurance, and freight (CIF) imports.

a. Excluding the Czech Republic, Hungary, Luxembourg, and Poland.

b. The Republic of Korea joined the OECD in December 1996.

*Source:* World Bank estimates, IMF Government Finance Statistics, and International Financial Statistics.

## Annex 1.C Time-Release Methodology

One of the most widely used performance indicators to measure customs effectiveness is the time it takes for customs to release goods.[20] For many years, customs reforms were launched without proper assessment of their impact. Various customs authorities publish their release times and the WCO has issued a methodology to measure release times so that the findings are comparable across countries.

The chain of processes that imports go through from the time of their arrival in a country to their release can be shown in 11 discrete steps

---

20. This appendix was written by Gael Raballand, Economist, Trade Department, World Bank.

**BOX 1.C.1    The Steps to Release Goods from Time of Arrival**

| Steps | Customs Participation |
|---|---|
| 1. Arrival of the goods | |
| 2. Unloading of the goods | |
| 3. Delivery to a customs area, where goods are generally temporarily stored | yes |
| 4. Lodgment of the declaration | yes |
| 5. Payment of duties and duty discrepancies (can take place after step 9) | yes |
| 6. Acceptance of the declaration | yes |
| 7. Documentary control | yes |
| 8. Physical inspection | yes |
| 9. Control of other agencies such as standards or phytosanitary | |
| 10. Goods released by customs | yes |
| 11. Actual removal from the port, airport, or land border post premises | |

*Source:* Author.

(box 1.C.1). This articulation may differ somewhat among countries, but almost all the events are present in every country. The type of goods being imported also has an effect on the process being followed.

Measurement of time release is a worthwhile exercise as it can establish a pre-reform benchmark and thus help in assessing progress made by modernization initiatives. In addition, it permits comparisons across countries, but only if the methodology adopted is identical.

Two different approaches can be taken regarding this issue: an overall trade logistics perspective and a more customs-oriented perspective.

### The Trade Logistics Perspective

From the overall trade logistics perspective, it is important to take into account the whole process. Indeed, from an importer's point of view, it is the overall time that the goods are detained before release that affects the transaction costs. The measurement should consider the time duration from arrival of the goods into the border post until they are physically released. This would measure the effectiveness of all operators involved in this transaction, including port authorities, warehouse management, control agencies, brokers, customs, the banking sector, and so forth. Such an analysis was undertaken in the Philippines, Japan, and in the

context of the TTFSE (Trade and Transport Facilitation in Southeast Europe) program.

Without distinguishing the causes of the delay in the release of goods, the TTFSE, for instance, adopted a "black box" approach, measuring the time releases from arrival to physical release. This allows data to be compared across different countries in Southeast Europe, but is best used to compare performance over time in a given country or border station. This effectiveness measurement was complemented by other indicators that measured the efficiency of customs operations such as the revenue collected per staff and the number of declarations per staff.

Another approach for obtaining data on trade facilitation is through firm surveys. Such data are generally less reliable as they reflect subjective opinions about time release rather than objective measurements. As a result, a large standard deviation among respondents results. Moreover, due to the costs of conducting this type of survey, they are only available from time to time without any real possibility of comparisons over time. One example of this type of study is the World Business Environment Survey.[21]

---

21. The World Business Environment Survey is the only large source regarding firm surveys' time-release data. A large-scale survey of more than 10,000 firms was conducted in 80 countries in 1999–2000 on many aspects of the regulatory environment (World Bank 2002).

*The Customs-Oriented Approach*

The time-release study could detail the time it takes for each of the steps identified in box 1.C.1 for which customs bears the sole responsibility. Such a study would suggest where bottlenecks exist and how they can be eased by actions and initiatives in which customs has primary authority.

Some estimates of time release related solely to customs are available, but they cannot be fully compared across countries because of methodological differences in their compilation. This is generally due to the local nature of customs procedures and a lack of harmonization of the measurement methodologies. For instance, in Bolivia, time measurement starts when the declaration is lodged in the ASYCUDA system even if the broker could have arrived many hours earlier and may have tried to submit his declaration, but with errors. In the case of the Philippines, the first step measured is "the arrival to lodgment," which includes the unloading as well as the processing and issuance of the import permit by noncustoms agencies. This step is, by far, the longest step in the Philippine procedure: 60 percent of the total release time in the case of seaport and 72 percent in the case of airports is taken up by the time lapse between the arrival of the goods and the lodgment at customs. It is unclear whether this delay is due to port inefficiency or to other controlling agencies' involvement.

To disentangle the responsibility of various actors within customs, one could measure the time between the different customs-related steps. To promote standardization of these measurements, WCO issued a guide to measure the time release and the World Bank, in partnership with WCO, is developing software that will provide an objective basis for this measurement (WCO 2002). The new software is expected to be fully compatible with the various automated customs management systems currently in operation. This tool should permit the measurement of time-release data in a manner that would be fully comparable across countries.

*Some Illustrative Results*

Time release may differ among different types of products, depending on what control agencies are involved, port of entry (airport or seaport), country of origins, and which verification channels (green, yellow, or red) the goods are assigned to after risk analysis has been performed. The whole logistical process can be assessed, and detailed customs-oriented information can be compiled.

In the case of the Philippines, the study calculates release time for goods that enter using different verification channels (green, yellow, and red lanes), broad commodity classifications, commodity value, country of origin, arrival location (port or airport), mode of payment, VAT exemption, exemption from payment of duties, lodgment days, mode of lodgment (electronically or not), and period of lodgment (UPECON 2003). (See box 1.C.2.)

---

**BOX 1.C.2   The Philippines Time-Release Study: An Example to Follow**

The Philippine customs authority has published detailed data on time release. The study distinguishes differences along selectivity status (color lanes), commodity class, commodity value, country of origin, arrival location (port or airport), mode of payment, VAT-exempted or not, exemption from payment of duties, lodgment days, mode of lodgment (electronically or not), and period of lodgment within a day.

In most cases, intuitions were confirmed. For instance, time release in ports is longer than in airports, and textile products and motor vehicles are cleared faster than food items (102 and 109 hours respectively, compared to 119 hours, probably because of the intervention of control agencies).

This type of study can also raise issues for further inquiry. For instance, by country of origin, Chinese goods should take longer to release than goods imported from ASEAN countries due to the fact that most Chinese goods enter the red lane and there is preferential treatment for imports from ASEAN countries due to membership in the Asian Free Trade Association (AFTA). On the contrary, it was found that the time to clear goods from ASEAN countries is longer than for goods coming from China (136 hours compared to 98 hours). The total customs processing time was shorter for Chinese goods in comparison with ASEAN goods (23 hours instead of 35 hours).

*Source:* UPECON 2003.

Several other studies suggest that time release differs for different types of products. For agro-products, time release was almost 40 percent longer when controlling agencies (other than customs) are involved. The port of entry also affects time release as airports are usually better organized than seaports, and can handle different categories of cargo that tend to make cargo clearance less complicated. In the case of Tema port in Ghana, it was calculated that 44 percent of the clearances occur within two days whereas at the airport 90 percent of the goods were cleared in 24 hours. Even among ports in the same country, time release can differ. In Morocco in September 2003, it was reported that the average time release was 31 minutes at Tangier port, but 50 minutes at Agadir port (Morocco government). In Bolivia, it was assessed that between the most efficient border post (Pisiga, at the Chilean border), and the least efficient (Yacuiba, at the Argentinean border), the average time release was almost 30 times lower in Pisiga than in Yacuiba (Mendora 2003). On the basis of this study, customs authorities identified some administrative measures to streamline the process in some border posts.

The Bolivia study also identifies differences in clearance time by the types of inspections to which goods are subject. After lodgment declaration, three possible actions have been defined: green for immediate release, yellow for documentary control, and red for physical inspection of goods. From a survey conducted from January to June 2003, average time release for a cargo assigned to the green lane was 39 minutes, 49 minutes for the yellow lane, and 71 minutes for the red lane.

### Conclusion

Time-release data represent a powerful performance assessment tool that enable the measurement of the effectiveness of customs services and the monitoring of progress.

They permit the creation of a detailed diagnostic of the time it takes to process goods and an examination of differences across different types of commodities, ports, and import regimes. They may also contribute to the monitoring of the impact of any customs reform. In addition, they can help to identify potential corrective actions.

## Annex 1.D Physical Inspection as an Element of Risk Management

There is a tendency in recent customs projects to use the rate of physical inspections as a shorthand indicator for trade facilitation. Doubtless, the trading community likes this indicator and wants to see it drop, as physical inspections can be intrusive, time consuming, and costly. Yet, the rate of physical inspections should only be thought of as a valid performance indicator when considered in the wider context of risk management used on the part of customs. At the margin it is possible to have no inspections and maximum trade facilitation, at the cost of serious revenue erosion. This annex provides some further clarification on the use of risk management in the context of physical inspection of cargo, and can also be read as a complement to chapter 5. A fuller treatment of this subject can be found in the WCO Risk Management Guidelines that can be found at www.wcoomd.org.

The rate of physical inspection is only one of a set of risk containment strategies and should be evaluated in the context of other strategies such as anti-smuggling, valuation, or rules of origin inspections. While physical inspection plays a role in these strategies, much of the risk containment strategy will depend on other customs interventions, many of which can take place after the goods have been released.

The rate of physical inspection may be useful as a performance indicator if applied in conjunction with the performance of revenue mobilization. A reduction in the rate of physical inspection that coincides with a stable or improved revenue performance suggests that trade facilitation (implied by the lower inspection rate) did not come at the expense of revenues. It suggests that the inspection rate is targeted at the most risky shipments and is well executed, involving more than just opening the tailgate of a container. Inspections, of course, can be better conducted if they are fewer and undertaken by better-trained staff.

### Selectivity in Physical Inspection

The use of selectivity for cargo inspection is only an application of the general principle of selectivity in control at the border, for documentary control, or for post-clearance audits. The principles involved are the same and consist of establishing a combination of risk indicators, weighing them, and, finally, applying them systematically to trade transactions to select those transactions that are to be subjected to a particular type of control. This combination of risk indicators can be called a risk profile.

The quality of the risk profile depends, of course, on the data that are used to draw up the profile. Intensive use of IT and data mining has, in recent times, greatly enhanced the possibility of preparing relevant profiles. Modern IT can periodically update the risk profiles of transactions to ensure that profiles adjust to changes in trade patterns or to seasonality (for example, in Morocco the risk profile is adjusted during periods prior to Ramadan when large amounts of luxury food products are imported). However, these profiles cannot be better than the data on which they are based. These data are drawn from customs declarations (HS, value, origin), tariff rates, and inspection results. Only when these data are available can a systematic risk profile be established. Even then, the incidence of smuggling and bribery are not represented in these databases, suggesting the data's limitations. Many customs administrations do not have these data or do not have them in a format that can be extracted properly.

Risk coefficients for particular shipments are determined by, among other factors, the classification of goods, origin of the goods, the traders involved, and the mode of transportation. Certain tariff lines attract high duties and there is a risk that traders will record erroneous classification or undervalue the goods to reduce their duty liability. Some goods originate in countries that attract preferential rates, prompting some traders to fake the origin of their imports. Some countries of origin or transshipment have a record of providing fraudulent, or doctored invoices. Some traders have a documented track record of infractions while others have given proof of good fiscal behavior and have no or minimal recorded violations of the Customs Code (authorized traders). Customs can apply this computer-generated risk profile to individual shipments and assign a risk coefficient on a scale of 0 to 100. Zero means that the transaction involves no risk to any of the customs objectives and 100 means that the transaction is certain to contravene some regulatory

provisions. Ratings in between convey the degree of risk of the transaction to customs objectives and alerts customs to the degree of care that is recommended to minimize these risks. A refined search of the risk coefficient can also provide the main reason for the particular risk coefficient rating and the particular control that should be activated. Such controls may include physical inspection.

Using the IT system, customs can gear its level of inspection to the risk that it is willing to accept in clearing goods. If customs decides that it can accept a 5 percent risk that the goods violate a regulatory prescription, only those transactions that the model suggests would exceed this level of risk will be inspected. Analysis and experience will suggest what overall level of inspection this entails. With everything else constant, striving for lower levels of inspection implies accepting higher degrees of risk. These tradeoffs can be calculated using modern IT systems. The model that activates the transaction-specific selectivity decision can be easily made to interface with the existing automated customs management systems, hence making the application of risk management techniques a matter of customs routine.

### Evaluation of the Selectivity Model

The performance of the selectivity model should be monitored and evaluated on an ongoing basis. This implies that the inspection reports would be validated and systematically entered into the IT system and compared to the inspection reports of transactions selected on a random basis. Only when the inspections based on the selectivity model yield better results than the inspections based on random sampling does the model make a valuable contribution to risk management. This applies to physical inspections as well as to other control instruments.

### Conclusion

The rate of physical inspection may be a useful performance indicator if used in conjunction with other performance indicators. In all cases, this rate must be analyzed along with revenue performance during the period when the physical inspection rates change.

Much would be gained if, by focusing on this performance indicator, project managers and policymakers were to address the complex issue of risk management more forcefully.

## Annex 1.E Checklist of Guidelines to Define a Customs Modernization Strategy

The following guidelines can be useful in developing and managing a customs modernization strategy.

### Identify the Main Components of the Modernization Based on the Findings of the Diagnosis

- Determine the focus of the reform, key measures, phasing, and sequence.
- Identify departments within customs or outside agencies affected by the process.
- Decide whether the problem involves reorganization or staffing issues and identify the key strategic steps to deal with these organizational and human resources issues.

### Describe the Enabling Environment

- Develop a matrix showing, by core function, who is in charge of which activity. In particular, the matrix should take into account what activities are to be undertaken by customs. These should include activities dealing with organization, personnel, clearance, brokers, transit, IT, control, prosecution, transport, insurance, and financial practice. The matrix should also include, in addition to those activities undertaken by customs, those that are undertaken by other government departments and agencies such as finance, commerce, transport, interior, industry, health, justice, Chamber of Commerce, and foreign affairs, as well as activities undertaken by the private sector and those resulting from international agreements.
- Develop a process flow chart showing the interactions between agencies and points of friction.

### Test the Commitment of the Government or the Administration

- Organize a brainstorming session within customs to determine where the administration

wants to go, and phase a strategic action plan that is not a shopping list.
- Validate the strategy either at the level of the Minister of Finance or at other government levels.
- Identify signals of political commitment, including a sustainable financing plan (both national budget and donor funding) that will be crucial for the sustainability of the reform.
- Ensure that all other stakeholders (for example, other ministries or agencies and private sector representatives) are on board.

### Check What the Other Donors Are Doing

- Develop a matrix of donor intervention and plans.
- Carry out a summary gap analysis in terms of outside support for the reform.
- Identify areas that need to be the focus of the forthcoming initiatives and request for external support.
- Establish a donor coordination mechanism.

### Appoint a Change Management Unit

- Designate staffs or an organizational unit that will monitor the entire modernization process.
- Identify a champion that is committed to the reform and is well connected with the various stakeholders.
- Ensure that staffs responsible for implementing the reform are released from their other duties and have adequate accommodation.
- Establish a project steering committee, including other donors and private sector representatives.

## Further Reading

The word *processed* describes informally reproduced works that may not commonly be available through libraries.

Inter-American Development Bank. 2001. *Customs Best Practices in East Asia and Latin America.* Washington, D.C.

Keen, Michael, ed. 2003. *Changing Customs: Challenges and Strategies for the Reform of Customs Administration.* Washington, D.C.: International Monetary Fund.

Lane, Michael. 1998. *Customs Modernization and the International Trade Superhighway.* Westport, Conn.: Quorum Books:.

World Customs Organization. 2003. *Risk Management Guide.* Brussels. www.wcoomd.org/ie/En/search/search.html.

———. 2003. "Capacity Building in Customs." Brussels. Processed. www.wcoomd.org/ie/en/Past_Events/Past_events .html.

## References

The word *processed* describes informally reproduced works that may not commonly be available through libraries.

APEC Economic Committee. 2002. "Measuring the Impact of APEC Trade Facilitation on APEC Economies: A CGE Analysis." Singapore.

Barbone, Luca, Luc De Wulf, Arindam Das-Gupta, Anna Hanson. 2001. "World Bank Projects in the 1990s with Tax or Customs Administration Reform Components: A Review." Tax Policy and Administration Thematic Group. Washington, D.C.: World Bank. econ.worldbank.org/docs/964.pdf.

Bernardo, Antonio. 2003. "Trade Enhancement Initiatives in the Philippine Customs Service." Presentation at the World Customs Organization 101st/102nd Session of the Customs Cooperation Council. June 26–28. Brussels.

Ebril, Liam, Janet Stotsky, and Reint Gropp. 1999. "Revenue Implications of Trade Liberalization." IMF Occasional Paper 180. International Monetary Fund: Washington, D.C.

Gill, J. B. S. 2000. "A Diagnostic Framework For Revenue Administration." World Bank Technical Paper No. 473. Washington, D.C.: World Bank.

Hinkle, Lawrence, Alberto Herrou-Aragon, and Keiko Kubota. 2003. "How Far Did Africa's First Generation Trade Reforms Go?" Africa Region Working Paper Series, No. 58a. Washington, D.C.: The World Bank.

Holl, John. 2002. *Customs-related Technical Assistance for Trade Capacity Building.* Nathan Associates report prepared for the USAID. Arlington, Va.

International Chamber of Commerce. 2002. "Customs Guidelines." www.iccwbo.org.

Keen, Michael, ed. 2003. *Changing Customs: Challenges and Strategies for the Reform of Customs Administration.* Washington, D.C.: International Monetary Fund.

Lane, Michael. 1998. *Customs Modernization and the International Trade Superhighway.* Westport, Conn.: Quorum Books.

Mendoza, Jaime, and Jose Eduardo Gutierrez. 2003. "A Methodology to Measure the Time Required for the Release of Goods." Working Paper 01/03. Aduana Nacional de Bolivia. Bogota.

Moroccan Government. Administration des Douanes et Impôts Indirects. *Délai de dédouanement,* available at www.douane.gov.ma (click on Universitaire, then Chiffres clés).

Nathan Associates. 1996. "Findings, Conclusions and Recommendations." *Research of the Quality Control System in Egypt,*

*Volume I.* Prepared for the Government of Egypt. Arlington, Va.: Nathan Associates Inc. http://www.economy.gov.eg/Download/02)%20Quality%20Control%20System/Quality%20Control%20System-English.pdf.

———. 1998. "Pilot Study for Pre-certification of Imported Products." Study Prepared for The General Organization for Export and Import Control. Ministry of Trade and Supply, Government of Egypt. Arlington, Va.: Nathan Associates Inc. www.economy.gov.eg/Download/07)%20Pre-Certification%20of%20Imports/Pre-Certification%20of%20Imports-English.PDF.

OECD. 2003. *Trade Facilitation Reforms in the Service of Development.* Trade Directorate, Trade Committee. Document number TD/TC/WP (2003) 11/Final. Organisation for Economic Co-operation and Development: Paris.

Raven, John. 2001. "Trade and Trade Facilitation, A Toolkit for Audit, Analysis and Remedial Action." World Bank Discussion Paper No. 427. Global Facilitation Partnership for Transportation and Trade. Washington, D.C.: World Bank.

Steenlandt, Marcel, and Luc De Wulf. 2004. "Morocco." In Luc De Wulf and Jose Sokol, eds. *Customs Modernization Initiatives: Case Studies.* Washington D.C.: World Bank.

UNECE (UN Economic Commission for Europe). 1982. "International Convention on the Harmonization of Frontier Control of Goods." Inland Transport Committee. Geneva. www.unece.org/trans/conventn/harmone.pdf.

UPECON Foundation. 2003. "The Study on Measurement of the Time Required for the Release of Goods in the Republic of the Philippines." Manila. Processed.

World Bank. 1996. "Global Economic Prospects and the Developing Countries: 1996." Washington, D.C.

———. 2002. *World Business Environment Survey.* Washington, D.C. www.worldbank.org/privatesector/ic/ic_ica_resources.htm.

———. 2003. *Global Economic Prospects 2004: Realizing the Development Promise of the Doha Agenda.* Washington, D.C.

———. 2004. "TTFSE Progress Report 2003." Washington, D.C. www.seerecon.org/ttfse

WCO (World Customs Organization). 2002. "Guide to Measure the Time Required for the Release of Goods. Brussels." www.wcoomd.org/ie/En/Topics_Issues/FacilitationCustomsProcedures/facil_time_release_study.htm.

———. 2003. *Risk Management Guide.* Brussels.

Zarnowiecki, Michel. The World Bank.

# HUMAN RESOURCES AND ORGANIZATIONAL ISSUES IN CUSTOMS

*Luc De Wulf*

Customs is a unique organization among government agencies in that it is neither a domestic agency nor an international agency. It is poised on the international borders,[1] not only as an expression of a nation's sovereignty, but also as the nation's guard against external threats to health, safety, and the environment; protecting (for better or for worse) domestic industry and collecting revenue to support the government. It must be aware of the border implications of national priorities concerning domestic crime, immigration, labor, the economy, and agriculture. At the same time, it must maintain an awareness of international issues and their potential impact on the nation, and it must be knowledgeable about national obligations to trade and transport treaties and conventions. In many ways, customs organizations relate more closely with their counterparts in other countries than they do with other agencies in their own government. They frequently look to customs administrations internationally and in neighboring countries for assistance and for ideas on how to improve operations or enforcement, as well as to exchange information on emerging threats.

---

The contributions of Michael Lane and the assistance of Melanie Faltas are gratefully acknowledged.

1. At a different plane, the "international" position of customs is due to two factors. It deals with international trade and, in doing so, follows internationally agreed on methods, practices, and instruments. It is the commonality of their vocational practices, a shared understanding of concepts, and an obligated harmonization of processes and procedures that makes customs international. A substantial part of customs legislation is developed in multilateral organizations like the World Customs Organization (WCO) in the form of conventions. In many cases, domestic legislation conforms to these international conventions.

The first section of this chapter deals with the modern management of human resources (HR) in customs. The second section addresses issues related to the more traditional customs organization, while the third and fourth sections discuss two recent organizational issues that have received considerable attention in recent years: Autonomous Revenue Authorities (ARAs) and management contracts. The final section provides operational conclusions and recommendations. The annexes provide checklists for issues of human resources management, management contracts, and ARAs.

## Human Resources: An Organization Is Only as Good as Its Staff

Good management of human resources is probably the single most important issue that affects the efficiency and effectiveness of customs, irrespective of its organizational structure. This cannot be overemphasized as all aspects of customs management and customs clearance, including the application and maintenance of modern information technology (IT), will require that staff is qualified to operate the existing systems efficiently and to prepare the existing services for the introduction of new processes and techniques. In doing so, staff must be attuned to developments in international trade logistics and must adjust to shifts in emphasis with respect to customs' mandate.

Historically, customs work consisted of the manual labor of inspecting cargo, vessels, and passengers, and patrolling long stretches of border between ports of entry. Customs management was close to higher ranking government officials, while its staff was often poorly educated, trained, and compensated. This arrangement undermined professionalism and integrity in customs.

Increasingly, government services are being held to higher standards. The imperatives of a globalized economy on customs have become clear. A modern customs administration, responsible for protecting and representing the government at its country's borders and ports, must use a professional workforce and an enabling technology to accomplish its mission. Managing human resources at customs can be broken down into several phases:

- defining the desired staff profile
- establishing a recruitment process that ensures that customs has the desired staff on board

- training incumbent staff to maintain skill levels
- ensuring that the compensation package enables customs to motivate and retain staff
- ensuring that poor performance and integrity failures are promptly sanctioned.

### Staff Profile

A modern customs administration needs to define the profile of its desired staff. The general educational background of all staff should be sufficiently high to ensure that they can acquire and maintain the skills required by a customs service. Such skills are bound to change over time and will increasingly require expertise in accounting, intelligence gathering, finance, investigation, analysis, training, planning, and HR management. All these functions will increasingly adopt procedures that rely heavily on the use of IT. Modern workflow analysis should be used to determine the desired distribution of personnel across the various skill categories.

Some of the major services required of customs, and the professional qualifications essential to fulfilling these requirements, include the following:

- *Enforcement of domestic laws and regulations at borders.* These laws and regulations should comply with all international customs conventions and standards to which the country has subscribed. Hence, staff should stay informed about developments in international trade negotiations and the requirements of globalization. Staff need adequate legal expertise to internalize the developments in the trading and international customs community and to translate them into domestic legislation.
- *Implementation of modern customs clearance processes.* With heavy IT input, modern risk assessment is based on modern intelligence gathering techniques to facilitate trade and to be attuned to private sector trade logistics advances. Expertise is required in IT as is the ability to perform risk analysis and postclearance audits.
- *Maintenance of open communications with the trading community.* Customs must ensure that the trading community has full information regarding its obligations and that the trading community's views are taken into account in decisionmaking at customs. Communication

skills are required, but operational interface with the trading community must be conducted at arm's length.

- *Enforcement of laws relating to intellectual property rights, security, drug trafficking, and, eventually, labor and human rights.* While labor and human rights may not be the national priority, the need to enforce such legislation may emerge depending on the outcomes of future trade negotiations. This requires the capacity to integrate the agendas of other agencies into customs procedures.
- *Collection and dissemination of international trade statistics* requires IT expertise and an awareness of the importance of statistics for economic decisionmaking.
- *Management of customs' HR* requires sound human resources management and human resources development expertise.

### Recruitment

Adjusting the existing staff profile to the desired one is frequently a gradual process. As the older staff retires, new staff has to be recruited not only for replacement but also to provide for any expansion in service. The recruitment effort should be a systematic one and could involve the announcement of job vacancies. Such announcements should clearly state the desired qualifications of the new staff, such as academic background, previous work experience, and so forth, and should clearly describe the recruitment process. Transparency in the recruitment process is important as this will set the standard for a new career at customs and curb the tendencies for favoritism and clientelism that often plague recruitment in the public sector.[2] Public advertising of vacancies as well as participation in job fairs and visits to schools of higher learning are recommended to ensure that qualified people apply for the adver-

tised jobs. Potential recruits should be subjected to stringent background investigations performed by trained investigators who might interview neighbors, associates, and previous employers. Checks of police records should be performed, as well as credit and bank account checks to assess the extent and sources of income. Entry requirements would include testing for the specific skills and aptitudes. Human resources management staff in customs could undertake these tasks in-house or could turn to recruitment professionals. New recruits should be advised that a career in customs involves rotation to enhance multifunctionality and to avoid the development of potentially unsavory relationships with the local trading community.[3] New recruits with no prior experience in customs-related work should undergo intense training and testing to prepare them for their new assignments. If successful, they should undergo a probationary period before being confirmed as customs staff. Such probationary periods often last a full year, during which the employee can be terminated for unsatisfactory performance or disciplinary problems without the complex recourse to appeals and administrative tribunals. Following this probationary period and satisfactory performance evaluation, the trainees should be confirmed. Relying on transparent performance criteria aids supervisors and enhances the transparency of the recruitment process.

Most customs organizations traditionally rely on the recruitment of young candidates who are then schooled in the best practices of the customs service through a combination of academic and on-the-job training. However, modern customs practices require staff to possess expertise that cannot easily be attained through training within the customs service. Expertise in IT and in accounting, which are increasingly required to perform post-clearance audits, are only two examples. Recruitment procedures and compensation scales need to be sufficient to attract staff with these specialized skills. When qualified applicants are not available, it is possible at times to sidestep these civil service restrictions by offering attractive consultant contracts. This practice has its downside though, as it could easily demoralize customs staff in general and could present the problem of staff continuity in specialized assignments.

---

2. As was the case in the 1880s in the U.S. Customs, it is known that potential candidates for positions in customs in some countries have paid for the appointment at prices that at times were a multiple of the annual salary. In Bolivia, for instance, before the recent reform, some customs officials worked "pro bono" and compensated themselves in the process of executing their tasks. High-level officials also are known to have interfered frequently in the appointment of family members or members of their ethnic groups—practices that undermine the recruitment process and create allegiances that are alien to the performance of the duties of customs officials.

---

3. In both Zambia and Morocco, for instance, staff rotation has become part and parcel of a career in customs.

The process of retirement and the recruitment of new staff will be a slow one if desired profiles of new staff differ substantially from the profile of those still on board. At times management may want a faster staff reprofiling. This was the case when ARAs were introduced and drastic changes in staffing were undertaken. (Details are provided in the Autonomous Revenue Authorities section.)

Box 2.1 provides some details of the process followed in Bolivia.

### Training

In-service training should be a major responsibility of the HR team at customs. The demands of globalization and the rapid adoption of IT in the various

---

**BOX 2.1     Staff Renovation in Bolivian Customs**

Prior to reform, staffing at Bolivia's customs administration was characterized by a large number of pro bono personnel working without a specific position or salary, appointments based on political recommendations rather than on individual merit, high turnover of personnel, low salaries, and an absence of training. As part of the government's overall reform of its whole administration, customs was selected as a pilot on the basis of the recently adopted Civil Service Statute and Civil Service Program. Human resources management reform was an essential element in helping customs become an efficient and transparent organization, while significantly reducing corruption.

The selection and hiring of personnel was to be based on transparent and competitive processes. All positions became open to public competition; all positions filled by staff who were not competitively selected were given provisional status; all pro bono staff positions were eliminated. Specialized firms were hired through public bidding to undertake the selection process. Customs benefited from the prestige of the independent firms, and misgivings concerning the transparency of the process were avoided. At the same time the HR Department developed a new market-based wage system that offered competitive salaries.

Openings for top and medium level positions were published on October 30, 1999, and for professional and technical positions on April 16, 2000. The outcome of the first opening was negatively affected by lack of appropriate publicity and effort (which held the number of applications below expectations), the wrongful elimination of a number of applications for border positions, and the unreliable software system used. Because many positions remained unfilled, a third opening for top level and technical personnel was issued on January 14, 2001.

The selection process required a series of prior actions: defining the ideal profile of cus-

toms officers; quantifying staff requirements, set at slightly over 700 officers, of which 575 positions were open for application; and defining job profiles with minimum requirements of education, experience other than previous customs experience, and personal qualities. There were various evaluations of the candidates: curricular evaluation; technical and psycho-technical evaluation based on tests; and integral evaluation through interview. A minimum score was established for each position. Candidates were also screened to eliminate those who, as former or current officers, had been found guilty of violating internal customs regulations or of committing a felony. Once tests were graded, a short list of applicants to be interviewed was established. Following completion of the process, a report that included a short list of candidates with summaries of the results obtained in each of the examinations for each finalist was provided to customs to assist in making final evaluations. A final evaluation was conducted through a structured interview with the purpose of validating the information provided by the consulting firm, verifying that all requirements had been met, and determining the candidate's suitability for a specific position. The final evaluation was carried out by a committee selected by the Board of Directors, which submitted a report that included recommendations to the Board of Directors or General Management. Appointed staff members were required to undergo an evaluation period of three months before starting an administrative career.

All in all the process attracted 12,563 applicants, with 8,763 candidates fulfilling all requirements; 2,718 candidates passed the technical and psycho-technical tests; and, following interviews, 1,653 were short listed, 87 percent of whom were selected to join the customs administration.

*Source:* IDB 2001.

aspects of customs operations make ongoing training an absolute necessity. Experienced customs officers should be teamed up with professional trainers to offer such training.

In modern Customs, many promotions depend on successful completion of well-defined training programs and all staff must undergo annual training, agreed on with the HR department and with direct supervisors. Supervisors are evaluated with respect to the implementation of the agreed on training of their staff. Special training academies can be appointed for this purpose on a national or regional basis. Full advantage should be taken of the training provided by bilateral agencies, the WCO, and even preshipment inspection (PSI) companies, whose contracts often specify training obligations.[4]

### Staff Compensation

Staff compensation is a crucial factor in HR management. It should be sufficiently high to attract and retain staff with the necessary qualifications to start work at customs. However, overall staff salaries are often inadequate and the difference between the compensation of management and lower level staff is much narrower than what prevails in the private sector.[5] While compensation is not the only motivating factor for doing a good job, it certainly ranks high.[6] Developing *esprit de corps* and pride in the office are complementary motivators that are often not sufficiently emphasized. In recent years, for example, Moroccan customs has paid special attention to this factor and this initiative appears to have had some benefits.[7]

In most cases customs does not have much flexibility in setting salary levels and must adhere to the civil service pay scale. Frequently, fiscal stringency has caused this pay scale to lag substantially behind the prevailing pay scale for equally qualified staff in the private sector. This situation discourages staff and often leads them to seek out facilitation money. It is not unusual for the most valuable staff members to leave the service, often to use their acquired knowledge to work as brokers. Inside knowledge of the customs service and familiarity with customs staff can both facilitate trade formalities for their customers, and potentially undermine integrity. The integrity risk has led some countries to prevent customs staff from providing customs brokerage services for several years after ending employment with customs.

A partial solution to the salary scale rigidities is to provide bonuses to staff. While many customs services pay bonuses, only a few pay them in a way that enhances effectiveness and efficiency. To do so, bonuses must be large enough to begin to bridge the gap between what private sector workers earn (discounted for the job security in the public sector), and satisfy a number of stringent criteria. Bonuses must have internal and external legitimacy, and be objective, transparent, and easy to administer. In addition, they should be SMART, that is, *s*pecific, *m*easurable, *a*chievable, *r*elevant, and *t*imed (De Wulf 2004). However, ensuring that performance evaluations provide for adequate differentiation of staff performance is not easy. In Morocco, for instance, where a fully satisfactory note leads to payment of a bonus that equals 100 percent of base salary, the great majority of staff members receive an evaluation report that qualifies them for the maximum bonus amount.

Internal legitimacy requires that customs staff perceive the bonus system to be distributed justly, without favoritism, with transparency, and with possibilities for appeal. External legitimacy refers to the acceptability of the bonuses outside customs, a requirement for allocating the necessary budget resources that pay for these bonuses. In the absence of either internal or external legitimacy, the bonus system will not be sustainable. In Ghana, for instance, the higher salaries that customs staff received when the ARA was created could not be sustained because of opposition from other civil servants. It would appear that the strict conditions that need to be fulfilled for bonuses to compensate for low salaries pose substantial challenges for

---

4. In Ghana, the service agreements of the companies undertaking Destination Inspection Services include the delivery of a training program for the customs staff. That this program was signed with the Ministry of Trade and Industry and not with customs complicates the integration of the training with other similar customs initiatives. Even worse, it may undermine any initiative of customs to take full responsibility for its training program.

5. In Nepal, for instance, salaries of customs staff are only one-third those paid in the private sector; the base salary of the Director General is only 150 percent higher than the starting salary of a gazetted officer.

6. Interesting background on this issue can be found in Van Rijckeghem and Weber (1997).

7. For details see Steenlandt and De Wulf (2004).

design and implementation, making such systems risky and in need of close monitoring.

An alternative to providing substantial bonuses would be to put revenue staff on a higher pay scale than the rest of the civil service, in light of the crucial importance that resource mobilization plays in running the government. Better pay would also protect customs staff somewhat against the temptations of accepting bribes from traders.[8] A higher pay scale would need to be combined with overall customs reforms that provide guarantees of enhanced effectiveness and efficiency.

Some customs services have adopted a more drastic solution to the inadequacy of staff compensation by creating ARAs that initially paid salaries that were competitive with those paid in the private sector, or with those given to the best paid civil servants.

Performance-related salary increases and promotions are also important factors for motivating staff. Yet both are often constrained by rigid promotion policies that are commonly applied to all civil servants and that are highly dependent on seniority. Noteworthy exceptions do exist. In Mozambique, for instance, staff performance is assessed on a quarterly basis during the two-year practical training period, and is closely monitored afterward by an internal audit. In Angola, an annual appraisal system is intended to match staff skills to job descriptions and to properly identify candidates for senior positions.

The state of infrastructure, both for work and for housing, particularly at outlying customs posts, also affects work ethic and morale. Often such infrastructure has suffered from years of neglect due to budget constraints. The poor outpost housing infrastructure in many border posts leads staff to go to great lengths to avoid such postings, which often are considered to be unfair hardship or even penalty assignments. In Zambia and Tanzania, customs reforms included upgrading infrastructure, a feature that was greatly appreciated by staff.

### Integrity and Sanctions

Modern customs clearance practices—based on intensive use of IT as well as adequate staff compensation—will play the determining role in countering integrity problems. However, experience has shown that this is not sufficient to completely eradicate corrupt practices. Hence, any HR policy must clearly spell out how to deal with these issues. Chapter 4 deals explicitly with the issue of integrity in customs, so some brief remarks must suffice here. Staff should be made fully aware that corrupt practices and slacking behavior will not be tolerated. Disciplinary actions could be made explicit in the personnel manual. Such actions could range from admonishment, to skipping salary adjustments and bonus payments, to dismissal. Dismissal from the service should not be used lightly and safeguards should be put in place to ensure that disciplinary actions are meted out in an unbiased manner. Official reaction to accusations of corruption should be prompt, both to clear unjustified accusations and to avoid lengthy delays between offense and penalty. Sanctions that include dismissal from the service can be a powerful enforcer of discipline when staff compensation is good and unemployment is high.[9]

## Customs Organization and Organizational Placement

A highly motivated and competent staff can make almost any organization work and can overcome a plethora of organizational obstacles; but a good organizational structure will help greatly. Even a perfect model of organizational design and efficiency, should it exist, would not survive if the employees are not competent, qualified, trained, and motivated. An ideal organization is not static. Public and private sector organizations modify their structures continually to address new challenges, changes in workload, geographic expansion, competition, the introduction of new technology, and innovation. A customs administration is no exception and often struggles to find an ideal organization to match the constantly changing customs environment. However, reorganization is not a panacea. Frequently, it is used as an excuse to disguise an inability to identify the root cause of poor performance. Reorganization can be disruptive and

---

8. Higher salaries for staff often impart greater social responsibility toward the larger family or clan, thereby not reducing, but increasing, the "need" to take bribes to live up to these greater responsibilities and new status in the traditional hierarchy (Fjeldstad, Kolstad, and Lange 2003).

---

9. As it is, the punitive mechanism that customs management may employ in some countries is hamstrung by corruption in the legal system.

could divert attention away from the ongoing work of the agency.

This section presents the traditional way that customs has been organized together with some minor variations on that theme.

### Internal Organization

Traditionally, customs organizations are structured as a department of the Ministry of Finance (MOF) and are fully accountable to the MOF for their operations and results. The overarching responsibility of customs is to raise fiscal revenue as prescribed by the budget. In doing so, it should ensure that customs procedures and policies are uniformly and consistently applied across the various points of entry and modes of transport. At times, customs has somewhat greater autonomy than other agencies or other ministerial departments, generally due to its responsibilities as border guard, as well as its responsibility to deal with noncompliant traders and smugglers. Given the nature of its responsibilities, the organizational structure of customs is decentralized, consisting of headquarters (HQ) and regional and local offices. HQ's responsibility is to develop operational policy and procedures—including the use of IT—that aim for effectiveness and efficiency and compliance with international agreements related to the World Trade Organization. HQ monitors the activities of the decentralized offices and is responsible for personnel policy, including recruitment, compensation, training, and enforcement. Regional offices oversee the activities of the local offices in their jurisdiction, while local offices are generally the point of contact with the international trading community and other customs administrations. Essentially, the staff at the local offices decide on the level of verification that is required when processing a declaration and releasing goods, as well as the effectiveness and efficiency of this process (Castro and Walsh 2003).

In addition to the traditional departments (legal, procedures, valuation, IT, law enforcement, field operations, international cooperation, corporate services, personnel, audit) many modern customs administrations are adding a department responsible for maintaining relations with the private sector—to solicit concerns, explain the procedures, and provide for an ombudsman when controversies arise with international traders. Importers, exporters, carriers, and customs brokers or forwarders also require an independent appeals process to provide an avenue for appealing decisions that they believe are in error or are inconsistent with international customs practices. This institutionalized openness to the private sector can help build the necessary trust between the private sector and customs, trust that will benefit all concerned.

Some customs administrations recognize that a relatively small number of taxpayers are responsible for a large share of the total import duties and have adjusted their internal operations to provide special services for large taxpayers. This is in line with the provisions of the Kyoto Convention that permits "authorized" importers to obtain faster release of their cargo; that is, traders that conform to certain criteria of transparency and honesty benefit from easier customs procedures, with the proviso that post-release audits can be undertaken. The Egyptian Model Customs and Tax Center, for instance, is equipped to process all customs and tax declarations of a select group of large enterprises (about 200 at the end of 2003) that account for a large share of total trade and tax payments. In fact, this center operates a single window for them where new and efficient procedures have been introduced.

### Customs' Position in the Overall Government Structure

The MOF has traditionally been the government organization in which customs resides and that provides oversight and direction in view of its primary mission of revenue collection. It has been argued that this does not have to be so, especially in light of customs' changing responsibilities. Over time, customs' role in trade facilitation supersedes that of revenue mobilization in many countries; and there is an increasing rationale for the Ministry of Commerce to assume a greater supervisory role for customs. With enhanced concerns for security, the United States has placed customs inside the Department of Homeland Security, while Canada has placed customs within the Public Safety and Emergency Preparedness Ministry. In Australia, the Department of Trade and Customs was the first Commonwealth Government department established after the Federation of the Australian States in 1901. Australian customs has since been linked with a number of ministerial portfolios—trade, excise, business, consumer affairs, science, industry, commerce, and justice—based on the changing priorities of government. It now lies in the Justice and Customs portfolio, reflecting the government's desire to ensure effective cooperation between all federal law enforcement and security agencies.[10] The placement of customs under one ministry or the other is, at the end, a decision that could be reached rationally given the unique administrative structure and economic circumstances of the country, as well as the mission assigned to customs by the government. One might keep in mind, however, that the reorganization of departments or the relocation of the agency to another department or ministry often is a favorite activity of government reformers, but one that certainly has, in the absence of real reform initiatives, little or no effect other than guaranteed internal and external disruption. Whatever the organizational context of customs, it is crucial that customs

- operates with adequate funding and staffing
- operates under correct oversight to ensure that rules and regulations are respected
- has a personnel system that enables it to recruit, train, and develop a professional workforce and the authority to remove corrupt or incompetent employees and to keep them removed
- operates with adequate autonomy in personnel and operational matters
- provides an appeals process for the trade community
- is held accountable for meeting performance goals.

### Advantages of Merging Customs with Other Revenue Agencies

In the 1990s, several countries merged customs with other revenue departments, in the hope of enhancing the efficiency as well as the effectiveness of revenue collection. The intuitive reason for such a merger is that there must be economies of scale to be exploited by combining the personnel, legal, and administrative functions of each of these departments, which, in

the final analysis, deal with many of the same tax payers (PLS RAMBOLL 2001).[11]

The PLS RAMBOLL (2001) study reviewed the experience of Denmark, Canada, Colombia, the Netherlands, and Latvia in integrating their tax and customs agencies.[12] It notes two different motives for the integration initiatives: to increase the *effectiveness* (the Netherlands, Latvia, and Colombia) or the *efficiency* (Denmark, see box 2.2) of revenue collection, or both (Canada). Effectiveness refers to the way the revenue is collected—amounts of revenue raised and the level of fraud, fairness, compliance, and so forth—while efficiency refers to the private and public resources spent on each unit of revenue raised.[13]

The reforms in the Netherlands aimed at greater effectiveness. High tax rates in the 1970s resulted in a greater incidence of tax avoidance and fraud, while prosperity led to a growth in the number of taxpayers. The tax legislation had also become more complex, indicating a need for better taxpayer services, which the government believed could be better provided with the integration of the revenue and customs departments. The merger of the customs and tax institutions in Denmark aimed at increased efficiency. It was the flagship of the government's antibureaucracy reform and enjoyed considerable political support. Before the merger, Denmark had a relatively high number of staff in the tax and customs administrations. Reducing the number to a level comparable to those of similar countries, such as Sweden and Norway, was fundamental to lowering collection costs.

The merger of the Canadian tax and customs administrations was undertaken to rationalize the

---

10. In addition to customs, the Justice and Customs portfolio includes the Australian Crime Commission, the Australian Federal Police, and AUSTRAC (Australia's anti-money-laundering regulator and specialist intelligence unit).

11. The discussion in this section draws on the findings of this study.

12. The merger of customs with revenue is also under consideration in the United Kingdom. As noted by the press on the Treasury Report on the subject, the main benefit of the merger is expected to come from reduced compliance costs for businesses as companies could deal with a single tax authority.

13. This study did not cover the merger of domestic tax offices and customs in a number of countries in the Americas, including Argentina, Brazil, Canada, Mexico, Guatemala, Colombia, Honduras, Peru, and República Bolivariana de Venezuela as the business processes of these agencies have converged. The tendency to unify the tax collection agencies has been stronger in cases where the share of the value added tax (VAT) on imports with respect to total revenues is high and in cases in which control of other taxes depends on VAT declarations.

---

**BOX 2.2   Denmark: Integration of Customs and Tax Administration**

The motive behind the integration of the customs and tax administrations in Denmark was to considerably increase efficiency. The strategy centered on full integration of the tax and customs administrations at all levels to reduce administrative costs. This strategy was also in line with the integration into the European Union (EU), which resulted in the reduction of tariff revenues as a source of fiscal revenues. The strategy included a number of rationalization measures:

- a reduction in number of combined staff in the two agencies—from 6,742 employees in 1989 to 5,846 in 1992 and 5,643 in 2000
- the design of an ambitious, integrated IT system, integrating all revenue collection systems into one

- a massive reduction in the number of local offices, merged into a few regional offices
- the establishment of a flat organizational structure, which reduced the number of management levels and delegated responsibility to lower levels
- the implementation of a number of new public management tools, such as contract management between central and regional offices, contracts between the ministry and the office managers, focus on core activities and reduction of support activities, and a massive focus on value-based management.

*Source:* PLS RAMBOLL 2001

---

collective revenue administration, partly to make it more efficient and partly to improve customer service. The merger was also a response to demands at that time for a more federal government structure. The reorganization affected virtually all aspects of the political and administrative setup of the new organization, to secure maximum advantages and benefits. At the political level, the posts of Deputy Minister for Taxation and Deputy Minister of Customs were merged into one position. New legislation was introduced to integrate the two sets of statutes and to merge existing legislation. The former 23 overlapping regions were reduced to 6 consolidated regions performing all functions of the tax and customs administration at the regional level. The HQs of the two former departments were consolidated into one, which was organized into a series of business lines supported by corporate services. A major staff development program was initiated, while IT and other support systems were consolidated into joint systems. Until recently, only the Customs Border Services remained a separate entity—all other aspects of the work of the former departments and regional offices have been organizationally and operationally integrated. This organizational structure was revised again in 2004, when customs was integrated into the Public Safety and Emergency Preparedness Ministry.

The case studies suggest that the success of any merger will depend greatly on the preparations preceding the merger, the political support it receives,

and the involvement of stakeholders—taxpayers as well as staff of the different agencies. In the Netherlands, the success of the merger was attributed to a large extent to sound preparatory work that started in the 1970s. The actual implementation took five years, from 1987 to 1992. In Colombia, however, preparation and political support for the merger were weak, and the results less than positive. In Canada, staffs were intimately consulted and many contributed to drafting new legislation and the rollout of the merger. The presence of a strong, politically well-connected champion heading the merger also helped greatly.

Clear from these initiatives is that a merger must fully account for the fact that substantive procedural differences between the customs and tax departments create asymmetries that will need to be accommodated in the unified institution. Tax collection operates on the basis of self-assessment and after-the-fact control, which allows tax-related data to be batched. Customs procedures require payment and control to take place simultaneously, through self-assessment combined with post-release audits. Also, customs operations are strictly guided by the need to release cargo promptly, adding a unique dimension to the overall customs operation, one that is not shared by other tax departments.

It is arguable that the effectiveness of the revenue services does not necessarily require a large degree of integration between the operations of the tax and customs authorities. The case studies illustrate that a full merger of the two institutions may, in fact, impede the goal of increasing effectiveness. A joint focus on the operational aspects, a cross-institutional focus on target groups, and coordinated legislation and planning may serve the purpose of enhanced effectiveness and efficiency. A merger of the physical organizations (shared personnel, organizational culture, infrastructure, and IT systems), though, requires tremendous effort on behalf of the political and administrative leadership, staff, and the stakeholders (vested interests, clients) of the agency—an effort that may in the end be counterproductive. This was the case in Colombia. At times it also threatened to imperil the merger in Denmark. Recently, Latvia decided to roll back its merger efforts. For this reason, it is vital that governments are clear on the motive behind the integration process, and that strategies chosen for implementation are in harmony with the motive.

## Autonomous Revenue Authorities

The emergence of ARAs[14] can be traced to the Executive Agency model that was introduced in the late 1980s in the United Kingdom.[15] Such agencies were to operate more like private businesses than like government agencies. Government would make policies and assign responsibility for the execution of these policies to agencies that would have greater autonomy and accountability in their day-to-day activities. This approach also gave the illusion that government had become smaller, a major objective of the political parties in power in those days. The agency approach was then modified and applied to the departments of the MOF in charge of revenue mobilization. Their proclaimed advantages of operating along ARA lines were that

- As a single purpose agency, separate from the MOF, it could focus on a single task.
- With autonomy, it could free itself from political interference in day-to-day activities.
- Freed from civil service constraints, it could establish its own personnel policies to enhance effectiveness and efficiency.

In sum, the ARA was to be granted greater accountability, but was also provided with greater operational flexibility, and shielded from political or other interference. It would be misleading to say that accountability was totally absent before the ARAs; however, accountability was either poorly managed or customs was able to deflect accountability by stating the restrictions under which it was forced to operate.

The creation of ARAs provided traders and taxpayers with greater assurance that the new initiatives to improve effectiveness and efficiency were serious efforts by the government and that they would be rather difficult to undo. Traders and taxpayers were thus expected to react with better compliance.

ARAs now operate in a number of countries in Latin America and Africa[16] and were largely introduced with Department for International Development (DFID), International Monetary Fund (IMF), and World Bank support. Some have been operational now for more than 10 years. In all these countries, the main reason for introducing ARAs was to mobilize a larger share of fiscal revenues. Rampant corruption in the revenue departments was often identified as the major reason that revenue mobilization was totally inadequate, and why efforts to reform the revenue agencies had yielded no appreciable results. Hence, it may be instructive to review whether the experience of establishing ARAs has lived up to the initial expectations, and what lessons can be learned from them. In this review the focus is on customs operations, even though these are intimately intertwined with the operation of the ARAs that combine customs with direct and indirect taxation.

### Management Structure and Responsibilities

In all cases, ARAs combine the customs department, the direct taxation department, and the indirect revenue departments into one authority. In Latin America, ARAs are headed by a chief executive

---

14. The term Autonomous Revenue Authority is used here, but can refer to various degrees of autonomy.

15. Much of the argument developed in this section draws from Talierco (2002), and Fjeldstad, Kolstad, and Lange (2003).

16. Colombia, Ethiopia, Ghana, Kenya, Lesotho, Malawi, Mexico, Peru, Rwanda, South Africa, Tanzania, Uganda, República Bolivariana de Venezuela, Zambia, and Zimbabwe. The degree of autonomy varies across countries and functions.

officer (except in Mexico), while in Africa and Asia most ARAs are headed by a board of directors. Invariably the Minister of Finance appoints the head of the board, and the board members represent the MOF and other public sector agencies. Some boards (in Zambia, for example) include private sector representatives. In Uganda the Uganda Manufacturers Association received a seat on the board in 1998. The day-to-day management of the ARAs that have a board of directors rests with a commissioner or the chief executive officer. The ARA is entrusted with the administration of taxes (customs, direct, and indirect), but at times is given responsibility for tax policy. This mixing of tax policy with administration responsibilities has been confusing and has raised conflicts. It was retracted in several ARAs (in Uganda in 1998, for example). The ARAs are given varying amounts of flexibility to run the agencies, particularly with respect to personnel matters, as well as financial management and operational issues, including the introduction of IT.

ARA operations are designed to be shielded from political interference to counter the tendency of politicians and government officials to appoint its political supporters and to use and misuse the information held by tax authorities to advance political, personal, and tribal objectives. Such interference has, in the past, strained the relationship between the taxpayers and the tax administration in a major way (Talierco 2004, 2002).

In several cases governments have chosen to appoint expatriate managers as commissioners of the ARAs or as deputy commissioners for customs, VAT, or direct taxes. This has been the case in Uganda, Rwanda, and Ethiopia, where a Ghanaian tax administrator, familiar with the Ghana Revenue Authority at times held the post of commissioner.

In Zambia, after a few years of tentative reforms four expatriate experts were appointed in 1997 to head the Zambia Revenue Authority (ZRA). Currently, an expatriate expert again heads the Uganda Revenue Authority. At the outset the practice of asking expatriates to run the ARAs was a means of securing technical expertise and management skills not otherwise immediately available in the domestic market. Also, there was, at times, a perceived need to resist pressures for special consideration, which may be hard for managers who are a part of the community they serve to resist. At the initial stages expatriate managers served as a buffer zone through which the authority could establish its identity and ethos.[17]

### Financial Autonomy

Greater budget autonomy meant that the ARAs gained some freedom in the use of their budgets without detailed scrutiny from the MOF for each expenditure, a stifling practice in many countries. Also, some have gained greater autonomy in procurement matters. The size of the ARA and customs budget can be set on an annual basis after detailed discussion with the MOF, either as a fixed percentage of total revenue or as a variable percentage based on revenues collected—variables that can be defined at the time of the creation of the ARA.[18] The latter variant was introduced as an incentive measure. In Peru this share was set at 3 percent of customs revenue collections, but customs is also allowed to charge fees for services. There is no nominal upper limit to the total revenue. Customs is free to use the revenue as it likes, but must use one-third for investment. At times customs receives a premium, to be shared between staff and ARAs, for exceeding the revenue target. This provides an incentive only if the revenue target is set at a realistic level. In practice this has not always been the case, and revenue targets were at times set at unrealistically high levels, when the MOF and foreign donors overruled more realistic estimates made by the ARA (box 2.3). ARAs may, however, have a tendency to underestimate revenue potential to capture bonus payments. When the agreed on budget share is retained from revenues raised (as in the case of Peru) the budget autonomy is safer than when these budget resources must pass through budgetary allocations approved by the MOF and parliament.

---

17. Comments made by Darryl Jenkins, who for four years was Commissioner of the ZRA.

18. The Kenya Revenue Authority receives 1.5 percent of collections, and an additional 3 percent of the difference between actual collections and the collection target for a three month period, subject to a maximum of 2 percent of collections (Talierco 2004).

**BOX 2.3    Revenue Targets and Autonomy: Illustrations from Tanzania and Uganda**

Neither the Tanzania Revenue Authority (TRA) nor the Uganda Revenue Authority (URA) has autonomy in setting revenue targets. This has important implications for both staff motivation and tax collection priorities. Foreign donors, particularly the IMF, are actively involved in setting annual revenue targets, as is the MOF. The tax-to-GDP targets are announced in the budget speeches, and are written into the Policy Framework Papers that the government cosigns with the IMF.

While the MOF and the IMF publicly agree about revenue targets in both Tanzania and Uganda, many staff members of the TRA and URA complain about their own lack of influence in setting the revenue targets. Both TRA and URA staff consider the budget targets unrealistically high, based on expenditure needs rather than revenue potential. Others point out that the international comparison of tax shares frequently used to argue for the existence of large untapped revenues, and hence for the legitimate expectations of better TRA and URA performance, has a shaky empirical basis. First, GDP figures themselves are subject to discussion. Second, straight tax share comparisons fail to take into account the differences between countries with respect to economic structure (for example, the size of small scale agriculture and the extent of the mining sector), income per capita, urbanization, tax policies, and so forth.

The focus of the MOF and the IMF on short run revenue maximization also translates directly into a TRA and URA concentration on the larger known taxpayers, as reflected in the establishment of large taxpayers' departments that draw resources from the other revenue collecting departments within the revenue authorities. Hence, the targets have substantial influence on the way the revenue authority allocates its internal resources as well as on staff morale.

In Uganda, the relations between the MOF and the URA have deteriorated over the years as the URA has failed to meet its targets. The MOF and the URA frequently have quite different views about revenue collection targets and their analytical basis. On the one hand, the MOF regards itself as the key tax policymaker. On the other hand, the URA has the administrative expertise without which realistic target setting and tax policy cannot be accomplished.

In contrast, the relations between the MOF and the TRA seem to be more harmonious. This may be due to the special policy role the Research and Policy Department plays in the TRA, of setting revenue targets for the revenue departments once the total tax revenue budget has been agreed on with the Ministry. This arrangement indicates a strengthening of the tax bureaucracy at the expense of politicians. There is, of course, the issue of moral hazard when the tax collection agency becomes involved in the process of setting its own performance targets.

*Source:* Fjeldstad, Kolstad, and Lange 2003; Therkildsen 2003.

Greater financial autonomy sometimes frees the ARA from strict supervision of procurement. For instance, in Zambia, prior to the ARA all procurement had to go through the Ministry of Supply, with the Tender Board involved for procurements that exceeded a certain limit. The present procurement regulations for the ARA have abolished the intervention of the Ministry of Supply, but maintained the requirement to involve the Tender Board for larger contracts. This procedure substantially speeds up the overall procurement process.

### Human Resources

Freedom from restrictive civil service rules for recruitment and compensation of staff is one of the major advantages of ARAs.[19] However, not all ARAs have the same powers over their staff. Peru's revenue service SUNAT has full power and needs to consult with no other authority regarding the recruitment and firing of its staff. Autonomy over staffing matters is much more lacking in Ghana. Many ARAs, at their creation, took advantage of the opportunity to renew their staffing. Bolivia took a

---

19. Nepal is presently considering creating an ARA, first at internal revenue and later at customs. This would, among other benefits, remedy the present situation where the Public Service Commission assumes all personnel responsibility for customs: it identifies potential staff, holds entry examinations, selects staff, and allocates them to departments. It is also responsible for promotions, the performance appraisal system, filling vacancies, and disciplinary matters.

systematic approach to ensure that its staff corresponded to the desired professional and integrity profile (see box 2.1). Peru and Tanzania also implemented a drastic policy of staff renewal at the creation of the ARA. Zambia was less successful as the new recruits were selected from a list provided by the MOF, so the process was not as free as it could have been from regional and ethnic considerations. The Kenya Revenue Authority did forgo the opportunity to change its staff. In Uganda, most of the revenue administrations' staff retained their positions when the URA was created. Staff renewal is expensive as staff must be bought out (in Peru, for example, staff that resigned received three years compensation for a total of US$1 million, plus US$1 million of pension improvements) and new staff must be offered competitive compensation. Not all ARAs have used their newly gained autonomy to embark on a sustained training program, thereby undermining somewhat the quality enhancement they gained by revamping the recruitment procedures.

In several cases, the staff renewal process was used to upgrade the overall skill mix of staff. For example, in 1991, out of 4,000 staff members in Peruvian customs, only 2 percent had a university degree and a considerable proportion were unsalaried assistants, living solely on tips and gifts. By 2000, 55 percent of the staff had university diplomas and the pro bono staff category had disappeared.

### Compensation

Staff salaries were increased substantially in all ARAs with the express objective of being able to recruit and motivate qualified personnel. This was particularly important in attracting staff with expertise in IT, finance and budgeting, investigation, and accounting. Policies with respect to promotions and salary advances were also made more flexible and could be brought in line with staff performance. Better salaries were also intended to reduce corruption, as well-paid staff are less likely to engage in corrupt practices, given the lesser need to seek out bribes to supplement their official salaries to sustain their families. Also, when fired for corruption, it is more of a penalty to lose a high paying job than to lose a poorly paid job. In Peru, for instance, salaries were increased by a factor of 10, while in Tanzania the salaries were set at a level

that was 10 times that of the civil service. In Ghana and Uganda, staff salaries were brought in line with those paid at the central bank, which in Uganda was eight to nine times the level of salaries paid in the civil service. Salary adjustments also allowed for greater differentiation between higher-level and lower-level staff, akin to what is practiced in the private sector.[20]

### Lessons from Experience

Now that ARAs have been operating in the developing world for about 20 years, some factors can be isolated that, if given proper attention, contribute to their success.

- *Political support.* The ARAs that proved most successful were those that benefited from high-level political support. Where political support wavered, the experiments were less successful.
- *Autonomy.* When MOF appointees dominate the board of directors, the ARA has less operational autonomy, and some degree of micromanagement by the board, including in selection of positions, may emerge (URA, for example). It would appear that having private sector representatives on the board makes customs more attuned to private sector concerns. There is the danger, though, that those private sector representatives are not fully independent of the public sector, and may have been selected for their party or social affiliations. Political interference is always a risk, particularly with respect to staff appointments. With higher staff compensation such interference becomes more tempting. Political interference may also take place in seeking preferential treatment for individual traders and cargo, or in providing exemptions (Fjeldstad, Kolstad, and Lange 2003). In Uganda, the MOF is seen as dominating the board, thus undermining the autonomy of the URA (Therkilsen 2003).
- *Compensation levels.* Some ARAs have encountered serious difficulties in maintaining their

---

20. At the URA in 2000, the top-level wages were 34 times the lower-level wages, a differentiation that led to resentment when a 10 percent bonus was granted and staff focused on the absolute value of these bonuses given to top-level staff, which was a multiple of the total salary of low-level staff (Fjeldstad, Kolstad, and Lange 2003, p. 15).

competitive compensation levels. In Uganda, the premium over civil servants' salaries fell from a multiple of about eight to nine in 1991 to a multiple of four to five at present. In Tanzania, many years of salary freezes also caused an erosion of the salary premiums paid to staff. In Ghana, too, salaries at the ARA have, over the years, not kept up with inflation and with the increases in private sector compensation packages. Much could be gained by having a clear compensation policy, the application of which is periodically monitored by independent auditors. Also, fraud that goes beyond "facilitation money" can hardly be stemmed with good wages, as the size of bribes can often represent a multiple of the annual salaries of staff. It is thus important to ensure that good wages are backed with effective disciplinary action for poor performance and bribery. In the absence of such discipline, good wages can replace poorly paid corrupt staff by well paid corrupt staff—not much of a gain.

- *Revenue generation.* Establishing ARAs seems to have helped to mobilize larger revenues, certainly in the first years of their existence. However, such success has not always been sustained.
- *Integrity.* Corrupt networks can easily reestablish themselves after one year (often at the end of the probationary period for new staff) (Fjeldstad, Kolstad, and Lange 2003). The Commissioner of the URA noted in 2003 that "corruption is the number one problem."

The experience so far has shown that providing customs with greater operational autonomy can substantially contribute to enhancing its effectiveness and efficiency. This deserves to be studied as an option for modernizing customs. However, the experience so far also shows that autonomy is only a facilitating condition, not a solution for all problems facing customs. Results are best when customs uses its autonomy to engage in a full modernization initiative (such as in Peru), and where autonomy is respected over the years. The results are weakest, and even unsustainable, when customs delays this modernization process. In both Ghana and Uganda, for instance, the introduction of computerized customs operations and the associated simplification of procedures and effective staff training was delayed for more than 10 years after the creation of the ARAs, and prevented the ARAs from fully reaping the benefits of their greater autonomy.

## Management Contracts

Contracting with private parties to assist governments in the collection of taxes is not new.[21] History abounds with examples of tax farming, under which the taxation function itself was given under contract to a private citizen or a group of citizens. Typically the contract was limited in time, granted as a favor, and later sold to the highest bidder, who was entitled to keep any revenues raised above the contracted amount. Tax farming occurred in Egypt, Rome, Great Britain, and Greece. When first introduced in France during the 13th and 14th centuries, there were hundreds of tax farms, which were allocated using competitive auctions. By the 1680s, however, there was a single tax farm monopoly known as *La Ferme Générale* responsible for collecting all indirect taxes in France. Historians typically portray the members of *La Ferme Générale* as massively corrupt and estimate that less than half the money collected from French citizens ended up in the French treasury. When La Ferme Générale was abolished in 1791, 30 members were guillotined, a clear sign of the aversion of the new regime to this type of tax collection.[22] Another example of relying on the private sector to assist in levying taxes, albeit a much more limited one, is the practice of contracting preshipment enterprises to assist customs in the determination of the value of imports (see chapter 8).

Today's management contracts are quite different from either of these two practices. They also differ from the Build, Operate, and Transfer (BOT) contracts mostly used in infrastructure operations, where private parties invest in and manage structures for an agreed on period, and from the Build, Operate, and Own (BOO) contracts under which enterprises run public facilities or public utilities to reap efficiency gains through the application of management expertise.

Management contracts in customs services are a drastic approach to customs modernization, and

---

21. This section draws heavily on the Mozambique case study by Mwangi (2004); Hubbard, Delay, and Devas (1999); and documentation provided by Crown Agents.

22. In 12th century Morocco, the rulers granted tax-farming privileges to Christian and Jewish traders, as they were in the best position to extract tribute and customs fees from foreign traders, and the ruler trusted them more than his national officials, whom he suspected of massive fraud. This practice continued at least until the 17th century (Administration des Douanes et Impots Indirects 2001, pp. 101, 121).

have dual objectives. In contrast to tax farming, only the management of the government's taxation function is privatized. A contractor's responsibilities are twofold: First, it must manage the customs service and ensure that its major responsibilities are implemented effectively and efficiently; often the prime interest is in revenue generation, but trade facilitation comes a close second. Second, the contractor is to train national staff to take over the full set of responsibilities of customs within a given time frame. In return, the contractor is paid a fixed compensation, possibly complemented by a performance-related payment. Any evaluation of such management contracts must keep these dual objectives in mind—raising revenue and building a national customs service. Also, any assessment of the cost of the management contract must consider not only what it costs to run customs during the period of the contract, but what resources would have been required to attain these objectives through other, maybe less drastic, approaches. Such evaluation is complicated by the fact that the cost and effectiveness of alternative approaches are not observable variables.

The practice of using management contracts has so far been limited to Mozambique and Angola,[23] but it is a customs development model that is receiving increasing attention, and several other countries are actively looking into this approach. The main features of the management contract approach is discussed using the Mozambique contract as an example, as this is the most complete application of the management contract approach and has been in place long enough to provide useful lessons.

In the mid-1990s, the government of Mozambique (GOM) saw the need to modernize its Customs Services, which, as a result of many decades of civil war, were dysfunctional and thus unable to undertake revenue mobilization and trade facilitation responsibilities. Bilateral and multilateral development partners supported this initiative and accompanied it with advice and financial resources. GOM made the bold decision to grant a management contract to run customs and to prepare national authorities to assume full responsibility for customs operations at the end of the management contract. In 1995, GOM created a Technical

Unit to Restructure Customs to manage the proposed reform and the tendering for consultant services, as well as to oversee the implementation of the contract and the necessary changes in customs legislation. The Technical Unit was also to coordinate with all other government agencies involved in trade and customs issues. Following a process of competitive bidding (25 organizations tendered) Crown Agents (CA) was granted a three-year management contract. The contract specified CA's responsibilities:

- take over the complete management of customs and bring on board key customs officials to perform the contracted functions in accordance with the local employment laws
- train national customs staff to take over from CA at the end of the contract
- fully implement customs legislation and exchange regulation
- maintain customs' assets in good order and prepare an effective asset inventory
- procure and maintain equipment allocated to the reform project.

The initial contract was for US$37 million, 43 percent of which was paid by DFID. At the outset of the reform, CA appointed 60 experienced expatriate customs staff to take up managerial and training positions. CA gradually introduced its proprietary customs information system and managed the restaffing program, redesigned customs procedures, and assisted in preparing the new legislation. The contract was extended twice (for three years in 1999 and for two years in 2003, at which time there were only 11 CA staff members working on the project). The extension of the contract in 2003 specified that CA was to assist in the merging of the revenue function of customs, VAT, and direct tax by 2005 and in the preparation for the establishment of an ARA. The major reason for these extensions was that the national management team was still fragile, because a number of management positions had not yet been filled and the restaffing was still not complete. Integrity problems were found to be very resilient to change and strict application of the new customs procedures needed to be more firmly rooted.

From both revenue and trade facilitation angles the results achieved have been impressive. However, the handover to national customs authorities was

---

23. Crown Agents (CA) signed a management contract with the government of Angola in 2000 and initiated its activities in 2001.

much slower than expected and corruption problems are still a major issue.

- *Revenue performance.* Revenues rose from US$105 million in 1996—the year before the CA contract—to US$233 million in 2002, suggesting that the project had essentially paid for itself. In 1996–99 the average annual revenue increase over the 1996 revenues was four times the cost of the CA project.
- *Release times.* Customs release times also gradually improved and by 2003 the majority of qualifying goods were cleared within 48 hours and most were cleared in 24 hours. In 2000, the average clearance time was estimated at 18 days, and was still as high as 8 days in mid-2002. All in all, it is estimated that clearance times are now 40 times faster than before the reforms.
- *Management handoff.* The initial contract seriously underestimated the complexity of handing over customs management, causing several contract extensions. Also, the staff renewal process (80 percent of the staff was to be replaced) was delayed because of national legislation and was still not completed by mid-2003.
- *Corruption.* Corruption still plagues the customs operations, in part because strict adherence to the new customs procedures is still inadequate.

The CA contracts in Mozambique and Angola can be checked against best practices for management contracts for public service, which specify that payment to the contractors should be performance related and that interference by the government in daily management should be minimal. The complexity[24] and novelty of the operation, both for GOM and for the contractors; the uncertainty surrounding the whole project; and the multiple objectives of the project made it difficult to realistically assess whether the outcomes were achievable. Further complications arose from the poor state of information systems to provide both before-the-fact benchmarks and progress indicators. Also, few contractors were available that could provide assurance that they could undertake the task for which they were bidding, so that competition could not be

exploited to its fullest extent to adjust the contract terms. It is therefore not surprising that the role of performance-related compensation to the contractor was small in the overall compensation agreement. GOM did fully support the project and provided the necessary logistical and moral support and did not interfere with the day-to-day operations of the customs services. This hands-off approach enabled the contractors to devote themselves to implementing their commitments.

All in all, the management contract approach is a bold approach and appears to be a workable one in circumstances where alternative approaches are less promising and where quick results on the revenue front are highly desirable. However, it is still a rather new approach to customs modernization in extraordinary circumstances. The jury is still out with respect to the sustainability of the reforms and the full transfer to the national customs. It would appear that eventual new initiatives along these lines should be custom designed and should take local circumstances into account, including the availability of trained local staff and the functioning of customs in premodernization years. These factors will be featured in a good diagnostic analysis that should precede any negotiation with external service providers. Similarly, such diagnostic analysis should define specific performance criteria for the service providers. Any contract with service providers should contain clear milestones for the transfer to national customs authorities, a precondition for sustainability of the reform.

## Operational Conclusions

The task of customs is becoming increasingly complex given the sharp increase in trade, the greater sophistication of traders, and the multiple and shifting objectives imposed on customs. Uniformity of customs operations across the territory and across cargo categories is important, and speedy release of goods is crucial to the competitiveness of traders. There is also a need to adhere to international standards on value and classification, as well as regional standards on rules of origin. It is thus obvious that customs organizations need to adjust to these challenges, manage staff and procedures accordingly, and find the organizational formula best suited for their particular circumstances.

---

24. The agreed on program plans were made up of 700 specific but related task areas, some of which had 20 subcomponents.

Four summary conclusions are in order:

- Good HR management is the linchpin to effective and efficient customs management. This is too often neglected, and the delivery of services, in all its dimensions, all too often suffers while integrity problems persist. The management of human resources is multifaceted. It includes recruiting, training, staff compensation and promotion, as well as enforcement. None of these tasks is easy, and often must be implemented in a constrained environment. Budgets are tight and civil service rules give little leeway to the HR staff in customs. These difficulties should not discourage the investigation of new initiatives, and field studies do suggest that within these constraints much more attention should be given to HR issues, and generous payoffs can be expected. Strengthening the HR department would often be a good beginning.
- Recent examples of ARAs are promising. They can free customs from rigid civil service rules, give them more budgetary and financial autonomy, and generally provide greater flexibility in operational matters. However, experience has shown that creating an ARA is no guarantee for improved customs services. It does not replace a modernization program that should include, at the very least, the introduction of simplified procedures, the strict enforcement of integrity policies, and the introduction of advanced IT systems. Aside from providing higher wages initially and weeding out some staff from the old system, modern HR policies must be maintained—otherwise all progress achieved will quickly erode. This includes avoiding the erosion of the compensation premiums granted at the creation of the ARA. ARAs should also pay full attention to training, and have diligent recruitment policies. The institution's autonomy should also be protected from undue interference from the MOF.
- Management contracts can improve customs operations if they are well designed and monitored. So far these management contracts have largely been tested in special circumstances. In both Mozambique and Angola, the countries emerged from many years of civil strife and from dysfunctional public administrations. Engaging private service operators in those countries had

the advantage of substantially improving the revenue performance in the short run under difficult circumstances. The track record for transferring management capabilities to nationals is still being tested, but initial reports suggest that this has proven more difficult than initially imagined. It certainly has taken more time than envisioned at the start of the exercise. New management contracts may pay special attention to identifying performance-based remuneration and to building up the necessary information systems to monitor the performance indicators.
- Whatever the organizational model chosen, governments must provide customs with the resources required to permit customs to operate effectively and efficiently.

## Annex 2.A Human Resources Checklist

This chapter makes the point that human resources management is probably the single most important issue affecting the ability of customs to achieve its assigned objectives effectively and efficiently.

Without providing an exhaustive list of issues that would need to be looked into to assess the availability of these human resources and the quality of HR management, there are a few priority areas that could be investigated as starting points for more in-depth investigation.

- *Skill mix.* Obtain information on the skills and qualifications of customs staff and compare this with the skill mix required to enable the implementation of the near- and medium-term modernization program.
- *Human Resources Department.* Does the HR Department have a strategic vision? How is it staffed? What are its activities in the fields of recruitment, training, and career planning?
- *Recruitment.* What is the present recruitment process? Is customs or a Civil Service Ministry in charge? Does customs have a forward-looking recruitment program so it can adjust its skill mix over time, and do the present recruitment practices enable it to implement this program?
- *Training.* What is the training program at customs? Is there a dedicated training institute? Are the staff and curriculum attuned to the modernization process? Is training provided for staff on board or only for new recruits?

- *Compensation.* Is compensation at customs guided by the same rules that apply to the rest of the civil service?
- *Level of compensation.* How does compensation at customs compare with compensation in the rest of the civil service, and with the private sector? Does entry level compensation provide a living wage?
- *Bonus and salary supplements.* Is there a system of bonuses and premiums that supplements basic wages? Are these additional compensation packages distributed equally to all staff or do they provide an incentive for good performance? Is the system of bonuses SMART (specific, measurable, achievable, relevant, and timed)?
- *Additional employment benefits.* Do staff have access to housing, health care, or pension benefits?
- *Career management.* Is advancement based on seniority or performance? What rules exist for mobility (geographic and across services)? Are the rules transparent?
- *Enforcement of discipline.* Is there a clear code of conduct and a stipulated system for sanctions? What are the internal disciplinary processes and do they function in a transparent and timely manner?
- *Staff satisfaction survey.* Is there a periodic survey to assess staff satisfaction? What was management's reaction to the survey if such a survey was performed?

### Annex 2.B Management Contracts Checklist

Modern management contracts are a relatively new approach to customs modernization. Under such contracts a private firm manages customs and prepares the national customs authorities to take over at the end of the contract. These contracts have so far been largely undertaken in countries recovering from civil war and where the civil service is extremely weak. Issues that deserve close attention when considering management contracts include the following:

- A good diagnostic study should establish the present practices and the difficulties that prevent modern customs practices from being implemented. This diagnostic assessment should address whether the present situation is amenable to correction using the traditional technical assistance approach, or whether the situation warrants a more unconventional approach such as management contracts.
- A transparent and competitive tendering process for the management services should be opened, and a careful exercise for prequalification should be undertaken.
- A good description of the tasks tendered (management and transferring capacity) should be provided.
- The contract should adhere to well-defined procurement rules, with emphasis on transparency and clarity of services rendered.
- Details on expected performance criteria (revenue, trade facilitation, efficiency, and effectiveness) and possible benchmarks should be provided.
- Responsibilities for ultimately transferring management functions to nationals should be clearly defined.
- Availability of financial and oversight support for the duration of the contract should be investigated.

### Annex 2.C Checklist for Autonomous Revenue Agencies

The issue is frequently raised as to whether transforming an existing customs organization into an ARA should be considered as part of the solution to modernizing a customs administration in a given country. When considering this option, it is worthwhile to contemplate the following issue: What major reasons prevent customs from attaining its objectives as effectively and efficiently as desired? The response to this question will be derived from the diagnostic study.

The major advantage that an ARA provides is greater autonomy in matters of human resources (salaries, staff renewal at the outset to ensure that the desired skill mix is available, career management from recruitment through retirement) and in the determination of its budgetary envelope, and the ease with which these resources can be used both for recurrent and investment purposes.

To the extent that the shortcomings of a customs administration derive from these issues it will be important to see if, within the specific country circumstances, the promises of an ARA can be realized. The issues to consider include the following:

- Is the political support present to engage in staff renewal at the outset? This may include declaring all positions vacant and recruiting new staff in a transparent manner.
- Is it possible to introduce a credible and transparent method to select those that the new administration wants to attract?
- Are there financial resources available to provide termination packages for staff not selected for the new organization?
- What are the chances that a different and higher salary scale will be provided to the staff of the ARA and that this pay differential with the other civil services will be sustained? What is the power of the civil service unions—or of similar organizations—to prevent such differentiation in compensation?
- What are the chances that the necessary financial resources will be forthcoming and sustained to permit the payment of salary premiums to ARA staff?
- Would the MOF be willing to grant the financial autonomy implied by an ARA? Would this extend to the investment budget?
- Is there a tradition of micromanagement and interference by the MOF that could impede the independence of the ARA?
- What assurance is there that the board of the ARA will have sufficient autonomy to make the necessary decisions beneficial to the operation of the ARA?
- Is the process of selecting the board and the ARA manager likely to provide good managers?

If these shortcomings are derived from other issues such as lack of automation, major integrity problems, or complex and nontransparent procedures, then it will be important to see to what extent

- new and independent management will tackle these issues
- international donor organizations are willing to assist the ARA in its initial years to engage in these basic reform issues, either with advice or with financial support

- the likelihood exists that the proposed ARA management either has a modernization vision or will be open to acquiring such a vision.

Clearly, if the motive for the introduction of the ARA rests solely on the possibility of providing higher salaries to ARA staff, it is unlikely that the creation of an ARA will promote the modernization agenda.

## Further Reading

Castro, Patricio, and James T. Walsh. 2003. "The Organization of Customs Administration." In Michael Keen, ed. *Changing Customs: Challenges and Strategies for the Reform of Customs Administration.* Washington, D.C.: International Monetary Fund.

De Wulf, Luc. 2004. "Salary Bonuses in Revenue Departments: Do They Work?" PREM Note 84. Poverty Reduction and Economic Management Network. Washington, D.C.: World Bank.

Fjeldstad, Odd-Helge, Ivar Kolstad, and Siri Lange. 2003. *Autonomy, Incentives and Patronage, A study in Corruption in the Tanzania and Uganda Revenue Authorities.* Development Studies and Human Rights. Michelsen Institute. Oslo, Norway. www.cmi.no/publications/publication.cfm?pubid=1688.

Taliercio, Robert. 2004. "Administrative Reform as Credible Commitment: The Impact of Autonomy on Revenue Authority Performance in Latin America." *World Development* 32(2): 213–32.

## References

The word *processed* describes informally reproduced works that may not commonly be available through libraries.

Administration des Douanes et Impôts Indirects. 2001. *La Douane Marocaine a Travers l'Histoire.* Rabat.

Castro, Patricio, and James T. Walsh. 2003. "The Organization of Customs Administration." In Michael Keen, ed. *Changing Customs, Challenges and Strategies for the Reform of Customs Administration.* Washington, D.C.: International Monetary Fund.

De Wulf, Luc. 2004. "Salary Bonuses in Revenue Departments: Do They Work?" PREM Note 84. Poverty Reduction and Economic Management Network. Washington, D.C.: World Bank.

Fjeldstad, Odd-Helge, Ivar Kolstad, and Siri Lange. 2003. *Autonomy, Incentives and Patronage, A study in Corruption in the Tanzania and Uganda Revenue Authorities.* Development Studies and Human Rights, Michelsen Institute, Oslo, Norway. www.cmi.no/publications/publication.cfm?pubid=1688.

Hubbard, Michael, Simon Delay, and Nick Devas. 1999. "Complex Management Contracts: The Case of Customs Administration in Mozambique." *Public Administration and Development.* 19(2):153–163.

IDB (Inter-American Development Bank). 2001. "Institutionalizing Human Resources Management in Bolivia's Customs Administration." In *Customs Best Practices in East Asia and Latin America.* Washington, D.C.

Mwangi, Anthony. 2004. "Mozambique." In Luc De Wulf and José B. Sokol, eds. *Customs Modernization Initiatives: Case Studies.* Washington, D.C.: World Bank.

PLS RAMBOLL. 2001. *Supporting Institutional Reforms in Tax and Customs: Integrating Tax and Customs Administrations.* Study prepared for the World Bank and supported by the Danish Governance Trust Fund. Washington, D.C. www1.worldbank. org/publicsector/tax/Taxandcustoms-finalreport.doc.

Steenlandt, Marcel, and Luc De Wulf. 2004. "Customs Pragmatism and Efficiency: Philosophy of a Successful Reform: Morocco." In Luc De Wulf and Jose Sokol, eds. *Customs Modernization Initiatives: Case Studies.* Washington D.C.: World Bank.

Talierco, Robert. 2002. *Designing Performance: The Semi-Autonomous Revenue Authorities in Africa and Latin America.* draft. Washington, D.C.: World Bank. Processed.

———. 2004. *Organizational Design Profiles of Semi-Autonomous Revenue Authorities in Developing Countries.* Washington, D.C.: World Bank. www1.worldbank.org/publicsector/tax/autonomy.html.

Therkildsen, Ole. 2003. "Revenue Authority Autonomy in Sub-Saharan Africa: The Case of Uganda." Paper presented at the Workshop on Taxation, Accountability and Poverty at the Annual Conference of the Norwegian Association for Development Research (NFU) "Politics and Poverty." Oslo. October 23–24.

Van Rijckeghem, C. V., and B. Weber. 1997. "Corruption and the Rate of Temptation: Do Low Wages in the Civil Service Cause Corruption?" Working Paper WP97/73. Washington, D.C.: International Monetary Fund.

# LEGAL FRAMEWORK FOR CUSTOMS OPERATIONS AND ENFORCEMENT ISSUES

*Kunio Mikuriya*

Customs plays a crucial role in trade operations and revenue collection, and it directly affects the private rights and obligations of citizens. Customs is also expected to play an active role in protecting society and national security from cross-border movements of prohibited or restricted goods, including illicit drugs, counterfeit goods, endangered species, and weapons of mass destruction. Consequently, customs operations require a solid legal framework within which duties can be discharged. Without an effective legal framework that guarantees transparent, predictable, and prompt customs procedures, the international private sector will find it highly cumbersome to conduct busi-

ness with or to invest in a country in a competitive international business environment. It is, therefore, of critical national interest for every country to maintain its customs activities at high levels of effectiveness buttressed by a legal system that meets internationally accepted standards.

In response to dramatic increases in trade volume and heightened requirements for security, many customs administrations are reviewing their operations in the context of international standards and best practices to assess the need for introducing legal reforms. Modernization of customs laws, regulations, and supporting legal systems is essential for modern customs administrations to cope with the increasing demands for their services. The International Convention on the Simplification and Harmonization of Customs Procedures (entered

Many thanks to Ms. Mashiho Yuasa, law student at the University of Michigan Law School, for her help in research.

---

**BOX 3.1    An Example of Obsolete Customs Legislation**

When Yugoslavia broke apart in the early 1990s, the newly independent republics inherited the Yugoslav Customs Code, which was, by socialist standards, considered to be relatively user oriented. However, the shortcomings of the Yugoslav Code became rapidly apparent.

Designed for foreign trade exchanges largely managed by the state or state-run entities, it did not envisage the rapid surge in the number of operators. Procedures that were designed for established corporations were no longer applicable. For example, deferred payment was no longer realistic until the reliability of new market entrants had been assessed. In addition, the old code was too detailed and quite bureaucratic. It went to the extent of determining the opening hours of customs offices, which was unrealistic in a rapidly changing economic environment. In an attempt to be user friendly, the old code arbitrarily set the maximum time allowed for customs to clear goods. In the new market economy, customs had to deal with experienced traders and novice importers within the same amount of time. As a result, officials did not have the time to properly examine suspicious transactions, as the prevailing impression was that, as all goods should be cleared in five hours, declarations could be held up by prolonged examination of any one transaction. Worse, the Yugoslav Code made it mandatory to inspect every consignment, thus preventing the introduction of selective examinations.

From the penal side, the code made a distinction between individuals and legal entities. In theory, penalties for legal entities that committed customs fraud were higher than those for individuals. This did not make much sense in a market economy environment, and it led to numerous disputes when the smaller businesses started getting involved in duty evasion, as it was not clear if the company or an individual had committed the offense.

*Source:* Zarnowiecki 2003.

---

into force in 1974 and revised in June 1999), also known as the Revised Kyoto Convention, provides an excellent blueprint for such reforms (WCO 1997).

The Revised Kyoto Convention was developed to standardize customs policies and procedures worldwide. It embodies best practices of national legislation around the world, and its implementation would enable countries to meet international commitments concerning trade and border procedures, including the rules of the World Trade Organization (WTO).[1] At the same time, the Convention enables each country to tailor its policies and procedures to meet its unique legal, political, cultural, and societal requirements. Other customs legislation, such as the Customs Code of the European Community (the EU Code), is closely aligned with the Convention (European Union 1992).

This chapter discusses the need to modernize customs legislation in the context of international legal standards and examines possible difficulties in its implementation and enforcement. The chapter also briefly touches upon other legal instruments that complement existing international legislation. The first section focuses on the need for modern customs legislation. The second section provides a brief overview of the Revised Kyoto Convention. The third section discusses the process of preparing a modern Customs Code while the fourth section reviews the potential obstacles to a modern Customs Code. The fifth section discusses the process of enforcing customs law. The sixth section focuses on model legislation for intellectual property rights. The final section summarizes the main operational implications of the chapter.

## The Need for Modern Customs Legislation

The realities of modern international trade have made it necessary to modernize customs legislation in many countries. Outdated customs laws constrain social and economic progress by acting as significant nontariff trade barriers (box 3.1). They prevent effective revenue collection, discourage foreign trade and investment, and potentially threaten social and national security.

---

1. For example, General Agreement on Tariffs and Trade (GATT) 1994, Articles V, VIII, and X, and Agreement on Implementation of Article VII of GATT 1994 (WTO Valuation Agreement). GATT 1994 Article V discusses transit; Article VIII, fees and formalities; and Article X, publication and appeals.

Outdated customs legislation typically includes one or more of the following characteristics:

- no comprehensive body of customs-related legislation that establishes the clear competence of customs
- noncore customs elements
- inadequate provisions for complying with international commitments, including WTO agreements
- insufficient transparency and predictability reflected in the failure to provide basic information on matters such as rules, decisions, consultation mechanisms, and adequate appeals processes
- complex or redundant customs formalities that delay clearance and create opportunities for unnecessary discretionary interventions
- no provision for selective verification of cargo based on risk management, resulting in reliance on the 100 percent examination of consignments, which hinders customs from deploying its limited resources in an efficient and effective manner
- prohibition of advance lodgment of information or goods declaration[2] or post-clearance audits[3]
- no provision for automation or electronic communication
- ambiguous provisions that bestow customs officers with excessive discretionary power
- inadequate authority for customs to achieve its enforcement and compliance goals.

A solid and modern legal framework is the foundation of effective customs operations. Such a framework should provide for customs-related legislation to accomplish the following:

- establishes the competency of customs authorities to administer and enforce customs laws, develop administrative regulations, adjudicate or settle cases, and make decisions on customs administrative matters
- promotes transparency and predictability (for example, timely dissemination of information,

advance rulings, independent audit, appeals processes)
- provides for modern customs systems and procedures (risk management, audit-based control, and adequate automation)
- simplifies customs procedures (simplified declaration, advance lodgment, and so forth)
- encourages cooperation with other customs administrations and with other governmental organizations
- provides for partnership with the private sector (formal consultations, for example)
- promotes customs integrity (clear rules that do not allow excessive discretion, unambiguous specifications of customs' officers authority and obligations, and so forth)
- provides for penalties proportional to the gravity of the offense (that is, penalties should be sufficiently strong to deter customs violations and promote compliance but should not be unjustly severe, especially when violations are minor—from the revenue and enforcement perspectives—and nondeliberate)
- is accessible to the public
- meets international standards.

## The Revised Kyoto Convention

Since its inception in 1952,[4] the World Customs Organization (WCO) has been working to develop modern principles that would buttress effective customs administrations by examining customs policies and practices worldwide, cooperating with its member administrations, and working with trade communities and international agencies. The early efforts for simplifying and harmonizing customs procedures culminated in the Kyoto Convention, which was adopted by the WCO in 1973 and entered into force in 1974. Globalization, rapid transformation of international trade patterns, and advances in information technology (IT) since then have compelled the WCO and its members to review and update the Convention. The resultant revision of the Convention, known as the Revised Kyoto Convention, reflects the economic and technological

---

2. An essential basis for intelligence-based risk management.

3. An important element for the effective implementation of the WTO Valuation Agreement.

4. Established as the Customs Cooperation Council (CCC) in 1952; the current name, the World Customs Organization, was adopted in 1994.

changes and incorporates best practices of member administrations. The Revised Kyoto Convention was adopted by 114 customs administrations attending the WCO's 94th Session in June 1999.

### Elements of the Revised Kyoto Convention

The Convention is an international instrument designed to standardize and harmonize customs policies and procedures worldwide. Customs processes based on national customs legislation that are consistent with the Convention will enable customs to process imports, exports, and international travelers more smoothly. Elimination of divergent customs procedures and practices around the world will permit international businesses to meet their customs obligations effortlessly. Additionally, the Convention can serve to implement customs-related principles developed by the WTO, such as Articles V, VIII, and X of the GATT of 1994.

The Convention consists of the Body of the Convention, the General Annex, and the Specific Annexes.[5] The main Body of the Convention is a concise 14-page document that sets forth in its Preamble the key principles of modern customs administrations, and refers to the General Annex and Specific Annexes that are constituent parts of the Convention. The Articles of the Convention provide clear rules of accession to and administration of the Convention. The Preamble of the Convention states the following as guiding principles:

(a) application of customs procedures and practices in a predictable, consistent, and transparent manner

(b) provision of information on customs laws, regulations, procedures, and practices

(c) adoption of modern techniques, such as risk management and maximum practicable use of IT

(d) cooperation, where appropriate, with other national authorities, other customs administrations, and the trade community

(e) implementation of relevant international standards

(f) provision of easily accessible administrative and judicial review to affected parties.

The General Annex contains the core customs policies and procedures, and the Specific Annexes cover the individual customs procedures and practices relating to import, export, transit, processing, and enforcement measures. The Convention mandates countries to accede to the provisions in the General Annex and requires them to automate data systems, cooperate on trade, implement risk management techniques, and create a mechanism to maintain and update the Convention. The Specific Annexes contain recommended practices. In addition to these legal documents, there are detailed guidelines and best practices to assist countries in understanding how to implement the Convention.

Forty of the contracting parties to the existing Convention must ratify the Protocol of Amendment for the Revised Convention to enter into force. Thus far, 35 contracting parties have ratified it[6] while others are in the process of completing their national procedures.[7] Many countries have already reviewed their national legislation based on the Revised Kyoto Convention, without waiting for its formal entry into force.

### Overview of the Convention

The Convention presents a comprehensive set of over 600 legal provisions outlining basic principles for all customs procedures and practices.[8]

**The General Annex**    The General Annex stipulates the core principles for all customs procedures and practices to ensure that these are uniformly applied by customs administrations. These principles include the following: (a) standardization and simplification of goods declaration and supporting documents, (b) minimum necessary control, (c) risk management and audit-based control, (d) fast

---

5. The WCO gives the text of the Body of the Convention and the General Annex and Specific Annexes on its Web site. The full legal text of the Convention and the implementation guidelines can be purchased from the WCO at www.wcoomd.org/ie/En/Topics_issues.

6. Algeria, Australia, Austria, Belgium, Bulgaria, Canada, China, Czech Republic, Denmark, European Community, Finland, France, Germany, Greece, Hungary, Ireland, Italy, Japan, Republic of Korea, Latvia, Lesotho, Lithuania, Morocco, Netherlands, New Zealand, Poland, Slovakia, Slovenia, South Africa, Spain, Sweden, Switzerland, Uganda, United Kingdom, and Zimbabwe.

7. The Council of the European Union, for its 15 member states, in March 2003, and the President of the United States in May 2003, approved the Convention.

8. These provisions include Standards, Transitional Standards, and Recommended Practices. Standards must be implemented within 36 months of ratification, while Transitional Standards have a 60 month implementation period. Reservations are permitted to recommended practices in Specific Annexes.

track procedures for authorized persons and entities, (e) coordinated interventions with other agencies, (f) maximum use of IT, (g) transparency and predictability, and (h) availability of appeals processes.

The General Annex covers the main customs functions in its Definitions, Standards, and Transitional Standards, all of which have the same legal value. The Convention mandates the acceptance of the General Annex for accession. No reservations are permitted. The General Annex is divided into 10 chapters.

*Chapter 1: General Principles.* This chapter expresses the two driving principles of the Convention, which are the simplification and harmonization of customs procedures. It stipulates that the provisions in the General Annex must be implemented in national legislation in the simplest possible form and that customs administrations should cooperate with the trade community.[9]

*Chapter 2: Definitions.* This chapter provides the definition of terms related to the different level of obligations and the structure of the Convention.

*Chapter 3: Clearance of Goods.* This chapter articulates various provisions aimed at simplifying clearance procedures.[10] It prescribes the obligation of customs to establish customs offices and designate business hours; the qualification of declarants, their rights, and their duties; the creation of simplified information requirements for goods declarations and other documents; and the establishment of expeditious procedures for examination, assessment, and collection of duties and taxes, and release of goods. It stipulates coordinated intervention with other government agencies and customs agencies[11] and establishes procedures to be applied in cases of inadvertent errors and minor offenses.[12]

*Chapter 4: Duties and Taxes.* This chapter outlines provisions aimed at achieving transparency, predictability, and simplification of customs' revenue collection procedures that require national legislation to specify conditions, timing, and methods of duty and tax payment.[13] It provides for deferred payment and repayment.[14]

*Chapter 5: Security.* This chapter contains the basic principles necessary to achieve transparency, predictability, and simplicity of customs practices pertaining to security (that is, pledges, guarantees, and the like to secure correct payment of duties). National legislation must enumerate the cases in which security is required and must specify the forms of security and the amount of security.[15] It also advocates that the amount of security must be as low as possible and must not exceed the amount that is potentially chargeable for payment of duties and taxes. In addition, it recommends that security should be discharged as soon as possible.[16]

*Chapter 6: Customs Control.* This chapter first states that all goods entering or leaving customs territory are under customs' control.[17] It then outlines recommended customs procedures to enhance customs control, based on modern techniques and technologies such as the use of risk analysis and risk management, audit-based control, cooperation with other customs administrations and the trade community, IT, and e-commerce.[18]

Facilitation of international trade is one of the most important objectives of the Convention, and modern customs procedures are the key to achieving this goal. Risk management, for example, expedites the clearance of legitimate shipments while maintaining appropriate border control by identifying high-risk cargo. It entails a shift from 100 percent examination of documents and consignments to selective inspections. Such a program will enable a customs administration to optimize the use of its resources and allow the establishment of a fast-track program in which approved traders with good compliance records (as "authorized

---

9. Standards 1.2–3.

10. For example, Standard 3.12 states that information required on goods declarations must be limited to data necessary for assessment of duties and taxes, compilation of statistics, and application of customs law, and Standard 3.38 limits samples drawn for examination purposes to the smallest possible quantity.

11. Transitional Standard 3.4 outlines joint operations at common borders by neighboring customs administrations, and Transitional Standard 3.5 advocates coordinated inspections of goods with other government agencies.

12. Standard 3.39 stipulates that customs must not impose substantial penalties for inadvertent errors and errors without evidence of fraud or gross negligence.

13. Standards 4.1–3, 5–11, 13.

14. Standards 4.15–24.

15. Standards 5.1–2.

16. Standards 5.6–7.

17. Standard 6.1.

18. Standards 6.3–8 and Transitional Standard 6.9.

persons")[19] can obtain the release of cargo with minimum customs intervention. Likewise, the introduction of audit-based control complements risk management and is an essential element of the effective implementation of the WTO Valuation Agreement (WTO 1994c and 1994d). Other customs administrations and the trade community are indispensable partners for an effective risk-management program because they can be consulted about latest trade practices.

*Chapter 7: Use of Information Technology.* Application of IT is another important requirement of the General Annex to simplify and harmonize customs procedures and facilitate trade. This chapter obligates customs administrations to apply IT to support operations where it is cost-effective and efficient for customs and for the trade community.[20] The chapter mandates new or revised national legislation to provide for electronic alternatives to paper-based documentation requirements, electronic as well as paper-based authentication methods, and the right of customs administrations to retain information and, as appropriate, share it with other customs administrations through electronic means.[21] It also states that customs administrations must develop information technology in consultation with all relevant parties.[22] The Guidelines for this chapter provides some information that might help customs determine how to improve the services it provides to its clients and trading partners through the use of information and communication technologies.

*Chapter 8: Relationship Between Customs and Third Parties.* This chapter provides for third parties, and states that persons or entities will have the option of doing business with customs directly or through a third party.[23] Third parties will have the same rights as parties on whose behalf they act.[24]

*Chapter 9: Customs Information, Decisions, and Rulings.* This chapter lists key principles for customs to achieve transparency and predictability of their procedures and practices, through the publication of laws, regulations, judicial decisions, and administrative rulings. Implementation of the standards outlined in this chapter is critical for meeting the requirements of Article X of GATT 1994.[25] For example, it stipulates that information pertaining to customs law must be readily available and that any changes must be made available well in advance of the changes entering into force.[26] Customs administrations must provide "as quickly and as accurately as possible" specific information requested by an interested party as well as any information they consider pertinent to the party without sacrificing confidentiality.[27] Adverse customs decisions must provide reasons and must advise of the right of appeal. Furthermore, customs administrations must issue binding rulings upon request.[28]

The guidelines to this chapter provide detailed information for administrations to set up their procedures for publication of information. They include quality and clarity of information, trade consultation, exhibitions, enquiry offices, availability of tariff information, liability of information provided, explanation of the concept of freedom of information, procedures for issue, and notification and annulment of binding rulings by customs.

*Chapter 10: Appeals in Customs Matters.* The right of appeal also ensures transparency and predictability of customs procedures and practices. It protects individuals against decisions of customs that may not be in compliance with national laws and regulations. It also safeguards against omissions by customs. Furthermore, the reviews of challenged decisions or omissions and subsequent verdicts by a competent authority guarantee uniform application of the laws and regulations. The provisions in chapter 10 provide for a multistage appeal process and an independent judicial review as a final avenue of appeal. Specifically, chapter 10 requires national legislation to provide for a right

---

19. "Authorized persons who meet criteria specified by the Customs, including having an appropriate record of compliance with Customs requirements and a satisfactory system for managing their commercial records." (Transitional Standard 3.32).

20. Standard 7.1.

21. Standard 7.4.

22. Standard 7.3.

23. Standard 8.1.

24. Standard 8.4.

---

25. Article X of GATT 1994, Publication and Administration of Trade Regulations, requires publication before enforcement of all laws, regulations, judicial decisions, and administrative rulings affecting imports and exports as well as measures that impose a new or more burdensome requirement, restriction, or prohibition on imports, or on the transfer of payments.

26. Standards 9.1–2.

27. Standards 9.4–6.

28. Standards 9.8–9.

of appeal in customs matters and gives anyone affected by a customs decision such a right.[29] An initial appeal will be made to the customs, and the appellant has a right to further appeal to an independent authority and finally to a judicial authority.[30] Compliance with the Standards in chapter 10 is an essential step toward meeting the requirements of Article X of GATT 1994.[31]

**Specific Annexes**   There are 10 Specific Annexes covering individual customs procedures and practices. Acceptance of the Specific Annexes is not obligatory for accession to the Convention. However, the WCO recommends that contracting parties at least accept the Specific Annexes on importation for home use,[32] those for export, and those regarding formalities prior to lodgment of goods declaration,[33] as well as those for warehouses,[34] transit,[35] and processing.[36] Reservations are permitted in Recommended Practices in the Specific Annexes, but contracting parties must review their reservations every three years.

---

29. Standards 10.1–2.

30. Standards 10.4–6.

31. Article X of GATT 1994, Publication and Administration of Trade Regulations, also requires appeal procedures. Members must "maintain or institute judicial, arbitral or administrative tribunals or procedures for the purpose, *inter alia*, of the prompt review and correction of administrative action relating to Customs matters" providing for uniform, impartial, and reasonable administration of laws, decisions, and rulings affecting import and export.

32. Annex B: The minimum specific requirements for the clearance of goods for home use (chapter 1), the requirements for the clearance of goods for home use that were exported and are being re-imported in the same state (chapter 2), and the circumstances and conditions in which relief from import duties and taxes may be granted for certain goods declared for home use (chapter 3).

33. Annex C deals with outright exportation as opposed to temporary exportation.

34. Annex D: Customs procedures for warehousing (chapter 1) and in free zones (chapter 2). These procedures facilitate trade by waiving or deferring payments of duties and taxes.

35. Annex E outlines customs procedures and practices related to goods traveling through multiple customs offices within a single customs territory (national transit) or multiple customs territories (international transit). These provisions on international transit provide for technical and operational means to meet requirements set out in GATT Article V.

36. Annex F describes customs procedures and practices that a country might use to promote its economy and trade by providing total or partial relief of duties and taxes.

**Guidelines**   One of the outstanding features of the Convention is the existence of comprehensive implementation guidelines that have been developed to provide, in the General Annex and Specific Annexes of the Convention, detailed explanations of all chapters, except for the chapter on Definitions. These guidelines are not part of the legal text of the Convention, but are rather designed to offer explanations of the provisions of the Convention, and to provide examples of best practices or methods of application and future developments. They must be read in conjunction with the legal text contained in each chapter of the annexes. The guidelines are constantly updated to provide information on new and modern practices.[37]

## Preparing a Modern Customs Code

The Revised Kyoto Convention can serve as a guiding principle for preparing a modern Customs Code. While countries can sign on to the Convention as a means to modernize a Customs Code, it is, in fact, not the only way to implement a modern one. Another option would be a phased introduction of the principles and practices contained in the Convention, taking into account the local environment and capacity.

### Obligations Under the Revised Kyoto Convention

Contracting parties are obligated to bring into force, nationally, the standards, transitional standards, and recommended practices that they have accepted. Standards must be implemented within 36 months of ratification, while transitional standards have a 60-month implementation period. Such regulations are not necessarily restricted to customs legislation and may apply to official notifications, charters, or ministerial decrees, or similar instruments. Customs administrations are obliged to ensure that their regulations are transparent, predictable, consistent, and reliable.

Contracting parties' national legislation must include at least the basic rules from the General Annex, with detailed regulations for their implementation; no reservations are permitted. In

---

37. For example, the guidelines for chapter 7 were revised in March 2003 to take account of developments in the area of information and communication technology since 1999.

addition, contracting parties may accept all or a number of Specific Annexes and chapters upon accession to the Convention. The WCO considers it desirable for contracting parties to accept the Specific Annexes on importation, exportation, warehouses, transit, and processing. Although the guidelines are not legally binding, customs administrations may adopt and implement those best practices that are most suited to their particular environment.

In addition to legislative measures, contracting parties must provide facilities, personnel, and equipment to realize the objectives of the Convention. Such infrastructure is indispensable particularly in the areas of IT, risk management, and audit-based controls.

### Practical Guide to the Modernization of Customs Codes

A customs administration might take the following steps to prepare for the implementation of the Convention into its legislation. It could organize a working group, consisting of headquarters and field officials, under the presidency of a high ranking official. Typically, some headquarters specialists (including IT) would be involved in major policy matters (such as procedures, investigations) or technical matters (such as valuation and origin, as well as legal matters). This group would meet at the very early stages of reform planning, and each member would be expected to provide a list of what he or she would like to see in the laws as the outcome of new legislation, what the current legislation does not allow, and how he or she would like to see customs evolve. At the same time, someone from the legal department's staff would review the existing laws that affect customs work. It would be essential to identify, as far upstream as possible, all the legislation relating to other relevant government agencies, including those dealing with offenses that might affect customs operations, and to determine whether the legislation would require adjustments to the relevant articles, cross-referencing in the customs law, or repealing. It would also be important to know if the customs law supersedes other previous legislation.

The customs administration also could do the following:

- Obtain support from appropriate quarters (the executive and legislative branches, various groups within the customs administration, members of the trade community, WCO, the donor community, and so on). Consultations with the trade community at this stage are particularly important.

- Check whether proper legal authority, such as the authority to make administrative regulations and the ability to provide technical input to the legislative branch, is accorded to the customs administration for the purpose of issuing a new code. Some customs administrations may need to obtain additional or new legal authority to effectively and efficiently implement the Convention.

- Use the provisions of the Convention or other national legislation aligned to the Convention, such as the EU Code as a checklist (for an example, see box 3.2). It should compare the current customs laws to the provisions in the General Annex and Specific Annexes and identify provisions that must be added, repealed, replaced, or modified. During this stage, it should study the national legislation of other countries and consult with other customs agencies to learn from them.

- Identify provisions that must be enacted as statutes by the national legislature.

- Identify provisions that are better suited for customs regulations, administrative guidelines, official notices, and so forth.

- Identify obstacles to successful implementation of a modern code through legislation.

- Determine how each provision should be implemented. It must be recognized that each provision can be implemented in a variety of ways. An effort should be made to choose a method of implementation that will suit the environment in which a particular customs authority operates. Morocco's revision of its Customs Code, in line with the Revised Kyoto Convention, presents a good example of this practice (see box 3.3).

## Potential Obstacles to Customs Modernization

Customs modernization efforts sometimes fail despite the good intentions and hard work of customs administrations. Certainly, the customs community and the international donor community

---

**BOX 3.2   Sample Checklist to Identify Provisions Requiring Amendment or New Legislation under the Revised Kyoto Convention**

Under the Revised Kyoto Convention it is possible to have in place a sample checklist that identifies provisions requiring amendment or new legislation. The following two provisions provide a good example for a sample checklist:

**3.34 Standard.** "When scheduling examinations, priority shall be given to the examination of live animals and perishable goods and to other goods that Customs accept are urgently required."

This provision requires that customs must examine urgent required goods without delay to avoid loss or deterioration of the goods. To fulfill this requirement, customs should, subject to the availability of resources, examine perishable goods, live animals, or goods that are urgently required, outside their normal hours of business or at a place other than the customs office where the goods declaration was lodged. In this regard, the national statutes and regulations that deal with the subject matter of the standard should be listed. It would also be important to write down whether the existing statute or regulation must be modified or replaced or whether new legislation is necessary. Useful resources,

other government departments to be consulted, and any other concerns should also be listed.

**3.35 Transitional Standard.** "If the goods must be inspected by other competent authorities and the Customs also schedules an examination, the Customs shall ensure that the inspections are coordinated and, if possible, carried out at the same time."

While the ideal situation is a single examination coordinated and conducted by the authorities concerned at the same time, this provision does not require customs to take special actions to ensure this situation. It requires that customs establish effective communications with other competent authorities and where possible to carry out their examination at the same time as the other authorities. However, in the interest of cost-effectiveness and efficiency to both governments and the trade, customs may give consideration to re-engineering its clearance process, which could result in the establishment of an inspection service or compliance verification process that is integrated with that of the other competent authorities.

*Source:* WCO 2000.

---

have learned the lesson that "one-size-fits-all" solutions do not work. Successful modernization of customs legislation requires attention to the unique political and legal tradition, social and cultural climate, and administrative or organizational structure in which a particular customs administration operates.

### Legal Tradition

Legal research by Victor Thuronyi (1996) has identified integration as one of four essential criteria for well-drafted legislation. Thuronyi defines integration as "the consistency of the law with the legal system and drafting style of the country" (p. 72). Indeed, when drafting new legislation, the drafter must be mindful of the legal tradition of the country. At the most general level, legal systems are classified in two broad groups: civil law and common law. Civil law is based on written legal codes arrived at through legislation, edicts, and so forth, whereas common law is based on the precedents

created by judicial decisions over time. Under the civil law system, legislation tends to be drafted in the form of broad statements of principles whereas common law legislation tends to be much more detailed. However, these sweeping characterizations are generally of limited use. To draft new, successful customs laws that are amenable to the unique legal tradition of a country, the drafter must look more closely at the country's traditional drafting style, organization of laws (for example, a single code vs. separate laws), practices of administrative and judicial interpretation, and choice of legal instruments.

### Drafting Styles

Thuronyi insists that a country's laws must be "consistent in appearance and style in order to facilitate understanding and interpretation of the laws and to maintain the dignity of the legislative process" (Thuronyi 1996, p. 89). At the same time, when drafting new customs legislation the drafter should

---

### BOX 3.3    Morocco's Adoption of the Convention: A Success Story

Morocco revised its customs law in 1997 and has become one of the first countries to adopt the Revised Kyoto Convention. The Moroccan Customs Administration attributes its successes to (a) its efforts to analyze and understand its operating environment, to form partnerships with the trade community, and to cooperate and consult with other government agencies; (b) a pragmatic approach aimed not only at developing a new law, but also at avoiding pitfalls common in any procedural improvement; and (c) involvement of all customs staff members. Its efforts raised awareness among the staff that the legislation's ultimate goal was to improve its procedures to fulfill its missions, including economic development.

The Moroccan Customs Administration aimed to adapt its legislation to national and international environments. The latest review of customs legislation was no exception. The administration consulted all relevant ministerial departments and private sector representatives. As a result, the Moroccan customs legislation is in harmony with all other national legislation. For example, customs penal provisions are consistent with the national penal code and include a number of common principles such as the principles of good faith, extenuating circumstances, and supervisory authorities of administrative officers.

The Moroccan Customs took leadership in implementing the Revised Kyoto Convention, and encouraged other government departments to review their border procedures. The Moroccan Customs began the process by first implementing essential provisions within the Customs Code and then proceeding to supplement them with explanations and clarifications in the form of administrative instructions such as circulars and notes. The Moroccan customs law provides for close cooperation with other relevant government agencies. This is particularly vital in health and agricultural controls and enforcement and information exchanges among law enforcement organizations. The customs law defines the principle of cooperation whereas regulations specify terms and conditions for such cooperation.

For some years the Moroccan Customs has been pursuing a decentralization policy, giving regional authorities the power to make certain decisions without consulting headquarters. A strong communication network was built to give frontline officers all the instruments, including authorizations, and instructions necessary to deal with a wide range of customs matters. Only when cases of major importance arise, when interpretation of legislative texts is required, or when arbitration is requested, is the central administration consulted. When a case requires legislative interpretation, customs prepares a general note to ensure consistent application of the law nationwide.

*Source:* Steenlandt and De Wulf 2004.

---

conscientiously consider the advantages and disadvantages of the country's traditional drafting style, for possible improvement. For example, statutes in the English-speaking world have a reputation for being excessively complex and difficult to understand. This is partly because drafters in these countries have inherited the traditional style of legislative language used in the United Kingdom in the 19th century (Turnbull 1993). However, the complexity of the legislative language was also a result of a strong need for precision. Turnbull believes that precision can be accomplished without unduly sacrificing simplicity and clarity. Simple clarity and precision are both extremely important for a country's customs legislation to achieve transparency and predictability. A customs law must be simple and clear so that nonlegislators and nonlawyers,

such as frontline customs officials and traders, can understand it. Simultaneously, customs law should be precise to minimize opportunities for excessive administrative and judicial discretion.

### Organization

A single consolidated Customs Code—a document containing all the customs laws—has many advantages over customs laws spread over many documents. For example, such a code promotes compliance because it is easier for a trader to find applicable laws and regulations in a single code than in multiple documents (Thuronyi 1996). It also helps to maintain consistency within the customs laws because legislators are more likely to work under a common guiding principle within a single code. A code is also easier to amend than multiple laws because "amendments are automatically consolidated into" the code itself (Renton 1975, pp. 76–84). This is desirable because it is hard to determine precisely what the law is if amendments do not repeal or replace previous laws clearly (Thuronyi 1996).

However, a truly consolidated Customs Code is perhaps a rarity. Many countries organize laws related to customs into two major legal documents: one dealing with the tariffs, duties, and taxes, and another concerning customs procedures.[38] Many customs-related laws and regulations are also found in the laws enacted to promulgate international treaties and agreements.[39] Moreover, it is almost inevitable for provisions relevant to the customs administration to be contained in separate laws, because in practice customs has authority to enforce legislation other than revenue laws (see Enforcement of Customs Laws in this chapter). Furthermore, because many of the legal provisions relevant to customs are procedural they are almost inevitably included, at least in part, in the general rules for criminal or administrative procedure, rather than in a Customs Code. Thus, even if a Customs Code is organized to include customs-related provisions on as comprehensive a basis as feasible, there will inevitably be a need for coordination with provisions that are found outside this code. Separate laws can be organized in an effective manner by cross-referencing and eliminating duplicate provisions (Thuronyi 1996). Particular attention must be paid when provisions related to a single customs duty or procedure are included in more than one piece of legislation or placed within noncustoms law, because such provisions are difficult to comply with, enforce, and amend.

### Administrative and Judicial Interpretation

It is generally agreed that statutes under common law tradition are detailed and that the courts interpret them narrowly. In contrast, statutes in civil law countries are broad, outlining general principles only and leaving details for other mechanisms, including the courts, to fill in. Such generalizations are of limited use because, in reality, some civil law countries have statutes that are as detailed as those in common law countries (Turnbull 1993). However, it is prudent to understand how officials and judges traditionally apply customs laws in a given country and to attempt to draft new customs legislation accordingly. The drafter should learn how customs officials and judges interpret a provision of the customs law, whether a legislative or administrative guideline is available, whether precedents are relied upon, and whether officials and judges enjoy a certain degree of discretionary power. However, the drafter should be cognizant of weaknesses of the traditional approach. Customs officials should not be allowed excessive discretion in interpreting customs laws because transparency and predictability of the customs procedures cannot be achieved under such circumstances. Customs laws also require some degree of flexibility. Excessively rigid applications of customs laws would result in unnecessary steps in customs procedures, particularly in relation to minor violations or disputes, and would burden traders, customs, and judicial systems.

### Choice of Legal Instruments

A wide variety of legal instruments are available for WCO member countries to implement modern customs principles. A government can enact customs legislation as statute, administrative guidance, official notification, charter, ministerial decree, schedule, and so on. For example, Moroccan customs laws are organized in two documents. The first document is the Code on Customs and Indirect Taxation, composed of decrees and decisions by the Minister of Finance. The second document is the Customs and Indirect Taxation Regulation that explains customs legislation and regulations and contains all the Notes and Circulars.

Selecting an appropriate legal instrument to match the purpose of a given provision is important. Thuronyi (1996, p. 86) states that it is not "appropriate to try to provide all the necessary details" in a statute because (a) it would make the statute "unduly lengthy and difficult to understand,"

---

38. For example, the EU has the Common Customs Code and Implementation Regulations dealing with Customs procedures and the European Union Tariff Code. Each member country has its own laws on customs enforcement, penalties, and appeals processes.

39. Japan, EU, and others, for example. When a provision of a convention or other international agreement cannot be implemented within the Common Customs Code, the EU makes an entry into the code referring to the provision.

(b) the legislature "cannot foresee all situations," and (c) statutes are more difficult to modify than other legal instruments. Furthermore, customs agencies are often a more suitable entity to make detailed rules because they have information and expertise, they are less vulnerable to political and other outside pressures, and they can react more quickly to new problems (Stein, Mitchell, and Mezines 2003). Some advocate that details should not be crystallized in the form of statutes because the resulting rigidity is potentially harmful to the practices of fair and speedy agencies (Jackson 1941).

In general, essential provisions must be enacted as laws while details that require frequent amending are better suited for administrative regulations. However, it should be noted that such determinations largely depend on "the practice in the particular country and on politics" (Thuronyi 1996, pp. 86–87). For example, Thuronyi states that how much power over detail the legislature is willing to delegate to an administrative agency often dictates the choice of legal instruments. Time is also one of the most obvious determinants for whether a given detail is included in a statute because the total time available to the legislature for lawmaking is limited (Jackson 1941, p. 14). Finally, Thuronyi points out that leaving details on which consensus is hard to reach to administrative regulations is a political tactic employed to ease passage of a bill.

### Determination of Which Principles to Implement and How to Implement Them

A customs administration must decide carefully which reform principles to implement. A modern reform principle can be implemented in a variety of ways; however, not all options suit the operating environment of the particular customs administration. For example, trade facilitation through a paperless customs procedure may be promoted by an incentive to use e-documents or by a mandate accompanied by a sanction. The choice between these two options should be based on careful consideration of the e-commerce environment in which a particular customs administration finds itself. A high level of compliance may be achieved by a system of penalties for customs violation alone or in conjunction with more subtle incentive measures such as the granting, denial, or withdrawal of

expedited clearance privileges. Before deciding which measure to implement, however, the capacities of the customs organization, including its commercial integrity and efficiency, must be examined carefully (Raven 2001).

### Interaction with Other Government Entities

Customs often enforces a wide range of laws besides customs law. For example, the United States Customs and Border Protection enforces numerous laws and international treaties and agreements in diverse fields from agriculture to national defense.[40] Customs also routinely cooperates with other government agencies, sometimes sharing facilities at national borders. Therefore, successful customs legislation must provide for the interdependence of multiple government entities. Consultations between customs and other departments are vitally important to eliminate duplicate and inconsistent legislation. To achieve simplification of customs and other border procedures, it is desirable for customs to enforce laws on border procedures or for customs to cooperate closely with other concerned departments and agencies.[41] Otherwise, border controls by multiple government organizations are likely to result in ineffective and inefficient border procedures and corruption. Customs in some market transition economies in which borders had been managed by military force with little external trade have experienced such difficulties. Cooperation is particularly important when laws are being made on border procedures in which customs generally lacks expertise, such as agricultural or health inspections. On such occasions, customs might get involved to ensure simple, coordinated border inspections.

---

40. According to its Web site, the United States Customs and Border Protection enforces laws on agriculture, alien and naturalization, banks and banking, census, commerce and trade, conservation, copyrights, crimes and criminal procedures, customs duties, food and drugs, foreign relations, internal revenue, intoxicating liquors, money and finance, navigation, patents, postal service, public building and property, public land, railroads, shipping, telegraphs and telephones, territories and insular possessions, transportation, war and national defense, and international treaties, statutes, and agreements (United States Customs and Border Protection 2003).

41. Raven (2001) states that it has been generally accepted that convergence of frontier controls in a single administrative agency, usually customs, is highly beneficial.

*Translation*

When drawing on a model code, the drafter must be careful of the hazards of translation. Frequently, a legal concept does not accurately translate from one language or legal system to another. The target culture might not have an equivalent legal concept. For example, not all languages have an equivalent word for "audit." The drafting team should take care to understand what a particular concept represents in the original language and provide a description, definition, or explanation to prevent misunderstandings.

## Enforcement of Customs Laws

Every customs administration has enforcement duties. However, the scope of the responsibility and authority differs widely from one administration to another. Some customs agencies have vast powers to enforce customs laws and regulations. In some countries, customs derives enforcement powers from its penal codes, and these powers are not confined to matters related to customs law. At the other end of the spectrum, some customs agencies play more limited roles. They enforce the customs law related only to revenue collection by "the inspection of goods and the classification and valuation of merchandise" (Lane 1998, p. 78). Because of the increasing need to fight customs fraud (intellectual property rights violations, revenue fraud, and transshipment, for example), narcotics trafficking, money laundering, and export violation (trafficking in weapons and munitions, among others), those customs agencies with limited powers might require a greater range of enforcement authority.

The WCO's Expert Working Group on commercial fraud recommends the following set of enforcement powers (WCO 2004a):

- examination (compliance with the customs law)
- right of search (illegal importation and exportation)
- sampling
- seizure
- right to access documents
- post-import and post-export audit
- detention or arrest
- charge
- prosecution

- restraint of assets
- exchange of information
- inquiries on behalf of other customs administrations.

Proponents for greater enforcement authority and responsibility for customs offer two reasons: (a) efficiency and effectiveness and (b) morale of customs officers. First, customs is uniquely situated to enforce customs and other laws in border regions because it has the infrastructure to examine goods and people that move across the borders. It also has familiarity with cross-border activities. Risk management tools, information technology, and cooperation with other government agencies and other customs administrations would enhance customs' abilities to enforce customs and other laws at the borders because these tools would enable the agencies to assess threats and deal proactively with possible violations. Therefore, it is efficient and effective to assign appropriate authority to customs agencies to enforce customs and other laws related to cross-border violations.

Second, the advocates of a substantial enforcement role for customs also claim that customs officers should be given the authority to search, detain, arrest, seize, and investigate people, goods, and means of transportation as related to actual or suspected customs violations because limiting customs' enforcement powers to revenue collection would demoralize customs officers (Zarnowiecki 2003). They believe the practice of handing over the investigation to another government agency such as the police would discourage customs officers from discovering violations at the borders in the first place because this would, in many cases, result in a loss of incentives, such as additional salary benefits and social recognition, for customs officers. They fear that such demoralization would decrease customs' effectiveness and weaken customs' integrity.

The Revised Kyoto Convention deals with enforcement issues specifically in Annex H, which sets out standards and recommended practices to ensure fairness, speed, consistency, transparency, and predictability of enforcement of customs laws while aiming for minimal disruption to trade and travel. The annex deals with the definition and investigation of breaches of the customs law and with customs' role in the administrative settlement of offenses. This annex, however, does not cover all the activities that customs usually engages in when dealing with customs and other cross-border offenses because many of those activities are beyond customs laws and regulations. Investigation and administrative settlement, however, are two topics in this area that must be covered specifically in the customs legislation. The Convention does not limit the powers granted to customs under individual national legislation. Instead, it acknowledges diversity in the scope of customs enforcement powers among its member nations.

Specifically, which enforcement powers to grant to customs officers must be determined in light of the country's constitution, legal system, and institutions. Yet, regardless of the number of enforcement authorities and their scope of responsibilities, it is important for each customs administration to use risk management tools, information technology, and cooperation with other government agencies and other customs administrations to achieve fair, speedy, and consistent customs enforcement in accordance with the principles of the Convention. The WCO offers information and training in customs enforcement and is a good source of information on enforcement modernization and reforms.[42]

## Model Legislation for International Property Rights

The Revised Kyoto Convention is the most comprehensive international instrument designed to harmonize and simplify customs procedures and practices. However, there are other instruments devised to support the Convention. The WCO is continually developing new tools and initiatives to respond to changes surrounding customs operations. Such tools and initiatives are designed to be compatible with and complementary to the Convention.

It is necessary for customs laws and institutions to keep pace with the government's international commitments. One such example is the enforcement of intellectual property rights, required by the Agreement on Trade-Related Aspects of Intellectual Property Rights (TRIPS Agreement) (WTO 1994b).[43] The WCO Intellectual Property Rights

(IPR) Model Legislation is being developed to help member administrations enact border measures designed to protect intellectual property rights, without interfering with legitimate trade (WCO 2004b).[44] This model legislation is intended to provide guidance to those customs administrations that are implementing intellectual property rights legislation for the first time and to those conducting legislative reviews or reforms. It will help customs meet the standards set in the TRIPS Agreement. However, the IPR Model Legislation is not binding upon members and goes beyond the minimum standards required in the TRIPS Agreement. The WCO first developed the IPR Model Legislation in 1988. Since then the model legislation has undergone two revisions, and the WCO aims to keep it up-to-date through regular revisions, incorporating best practice and keeping in line with the suggestions of the World Intellectual Property Organization. Box 3.4 describes the process of modernizing the Russian Federation customs legislation.

## Operational Conclusions

Several key operational implications derived from this chapter stand out.

- Customs' efforts to modernize legislation should strive to achieve international legal standards. The Revised Kyoto Convention embodies best practices of national legislation around the world. In particular, it enables each country to meet international commitments concerning trade and border procedures, including the agreed on rules of the WTO. It also enables each country to tailor its policies and procedures to meet its legal, political, cultural, and societal requirements.
- Implementing a Customs Code aligned with the principles of the Revised Kyoto Convention would allow for sufficient transparency and predictability based on providing basic information on matters such as rules, decisions, consultation mechanisms, and adequate appeals processes. It would eliminate complex or redundant customs formalities that delay clearance and create

---

42. World Customs Organization, www.wcoomd.org.

43. Articles of TRIPS relevant to customs are 51–60 in Section 4 Special Requirements Related to Border Measures.

44. The latest text is available on the WCO IPR-related Web site http://www.wcoipr.org.

## BOX 3.4   Modernization of Customs Legislation in the Russian Federation

In 1993, the Russian Federation committed itself to unifying its customs legislation and implementing the rules accepted worldwide. In 2003 a new Customs Code was adopted; it entered into force on January 1, 2004. The new law is based on the Revised Kyoto Convention, as well as on customs legislation of Russia's key trading partners.

In the new Customs Code, account has been taken of the WTO requirements stipulated in Article I "General Most-Favored-Nation Treatment," Article V "Freedom of Transit," Article VII "Valuation for Customs Purposes," Article VIII "Fees and Formalities connected with Importation and Exportation," Article X "Publication and Administration of Trade Regulations" of the GATT, TRIPS, the Agreement on Rules of Origin, and the Agreement on Implementation of Article VII.

The new Customs Code aims to eliminate excessive administrative restrictions on foreign trade, establish clear and consistent rules for economic operators with regard to transborder movement of goods, as well as reduce the administrative discretion of customs officials and the inordinate number of bylaws and administrative instructions, which had had a negative impact on the clarity and transparency of customs operations. The final draft of the code was prepared in close cooperation with the business community. A review of an initial draft of the new code was initiated by the Russian Union of Entrepreneurs. A working group consisting of representatives from the business community, the State Customs Committee, the Ministry of Finance, and the Ministry of Economy developed joint proposals for amendments to the final reading of the draft code in the Duma. This process made it possible for the different groups to compromise on many issues. The state has taken significant innovative measures to meet the needs of traders, as well as those of ordinary citizens, crossing the border.

The legal and enforcement powers of customs are clearly spelled out while the conditions to speed up the customs procedures (pre-entry declaration, specific simplified procedures, use of a single classification code, and so forth) have been clarified. The new code envisages a broad application of IT, electronic customs control, and customs clearance. The process of streamlining and simplifying customs formalities was conditioned by the shift from full physical examination of all goods to a system of selective inspections based on risk assessment and risk analysis. This shift is expected to facilitate international trade and provide reliable customs control while ensuring efficient handling of customs resources. Implementation of the code is expected to change the relationship between customs and the business community, which will increasingly be based on the principle of cooperation and consultation. This approach is consistent with the new concept of governing the state, that is, a dialogue between the government and the business community, and reflects the approach recommended by the WCO. The approach permits the exercise of public control while taking into account the needs of the business community and ensuring openness and transparency of the legislation.

While this legislation is a considerable step in the right direction, the code still contains ambiguities that could lead to substantial discretion in customs operations. How it will actually be implemented needs to be observed carefully by both the customs administration and the trade community. Based on the experience of implementing a new Customs Code, there might arise a need to adjust or improve the Customs Code itself or the way it is implemented. It is therefore critical to maintain consultations between the customs administration and the trade community to follow the implementation procedures recommended by the Customs Code.

*Source:* Based on contributions from Leonid Lozbenko, First Deputy Chairman, State Customs Committee of the Russian Federation 2003.

opportunities for unnecessary discretionary interventions. Also, the legislation would provide for selective verification of cargo based on risk management. It would allow for advance lodgment of information or goods declarations and post-clearance audits. It would also ensure the legal framework for automation, including that of electronic communication; avoid ambiguous provisions that give customs officers excessive

discretionary powers; and grant adequate authority for the customs administration to achieve its enforcement and compliance goals.

- Governments need to have in place a development strategy that provides a clear view of the customs administration's role, particularly taking into account how it will address these needs while achieving and maintaining international standards in its customs legislation.

- As a practical way to modernize the Customs Code, it is critical for a customs administration to maintain consultations with the trade community.
- The provisions of the Revised Kyoto Convention can be used as a checklist to make a point-by-point comparison between best practices and what exists in the current code. It is also highly recommended that the national legislation of other countries be studied and that other customs agencies be consulted to learn from their experience. Once the gaps in the current code are identified, the remedies to the problem—based on international standards and tailored to country-specific needs—should be proposed as new legislation.
- To be functional and effective, the proposed legislation must fit into the local culture and the national legislative framework, and should be supported by sufficient judicial capacity.
- Modern customs legislation should strive to put in place a comprehensive body of customs-related laws that establish the clear competence and enforcement powers of customs.

## Further Reading

Lane, Michael. 1998. *Customs Modernization and the International Trade Superhighway*. Westport, Conn.: Quorum Books.

Thuronyi, Victor. 1996. "Drafting Tax Legislation." In Victor Thuronyi, ed. *Tax Law Design and Drafting*. Washington, D.C.: International Monetary Fund.

World Customs Organization. 1997. *Text of the Revised Kyoto Convention*. Brussels. www.wcoomd.org/ie/En/Topics_Issues/FacilitationCustomsProcedures/Kyoto_New/Content/content.html.

## References

De Wulf, Luc, and José B. Sokol, eds. *Custom Modernization Initiatives: Case Studies*. Washington, D. C.: World Bank.

European Union. 1992. *Council Regulation (EEC) No 2913/92 of 12 October 1992 establishing the Community Customs Code*. Brussels. europa.eu.int/smartapi/cgi/sga_doc?smartapi!celexapi!prod!CELEXnumdoc&lg=EN&numdoc=31992R2913&model=guicheti.

Jackson, Justice Robert H. 1941. *Attorney General's Report on the Administrative Procedure Act*. Washington, D.C.: United States Department of Justice.

Lane, Michael. 1998. *Customs Modernization and the International Trade Superhighway*. Westport, Conn.: Quorum Books.

Raven, John. 2001. *Trade and Transport Facilitation*. Discussion Paper No. 427. Washington, D.C.: World Bank.

Renton, David. 1975. *The Preparation of Legislation: Report of a Committee Appointed by the Lord President of the Council*. House of Commons. Preparation of Legislation Committee Sessional Papers. Volume xii, Cmnd. 6053, pp. 76–84; London: HMSO.

Steenlandt, Marcel, and Luc De Wulf. *Custom Pragmatism and Efficiency: Philosophy of a Successful Reform*. Morocco.

Stein, Jacob A., Glenn A. Mitchell, and Basil J. Mezines. 1977. *Administrative Law*. Washington, D.C.: Matthew Bender.

Thuronyi, Victor. 1996. "Drafting Tax Legislation." In Victor Thuronyi, ed. *Tax Law Design and Drafting*. Washington, D.C.: International Monetary Fund.

Turnbull, Ian. 1993. *Plain Language and Drafting in General Principles*. Australian Office of Parliamentary Counsel. Canberra. www.opc.gov.au/plain/docs/plain_draftin_principles.doc.

United States Customs and Border Protection. 2003. *Summary of Laws Enforced by CBP*. Washington, D.C.: United States Department of Homeland Security. www.Customs.ustreas.gov/xp/cgov/toolbox/legal/summary_laws_enforced.

WCO (World Customs Organization). 1997. *Text of the Revised Kyoto Convention*. Brussels. www.wcoomd.org/ie/En/Topics_Issues/FacilitationCustomsProcedures/Kyoto_New/Content/content.html.

———. 2000. "The Revised Kyoto Convention, General Annex Guidelines, Chapter 3 Clearance and other formalities, Part 6 Checking the Goods declaration." Brussels.

———. 2004a. "Commercial Fraud Manual for Senior Customs Officials." Brussels.

———. 2004b. "Model Provisions for National Legislation to Implement Fair and Effective Border Measures Consistent with Agreement on Trade-related Aspects of Intellectual Property Rights." www.wcoipr.org.

WTO (World Trade Organization).1994a. "Agreement on Implementation of Article VII of the General Agreement on Tariffs and Trade." Geneva. www.wto.org/english/docs_e/legal_e/20-val.pdf.

———.1994b. "Annex 1C: Agreement on Trade-Related Aspects of Intellectual Property Rights." *Legal Instruments—Results of the Uruguay Round*. Vol. 31, 22I.L.M. 81. Geneva. www.wto.org/english/docs_e/legal_e/27-trips.pdf.

———. 1994c. "Decision on Texts Relating to Minimum Values and Imports by Sole Agents, Sole Distributors and Sole Concessionaires." WTO Document LT/UR/D-4/1. Geneva.

———. 1994d. "Decision Regarding Cases Where Customs Administrations Have Reasons to Doubt the Truth or Accuracy of the Declared Value." WTO Document LT/UR/D-4/2. Geneva.

Zarnowiecki, Michel. 2003. "Managing Integrity in Customs." Prepared for the International Anti-Corruption Conference. May 29–30. Seoul, Korea.

# INTEGRITY IN CUSTOMS

*Gerard McLinden*

In many developing countries, high levels of corruption drastically reduce the effectiveness of key public sector agencies. Customs administrations are no exception and are frequently cited as among the most corrupt of all government agencies. Given the vitally important role customs plays in revenue collection, trade facilitation, national security, and the protection of society, the presence of corruption in customs can severely limit a nation's economic and social prospects and national development ambitions.

This chapter describes the scope and nature of the corruption problem in customs and identifies a range of practical approaches that can be employed to address it. The chapter is designed to provide a comprehensive framework for analyzing the potential effectiveness of a range of anticorruption strategies and provides practical guidance and advice to customs officials, consultants, donors, and other stakeholders engaged in the identification and implementation of sound anticorruption and integrity development strategies.

Attempts to deal with corruption in the past have often been frustrated by well-intentioned but totally

The author gratefully acknowledges the contribution of Michel Zarnowiecki.

ineffective calls for the adoption of industrial countries' standards of administrative honesty, effectiveness, and efficiency or, perhaps, the adoption of quick fix solutions designed to work around rather than deal with the problem. Recourse to preshipment inspection services has at times been inspired by such motives. To effectively tackle the problem of corruption in customs, a comprehensive and sustainable approach that addresses the underlying causes and consequences is required. There are no quick fix solutions. Rather, a pragmatic and situation-specific approach is necessary—one that draws on the lessons learned from previous efforts around the world and that takes into account the fundamental issues of motive and opportunity.

The first section of this chapter provides an introduction to the nature of the corruption problem in customs and describes some important considerations to take into account when framing an effective anticorruption strategy for customs. It also provides an overall framework based principally on the work of scholars such as Robert Klitgaard. The second section reviews the international customs community's response to the problem and outlines a comprehensive 10-point framework for tackling corruption, as contained in the World Customs Organization's (WCO's) Arusha Declaration on Integrity in Customs. The section also provides some practical guidelines on how to develop, implement, and monitor a national customs integrity action plan and how to establish a process and sustainable culture of continuous improvement. A series of key issues and questions are included in a simple checklist for each of the 10 points (see boxes 4.1–4.7 and 4.9–4.11). The final section presents the key operational conclusions derived from the chapter.

## Consequences of Corruption in Customs

Customs plays a central role in every international trade transaction and is often the first window through which the world views a country. The implications of corruption in customs on a nation's capacity to benefit from the expansion of the global economy are obvious. Data obtained from the World Bank's Investment Climate Surveys indicate that 40 percent of firms included in the 80-country survey rate Customs/Trade regulation as a major or moderate constraint to business investment (World Bank 2003). As business and investment decisions by multinational companies are increasingly subjected to international competition, the presence of widespread corruption in customs can act as a major disincentive to foreign investment. In addition, corruption in customs takes on new significance in the current environment of heightened concern about the security of international trade. Sophisticated systems and procedures designed to detect weapons of mass destruction will offer little protection if they can be circumvented simply by bribing customs officials.

In many developing countries, customs' collections continue to represent a large portion of government revenue. Figures provided by the WCO suggest that in many countries customs collects over 50 percent of all government revenue (WCO 2003a), and delays in the processing of imports and exports can cause significant losses, increase the cost of doing business, affect the competitiveness of a country's firms, and scare away foreign investment. The presence of widespread corruption can, therefore, destroy the legitimacy of a customs administration and severely limit its capacity to contribute to government objectives. The adverse effects of corruption within a customs administration include the following:

- a reduction in public trust and confidence in government institutions
- significant revenue leakage
- a reduction in the level of trust and cooperation between customs and other government agencies and between customs and relevant counterparts in other countries
- low staff morale and *esprit de corps* (although this is both an effect and a cause)
- a reduction in the level of voluntary compliance with customs laws and regulations by the business sector
- a reduction in national security and community protection
- the maintenance of unnecessary barriers to international trade and economic growth
- increased costs, which are often borne by the poorest sectors of the community.

Most, if not all, customs functions are susceptible to corruption; however, the following activities are frequently cited as being particularly vulnerable as they provide both a motive for unscrupulous traders to circumvent customs regulatory requirements and an opportunity for corrupt customs officials to seek bribes. Table 4.1 lists a number of areas and examples

**TABLE 4.1 Customs Functions and Their Vulnerability to Corruption**

| Selected Customs Functions | Examples of Integrity Violations |
|---|---|
| Processing of import, export, and transit declarations | Soliciting or accepting payment to<br>• accelerate the processing of documents<br>• ignore the fact that some cargo listed on the manifest was not declared<br>• certify the exportation of fictitious exports or provide for a wrong HS classification<br>• permit goods in transit to be released for domestic consumption. |
| Assessment of origin, value, and classification of goods | Soliciting or accepting payments to<br>• permit under-invoicing of goods<br>• not challenge the declaration of goods under a different HS that attracts a lower tariff rate<br>• accept a false country of origin declaration, thus permitting the importer to benefit from a preferential tariff regime. |
| Physical inspection, examination, and release of cargo | Soliciting or accepting staff who would<br>• ensure that an inspecting officer is chosen who will take an accommodating approach to the inspection<br>• skip the inspection<br>• influence the findings of the inspection<br>• simply speed up the inspection. |
| Administration of concessions, suspense and exemption schemes, and drawback schemes | Soliciting or accepting payment to<br>• permit traders to release, for domestic consumption and without paying the required import duties, goods that entered under suspense regimes or goods made with inputs that entered under such regimes<br>• obtain a release of the bond that is to protect customs revenues in cases of temporary admission of imports without adequate documentation<br>• permit traders to claim excessive input coefficients for exports produced with inputs that benefited from the suspense regimes<br>• permit traders to claim drawbacks for fictitious exports<br>• permit importers to transfer imports that benefited from duty relief to nonauthorized users or for nonintended purposes, or permitting them to import such goods in excess of the amounts agreed to. |
| Conduct of post-clearance audits | Soliciting or accepting payments to influence the outcome of the audit findings. |
| Issuing of import licenses, warehouse approvals, and authorized trader status approvals | Soliciting or accepting payments to obtain these licenses and certificates without proper justification. |
| Processing of urgent consignments | Soliciting or accepting payments to obtain preferential treatment or speedy clearance. |

*Source:* Author.

where corruption can take place in customs. This list is not intended to be exhaustive.

Customs is vulnerable to corruption because the nature of its work puts its officials, even at junior levels, in situations in which they have sole authority and responsibility; in which they are authorized to make important decisions on the level of duty or taxes or admissibility of imports and exports; and in which careful supervision and accountability is difficult. In addition, they work face-to-face with members of the trading community who have a strong incentive to influence the decisions made by customs officials. High tariffs and complex regulations offer significant incentives for traders to try to reduce import charges and speed up transactions. That many officials are poorly paid is often a strong incentive to accept or solicit bribes in the execution of their duties.

## Types of Corruption in Customs

Irene Hors, of the Organisation for Economic Co-operation and Development (OECD) Development Centre, has identified three types of corruption that typically occur in the customs working environment and suggests that the strategies necessary to deal with the three types of corruption vary significantly (Hors 2001):

- routine corruption, in which private operators pay bribes to obtain the speedy completion of routine customs procedures
- fraudulent corruption, in which the trader or agent asks customs officials to turn a blind eye to certain illegal practices to reduce taxation liability or fiscal obligations
- criminal corruption, in which criminal operators pay bribes to conduct a totally illegal but lucrative operation, such as drug trafficking or the abuse of export promotion schemes.

Transparency International[1] (TI) takes a different approach and divides corruption into two broad types: petty corruption and grand corruption (TI 1997). Petty corruption is described as "survival" corruption—a form of corruption that is most

often pursued by relatively junior civil servants who may be grossly underpaid and who depend on small but illegal rents to feed and house their families and pay for their children's education. This corresponds closely with Hors' concept of routine corruption.[2] Grand corruption usually involves more senior officials and significant amounts of money. Like Hors, TI recognizes that different strategies are required to deal with the two types of corruption.

Without attempting to be exhaustive, it is useful to consider a further classification of corruption that has practical applications to the customs working environment, namely, bribery, nepotism, and misappropriation (Nye 1977).

Bribery in the customs context includes the payment of money to secure or facilitate the issuance or processing of licenses, clearances, and authorities; payment to alter or reduce duty or taxation liabilities; payment to ensure that officials turn a blind eye to illegal activities; and payment or kickbacks provided after the fact, to ensure that an individual successfully obtains a lucrative exemption from normal administrative formalities. Customs officials often have discretion over such disbursements and may be tempted to corruptly charge monopoly rents. For example, in the Philippines prior to the reforms of the late 1990s, customs officials seemed to consider that they had the right to obtain compensation for their services. Businesses had become accustomed to giving small bribes as part of their standard operating procedures. It was generally accepted that it was necessary to pay someone to "facilitate" even fully legitimate transactions, and to have the services of someone personally friendly with customs to avoid harassment. In Bolivia, before the reform of the late 1990s, many customs staff worked pro bono and had to find compensation by soliciting and accepting facilitation money—an officially sanctioned bribery system.

Nepotism in the customs context can include such behavior as the selection, transfer, or promotion of individuals or groups on the basis of an existing relationship rather than on merit; the awarding of lucrative customs appointments; and the allocation of scarce government resources to individuals on a nonmerit basis. Nepotism is most

---

1. Transparency International is a nonprofit organization based in Berlin with chapters in more than 60 countries. Its focus is on corruption prevention at the international and local levels. Its Corruption Perception Index is the most comprehensive quantitative indicator of cross-country corruption available.

2. The terms "routine" and "petty" are used to describe a particular form of corruption that is prevalent in many countries. The impact of such corruption is, however, far from inconsequential and is frequently extremely damaging and difficult to control.

often seen in the customs administrations of microstates or in larger administrations that have border posts that are geographically remote from headquarters. Under such circumstances, customs officials often develop close bonds with members of the small communities in which they live and work and find it extremely difficult to maintain an arms-length relationship with members of their extended family or with members of the social or ethnic groups to which they belong.

Misappropriation includes a wide range of behavior such as theft, embezzlement, falsification of records, and fraud. It can be seen at the individual, group, or organizational level. While this form of corruption has been reported in many industrialized countries, it is also a common factor in the customs administrations of many developing countries in which administrative controls or checks and balances are not always present and where systems to ensure appropriate supervision and audit of financial transactions are not well developed.

Corrupt behavior can range from the individual to the widespread and systemic. Many observers note that corruption in customs is often well organized into networks, with members of the networks sharing the obligation of distributing the profits from corrupt practices with colleagues and superiors. This safeguards and protects the network from outside intervention and disruption, rendering its eradication extremely difficult. Corruption can be initiated by either the client or the agent (it takes two to tango); can entail acts of omission or commission; can involve illicit or licit services; and can be practiced both inside and outside the organization (Klitgaard 1993, p. 221).

### Definition of Corruption

The World Bank and the WCO define corruption simply as "the misuse of public power for private benefit" (World Bank 2000). This definition focuses on the departure from, or contravention of, some form of public duty, and the provision or receipt of some form of improper inducement. Criminal and fraudulent corruption mostly takes place in secrecy, or at least without official sanction. Routine or petty corruption, however, is often practiced with little secrecy. It goes by such names as "facilitation money" or "tea money." While unlaw-

ful to accept such payments, in some countries this practice is so widespread and such a central element of the working relationship between customs officials and members of the business community that it has become a quasi-accepted practice. Frequently, the proceeds of the facilitation payments are pooled and shared among colleagues and supervisors, often according to a well-specified formula.

### An Analytical Framework for Understanding Corruption

A useful analytical framework to analyze corruption is proposed by Robert Klitgaard (1988).[3] Klitgaard suggests that corruption is most likely to occur when agents (individuals or groups) enjoy monopoly power over clients, when agents enjoy discretionary power over the provision of goods or services, and when the level of accountability is low. According to this framework, the probability of corruption occurring follows a simple equation:

**Corruption = Monopoly + Discretion − Accountability
(C = M + D − A)**

This framework has particular relevance for the customs environment where, due to an administrative monopoly, customs administrations are often the only agency with responsibility for certain administrative and regulatory functions; where customs officials, at even relatively junior levels, enjoy considerable discretionary decisionmaking power, and discharge important administrative functions; and where the level of supervision and accountability is often poor.

Klitgaard's framework has been influential in shaping the direction of the anticorruption efforts in several countries and has been used extensively in the development of the WCO's Revised Arusha Declaration on Integrity in Customs, as well as in a range of the WCO's integrity-related tools.

---

3. Klitgaard's conclusions accord closely with those of Irene Hors of the OECD Development Centre. Hors, drawing on the lessons learned from the anticorruption and modernization efforts in the customs administrations of three countries, concluded that the customs working environment is vulnerable to corruption because there is (a) a discretionary interface between customs officials and private sector operators, (b) a possibility for customs officials to operate within a network of accomplices, and (c) a lack of official controls.

Klitgaard's framework provides an overall conceptual basis for examining the critical issues involved in developing a sound anticorruption strategy.

Inspired by this framework, Klitgaard proposes the following range of corrective strategies. His strategies consist of five distinct but related steps. These include

- changing administrative systems to remove the corruption-inducing combination of monopoly power combined with officer discretion plus limited accountability
- selecting agents (in this case, customs officials) for incorruptibility as well as job-specific skills and educational qualifications
- changing the rewards and penalties mix facing agents and clients
- increasing the likelihood that corruption will be detected and punished
- altering attitudes toward corruption.

Klitgaard's strategies and examples of their practical application in the customs environment are illustrated in table 4.2.

## The International Customs Response

The vast majority of literature available on institutional or administrative corruption in developing countries can be described as problem reporting rather than problem solving. Beyond advocating the introduction of effective and efficient customs procedures, there is little material available that provides practical solutions to the problems associated with predicting, controlling, and eliminating corruption in public administration, particularly in the customs environment. In response to this, and in recognition of the fact that customs is often cited as one of the most corrupt sectors of government, the international customs community, through the WCO, commenced work in the mid to late 1980s to formulate a comprehensive integrity and anticorruption strategy. This work resulted in 1992 in the unanimous adoption by World Trade Organization (WTO) members of the Arusha Declaration on Integrity in Customs. Since that time, the Arusha Declaration has become the principal anticorruption framework for the WCO's 162 member customs administrations. But progress with stemming

corruption in customs had been slow. In reaction, the WCO called for a comprehensive review of the Arusha Declaration and its practical implementation in member administrations. This led to the preparation of the Revised Arusha Declaration that was unanimously endorsed by the WCO Council in June 2003.

The Revised Arusha Declaration on Integrity in Customs consists of 10 distinct but related elements considered essential for the development and implementation of a comprehensive and sustainable anticorruption and integrity enhancement program. It is consistent with the framework provided by Klitgaard and is closely aligned with a range of internationally agreed on customs instruments, standards, and best practice approaches, including the Revised Kyoto Convention. It is also designed to strike an appropriate balance between the positive strategies (reform and modernization, leadership, progressive human resources [HR] management policies, and so forth) favored by many within the international customs community and the repressive strategies (sanctions, controls, investigation, prosecution) promoted by others. The 10 elements of the Revised Declaration follow:

- Leadership and Commitment
- Regulatory Framework
- Transparency
- Automation
- Reform and Modernization
- Audit and Investigation
- Code of Conduct
- Human Resources Management
- Morale and Organizational Culture
- Relationship with the Private Sector.

Collectively, these 10 key elements are designed to reduce monopoly power and the inappropriate use of official discretion, and at the same time increase the level of practical accountability. They link directly to Klitgaard's equation and strategies outlined earlier in this chapter. In developing the Revised Arusha Declaration, the WCO was conscious of the different social, political, and economic circumstances faced by its member administrations. It therefore deliberately designed the Declaration to be nonprescriptive in nature. In other words, the Declaration provides a comprehensive conceptual framework, but the actual

**TABLE 4.2   Strategies to Reduce Corruption in Customs**

| Strategy | Practical Activities |
|---|---|
| Change administrative systems to remove the corruption-inducing combination of monopoly power combined with officer discretion plus limited accountability | • Reengineer administrative systems or procedures to enhance transparency and predictability<br>• Introduce competition or contestability in the provision of key services<br>• Contract out selected customs functions<br>• Introduce self-assessment to shift the onus of responsibility for compliance to client groups<br>• Introduce automation to limit official discretion and face-to-face contact between officials and clients, enhance transparency, and streamline customs procedures<br>• Implement job rotation and staff mobility schemes<br>• Increase transparency by publishing the criteria upon which officials are entitled to exercise official delegations |
| Select customs officials for incorruptibility as well as job-specific skills and technical competence | • Widen the selection criteria for customs recruitment to include integrity-related factors<br>• Introduce merit as the key criteria for recruitment and promotion<br>• Carefully screen potential employees, including references from previous employers or educational establishments and background checks of potential criminal record<br>• Recruit senior officials who are known for their integrity from other agencies and the private sector |
| Change the rewards and penalties mix facing agents and clients | • Evaluate the present remuneration levels and conditions of employment to ensure competitive conditions<br>• Provide nonsalary benefits that are difficult to obtain elsewhere<br>• Restructure bonus or rewards systems to reinforce positive behaviors and, where needed, increase these rewards<br>• Introduce performance management and appraisal systems<br>• Encourage and reward officials who identify vulnerabilities in administrative systems and procedures<br>• Increase penalties to provide a disincentive to engage in corrupt behavior<br>• Ensure that penalties are calibrated to correspond to the offense<br>• Ensure that all officials, regardless of rank, are subject to the same penalties |
| Increase the likelihood that corruption will be detected | • Undertake a thorough analysis of customs' administrative systems and controls to identify vulnerable points<br>• Rely on client and general public for information<br>• Assess issues such as internal controls, reporting relationships, staff competence, official delegations, and decisionmaking powers<br>• Identify which positions and activities carry an inherent risk of corruption and the adequacy of controls or safeguards in place<br>• Establish internal audit and investigation units to thoroughly investigate any information provided or allegations made<br>• Encourage officials and clients to report corruption to independent anticorruption agencies, and ensure confidentiality and anonymity for the information provided<br>• Ensure that punishments are meted out promptly, and vindicate staff from unjustified accusations; sanctions should be commensurate with the severity of the violation and sanctions should be made public to serve as examples for others |
| Alter attitudes of staff and traders toward corruption | • Instill *esprit de corps* in customs that will raise the moral costs of corruption<br>• Implement or improve professional development and training<br>• Introduce and promote a code of conduct; make this code widely available to staff and the public; consider making staff sign this code of conduct (upon recruitment or anniversary of appointment)<br>• Ensure that managers and supervisors lead by example<br>• Introduce a zero tolerance policy for acceptance of gifts<br>• Publicize the names of officials found guilty of corruption |

*Source:* Author, based on Klitgaard 1988.

implementation of each key element is up to individual customs administrations.

A similar, nonprescriptive philosophy has been employed for all other WCO integrity-related materials, tools and training, and technical assistance programs that were developed as part of the WCO Integrity Action Plan. For example, to assist member administrations to implement the provisions of the Revised Arusha Declaration and to develop a culture of continuous improvement, the WCO has developed an Integrity Development Guide, established an Integrity Resource Center, prepared a Model Code of Ethics and Conduct, and conducts a range of national and regional integrity seminars, workshops, and training programs. In all of these tools or programs, the onus is on individual customs administrations to develop and implement realistic programs that are based on their own needs and circumstances.[4]

A summary of the Revised Arusha Declaration's 10 key elements, together with a list of recommended actions, follows. Where possible, discussion of the key elements has been complemented by the introduction of country examples emanating from the experiences of the World Bank and other international organizations.

### Leadership and Commitment

A firm commitment at the highest political level to maintaining a high standard of integrity throughout customs is particularly important in societies where corruption is a widespread or systemic problem. The government needs to be aware of the steps that customs is taking, and customs should ensure that the government receives regular updates on progress through publications, briefings, verifiable performance indicators, and through the media. Effective integrity programs also require a high level of management support and leadership. It is important to set up clearly defined supervisory and decisionmaking structures and obligations.

A strong champion at both the political and customs management levels is essential. Frequent changes at the top of the administration prevent a clear signal from being sent out, and damage credibility, particularly with the private sector. An adequate political framework, strong commitment from the government, and support from the business community are essential. In Bolivia, Morocco, and Peru, strong political backing for the reform from the highest political authority and unwavering support from the business community were key factors in decreasing corruption. Feedback is also needed, and can be provided by performance indicators, user surveys,[5] and through consultation with the business community.

Experience in several countries suggests, however, that where corruption in customs has been a long-term feature of the customs–business environment it is extremely difficult for managers and supervisors to take a strong stance against staff engaged in corrupt practices that they themselves were engaged in at earlier periods in their careers. In such cases it may be useful to examine the feasibility of introducing a limited official amnesty. Such an approach must, however, be introduced as part of a comprehensive anticorruption strategy and should incorporate stiff new penalties for future breaches of integrity. Likewise, it should be accompanied by a widely publicized zero tolerance policy and a commitment to investigate and prosecute any future allegations of corruption. Care must be taken to ensure that officials understand that the amnesty is a "once only" opportunity to clear the slate.

Government actions are essential to demonstrating a commitment to combat corruption. Such actions may include the establishment of ombudsmen, supreme audit bodies, and anticorruption agencies. Such action however, can only become effective if laws are enforced adequately. In Hong Kong (China), the Independent Commission Against Corruption was successful because the agency was provided with independence, significant financing, direct citizen oversight, and considerable legal powers.

Box 4.1 reviews important questions to consider regarding top level commitment to eradicating corruption.

---

4. All WCO integrity-related tools are available on the WCO Web site www.wcoomd.org.

5. See www.seerecon.org/RegionalInitiatives/TTFSE/ for a description of performance indicators and surveys used in Southeast Europe under the World Bank–supported Trade and Transport Facilitation program.

**BOX 4.1   Leadership and Commitment: Key Issues and Questions**

Has high-level multipartisan support and political commitment to the fight against corruption been obtained?

Have the government and customs administration adopted a zero tolerance policy?

Are "big fish" as well as small ones investigated and prosecuted?

Are clear responsibilities, obligations, and accountability for all customs managers, supervisors, and staff established and understood?

Is promotion to managerial positions dependent on integrity performance?

Do senior managers and supervisors lead by example?

Are periodic surveys conducted to assess stakeholders' perceptions of customs' commitment to integrity?

Does customs lead or participate in wider all-of-government integrity initiatives?

Is appropriate priority afforded to the anticorruption strategy in corporate vision, mission, values, resource allocation processes, and strategic planning documents?

Has the use of an official amnesty been considered?

*Source:* Based on WCO 2003b.

### Regulatory Framework

Customs administrations should simplify their laws, regulations, administrative guidelines, and procedures so that customs duty assessment and clearance can proceed without undue delay and red tape. This often involves changing or restructuring current systems and procedures to reduce or eliminate pointless bureaucratic processes. In many cases this will involve elimination of nontariff regulations, unnecessary steps, or duplication in administrative procedures.

Possible strategies to minimize regulation include the adoption of internationally agreed on standards, including the Harmonized System (HS) Tariff Convention, WTO Valuation Agreement, Air Transport Association (ATA) Carnet Convention or Istanbul Convention, WTO Trade-Related Aspects of Intellectual Property Rights (TRIPS) Agreement, and WCO Revised Kyoto Convention on the Harmonization and Simplification of Customs Procedures. In this regard, Bolivia, Cameroon, Morocco, Mozambique, Peru, and Turkey have all adopted new Customs Codes that have allowed the introduction of new and simplified procedures more in line with evolving business practices. Barriers to the free flow of goods, such as nontariff regulations on quotas, import licenses, and permits, should also be reduced or rationalized to the fullest extent. Where possible, the number of tariff rates should be moderated.

The rationalization of both tariff and nontariff barriers extends beyond the policy responsibility of the customs administration. In this respect, customs should maintain a close relationship with other responsible agencies, for example, through regular interdepartmental liaison processes. A key initiative is the adoption of risk management principles to ensure that trade and travel risks are assessed, and to identify and investigate integrity risks within the organization (see annex 1.D for further comments on this subject).

Box 4.2 presents key questions for assessing customs' regulatory framework with regard to promoting integrity.

### Transparency

Transparency is a key issue for all customs administrations. Increasing accountability and maintaining an open and honest relationship with clients and stakeholders is crucial to maintaining public trust and confidence in the performance of customs functions. Clients must be able to expect a high degree of certainty in their dealings with customs authorities. This can only be achieved when customs laws, regulations, procedures, and administrative guidelines are made public, are easily accessible, and are applied in a consistent manner. Any deviations from laws, regulations, and discretionary power should be justified and documented for later review. In Pakistan, the lack of transparency in the design of a customs reform project where no diagnostic report was made public, and the lack of participation by supporting interests, clearly contributed to the project's failure to achieve its initial objectives (Hors 2001).

---

### BOX 4.2    Regulatory Framework: Key Issues and Questions

Have customs laws, regulations, administrative guidelines, and procedures been reviewed, harmonized, and simplified to reduce unnecessary duplication and red tape?

Has a process of continuous review and improvement of systems and procedures been introduced?

Has a tariff rates been moderated and the number of different rates of duty rationalized?

Has a formal process for the review and rationalization of exemptions and concessions been introduced?

Has a program of consultation and cooperation with other government agencies been established to examine means of rationalizing regulatory requirements?

Have internationally agreed on conventions, instruments, and accepted standards including the Revised Kyoto Convention, the WCO HS Convention, the WTO Valuation Agreement, the ATA Carnet Convention, and the WTO TRIPS Agreement, been implemented?

Do regional customs unions and economic groups adopt internationally agreed on standards and work toward regional harmonization of systems and procedures?

Does the administration actively participate in international benchmarking and information sharing initiatives?

*Source:* Based on WCO 2003b.

---

Administrative or judicial review should be available. In the first instance, such a review should be made on an internal basis. However, clients should also have access to an independent, external review. In developing or implementing appeal or review mechanisms, an appropriate balance should be struck between the need to make the process inexpensive, timely, and accessible and the need to ensure that it is not used inappropriately for frivolous appeals. Client service charters are a way to increase accountability and demonstrate customs' commitment to provide quality service to clients. Service standards should be challenging but realistic and should be fully supported by the organization's systems and procedures. Achieving a consistently high degree of transparency is not an easy task but it is vital to the development of a comprehensive integrity program.

The experience of the Zambian Revenue Authority (ZRA) provides a practical example of what can be achieved when a commitment to increased levels of integrity is made. The ZRA has introduced a number of positive initiatives designed to increase clients' awareness of customs rules and regulations. These include publication of information brochures and posters, development of a public Web site, and regular participation in public radio programs. In Morocco, the customs Web site contains the essential rules and regulations governing customs operations as well as data on international trade and various performance indicators, including detailed and regularly updated clearance times. In Peru, customs uses its Web site to make available to users and to the public in general, information on customs rules and regulations, and all its activities and programs, including the details of various customs declarations processed. In Turkey, legislative arrangements are updated on customs' official Web site and traders are provided with guidance on the formal procedures to be used for seeking advanced rulings on tariff and valuation. Internal transparency standards can be enhanced by maintaining a tracking and analysis system for compliments or complaints, ensuring that any complaints are examined and dealt with promptly, as in Morocco, and that an audit trail exists to enable monitoring of the exercise of officer discretion.

Box 4.3 provides examples of questions to raise when assessing the transparency of customs.

### Automation

Computerization of core customs processes can improve efficiency and effectiveness and remove opportunities for corruption. Well-designed and implemented systems can minimize unnecessary face-to-face contact between officials and clients and reduce opportunities for the improper exercise of discretion. Automated systems can also be configured to maximize the level of accountability and provide a reliable audit trail for later evaluation and

---

**BOX 4.3    Transparency: Key Issues and Questions**

Have customs laws, regulations, procedures, and administrative guidelines been made public and are they easily accessible?

Has the basis upon which customs officials are entitled to exercise their discretionary power been defined and are variations recorded for later review and monitoring?

Have administrative and judicial appeal mechanisms been established that allow customs decisions to be challenged?

Have advance tariff and valuation rulings systems been implemented?

Have Customs Service Charters and performance targets been established that are challenging but realistic and is the administration's performance reported to the public?

Does the administration use a range of media to publicize information, including brochures, posters, Web site, and the mass media?

Are all fees and charges publicized?

Have help desks been established to assist clients in complying with customs requirements?

*Source:* Based on WCO 2003b.

---

review. Automation can be used to eliminate the most vulnerable points in manual systems. Automation, however, is unlikely to assist the anticorruption effort if it is not combined with other reform measures. For example, the introduction of an automated entry processing system will certainly reduce the opportunities for customs officials to seek illegal payments for making certain decisions; but it may also simply result in shifting the point of corruption to a part of the process that is not automated. By way of example, in the case of cargo clearance, the point of collection of illegal fees could simply shift from the duty assessment phase to the cargo examination or delivery phase.

Automated systems can be vulnerable to attack and manipulation from both inside and outside the organization. This is a particular threat in many developing countries where access to skilled and professional IT experts may be extremely limited. For instance, field work of World Bank staff highlight some of these. In one case, the system of random allocation had been implemented to break the unhealthy relationship that had developed between traders and officers; but customs staff learned how to manipulate the system by running the software until a "suitable" officer was selected. In another case, the main software introduced to handle the processing of declarations and computation of duties was manipulated by officers to maintain parallel registers. In another case, cars exiting the port illegally were found to possess fake declaration forms, produced using official systems and procedures.

Tight security checks should be undertaken and appropriate supervision and accountability systems established, particularly when external consultants or contractors are involved. Where sensitive information is stored on automated systems a suitable audit trail needs to be established to protect the information and identify any officials who may access information for private or inappropriate purposes.

Customs must respond to changing international trade practices that increasingly involve the use of electronic commerce. The electronic service delivery of customs functions improves efficiencies within the organization and the trading community and provides a mechanism to reduce the opportunity and incentives to engage in corrupt behavior. The experience of the Philippine Bureau of Customs is illustrative of the capacity of automation to drastically improve efficiency and eliminate opportunities for corruption. Prior to automation, processing customs declarations involved the submission of numerous documents logged in 20 separate registers, more than 90 separate steps, and more than 40 signatures. Automation, coupled with a range of supporting reforms, has resulted in a significant reduction in clearance times. It has also significantly reduced the opportunities for face-to-face contact between customs officials and traders and the inappropriate use of official discretion.

Important questions to consider in reviewing the role of automation in corruption prevention efforts are in box 4.4.

---

**BOX 4.4 Automation: Key Issues and Questions**

Have automated systems for declaration processing and cargo reporting been introduced based on the IT guidelines contained in the Revised Kyoto Convention and the WCO Data Model?

Have the systems been designed to do the following:

- incorporate appropriate risk assessment and selectivity capabilities
- minimize the need for officials to exercise discretionary authority
- minimize face-to-face contact between customs officials and traders
- record any variations or exercise of discretionary powers for later review and audit

- accommodate automated payment or electronic funds transfer systems?

Is the IT infrastructure appropriately managed and has adequate provision been made for ongoing hardware and software maintenance and replacement?

Have appropriate provisions been made to secure the systems from internal or external manipulation?

Have appropriate provisions been made to ensure the effective integration of manual and automated systems?

*Source:* Based on WCO 2003b.

---

### Reform and Modernization

Corruption typically occurs in situations where outdated and inefficient practices are employed and where private sector operators have an incentive to attempt to avoid slow or burdensome procedures by offering bribes and paying facilitation fees. Customs administrations should reengineer or reform and modernize systems and procedures to eliminate any perceived advantages that might be obtained through circumventing official requirements. Such reform and modernization initiatives should be comprehensive in nature and should focus on all aspects of customs operations and performance.

This conclusion was also reached by Hors in summarizing the outcome of a series of studies into the reform initiatives that had been undertaken by three customs administrations. She suggests that there is a need to identify those points in the customs system that provide special opportunities for corruption and to eliminate or reengineer customs systems and procedures to reduce the opportunities for corruption and provide less incentive for private sector personnel to pay bribes to customs officials (Hors 2001). The International Chamber of Commerce (ICC) also notes that increasing overall efficiency and effectiveness is the most appropriate approach to tackling corruption in customs administrations (ICC 1997).

Reform and modernization of a customs administration should be based on a comprehensive diagnosis of its needs and should be tailored to the individual circumstances and aspirations of the administration concerned. A sound reform and modernization program should focus on simplifying and harmonizing systems and procedures, be comprehensive in nature, address all customs roles and responsibilities, involve all key stakeholders, focus on developing local ownership, be sustainable in the longer term, and have sufficient resources to ensure effective implementation. The preparation of a corruption risk map can be a useful element of this process.

Customs administrations should be regarded by governments as important national assets and tools for trade facilitation, revenue collection, community protection, and national security. Comprehensive reform and modernization programs should focus on achieving improved performance in each of the following core customs areas:

- Leadership and strategic planning
- Organizational and institutional framework
- Resources (human, financial, and physical)
- External cooperation and partnership
- Good governance
- Customs systems and procedures
- Legal framework
- Change management and continuous improvement
- Information technology
- Management information and statistics.

In Bolivia, Cameroon, Morocco, Mozambique, Peru, the Philippines, Turkey, and Uganda, the reform programs generally covered issues relating to all components of customs administration, including the legal framework, systems and procedures, IT, strategic management, personnel, and organizational structure.

The Peruvian Customs provides an excellent example of what can be achieved through the implementation of a comprehensive reform and modernization program. In 1963, Peruvian Customs was characterized by corruption and incompetence. The reform process involved firing corrupt employees, conducting tests of competence, training, hiring new professionals, establishing standards for cargo clearance, tariff simplification, and establishing reduced duty rates. Over a five-year period, staffing was reduced by 30 percent and cargo clearance time was reduced from 15–30 days to 1–2 days. As a result, imports doubled and revenue collections quadrupled (Lane 1998). In the case of Morocco, improving integrity was not included as a specific priority in their reform and modernization program, but rather, was achieved as a positive byproduct of the program.

Box 4.5 reviews questions crucial to determining the role of modernization in battling corruption in customs.

### Audit and Investigation

Mechanisms to detect corruption and identify and reduce organizational vulnerabilities are primary elements of any effective corruption prevention strategy. Regardless of the severity of penalties pro-vided, they will offer little deterrence if the probability of detection and prosecution is low. Internal and external audits can review processes and procedures with the aim of focusing on high risk areas. Audits also provide an independent opinion regarding the efficiency and effectiveness of customs procedures and controls. The audit process should include internal check programs, random sampling, and on-the-spot checks. To prevent collusion between customs officials and clients and to avoid clients anticipating customs actions, a task force comprising staff from different work areas may be set up to conduct unannounced special operations or checks at various high risk customs posts at irregular intervals. On-the-spot inspections should be conducted frequently enough to provide a real deterrent to corrupt behavior.

The development of a comprehensive risk map, which identifies functional areas and processes that are most vulnerable to corruption, can usefully guide the audit opportunities. The risk map should be administration-specific and cover all functional areas and key processes. Staff closely involved in each of the functional areas should participate in the preparation of the risk map. Likewise, private sector operators should be consulted to identify their perspective on the most vulnerable parts of the customs system, the key concept being that the staff and clients most closely involved in particular customs processes are best equipped to identify particular vulnerabilities and to devise corrective strategies.

The organization should have the necessary resources to follow up and investigate any allegations or information provided. Mechanisms should

---

**BOX 4.5   Modernization of Customs: Key Issues and Questions**

Is customs regarded by the government and the business sector as a key national asset and tool for trade facilitation, revenue collection, community protection, and national security?

Is customs ranked high on the list of government priorities for international donor assistance?

Has a comprehensive and long term reform and modernization program been established that is

- adequately resourced, with roles and responsibilities clearly defined

- based on an accurate diagnosis of needs
- focused on simplifying and harmonizing systems and procedures
- well supported by all stakeholders including staff
- effectively coordinated and managed at the local level
- based on sound performance data and objective performance measures?

*Source:* Based on WCO 2003b.

## BOX 4.6    Audit and Investigation: Key Issues and Questions

Have effective monitoring and control mechanisms been established, including internal audit functions and internal check responsibilities?

Is the administration subject to regular and professional external audits?

Does the administration develop and maintain a strategic audit plan that identifies priorities and ensures that audit findings and recommendations are implemented?

Are staff working in audit and investigation areas appropriately qualified to undertake their tasks?

Has an internal investigation or internal affairs unit been established to promptly investigate allegations of corruption?

Has a detailed risk map of the administration been developed to identify particular vulnerabilities and devise appropriate corrective strategies?

Does the administration make use of the appropriate independent anticorruption authorities to deal with large-scale cases or allegations against senior officials?

*Source:* Based on WCO 2003b.

---

also be in place to encourage staff and stakeholders to report corrupt practices, including confidentiality provisions. For example, there should be a channel for staff to report corrupt practices directly to the most senior level, bypassing their immediate supervisors. Along these lines, in 2002 the Commissioner of the Ugandan Revenue Authority established a confidential e-mail address and telephone number to allow staff to report corrupt practices and officials. Customs managers and clients should promote recourse to independent anticorruption agencies as a means of demonstrating the organization's commitment to tackling corruption. In recent years the Hong Kong Customs and Excise Department has worked closely with the Independent Commission against Corruption (ICAC) to strengthen the level of integrity within the organization. In addition to investigating serious allegations against customs personnel, ICAC has provided training to customs officials and has done much to increase the level of public confidence in the customs administration.

Staff allocated to audit and investigation work should be appropriately skilled and qualified for the role they are to perform. In recognition of the skill requirements necessary to undertake effective internal audit and investigative work, the Australian Customs Service outsourced its internal audit function to a private audit company. Likewise, an experienced former Australian Federal Police officer was selected to head its Internal Affairs Unit. The organization does, however, maintain effective control through a national audit committee made up of members of the senior management team and through the development of an annual audit plan that specifies the priorities for the coming year. It

also relies on external audit, which is provided by the Australian National Audit Office.

Box 4.6 outlines important questions about the role of audit and investigation in eliminating corruption.

### Code of Conduct

A key element of any sound integrity program must be the development, issuance, and acceptance of a comprehensive code of conduct that sets out, in very practical and unambiguous terms, the standards of behavior and conduct required of employees and all customs officials. An effective code of conduct also provides a guide to solving ethical issues for those working in customs and those who have dealings with customs officials. The content of the code should be regularly reinforced to staff.[6]

To assist customs administrations in developing appropriate codes of conduct, the WCO has prepared a Model Code of Ethics and Conduct[7] that sets out the following key elements:

---

6. Within the framework of the Free Trade Area of the Americas, trade ministers discussed customs-related issues in Latin America and the Caribbean. Participants followed up on work undertaken since 2001 on a new code of conduct for the region, which was designed to be more robust than existing codes around the world. The code seeks to be wide in scope and definite in its provisions and places emphasis on prevention rather than punishment. The code also establishes an independent monitoring authority and provides a role for civil society. The Inter-American Development Bank, which is financing the initiative, is requiring all Latin American countries without a code of conduct for customs officers to implement this new code. It has already been implemented in Honduras, Paraguay, St. Vincent and the Grenadines, Dominica, and Grenada. See www.regionaladuanas.org

7. See the WCO Web site at www.wcoomd.org.

- *Personal responsibility.* Explains the personal responsibilities and obligations that all officials have to comply with the provisions of the code.
- *Compliance with the law.* Explains the need for officials to operate within the appropriate legal framework.
- *Relations with the public.* Explains the need for officials to maintain professional standards of service and behavior in their dealings with the public.
- *Acceptance of gifts, rewards, hospitality, and discounts.* Explains the rules and circumstances associated with the acceptance and rejection of offers of gifts, rewards, hospitality, travel, and discounts.
- *Avoiding conflicts of interest.* Explains the rules associated with officials participating in commercial enterprises, holding shares, being involved in government contracts and tendering, and engaging in other paid employment.
- *Political activities.* Explains the rules associated with officials engaging in political activities such as fundraising, elections, and commenting on government decisions and policy.
- *Conduct in money matters.* Explains the rules associated with managing private financial matters and the handling of official funds.
- *Confidentiality and use of official information.* Explains the rules for the care of official information, documents, records, and so forth, whether paper-based or stored electronically.
- *Use of official property and services.* Explains the rules associated with the use and care of official assets and property.
- *Private purchases of government property by staff.* Explains the rules associated with officials purchasing government property such as seized or forfeited goods.
- *Work environment.* Explains the need to foster a healthy, safe, and productive working environment and covers issues such as fairness and nondiscrimination, occupational health and safety, misuse of drugs and alcohol, smoking, standards of dress, and security.

Several customs administrations, including the Czech Republic and Turkey, have used the WCO's Model Code of Conduct to develop their own codes of conduct.

Issues and questions regarding the role of a code of conduct are contained in box 4.7.

### Human Resources Management

Staff remuneration and career management are key HR issues that can seriously affect integrity in customs.

**Staff Remuneration**    A key element in any effective integrity strategy is managing the personal integrity of staff. People management is just as important as the reform of systems and procedures. Human resources (HR) policies should not only be aimed at recruiting and firing staff, but also improving staff skills and providing a work environment that recognizes and supports the efforts of staff. (See chapter 2 for further information on HR management issues in customs.)

Providing appropriate conditions of employment and, in particular, remuneration that includes bonuses and rewards for good performance, and that can sustain a reasonable standard of living, are

---

### BOX 4.7    Code of Conduct: Key Issues and Questions

Has a comprehensive code of conduct compatible with the WCO model been adopted?

Are the contents of the code clear and unambiguous and the penalties for noncompliance understood by staff?

Are all managers and supervisors required to lead by example or is there "one rule for us and another for you?"

Are all staff required to read, understand, and endorse the code?

Is prompt and appropriate action taken to redress any breaches of the code that are identified?

Has a periodic review process been established?

Were staff and clients consulted during the development of the code?

*Source:* Based on WCO 2003b.

## BOX 4.8    Are Low Salary Levels Really a Factor?

Based on the results of a study into the customs administrations of three developing countries, Irene Hors of the OECD Development Centre identified low salary levels as a contributing factor in the development of corruption within one East Asian customs administration. She noted that salary levels for junior officials had not taken account of inflation and increases in the cost of living, and that employees living within their salaries simply could not rent houses or educate their children. She did, however, question the link between remuneration and corruption at higher levels in the customs hierarchy. In this respect she noted that among senior officials, who sometimes enjoyed relatively generous levels of salary and working conditions, ostentatious living and extravagant expenditures had become the norm and that the officials' behavior had become conditioned by the behavior of a wider elite, which customarily indulged in illegal activities and paraded excessive riches. She concluded by noting that there is probably a continuum of gradually changing situations between officers who are practically obliged to engage in corruption to provide for basic needs and those who are drawn to bribery by the pressures of social emulation and greed.

Fjeldstad, Kolstad, and Lange (2003), drawing on the experiences of Uganda and Tanzania, where wage rates and conditions of employment were increased significantly following the adoption of the ARA model, suggest that even with relatively high wages and good working conditions corruption may continue to thrive as pay rates can never effectively compensate officials for the amount they can gain through bribery. Moreover, if wage increases are granted but subsequently not maintained in real terms, then the increases may in fact result in less effort and more corruption than if wages had remained constant. Increased pay may also imply more extensive social obligations resulting in a net loss to the employee. Likewise, in the civil service context, wage increases in one department could result in officials in other agencies viewing their own remuneration as unfair with detrimental consequences for wider civil service morale. They conclude that without extensive and effective monitoring and an overall program of modernization, wage increases may simply produce a highly paid but also highly corrupt administration.

*Sources*: Hors 2001; Fjeldstad, Kolstad, and Lange 2003.

crucial. Indeed, severe penalties applied to breaches of a code of conduct are more likely to be accepted in circumstances where the difficult working environment and required levels of integrity are recognized in the base level of remuneration. However, levels of remuneration all too frequently are extremely low in customs. In Cambodia, for instance, the average annual civil service salary, at US$0.60 per day, is well below private sector pay, even for unskilled workers, and creates severe pressures to engage in additional income-generating activities just to meet basic household expenditures (World Bank 2001).

In recent years, several countries have established Autonomous Revenue Agencies (ARAs) as a means of improving the efficiency and effectiveness of customs, and in the process have significantly increased the level of remuneration paid to revenue officials without having to increase salaries in other sectors of public administration. However, in several instances these higher remuneration levels could not be maintained. (See chapter 2 and box 4.8.)

While the research on the long-term impact of public sector salaries is inconclusive, there is little doubt that staff will identify and exploit the many opportunities for illegal rent-seeking if customs officials are not provided with sufficient remuneration to provide a basic standard of living for themselves and their families. This is particularly the case for customs officials engaged in preventive, enforcement, or audit activities where discretionary powers are significant and the environment is not conducive to effective supervision and accountability. In addition, remuneration should be geared to take into account the sometimes dangerous and difficult working conditions and associated hardships faced by customs officials, particularly in remote border stations.[8] Anticorruption programs that fail to address this issue are likely to fail in the longer term. In essence, better salaries can begin to

---

8. For example, in many former socialist countries, border police officers are paid on average 30 percent more than customs officials performing similar duties.

address corruption problems that stem from need but not from greed.

**Recruitment and Staff Selection**    Recruitment and staff selection procedures should be based on merit and should focus on selecting staff for their incorruptibility as well as their academic, professional, or technical competence. The importance of appropriate recruitment and selection policies is clearly demonstrated in surveys conducted by the World Bank in Albania, Georgia, and Latvia. The surveys demonstrate that bureaucrats are willing to pay for appointment to agencies that are regarded as the most corrupt, and for promotion or deployment to positions in which they are able to obtain illegal rents based on the exercise of official discretion.[9] The administrative processes associated with recruitment and promotion should be fair, objective, and free of bias. Recruitment and promotion committees should be composed of independent members selected from different areas of the organization. Such an approach reduces the chances of nepotism and corruption.

Some countries and customs administrations have adopted drastic measures to improve the quality and integrity of their staffs, including firing a significant percentage of officials. Evidence suggests, however, that while such drastic approaches can deliver short-term gains, the benefits are invariably short lived if not supported by wider reform initiatives. Moreover, the maintenance of such policies is resource intensive and difficult to sustain in the longer term. An additional factor that needs to be considered is the impact that the departure of a large number of experienced officials will have on the wider customs–business relationship. Experience in several countries suggests that many customs officials sacked in large-scale staffing purges readily find work on the other side of the counter working for customs brokers and in the import/export sector leading to an extension of existing unofficial networks.[10] The

conclusion, therefore, is that the operational environment for customs work, rather than individual officials, determines the level of corruption. Care needs to be taken when introducing new legislation and HR management policies to ensure that increased managerial freedom to hire and fire is not used to enable politically motivated firings or to introduce a level of job insecurity that simply encourages officials to seek short-term financial gain rather than build long-term careers.

**Mobility and Random Job Assignments**    Enhancing staff mobility can substantially augment integrity. Job segregation can also be limited so that a number of officials are able to discharge the same discretionary functions. This will ensure that clients do not have to deal with only one official who can abuse discretionary power. In cases where examinations or inspections need to be undertaken, allocation to individual officials may be made on a random rather than on a commodity, industry, or geographic basis. The performance of examinations or inspections can also be subject to regular peer and independent reviews. Many countries do, however, face significant difficulties in introducing staff rotation or mobility schemes. Issues such as cost, available housing, and education opportunities at regional offices or remote border posts prevent the introduction of appropriate mobility schemes. In such cases it is important to look at opportunities for job segregation and mobility within the regional office or border post.

**Training**    Education and training play a major role in the fight against corruption in two ways. First, they provide staff with appropriate professional development, thus increasing technical competence and reducing reliance on informal on-the-job training. While on-the-job training is important, care needs to be taken to ensure that it is both positive and structured and does not inadvertently reinforce certain inappropriate practices that have developed over time. Second, education and training provide regular opportunities for the organization to reinforce the integrity and anticorruption message. This is particularly appropriate when an organization is introducing a formal code of conduct.

9. World Bank surveys of 218 public officials in Latvia, 350 public officials in Georgia, and 97 public officials in Albania (Kaufman, Pradhan, and Ryterman 1998).

10. In addition, the firing of large numbers of staff and their replacement by a group of new and more qualified officials has sometimes resulted in the reemergence of corruption on a more sophisticated scale and increased incentives to bribe based on insecurity of employment tenure.

---

**BOX 4.9    Human Resources: Key Issues and Questions**

Has a comprehensive and strategically focused HR management strategy been introduced incorporating sound polices on

- recruiting and retaining the right people
- developing and improving professional competencies and skills
- recognizing and supporting integrity efforts?

Is staff remuneration comparable to similar public or private sector positions and sufficient to allow a reasonable standard of living?

Have procedures been established that can identify and support staff with financial difficulties?

Are objective and merit-based selection processes employed that identify personal integrity as well as academic or technical competence?

Are procedures in place to ensure appropriate security vetting for potential staff during recruitment, and for existing staff periodically?

Are selection committees impartial and made up of officials from different work areas?

Has a staff transfer or rotation policy been implemented with clear and unambiguous rules on the regular movement of staff from high-risk positions?

Have all high-risk positions and functions been identified and systems and procedures modified to limit the exercise of official discretion?

Are appropriate informal and formal training and professional development opportunities provided to build technical competence and promote integrity?

Are the administration's code of conduct and the individual responsibilities of officials regularly reinforced during training and professional development programs?

Has a performance appraisal system been implemented that is fair, regular, monitored, and periodically reviewed?

Are managers and supervisors required to actively manage staff performance and performance issues?

Are managers and supervisors held responsible for the integrity performance of officers under their control?

*Source:* Based on WCO 2003b.

---

**Performance Evaluation**    A performance appraisal and management system concerns the day-to-day management of people and their performance. Regular appraisals tied to compensation reviews encourage staff to take responsibility for maintaining high levels of integrity. Performance appraisal can encourage staff to participate in activities designed to reduce or control corruption, and reward those who have been able to identify methods by which corruption can occur and for suggesting improved control mechanisms. The reward system may include nonmonetary rewards such as transfer, training, travel, praise, and publicity to further encourage positive behavior. The appraisal system should be designed to optimize staff performance in the long term. Performance appraisal should be undertaken on a regular basis. Management should be held accountable for the performance of staff and should actively handle performance issues.

Box 4.9 contains issues and questions critical to the HR function's role in promoting integrity.

*Morale and Organizational Culture*

Corruption is most likely to occur in organizations in which morale or *esprit de corps* is low and customs personnel do not have pride in the reputation of their administration. Customs employees are more likely to act with integrity when morale is high, if HR management practices are seen as being fair, and if there are reasonable opportunities for career development and progression for all well-performing officials.[11] Employees at all levels should be actively involved in the anticorruption program and should be encouraged to accept an appropriate level of responsibility for the integrity of their administration. Integrity must be regarded as everyone's responsibility and obligation.

---

11. It is often suggested that experienced customs officials who are prevented from further career advancement or promotion by, for example, the lack of prescribed academic qualifications are the most likely to engage in corrupt behavior and, due to their extensive experience, the most unlikely to be detected.

Corruption is often not restricted to customs, but a phenomenon that is prevalent in the society as a whole. Integrity campaigns in customs must be fully cognizant of this and are likely to be most efficient if they are part of a nationwide anticorruption effort. Such campaigns will raise the moral costs of corruption, but will require that appropriate changes in the organizational culture be implemented for the changes to last.

Certainly, while politicians and senior customs officials regularly denounce corruption in all its forms and openly describe it as a significant obstacle to development, there is often a huge gulf between the rhetoric and reality. Some observers note that corrupt practices are often not linked to shame and people who engage in them conduct their activities with a clear conscience. Moreover, there may be no social stigma for being dismissed from one's position due to corruption. The issue of culture and its acceptance of corruption extends beyond individual customs administrations to whole societies and regions. It is frequently argued that the traditional social norms that govern the conduct of public office in industrialized countries are quite different from those that govern the behavior of officials in many developing countries. In many developing countries there exists a gap between law (as imposed by Western and Alien standards) and informal social norms (sanctioned by prevailing social ethics) i.e., there is a divergence between the attitudes, aims, and methods of government of a country and those of the society in which they operate (Caiden and Caiden 1977).

Many traditional societies value kinship and reciprocity, which serve important social functions, such as the provision of an informal insurance network during times of need. The majority of those engaging in corrupt behavior, however, do so for self-serving reasons, and rarely to benefit others. This fact is not lost on the majority of countries and cultures, which decry most forms of bribery, fraud, extortion, embezzlement, and most forms of kickbacks on public contracts (Klitgaard 1988).

In crafting an appropriate anticorruption program it does, however, seem prudent to consider the impact of social norms and cultural traditions and to incorporate specific strategies to deal with any particular issues that are identified. For example, in a number of small Pacific Island states where familial and community links are particularly strong, a customs IT system was introduced that automatically allocated declaration processing, cargo examination, and customs broker inquiries on a random basis, thus preventing any potential embarrassment that might ensue from officials having to deal with members of their own linguistic or cultural group.

Box 4.10 reviews key questions regarding the place morale has in promoting integrity.

### Relationship with Private Sector

Client groups can play an important role in controlling corruption. After all, many forms of corruption require the active involvement of external partners such as importers, exporters, transport providers, and customs brokers. Therefore, an effective anticorruption strategy will need to secure the active and wholehearted support of the business sector. Experience has shown, however, that such cooperation is often difficult to obtain and even more difficult to sustain as long as individual

---

**BOX 4.10  Morale and Organizational Culture: Key Issues and Questions**

Are staff encouraged to participate in project teams to identify high-risk areas and suggest changes to existing systems and work practices?

Are staff satisfaction surveys conducted? Are the results analyzed and acted upon?

Are all breaches of integrity dealt with promptly and investigation results made available to staff and the public?

Is the administration willing to undertake a process of self-assessment and participate in international integrity activities and initiatives?

Is customs regarded as a good employer? Do customs officials take pride in working for customs?

Has effective whistle blower legislation been introduced to protect officials who report corrupt behavior?

*Source:* Based on WCO 2003b.

traders are willing to pay a bribe to obtain a commercial advantage relative to their competitors.

Customs brokers, who assist importers and exporters in working through a range of complex administrative regulations and procedures, are usually the main points of contact with customs. In the absence of modern customs systems and procedures, brokers are required to work on a day-to-day basis with customs officials. They are often the conduits through which bribes are demanded and paid, and added to the brokerage fees. Anecdotal evidence suggests that brokers regularly inflate the amount of the bribes paid and reimbursed by their clients, and keep the excess for themselves. This practice provides brokers with a strong economic incentive to perpetuate a cycle of corruption.

The need for the business sector to take responsibility for its own ethics is acknowledged by the ICC Rules of Conduct. Article 5 of the ICC Rules sets out the principles governing the responsibilities of enterprises in relation to official corruption (ICC 1999). It states that the Board of Directors or other bodies with ultimate responsibility for the enterprise should take reasonable steps, including the establishment and maintenance of proper systems of control, aimed at preventing any payments being made by or on behalf of the enterprise that contravene the Rules of Conduct; periodically review compliance with the Rules of Conduct and establish appropriate reports for the purpose of such review; and take appropriate action against any director or employee contravening the Rules of Conduct. Directors of multinational companies should also monitor the extent to which management ensures that, throughout the enterprise, staff adhere to the OECD anticorruption convention.

Joint customs–business anticorruption task forces and committees could be excellent means of achieving the desired level of cooperation and commitment in the fight against corruption. Such committees provide an important vehicle for customs administrations to clearly communicate the standards of behavior expected of clients and for clients to provide practical examples of the administration's most vulnerable points. They can also establish practical mechanisms that encourage traders to report customs officials who demand bribes. Clear performance standards and client service charters may provide a useful starting point and a practical monitoring mechanism. The Indian Customs' Central Board of Customs and Excise has established a special vigilance Web site to allow clients to report complaints or allegations of misconduct. Each complaint or allegation is directed to an appropriate senior manager for action, and time frames for resolution are established and monitored. While functioning as a mechanism to register complaints with respect to customs operations, the mechanism can be made to serve as a platform for public–private sector dialogue.

Box 4.11 presents key questions concerning integrity and the relationship between the private sector and customs.

### Implementation of the Strategy

The WCO has developed a road map for assessing the quality of the integrity programs employed by customs administrations. The WCO's Integrity Development Guide provides an ongoing process of review and improvement of integrity strategies and includes a component of self-assessment and action planning.

---

**BOX 4.11    Relationship with the Private Sector: Key Issues and Questions**

Has a client service charter incorporating objective performance standards been established?

Have formal cooperative agreements and practical consultative mechanisms been established to foster open, transparent, productive relationships with the private sector?

Has a joint customs–business task force been established to address integrity issues and identify practical solutions?

Has a communication strategy been developed that supports the prompt provision of information and promotes the achievements of customs?

Are private sector operators encouraged to report incidences of corruption? If allegations are made, are the sources protected?

*Source:* Based on WCO 2003b.

As a starting point it is particularly useful to undertake a comprehensive assessment of the current situation.[12] Once a comprehensive diagnostic assessment has been conducted, it is then necessary to establish priorities and agree on the content of a national integrity action plan. Priorities can be established based on the following criteria: importance, urgency, consequence of failure, probability of obtaining executive and staff commitment, impact, national and international obligations, ease of implementation, and cost. Once the priority-setting process has been completed it is useful to develop a detailed implementation plan with realistic time frames for implementation, responsible officials, and verifiable performance indicators or measures.

To ensure that the results of the action planning process are well understood and accepted by senior executives and embraced by the majority of the organization's staff, it is important to develop practical information as well as a comprehensive marketing strategy. The action plan must be closely monitored to assist customs administrations in assessing and adjusting their individual integrity strategies. The action plan can best be monitored through the use of performance indicators. These could include the following: results of client and stakeholder satisfaction surveys, number of complaints or allegations against customs personnel, number of successful investigations or prosecutions for integrity breaches, positive or negative media coverage of integrity in customs, reports by international agencies, number and nature of ombudsman complaints, number of complaints by the traveling public and customs brokers or importers, results of internal and external audits, achievement of performance targets or client charter standards, and increases or decreases in operational performance statistics.

## Operational Conclusions

There is little doubt that the customs working environment makes it vulnerable to corruption. However, the critically important role played by customs

requires governments and the business community to tackle the problem in a meaningful way. The international customs community has acknowledged the problem and has developed a range of tools and programs to deal with it in a positive and pragmatic way. The Revised Arusha Declaration on Integrity in Customs sets out a comprehensive approach to dealing with the problem and has been endorsed by the 162 members of the WCO.

In looking to implement the 10 key elements of the Revised Arusha Convention, experience suggests that a good starting point is the performance of a comprehensive assessment of the current situation. The key issues and questions contained in this chapter provide a practical guide or checklist for this process (see boxes 4.1–4.7 and 4.9–4.11). Once the assessment is complete it is then helpful to establish realistic priorities and agree on a series of practical objectives and activities. These then form the basis of a national integrity action plan. Customs officials at all levels need to be involved in the diagnostic process, the identification of priorities, and the development of the action plan. The plan should outline a range of specific objectives, key activities, responsible officials, and verifiable performance indicators or measures of success.

Customs administrations do not, however, operate in a vacuum. They typically take policy and operational direction from the government of the day and interact with a wide range of stakeholders from both the public and private sectors. Much can therefore be gained by taking a whole-of-government approach to fighting corruption and by aligning the customs strategy with existing or future national anticorruption campaigns. However, if this is not possible, customs must be prepared to act independently and decisively to control and minimize corruption.

Most corrupt transactions that occur within the customs environment involve the active or passive participation of the private sector. The private sector must, therefore, be actively involved in and committed to identifying and implementing practical solutions.

A vitally important element of such a strategy is the comprehensive reform and modernization of customs to eliminate the incentive for private sector operators to seek means of circumventing normal regulatory requirements. In this sense, the Revised Kyoto Convention is one of the most

---

12. To assist this process, the WCO has developed a series of detailed diagnostic questions relating to each of the 10 elements of the Revised Arusha Declaration. These questions are incorporated in the WCO's Integrity Development Guide, which is available on the organization's Web site www.wcoomd.org.

effective tools available to address corruption problems in customs. Its provisions provide for less discretion and greater accountability. The adoption of an integrity strategy without modernized customs procedures will only provide a short-term remedy and will not be sustainable in the longer term. Indeed, many senior customs officials are convinced that if a customs service adopts modern procedures in line with the Revised Kyoto Convention, makes effective use of IT, pays its staff a competitive wage, and enjoys a cooperative relationship with the private sector, then it has done much of the work required to ensure integrity.

An anticorruption strategy in customs must be developed as a coherent package of mutually sustaining measures. The motives for engaging in corruption are complex; therefore, strategies should be designed to address both motive and opportunity. It is important to strike a balance between positive preventive strategies and repressive ones. In any case, customs administrations must focus on the thorough investigation of allegations of corruption and the enforcement of penalties irrespective of the position or influence of the individuals involved. The strategies contained in box 4.12 draw on lessons learned from several customs reform programs undertaken throughout the world, and demonstrate the need to address both motive and opportunity for corruption through a comprehensive strategy.

In conclusion, the effective control and elimination of corruption in customs is not an easy task. No quick fix solutions currently exist. To achieve sustainable results, customs administrations need to do the following:

- obtain the wholehearted support of their governments, the business community, and a range of other stakeholders
- undertake a comprehensive diagnosis of their current integrity problems and strategies
- collect appropriate baseline data and establish realistic verifiable performance indicators
- develop a comprehensive integrity action plan based on each of the 10 elements of the Revised Arusha Declaration
- continually evaluate and review results and establish an ongoing improvement process
- commit to sharing the results of their efforts
- most important, assign appropriate responsibility for the administration's anticorruption program to all managers, officials, and clients.

## Further Reading

Andvig, J. C., and O. Fjeldstad. 2000. *Research on Corruption: A Policy Oriented Survey*. Chr Michelsen Institute and Norwegian Institute of International Affairs. Oslo. www.cmi.no/research/project.cfm?proid=272.

Hors, Irene. 2001. *Fighting Corruption in Customs Administration: What Can We Learn from Recent Experiences*. OECD

---

**BOX 4.12  Lessons Learned from Customs Reforms to Control Corrupt Behavior**

The primary lesson learned from customs reform in transition countries and other parts of the world is that efforts to control the potentially corrupt behavior of customs officials require a comprehensive strategy to reduce the motive and opportunity for corruption. As summarized below, these lessons of experience have been incorporated in Bank projects through the integrated strategy to promote integrity.

**Measures Addressing Motive**

- Elite ethos and *esprit de corps*
- Positive career development
- Incentives for high performance
- Competitive pay and transparent reward system
- Stronger supervision and controls
- Sanctions for corruption
- Independent appeals mechanism
- Stakeholder surveys

**Measures Addressing Opportunity**

- Lower rates, less exemption
- Computerization
- Inspection based on risk analysis
- Arms-length transactions and reduction in discretionary authority
- Transparent clearance requirements
- Rotation of officers
- Functional organization
- Internal anticorruption strategy and audit

*Source*: Gill 2001.

Development Centre, Technical Paper No. 175. Paris: OECD. www.oecd.org/dataoecd/60/28/1899689.pdf.

ICC (International Chamber of Commerce). 1997. *International Customs Guidelines*. ICC Publication No. 587 (E). New York: ICC Publishing. www.iccwbo.org

Kaufmann, D. 1999. "Economic Reforms: Necessary But Not Sufficient to Curb Corruption?" In R. Stapenhurst, and S. J. Kpundeh, *Curbing Corruption: Toward a Model for Building National Integrity*. Economic Development Institute. Washington, D.C.: World Bank.

Klitgaard, R. 1998. *Controlling Corruption*. Berkeley: University of California Press.

Sparrow, Michael. 2000. *The Regulatory Craft*. Washington, D.C.: Brookings Institution Press.

## References

The word *processed* describes informally reproduced works that may not commonly be available through libraries.

Caiden, G. E., and N. J. Caiden. 1977. "Administrative Corruption." *Public Administration Review* 37(3): 301–309.

Fjeldstad, Odd-Helge, Ivar Kolstad, and Siri Lange. 2003. *Autonomy, Incentives, and Patronage: A Study in Corruption in the Tanzania and Uganda Revenue Authorities*. Development Studies and Human Rights. Oslo, Norway: Michelsen Institute.

Gill, J.B.S. 2001. *Customs: Developing an Integrated Anti-Corruption Strategy*. World Bank Institute. Draft Monograph. Washington, D.C.: The World Bank.

Hors, Irene. 2001. "Fighting Corruption in Customs Administration: What Can We Learn from Recent Experiences?" OECD Development Centre Technical Paper No. 175. Paris: OECD.

ICC (International Chamber of Commerce). 1997. "International Customs Guidelines." ICC Publication No. 587 (E). New York: ICC Publishing.

———. 1999. *Fighting Bribery: A Corporate Practices Manual*. New York: ICC Publishing.

Kaufman, Daniel, Sanjay Pradhan, and Randi Ryterman. 1998. "New Frontiers in Diagnosing and Combating corruption." PREM Note No. 7. Washington, D.C.: World Bank.

Klitgaard, R. 1988. *Controlling Corruption*. Berkeley: University of California Press.

———. 1993. "Gifts and Bribes." In R. J. Zeckhauser, ed. *Strategy and Choice*. Cambridge: MIT Press.

Lane, M. H. 1998. "Customs and Corruption." Working paper. Transparency International. Processed.

Nye, J. S. 1977. "Corruption and Political Development: A Cost Benefit Analysis." *American Political Science Review* LXI(2): 417–427.

TI (Transparency International). 1997. *TI Sourcebook—Confronting Corruption: The Elements of a National Integrity System*. Berlin. www.transparency.org/sourcebook/.

World Bank. 2000. *Helping Countries Combat Corruption*. Operational Core Services, Poverty Reduction and Economic Management Network. Washington, D.C.

———. 2001. "Cambodia Integration and Competitiveness Study." International Trade Department. Prepared for the Integrated Framework for Trade-Related Technical Assistance. Poverty Reduction and Economic Management Network. Washington, D.C.

———. 2003. Investment Climate Survey Database. Washington, D.C.

WCO (World Customs Organization). 2003a. *Annual Survey to Determine the Percentage of Government Revenue Provided by Customs Duties*. Document No. NC0665. Brussels.

———. 2003b. "Integrity Development Guide; Self-Assessment and Evaluation." Brussels.

# 5

# MANAGING RISK IN THE CUSTOMS CONTEXT

*David Widdowson*

In recent years the international trading environment has been transformed dramatically in terms of the manner in which goods are carried and traded, the speed of such transactions, and the sheer volume of goods now being traded around the globe. This, together with mounting pressure from the international trading community to minimize government intervention, has caused customs authorities to place an increasing emphasis on the facilitation of trade.

In an effort to achieve an appropriate balance between trade facilitation and regulatory control, customs administrations are generally abandoning their traditional, routine "gateway" checks and are now applying the principles of risk management, with varying degrees of sophistication and success.

This chapter examines the basic principles of risk management and identifies practical ways of putting the theory into practice. The first section discusses the importance of managing risk in customs. The second section examines the two key objectives of customs—facilitation and control. The third section identifies risk management as the means of achieving a balanced approach to facilitation and control. The fourth section deals with managing compliance and describes a risk-based compliance management strategy. The fifth section concentrates on putting the theory to practice and thus draws together the various elements of a risk management style to provide a structured approach to the management of compliance. The sixth section links compliance assessment with trade facilitation. The next section provides an example of risk management. The final section summarizes the chapter's main conclusions.

David Widdowson is Chief Executive Officer, Centre for Customs and Excise Studies and Adjunct Professor, School of Law, University of Canberra, Australia.

## The Importance of Managing Risk

The concept of organizational risk refers to the possibility of events and activities occurring that may prevent an organization from achieving its objectives. Customs authorities are required to achieve two primary objectives—provide the international trading community with an appropriate level of facilitation, and ensure compliance with regulatory requirements. Risks facing customs include the potential for noncompliance with customs laws such as licensing requirements, valuation provisions, rules of origin, duty exemption regimes, trade restrictions, and security regulations, as well as the potential failure to facilitate international trade.

Customs, like any other organization, needs to manage its risks. This requires the systematic application of management procedures designed to reduce those risks to ensure that its objectives are achieved as efficiently and effectively as possible. Such procedures include the identification, analysis, evaluation, treatment, monitoring, and review of risks that may affect the achievement of these objectives.

Sound risk management is fundamental to effective customs operations, and it would be true to say that all administrations apply some form of risk management, either formal or informal. Drawing on intelligence, information, and experience, customs has always adopted procedures designed to identify illegal activity in an effort to reduce its risks. The more traditional procedures include physical border controls over the movement of goods and people consisting of documentary checks and physical inspections aimed at detecting illicit trade. The introduction of such controls constitutes a form of risk management, but not necessarily an effective or efficient one.

Recently, the increasing complexity, speed, and volume of international trade, fueled by the technological advances that have revolutionized global trading practices, have significantly affected the way customs authorities carry out their responsibilities. As a consequence, many administrations have implemented a more disciplined and structured approach to managing risk. This has also helped them to increase the efficiency of their operations and to streamline their processes and procedures, minimizing intervention in trade transactions and reducing the regulatory burden on the commercial sector.

## Facilitation and Control

The two key objectives of customs are commonly referred to as "facilitation" and "control." In seeking to achieve an appropriate balance between trade facilitation and regulatory control, customs must simultaneously manage two risks—the potential failure to facilitate international trade and the potential for noncompliance with customs laws. The application of risk management principles provides the means of achieving this balance.

Note that the phrase "facilitation *and* control" has been used in this context, rather than the phrase "facilitation *versus* control." It is a commonly held belief that facilitation and control sit at opposite ends of a continuum, and it is not uncommon for commentators to refer to the apparent "paradox" of achieving both facilitation and control. It is often assumed that, as the level of facilitation increases, the level of control decreases. Similarly, where regulatory controls are tightened, it is commonly assumed that facilitation must suffer. This is an extremely simplistic view, as it assumes that the only way a process may be facilitated is by loosening the reins of control. Such a contention is fundamentally flawed, because the concepts of facilitation and control represent two distinct variables, as depicted in the matrix in figure 5.1.

The top left quadrant of the matrix (high control, low facilitation) represents a high-control regime in which customs requirements are stringent, to the detriment of facilitation. This may be described as the red tape approach, which is often

**FIGURE 5.1  Facilitation and Control Matrix**

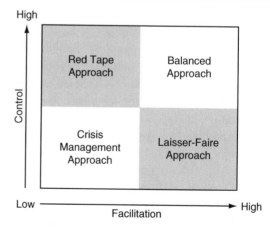

*Source:* Author.

representative of a risk-averse management style. In most modern societies such an approach is likely to attract a great deal of public criticism and complaint, due to the increasing expectations of the trading community that customs intervention should be minimized.

The bottom left quadrant (low control, low facilitation) depicts the approach of an administration that exercises little control and achieves equally little in the way of facilitation. This crisis management approach is one that benefits neither the government nor the trading community.

The bottom right quadrant (low control, high facilitation) represents an approach in which facilitation is the order of the day, but with it comes little in the way of customs control. This *laisser-faire* approach would be an appropriate method of managing compliance in an idyllic world in which the trading community complies fully without any threat or inducement from government, because such an environment would present no risk of noncompliance.

Finally, the top right quadrant (high control, high facilitation) represents a balanced approach to both regulatory control and trade facilitation, resulting in high levels of both. This approach to compliance management maximizes the benefits to both customs and the international trading community. It is this approach that administrations should be seeking to achieve.

## Achieving a Balanced Approach

Effective application of the principles of risk management is the key to achieving an appropriate balance between facilitation and control. As the use of risk management becomes more effective (for example, more systematic and sophisticated), an appropriate balance between facilitation and control becomes more achievable. Thus, those administrations that are able to achieve high levels of both facilitation and control (the balanced approach quadrant of the Facilitation and Control Matrix) do so through the effective use of risk management. Similarly, administrations in a state of total crisis management (that is, zero facilitation, zero control) would essentially be adopting a compliance management strategy that is devoid of risk management.

However, any movement away from a state of total crisis management implies the existence of some form of risk management. For example, recognizing that risk is the chance of something happening that will have an impact on organizational objectives, a regulatory strategy that achieves some degree of control, however small, represents a method of treating potential noncompliance with customs laws. Equally, a strategy that achieves some degree of facilitation represents a method of treating the potential failure to facilitate trade. This relationship is depicted in the three-dimensional Compliance Management Matrix in figure 5.2.

## Managing Compliance

The customs role is, therefore, to manage compliance with the law in a way that ensures the facilitation of trade. To achieve this, many administrations have already implemented compliance management strategies that are based on the principles of risk management.

The Compliance Management Matrix provides a useful conceptualization of the interrelationship between facilitation, regulatory control, and risk management. The next step is to identify the components of a risk-based compliance management strategy.

The underlying elements of such a strategy are summarized in table 5.1, which compares key elements of a risk-management style of compliance management with the more traditional gatekeeper style, which is typically characterized by indiscriminate customs intervention or a regime of 100 percent checks. Similarly, payment of duties and other taxes is a prerequisite for customs clearance under the gatekeeper model, and such clearance is invariably withheld until all formalities and real-time transactional checks are completed. A risk management approach, however, is characterized by the identification of potentially high-risk areas, with resources being directed toward such areas and minimal intervention in similarly identified low-risk areas. Such regimes adopt strategies that break the nexus between physical control over goods and a trader's revenue liability, and permit customs clearance to be granted prior to the arrival of cargo.

The various elements of each style of compliance management can be broadly grouped into four main categories—a country's legislative framework, the administrative framework of a country's customs organization, the type of risk management

**FIGURE 5.2 Compliance Management Matrix**

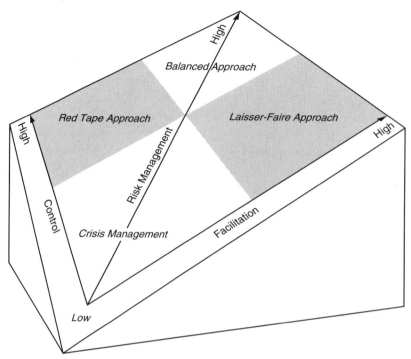

*Source:* Author.

framework adopted by a country's customs organization, and the available technological framework. Collectively, the four categories represent key determinants of the manner in which the movement of cargo may be expedited across a country's borders, and the way that customs control may be exercised over such cargo.

An appropriate legislative framework is an essential element of any regulatory regime, because the primary role of customs is to ensure compliance with the law. Regardless of the compliance management approach that it is supporting, the legislative framework must provide the necessary basis in law for the achievement of the range of administrative and risk management strategies that the administration has chosen to adopt. For example, an appropriate basis in law must exist to enable customs to break the nexus between its physical control over internationally traded goods and the revenue liability (that is, customs duty and other taxes) that such goods may attract. This does not necessarily imply, however, that such a differentiation must be explicitly addressed in the relevant statutory provisions. For example, if the legislation itself is silent on the relationship between customs control over cargo

and revenue liability, sufficient scope is likely to exist for administratively flexible solutions to be implemented.

Underpinned by the relevant legal provisions, the various elements of the administrative and risk management frameworks employed by customs essentially reflect the underlying style of compliance management being pursued by the administration, with an increasing use of risk management principles as the administration moves away from the traditional, risk-averse gatekeeper style of compliance management to a more risk-based approach.

The available technological framework represents an enabler that, while not critical to the achievement of a risk management style, serves to significantly enhance an administration's ability to adopt such a style.

**Putting the Theory into Practice**

The Risk-Based Compliance Management Pyramid (figure 5.3) draws together the various elements of a risk management style (that is, those on the right side of table 5.1) to provide a structured approach to the management of compliance. It provides a

**TABLE 5.1 Compliance Management Styles**

| | Traditional Gatekeeper Style | ↔ | Risk Management Style |
|---|---|---|---|
| **Legislative Framework** | Legislative base provides for a "one size fits all" approach to compliance management | ↔ | Legislative base provides for flexibility and tailored solutions to enable relevant risk management and administrative strategies to be implemented |
| | Onus for achieving regulatory compliance is placed solely on the trading community | ↔ | Legislative base recognizes responsibilities for both government and the trading community in achieving regulatory compliance |
| | Sanctions for noncompliers | ↔ | Sanctions for noncompliers |
| **Administrative Framework** | "One size fits all" compliance strategy | ↔ | Strategy dependent on level of risk |
| | Control focus | ↔ | Balance between regulatory control and trade facilitation |
| | Enforcement focus | ↔ | Dual enforcement–client service focus |
| | Unilateral approach | ↔ | Consultative, cooperative approach |
| | Focus on assessing the veracity of transactions | ↔ | Focus on assessing the integrity of trader systems and procedures |
| | Inflexible procedures | ↔ | Administrative discretion |
| | Focus on real-time intervention and compliance assessment | ↔ | Increased focus on post-transaction compliance assessment |
| | Lack of or ineffective appeal mechanisms | ↔ | Effective appeal mechanisms |
| **Risk Management Framework** | Indiscriminate intervention or 100 percent check | ↔ | Focus on high-risk areas, with minimal intervention in low-risk areas |
| | Physical control focus | ↔ | Information management focus |
| | Focus on identifying noncompliance | ↔ | Focus on identifying both compliance and noncompliance |
| | Post-arrival import clearance | ↔ | Pre-arrival import clearance |
| | Physical control maintained pending revenue payment | ↔ | Breaks nexus between physical control and revenue liability |
| | No special benefits for recognized compliers | ↔ | Rewards for recognized compliers |
| | **Risk Management Enablers** | | |
| **IT Framework** | Legislative provisions provide the trading community with electronic as well as paper-based reporting, storage, and authentication options. Such provisions should enable regulators to rely on commercially generated data to the greatest extent possible. Appropriate communications and information technology infrastructure to provide for automated processing and clearance arrangements. Regulators should seek to achieve maximum integration with commercial systems. Consultative business process reengineering prior to automation. | | |

*Source:* Author.

logical framework for demonstrating how various types of risk-based strategies, including nonenforcement strategies such as self-assessment, may be used to effectively manage compliance.

Fundamental to this approach is the need to provide the commercial sector with the ability to comply with customs requirements. This involves establishing an effective legislative base (the first tier of the pyramid) and an appropriate range of client service strategies (the second tier), including effective consultation arrangements and clear administrative guidelines. Such strategies are necessary to provide the commercial sector with the means to achieve certainty and clarity in assessing liabilities and entitlements.

At the third tier of the pyramid, the elements of compliance assessment come into play, including risk-based physical and documentary checks,

**FIGURE 5.3    Risk-Based Compliance Management Pyramid**

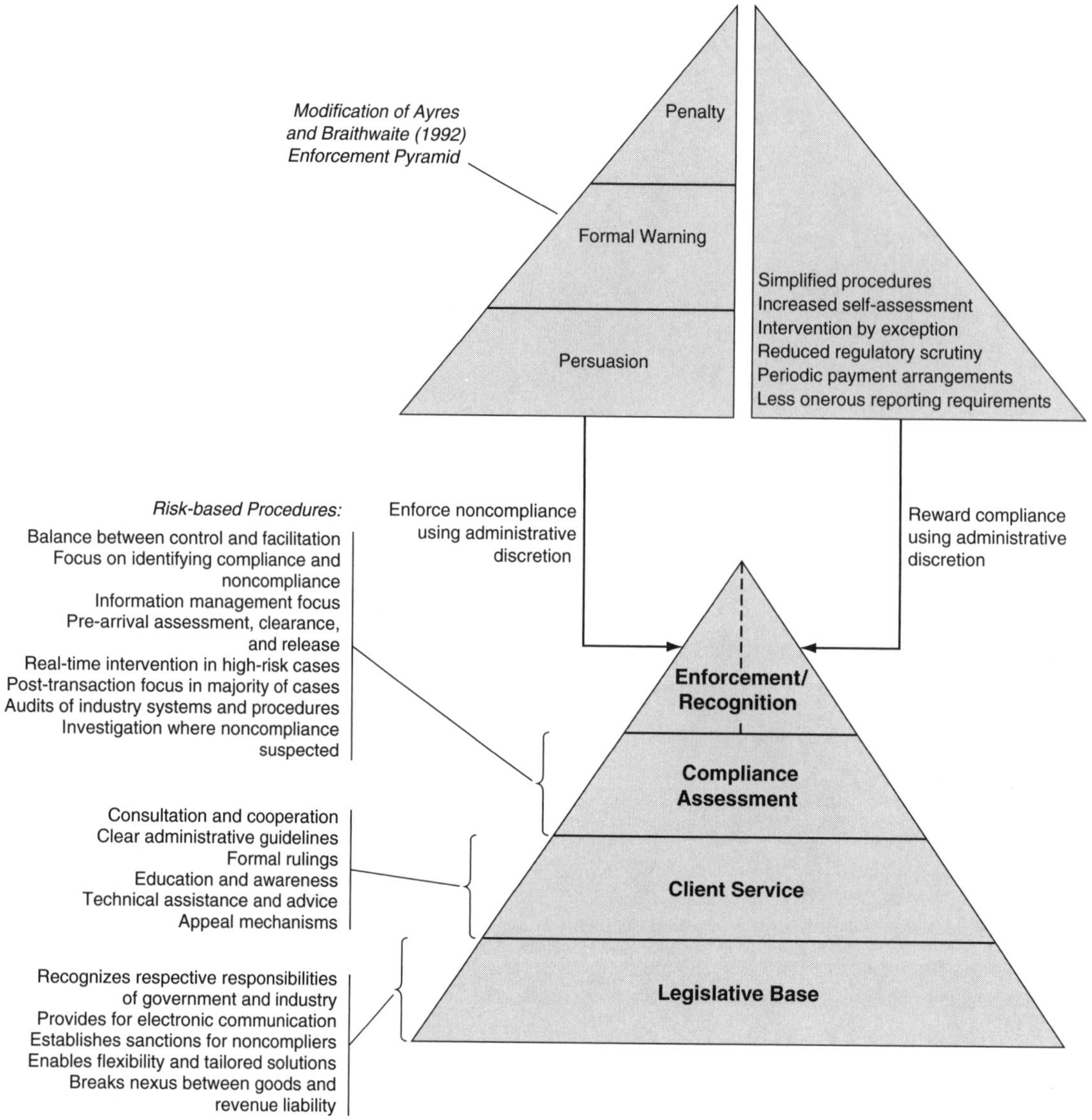

Modification of Ayres
and Braithwaite (1992)
Enforcement Pyramid

Penalty

Formal Warning

Persuasion

Simplified procedures
Increased self-assessment
Intervention by exception
Reduced regulatory scrutiny
Periodic payment arrangements
Less onerous reporting requirements

Enforce noncompliance
using administrative
discretion

Reward compliance
using administrative
discretion

*Risk-based Procedures:*

Balance between control and facilitation
Focus on identifying compliance and
noncompliance
Information management focus
Pre-arrival assessment, clearance,
and release
Real-time intervention in high-risk cases
Post-transaction focus in majority of cases
Audits of industry systems and procedures
Investigation where noncompliance
suspected

**Enforcement/
Recognition**

**Compliance
Assessment**

Consultation and cooperation
Clear administrative guidelines
Formal rulings
Education and awareness
Technical assistance and advice
Appeal mechanisms

**Client Service**

Recognizes respective responsibilities
of government and industry
Provides for electronic communication
Establishes sanctions for noncompliers
Enables flexibility and tailored solutions
Breaks nexus between goods and
revenue liability

**Legislative Base**

*Source:* Author.

audits, and investigations. Such activities are designed to determine whether a trader is in compliance with customs law, and these are discussed in more detail in the next section.

At the peak of the pyramid are strategies to address both identified noncompliers and recognized compliers. Strategies for the identified noncompliers include a range of enforcement techniques (see Ayres and Braithwaite 1992), while strategies for the recognized compliers include increased levels of self-assessment, reduced regulatory scrutiny, less onerous reporting requirements, periodic payment arrangements, and increased lev-

els of facilitation (see Industry Panel on Customs Audit Reforms 1995 and Sparrow 2000).

In assessing the level of compliance, customs will encounter two situations: compliance and noncompliance. The noncompliance spectrum will range from innocent mistakes to blatant fraud. If the error nears the fraudulent end of the spectrum, some form of sanction will need to apply, including administrative penalties or, in more severe cases, prosecution and license revocation.

Before determining the need for, or nature of, a sanction, however, it is important to identify the true nature of the risk by establishing why the error has occurred. For example, the error may be the result of a control problem within the company due to flawed systems and procedures, or it may be the result of a deliberate attempt to defraud. It also may be that the relevant legislation is unclear or the administrative requirements are ambiguous. The type of mitigation strategy that customs should employ to ensure future compliance will depend on the nature of the identified risk. Unless the error is found to be intentional, it may be appropriate to address systemic problems within the company, or to provide the company (or perhaps an entire industry sector) with advice on compliance issues, or provide formal clarification of the law through binding rulings or other means (Widdowson 1998).

In this regard, it is important to recognize that different solutions will be required to address honest mistakes on the one hand, and deliberate attempts to evade duty on the other. For example, industry familiarization seminars and information brochures may adequately address errors that result from a lack of understanding of the relevant regulatory provisions. However, if someone is actively seeking to commit revenue fraud, seminars and information brochures will have absolutely no impact on their activities. Indeed, such members of the trading community are likely to have an excellent understanding of their obligations and entitlements. To treat the risks posed by such individuals (or organizations, for that matter), a rigorous enforcement approach is likely to be required.

## Compliance Assessment and Trade Facilitation

In applying the principles of risk management to the day-to-day activities of customs, one of the most critical areas is that of compliance assessment—determining whether an entity or transaction is in compliance with regulatory requirements. This represents the third tier of the Compliance Management Pyramid in figure 5.3. When developing strategies to assess compliance, it is important to consider a key principle of the Revised Kyoto Convention—that customs control should be limited to what is necessary to ensure compliance with the customs law (WCO 1999). Administrative regimes should be as simple as practicable, and should provide the trading community with cost-efficient ways of demonstrating compliance with the law.

This principle applies to a range of customs controls, including physical control over goods, information requirements, timing and method of reporting, and timing and form of revenue collection. The use of documentary controls (information management) to monitor and assess compliance generally represents a far less intrusive and hence more facilitative approach than the use of physical controls. Similarly, post-transaction audit generally represents a more facilitative method of verification than checks undertaken at the time of importation or exportation.

For many developing countries, however, the task of introducing risk-based strategies can be daunting, particularly for those administrations that do not yet have the capacity to undertake post-transaction audits, or that currently rely heavily on manual processing systems. While it is clear that such impediments will limit the effectiveness of any risk-based strategies, applying a risk management approach to existing manual systems will prove far more effective and efficient than continuing to apply a gatekeeper approach to those same systems. For example, despite the fact that an administration may undertake all customs examinations and assessments at the time of importation, there is nevertheless an opportunity to replace an indiscriminate or random method of examining goods with one that takes account of the potential risks. Similarly, it is quite possible to apply documentary checks prior to the arrival of goods despite the fact that manual methods of processing are employed.

A case in point is Sri Lanka, which was successful in introducing pre-arrival screening and clearance for air express consignments prior to the availability of its automated systems. This consisted of a combination of manual documentary assessment, selective examination, and the establishment of x-ray facilities to address the potential risk of misdescription. Consolidated manifests were manually submitted to customs prior to aircraft arrival, together with advance copies of air waybills and invoices. These were manually screened by customs to identify potentially high-risk shipments (based on intelligence, emerging trends, the previous compliance record of consignees and consignors, and so on). Any consignments that were considered to be high risk were identified for further examination upon arrival, together with certain dutiable and restricted goods that were held pending formal clearance. All

---

### BOX 5.1    Managing Risk: Customs Valuation

Following its adoption of the WTO Valuation Agreement, customs needs to ensure that importers comply with the new provisions. Its task is therefore one of *compliance management.* To effectively manage compliance, it decides to follow the principles of *risk management,* which require it to identify, analyze, evaluate, and treat risks to the achievement of its objectives. In this case, the overriding *risk* is that traders fail to comply with the valuation provisions.

To accurately *identify the risk,* customs considers in further detail what could happen that may result in incorrect valuation, and how such an event could occur. One such risk is undervaluation due to certain traders deliberately failing to declare the cost of assists (includes materials, tooling, or other costs provided by an importer to a foreign producer). Customs then *analyzes the risk* by determining the *likelihood* of it occurring and *the consequence* if it was to occur. Its next step is to *evaluate the risk* by determining

whether it is an acceptable risk—that is, does customs need to do anything about it? (Some prefer to use the term *risk assessment* in lieu of *risk evaluation.* Others use the term *risk assessment* to describe the combined process of *risk analysis* and *risk evaluation.*)

Customs decides to *treat the risk,* and determines that the best way is to *target* shipments that are likely to include undeclared assists. Based on its research, customs identifies a number of criteria or *risk indicators* (for example, type of goods, supplier, consignee, origin) that, collectively, are likely to indicate a potential nondeclaration of assists. When combined, these indicators represent a *risk profile* that customs uses to select suspected *high-risk* consignments. Such *selectivity* ensures that *low-risk* consignments are facilitated.

*Source:* Author.

---

other consignments (that is, low-risk shipments) were available for delivery on arrival.

Administrations that have adopted a risk-based approach to compliance management, regardless of whether their systems are automated, are also selective in their use of the broad range of controls that are available to them. In being selective, they recognize that individual members of the trading community present customs with varying levels of risk in terms of potential noncompliance with relevant laws. For example, traders with a good record of compliance are unlikely to require the same level of scrutiny as those with a history of poor compliance. Consequently, if a trader is judged to be relatively low risk, customs may reduce its level of regulatory scrutiny and place greater reliance on the company's self-assessment of compliance.[1] This particularly effective strategy is a commonly used method of recognition, and forms the right half of the peak of the Compliance Management Pyramid.

Risk-based compliance management results in a situation where low-risk traders are permitted to

operate under less onerous regulatory requirements and may anticipate little in the way of customs intervention, and therefore receive relatively high levels of trade facilitation. Transactions of high-risk traders, however, are more likely to be selected for higher levels of customs intervention and control. Customs intervention for high-risk traders may include documentary checks or physical examinations at the time of importation or exportation, higher levels of audit activity, physical controls at manufacturing premises, and relatively high security bonds. In all cases, however, the level and type of intervention should be based on the level of identified risk.

### Risk Management: An Example

Sometimes confusion arises over the terms used to describe the management of risk, and often terms are used interchangeably. The simple scenario in box 5.1 of a country that recently accepted the WTO obligation on valuation is designed to clarify the more common terms.

### Conclusion

Effective risk management is central to modern customs operations, and provides the means to achieve an appropriate balance between trade facilitation

---

1. Allowing low-risk traders to self-assess their revenue liability does not imply that no customs checks will be made. It does, however, imply that a decision to clear the goods will generally be made on the basis of the traders' own assessment of their liability or entitlement.

and regulatory control. The principles of risk management can be applied by all administrations, regardless of whether they operate manual or automated systems, if they adopt strategies that incorporate the key elements of a risk-based approach to compliance management.

To manage risk effectively, administrations must gain a clear understanding of the nature of risks to the achievement of their objectives and devise practical methods of mitigating those risks. Finally, there needs to be a demonstrated commitment from the highest level of the organization to support the transition to a risk-based approach to compliance management.

## References

Ayres, Ian, and John Braithwaite. 1992. *Responsive Regulation: Transcending the Deregulation Debate.* New York: Oxford University Press.

Industry Panel on Customs Audit Reforms. 1995. *Looking to the Future—Compliance Improvement, Report of the Industry Panel on Customs Audit Reforms.* Canberra: Australian Customs Service.

Sparrow, Malcolm. 2000. *The Regulatory Craft.* Washington, D.C.: Brookings Institution Press.

Widdowson, David. 1998. "Managing Compliance: More Carrot, Less Stick." In Chris Evans and Abe Greenbaum, eds. *Tax Administration: Facing the Challenges of the Future.* Sydney: Prospect.

World Customs Organization. 1999. *International Convention on the Harmonization and Simplification of Customs Procedures (as amended),* General Annex, Standard 6.2. Brussels.

# PART II

# LESSONS FROM A SELECT SET OF CUSTOMS REFORM INITIATIVES

# 6

# POLICY AND OPERATIONAL LESSONS LEARNED FROM EIGHT COUNTRY CASE STUDIES

*Paul Duran and José B. Sokol*

## TABLE OF CONTENTS

## LIST OF TABLES

## LIST OF BOXES

The focus of this chapter is the customs reform and modernization programs in eight developing countries—Bolivia, Ghana, Morocco, Mozambique, Peru, the Philippines, Turkey, and Uganda[1]—with a view to drawing lessons that could be useful in formulating reform programs for other countries. The country case studies were assigned to customs experts and consultants who either participated in the reform processes in the countries reviewed or who, in their professional experience, had accumulated significant technical knowledge of customs reform and modernization processes in a worldwide context.

Countries were selected that would present initiatives from different continents, with their respective special reform outlooks, and that would yield interesting insights.

Initiated within the framework of an institutional reform covering the entire government and

---

1. The country case studies were performed by the following consultants: Bolivia (Flavio Escobar), Morocco (Marcel Steenlandt and Luc De Wulf), Mozambique (Anthony Mwangi), Peru (Adrien Goorman), the Philippines (Guillermo L. Parayno Jr.), Turkey (M. Bahri Oktem), and Uganda (Luc De Wulf). The Ghana report (Luc De Wulf) was commissioned by the World Development Report team of the World Bank.

with strong leadership provided by the vice president, customs reform in *Bolivia* aimed at its total transformation. One of the key elements of the reform was complete staff renewal designed to rid the service of deeply embedded corruption.

The study of the *Ghana* experience is quite different from the other country studies. It was undertaken initially as a case study of reform that would improve the investment climate. It clearly illustrates how introducing information technology (IT)—even in the absence of a comprehensive customs reform—can strengthen revenue mobilization and speed up the clearance of cargo.

While not codified in a detailed action plan, *Morocco's* program of customs reform and modernization reflected a comprehensive vision and covered all aspects of customs from its organization to its operation. Reform actions were undertaken in a deliberate and pragmatic process.

In *Mozambique,* the most significant characteristic of the reform was the willingness to rely extensively on external consultants for management and implementation of the reform, and for the valuation of imports and exports for customs purposes. This unusual approach was adopted in the midst of rebuilding a government service that was totally destroyed after many years of war.

In *Peru,* customs reform and modernization was high on the agenda of the president, who provided strong political support throughout the reform process. Customs was vested with full ownership, and maintained the necessary continuity to see the process through to its completion.

Decisive factors in the success of the reform in the *Philippines* during 1992–98 included strong top-level political backing; strong, able, and sustained operational leadership; ownership of the reform by the head of customs; and support that included some funding by private sector users of customs services. Among its weaknesses was a failure of commitment from the staff arising in part from inadequate compensation—a problem that could not be addressed because the Philippine Bureau of Customs lacked authority and funding.

Customs reform and modernization efforts in *Turkey* were dominated by two goals: bringing customs legislation and administrative structures in line with European Union (EU) standards in the context of a customs union with the EU, and the automation of customs procedures. The establishment of an independent Modernization Project Unit with strong political support and steady management was a critical element in the effective coordination of automation activities.

In *Uganda,* customs reform has been a long-term process. Started in 1990–91, its main aim was to strengthen revenue mobilization and to combat corruption.

In addition to the experiences of the country studies, reference is occasionally made to the experiences of interesting customs reform and modernization processes in *countries of Southeastern Europe,*[2] where the Bank supported border infrastructure and institutional modernization to facilitate legitimate trade and fight smuggling and corruption. Such efforts address customs reform from the perspective of the end-user—the trading community—and cover a broad spectrum of activities, including interagency cooperation, enforcement, private sector relations, infrastructure rehabilitation, and revenue collection. Corruption issues are addressed through procedural and organizational reforms.

The country case studies were undertaken based on a common approach to ensure comprehensiveness and comparability. Five areas of the reform process were targeted:

- The background of the reform and modernization process, its economic and institutional context, factors leading to reform decisions, supporters, objectives and design, and financial and technical support.
- Issues in the reform process.
- The reform measures themselves, covering legislation; management changes; staff-related questions such as pay, selection, training, integrity, and corruption; information technology; valuation; experience with preshipment inspection; special import regimes; and selectivity in pre- and post-release control.
- Reform outcomes including impact on fiscal performance, trade facilitation, anticorruption, staffing and workload, and conformance to international standards. Where available, quantitative

---

2. The Trade and Transport Facilitation in Southeast Europe Program (TTFSE) is an integrated approach to customs and border management issues, involving eight countries (Albania, Bosnia and Herzegovina, Bulgaria, Croatia, Macedonia, Moldova, Romania, and Serbia and Montenegro).

performance indicators receive attention as do user reactions.

- The lessons that each of these studies contain and the judgment pertaining to the sustainability of these modernization initiatives.

Reform and modernization in the case study countries aimed at transforming customs into a professional administration. Whereas most countries pursued several objectives encompassing facilitating trade, raising revenue, and protecting the economy against harmful practices, in others the scope was more limited with emphasis on a particular area. In all cases, reform efforts were supported by external technical and financial assistance.

To provide a firm foundation to the reform process, most countries adopted a new Customs Code, adapting legal provisions to the needs of international trade practices and the application of IT. The reform of customs services included changes in the structure, organization, or status of customs administrations. In several countries, customs was given administrative autonomy, which provided flexibility in adopting a structure and in developing procedures most suited to discharging its tasks. In a few countries, customs also obtained financial autonomy.

To distill the experiences of the countries reviewed into usable lessons, this chapter is organized as follows: The first section provides background information on the economic performance, economic policies, and reforms, relative size, and degree of integration of the countries reviewed. The second section gives an indication of the principal reform objectives, their main design features, and the donor financial and technical assistance that supported them. The third section contains a detailed review of the reform components, covering the Customs Code, management changes, personnel issues (including integrity), IT, customs control, and measures for trade facilitation and for safeguarding revenues. The fourth section evaluates the outcome of the reforms, assessing their impact on customs in the areas of revenue generation, enforcement, integrity, customs clearance time, and the reaction of users of customs' services. Finally, the fifth section derives the lessons of country experiences and identifies factors that are critical for designing and undertaking successful reform programs.

## Main Characteristics of the Countries Case Study

The design, enactment, and implementation of major customs reforms in the countries reviewed were influenced by concerns within the countries for improving economic management and increasing the incomes of their population, ongoing economic reform efforts, and the possibility of expanding trade links with other countries.

### Economic and Population Characteristics

Wide differences were recorded in the countries reviewed in terms of the size of their economies, population, level of development, and recent economic performance (see table 6.1). Yet these factors did not influence any country's commitment to reform or its pace. Gross domestic product (GDP) levels range from close to US$200 billion for Turkey to less than US$4 billion for Mozambique. With 77 million inhabitants, the Philippines has the largest population of all eight countries reviewed, followed by Turkey with 65 million. Bolivia is the smallest of the group with 8 million inhabitants.

In terms of GDP per capita, Mozambique lies at the lower end of all countries reviewed with US$216, Turkey at the highest end with US$3,052. A wide variance of growth rates was also recorded. In some countries, the reforms contributed to higher growth rates during 1996–2001 than those achieved during 1990–95. Mozambique grew at 9.0 percent per year on average, followed by Uganda at 5.8 percent, and Morocco at 4.1 percent. Peru and Turkey had the lowest growth rates of all, at 2.2 percent.

### Fiscal Performance

Reliance on import taxes[3] as a source of revenue was relatively higher for most countries prior to the introduction of the reforms (see table 6.2), with import taxes as a share of tax revenue amounting to more than 30 percent in five countries and around 20 percent in two. Customs duties as a share of tax

---

3. Customs revenue is the sum of import values multiplied by tax rates applicable to imports, less tax exemptions (some mandated by international agreements, others by local legislation, for example, certain sectors, new investment, or other). Revenue changes when either tax rates or import values change. The latter changes because of changes in GDP, import prices, institutional valuation capacity, and contraband volumes.

**TABLE 6.1   Basic Economic Data, 2000**

| Country | GDP (Millions of US$) | Population (Millions) | GDP per Capita (US$) | GDP Growth (Annual average in percent) | |
|---|---|---|---|---|---|
| | | | | 1990–95 | 1996–2001 |
| Bolivia | 8,356 | 8 | 1,003 | 4.2 | 3.1 |
| Ghana | 4,977 | 19 | 340 | 4.3 | 4.2 |
| Morocco | 33,345 | 29 | 1,162 | 1.6 | 4.1 |
| Mozambique | 3,813 | 18 | 216 | 3.1 | 9.0 |
| Peru | 53,466 | 26 | 2,061 | 3.8 | 2.2 |
| Philippines | 74,733 | 77 | 975 | 2.8 | 3.5 |
| Turkey | 199,267 | 65 | 3,052 | 4.3 | 2.2 |
| Uganda | 5,891 | 22 | 265 | 7.0 | 5.8 |

*Source:* World Bank data.

**TABLE 6.2   Revenue Performance Before and After Customs Reforms**

| | Bolivia | Ghana[a] | Morocco | Mozambique | Peru | Philippines | Turkey | Uganda |
|---|---|---|---|---|---|---|---|---|
| | (Percent of Tax Revenue) | | | | | | | |
| **Customs duties** | | | | | | | | |
| Before reforms | 10.5 | 16.9 | 17.0 | 22.5 | 10.7 | 26.9 | 3.7 | 10.0 |
| After reforms (2001) | 8.2 | 14.1 | 14.2 | 17.2 | 11.6 | 10.9 | 1.0 | 12.9 |
| **Import Taxes** | | | | | | | | |
| Before reforms | 39.8 | 38.4 | 45.4 | 31.6 | 20.6 | 35.3 | 15.3 | 22.3 |
| After reforms (2001) | 34.4 | 35.2 | 42.2 | 45.4 | 37.2 | 20.5 | 14.0 | 33.7 |
| | (Percent of GDP) | | | | | | | |
| **Tax revenue** | | | | | | | | |
| Before reforms | 11.5 | 16.3 | 21.6 | 9.8 | 10.8 | 14.7 | 15.2 | 7.8 |
| After reforms (2001) | 13.2 | 20.2 | 22.7 | 11.5 | 12.3 | 14.0 | 22.3 | 12.3 |
| **Customs duties** | | | | | | | | |
| Before reforms | 1.2 | 2.8 | 3.7 | 2.2 | 1.2 | 4.0 | 0.6 | 0.8 |
| After reforms (2001) | 1.1 | 2.9 | 3.2 | 2.0 | 1.4 | 1.5 | 0.2 | 1.6 |
| **Import taxes** | | | | | | | | |
| Before reforms | 4.6 | 6.2 | 9.8 | 3.1 | 2.6 | 5.2 | 2.3 | 1.7 |
| After reforms (2001) | 4.5 | 7.1 | 9.6 | 5.3 | 4.4 | 2.9 | 3.1 | 4.1 |

*Note:* Period before reform refers to following years: Bolivia, 1996; Ghana, 2000; Morocco, 1996; Mozambique, 1996; Peru, 1990; the Philippines, 1991; Turkey, 1994; and Uganda, 1990–91.
a. For Ghana, the year after reforms is 2003.
*Sources:* De Wulf and Sokol 2004. Data provided by national customs; World Bank database; International Monetary Fund International Financial Statistics; and Government Finance Statistics Yearbook, various issues; and IMF, various Country Reports.

revenue lies between about 4 percent and 27 percent. The tax-revenue-to-GDP ratio is in the range of about 8 percent to 22 percent.

At the outset of the reforms, tax revenue was rather low as illustrated by tax-to-GDP ratios of less than 10 percent in Uganda and Mozambique, and in the low to mid-teens in Peru, Bolivia, the

Philippines, and Turkey (table 6.2). Following the reform, the tax-revenue-to-GDP ratio increased in all countries, except the Philippines. Moreover, import taxes became an important tax handle in most countries.

During the period from the outset of the reforms through 2001, the import-tax-to-tax-revenue ratio rose sharply in a number of countries (to 34 percent in Uganda, 45 percent in Mozambique, and 37 percent in Peru) owing to the introduction of the value added tax (VAT). The fall of this ratio in other countries (to 34 percent in Bolivia and 21 percent in the Philippines) reflected the sharp drop of customs duties in tax revenue, resulting from customs duty rate cuts.

### Overall Reform Context

In several countries, the implementation of customs reforms was coordinated with trade liberalization policies, themselves often part of a broader economic reform program. Between 1988 and 1991, Bolivia reduced its general import tariff rate from 20 percent to 5 percent on capital goods and 10 percent on other goods. In Peru, the average nominal tariff declined from 46.5 percent in 1990 to 13.5 percent in 1997 and 11 percent in 2000. The acceleration of trade reform in the Philippines reflected the country's compliance with commitments under the World Trade Organization (WTO), and the regional groups Asia-Pacific Economic Cooperation (APEC) and Asian Free Trade Association (AFTA). Uganda moved to two nonzero rates of 7 percent and 15 percent in 1995. In Mozambique, the average tariff rate declined from 15.7 percent in 1998 to 13.0 percent in 2001.

In Bolivia, Peru, and Turkey, customs reforms formed part of a broad program of policy and institutional reform that covered other government units or even the whole administration. Reform was either directed at the general structure of government or focused on specific aspects, such as personnel management. In Bolivia, personnel management reform was part of an administration-wide civil service reform, with customs selected as the initial reform area. Other aspects of the reform touching on the administrative structure of customs were also part of the administration-wide reform program, including contraband control.[4]

---

4. To control contraband, most customs administrations have a police-like law enforcement unit. Some countries delegate this function to law enforcement agencies, such as the general police force or special border police (Chile and Argentina, for example). The control of contraband poses many complex issues, including determining the best arrangements to address it, the optimal number of personnel to be assigned to the task in relation to import volume and kilometers of borders, and so forth, which are beyond the scope of this review.

In 1990, Peru carried out a complete overhaul of the central government and all public institutions, including customs. In Turkey, customs reform was part of the reform requirements for membership in the customs union with the EU. The reorganization of customs was also an integral element of Turkey's government-wide administrative reform.

In Morocco, customs modernization was directed at enhancing the country's external competitiveness, a clearly perceived necessary condition to fulfill the country's ambition of fuller integration of its economy into the world economy, as reflected in its broader commitments under the WTO and the association agreement with the EU. In Southeast Europe, customs reform under the TTFSE program was designed to combat corruption and smuggling, and improve border processing and decrease delays. The ultimate objective was to achieve compatibility with EU standards, thus facilitating the accession process. In Mozambique, customs reform became part of the government's effort to reconstruct its war-torn economy and resulting total lack of effective administrative capacity.

In Mozambique, Morocco, the Philippines, and Uganda,[5] customs was the single targeted institution for reform. In Ghana, customs modernization was part of the government trade policy reforms being enacted to implement the government vision for a Ghana that is open to the rest of the world.

### Regional and Preferential Arrangements

All case study countries are members of one or more regional or bilateral preferential arrangements in the form of a customs union or full-fledged or partial free trade arrangement. In some countries, membership in a regional arrangement has been a positive factor providing an impetus for customs reform either through the adoption of modern regulations as in the case of Turkey, or of best practices jointly with other countries, such as the Philippines in APEC or Southeast European countries in the EU.

The management of effective transit trade requires good cooperation between the various countries affected. A regional approach to this

---

5. In Uganda, the reform created an Autonomous Revenue Agency (ARA) that encompasses Customs and Domestic Taxation as two separate departments.

matter has many advantages. For example, Mozambique is a member of the Cross-Border Initiative (CBI) and Southern African Development Community (SADC), both of which provide for free trade among members except for raw materials. Mozambique has entered into several bilateral preferential trade agreements, especially with African countries, and trade protocols governing transit trade. Turkey has signed free trade agreements with the European Free Trade Association (EFTA) and a number of central and eastern European countries similar to EU agreements with those countries. In Southeast Europe, the reintroduction of the Transport International Routier (TIR) regime across Serbia was a key element of trade facilitation.

A problem in the implementation of the Common Market for Eastern and Southern Africa (COMESA) in Uganda is a result of the incidence of fraud in the certificates of origin and the low level of effective cooperation of customs authorities in the various countries that substantially increases the cost of transit. Ongoing discussions with Kenya and Tanzania to revive the East African Community could help alleviate problems for Uganda's importers at the Kenyan and Tanzanian borders.

## Customs Reform Experiences

Before undertaking the reforms reviewed here, customs administrations in the sample countries shared a number of weaknesses. In general, clearance procedures were tedious and costly in terms of required documentation and procedures, resulting in lengthy clearance times. Clearance procedures often included redundant verifications and multiple steps that lacked business rationale and whose objectives were overtaken by modern business practices. Also, in most cases all shipments were subject to physical inspection, and procedures were largely paper-based and inadequately supported by customs IT. In several countries (Bolivia, Mozambique, the Philippines, and Uganda) corruption and smuggling were major problems. In Southeast Europe, as in most transition countries, the situation was further complicated by the need to move customs from its traditional role in a socialist environment of statistical regulation and passenger control to a more trade-oriented activity. This was a serious challenge, as the administrations had to cope, in a very short time, with a rapidly expanding

private sector. The latter consisted of often unreliable or unknown operators and the customs administrations did not have the resources, organization, or training to manage that fundamental change. In Ghana, customs clearance procedures were time consuming, error prone, and did not provide a transparent method to audit whether, in fact, all cargo had been declared.

### Customs Reform Objectives

The main reform objectives included strengthening revenue-generating capacity, enhancing trade facilitation, and combating smuggling and corruption. Most countries pursued several objectives, although in some the initial emphasis on one objective shifted during the reform process as sufficient progress was achieved and its urgency declined. Among the factors determining the choice of objectives were the initial state of customs services and the economic policy objectives of the government, especially in the fiscal and trade policy areas.

In countries with a comprehensive reform program, the objective was to set up a fully professional, efficient, and integrated administration, which would become an effective instrument of fiscal and trade policies by ensuring proper revenue collection, minimizing trade costs, and protecting the economy from harmful practices. These were the broad reform objectives instituted in Mozambique, Morocco, Peru, and the Philippines. While at the beginning of the reform process the primary objective in the Philippines may have been revenue generation, improving trade facilitation and the business and investment environment by streamlining the customs bureaucracy gained prominence in the reform. In Turkey, the aim of the reform was to enhance trade facilitation and contribute to Turkey's integration into the European Community (EC). This was also the case in Southeast Europe. In Uganda, the reform focused primarily on increasing government revenue and combating corruption, with less emphasis on trade facilitation.

In Peru and the Philippines, the reform was triggered by declining or stagnating government revenues. The revenue-related problems became particularly severe in Peru, which was then facing an economic crisis, and in the Philippines, where there were serious revenue leakages. In other cases the severity of corruption was the main driver for reform (in Bolivia), or a strong contributing factor to the decision to reform (in Mozambique, the Philippines, and Uganda). In some countries, broader institutional changes or external requirements led to customs reform, such as the economic programs supported by the International Monetary Fund (IMF) and the World Bank in Mozambique (see box 6.1). Easing constraints on trade imposed by customs led representatives of the trading community to place trade facilitation high on the agenda of the customs reform in Morocco and in Turkey. In Ghana the customs modernization process arose because of lagging foreign direct

---

### BOX 6.1 Implementation of Customs Reform in Mozambique

Faced with the run down state of customs the Mozambican authorities chose to enter into a managing contract with an outside agency to rebuild its customs department. The authorities were fully aware that it would be difficult to break out of the grip of firmly entrenched smuggling rings from within. Under these circumstances, and with a view to supplementing the shortage of domestic experienced staff, the Technical Unit for Restructuring Customs (UTRA) invited external service providers to manage customs and implement key parts of the customs reform process initiated in 1995. The outside agency had both short-term objectives aimed at increasing recurrent revenue collection, and long-term goals focused on capacity building. The outside agency's major assignment was to take over the complete management of customs, including training, appointing key customs officials to perform the contracted functions, supervising external trade operations subject to customs legislation, preventing fraud and evasion of taxes, and procuring and maintaining equipment assigned to the reform project, such as data processing software and hardware. However, the authorities went into these arrangements with a gradual approach.

Through an international bidding process, Crown Agents (CA) was awarded a three-year contract covering 1997–99. Operational management began in May 1997 following agreement on proposed work plans for each of the areas to be implemented during the contract. A senior consultant of CA was appointed Delegated Manager of Customs. The process of change management implemented by CA was overseen by a steering committee made up of representatives of UTRA, IMF, World Bank, and the Department for International Development (DFID), which was supporting the project with financial and technical assistance. In addition, there were annual reviews of progress to measure the project against original objectives. However, the envisaged timetable for phasing out the contribution to be made by CA proved optimistic, in part because the original assumptions of the project, such as those related to revenue gains and expected staff replacement needs, were too aggressive. By the end of the contract some of the anticipated outcomes had not been achieved, as the newly appointed Mozambican senior managers were not ready to assume their full managerial responsibilities. Also, some of the operational procedures and information systems were not sufficiently established.

Following a comprehensive contract compliance review carried out by DFID, the government approved an initial six-month contract extension, followed by a further contract of three years through mid-2003 to consolidate the reform. During the extension, the role of CA changed from execution to supervision and mentoring, except in the areas of intelligence, staff irregularities, audit, and anticorruption. CA was to advance the improvements made in customs services and introduce the necessary systems and procedures. The number of CA consultants was to be reduced from 47 in mid-2000 to 11 in mid-2003. Since then, a further extension through mid-2005 was agreed on, as more time was needed for the handover of responsibilities to senior managers. Despite limited progress in reducing corruption and a further need to tackle smuggling on a sustainable basis, the role of CA is generally seen as beneficial in implementing customs reform and reorganization. The test of the overall success of engaging an external manager will be provided by the sustainability of customs operations carried out by a domestically run agency once CA's intervention is fully phased out.

The above experience underlines the importance of having both a full diagnostic as well as a detailed feasibility study of the management tasks entrusted to an outside agency before a contract is agreed on. This would reduce the possible need for repeated extensions, while a somewhat more flexible contract length could be useful for tasks related to capacity building.

*Source:* Mwangi 2004.

investment despite the fact that much of the policy reforms had been accomplished. In all cases, trade facilitation initiatives were subjected to the requirement that the role of customs in revenue generation was not to be undermined.

### Sponsorship and Political Backing

The impetus for the reform differed across countries. In several countries it originated from the highest authorities, which in some cases provided strong and sustained political backing. In Peru and the Philippines, the reforms were direct initiatives of the presidents, who protected the reform and its leadership against political and administrative obstacles. In Bolivia, the leadership of the institutional reform program covering customs was vested in the vice president. In Morocco, support measures for foreign trade, including improving customs, had been called for by the late King Hassan II and demanded by the trading community; the reforms benefited from strong support from the King. In Uganda, the main reform sponsor was the Minister of Finance (MOF), while the State Minister for Customs played the leading role in spearheading the reform in Turkey. In Ghana, the reform drive benefited from the strong personal support of the Minister of Trade, while the MOF supported it because of the prospects it offered to strengthen the Customs Service and raise larger budget revenues.

### Design

In Bolivia, Peru, the Philippines, and Turkey, the reforms were part of a comprehensive master plan that covered all aspects of customs operations and administration, including the overhaul of systems and procedures, in-depth reform of services with upgrading and redeployment of staff, automation of the clearing process, post-release control and audit processes, and extensive IT use. In other countries the approach was pragmatic, moving forward with successive measures with either full or limited coverage of reform components. In Morocco, the reform was not contained in a master plan, but proceeded on the basis of a pragmatic approach with measures that were implemented in a piecemeal fashion, building upon successes achieved. In Southeast Europe, the customs reform package was totally integrated in a trade facilitation

objective supported by numerous external organizations (EU, Stability Pact, South East Cooperation Initiative). It resulted in a comprehensive project design. It included the private sector and involved other agencies operating in the border areas. In Ghana, the reforms were driven by a vision of converting Ghana into a gateway for West Africa to the rest of the world.

In some countries the reform entailed providing greater operational autonomy to customs. In Uganda, the reform centered on the activities of the independent Uganda Revenue Authority (URA), which was created in 1991 and endowed with substantial management flexibility to improve staff quality, compensation, and discipline. In Peru, SUNAT (the merged Inland Revenue and Customs Administration agency) focused on effective management of human, budgetary, and physical resources; and the introduction and implementation of modern administrative and control procedures and systems. In Turkey, the customs modernization project was directed at harmonizing procedures and regulations in line with those in effect in the EU, and at upgrading computer support for customs operations to enhance overall efficiency.

There were notable differences among countries in the design and implementation of the reforms. In Morocco, Peru, and the Philippines, the reforms were under full control of the customs administration. In other countries special units were set up to formulate and implement the reform, for example, the Technical Unit for Restructuring Customs (UTRA) in Mozambique. In Bolivia, the reform program was conceived by a group of high-ranking officials, including the Minister of the Treasury, but implemented by customs. In Southeast Europe, a Regional Steering Committee that comprised a National Coordinator per country further supervised the reform process. Each National Coordinator (usually the MOF or the Director General of Customs) was nominated by the government to represent all the agencies and bodies involved in cross-border trade.

The customs reforms were usually carried out over several years. In most countries a frontloading of major institutional changes was followed by a period of consolidation during which the changes were fully absorbed and their implementation carefully monitored, while accompanied by further reforms, as in Peru. In others, reforms were more gradual and phased in over time, as in Mozambique, where a major overhaul of customs staff was undertaken.

### Donor Assistance

All reforms in the country case studies were supported by external assistance, but the scope of this assistance varied substantially across countries. In all countries except Uganda and Peru, the IMF and the World Bank provided technical assistance, advising on certain aspects or on overall reform requirements. In Turkey and the Philippines, World Bank support focused on IT and automation of procedures, in addition to advice on the whole reform process. In Turkey, World Bank financing covered the costs of automation studies, their implementation, and equipment acquisition. The IMF supported the reform initiative by posting a resident adviser in the organizational structure of customs in 1996–97 and by assisting in the selection and supervision of an IT adviser for the World Bank–financed project in 1997–99. In the Philippines, the World Bank financed the services of UNCTAD (United Nations Conference on Trade and Development) for the implementation of the new customs information systems (ASYCUDA++) and of the computer hardware. In addition, the IMF proposed an 11-point action program for reform in 1991, which was followed up by posting two resident advisers. In Southeast Europe, the TTFSE projects were cofinanced by the Bank and the United States, with the Bank funding the infrastructure and IT components, and U.S. Customs providing technical assistance. In Ghana, customs modernization formed part of World Bank support for the Ghana Gateway Project.

In Mozambique, the World Bank provided financing for UTRA while the IMF provided a legal specialist. Mozambique also received significant grant support from the United Kingdom's DFID for engaging Crown Agents in the implementation of its whole reform process, including the assumption of executive functions. In Bolivia, where the design of the reforms benefited from IMF assistance, the World Bank financed the new human resources administration. Bolivia also received Inter-American Development Bank (IDB) financing for a new technology system, while the Nordic Fund for Development and several European countries provided grants. The reform in Peru was supported by several IDB loans spread between 1991 and 1999 that financed nearly every step of the customs reform program. Also, IDB experts assisted in the design, implementation, and monitoring of the program. In Uganda, DFID supported setting up URA, including providing an external adviser with line managerial responsibilities. Although Morocco's reform benefited from the outset from technical assistance provided by the French government and the IMF, it financed the implementation of its reforms with domestic resources.

## Components of Customs Reforms

The reform programs generally covered issues related to all components of customs administration, including the legal framework, management, human resources, IT, and customs procedures, particularly those related to valuation and physical inspection.

### Customs Code

In all countries, except Ghana, Uganda, and the Philippines, a new Customs Code covering procedures, customs services, and status of personnel was adopted to provide a firm foundation to the reform process. In Morocco, the Customs Code was revised at the end of the 1990s and was made fully consistent with the Revised Kyoto Convention.[6] In some countries the reform program replaced an old and obsolete code that had become an obstacle to the introduction of new procedures more in tune with changed business practices. Implementing regulations and other legislative changes, including those in the Penal Code, were introduced. In Southeast Europe, new customs legislation was introduced to replace the overregulating socialist laws.[7]

---

6. The Morocco Code revisions include a clarification that permits risk-based verification instead of 100 percent physical verification, and a provision for minor sanctions for inadvertent errors in the customs declaration. Also, a variety of regulations that were issued over the years were consolidated in the new code.

7. While at first the legislative changes consisted of copying the EU Customs Code, it rapidly became obvious that the code was not addressing matters pertaining to national sovereignty such as enforcement, organization, and penal provisions and thus was not applicable on its own. In addition, there were serious discrepancies between the EU-inspired customs legislation and the rest of the countries' laws and regulatory frameworks, which led to its inapplicability, especially in the enforcement area.

In the Philippines, a large number of laws and regulations were issued, mainly in the areas of the automated customs operating system, the control system, and the structure of the customs department. In Turkey, the EC Customs Code, which also covered customs administrative procedures, became part of the domestic legislation. Following the adoption in Peru of a new general customs law, subsequent legislative changes were consolidated and the general customs law was updated in 1996. In Uganda, the East African Customs Act from the 1960s remained in effect. The authorities have accepted the Revised Kyoto Convention, which implies that they have to adjust the existing legislation.

### Customs Management

All reform plans provided for management changes, changes in the status of the customs administration and its personnel, and changes in the structure or organization of the services concerned. Staffing changes were the key elements in some programs.

In Morocco, management changes focused on a functional and territorial reorganization, including the redistribution of tasks between central and regional authorities, and a more pronounced decentralization. This reorganization is being assessed on an ongoing basis and adjusted in a flexible manner. With the shift away from physical inspection to post-release control, staff have been reassigned and trained for new assignments.

The reform in Mozambique reflected a bold approach. Given that customs and most of the civil administration were severely dysfunctional following years of civil strife, the government assigned most of the key operational management functions to external consultants (see box 6.1). The program called for significant staff renewal. In addition, a specialist valuation team was set up, supported by a software valuation module and a visiting control team.

In Bolivia, Peru, and Uganda, management reforms included granting administrative and management autonomy to customs, and providing greater autonomy on matters of personnel policy, recruitment, training, and, subject to approval, remuneration. In Uganda, the Uganda Revenue Authority (URA) was created in 1991 as an independent authority with the responsibility of collecting and accounting for all domestic and foreign

trade taxes. Subsequently, further measures were taken to strengthen management and its independence in response to a perceived decline in performance. These measures included the appointment of a new board and senior managers, and a clarification of the relationship between the board, management, and the Ministry of Finance. URA was no longer responsible for advising the government on tax policy issues, but was charged with advising the MOF on the revenue implications and tax administration aspects of tax policy changes.

In Macedonia, the placement of customs under the Ministry of Finance (customs previously reported to parliament and the government) was inefficient at first as there was no integration with the ministry, only the addition of an extra layer of bureaucracy.

In Peru, full autonomy allowed customs to adopt a structure and develop its own procedures to discharge its tasks with clearly established functions for each organizational subdivision and unit.[8] The reforms in Bolivia, Peru, and Uganda included a large-scale personnel changeover. In these three countries the reforms provided for greater budgetary autonomy, as they were given (or promised) a share of customs revenue to cover operating and capital outlays independent of the government budget. While URA's budget was to receive 2–4 percent of collected revenues, the actual budget allocation was lower.

In Turkey, a number of inefficient offices were closed, customs and enforcement services were integrated under single regional directorates, and operational responsibilities were delegated to regional and local offices, while a number of regional directorates were eliminated. In the Philippines, a group responsible for the development of IT in customs was set up, and a valuation center and library were created charged with the development, maintenance, and dissemination of the department's database on values. In Ghana, the customs management system that had been designed for Mauritius and that was smoothly interfacing with the initial TradeNet[9] from Singapore was adopted. As part of

---

8. Customs prepares proposals for customs legislation changes; it has no role in tax legislation and policy.

9. The Singapore TradeNet links multiple parties involved in external trade, including 34 government agencies, to a single point of transaction for most trade-related transactions.

the arrangement, a company was created and charged with the implementation of the TradeNet and the Ghana Customs Management System (GCMS) for the Customs Excise and Preventive Services (CEPS). However, CEPS remains a rather outmoded and inefficient organization. Its organizational structure reflects serious shortcomings that prevent it from fully internalizing the ongoing reforms and taking advantage of the possibilities offered by the modern customs process in place.

In most transition countries (despite statistical data pointing to an overabundance of clearance stations) the tendency was to maintain as many clearance offices as possible because of political pressures and vested interests.

### Human Resources

The experiences recorded in all case study countries have shown that customs reform can only succeed with competent staff who internalize the objectives of the reform. It was also generally acknowledged that adequate compensation was necessary to motivate staff and tackle the thorny issue of integrity. The integrity issue has serious implications for staff recruitment policies, training, and compensation. The scope of human resources reform in the countries reviewed also depended on the degree of autonomy granted to customs administrations in personnel policy matters. Human resources issues are addressed in detail in chapter 2.

Salary increases have been a critical element of most reform initiatives. Better pay allowed the recruitment and retention of competent staff, enhanced operational efficiency, and countered the need to supplement low official salaries through corrupt practices. Salaries were raised at the outset of the reform in Bolivia, Mozambique, Peru, and Uganda, with the largest increase made in Peru (600 percent), where salary levels of financial institutions were matched and the salary scale was shifted from the public to the private sector. Upon gaining autonomy, Uganda's URA raised salaries to a level compatible with that of the highest paid civil servants—those at the Central Bank—and a comprehensive set of performance bonuses was introduced. However, real salaries slipped because of inflation. By 2002, URA's remuneration ranked only 17th at the national level, some 40 percent lower than that at the Central Bank. The system of

salary bonuses, which was based on meeting revenue targets, did not achieve its objective, as bonuses were either not paid out despite meeting the revenue target, or because the target was set at unrealistic levels. In Ghana, a similar situation prevailed. When the independent revenue authority was created, salaries were set at highly competitive levels, but the premium over general civil service salaries eroded over time.

In Mozambique, new salary levels in customs were made comparable with those prevailing in the private sector. Part of the remuneration consisted of a variable customs allowance based on performance and merit. Also, a pension plan was introduced and the health insurance system improved. In Bolivia, where salary increases ranged from 22 percent to 73 percent, there were also monetary incentives for group performance. In Peru, productivity bonuses were linked to expected results established in an operational plan, with individual shares based on performance. The strict application of civil service salaries to customs staff prevented any overall salary adjustment from being introduced in Morocco, the Philippines, or Turkey during the reform process. However, there was greater flexibility in terms of providing overtime compensation, or year-end bonuses. In Morocco the prevailing, rather generous, bonus system was made more egalitarian and was extended to include staff involved in front-line activities.

Most reforms recognized that training must be provided on a continuous basis to update staff on ongoing developments in the customs administration, including the elements of reform and modernization programs being implemented. In all countries, except the Philippines, training was included in the reform program, although with varying degrees of coverage. In Bolivia, Mozambique, and Peru, where preshipment inspection (PSI) companies were hired, the PSI companies were required to offer training in the area of valuation. In Bolivia, new staff regulations required a minimum of annual training, which was taken into account for performance evaluations. In Morocco, the training academy was restructured. However, because of a general hiring freeze the academy is largely used for continuing education of customs staff and training of staff from French-speaking Sub-Saharan customs administrations.

In Albania, the EU-supported Customs Assistance Mission (CAM-A) developed a comprehensive staff management policy that included recruitment, career development, performance evaluation, and reward systems. Initially run by CAM-A, the system was subsequently handed over to customs management and proved to be sustainable.

### Integrity and Corruption Issues

Integrity and corruption issues were central in Bolivia, Mozambique, Peru, the Philippines, and Uganda. Most reform initiatives recognized that efforts to address corruption would benefit from simplified and streamlined procedures that would lead to increased transparency in customs operations and fewer contacts between traders and staff. Reliance on IT to manage customs processes reduced the scope for discretion as it cut down on face-to-face relations between importers and customs officials. In addition, several countries put in place specific measures to enhance integrity. Integrity issues are discussed in more detail in chapter 4.

A Code of Conduct or Code of Ethics was introduced in Bolivia, Mozambique, Peru, and Turkey. In Bolivia and Mozambique, staff is required to sign an integrity commitment. The URA requires management staff to complete an assets declaration form and to notify URA of all substantial changes in asset ownership. Other initiatives undertaken by Uganda are outlined in box 6.5 in the context of results of the reform. Similarly, the Peruvian customs authorities can request presentation of a sworn declaration of income and assets. In Turkey, a circular on ethical conduct was issued in 2001. It clearly defines bribery and spells out how staff should react when faced with corrupt practices. The World Customs Organization (WCO) Model Code of Conduct largely inspired Turkey's code.

In the Philippines, a series of legislative changes were introduced to enhance detection capabilities and chances of successful prosecution in corruption cases. Procedures to detect staff misconduct were improved in Mozambique as well. In Bolivia and Peru, the recruitment process includes background checks of applicants with a view to ensuring honesty.

As members of the WCO, all case study countries are signatories of the 1993 WCO Arusha Declaration and signed on to the Maputo Declaration on customs integrity.[10]

### Information Technology

In most of the case study countries, reliance on computerized processes was low. In some countries, customs administrations lacked substantive IT support (Bolivia and Mozambique) or operated systems that had nearly outlived their usefulness (Morocco) or were inadequate (Turkey and Uganda), with the result that many operations were still undertaken manually, with all the inefficiencies associated with such work processes.

Upgrading IT and increasing its use significantly have been critical customs reform components because they make it possible to establish an automated clearance process from submission of the cargo manifest and customs declaration to the release of goods. IT also facilitates the implementation of control systems based on risk-assessment, allowing selectivity in physical inspections, post-release controls and audits, and a tightening of revenue control. Upgraded IT also contributes to shortening the time of customs clearance and improves the efficiency of operations. A detailed discussion of the basic characteristics required for good customs IT is included in chapter 13.

Peru developed an integrated computerized system encompassing all customs operations and regimes, control functions, statistics, and management. The clearance process was fully automated, including selection of inspections and post-release checking. Significant progress was also achieved in Morocco, the Philippines, and Turkey. In 1996, Morocco restructured its information directorate as part of the reform program and gradually introduced the main customs functions and operations into its computer system. A major renewal of the computer system is scheduled during 2003–2004. The systems in place became outdated and the hardware became increasingly difficult to maintain; a totally upgraded system is now being rolled out.

---

10. For details see chapter 4. To strengthen customs' integrity, the Arusha Declaration calls for a simplified trade regime, streamlined and transparent procedures, automated processes, appropriate personnel policies, and effective audits. To assist member countries, a work group developed an Integrity Action Plan adopted in 1999.

---

**BOX 6.2   Information Technology in Turkey**

The computerization of customs offices and automation of customs procedures was a key component of Turkey's customs modernization program. Automation activities were coordinated by an independent Modernization Project Unit set up in 1997, with a senior official responsible for technical aspects.

A software system named BILGE (Computerized Customs Activities) was developed on the basis of SOFIX software purchased from France, which was adapted to the needs of Turkey's customs. The system consists of four modules: a summary declaration module, a detailed declaration module, an accounting module, and an integrated tariff module. In a successful pilot operation, BILGE was initially installed at the Istanbul Customs Directorate in July 1998. Since then, BILGE has been set up at 65 customs offices, realizing some 99 percent of all transactions. Procedures carried out electronically using BILGE include cargo, import, and export declarations; transit and warehousing procedures; tax collections; and risk analysis and control methods. Declarations can be registered with customs through kiosks located at customs offices,

electronic data interchange (EDI), and the Internet. Started at the Istanbul Customs Directorate in August 1999, applications of EDI rose rapidly, representing some 50 percent of all electronic declarations in mid-2003. All automated customs offices are connected with each other and customs headquarters via local area and wide area networks.

In addition to customs transactions, foreign trade regulations and data related to customs performance are entered into BILGE. Export and import declaration details are provided electronically to the State Institute of Statistics, allowing for timely compilation of trade statistics. Comprehensive training on the computerized customs procedures was offered to customs officials and to some 15,000 traders free of charge. Other software systems used by customs in Turkey include Vehicle Tracking Program, TIR/Transit Control, and Customs Data Warehouse. Customs Data Warehouse stores all information from BILGE and other systems, and feeds into a customs valuation database.

*Source:* Oktem 2004.

---

In the Philippines, where the tax computerization program provided strong impetus to the reform, many procedures were brought into the automated customs operating system. By 1997 nearly all segments of the clearance process had been automated, assisted by a risk assessment and selectivity program made possible by using UNCTAD's ASYCUDA++ software. In Turkey, the automation of customs operations was a key component of customs modernization (see box 6.2).

Since the initiation of its reform program in 1991, Uganda has gradually upgraded its customs IT through various stages. The installation of ASYCUDA version 2 software, begun in 1997, allowed randomly selected officials to execute the physical cargo verification and helped in the compilation of statistics, but proved difficult for data retrieval and did not provide risk management. As is often the case in the process of implementing computerized customs management systems, staff trained in the operation of these systems were assigned to other tasks, preventing customs from reaping the full benefits of automation. In light of these experiences, the URA recently installed the

ASYCUDA++, with UNCTAD providing improved training.

Beginning in 1998, the Mozambique customs administration gradually introduced the Trade Information Management System software (owned by CA, which was managing customs at the time) to support its customs clearance processes. The roll out program of the various process functions accommodated the capabilities of staff to adopt the process. Since the end of 1999, clearance of goods has been computerized throughout the country. In Ghana, the Ghana Community Network (GCNet) was, from the outset, the cornerstone of a vision to connect all members of the trading community in an electronic data exchange system. The software in place had been grossly underutilized and poorly maintained, adding little value to the current procedures. The rollout of advanced EDI (Electronic Data Interchange) and a new computerized customs management system was initially plagued with problems, but these were eventually addressed and legislation to permit automation of the customs operation was enacted in July 2002. The system is now fully operational.

*Valuation Issues*

Proper valuation is essential for the predictability and transparency of customs transactions. All case study countries are members of the WTO and thus have committed themselves to implement the WTO valuation principles under the WTO Agreement on Customs Valuation (ACV). Most of the countries reviewed officially adopted the ACV during their customs reform. The Philippines began implementing the ACV in 2000, following the conclusion of its reform program. The ACV requires customs officers to change their valuation procedures and renders challenging invoice prices more difficult than under prior valuation practices. Reform programs, therefore, call for a strengthening of customs capabilities in valuation assessment. Because the ACV requires that priority be given to adopting the transaction value for customs valuation purposes, customs officers now have to gather more evidence or justification if they are to challenge the declared or invoice value.[11]

Implementing the ACV has proven to be difficult in a number of countries. Implementation problems include the frequent use of false invoices that grossly undervalue the merchandise and insufficient training of staff to challenge the invoices.[12] Also, the growing trade in second-hand goods as well as trade undertaken by the informal sector, where poor or no records are kept, renders post-clearance inspections impractical. In practice, several customs administrations continue to rely, to various degrees, on price lists that are rarely shared with the trading community and that, at times, are inadequately updated.

In all case study countries, the reform program paid attention to the valuation function. To assist in the valuation of imports, Bolivia, Mozambique, Peru, and the Philippines resorted to the services of PSI companies. Elements of Peru's program of PSI-assisted import verification are provided in box 6.3. Uganda first adopted a PSI program but later discontinued these services for a variety of reasons, including claims that the PSI company did not provide the staff training agreed to in the contract,

particularly in developing a valuation database. In general, recourse to PSI companies was initiated to safeguard revenue since revenue leakages were often related to undervaluation and fraud. This was intended to be a temporary measure to allow customs administrations to build up their capacity. Services of PSI companies typically include import verification covering quantity, quality, value, and customs classification.

There are differences among countries in the evaluation of PSI services. While in several countries the revenue generation and dissuasion of fraud experiences appear to have been positive, the PSI companies' performance in improving national capacity in customs valuation has often been questioned.[13] Lack of cooperation between PSI companies and customs departments was noted in Uganda, where customs often relies on a parallel value database rather than on current PSI data. Insufficient use of the information generated by PSI providers undermined the effectiveness of their services in the absence of a systematic reconciliation between PSI data and that used to calculate import duties. It was often not clear what use was made of the PSI-provided information. Peru is an exception as PSI valuation information is fully used by customs. The PSI company operating in Mozambique also assisted customs staff in training on transaction value and delivered a software module on valuation. A problem noted in the Philippines was the circumvention of PSI-conducted inspections.[14]

The reform program strengthened the valuation function in customs departments, including by setting up value databanks. In Peru, a databank set up in 1992 was developed on the basis of inspection certificates and verification reports issued by the PSI provider. A valuation unit was also established

---

11. For an in-depth discussion of valuation, as well as for more details on this issue, see chapter 8.

12. Invoices are the easiest documents to forge. Unlike bills, bonds, shares, or any other securities or lending instruments, invoices have no security measures.

13. There are both advantages and disadvantages of hiring PSI companies. It is the duty of the government authorities to clearly define their roles and responsibilities, as well as to closely monitor performance. A related issue is at which stage in the valuation process should PSI companies enter? In most countries they enter at the first stage, that is, assisting in or undertaking valuation activities. In Mexico, however, they enter at the second stage, after a customs officer has valued and classified the goods. Hence, they check the importer's declaration and the customs officer's effectiveness and honesty.

14. Such actions may involve splitting up or undervaluing shipments to remain below the threshold set for inspections, and abusive recourse to suspense regimes such as transit and temporary admission (Parayno 2004).

---

**BOX 6.3   Import Verification in Peru**

At the outset of its customs reform in 1991, Peru introduced the Import Verification Program (IVP). The government resorted to external assistance in view of customs' failure to effectively conduct the verification of import shipments for purposes of assessing duties to be collected. This action was also seen as a way to outsource an administrative function to the private sector, in line with the reform's objectives. Under the IVP, importers are required to submit shipments for verification by an authorized PSI company before the goods are shipped from the country of exportation. Between 1991 and 1999, when the Brussels Definition of Value was in effect, the verification resulted in a certificate of inspection-covering the nature, quantity, value, and tariff classification of the goods. These data were to be declared by the importer and formed the basis for the payment of duties. Customs verified the consistency of the import shipment with the data on the certificate of inspection.

When implementation of the ACV under the WTO became effective in 2000, PSI services were used to provide an indicator of risk rather than a dutiable value. Accordingly, under IVP procedures, instead of certifying the usual competitive price, PSI companies issue verification reports in which they state the observed value based on inspection of the shipment and price comparisons. The importer can either declare the transaction value or the observed value. Reasonable doubt can be generated when the declared value is lower than the observed value in the report. While the verification reports contain the tariff code, the importer can declare a different code, with discrepancies resolved by customs. About 80–85 percent of import shipments are subject to PSI intervention; imports valued below US$5,000 and some other categories are exempt. The cost of the IVP amounts to some US$45 million per year.

The IVP has made valuable contributions to improving customs in Peru. In addition to providing duty assessments at the beginning of the reform when customs capacity was deficient, it provided most of the price information that allowed customs to create and build up its valuation data bank, had a dissuasive impact on fraud, and contributed to the training of valuation officers. Between 1992 and 2002, some 1.3 million inspection certificates and verification reports were issued by the PSI companies; these reports were the main source of the 40,000 entries contained in the data bank as of March 2002.

*Source:* Goorman 2004.

---

in Mozambique, while that in Morocco was reinforced. In Uganda, the staff responsible for valuation has been given special training, and steps are under way in Turkey to extend the electronic database to customs valuation information. In several countries, declared values are investigated under risk-based post-release verification systems, making use of valuation databases, price reference data including information from other declarations and supplier catalogues, statistical analyses, surveys, and international market studies. However, in Ghana, given CEPS' limited capacity in customs valuation, strengthening customs valuation has become a key and immediate priority to support customs officers in charge of documenting compliance checks. In the meantime, the services of four destination inspection companies are being relied upon.

*Physical Inspections*

Before the reforms, most countries performed 100 percent physical inspection on all incoming imports, resulting in major clearance delays. All customs reform and modernization programs now aim to reduce the frequency of physical inspections to streamline and shorten the clearance process. In some countries, the new Customs Code sets a maximum share of shipments subject to physical control (20 percent in Bolivia and 15 percent in Peru). In Turkey, customs endeavors to reduce the physical inspection rate to 15 percent for imports. In Southeast Europe, 100 percent inspection was mandated by law. Even when the legislation was amended, customs continued to carry out systematic inspections, largely for fear that subsequent reexaminations by the police of the same consignments would lead to the detection of unspotted irregularities. This stalled the proper deployment of service examinations for many years.

A system of risk assessments provides the basis for selectivity in physical inspections. Risk criteria typically include the origin of goods, importer track record, type of goods, trade patterns, misclassification incentives, and shipment value. The system chooses shipments for one of the three established color-coded channels. Goods selected for the red channel undergo physical and documents inspection, those designated to the yellow or orange channel are subject only to document control, while goods assigned to the green channel benefit from immediate release.

A risk assessment module of the computer software system automated the selection process in Peru, the Philippines, and Turkey. In cooperation with the PSI company, customs in Mozambique moved to a risk-based approach to select goods for inspection. A small percentage of goods were still randomly selected for inspection.[15] When selectivity was introduced in Turkey in 1998, goods directed to the yellow channel could still be made subject to physical inspection depending on the judgment of the customs officer. Before the initiation of the reform program in the Philippines, it was decided that inspections abroad by the PSI company constituted sufficient compliance with inspection requirements. This was followed by the introduction of selectivity in physical inspections, which became effective early under the reform program. Selective controls were one of the first elements of the reform program introduced in Morocco and have greatly contributed to the drastic reduction of clearance time. In Bolivia, the selection of shipments for physical inspections is totally random. Customs management in Uganda is working on the introduction of a risk-based inspection system. Ghana's risk assessment system results in the great majority of goods being selected for physical inspection. This is, to a large extent, due to the broad categories of goods that are subjected to mandatory inspection by the Ghana Standards Board.

### Revenue and Trade Facilitation

The challenge faced by all case study countries has been to achieve the trade facilitation objective without undermining the revenue mobilization function of customs services, which is the most important motive for undertaking the customs reforms. As there were indications that trade liber-

alization measures would tend to reduce revenues from international trade transactions, a special effort was made to enhance the revenue-generating capabilities of customs. Improvement of procedures and simplification of formalities have reduced the frequency of physical inspections, while automation of operations has streamlined overall customs procedures. These measures are in line with the overall Revised Kyoto Convention objectives of simplification and harmonization of customs procedures. The continued implementation of the convention's objectives will reduce the incidence of smuggling, enhance overall integrity, lead to increased budget revenue, and reduce transaction costs for traders.

Efforts to upgrade staff integrity and qualifications brought about in part by more selective recruitment and improved training, and strengthening and expanding of post-release controls and audits to keep smuggling in check, would contribute to safeguarding revenue.

In several countries, customs clearance is now conducted under automated uniform procedures, from manifest submission to the release of shipment. Peru has put in place an advance clearing system for importers in good standing. In Turkey, simplified procedures were introduced, including a waiver of some document requirements (sales invoice, certificate of origin, and movement certificate) for companies satisfying certain conditions. In Uganda, further streamlining took place in early 2002, including processing of trucks, forwarding of border documentation to the central customs office, a single verification of shipments, inspection of second-hand cars, and the gradual introduction of Direct Trader Input (DTI). In Morocco, procedures for the temporary admissions regime were substantially improved. In Macedonia, the management of licenses and quotas is handled by customs through a totally transparent World Wide Web application based on a first-come first-served principle that eliminates negotiations between importers and government officials.

For most countries the development of a strong audit system constitutes a major instrument in safeguarding revenue. This requires the enhancement of intelligence and information gathering and analysis, which also helps to combat smuggling. In Peru, an intelligence unit was included in the structure of the audit department, while in Uganda the

---

15. Random selection of shipments for physical inspection under a system of general risk-based selection is used to test the robustness of the system, especially the effectiveness of selected risk factors.

program called for increased support for the investigation department. In Morocco, the reform program also recognized the need for a significant upgrading of intelligence activities. In Morocco and Uganda, a territorial redeployment of manpower with more efficient control procedures and increased checkpoints was part of the restructuring of customs services with a view to combating the circumvention of customs border controls.

A new payment control system in Peru provides tight control of payments made electronically or otherwise. In the Philippines, the establishment of a data security system ensures the protection of payments of duties to banks and their transmission to customs. Also, the introduction of online release systems helps avoid the illegal release of shipments from customs custody by using spurious documents. In Mozambique, measures to safeguard revenue include a tightening of duty exemptions controls, a closer monitoring of movements in and out of free zones supported by computerized records, and the enforcement of security arrangements for temporary admission regimes. In addition, new transit procedures have been introduced and guarantee centers established.

## Outcomes of the Reform Programs

Under ideal circumstances, effectiveness and efficiency indicators should be used to measure whether the reforms have achieved their objectives. Partial indicators were used and these measure the impact of the modernization efforts on revenue generation and on customs clearance time for imports. Surveys of customer satisfaction could also be used as important gauges of success.

### Fiscal Performance

The impact of customs reforms on tax revenue is an outcome of two separate factors. First, streamlined customs clearance procedures, together with strengthened enforcement and higher compliance, can lead to higher collection rates for a given level of imports by reducing revenue-reducing acts of corruption and smuggling opportunities. Second, good customs procedures, combined with trade liberalization measures, reduce the cost of imports and will lead to higher imports for a given level of GDP. The combined effect of these two factors will

affect the contribution of trade taxes to budget revenue. Anticipating that the share of trade taxes in the overall revenue structure is likely to fall as a proportion of total revenue as a country's taxable economic base expands, and certainly with trade liberalization, most countries have also strengthened their domestic tax systems mainly by introducing a VAT.

Tariff reductions made in conjunction with customs reform positively affected trade, but initially had an adverse impact on customs duties in the countries reviewed. The reform often replaced sales taxes by the VAT. Higher VAT rates accompanied the cuts in import tariffs, and raised import revenues other than customs duties for a given level of imports.

The actual outcome of the reforms indicates that the import taxes-to-GDP ratio increased the most in Ghana, Mozambique, Peru, and Uganda, while registering the largest decline in the Philippines (see table 6.3). In Mozambique and Peru, the improved revenue performance resulted from the increase in the ratio of import taxes other than customs duties to imports, assisted in Peru by a higher imports-to-GDP ratio. In Turkey, the rise in the import taxes-to-GDP ratio, which was more limited, reflected a substantial increase in the import ratio in the face of a limited reduction in import tariffs. In Uganda, all factors, including an increase in the ratio to imports of customs duties and other import taxes, and a higher imports-to-GDP ratio, made positive contributions. In Ghana, the increase in the import taxes-to-GDP ratio was fully due to a rising import taxes-to-imports ratio while the imports-to-GDP ratio declined. Clearance times and revenue performance exceeded expectations from early 2001 to mid-2003. The Treasury has benefited from accelerating revenues and more rapid access to tax payments.

When measured in relation to GDP, the decline in receipts from customs duties in Bolivia, Morocco, and Turkey, as well as the increases in Peru and Uganda, amounted to less than 1 percentage point. In the Philippines, the drop was 2.5 percentage points of GDP, largely due to a reduction in tariff rates.

### Enforcement

There are indications that important progress has been achieved in reducing smuggling in Peru and

**TABLE 6.3 Revenue and Import Performance Before and After Customs Reforms**

| | Bolivia | Ghana[a] | Morocco | Mozambique | Peru | Philippines | Turkey | Uganda |
|---|---|---|---|---|---|---|---|---|
| | (Percent of Imports) | | | | | | | |
| **Customs duties** | | | | | | | | |
| Before reforms | 5.4 | 4.6 | 13.5 | 8.0 | 12.3 | 13.9 | 3.2 | 3.4 |
| After reforms (2001) | 5.1 | 6.2 | 9.5 | 7.5 | 10.6 | 3.4 | 0.8 | 5.4 |
| **Import Taxes** | | | | | | | | |
| Before reforms | 20.5 | 10.5 | 36.2 | 11.2 | 23.0 | 18.2 | 13.0 | 7.5 |
| After reforms (2001) | 21.4 | 15.4 | 28.4 | 19.7 | 33.1 | 6.4 | 10.9 | 14.2 |
| | (Percent of GDP) | | | | | | | |
| **Imports** | | | | | | | | |
| Before reforms | 22.4 | 59.6 | 27.0 | 27.6 | 11.1 | 28.6 | 17.8 | 23.4 |
| After reforms (2001) | 21.2 | 46.2 | 33.7 | 26.6 | 13.3 | 45.3 | 28.4 | 29.1 |
| **Customs duties** | | | | | | | | |
| Before reforms | 1.2 | 2.8 | 3.7 | 2.2 | 1.2 | 4.0 | 0.6 | 0.8 |
| After reforms (2001) | 1.1 | 2.9 | 3.2 | 2.0 | 1.4 | 1.5 | 0.2 | 1.6 |
| **Import taxes** | | | | | | | | |
| Before reforms | 4.6 | 6.2 | 9.8 | 3.1 | 2.6 | 5.2 | 2.3 | 1.7 |
| After reforms (2001) | 4.5 | 7.1 | 9.6 | 5.3 | 4.4 | 2.9 | 3.1 | 4.1 |

*Note:* Period before reform refers to following years: Bolivia, 1996; Ghana, 2000; Morocco, 1996; Mozambique, 1996; Peru, 1990; the Philippines, 1991; Turkey, 1994; Uganda, 1990–91.

a. For Ghana, the year after reforms is 2003.

*Sources:* Luc De Wulf and José B. Sokol 2004; data provided by national customs; World Bank database; International Monetary Fund; International Finance Statistics; Government Finance Statistics; Balance of Payments; and Direction of Trade Statistics Yearbook, various issues; and International Monetary Fund, various country reports.

Uganda. Such efforts have been less successful in Bolivia and Mozambique. To enhance enforcement a number of initiatives have been pursued, including preventive inspections; expanded audit units; cooperation with other authorities, including the police and private entities; and improved intelligence and information. In some countries the lack of a central database for enforcement purposes and the difficulties in adapting inspections to automated clearance procedures have impaired enforcement efforts.

In Bolivia the reforms helped reduce smuggling, especially of commodities of mass consumption; however, problems remain in small-scale smuggling, which benefited from much softer enforcement rules. At the same time, under the new enforcement system in Mozambique, seizures of illegally imported goods have increased substantially. There is a commonly shared perception that smuggling has increased because of the growing importance of the informal sector in cross-border activities. In Peru, preventive inspections and other actions to

combat smuggling are taken by customs in cooperation with other public and private entities, including the national department for fraud prevention and border control. Customs also more than doubled the number of auditors in recent years. Although there are signs in Uganda that fraud is declining, the incidence of fraud remains high. A detailed audit suggests that up to 70 percent of the sampled invoices are false or spurious, substantially complicating the assessment of correct customs duties. Also, the removal of PSI intervention in 2000 was not accompanied by a strengthening of valuation capabilities.

In Turkey, control units are concerned that reduced physical controls could weaken enforcement because of insufficient access by enforcement staff to the central customs database and difficulties in adapting inspection to automated clearance procedures. Regional directorates also seem to lack the proper sources of data for customs valuation. In Morocco, efforts are continuing to centralize and streamline intelligence gathering and processing. In Southeast Europe, where customs had traditionally no other responsibility than manning approved border crossings, enforcement was considered for a long time to be the exclusive prerogative of the border police. This resulted in the misconception that the border police were in fact in charge of monitoring customs activities to detect corrupt practices. It destroyed cooperation between the two agencies, and created an unhealthy climate of suspicion that further encouraged customs to compensate for frustration through increased corruption. The situation gradually changed when legislation was amended and when political decisionmakers became more aware of the new role of customs in a market economy environment.

### Clearance Time and the View of Traders

Customs clearance time has been reduced in all case study countries (table 6.4). Selectivity in physical inspection is a major factor explaining the shortening of customs clearance time. Obviously, cargo that is channeled through the green line will clear faster than other cargo. Note, however, that the data reviewed are not fully comparable among countries due to differences in recording methodologies and the precise sequence of transactions required before cargo clearance. Although customs clearance has become faster, the period between the arrival of goods in port and their exit is often still excessively long because of the time needed for other procedures, including health, safety, and quality controls, and because of slow port operations.

During the first half of 2003, customs clearance in Bolivia required 53 hours on average from the time of registration of the import declaration to the exit of the goods from the customs warehouse. Excluding the time elapsed between the inspection and control and the exit of the shipment, the average time amounted to 37 hours. Although data on release times are not published, they are readily available to

**TABLE 6.4 Customs Processing Times**
(hours and minutes per shipment)

| | General | Green Channel[a] | Yellow Channel | Red Channel | Period |
|---|---|---|---|---|---|
| Bolivia | 53:06 | 39:25 | 49:05 | 70:48 | Jan.–June 2003 |
| Ghana KIA Airport | | 75 percent clearance the same day | | | |
| Ghana Tema Port | | 44 percent clearance in two days | | | |
| Morocco | 0:37 | | | | March 2003 |
| Mozambique | 8 days | | | | mid-2002 |
| Peru | | 1:00–2:00 | 12:00 | 24:00 | 2002 |
| The Philippines | | 18:20 | 22:50 | 19:29 | Dec. 1997 |
| Turkey | | In 24 hours: 71.5 percent of imports | | | 2002 |
| | | In 48 hours: 82.5 percent of imports | | | |
| Uganda | | Up to one week | | | |
| | | Under simplified procedures: Single item cargo: one day | | | 2002 |
| | | Mixed cargo: three days | | | |

*Note:* Customs processing time is the clearance time for imports through single window facility; not including operations before and after single window formalities. The data reviewed are not fully comparable among countries in view of differences in recording methodologies and the precise sequence of transactions required before cargo clearance. For detailed information on clearance times see annex 1.C.

a. While it appears that it takes 39 hours to clear merchandise that has been slated for green channel, the clearance time for this channel is zero. Once the system assigns green to an import declaration, it immediately clears it with no further ado. That is precisely the essence of the green channel. Thirty-nine hours is the average time that the importer or its customs agent takes from the moment he or she registers the declaration in the system until it picks up the merchandise, but it has nothing to do with the time that customs takes to authorize the goods.

*Source:* Customs authorities; De Wulf and Sokol 2004.

the authorities, underlining the effectiveness of the ASYCUDA++ program in compiling the data, which include a detailed breakdown of the time required for the various steps of the clearance process and for each of the color channels.

Morocco's customs reduced clearance time on average from one hour and 45 minutes in December 2001 to 37 minutes in March 2003. However, because of controls and procedures instituted by other agencies, a container requires on average more than 10 days before it can leave the port area. Morocco is the only one of the case study countries reviewed that systematically publishes such data on its own. By introducing transparency in the availability of customs data it not only puts pressure on its own operations to further improve efficiency, but also clarifies the role of the other agencies in overall clearance delays. This may lead them to introduce speedier work procedures.

Substantial progress has also been reported in Mozambique. By mid-2002, the time between filing a declaration and the posting of the release permit had been brought down to 8 days from 18 days as recently as 2000, and 20 days before the reform. Customs clearance in Peru now averages between 24 hours for the red channel to 12 hours for the orange channel, and one to two hours for green channel passage. In the Philippines, the average clearance time ranges from 18 hours to 23 hours for imports with DTI, depending on the channel. In Turkey, 72 percent of imports are cleared within 24 hours, and 83 percent within 48 hours. With the introduction of simplified procedures in Uganda, customs clearance for single item cargo takes one day and for mixed cargo three days.

In Southeast Europe, clearance times were halved on average following two years of project implementation. From a high of up to five hours of average waiting time for trucks at the borders next to the Balkans, implementation of the TTFSE program allowed for a significantly reduced waiting time compared to—a still high—two hours crossing.

In Ghana, average clearance times at the KIA airport have dropped from three days to four hours and customs document reviews, which used to take 24 hours, now take minutes on average. At the Tema port, clearance times have been reduced from a week on average to days. Currently 14 percent of goods are cleared on the same day, 30 percent take

between one and two days, 45 percent take between two and five days, and 11 percent of clearances take more than five days (often problematic cargo). Customs documents review takes on average 15 minutes instead of 24 hours while bank payments only take 10 minutes compared to a few hours before GCNet was fully operational.

Reactions to customs reforms from the users of customs services have generally been favorable. There has been widespread agreement that overall customs performance has improved, and that the incidence of corruption has declined. In some countries the initial opposition of traders to reform disappeared and gave way to approval when gains from the reform became noticeable. In countries where customs sought closer cooperation with the private sector, the new openness was widely appreciated. However, users emphasize that customs modernization is an ongoing process that needs to continue and keep up with modern trade practices. In Southeast Europe, a new partnership between customs and the private sector materialized through the creation of "Pro-Committees," which were supported through SECI and the Stability Pact.

In Bolivia, users feel that in some sectors the incidence of physical inspections is still high and small-scale smuggling remains widespread. They would like to see improved coordination between customs and warehouse operators, and extended hours for customs operations. In Morocco, the willingness to listen and the new openness of the Customs Directorate in reporting on customs reforms has been greatly appreciated by the trade community, and is reflected in periodic customer surveys, the results of which are published. (More detail on the cooperation between customs and the private sector in Morocco is in box 6.4.) Traders in Mozambique agree that the reforms have made substantial progress, but are looking forward to the promised introduction of electronic customs declarations and duty payments. The practice of customs to consult with them is very much appreciated.

Following initial opposition by vested public and private sector interests in Peru, both have come to view the reform as highly successful in the areas of trade facilitation and revenue generation. With respect to the reforms undertaken in the Philippines, press reports were generally favorable and trade

---

**BOX 6.4    Customs Cooperation with the Private Sector in Morocco and the Philippines**

A significant factor in the successful implementation of customs reform in Morocco was the active participation of private sector partners in the preparation of the reforms, and the openness of customs to private sector concerns, reflecting a dedication to transparency, efficiency, and partnership. This openness, focusing on quality service delivery and willingness to listen to the concerns of traders, has been widely appreciated by economic agents.

During the preparations for the implementation of the ACV in 1998, customs was particularly concerned that traders were fully informed of the new approach to customs valuation. Customs provided full information on the new principles and the risk assessment–based verification process that it would adopt, thereby facilitating the transition to the ACV. In general, customs placed great emphasis on trade facilitation measures in line with the Revised Kyoto Convention. Changes in procedures were introduced following consultations with private sector representatives. The management of the temporary admission system and drawback systems are only two examples of this fruitful dialogue. In the same spirit, customs has established a specialized service of business advice to enterprises, and provides direct assistance by telephone and electronically.

Even though there was no consultation on reform measures in the Philippines, the business sector provided substantial material and financial assistance to customs in the reform process, including setting up an online system for securing final release of shipments from ports and warehouses, and introducing encryption technology for the electronic transmission of payments data and the advance submission of manifest information. It also participated in managing a number of steps in customs clearance operations.

*Source:* Steenlandt and De Wulf 2004; Parayno 2004.

---

representatives registered their satisfaction with the improvement in customs operations. However, by the late 1990s the much-hailed results of the reforms had not been sustained and customs services were again criticized as inefficient and corrupt. One reason for this backtracking was the erosion of political support for the reforms. At present, efforts are under way to restore the previous degree of satisfaction with the reform outcomes. In Turkey, in a small survey of traders, 70 percent recorded that they were satisfied with the progress made in modernizing customs clearance processes. In Uganda, relations between customs and the private sector are seen as satisfactory and cooperation has improved as a result of the reforms. Private sector operators would welcome further progress, particularly in the areas of transparent use of price lists for valuation, the introduction of customs clearance at the border or in ports in Kenya and Tanzania rather than in Kampala, and greater emphasis on risk-based control procedures.

In Ghana, the reforms showed that private–public sector partnerships work. GCNet anchored the reforms and ensured continuity and focus on the reform objectives during a period of political transition, and at a time when no other local organization had the wherewithal to effect such a drastic transformation of trade and customs procedures.

### Anticorruption Measures

In several countries where the incidence of corruption was high, targeted measures under the reform programs have resulted in reduced corruption and enhanced staff integrity. Greater reliance on computer support in customs operations has resulted in greater transparency in those operations. In Peru, Mozambique, and especially Bolivia, staff renewal at the outset of the program enabled customs to remove corrupt personnel. The more limited staffing changes in Uganda, together with the rather timid use of other instruments to fight corruption, may have contributed to more modest progress in improving integrity than in other countries (box 6.5).

In Bolivia, where the eradication of corruption was central to government reform, the nearly complete changeover of staff resulting from subjecting all staff to new competitive recruitment was the first step in the reform process. At the time of the review it was estimated that 90 percent of the staff was new. There is a widespread view that this has

## BOX 6.5 Addressing Corruption in Uganda's Independent Revenue Authority

Efforts to fight corruption were high on the reform agenda at the creation of the URA. There was a general perception, shared by its management and by private sector operators, that the incidence of corruption in customs staff was high. The anticorruption campaign in customs was in line with efforts to stem corruption in the public sector, efforts that led to the creation of a Ministry of Integrity headed by a forceful minister.

The anticorruption campaign in URA had several aspects. At the outset, URA provided salaries that competed with the best of the public sector or even those of the private sector. Alone among government units and autonomous agencies, URA requires all staff members to fill out an "Asset Declaration Form," to be updated for significant changes in family status or in asset ownership. Automation of customs processes was strengthened and recently ASYCUDA++ was introduced. An anticorruption campaign is publicized in customs offices with "in your face" messages (for example, "Corruption Stops Here" signs posted at the doors of managers).

More recently URA launched other initiatives in the anticorruption campaign and created an Ethics and Integrity Committee, elected ethics counselors who would be responsible for a series of anticorruption initiatives, and started working on a code of ethics (which is still in the draft stage and could benefit from application of the WCO Model Integrity Code). The URA Commissioner made a well-publicized initiative to reinvigorate the anticorruption campaign. (He promised strong measures, including firing combined with the possibility to submit voluntary resignations with impunity, and a confidential e-mail address and telephone number to report corruption.) Responses to these initiatives would benefit from greater follow up. Yet, some early success was achieved when several URA managers were arrested for fraudulently benefiting from a drawback scheme.

*Source:* De Wulf 2004.

substantially contributed to lowering corruption. With improved procedures to detect staff misconduct, Mozambique has stepped up the number of cases investigated and resulting staff dismissals. In the recruitment of senior managers and of those appointed to sensitive positions, background and integrity checks are undertaken. With the targeted upgrading in quality of staff under the reform, 60 percent of the initial staff has been removed, thus providing the opportunity to strengthen integrity. However, the incidence of staff misconduct remains high and the process of disciplinary action lengthy.

At the outset of the reform program in Peru, about 60 percent of the staff was removed through "voluntary departure," while those not leaving were subjected to external tests, and corrupt personnel were dismissed. The modernization of customs in the Philippines initially was successful in stemming corruption, but since the late 1990s the situation reversed itself and traders again came to view customs as one of the most corrupt public services in the country.

## Lessons Learned

Several factors played a key role in ensuring the success of the reforms in the case countries studied. These are summarized in chapter 1 and discussed here.

Good customs operations consist of coherent and interlocking sets of processes. An overall customs reform program has a greater chance of yielding effective and sustainable results than partial reforms. In countries with successful reforms, feasible measures were successively and progressively introduced within an overall vision to establish a modern customs organization.

Political support was essential for the success of the reforms. Continuity in leadership is important in carrying out reforms; continuity in management is important in sustaining them. Strong and stable leadership with an opportunity to see the implementation through to completion proved to be essential for success.

Sustainability requires continued political commitment. Even when successful reforms become firmly embedded in a country's administrative and institutional framework, their endurance is subject to risks. These include changes in policy direction, weakening of political support, and changes in the reform leadership or management of customs, all of which can stall the reform or reverse its course. Other risks include lack of political commitment, inadequate funding for staff compensation and the maintenance of IT infrastructure, changing customs-funding rules, and political interference in personnel management. When reforms clearly benefit both private traders and the Treasury, they create their own advocates, thus reducing the chances of backsliding.

The reform must be realistic and consist of reform measures that can be implemented. The early strengthening and stepped up application of IT-based customs processing is essential for a successful reform. Full automation of clearance procedures and the establishment of risk-based control and audit systems critically depend on the proper use of IT. These actions set the stage for streamlining and simplifying customs procedures to speed up the clearance process and reduce physical inspections. They also help reduce contacts between customs staff and traders, thus reducing the possibility of discretionary and accommodating decisions that engender corruption.

A good funding strategy is needed to ensure the success of a reform. Donor support and coordination was critical for launching and implementing the reforms in all of the eight case study countries. Domestic funding, complementing foreign financing, was also important in ensuring the success of the reforms. This was even more acute in countries where a culture of management by objective had to be substituted for that of management by institution. Donor coordination at the diagnostic level is also important.

Coordination with other agencies is essential to reap the full benefits of the reforms. In no case was it possible to document that trade facilitation was able to extend effectively beyond customs, but some reform initiatives explicitly include such objectives in medium- to long-term work programs. Such coordination with other agencies is essential so that inefficiencies in obtaining import authorizations related to health, safety, and other purposes—which can significantly delay the processing of trade operations—can be rooted out.

Customs reforms need the support of customs staff and other stakeholders. Just as the autonomy of customs administrations can facilitate the implementation of reforms, it can also strengthen the dedication of staff to high performance standards. The administrative autonomy of customs also contributes to the achievement of reform objectives. Ideally, customs administrations should receive as much autonomy as possible in their administration and operations, and should be provided with an adequate budget to effectively and efficiently undertake their functions. They should also be provided with clear evaluation criteria.

The personnel policies of customs were a major factor in enhancing quality and integrity of staff. Personnel reform contributed to successful customs modernization programs, particularly in countries that proceeded with a large-scale changeover of personnel and where existing staff had to go through the same recruitment process as new applicants and were also offered incentives to leave. Salary upgrades were designed to attract and maintain qualified personnel, as well as to strengthen integrity and financial autonomy. A major element of these new policies was also the introduction of WTO-compatible declaration processing fees, which enabled customs to earmark sufficient resources to maintain their new, modernized systems.

Cooperation between customs and private sector operators was a significant factor in the success of the reform programs. The change in the orientation of customs from a nearly exclusive emphasis on its role as enforcer and collector to one of provider of services, incorporating effective service delivery with its revenue mobilization responsibilities, requires strong support from the trade community. Such support can be sustained by a deliberate outreach program to the private sector, including periodic high-level consultative meetings. However, the full transparency of regulations, performance indicators, and statistics, will be most important in convincing the trade community.

Using clear performance indicators to monitor the progress of reform is essential not only to evaluate progress, but also to adjust the reform measures to changing circumstances without losing sight of the big picture. Customs clearance time was reduced in all the case study countries reviewed. Green channel designations as well as the incidence of physical inspections are good indicators for monitoring clearance time and must be evaluated within the context of the application of risk management principles.

## Further Reading

The various case studies referred to in this chapter are published in Luc De Wulf and José B. Sokol, eds. 2004. *Customs Modernization Initiatives: Case Studies.* Washington, D.C.: The World Bank, which is issued as a companion volume to this publication.

Molnar, Eva. and Lauri Ojala. 2003. "Transport and Trade Facilitation Issues in the CIS-7, Kazakhstan and Turkmenistan." Washington, D.C.: The World Bank.

World Bank. 2002. "Trade and Transport Facilitation in Southeast Europe Program." Washington, D.C. www.seerecon.org/ttfse.

## References

De Wulf, Luc. 2004. "Uganda." In Luc De Wulf and José B. Sokol, eds. *Customs Modernization Initiatives: Case Studies.* Washington, D.C.: The World Bank.

Goorman, Adrien. 2004. "Peru." In Luc De Wulf and José B. Sokol, eds. *Customs Modernization Initiatives: Case Studies.* Washington, D.C.: The World Bank.

Mwangi, Anthony. 2004. "Mozambique." In Luc De Wulf and José B. Sokol, eds. *Customs Modernization Initiatives: Case Studies.* Washington, D.C.: The World Bank.

Oktem, M. Bahri. 2004. "Turkey." In Luc De Wulf and José B. Sokol, eds. *Customs Modernization Initiatives: Case Studies.* Washington, D.C.: The World Bank.

Parayno, Guillermo L. Jr. 2004. "The Philippines." In Luc De Wulf and José B. Sokol, eds. *Customs Modernization Initiatives: Case Studies.* Washington, D.C.: The World Bank.

Steenlandt, Marcel, and Luc De Wulf. 2004. "Morocco." In Luc De Wulf and José B. Sokol, eds. *Custom Modernization Initiatives: Case Studies.* Washington, D.C.: The World Bank.

# 7

# TWO DECADES OF WORLD BANK LENDING FOR CUSTOMS REFORM: TRENDS IN PROJECT DESIGN, PROJECT IMPLEMENTATION, AND LESSONS LEARNED

*Michael Engelschalk and Tuan Minh Le*

## TABLE OF CONTENTS

The authors gratefully acknowledge the research assistance provided by Patricia Laverley (OED PK) and Gonzalo Salinas (OEDCR). They wish to thank Yvonne M. Tsikata (OEDCR), Gianni Zanini (WBIPR), and Michel Zarnowiecki (ECSIE) for their valuable comments and suggestions received over the course of the development of this chapter.

## LIST OF TABLES

## LIST OF FIGURES

## LIST OF BOXES

Over the past 20 years the World Bank has provided substantial support for reforming customs administrations in developing countries. While this support was seldom provided in the form of customs-specific technical assistance operations, many projects in trade facilitation, infrastructure, and public sector included customs reform components. In addressing customs reforms, the Bank has accumulated a significant amount of knowledge and experience, which should be used in designing new projects as well as in improving existing ones.

The chapter is structured as follows: The first section, Bank Assistance in Customs-Related Projects, summarizes the level, format, and regional distribution of World Bank lending for customs reform. The analysis is based on the project database (Trade Assistance Evaluation Project Database—TAEPD) compiled by the World Bank's Operations Evaluation Department (OED) and project-specific documentation including staff appraisal reports (SARs), project appraisal documents (PADs), implementation completion reports (ICRs), and OED evaluation summaries.[1] The second section, Pre-Project Diagnostic Work and Project Design, provides a detailed discussion of issues, trends, and patterns in setting objectives, selecting performance indicators, and defining project activities. The third section, Project Implementation and Outcomes, identifies key problems in diagnostic work, project design, implementation management, and supervision that affect final project outcomes and sustainability. The concluding section discusses the design and process issues of projects with customs reform activities and draws key lessons for future Bank operations to support customs modernization.

## Bank Assistance in Customs-Related Projects

The World Bank has been active in providing support for customs reforms in all geographical regions. A variety of lending instruments was used for these assistance projects, and the distribution of projects differed across region.

### Rationale and Lending Instruments

World Bank customs modernization activities have generally been part of broader reform programs to facilitate trade, support general revenue mobilization, enhance public finance management, strengthen public sector human resources management, support infrastructure development, or enhance competitiveness. In many cases, customs is just a small component in a complex reform program.[2] At the other extreme, in very few cases, such as the Russian Customs Development Project (RCDP), customs reform has been the sole focus of an operation.

---

1. See also, Operations Policy and Country Services 2003, and OED 2004.

2. A typical example is the Economic Recovery Credit Project (Chad), which lists among its various objectives "reinforcement of the Customs Office through training programs and the provision of equipment and materials." The project document, however, does not offer any specific plan for implementation nor does it offer a detailed cost allocation among different components of the project.

Customs reform components are embedded in investment and technical assistance loans (TALs) as well as in structural adjustment loans and credits (SALs). In the case of a technical assistance (TA) operation, the project document specifies the allocation of funds to each particular project component. Structural adjustment operations are generally designed to provide financial support for a policy program such as in fiscal reform or public resource management. The operations do not require an in-depth specification of project components nor do they specify the allocation of the funds to different components. Given the different nature of SALs, the following analysis focuses solely on the Bank's TA components to distill lessons for future customs modernization activities.

### Scope and Distribution of Bank Assistance

During 1982–2002, the Bank engaged in 117 projects with a customs reform component; 38 of these were TA projects and 29 were SALs. Annex 7.A summarizes the distribution of these projects across regions and periods.

In the SALs with customs components, two-thirds of the policy reforms retained were trade related, while one-third were public finance related. With respect to the customs-related components, 75 percent aimed at process simplification, 16 percent at improvements in legislation, and 9 percent at human resources development.

The customs-related conditionalities and scope of activities included in the SALs vary widely from the very specific to the most ambitious. Some SALs developed specific conditionalities related to specific customs procedures and operations (Georgia Third Structural Adjustment Credit Project, Jordan Third Economic Reform and Development Loan Project, and Morocco Policy Reform Support Loan Project), specific aspects of human resources management and training (Haiti Second Technical Assistance Project, Tunisia Development of the Capacity to Administer Foreign Trade), revision of the Customs Code (Nigeria Trade and Investment Policy Loan Project), and targets for simplification of procedures to facilitate trade (Morocco Second Industrial and Trade Policy Adjustment Loan Project). Some SALs imposed broad and ambitious conditions for customs modernization, such as strengthening customs administration (Sao Tome and Principe Strengthening Planning Budgeting

Implementation and Control Project, Cambodia Economic Rehabilitation Credit Project) or strengthening the role of government in quality control of imports (Senegal Agricultural Sector Adjustment Credit Project). For the purpose of this chapter, we do not particularly analyze the 79 SALs in the database because SAL conditionalities are difficult to monitor in their linkage with TA provided, and the Bank's expertise is in general not explicitly tested in SALs.

Table 7.1 shows the allocation of approved TA operations (approximately US$309 million in total) toward customs-specific components by period and by region. The RCDP by itself attracted US$140 million—more than 45 percent of the total of financing for Bank customs-related projects. With or without the RCDP, Europe and Central Asia (ECA) countries far outweighed any other region in attracting Bank funds. The ECA region attracted about US$213 million with the RCDP included (approximately 69 percent of the total customs-related TA lending of US$309 million), and US$73 million without the RCDP (or 43 percent of total lending).

Table 7.2 depicts the distribution of the 38 TA operations with customs components by five project categories: customs-specific, trade-related, infrastructure, public finance, and others. The single customs-specific project, the RCDP, drew the highest share of the total approved loans for customs components (45 percent), whereas the customs activities embedded in infrastructure projects obtained the lowest share (3 percent of the total amount of customs loans with the RCDP, and 5 percent of the total without it). Public finance reform projects attracted the second highest share (32 and 59 percent of the total approved loans for customs, with and without the RCDP, respectively), followed by trade-related projects (16 percent and 30 percent with and without the RCDP). Except for the RCDP, public finance and trade-related projects are ranked second and third, respectively, in terms of average customs project amounts (column 4) and the share of customs operations in the total Bank-approved operations by project category (column 5).

### Pre-Project Diagnostic Work and Project Design

Bank project documents provide detailed information on the pre-project diagnostics and project

**TABLE 7.1   Approved Amounts for Customs Components of Technical Assistance Projects, 1982–2002**
(amounts in US$ million; shares in percent)

| Fiscal Year Region | 1982–86 Amount Approved | Share | 1987–91 Amount Approved | Share | 1992–96 Amount Approved | Share | 1997–2002 Amount Approved | Share | 1982–2002 Amount Approved | Share |
|---|---|---|---|---|---|---|---|---|---|---|
| Sub-Saharan Africa | 0.24 | 8 | 8.63 | 86 | 5.29 | 7 | 11.67 | 5 | 25.8 | 8 |
| East Asia and Pacific | | | | | 20.3 | 26 | 1.1 | 1 | 21.4 | 7 |
| Europe and Central Asia[a] | | | 0.3 | 3 | 48.2 | 62 | 164.5 | 75 | 213.0 | 69 |
| Latin America and Caribbean | 2.6 | 92 | 1.15 | 11 | | | 22.0 | 10 | 25.7 | 8 |
| Middle East and North Africa | | | | | 3.82 | 5 | 9.0 | 4 | 12.8 | 4 |
| South Asia | | | | | | | 10.45 | 5 | 10.5 | 3 |
| Total | 2.8 | 100 | 10.1 | 100 | 77.6 | 100 | 218.7 | 100 | 309.2 | 100 |

a. The RCDP was approved in 2002 in the amount of US$140 million.
*Source:* Authors based on World Bank database.

design. To track the evolution in pre-project diagnostics, the 1982–2002 review period is divided into two subperiods, 1982–93 and 1994–2002. The rationale for the time breaking point is two-fold: Because the OED database does not have any investment or TA projects with customs components during 1982–84, the natural break point that evenly divides the 1985–2002 period is 1993–94. Also, a number of projects with substantial customs components, such as Turkey Public Financial Management, RCDP, and Trade and Transport Facilitation in Southeast Europe (TTFSE), were approved after 1993, and this offers an opportunity to analyze any shift in the Bank's approach to assistance of customs reforms.

*Pre-Project Diagnostic Framework*

Proper pre-project preparation and diagnostic work are critical for devising reform options, and determining project priorities and appropriate sequencing of activities. Several tools are available to support pre-project diagnostic work (see chapter 1).

Basically, a comprehensive diagnosis should use both quantitative and qualitative indicators and look at the effectiveness and efficiency of the institution, institutional design and management, and the institutional and economic environment of the customs administration.

The review of Bank operations reveals, however, that a significant number of TA operations lack substantive diagnostic analysis. While the level and comprehensiveness of pre-project diagnosis depend on the scope of the project envisaged, an institutional analysis is essential even for small projects that address only specific elements of customs management and operations. However, out of a total of 38 TA projects with a customs reform component in the OED database, only 20 projects (or less than 53 percent) were designed on the basis of an institutional diagnosis. Across the projects that were designed following a pre-project diagnosis, the approach to identifying institutional weaknesses, as well as reform needs and priorities, differed widely. This indicates that project preparation and design

**TABLE 7.2   Distribution of Approved Operations with Customs Component by Project Category, 1982–2002**
(amounts in US$ million; shares in percent)

| Project Category | Total Amount Approved (Customs and Non-Customs Activities) [1] | Number of Projects [2] | Approved Amount Allocated for Customs [3] | Average Customs Amount per Project [4]=[3]/[2] | Share of Customs Operations in Total Approved Operations by Project Category [5]=[3]/[1] | Share in Total Amount Allocated for Customs | |
|---|---|---|---|---|---|---|---|
| | | | | | | With RCDP[a] [6] | Without RCDP[b] [7] |
| Customs-specific (RCDP) | 140.0 | 1 | 140.0 | 140.0 | 100.0 | 45.0 | |
| Trade-related | 277.8 | 14 | 50.9 | 3.6 | 18.0 | 16.0 | 30.0 |
| Infrastructure | 210.5 | 5 | 8.6 | 1.7 | 4.0 | 3.0 | 5.0 |
| Public finance | 229.2 | 7 | 100.0 | 14.3 | 44.0 | 32.0 | 59.0 |
| Others | 127.9 | 11 | 9.6 | 0.9 | 8.0 | 3.0 | 6.0 |
| Total (with RCDP) | 985.4 | 38 | 309.2 | 8.1 | 31.0 | 100.0 | |
| Total (without RCDP) | 845.4 | 37 | 169.2 | 4.6 | 20.0 | | 100.0 |

a. The share is estimated in the total approved operations for customs including the RCDP (US$309.2 million).
b. The share is estimated in the total approved operations for customs without the RCDP (US$169.2 million).
*Source:* Authors based on World Bank database.

were largely ad hoc and lacked a common methodological framework. Table 7.3 summarizes the scope of the diagnostic analysis of the 20 projects with a pre-project diagnosis.[3] Box 7.1 offers three project-specific cases.

While all 20 projects provided some kind of qualitative diagnostics, in very few cases was a quantitative analysis carried out to probe the strengths and weaknesses of customs administrations, especially regarding effectiveness, efficiency, and integrity. However, pre-project diagnostics improved over time, especially in the case of the most recent projects (those projects approved in the late 1990s and early 2000s).

Customs reform covers much more than just customs administration. More than half the projects in the sample evaluated the legislative framework for customs operations, ongoing or planned

customs reform strategy, organizational structure and functions, implementation of the harmonized system, customs rules and procedures, the status of automation, and office facilities. The depth of the analysis was, however, not uniform across projects and assessment areas. For example, almost all projects with diagnostics examined the existing customs laws and regulations (95 percent), while a significantly lower share analyzed more specific issues such as the implementation of the harmonized system (60 percent) or the complexity of rules or procedures (70 percent). The fact that a substantial share of project preparation activities (65 percent) included a diagnosis of the existing IT infrastructure and automation plans reflects the generally high share of IT-related costs in the customs components of the TA projects.[4] Interestingly, there was far less analysis of the system of inspection of goods

---

3. The structure of table 7.3 follows Lane's (1998) framework for the assessment of fundamentals in customs administration as well as Gill's (2000) diagnostic guidelines for revenue administration.

4. For example, the share of IT costs in customs modernization in the Philippines Tax Computerization Project and in the Turkey Public Finance Management Project account for approximately 52 percent and 82 percent of the total costs of the customs components, respectively.

**TABLE 7.3  Pre-Project Diagnostic Analyses in Technical Assistance Projects, 1982–2002**
(number of projects, shares in percent)

| | 1982–93 | | 1994–2002 | | 1982–2002 | |
|---|---|---|---|---|---|---|
| | Number of Projects | Share[a] | Number of Projects | Share[b] | Number of Projects | Share[c] |
| **Total Number of Projects with Diagnostic Analyses** | 3 | | 17 | | 20 | |
| **Diagnostic Areas** | | | | | | |
| **Institutional Environment Assessment** | | | | | | |
| General diagnostics of customs laws and regulations | 3 | 100 | 16 | 94 | 19 | 95 |
| Planned or ongoing customs reform strategy | 3 | 100 | 16 | 94 | 19 | 95 |
| Customs administration indicators | | | | | | |
| **Effectiveness** | | | | | | |
| Service time indicators | 0 | 0 | 9 | 53 | 9 | 45 |
| Organizational structure and functions | 1 | 33 | 13 | 76 | 14 | 70 |
| Availability of risk management practice | 1 | 33 | 3 | 18 | 4 | 20 |
| Number of arriving passengers | 1 | 33 | 0 | 0 | 1 | 5 |
| Tonnage cleared | 1 | 33 | 0 | 0 | 1 | 5 |
| Ratio of taxes and duties collected to GDP (buoyancy) | 1 | 33 | 4 | 24 | 5 | 25 |
| Revenues-collected-to-potential-revenue ratio | 1 | 33 | 0 | 0 | 1 | 5 |
| **Efficiency** | | | | | | |
| Estimated administration costs per transaction | 1 | 33 | 0 | 0 | 1 | 5 |
| Implementation of harmonized system (HS classification system) | 0 | 0 | 12 | 71 | 12 | 60 |
| Number of office staff | 2 | 67 | 2 | 12 | 4 | 20 |
| Size of trade | 1 | 33 | 5 | 29 | 6 | 30 |
| Valuation procedures | 0 | 0 | 3 | 18 | 3 | 15 |
| Complexity of rules or procedures | 2 | 67 | 12 | 71 | 14 | 70 |
| Automated customs procedures | 2 | 67 | 11 | 65 | 13 | 65 |
| **Customs Expertise (Human Resources Development)** | | | | | | |
| Recruitment processes (selection of administration management) | 1 | 33 | 2 | 12 | 3 | 15 |
| Training (formal or on-the-job) | 1 | 33 | 8 | 47 | 9 | 45 |
| **Integrity** | | | | | | |
| Office facilities | 2 | 67 | 11 | 65 | 13 | 65 |
| Code of conduct (code published or discussed) | 0 | 0 | 4 | 24 | 4 | 20 |
| Availability of merit-based promotion | 0 | 0 | 3 | 18 | 3 | 15 |
| Pay and benefits | 2 | 67 | 3 | 18 | 5 | 25 |
| Internal control and audit | 0 | 0 | 2 | 12 | 2 | 10 |
| Description and evaluation of methods to detect corruption and ensure integrity | 0 | 0 | 9 | 53 | 9 | 45 |

a. Share of the total number of TA projects with diagnostic analysis for 1982–93 (3 projects total).
b. Share of the total number of TA projects with diagnostics for 1994–2002 (17 projects total).
c. Share of the total number of TA projects with diagnostics for 1982–2002 (20 projects total).
*Source:* Authors based on World Bank database.

## BOX 7.1    Diagnostic Framework—Three Project-Specific Cases

The **Tanzania Tax Administration Project** (approved fiscal year 1999; total approved amount US$40 million) confined its diagnostics to the qualitative analysis of the problems or weaknesses in the customs administration, but did not offer detailed quantitative assessments of its efficiency and effectiveness. The project specifically assessed institutional weaknesses related to poor management, weaknesses in human resources development, cumbersome documentary requirements coupled with bureaucratic and discretionary paper-based procedures, lack of physical infrastructure and equipment, outmoded legislative or regulatory base with inadequate authority and penalty structures, and ineffective enforcement practices that rely largely on physical inspection despite the use of a preshipment inspection (PSI) company.

The **Philippines Tax Computerization Project** (approved fiscal year 1993; total approved amount US$63 million) and the **Russia Customs Development Project** (approved fiscal year 2003; total approved amount US$140 million) offer examples of more comprehensive diagnostics. The diagnosis in the Philippines Tax Computerization Project was based on an International Monetary Fund (IMF) analysis for a customs reform action plan. Additional diagnostic work initiated by the Bank resulted in supplements to the IMF recommendations for the action plan. The project analyzes the existing revenue system and the institutional capacity of the revenue administration. It studies the historical background and the overall reform context of the computerization project, as well as describes the status of computerization in customs and the tax administration. It also supplements the analysis of the institutional capacity with statistics on performance of customs and the tax administration. The specific statistics on customs include number of staff, taxes collected by the Bureau of Customs (BOC), expenses, number of passengers (total and per BOC staff), net tonnage cleared (total and per BOC staff), trade flows (imports and exports values), and tax efforts (defined as the share of tax collection in gross domestic product).

For the RCDP, the Bank project team developed jointly with IMF customs experts a project-specific diagnostic questionnaire. It was sent to the State Customs Committee (SCC) before the beginning of the actual project design work. Information provided by the SCC was analyzed before the pre-appraisal of the project, and was supplemented by additional pre-project diagnostic work, using the diagnostic tools designed by the World Customs Organization (WCO) and the European Union (EU) Blueprints for Customs Administrations, in addition to Gill's diagnostic toolkit. Pre-project diagnosis covered all relevant areas ranging from the analysis of the project environment, commitment to reform, and stakeholder needs and expectations to an assessment of the needs for legal and regulatory changes, institutional effectiveness and efficiency, human resources and training issues, and integrity problems.

*Sources:* World Bank 1993b, 1999b, 2003.

and the application of a risk-based inspection system, although this is an important element of the overall computerization strategy (only 20 percent of projects assessed the existing risk management practices). In assessing the customs environment, the majority of projects eluded the diagnostics of valuation procedures, which was carried out in only 15 percent of project preparations.

Integrity and human resources management received relatively light treatment. Few projects explicitly analyzed the availability and quality of a code of conduct (20 percent), merit-based promotion (15 percent), or pay and benefit packages (25 percent). Only 10 percent of the projects offered a diagnostic of the internal control and audit systems, which form the core institutional settings for coping with incentives and opportunities for corruption. Instead, many projects limited their diagnostics to a general description of the availability of methods to detect corruption (45 percent), and a description of office facilities (65 percent). In assessing the expertise or status of human resources development, projects largely focused on training (45 percent) but bypassed the critical issue of recruitment processes, especially the process of management recruitment (15 percent).

Project sustainability has to be an important part of pre-project diagnosis. Several issues arise here. In addition to the government's commitment to implement the project, clarity is needed on how the operating costs of the agency will be financed after the project closes. This is particularly important for projects with a substantial IT component, projects with substantial investment in infrastructure, and projects supporting the introduction of a special bonus and incentive system for customs staff. In the case of the Philippines Tax Computerization Project, for example, the project team did not address the issue of the cost of ongoing maintenance and IT system upgrades until the project closure discussion. Government guarantees to allocate adequate funds to the BOC for replacing outdated hardware could not be obtained and the status of computerization deteriorated significantly after the close of the project.

The ability of the customs agency to attract and retain qualified staff is another key issue for the sustainability of a customs reform project. It will depend on the human resources management flexibility of the customs agency, in particular the flexibility to create a sufficient number of expert positions and to offer adequate compensation packages. Reform efforts to create a more professional customs agency cannot be successful if the agency does not have the flexibility to attract the necessary number of qualified and motivated staff. This has to be confirmed before the final design of the project.

Most of the projects reviewed neglected the quantitative diagnostics of effectiveness in customs administration. In addition, only one out of twenty projects with a diagnostic component analyzed the customs administration's cost per transaction, a critical indicator for efficiency in customs administrations. On the other hand, there was a clear evolution in the diagnostic work. Out of 26 TA projects undertaken during the period 1994–2002, 17 projects conducted some kind of diagnostics. This is in sharp contrast with the insignificant share of projects with diagnostics during 1982–93, where only three out of twelve TA projects had any kind of pre-project diagnosis. The juxtaposition of the shares of projects with individual indicators in the total number of projects with diagnostics in each subperiod reveals an improved quality of the diagnostics, except for the area of efficiency assessment. The diagnostics undertaken during 1994–2002 were significantly more comprehensive in probing the fundamental issues of customs operation and management, particularly service time indicators (53 percent in the second subperiod compared to none in the first), organizational structure and

functions (76 percent versus 33 percent), status of the implementation of the harmonized system (71 percent versus none), and complexity of rules and procedures (71 percent versus 67 percent). In addition, the second subperiod marked a substantial evolution in the integrity assessment.[5]

### What are Customs Projects Trying to Achieve? An Analysis of Project Objectives

Table 7.4 summarizes the customs-related objectives of the 38 TA projects reviewed. There are three broad project objectives for customs administration reform: revenue mobilization, minimization of burden on trade, and national security. More specific project objectives relate to specific project components or reflect a narrower project focus and are basically subcomponents of the three major functions of customs. They include objectives such as strengthening integrity or improving services to the trader community. Many projects list a number of detailed objectives instead of aiming at generally strengthening one or several of the core functions of customs. Some projects simply pursue the broad objective of strengthening the customs agency without mentioning specific effectiveness, efficiency, or integrity objectives.

Minimizing the burden on trade emerged as the main target of the 38 projects; more than half the projects during 1982–2002 broadly had trade facilitation as the core project objective. Ten projects identified revenue enhancement as the main objective. No project incorporated national security in its objectives, which is understandable given that national security is not part of the Bank's mandate. The cross-period comparison shows that the definition of broader project objectives of trade facilitation or revenue enhancement became more widespread in recent years compared to earlier Bank projects. While only 25 percent of projects identified trade facilitation as their main objective during 1985 to 1993, this share jumped to 65 percent for projects

---

5. Projects with pre-project diagnostics during 1982–93 seemed to focus more on the quantitative assessment of effectiveness in customs administration. Nevertheless, one should be aware of the major caveat in this cross-period comparison: the skewed distribution of the number of projects with pre-project diagnostics toward the second period, and the very small sample of just three projects with pre-project diagnostics in the first period tend to overestimate the diagnostics shares in the first period.

**TABLE 7.4  Summary of Objectives**
(shares in percent)

| Period | 1982–93 | | 1994–2002 | | 1982–2002 | |
|---|---|---|---|---|---|---|
| Objective | Number of Projects | Share[a] | Number of Projects | Share[b] | Number of Projects | Share[c] |
| Revenue enhancement | 1 | 8 | 9 | 35 | 10 | 26 |
| Trade facilitation | 3 | 25 | 17 | 65 | 20 | 53 |
| Security | 0 | 0 | 0 | 0 | 0 | 0 |
| Strengthening customs agency | 8 | 67 | 19 | 73 | 27 | 71 |
| Integrity | 1 | 8 | 3 | 12 | 4 | 11 |
| Improving compliance | 1 | 8 | 11 | 42 | 12 | 32 |
| Improving trader services | 0 | 0 | 13 | 50 | 13 | 34 |
| Participation of stakeholders | 0 | 0 | 0 | 0 | 0 | 0 |

a. Share of TA projects during 1982–93 reviewed (12 projects).
b. Share of TA projects during 1994–2002 reviewed (26 projects).
c. Share of TA projects during 1982–2002 reviewed (38 projects).
*Source:* Authors based on World Bank database.

designed between 1994 and 2002. Similarly, only 8 percent of projects designed between 1982 and 1993 specified revenue enhancement as a core project objective. The related share was 35 percent for projects designed between 1994 and 2002. Bank TA projects thus seem to reflect and react to the growing awareness in recent years among policymakers in developing countries of the importance of trade facilitation in general and the importance of customs reform for trade facilitation.

The fact that the majority of projects (27 out of 38 projects, or 71 percent) during 1982–2002 listed the global—and somewhat vague—objective of "strengthening of the customs agency" as a key project objective indicates a certain reluctance to commit to more specific and measurable outcomes.[6] However, more recent Bank projects designed between 1994 and 2002 witnessed a dramatic change in the identification of more specific project objectives. Moreover, while no project set the improvement of services to the trader community as one of its targets during 1982–93, it became a key objective for half of the 26 TA projects during 1994–2002. No project identified mobilizing the voice and participation of the private sector, partic-

ularly the trader community, as sufficiently important to be highlighted as a separate project objective.

### Measuring Performance: The Design of Performance Indicators

Table 7.5 summarizes the coverage of benchmarks or performance indicators used to monitor implementation of the objectives as set out in the projects.[7]

Measuring performance was particularly weak in the case of projects designed before 1994. Only a single project designed between 1982 and 1993 listed any performance indicators. Performance measurement was limited to only two indicators, the release or import clearance time and the annual number of declarations per customs staff. Among more recent Bank projects, the RCDP, the Turkey Public Finance Management Project, the Tunisia Export Development Project, and the Trade and Transport Facilitation Projects in Southeastern Europe are the ones with the most comprehensive sets of performance indicators.

The selection of performance indicators depends on the objectives and coverage of the TA

---

6. Of the 27 TA projects that included the objective of strengthening the customs agency, seven listed this objective as the single objective for their customs administration reform components.

7. The listing is based on the set of indicators established in the Turkey Finance Management Project and in the seven Trade and Transport Facilitation projects in Southeastern Europe.

**TABLE 7.5   Performance Indicators**

| Period | 1982–93 | 1994–2002 | 1982–2002 |
|---|---|---|---|
| Indicator | Number of Projects | Number of Projects | Number of Projects |
| **Efficiency-Intended Results** | | | |
| Revenue collected per customs staff | 0 | 8 | 8 |
| Total customs agency costs compared to revenue collected | 0 | 7 | 7 |
| Salaries compared to revenue collected | 0 | 7 | 7 |
| Trade volume per number of staff | 0 | 8 | 8 |
| Annual number of declarations per customs staff | 1 | 9 | 10 |
| **Effectiveness-Intended Results** | | | |
| Release time (import clearance time) | 1 | 12 | 13 |
| Physical inspection and introduction of risk management | 0 | 14 | 14 |
| Trade community information | 0 | 4 | 4 |
| Irregularities per number of examinations | 0 | 8 | 8 |
| Surveyed occurrence of corruption/ integrity | 0 | 2 | 2 |
| More effective physical inspections | 0 | 4 | 4 |
| Rejection of incomplete or inaccurate declarations | 0 | 1 | 1 |
| Timely and accurate production of trade statistics | 0 | 2 | 2 |

*Source:* Authors based on World Bank database.

---

**BOX 7.2   Inadequacy of Performance Indicators: Project-Specific Cases**

The majority of the TA projects reviewed did not include any indicators for measuring project performance. For instance, the lack of performance indicators was highlighted in the OED evaluation of the Philippines Tax Computerization Project, which had a substantial customs reform component. A number of other projects did not provide an adequate set of performance indicators corresponding to the project objectives and activities. An additional problem faced in project supervision was the fact that project documents frequently did not offer any explicit time line for achieving the implementation benchmark.

The abstract below from the table entitled "Key performance indicators" shows the indica-

tor for the component "Resource mobilization" of the Armenia Second Structural Adjustment Technical Assistance Credit (approved fiscal year 1998; total approved amount US$5 million). The project included isolated efforts to computerize the State Tax Inspectorate and the Customs Department, but there was no ongoing or planned strategy for comprehensive reform of the customs administration. The project was not based on a diagnostic analysis to make sure that the proposed activity would have a tangible impact on revenue collection. As a consequence, the indicator is vague, mixes project output and outcome, and does not specify when the benchmark would be reached.

| Expected Outcomes/Impact | Key Performance Indicators | Monitoring Indicators and Supervision | Critical Assumptions and Risks |
|---|---|---|---|
| Customs declaration process fully computerized and payment system improved | Customs declarations and payments processed using computerized system | Customs department records | Implementation capacity of Customs department |

*Sources:* World Bank 1997a, 2000g.

---

**BOX 7.3    Designing a Comprehensive Set of Performance Indicators: The Case of Trade and Transport Facilitation Projects in Southeast Europe**

Seven countries in Southeast Europe (Albania, Bulgaria, Bosnia and Herzegovina, Croatia, Macedonia, Federal Republic of Yugoslavia, and Romania) participate in the regional program for Trade and Transport Facilitation. The program is aimed at modernizing customs administrations and other border control agencies. To facilitate coordination, a Regional Steering Committee (RSC) was established. Customs reform was identified as a core requirement to support EU accession, and organizational reforms were combined with the provision of infrastructure. EU customs reform blueprints and accession requirements provided the basis for the TA program.

A template of a comprehensive set of performance indicators was developed and uniformly applied to pilot ports in all participating countries (with the sole exception of the indicator on surveyed occurrence of corruption, which was only measured by one participating country—Albania). All indicators were devised on the basis of the existing situation in 1999 and specified for the subsequent four years. They included benchmarks for pilot sites clearance performance (for example, import clearance time in minutes, percentage of physical examination, proportion of times that trucks are cleared in less than 15 minutes, share of number

of irregularities in total number of examinations) and those to monitor efficiency and effectiveness-intended results (for example, average revenue collection per customs staff, share of salaries in revenue collection, average annual number of declarations per customs staff).

The fact that the TTFSE program included all border inspection agencies permitted the design of indicators that measure not only customs clearance time, but also total clearance time at the border. Projects focusing exclusively on customs operations will find it more difficult to work with these indicators. However, customs generally has a lead responsibility for coordination with other agencies in efforts to reduce import clearance time, and customs reform projects with a trade facilitation objective may find it useful to monitor the development of overall import clearance time throughout the implementation period of the project. This can be done by adding to the list of customs-specific key performance indicators a small number of broader trade facilitation indicators, to be monitored for information purposes only. This has been done before, in the RCDP, for example.

*Sources:* World Bank 2000a, 2000b, 2000c, 2000d, 2000h, 2001, 2002a, 2002b.

---

project. The broader and more comprehensive a customs reform project is designed to be , the more comprehensive the set of performance indicators needs to be. A narrow set of indicators, therefore, can be perfectly justified in the case of a limited TA project with narrow focus and objectives. However, of the 38 TA projects under review, only 17 (or approximately 45 percent) had any benchmarks for monitoring and evaluating project implementation and results. A majority of projects were designed without an appropriate set of performance indicators, and there was a wide variation across projects in terms of indicator coverage. Chapter 1 of this book suggests a number of good indicators for monitoring revenue enhancement. Box 7.2 provides some examples of incomplete sets of performance indicators, while box 7.3 highlights a good practice in designing a comprehensive set of indicators.

Table 7.5 shows that only a small set of the indicators on efficiency and effectiveness attracted the focal attention of the project teams. During 1982–2002,

out of 17 TA projects with performance indicators, more than half measured certain aspects of the improvement in customs service (or effectiveness-intended results) and efficiency in using customs staff for processing declarations. Thirteen projects presented benchmarks for the release or import clearance time, and 14 focused on the introduction of risk management practices, while 10 focused on the indicator of annual number of declarations per customs staff (efficiency-intended results). A number of other good efficiency indicators—specifically, average revenue collection per customs staff, average costs of customs administration in terms of revenues collected by customs, salaries-to-revenues-collected ratio, and trade-volume-to-staff ratio—attracted fewer than half of the Technical Assistance Loans (TALs) with performance indicators. An even longer list of critical indicators on effectiveness—such as trader service, number of irregularities-to-number of examinations ratio, and rejection of incomplete or inaccurate declarations—attracted a substantially low number of projects; this may reflect the lack of

**FIGURE 7.1  Institutional Environment Assessment Framework**

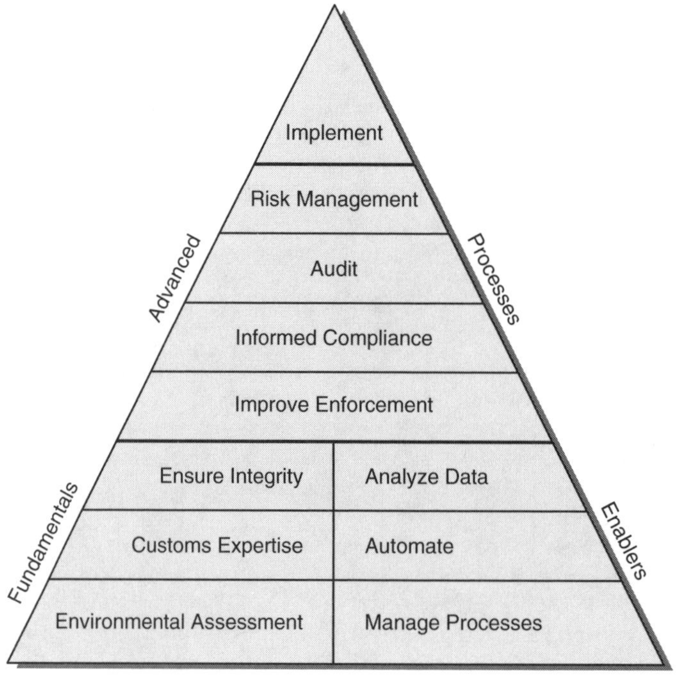

*Source:* Lane 1998.

effectiveness assessment in the pre-project diagnostics. It is critical to note that although a significant number of projects (10 out of 38 TA projects under review) set the objective for revenue enhancement (see table 7.4), none ever established a benchmark for monitoring.

### *Key Features of Project Design*

Customs modernization is a complex and continuous process. It requires long-term commitments and a proper strategy for capacity building, which involves the development of systems, procedures, and processes, as well as staff competencies. The Revised Kyoto Convention on simplification and harmonization of customs procedures has sketched the vision of a modern customs organization and has provided guidelines for a customs reform strategy.[8] In his book *Customs Modernization and the*

*International Trade Superhighway* (1998), Lane develops a comprehensive and practical framework for customs reforms. The framework shows a pyramidal structure with the base consisting of the reform fundamentals (environment, customs expertise, and integrity) and enablers (analyze data, automate, manage processes), the middle level incorporating advanced processes (risk management, audit, compliance, and enforcement), and the top containing implementation processes (figure 7.1).[9] In this chapter, we apply this analytical framework to survey the design of the Bank's TA projects between 1982 and 2002.

Table 7.6 summarizes the scope of customs modernization activities in Bank TA projects. It not only lists project areas and activities but also includes key issues in project implementation such as sequencing, implementation plan, and coordination between customs administration and other related institutions. The past two decades have seen a steady evolution in the Bank's strategy to modernize customs: The project scope became consistently more

---

8. The WCO developed the original Convention in 1974 and revised it in 1999 to adapt to the changing nature of global trade through the 1980s and 1990s. The Convention, formally referred to as the International Convention on the Simplification and Harmonization of Customs Procedures, contains the basic principles for a modern customs administration and offers a blueprint for customs reform.

---

9. One of the Bank's projects, the Ghana Trade and Investment Gateway Project, used this framework in formulating its customs reforms activities.

**TABLE 7.6  Comprehensiveness of Project Design**

| | 1982–93 | | 1994–2002 | | 1982–2002 | |
|---|---|---|---|---|---|---|
| | Number of Projects | Share[a] | Number of Projects | Share[b] | Number of Projects | Share[c] |
| **Legislative Environment** | | | | | | |
| New codes or legislation[d] | 0 | 0 | 15 | 58 | 15 | 39 |
| New tariff structure[e] | 1 | 8 | 11 | 42 | 12 | 32 |
| Valuation[f] | 1 | 8 | 3 | 12 | 4 | 11 |
| Part of planned or ongoing customs reform strategy | 3 | 25 | 16 | 62 | 19 | 50 |
| **Process Management** | | | | | | |
| Process simplification | 5 | 42 | 22 | 85 | 27 | 71 |
| Coordination with other import clearance agencies | 0 | 0 | 14 | 54 | 14 | 37 |
| Automation | 8 | 67 | 24 | 92 | 32 | 84 |
| Risk management | 3 | 25 | 18 | 69 | 21 | 55 |
| **Management/Human Resources Development** | | | | | | |
| Recruitment procedures | 0 | 0 | 6 | 23 | 6 | 16 |
| Training | 7 | 58 | 20 | 77 | 27 | 71 |
| Salaries | 1 | 8 | 10 | 38 | 11 | 29 |
| Promotion | 1 | 8 | 4 | 15 | 5 | 13 |
| Penalty | 0 | 0 | 4 | 15 | 4 | 11 |
| Code of conduct[g] | 0 | 0 | 4 | 15 | 4 | 11 |
| Other aspects of integrity (facilities, auditing) | 1 | 8 | 13 | 50 | 14 | 37 |
| Customs and revenue department integration[h] | 0 | 0 | 2 | 8 | 2 | 5 |
| Informing or educating stakeholders | 1 | 8 | 15 | 58 | 16 | 42 |
| Analysis of data for better compliance and facilitation | 0 | 0 | 12 | 46 | 12 | 32 |
| **Change Management Sustainability** | | | | | | |
| Benefit package or policy to retain good staff | 0 | 0 | 3 | 12 | 3 | 8 |
| Government budget commitment[i] | 0 | 0 | 9 | 35 | 9 | 24 |
| Implementation plan specified | 4 | 33 | 16 | 62 | 20 | 53 |
| Sequencing (explicitly or adequately presented) | 1 | 8 | 3 | 12 | 4 | 11 |
| Monitoring and evaluation (performance indicators) | 1 | 8 | 16 | 62 | 17 | 45 |
| Project appraisal (financial and economic appraisal) | 2 | 17 | 14 | 54 | 16 | 42 |
| Bank's cooperation with other donors in project preparation or implementation envisaged | 2 | 17 | 15 | 58 | 17 | 45 |
| Project supervision or management staffing involving IMF, WCO, or UN Conference on Trade and Development | 2 | 17 | 14 | 54 | 16 | 42 |

a. Share of total TA projects reviewed during 1982–93 (12 projects).

b. Share of total TA projects reviewed during 1994–2002 (26 projects).

c. Share of total TA projects reviewed during 1982–2002 (38 projects).

d. New code or legislation is part of the project or is issued in other related programs.

e. New simplified tariff structure is part of the project or adopted in a related program.

f. Including any mention of revising valuation system or of the role of PSI or the shift to ACV.

g. Issued as part of the reviewed project or in a related effort to modernize customs administrations.

h. The integration has either taken place or is part of the reviewed project. Two projects in the sample began when the customs and revenue departments were merged.

i. Government commitments include the budget, political will, or regional trade liberalization (for example, the Southeast European countries involved in Trade and Transport Facilitation projects).

*Source:* Authors based on World Bank database.

comprehensive during 1994–2002 compared to 1982–93. Despite this trend toward a more comprehensive approach, projects did not always give sufficient importance to certain core reform issues. Key reform issues that were often neglected are improvement of the legislative framework for customs operations, change management, efficient coordination between customs agencies and other import clearance agencies, integrity, and sequencing in project implementation.

The majority of projects failed to focus sufficiently on change management issues. Administrative reforms can only succeed in a legal and regulatory environment that permits their full implementation. A typical example is the introduction of a risk-based selective physical control system and of post-release audits, which in many countries are not possible under the existing Customs Code. However, only 15 out of the 38 TA projects in the sample (39 percent) mentioned the need for modernizing and revising customs legislation. Most projects did not cover valuation issues in their design: valuation was mentioned in only 11 percent of the projects, which means that the Tokyo Round and the GATT Agreement on Customs Valuation (ACV) of 1980 were generally neglected.[10] Interestingly, no projects in the database included a PSI-related component (either strengthening a PSI regime or phasing out PSI) in their design, although PSI regimes were in place in some of the client countries at the time of project design (the Philippines and Tanzania, for example).[11]

There were few projects targeted at change management and sustainability. For example, only three projects (8 percent) planned to design a benefit package or policy to retain good staff. The RCDP is distinguished as a project that dealt with this issue most thoroughly. The human resources component of the project emphasized developing and implementing proposals for improving the remuneration and nonmonetary benefits of customs staff and managers—the purpose was to improve the capacity of the State Customs Committee (SCC) to recruit and retain qualified staff.

It is interesting to note that just half of the projects linked the customs component with a planned or ongoing customs reform strategy. This may be explained to some extent by the fact that in other cases, the government had not been ready to embark on comprehensive customs reforms.

Except for the RCDP, no project referred to the original WCO or Revised Kyoto Convention in its proposed customs reform activities. The proposed reform procedures focused primarily on process simplification—including the introduction of post-release audits and account management (71 percent), automation (84 percent), and training (71 percent). Despite the high emphasis on automation, just slightly more than half of all projects targeted the introduction of risk management (55 percent); this implies that the objective of automation was not always well defined and sufficiently linked to other critical reform components. An interesting fact is that few projects addressed the issue that customs is only one of several agencies involved in the import clearance process. The impact of customs reform measures on the effectiveness of the overall import clearance process can be strengthened considerably by either supporting additional complementary reforms in other import clearance agencies or at least supporting better coordination between the agencies involved in import clearance. However, only 14 out of the 38 projects reviewed emphasized the need for simultaneous reforms of these institutions and better coordination of the clearance process. Box 7.4 presents the case of the Tunisia Export Development Project, which highlights an integrated approach for streamlining the interagency coordination for handling imports and exports. This was also a major objective in the Ghana Trade and Investment Gateway Project.[12]

The analysis also shows an imbalance in the coverage of the various human resources management issues. While more than two-thirds of the TA projects covered training needs, most projects missed other critical human resources–related determinants of both success and sustainability of customs reforms such as recruitment procedures (only listed in 16 percent of the TA projects), salary and benefit structure (29 percent), or career management

---

10. The ACV aims for a fair, uniform, and neutral set of standards for valuation to avoid the use of arbitrary or fictitious values.

11. The Tanzania Tax Administration Project identified the existing issues related to PSI in its diagnostics, but it emphasized the PSI-related activities only during supervision missions.

12. See De Wulf (2004).

## BOX 7.4    Integrated Approach in Process Management: The Case of the Tunisia Export Development Project

The customs reform component in this Bank-supported project (approved fiscal year 1999; total approved amount US$34.7 million) is targeted at promoting trade in general and export in particular, while revenue enhancement is not a specific reform objective. The reforms combine the introduction of Electronic Data Interchange (EDI) with process simplification, cooperation and partnership, risk management, and human resources development. It was proposed that the EDI server be developed as a center to transform the existing complex web of manually-based cross-connected exchange of information through forms and messages among trade stakeholders (customs, banks, shipping agents, traders, customs brokers, freight forwarders, Ministry of Commerce, and Port Authority)—shown in box figure 1—to a new direct connection–based interrelation among the trade stakeholders (see box figure 2).

The customs reform component was designed in three subsequent phases. The first phase targets the simplification of procedures for submission of shipping manifests. The second phase promotes real time automated processing in responses to customs declarations. Also, post-event auditing techniques and risk management are to be adopted. The third phase focuses on training customs officers to enable them to uniformly implement new procedures and regulations.

*Source:* World Bank 1999c.

**Trade document processing—present situation**

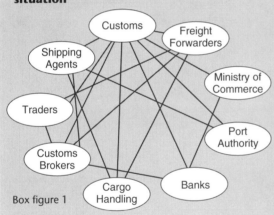

Box figure 1

**Trade document processing—after implementation of the component**

Box figure 2

(13 percent).[13] Considering that according to customer surveys customs administrations figure among the most corrupt government institutions in many countries, insufficient attention was given to integrity issues, which were not specifically addressed in the majority of projects. It was largely assumed that modernization of customs procedures would benefit integrity. Only 11 percent of the total TA projects reviewed included a revision of disciplinary measures and penalties to fight corruption and the development of a code of conduct

in their design; similarly, just 37 percent of the projects dealt with the introduction or improvement of the internal audit system.

While more than half the projects under review (53 percent) specified implementation plans, only 11 percent offered explicit and adequate sequencing of the reform activities. Very few projects actually provide an appropriate time line for implementation. A lack of focus on preparing an appropriate implementation plan can cause serious sequencing mistakes. In the Lebanon Revenue Enhancement and Fiscal Management Technical Assistance Project, for example, phase one of the ASYCUDA implementation was scheduled before the beginning of the business reengineering exercise, and

---

13. It is conceivable that the issue of salary cannot be easily resolved in isolation from overall civil service reforms or establishment of semi-autonomous revenue agencies.

---

**BOX 7.5    Increased Bank Emphasis on Coordination with Other Donors**

**Trade and Transport Facilitation Projects in Southeast Europe.** The customs modernization component in these projects was proposed as the least costly approach to complement the ongoing EU-supported customs reforms in these countries. The component used grants from the World Bank, EU, and the United States for most technical assistance. In the case of Bosnia and Herzegovina, the EU was committed to providing all technical support for customs reforms.

Donors were active in supporting the implementation and supervision of the projects. In particular, all donor representatives participated in the Regional Steering Committee (RSC) as observers in overseeing the overall implementation of the program. The active participation of the donors was to ensure that the customs modernization component would take full account of the ongoing reform efforts. In addition, the United Nations Economic Commission for Europe (UN-ECE) provided a secretary for each country RSC member to support the implementation of the program.

**Turkey Public Financial Management Project** (approved fiscal year 1996; approved amount US$62 million). The Bank and the IMF demonstrated close coordination from the proj-

ect design stage throughout the implementation stage. The Bank engaged the Fiscal Affairs Department (FAD) of the IMF to help with the implementation of the technical components of the customs modernization plan. FAD supervised the customs administration adviser, the information technology adviser appointed under the loan agreement, and the short-term advisers appointed to provide specific technical assistance. It was also agreed that FAD would make regular inspection missions (approximately every six months) and assist in assessing the pilot customs operation.

**Bangladesh Export Diversification Project** (approved fiscal year 1999; approved amount US$32 million). The government convinced the WCO that sufficient reform readiness existed to launch a WCO Customs Reform and Modernization Program for Bangladesh as part of the Export Diversification Project. The project planned to engage the WCO in customs administration staff training and UNCTAD in installation of ASYCUDA++ and related training.

*Sources:* World Bank 1995, 1999a, 2000a, 2000b, 2000c, 2000d, 2000h, 2001, 2002b.

---

training for ASYCUDA implementation was supposed to start only nine months after the launch of the first phase of ASYCUDA (World Bank 1994).

A cross-period comparison reveals consistent progress in project design, however. While almost all projects designed between 1982 and 1993 neglected the need for improving the legal and regulatory environment for customs operations, attention to such issues surged between 1994 and 2002. A substantially higher share of projects designed in the later period also paid sufficient attention to such crucial reform activities as process simplification (85 percent), automation (92 percent), and risk management (69 percent). Projects designed between 1994 and 2002 showed a significantly improved coverage of issues of coordination with other import clearance agencies, integrity, project evaluation, and customer service. Finally, the Bank's emphasis on cooperation, to various extents, with other donors in project preparation or implementation increased dramatically from 17 percent

during 1982–93 to 58 percent during the 1994–2002 (see box 7.5 for project-specific cases).

## Project Implementation and Outcomes

This section reviews 22 complete TA projects with customs components. Outcomes of the project implementation are presented and followed by an analysis of the factors that affect the outcomes and impacts of these projects.

### Project Implementation, Outcomes, and Issues

Evaluation work has two dimensions. The first deals with the lessons learned, and design and performance indicators are emphasized. A second phase should deal with the outcomes of projects reviewed, identifying elements that affect such outcomes. Of the 38 TA projects reviewed that were approved by the World Bank between 1982 and

**TABLE 7.7    Summary of Suggested Rating of Outcomes of Customs Activities**
(percent)

| | Closed Projects | Ongoing Projects |
|---|---|---|
| Projects with rated customs outcomes | 77 | 50 |
|    Moderately satisfactory (SAT) or better rating[a] | 50 | 38 |
|    Moderately unsatisfactory (UNSAT) or lower rating[b] | 27 | 12 |
| Projects with unrated customs outcomes[c] | 23 | 50 |
| Total | 100 | 100 |

a. Including High SAT, SAT, and Moderately SAT.

b. Including Moderately UNSAT, UNSAT, and Highly UNSAT.

c. Ratings could not be done due to various reasons, specifically lack of evaluation documents at the time the chapter was written; insufficient information from available documents; or customs component dropped during the implementation stage (for example, Ghana Economic Management Support Project).

*Source:* Authors based on World Bank database.

2002, 22 have been closed and permit a review of implementation and outcomes.[14] This analysis is based primarily on implementation complementation reports (ICRs) and OED evaluation reports, and to some extent, on project status reports (PSRs).[15] ICRs and OED evaluation reports use a uniform set of criteria for evaluation and cover pre-project preparation, design, implementation, institutional development impact, sustainability, and performance by the Bank and the borrower. An overview of specific definitions of criteria for OED evaluation reports is provided in annex 7.B.

We have also attempted to evaluate the implementation of customs components of ongoing projects. Our suggested rating of ongoing customs reform activities is based largely on internal documents such as mid-term reviews, internal memos, supervision reports, and PSRs. However, a substantial number of projects are not ready for such an evaluation, as they either were just newly approved and launched, or did not have sufficiently detailed reports on their implementation by the time this chapter was prepared.

Table 7.7 summarizes our suggested rating of customs components for both closed and active projects in the form of relative frequency. The results indicate that while the majority of rated customs activities were or are being satisfactorily implemented, a significant number of projects received low ratings.

To analyze the links between customs component outcomes and general issues of Bank quality at entry, and Bank and borrower performance, we attempted to estimate a number of correlation coefficients.[16] At the preliminary level, we estimate the correlation between the suggested rating of customs activities and the OED general rating of overall projects (panel A, table 7.8). Then we estimate the correlation of the suggested customs rating with the rating of quality of diagnostics and performance indicators—two proxies for the quality at

14. Our evaluation of the outcomes of the customs components are suggested in the sense that the evaluation is derived from the description of the implementation and outcomes of those components made in ICRs, OED evaluation, and PSRs. Our suggestive rating does not reflect the official rating by either the regions or OED. The rating is applicable to the outcomes of the customs components against their performance indicators if they are available or against their objectives as established in project documents.

15. Regions prepare ICRs for each lending operation using information and data from project preparation and appraisal as well as supervision reports. One of the objectives of ICRs is to "reinforce self-evaluations, including development impact assessment, by the Bank and borrowers" (Operations Policy and Country Services 2003, p. 2). OED, however, provides independent evaluation after the close of the project.

16. Quality at entry reflects the quality of the project design. The factors to be considered and rated include project concept, objectives, and approach during identification. The design is rated from various perspectives consisting of technical, economic and financial, environmental, poverty reduction and social, institutional, financial management, readiness of implementation, and assessment of risk and sustainability aspects. For a detailed description of the concept and criteria for rating of quality at entry, see "OED Evaluation Tools and Approaches" at www.worldbank.org/oed/oed_approach_summary.html.

**TABLE 7.8   Correlation Estimation: A Summary**

A. Correlation coefficients between suggested rating of customs outcomes and OED selective rating of projects overall (OED rating on both customs and noncustoms outcomes)

|  | General Project Outcomes | Bank Quality at Entry | Bank Supervision | Bank Overall | Borrower Overall |
|---|---|---|---|---|---|
| Customs outcome | 0.38 | 0.23 | 0.51 | 0.50 | 0.33 |

B. Correlation coefficients between suggested rating of customs outcomes and quality of diagnostics and performance indicators for customs components

|  | Diagnostics for Customs Components | Performance Indicators for Customs Components |
|---|---|---|
| Customs outcomes | 0.54 | 0.67 |

*Source:* Authors based on World Bank database.

entry—for the exclusive customs components (panel B, table 7.8). Annex 7.C explains the methodology and data for the correlation analysis. Table 7.8 shows positive but relatively weak correlation between the rating of the customs components and the OED general rating of the overall projects, Bank quality at entry, and borrower performance (the correlations range from 0.2 to 0.38). The coefficients of correlation between the customs component rating and Bank overall supervision and performance are somewhat higher (0.51 and 0.5, respectively).[17] The estimates may have been confounded by noncustoms components of projects, especially for the cases in which customs modernization is just a small part.

There is a relatively strong link between the quality of diagnostics and design of customs activities and their outcomes. Panel B, table 7.8 shows significant correlation between the suggested rating of outcomes of customs components and the two proxies for quality at entry of the customs components, specifically the quality of diagnostics and performance indicators (0.54 and 0.67, respectively). The results reaffirm the chain of impact from the quality of pre-project diagnostics to design to implementation of customs modernization activities embedded in the Bank-funded projects.

---

17. The results obscure the fact that there is strong correlation between outcomes of overall projects and their quality of design, Bank supervision, and Bank and borrower performance. For example, the correlation between general outcomes of projects and overall Bank quality at entry is robust at 0.9.

### Factors Affecting Outcomes and Impact

The outcomes and the institutional development impact of a project are dependent upon various factors, which, for the purpose of this analysis, are grouped into three major categories: (a) pre-project diagnostics and design, (b) appropriate project objectives and components, and (c) implementation and change management strategy. Some issues related to the sustainability of project outcomes are incorporated in the third category.

**Pre-Project Diagnostics and Design Problems**
The ICR and OED evaluation reports pinpointed a number of pre-project preparation and design problems leading to unsatisfactory implementation of some projects. These problems can be categorized as follows:

- *Noncomprehensive and isolated reform activities.* The review of the 38 TA projects indicates that the inclusion of customs components was largely consistent with the World Bank Country Assistance Strategies, or overall government development strategies, or both. However, some projects were targeted only at certain processes or organizational or human resources management issues without explicit coordination with specific planned or ongoing customs reforms in the borrowing country. Only 6 of the 22 completed projects, to different extents, linked the customs components with the countries' overall customs reforms. Such a piecemeal and isolated approach partly reflects the underestimation of the complexity of customs modernization, the lack of recognition of existing institutional barriers to reforms, and a lack of experience in designing customs reform projects.

- *Design mismatch between proposed reform activities and level of funding, and insufficient coordination with other donors.* Some projects proved to be too ambitious in their coverage in the face of a clear lack of funding. Project design and implementation became troublesome, especially when there were no apparent efforts to coordinate the technical assistance with other donors or to incorporate the project into a long-term Bank assistance strategy. Donor coordination was exercised in only 5 of the 22 closed projects.
- *Mismatch between project design and government interest.* In some cases, the government's objectives and interests were not properly taken into account in the project preparation and design. A government commitment to support the reforms was assumed, but assumptions in certain instances did not reflect the reality. As a result, lack of government commitment negatively affected the project even in the earliest stages of implementation.
- *Hurried preparation without proper analysis.* A number of projects were designed without diagnostic analysis or failed to pay attention to the proper sequencing of activities.

Box 7.6 illustrates the problems with some project-specific cases.

### Amendments to Objectives and Components

The review of the 22 closed TA projects reveals that, while a large majority of projects (65 percent) did not change specified objectives, more than half (approximately 55 percent) revised their components.[18] The revision of objectives or reshuffle of funding or modification of components of a project does not necessarily mean that the project design was inappropriate. There are basically two types of developments leading to a change in the set objectives or components. The first includes unexpected changes in the project environment regardless of the quality of the pre-project diagnostics and the

project design. The second is triggered during implementation and becomes necessary to adjust for poor component design. For the success and sustainability of a project, problems of the second type should be avoided, but it is nonetheless better to make necessary modifications to project components than to stick to an original bad design. Box 7.7 illustrates some specific issues that have caused the change of project objectives or components.

### Project Implementation and Change Management

The following main reasons have been identified for failures in project implementation and change management to sustain the outcomes of the project: (a) weak project management (by the Bank and the client government) and supervision;[19] (b) lack of ownership, commitment, and accountability; (c) inadequate coordination with other donors; and (d) lack of a change management strategy for sustainability. Box 7.8 illustrates major implementation management problems.

### Main Conclusions and Lessons for Future Bank Operations to Support Customs Modernization

Customs reform has been addressed in Bank projects from very different angles. Customs reform has been covered as one of many elements of investment and technical assistance or structural adjustment projects. Support for customs reform has been granted in the context of a broader public sector reform objective recognizing that customs is a major and powerful government institution, which in many countries faces serious integrity problems. Even with the reduction of trade taxes and tariff rates, customs remains a key institution for securing revenue collection, given its crucial role in administering the VAT. Customs reform has also been included in trade facilitation operations, given its importance in the export and import process. Finally, customs reforms have been included in infrastructure improvement projects, in particular port rehabilitation projects, to support the main objectives of these projects.

---

18. The shares are estimated on the basis of a subsample of 20 complete projects because the ICRs for two projects were still in progress when the chapter was written.

19. The review of the completed projects indicate some typical problems in the borrower's performance in customs modernization, including the lack of coordination between customs and other related agencies, and frequent change of customs management that puts continuity in efforts for reform at risk.

---

**BOX 7.6    Quality of Pre-Project Preparation and Design Matter:
Two Project-Specific Cases**

**Argentina Public Sector Management Technical Assistance Project** (approved FY86; approved loan amount US$18.5 million; customs reform component approved loan amount: US$ 2.4 million; suggested customs outcome rating: UNSAT). This project illustrates the mismatch between ambitious design and funding level. While all ratings of the project as a whole were favorable—except for the unsatisfactory rating of the borrower's performance—the customs component clearly failed. The ICR lists a number of problems:

- Defined project objective—strengthening the capacity of the National Customs Administration to collect import duties and export taxes, to simplify export procedures, and to provide a statistical base for monitoring exports—were overly ambitious while the level of commitment to real reform of the customs system was not apparent at the time. Funding was insufficient with just US$900,000, and the project was prepared without a clear mandate in government to carry out profound reforms.
- Lack of clarity of the initially proposed list of activities, substantive disagreements as to the appropriate direction for activities, and an early decision to use the French model as a reference for the reform of the Argentine Customs Administration, which met serious resistance from within the Coordinating Unit indicate a lack of careful preparation of the proposed activities and costs. The project failure was attributed to the narrowing of the scope of the project component to diagnostic activities and the preparation of a new program on the modernization and reorganization of Customs. A majority of funds were therefore reallocated. Ultimately, the project managed to absorb only US$77,616 for the automation of the National Customs Administration.

**The Philippines Tax Computerization Project** (Customs reform component approved loan amount: US$20.3 million; suggested customs outcome rating: SAT). The quality at entry for all project components was rated as unsatisfactory. Although the final outcome of the project for the customs modernization component was rated as satisfactory, the ICR and OED highlighted the following shortcomings in designing the customs activities:

- Underestimated the difficulties of customs software development and maintenance ventures for the BOC. The Staff Appraisal Report (SAR) failed to diagnose properly the risk in the overall project implementation. It discounted the risk that the project might not be able to retain adequately trained and qualified staff; instead, it predicted that massive training programs would lessen the risk. In addition, the SAR underestimated the institutional constraints (civil service salaries, for example) to the project implementation and sustainability.
- The SAR did not include performance benchmarks.
- The SAR underestimated the change management needed for an agency modernization effort of this large scale. Specifically, the SAR did not explicitly link the project with the need for each agency to modernize, reorganize, and reengineer business processes prior to computerization. Nor did it recognize the need to improve the quality and efficiency of communication among the Bureau of Internal Revenue, BOC, and the Department of Finance. It is particularly interesting that these problems occurred in the design process, even though the diagnostics clearly identified problems with administration and communication.

*Sources:* World Bank 1993a, 2000f, 2000g.

---

Comprehensive capacity-building projects targeting customs administrations specifically are the exception and not the rule in Bank operations. Bank projects tend to focus both in the pre-project diagnostics as well as in the project design on specific elements of customs organization, management, or processes. Project staff appeared insufficiently aware that organizational design, management, and procedural issues of other than the target elements are interrelated with, and dependent for their good operation on, a coherent set of process changes. Thus, these projects ran the risk of underestimating the complexity of customs reform and the comprehensiveness in the reform approach required to achieve sustainable results. A partial approach to customs reform, therefore, jeopardizes

## BOX 7.7 What Triggered the Modification of Project Objectives or Components

**Tanzania Port Modernization Project II** (approved fiscal year 1990; approved amount US$37 million; customs reform component approved loan amount: US$2.0 million;, suggested customs outcome rating: SAT). The main original objective of the project was to expand the physical, managerial, and operational capabilities of the Tanzania Harbors Authority (THA) to meet the traffic volume expected in the 1990s. The project was intended to provide technical assistance to customs for introducing a simplified documentation process, computerization, and training of customs officers. The project, however, revised its objectives for two reasons—the establishment of a new semi-autonomous revenue agency, the Tanzania Revenue Authority (TRA), and the promotion of regional integration that triggered the need to provide support for customs and transit controls. With the establishment of the TRA in 1994, the Development Credit Agreement in 1995 added a sentence highlighting the need for strengthening and streamlining the TRA. In addition, the project added an additional component for reforming the customs wing in the TRA, focusing on rehabilitation and strengthening of border stations and their computerization.

**Mozambique First Road and Coastal Shipping Project** (approved fiscal year 1992; amount approved: US$74.3 million; customs reform component approved loan amount: US$0.8 million; suggested customs outcome rating: SAT). The project modified its components during the implementation to reflect the new environment and to compensate for an omission of a key project component in the project design. Specifically, in 1994, following the establishment of a Customs Restructuring Technical Unit (UTRA) in the Ministry of Planning and Finance, the Customs and Trade Facilitation Activity, which was under the Small Ports and Coastal Shipping Component, emerged as a separate component managed directly by UTRA. The restructuring of customs operations required adequate staff training. However, a training component was omitted in the project design stage and therefore was added during project implementation. The modification contributed to the success of the customs component. All key performance benchmarks for customs as projected in the last Project Supervision Report were achieved, and import duty rates of collection increased from 6 percent in 1996 to 11 percent in 1999.

**The Philippines Tax Computerization Project.** The project added one objective to meet the new emerging demand for better communications: A system called FINLINK was set up for the Department of Finance to communicate with other government agencies responsible for tax collection and fiscal management (Bureau of Internal Revenue, BOC, Bureau of Trade, Central Bank, Land Registration Authority, and others).

*Sources:* World Bank 2000e, 2000f, 2000g, 2000i.

the expected efficiency and effectiveness gains in customs operations, and places sustainability at risk. Other weaknesses in the projects reviewed are related to the ad hoc nature of the diagnostic work, the insufficient attention given to performance indicators, inadequate attention to proper sequencing of project components, and commitment of government to provide adequate funding to sustain the project's achievements, particularly with respect to IT maintenance and upgrading. Projects too often considered customs as an isolated link in the trade logistics chain, so that progress achieved in customs often did not translate to overall trade facilitation given the dysfunctionalities of other trade-related agencies and infrastructure services.

The review highlights that project preparation and design have substantially improved in the

1990s, and there are a number of more recent customs reform projects that can serve as guides to good practice.

In 1999 the Bank's Tax Policy and Tax Administration Thematic Group published a Policy Research Working Paper on "Reforming Tax Systems: The World Bank Records in the 1990s." This paper includes a number of suggestions to improve Bank assistance for revenue administration reform, covering both tax and customs administrations. The suggestions given in this paper remain relevant and are repeated in annex 7.D. Based on this review it is now possible to add several other customs-specific recommendations:

• When preparing a customs reform TA project, the standards of the Revised Kyoto Convention

---

### BOX 7.8    Implementation Management Issues: The Case of the Senegal Development Management Project

The Senegal project (approved fiscal year 1988; approved amount US$17 million; customs reform component approved loan amount: US$2.2 million; suggested customs outcome rating: UNSAT) failed in all rating criteria in both ICR and OED evaluations. For the customs-specific component, the training of customs staff was conducted in an ad hoc manner in the absence of a needs assessment and a coherent policy to link training to job effectiveness. In addition to other design problems, especially the mismatch between the scope of the project and borrower commitment, multiple—and combined—shortcomings led to the poor project outcomes:

**Frequent changes in project management and poor supervision coordination.** Over the eight-and-half-years of the project, six different task managers were responsible for the project and 11 supervision missions were made with significant differences in the understanding of the project objectives.

**Poor quality of supervision assessment.** Weak supervision failed to catch problems and to suggest timely modifications. In fact, supervision ratings on development objectives and institutional development remained high in spite of serious problems.

**Inadequate action by Bank management.** During the implementation, Bank management ignored warnings from staff pointing at the lack of commitment of the government of Senegal; and failed to object to the continued favorable ratings on development objectives and institutional performance, while it became obvious that progress was slow and limited.

*Sources:* World Bank 1997b. OED Evaluation Summary 2004.

---

should be used to the extent possible as benchmarks for expected project results. As discussed in chapter 3, the Revised Kyoto Convention provides important guidelines for the design and operation of a modern and efficient customs organization.

- Diagnostic work would benefit from drawing on existing tools for the assessment of strengths and weaknesses of customs administrations.
- A comprehensive set of performance indicators with practical benchmarks must be developed to monitor project implementation. These indicators should cover both efficiency and effectiveness of customs reform activities.
- Customs is only one of several import and export clearance agencies. Reform projects should make an extra effort to include these other agencies in the analysis and investigate the possibilities of streamlining the overall clearance process. Improving the coordination between customs and other agencies would be a critical cost effective approach to enhance the clearance process and to strengthen enforcement.
- Specific, partial customs reform components of broader, noncustoms-focused TA projects can be justified. However, the project preparation and design need to make sure that a sufficiently comprehensive institutional diagnosis has been carried out, that the specific reform activities

supported by the project are linked to a more general and long-term customs reform strategy, and that the implementation of this component is adequately monitored.

- The Bank had until recently limited in-house expertise and staff capacity to prepare and supervise customs reform projects. Cooperation with other multilateral agencies with specific expertise in customs reform, in particular the IMF and WCO, should be strengthened to facilitate high quality project preparation and supervision. In fiscal year 2004, the Bank strengthened its in-house expertise in the customs area.
- To improve the chances of achieving sustainable outcomes, government commitment to finance follow-up costs after project closure, relating to IT and infrastructure maintenance and replacement costs in particular, should be sought early in the project preparation stage.
- Considering the high incidence of corruption in customs administrations, special attention must be given to designing an anticorruption strategy as part of a comprehensive customs reform TA project. Yet it should be recognized that integrity is not built by standalone integrity actions. Integrity is largely the outcome of the efficient application of good procedures consistent with the Revised Kyoto Convention. Integrity-specific modules of the project design need to be

dovetailed to this overall customs modernization model, and can make a substantial contribution.

- The importance of change management should not be underestimated and a sufficiently high budget should be allocated to change management activities.
- The borrower's political commitment at the top and commitment by the customs administration should be more clearly sought and expressed.
- Donor coordination in the design stage of a customs modernization and reform process has a very high payoff.

- The definition of an exit strategy is important to ensure sustainability of the reform. Once the moneys of an operation are fully disbursed, the Bank signs off and no additional resources for ensuring sustainability materialize. Therefore, it is critical to build bridges with the private sector to ensure sustainability of the reform process.

## Annex 7.A Distribution of Projects with Customs Components by Region, 1982–2002

**Table 7.A.1  Distribution of Projects with Customs Components by Region, 1982–2002**
(shares in percent)

Distribution of Technical Assistance Projects

| Fiscal Year | 1982–86 | | 1987–91 | | 1992–96 | | 1997–2002 | | 1982–2002 | |
|---|---|---|---|---|---|---|---|---|---|---|
| Region | Number of Projects | Share | Number of Projects | Share | Number of Projects | Share | Number of Projects | Share | Number of Projects | Share |
| Sub-Saharan Africa | 1 | 33 | 5 | 71 | 3 | 38 | 2 | 10 | 11 | 29 |
| East Asia and Pacific | | | | | 1 | 13 | 1 | 5 | 2 | 5 |
| Europe and Central Asia | | | 1 | 14 | 3 | 38 | 12 | 60 | 16 | 42 |
| Latin America and Caribbean | 2 | 67 | 1 | 14 | | | 2 | 10 | 5 | 13 |
| Middle East and North Africa | | | | | 1 | 13 | 1 | 5 | 2 | 5 |
| South Asia | | | | | | | 2 | 10 | 2 | 5 |
| Total | 3 | 100 | 7 | 100 | 8 | 100 | 20 | 100 | 38 | 100 |

Distribution of Structural Adjustment Projects

| Fiscal Year | 1982–86 | | 1987–91 | | 1992–96 | | 1997–2002 | | 1982–2002 | |
|---|---|---|---|---|---|---|---|---|---|---|
| Region | Number of Projects | Share | Number of Projects | Share | Number of Projects | Share | Number of Projects | Share | Number of Projects | Share |
| Sub-Saharan Africa | 1 | 20 | 7 | 37 | 13 | 45 | 8 | 31 | 29 | 37 |
| East Asia and Pacific | 1 | 20 | 1 | 5 | 3 | 10 | 1 | 4 | 6 | 8 |
| Europe and Central Asia | | | | | 2 | 7 | 10 | 38 | 12 | 15 |
| Latin America and Caribbean | | | 8 | 42 | 7 | 24 | 2 | 8 | 17 | 22 |
| Middle East and North Africa | 2 | 40 | 2 | 11 | 3 | 10 | 5 | 19 | 12 | 15 |
| South Asia | 1 | 20 | 1 | 5 | 1 | 3 | | | 3 | 4 |
| Total | 5 | 100 | 19 | 100 | 29 | 100 | 26 | 100 | 79 | 100 |

*Source:* Authors' calculations.

## Annex 7.B Selected Criteria for OED Project Evaluations

The following is a summary of the indicators use by OED (see OED 2004) for evaluating projects after completion, using an objectives-based approach.

*Relevance of Objectives.* The extent to which the project's objectives are consistent with the country's current development priorities and with current Bank country and sectoral assistance strategies and corporate goals (expressed in Poverty Reduction Strategy Papers, Country Assistance Strategies, Sector Strategy Papers, Operational Policies).

*Efficacy.* The extent to which the project's objectives were achieved, or expected to be achieved, taking into account their relative importance.

*Efficiency.* The extent to which the project achieved, or is expected to achieve, a return higher than the opportunity cost of capital at least cost compared to alternatives.

*Outcomes.* The extent to which the project's major relevant objectives were achieved, or are expected to be achieved, efficiently.

*Sustainability.* The resilience to risk of net benefit flows over time.

*Institutional Development Impact.* The extent to which a project improves the ability of a country or region to make more efficient, equitable, and sustainable use of its human, financial, and natural resources through (a) better definition, stability, transparency, enforceability, and predictability of institutional arrangements or (b) better alignment of the mission and capacity of an organization with its mandate, which derives from these institutional arrangements, or both. IDI includes both intended and unintended effects of a project.

*Bank Performance.* The extent to which services provided by the Bank ensured quality at entry and supported implementation through appropriate supervision (including ensuring adequate transition arrangements for regular operation of the project).

*Borrower Performance.* The extent to which the borrower assumed ownership and responsibility to ensure quality of preparation and implementation, and complied with covenants and agreements, toward the achievement of development objectives and sustainability.

## Annex 7.C Correlation Estimation

The correlation coefficient measures the association between two variables. It is unit free and hence insensitive to the unit of measurement of the two variables. The following formula is used to calculate the coefficient of correlation between $x$ and $y$ for a sample.

$$\rho_{xy} = \frac{\delta_{xy}}{\delta_x \delta_y}$$

Where, $\delta_{xy}$ is the sample covariance between $x$ and $y$, and is estimated as

$$\delta_{xy} = \frac{\sum (x_i - \mu_x)(y_i - \mu_y)}{N - 1}$$

(N is the number of observations in the sample, and $\mu_x, \mu_y$ are the means of $x$ and $y$ respectively.)

The standard deviations of $x$ and $y$, respectively, are $\delta_x$ and $\delta_y$. Note, a sample standard deviation of a variable ($x$, for example) is the square root of sample variance estimated as follows:

$$\delta^2 = \frac{\sum_{1}^{N}(x_i - \mu)^2}{N - 1}$$

To specify the relationship between outcomes of customs components and selected OED ratings of the general quality at entry and overall project implementation as well as the impact of quality of pre-project design and design of specific customs modernization activities on customs outcomes, we estimate a series of correlation. The data include (a) our suggested rating of outcomes of customs components and quality of diagnostics and performance indicators applicable to the customs components, and (b) OED rating of overall outcomes of projects, Bank quality at entry, Bank supervision, and overall Bank and borrower performance.

Our ratings of the outcomes of customs components, the customs diagnostics, and performance indicators are suggested on the basis of the project documents and any available Bank midterm review, internal memos, supervision report, project appraisal documents, ICR, or OED evaluation documents. The set of correlations between customs outcomes and the OED overall project rating is estimated from the sample of 22 completed projects. However, the correlation between customs outcomes and quality of customs diagnostics and performance indicators is estimated from the combined set of completed and ongoing projects. Projects with nonrated customs components are removed from the samples used to estimate correlation.

There are six levels of rating applicable for correlation estimation: highly satisfactory, satisfactory, moderately satisfactory, moderately unsatisfactory, unsatisfactory, and highly unsatisfactory. To estimate correlations, we assign numeric codes to the ratings that range from 1 to 6, with 6 given to a highly satisfactory rating and 1 given to a highly unsatisfactory rating. The coding is set consistently across all variables.

## Annex 7.D Reforming Tax Systems: The World Bank Record in the 1990s

The following excerpt from Barbone and others (1999) provides suggestions for improving World Bank assistance for revenue administration reform. The suggestions are relevant for both tax and customs reform projects.

### Diagnosis

1. Pre-project diagnostic work should be based on a comprehensive framework that pays sufficient attention to institutions in addition to traditional concerns of tax administrators. Ideally, a single but flexible framework should be adopted throughout the Bank.
2. Diagnostic performance measurement should be done, where possible, quantitatively according to standard indicators and against preferably cross-country benchmarks.
3. Pre-project work should also include a review (or citation) of the key determinants of good administration and project implementation.

### Design

4. Project design should be based on a strategic vision of the administration, and pay adequate attention to good governance, but should, nevertheless, be limited in scope given a country's implementation capacity. Alternative designs and sequencing should be analyzed and their rationale provided.
5. To generate long-term lessons, projects should specify hypotheses being tested.

### Performance Indicators

6. A standard set of outcome performance (effectiveness, efficiency, accountability) indicators for tax and customs administrators should be specified, to be drawn on for all projects.
7. Diagnostic work should give rise to pre-project base values of performance indicators for outcome assessment.
8. Outcome performance indicators for projects should not only permit project performance to be tracked, but should be chosen to permit hypotheses to be evaluated.
9. The use of taxpayer surveys should be an integral part of both diagnostic work and performance appraisal if not precluded by cost considerations.
10. Standard guidelines for quantitative input, process, and output indicators should be laid down and mandated.

### Appraisal

11. A standard, quantitative appraisal framework or tool needs to be developed for tax administration projects. If possible, this should be linked to an economic impact assessment, and a model such as the 1-2-3 model developed by DEC should be incorporated in this tool.
12. The tool should be designed to allow for risk assessment and sensitivity to key parameters like shadow values.

### Post-Project Evaluation

13. The use of performance indicators specified in the project is essential if the evaluation is to have comparability across projects.
14. The assignment of outcome, sustainability, institutional development, and Bank–borrower performance rankings should, as far as possible, be based on the quantitative indicators specified.

15. To facilitate the knowledge-gathering and hypothesis-testing role of projects (lessons learned), greater involvement of academic consultants could be desirable in diagnostic, design, and evaluation phases.

## Further Reading

Barbone, Luca, Arindam Das-Gupta, Luc De Wulf, and Anna Hansson. 1999. "Reforming Tax Systems: The World Bank Record in the 1990s." Policy Research Working Paper 2237. Washington, D.C.: The World Bank.

European Commission Directorate General XXI, Taxation and Customs Union. 1998. *Blueprints to Improve the Operational Capacity of Customs Administrations of Candidate Countries.* Brussels: European Commission.

Gill, Jit B. S. 2000. "A Diagnostic Framework for Revenue Administration." World Bank Technical Paper No. 472. Washington D.C.: The World Bank. Available at www1.worldbank.org/publicsector/tax/DiagnosticFramework.pdf.

Lane, Michael H. 1998. *Customs Modernization and the International Trade Superhighway.* Westport, Conn.: Quorum Books.

OED. 2004. *OED Evaluation Tools and Approaches.* Washington D.C.: The World Bank. Available at www.worldbank.org/oed/oed_approach_summary.html

Operations Policy and Country Services. 2003. *Guidelines for Preparing Implementation Completion Reports.* Washington D.C.: The World Bank. Available at http://opcs.worldbank.org/opcil/icrguide.html.

Raven, John. 2001. *Trade and Transport Facilitation—A Toolkit for Audit, Analysis and Remedial Action.* Washington, D.C.: The World Bank. Available at www.worldbank.org/transport/publicat/twu-46.pdf.

World Customs Organization. 1998. "*Integrity and Customs Administration: A Self-Assessment Guide, 'Putting the WCO Arusha Declaration into Action.'*" Malacca, Malaysia.

## References

Barbone, Luca, Arindam Das-Gupta, Luc De Wulf, and Anna Hansson. 1999. "Reforming Tax Systems: The World Bank Record in the 1990s." Policy Research Working Paper 2237. Washington, D.C.: The World Bank.

De Wulf, Luc. 2004. "TradeNet in Ghana: Best Practice in the Use of Information Technology." In Luc De Wulf and José B. Sokol, eds. *Customs Modernization Initiatives.* Washington, D.C.: The World Bank.

Gill, Jit B. S. 2000. "A Diagnostic Framework for Revenue Administration." World Bank Technical Paper No. 472. Washington D.C.: The World Bank. Available at www1.worldbank.org/publicsector/tax/DiagnosticFramework.pdf.

Lane, Michael. 1998. *Customs Modernization and the International Trade Superhighway.* Westport, Conn.: Quorum Books.

Operations Evaluation Department. 2004. "Evaluation Tools and Approaches." Washington, D.C.: The World Bank. www.worldbank.org/oed/oed_approach_summary.html.

Operations Policy and Country Services. 2003. *Guidelines for Preparing Implementation Completion Reports.* Washington, D.C.: The World Bank.

World Bank. 1993a. "Argentina Public Sector Management Technical Assistance Project." ICR Report No. 12124. June 30. Washington, D.C.

——— 1993b. "The Philippines Tax Computerization Project." Staff Appraisal Report, No. 11355-PH. Washington, D.C.

——— 1994. "Lebanese Republic Revenue Enhancement and Fiscal Management Technical Assistance Project." Report No. P-6374-LEB. June 10. Washington, D.C.

——— 1995. "Republic of Turkey— Public Financial Management Project." Report No. 14656-TU, vol. 3. Washington, D.C.

——— 1997a. "Armenia—Second Structural Adjustment Technical Assistance Credit." Project Information Document No. 5430. Washington, D.C.

——— 1997b. "Senegal—Development Management Project." Report No. 17247. Washington, D.C.

——— 1998. "Senegal Development Management Project." OED Evaluation Summary. February 24. Washington, D.C.

——— 1999a. "Bangladesh—Export Diversification Project." Report No. 19250. Washington, D.C.

——— 1999b. "Tanzania—Tax Administration Project." Report No. 17713. Washington, D.C.

——— 1999c. "Tunisia—Export Development Project." Report No. 18778. Washington, D.C.

——— 2000a. "Albania—Trade and Transport Facilitation in Southeast Europe Project." Report No. 20828. Washington, D.C.

——— 2000b. "Bulgaria—Trade and Transport Facilitation in Southeast Europe Project." Report No. 20036. Washington, D.C.

——— 2000c. "Croatia—Trade and Transport Facilitation in Southeast Europe Project." Report No. 20459. Washington, D.C.

——— 2000d. "Macedonia—Trade and Transport Facilitation in Southeast Europe Project." Report No. 20493. Washington, D.C.

——— 2000e. "Mozambique First Roads and Coastal Shipping Project." Report No. 20682. June 29. Washington, D.C.

——— 2000f. "Philippines Tax Computerization Project." ICR Report No. 20554. June 29. Washington, D.C.

——— 2000g. "Philippines Tax Computerization Project." OED Evaluation Report: August 16. Washington, D.C.

——— 2000h. "Romania—Trade and Transport Facilitation in Southeast Europe Project." Report No. 20407. Washington, D.C.

——— 2000i. "Tanzania Port Modernization Project II." Report No. 21559. December 28. Washington, D.C.

——— 2001. "Bosnia and Herzegovina—Trade and Transport Facilitation in Southeast Europe Project." Report No. 20714. Washington, D.C.

——— 2002a. "Russian Federation—Customs Development Project." Report No. 24232. Washington, D.C.

——— 2002b. "Yugoslavia—Trade and Transport Facilitation in Southeast Europe Project." Report No. 23888. Washington, D.C.

——— 2003. "Russian Federation Customs Development Project." PAD Report No. 24690-RU. March 12. Washington, D.C.

# PART III

# GUIDELINES ON ISSUES THAT AFFECT CUSTOMS' OPERATIONAL TRADE FACILITATION

# CUSTOMS VALUATION IN DEVELOPING COUNTRIES AND THE WORLD TRADE ORGANIZATION VALUATION RULES

*Adrien Goorman and Luc De Wulf*

## TABLE OF CONTENTS

## LIST OF TABLES

## LIST OF BOXES

The lack of understanding of customs valuation and of its supporting procedures are two of the

principal factors minimizing the efficiency of the customs administrations in many developing countries. The absence of effective customs valuation systems affects the outcome of a country's customs and trade policies, endangers its revenue

Special thanks for the valuable comments received from Ms. Lee Deegan of the Australian Customs and previously of the World Customs Organization.

mobilization performance, and aggravates integrity issues. Customs valuation systems have been the subject of international agreements because they can constitute barriers to trade. The World Trade Organization (WTO) Agreement on Customs Valuation (ACV) mandates the use of the ACV for all WTO members. The ACV establishes that the customs value of imported goods, to the greatest extent possible, is the transaction value, that is, the price actually paid or payable for the goods. Despite receiving substantial technical assistance (TA), many developing countries have not succeeded in adequately implementing the WTO valuation standard.

A full appreciation of the central issue of this chapter—the difficulties that many developing countries find in implementing the ACV, together with measures that could overcome these difficulties—requires a good understanding of the complex nature of customs valuation and the constraints developing countries face in the practice of customs valuation. This chapter, therefore, briefly notes the nature and significance of customs valuation systems and practices and their international standardization. It provides insights into the difficulties experienced by developing countries in customs valuation and in implementing the ACV. It also examines the type of measures that could contribute to effective valuation of import shipments. The first section highlights the significance of customs valuation and its historical development. The second section reviews the main characteristics of the ACV. The third section deals with the problem of ACV implementation in developing countries. The fourth section proposes measures to address these problems. The fifth section reviews the role of PSI services and other programs in the customs valuation area. The final section provides the key operational conclusions of the chapter.

## Significance and Historic Overview of Customs Valuation

Most import tariffs are based on *ad valorem* duties, that is, a rate expressed as a percentage of the value of the imported good. Customs valuation is the determination of the amount upon which the rate of duty is calculated.[1] While these rates are unambiguously fixed by statute in a tariff schedule, the declared value of imported goods may differ from transaction to transaction. This has three important implications for tariff policy. First, an importer may engage in underinvoicing and not declare the full value of the shipment to reduce his duty liabilities. Unless the underinvoicing is detected, government revenue is lost, and the importer receives an unfair advantage compared to its competitors. Second, governments can take advantage of the valuation system to increase or decrease duty liabilities for revenue or protective purposes, thereby offsetting tariff concessions made under multilateral or bilateral trade agreements. Third, undervaluation and overvaluation are used for capital flight.

For these reasons, a valuation standard is needed both at national and international levels to ensure that the correct duty is levied and a level playing field exists for all importers. It is also needed to enhance transparency and predictability of international transactions. Good valuation standards and practices enhance trade facilitation and contribute to the preparation of good trade statistics.

### *International Valuation Standards*

Customs valuation systems have been the subject of a number of international harmonization and standardization efforts. International efforts toward harmonization began in the early 20th century, but significant results did not come until the 1947 General Agreement on Tariffs and Trade (GATT). This Agreement was followed by the 1950 Convention on the Valuation of Goods for Customs Purposes, establishing the Brussels Definition of Value (BDV) and the 1979 Agreement on Implementation of Article VII of the GATT (ACV), resulting from the Tokyo Round. At the 1994 Uruguay Round, a decision (based on Article 17 of the GATT Valuation Agreement) was reached regarding the cases where customs administrations have reasons to doubt the truth or accuracy of the declared value.

---

1. When tariffs are based on specific duty rates, that is, a given amount of duty per unit of good, value does not have an impact on the duty. Thus, value determination is not needed for assessing duties, although valuation is required for statistical purposes and for nonduty charges.

**Valuation Principles: Article VII of the GATT**  The first significant international agreement on customs valuation was reached at the 1947 GATT negotiations that established principles to be adhered to by trading partners. These principles, embodied in GATT's Article VII, emphasize that customs value should not be arbitrary, fictitious, or based on value of indigenous goods. It should be real and based on the actual value of the imported goods or like goods. Customs value should derive from a sale or offer of sale in the ordinary course of business under fully competitive conditions. If the actual value is not ascertainable, customs value should be based on the nearest ascertainable equivalent of such value using prescribed criteria. These principles have remained the basis for customs valuation since then.

**Brussels Definition of Value**  The first international standard based on the GATT valuation principles, the BDV, was introduced in 1950. The BDV is based on the concept of "normal price"—the price that the goods would obtain under open market conditions between unrelated buyers and sellers under specified conditions of time and place. In practice, as the bulk of imports are the subject of a bona fide sale effected in conditions consistent with the terms of the definition, the transaction or invoice price can be taken as a valid basis for valuation for the majority of imports. The BDV recommends that the invoice price be used to the greatest extent possible. Where the invoice price cannot be used, such as with transactions that are not at arm's length, with goods on consignment, with importations by agents and concessionaries, or when the declared price is suspiciously low, customs can use another suitable basis to construe the normal price, using available information and taking into account the actual conditions relating to the transaction being valued. This flexibility is severely restricted under the ACV.

BDV acceptance represented substantial progress toward the international standardization of valuation systems. By 1970, about 100 countries applied the BDV (many on a de facto basis), and several economic associations had adopted it as their valuation standard—the European Economic Community (EEC), Customs Union of Central African States (UDEAC), and Caribbean Common Market (CARICOM). However, a number of important

trading countries (the United States and New Zealand, among others) did not adopt the BDV and continued to apply their own systems, largely based on the positive concept of value. Some others adopted the BDV when it was extended to cover FOB countries (Australia, for example) whereas Canada continued to use a fair market value in the export country, leading it to undertake investigations in the country of export. Moreover, the BDV itself was not always applied uniformly, and exporters complained about discretionary and unjustified rejection of the invoice price and uplifting of the declared value by customs. In addition, many countries relied on reference prices for protective purposes and for facilitating customs clearance without endangering budget revenues. Negotiations on customs valuation were therefore included in the negotiations on nontariff barriers at the Tokyo Round GATT negotiations (1973–1979).

**The Tokyo Round and the Agreement on Customs Valuation**  The purpose of the negotiations on customs valuation at the Tokyo Round was to arrive at a fair, uniform, and neutral standard of value that precludes the use of arbitrary or fictitious values, conforms to commercial realities, and does not act as a barrier to trade.[2] Following difficult negotiations between industrialized and developing countries, agreement was reached on a new valuation standard, the Agreement on Implementation of Article VII of the GATT.[3]

Developing countries entered the negotiations by fully supporting the EEC valuation draft proposals, mainly based on the BDV. But the EEC, following separate understandings with the United States, dropped its support for the BDV and opted for the positive concept of valuation. This concept provided that, with few exceptions, the value should be determined on the basis of the price actually paid or payable for the imported goods. The exceptions were listed, as were the five alternate methods that were to be applied in strict hierarchical order when the primary method, the transaction value, could not be applied.

---

2. The Tokyo Round objective was to achieve the expansion and ever greater liberalization of world trade through the progressive dismantling of obstacles to trade.

3. Generally referred to as the GATT Valuation Code (GVC) until the Uruguay Round, and since then as the ACV.

Developing countries objected strongly to the new proposal, particularly to its failure to provide sufficient authority to customs to reject transaction prices that were substantially out of line with those related to transactions in like goods when the difference is not accounted for. They argued that the draft agreement would not enable them to take action against underinvoicing, which was more prevalent in their countries than in developed ones. They also argued that adopting the ACV would increase the risk of fraud and would result in revenue losses. These objections were partly addressed by introducing provisions for special and differential treatment (SDT). The most important provision allowed the countries more time to fully implement the ACV. However, as membership in the GATT did not require member countries to implement the individual GATT codes, there was no obligation for members to introduce the valuation code.

### The Uruguay Round and the Decision on Shifting the Burden of Proof

The Uruguay Round negotiations led to the adoption of the "Decision regarding cases where customs administrations have reasons to doubt the truth or accuracy of the declared value" (Decision 6.1 based on Article 17, see annex 8.A). That decision came to be known as the SBP (shifting the burden of proof) and was appended to the ACV to clarify the intent of the original valuation provisions. The SBP determines that in cases where customs has reasonable doubts as to the truth or accuracy of the importer's declaration, the burden of proof could be shifted to the importer to prove that the declared value represents the total amount actually paid or payable for the goods. In this process customs discusses with the importer their reasons for doubting the declared value, allows the importer to respond, and informs the importer of their final decision. The decision may be that customs still has reasonable doubts, that is, it deems that the customs value of the goods cannot be determined on the basis of the transaction value, and thus proceeds to use the alternate valuation methods of the ACV, which must be followed in strict order.

### State of Implementation

All industrialized countries apply the ACV. The Uruguay Round made its implementation manda-

tory for all World Trade Organization (WTO) members.[4] Developing countries that had not yet adopted the ACV were given five years to introduce it, or until January 1, 2000, at the latest, under the SDT provisions of the ACV. For countries joining the WTO at a later date, the five-year period begins from their date of accession to the WTO. The WTO Committee on Customs Valuation may agree to an extension at a country's request.

Since the conclusion of the Uruguay Round, 58 developing countries have requested the five-year implementation delay.[5] Of these, only two introduced the ACV before 2000. The delay period expired for 29 countries on January 1, 2000, and for 25 more during 2000 and 2001. Twenty-two countries had been either granted an extension to the five-year delay or their request for extension was under consideration, and 13 countries implemented the ACV (with reservation as to the use of minimum values).[6] In addition, 23 countries, mostly among the poorer of the developing countries, neither invoked the five-year delay, nor notified the WTO about the passing of legislation. It thus appears that many developing countries have problems with implementation of the ACV despite substantial TA received.

## The Agreement on Customs Valuation: An Introduction

The ACV establishes that customs value should, to the greatest extent possible, be based on transaction value, that is, the price actually paid or payable for the goods being valued, subject to certain adjustments. Where the transaction value cannot be used because there is no transaction value or the price has been influenced by certain conditions or

---

4. Upon creation of the WTO (1994 Marrakesh Agreement), all WTO members were required to subscribe to all WTO Agreements, including the ACV.

5. From data obtained from various undated documents from the WTO Committee on Customs Valuation concerning the status of implementation of the ACV, including the extension situation as of August 31, 2002.

6. Several developing countries also had reservations related to the reversal of the order of Articles 5 and 6, the deductive and computed value methods (52 countries as of October 2001), and the three-year delay for application of the computed value method (46 countries as of October 2001).

restrictions, the ACV provides five alternate methods, to be applied in prescribed order. In summary, the ACV evaluation methods are as follows:

- *The transaction value (Article 1—Primary Method).* The price actually paid or payable for the goods when sold for export to the country of importation, subject to adjustments for certain costs and considerations in accordance with Article 8 of the ACV. The possible adjustments include commissions, containers, packing, certain goods and services, royalties, and license fees. Buying commissions are not to be included, and legitimate discounts to sole agents and sole concessionaries are to be accepted. Article 1 also stipulates that if the buyer and seller are related in business, this does not in itself constitute grounds for rejecting the transaction value. Such value needs to be accepted provided that the relationship did not influence the price.
- *The transaction value of identical goods (Article 2—First Alternate Method).* The transaction value of identical goods sold for export to the same country of importation at or about the same time, under a sale at the same commercial level and in substantially the same quantity, as the goods being valued.
- *The transaction value of similar goods (Article 3—Second Alternate Method).* The transaction value of similar goods sold for export to the same country of importation at or about the same time and under the same conditions as those for identical goods but with different definitional standards.
- *The deductive method (Article 5—Third Alternate Method).* Under this method, the customs value is based on the unit price at which the imported goods or identical or similar goods are sold in the greatest aggregate quantity in an unrelated party transaction, subject to the deduction of profits and certain costs and expenses incurred after importation.
- *The computed value method (Article 6—Fourth Alternate Method).* The value consists of the sum of the costs of materials and manufacturing, profits, and general expenses equal to that usually reflected in sales of goods of the same class by producers in the exporting country for export to the importing country.

- *The fallback method (Article 7—Fifth Alternate Method).* If the customs value of the imported goods cannot be determined on the basis of any of the previous methods, it shall be determined using "reasonable means consistent with the principles of the ACV." This implies that the previous methods should be applied in a flexible way. Article 7 prohibits the determination of value on the basis of

(a) the selling price of goods produced in the importing country
(b) a system based on acceptance of the higher of two alternative values
(c) the price of goods on the domestic market of the exporting country
(d) the cost of production other than the computed value as determined in line with the computed value method
(e) the price of the goods for export to a country other than the importing one
(f) minimum values
(g) arbitrary or fictitious values.

The ACV includes provisions concerning the treatment of transport and insurance costs, currency conversion, right of appeal, publication of laws and regulations concerning customs valuation, and prompt clearance procedures. It also stipulates that upon written request the importer has the right to a written explanation as to how the customs value was determined. It states that nothing in the ACV shall be construed as restricting the right of customs administrations to satisfy themselves as to the truth or accuracy of any statement, document, or declaration presented for valuation purposes. Provision is also made for administration, consultation, and dispute settlement, and for the establishment of two committees to oversee its implementation: the Committee on Customs Valuation at the WTO, and the Technical Committee on Customs Valuation under the auspices of the WCO.

### Special Provisions for Developing Countries

The ACV contains special provisions for developing countries. These stipulate that under certain conditions developing countries may do the following:

- delay ACV application for a maximum of five years and, under specified conditions, request an extension of that period

- delay application of the computed value method for a period of three years following their application of all other provisions
- using officially established minimum values, make a reservation to retain such values on a limited and transitional basis
- make a reservation to allow importers to reverse the order of application of the deductive method and the computed method of valuation, dependent on the approval of the customs administration
- make a reservation to value imported goods subject to processing after importation on the basis of the deductive method, whether or not the importer so requests.

An associated decision stipulates that developing countries experiencing problems with importations into their countries by sole agents and concessionaries may request a study of this question. The ACV also details the procedures that should be followed in cases where customs administrations have reasons to doubt the truth or accuracy of the declared value. The texts make it clear that these procedures should not prejudice the legitimate interests of traders.

### Implementation Requirements

Implementation of the ACV requires the establishment of a legislative and regulatory framework; a mechanism for judicial review; administrative procedures; organizational structure; and training. These requirements are summarized below and presented in more detail in annex 8.B.

**Legislation and Regulations**   ACV provisions must be incorporated into the national legislation. While legislative practice in a country may dictate the actual form of including the provisions, the valuation legislation should be comprehensive, covering the ACV and its Interpretative Notes as well as a number of specific provisions such as those concerning exchange rate conversion, right of appeal, release of goods before final determination of value, and treatment of transportation and insurance costs (FOB or CIF system).

**Valuation Procedures and Control**   The valuation function should be fully integrated into customs' overall operational structure and practices. This implies the following:

- It is the importer's responsibility to declare the import value in accordance with the ACV.
- Value checks should be limited and selective at the time of clearance, and shipments should not be retained because of value disputes, but cleared with reservation as to value and under security for additional duties that may be at stake.
- Selective post-release verification and audit will be applied with selection of goods or importer based on information from the risk management system.
- Customs needs to maintain a comprehensive information system and database. Information and data are needed to help detect cases of underinvoicing or overinvoicing, to compare values for application of Article 2 (identical goods) and Article 3 (similar goods), to develop and update the risk analysis and management system, and to enable the central and regional offices to respond to queries from the clearance offices.

### Organizational Structure and Training

The recommended organizational structure for valuation requires the establishment of a central valuation office complemented with regional and local offices as needed in relation to country size and the overall customs department organization. The central valuation office is to be responsible for establishing valuation policy, developing procedures, supervising correct and uniform implementation by all offices, ensuring adequate training, and monitoring international developments in valuation. It should develop a value database and could be made responsible for the value-related risk management system. The local and regional offices have an operational role. The complexity of the ACV and the control strategy (post-clearance review and audit) require the services of valuation specialists trained in value legislation and procedures and auditing of company accounts.

## ACV Implementation in Developing Countries

Many developing countries face serious difficulties in implementing the ACV. The major ones are discussed here.

### Lack of Ownership

As noted, empirical evidence indicates that the concerns of developing countries regarding the valuation system to be adopted in the WTO were not fully taken into account, and were even largely ignored. For instance, commitments made by the countries' Ministers of Commerce, who represent their countries at the WTO, were often poorly communicated to the countries' Ministers of Finance, who are responsible for implementing the ACV. As a result, the ACV was poorly internalized. The SDT provided some flexibility as to the timetable for ACV introduction, but was widely perceived as inadequate in taking into account the special difficulties of developing countries. Furthermore, poor internalization is also often reflected in inaccurate or incomplete incorporation of the ACV provisions into domestic legislation, resulting in the system no longer being WTO-compliant. This is the case, for instance, when the WTO requirement that the importers have the right to launch a complaint through their trade representative to the WTO is omitted.

### Revenue Loss

Developing countries are deeply concerned with revenue loss. Low taxpayer compliance and administrative inadequacies in customs make it difficult to effectively check underinvoicing. Underinvoicing becomes attractive to the importer because of the high level of taxes levied at the import stage. There is no empirical proof that supports this concern and knowledgeable observers point to countries that have implemented the ACV without suffering revenue losses. It is also difficult to determine such losses under the ACV because countries that have officially subscribed to it adopt valuation practices that deviate substantially from pure ACV ones, precisely to protect revenues. This issue frequently reappears at ACV discussions, reflecting the concerns of customs managers whose main responsibility is revenue performance, and whose job security is dependent on it. The heavy dependence on customs revenue (see annex 1.A) certainly has a bearing on their concerns that ACV implementation might lead to potentially significant revenue losses.[7]

For technical reasons the value of the ACV is lower than that of the BDV because it excludes buying commissions (when undertaken by the importer) and advertising from the dutiable value, and requires customs to accept legitimate discounts given to sole concessionaries, sole distributors, and sole agents.[8]

### High Tariff Rates

While tariff rates have been lowered in many countries within the context of multilateral and regional agreements, their average level remains substantially higher in developing countries than in developed ones. Data for 2001 show that in the Organisation for Economic Co-operation and Development (OECD) countries, average import duties amounted to 1.1 percent of the import

---

7. In March 1990, a Preferential Trade Area (PTA) proposal for changes to the ACV stated that ACV implementation would cause customs revenue to decline by nearly 10 percent unless the ACV was amended along the lines proposed by the 17 PTA member countries (WTO 1990). A 1996 informal study made by the Indian customs administration estimated revenue losses of Rs. 100 billion (about US$2.8 billion) on account of undervaluation. This study was the basis for setting up a new Directorate of Valuation in India in 1997 (*Source:* personal communication with Indian Delegation at WTO). A 2002 report on valuation fraud in China mentions 12 cases in which a total of US$1.5 million was lost (*Source:* Indian Delegation at WTO). Representatives of PSI companies confirmed that in their experience fake invoicing and undervaluation of shipments to developing countries occurs frequently.

8. A WCO study suggested that the adoption of the ACV by Organisation for Economic Co-operation and Development countries led to slightly lower customs value and customs duties compared with the BDV. (See Customs Cooperation Council 1985.) Australia estimated the reduction in revenue to be equivalent to a general reduction in duty rates of 2 percentage points. The EEC reported shrinkage in the overall taxable base, but of no particular significance to revenue. Finland estimated the loss of revenue to be less than 1 percent of all *ad valorem* duties and taxes levied by customs. Spain projected losses of 4 percent in the most sensitive commodity areas, but lower overall losses. Canada negotiated GATT tariff rate adjustments needed to maintain tariff protection of certain industries at the prevailing levels, but expected no significant revenue losses. New Zealand reported a loss of 0.25 percent of customs revenue.

value compared to 11.8 percent in non–OECD countries. For developing countries, the average collected tariff fell in the range of 7 percent to 17 percent. Even when the average tariff rate of a given country is relatively low, tariff peaks create incentives to undervalue imports of these goods. To the extent that the avoidance of high duty rates tends to contribute to tax evasion practices, underinvoicing becomes more attractive to importers in developing countries than elsewhere.

### Less Compliant Trading Environment

Often large shares of imports are accounted for by an informal sector that uses unreliable invoices, has poor bookkeeping standards or maintains no bookkeeping at all, has no fixed business address, or has frequent changes in the name of their businesses. Under these circumstances, valuation control based on post-release audit is hardly applicable. Customs officials in many countries are aware of the ease with which import invoices are falsified at the point of export or even produced in the destination country. Some of these falsified invoices are easy to detect. Others display a high degree of sophistication and are prepared by medium- and large-scale importers. Only a well-developed customs organization has a chance of detecting such fraud. Overreliance on invoices is often seen as complicating efforts to address the underinvoicing issue.

### Administrative Limitations

The administrative capacity to effectively implement the ACV system is lacking in many developing countries. The enormous variety of goods traded, widely differing prices for similar goods, continuously changing prices, as well as different levels of transaction and sale conditions complicate the correct valuation of imports. Much of the information needed to value a transaction is not readily available because it remains with the foreign supplier. For instance, cross-checking the outgoing invoices of the seller (exporter) with the incoming invoices of the buyer (importer) or performing simple checks such as determining the existence of the exporter is normally not possible or excessively cumbersome. That valuation fraud needs to be

dealt with not as a valuation matter but as a fraud investigation activity also presents implementation problems.

Applying the alternate methods of the ACV in strict order is burdensome, costly, and time consuming. It requires updated information on values of identical and similar goods, and information that is not readily available or that requires complicated calculations. To apply the computed value would require investigations in exporting countries, a procedure that is simply not feasible in most developing countries because of lack of budgetary resources and staff. Strict application of these rules would lead to clearance delays, particularly in cases where postclearance audits are not yet in place. As a result, many developing countries resort to the fallback method for a substantial part of their imports. Clearly, this is far from an ideal situation for a valuation system that was supposed to facilitate trade.[9]

The main developing country limitations stem from the following:

- inadequate value data and poor means of information gathering and communication that result in customs having little or no access to price information and little means to verify declared values
- heavy administrative constraints such as lack of qualified personnel; poor or nonexistent training facilities; and public service salaries, substantially lower than those in the private sector, that often do not pay a living wage, or are insufficient to attract the best
- limited and often ill-managed computerization with only statistical functions, or nonautomated clearance processes with too many manual functions and excessive room for discretion
- inadequate organization and poor management resulting in unavailability of operating manuals, poor hierarchical supervision, and weak or nonexistent internal audits, as well as inadequate management information systems, and unavailability of basic equipment

---

9. A 1999 World Bank publication had the following comments: "The prescribed Customs valuation system is inappropriate for the problems the least developed countries face, incorrect as a solution to their Customs valuation problems, incomplete as a solution to their Customs system problems. It is also incompatible with the resources they have at their disposal." (Finger and Schuler 1999, p. 24).

- complex SBP procedures—in case of reasonable doubt about the declared value, customs has to request further explanations and documents from the importer in support of the declared value, notify the importer in writing if requested, allow the importer to respond, and communicate its final decision in writing.

These differences have led to less than proper implementation in some of the countries that have introduced the ACV. Empirical evidence confirms that customs frequently does not comply with the requirement of informing importers on what grounds they dispute declared value, nor do they provide written justification for their claims. In other cases customs somehow misleads importers, telling them that if they do not increase declared values, the goods will not be released. This leads to conditional release and importers often have difficulties getting back their deposits. Altogether, there is a situation where importers know that their declared value will almost inevitably be challenged, so they are encouraged to underdeclare; and customs considers that all imports are therefore undervalued. This vicious circle should be broken, but little effort has been made so far in that direction. A frequent error made in many countries is the idea that physical examination is essential to verify value. In fact, valuation owes little to examinations, except in a few obvious cases where the characteristics of the goods are not adequately or sufficiently described in the documentation.[10] This affects the risk-management approach to customs.

### Doha Ministerial Conference

Developing country action for changing the ACV has continued within the framework of the WTO. Proposals for amendments to the ACV to better adapt it to the developing countries' trading environment and administrative realities were submitted to the Ministerial Conference at Doha (November 2001). The Doha Ministerial Conference issued the Decision on Implementation-Related Issues and Concerns that covers the exchange of information on export value between exporting and importing countries. (See annex 8.C.)[11] Implementation of this decision together with the submitted proposal is being negotiated or further studied in the appropriate WTO bodies.

## Toward Better Customs Valuation Practices

There are a number of policies and approaches that could lead to better customs valuation practices in developing countries. These would also protect revenue, provide for increased transparency, and minimize interference with trade flows. Some measures would require consideration at WTO and WCO levels, others would require TA, while the most important ones would require actions by the concerned governments.

### Addressing Ownership Questions

The lack of developing country ACV ownership arising from the historic neglect of their concerns cannot be fully overcome. However, there are ways to repair some of the damage. At the Uruguay Round negotiations, developing countries pressed for change with some results, including the SBP. This process should be continued. One way to do so would be for the developing countries to clearly formulate their challenges in implementing the ACV at the next WTO trade negotiations and to suggest practical approaches for implementing the spirit of the ACV. This could be initiated by identifying possibilities where customs authorities could assist each other with data exchanges and modernization

---

10. For example, when a tariff heading corresponds to brands of significantly different values.

11. Decision 8.3 "underlines the importance of strengthening cooperation between the customs administrations of Members in the prevention of customs fraud. In this regard, it is agreed that, further to the 1994 Ministerial Decision Regarding Cases Where Customs Administrations Have Reasons to Doubt the Truth or Accuracy of the Declared Value, when the customs administration of an importing Member has reasonable grounds to doubt the truth or accuracy of the declared value, it may seek assistance from the customs administration of an exporting Member on the value of the good concerned. In such cases, the exporting Member shall offer cooperation and assistance, consistent with its domestic laws and procedures, including furnishing information on the export value of the good concerned. Any information provided in this context shall be treated in accordance with Article 10 of the Customs Valuation Agreement." WTO (2001, pp. 5–6).

initiatives. Acting on proposals formulated at the Doha Conference should complement this. It would be essential for industrialized country WTO members to recognize that developing countries face real problems in implementing ACV provisions.

### Reforming the Tariff and Trade Regime

Incentives to underinvoice or otherwise evade duties originate mainly from high tariff levels and trade restrictions. Lower import taxes and a more liberal import regime would alleviate the problem of underinvoicing and resulting revenue loss. Strengthening the indirect tax regime (value added tax or VAT) could help make up for revenue loss arising from lower tariffs. VAT is also levied at the import stage and runs the risk of undervaluation, but any revenue loss can usually be recaptured when these transactions are taxed at later stages of the production and distribution chain through inland revenue or customs post-clearance audit. However, when these goods are not included in future taxed transactions (informal trade, for example), the sales tax proceeds are not recovered.

### Modernizing Customs Administration

The key action needed in modernizing a customs administration consists of designing and implementing a comprehensive customs modernization program. Customs valuation does not operate in isolation from the overall customs operational and management system. The ability to effectively undertake a valuation function is directly related to the administration's overall quality. A modernization program should include the following key elements:

- streamlining and computerizing operational procedures
- introducing modern clearance strategies, that is, selective checking based on risk analysis and management, and post-clearance review
- professionalizing customs through appropriate personnel recruitment, development, and management policies; better salaries; adequate and sustained training; and internal controls
- introducing modern forms of organization and management based on administrative, financial, and technical autonomy, coupled with accountability.

For a comprehensive modernization program along those lines to succeed, strong and sustained support from senior levels of government is essential. Furthermore, such programs should ideally be TA-oriented and implemented with the assistance of organizations experienced in undertaking customs administration reform projects. Some governments have also elected to temporarily use PSI services or PSI-like services to assist with price information gathering and also with the development of a database during the first years of the customs administration's implementation program.

### Strengthening the Organization and Infrastructure for Valuation

Effective ACV implementation requires an efficient customs administration, and any initiative to modernize customs should take this into account. When there are delays in undertaking comprehensive reform, the valuation function still can and should be strengthened. Such a thrust requires the following:

- provision of the necessary legislative framework, including in the area of foreign exchange conversion rates, treatment of transport and insurance costs (CIF or FOB system), right of appeal, and so forth
- development of value declaration and checking procedures, including self-assessment, selective checking, risk analysis and management, post-clearance review, and audit
- setting up a central valuation office and regional valuation offices, including post-clearance review or audit unit(s)
- training of valuation officers in the ACV system and in post-release review and audit procedures
- establishment of a value information system and database.

Providing importers with an advance ruling on valuation can also speed up the valuation procedure. Such a ruling can be obtained in advance when the importer submits transaction-related documentation to customs. Once granted a ruling, the importer notes the registration number of the ruling on his declaration at the importation stage, and no further valuation work needs to be undertaken, thus speeding up the clearance procedure.

*Establishing a Value Database*

Effective ACV implementation also requires customs to have information on prices to permit it to eliminate reasonable doubt on the accuracy of declared values and to derive the import value using the alternate valuation methods provided in the ACV. It is sometimes argued that when customs deals with an almost fully compliant trading environment in which the few cases of fake invoicing can be dealt with outside the valuation system (such as fraud cases) there would be no need for a valuation database. Yet quite a few developed countries still feel the need to equip their services with a valuation database. For developing countries in which, for a substantial share of imports, the invoice prices cannot be accepted out of hand as the true representation of the price actually paid or payable for the goods, the development of a computerized database is a priority, without which proper operation of the ACV system cannot be expected. A valuation database used as a source of information and guidance is compatible with ACV implementation; and the possibility of undertaking this on a regional basis should be explored.[12] Indeed, a database would allow customs to make more informed decisions and thus would enhance its capability to properly implement the ACV. However, experience has shown that these databases tend to evolve into minimum price lists, which is obviously contrary to the ACV.

The WCO is now preparing a document that will provide guidelines for the development and use of a national valuation database as a risk assessment tool. Some observers suggest that such a database could focus on the 100 most important imported items, and thus would cover the largest share of total imports. The creation of such a database should be within the means of nearly all developing countries. Possible sources for building up a database include the following:

- *Reliable, scrutinized, recent import declarations.* This is the primary source for building a database and should be supplemented with data from price lists, catalogues, trade publications,

market research, and various other sources. Good examples of such databases are the ones that the Peruvian and Pakistani customs authorities have on the Internet.

- *Certificates of verification from the PSI service providers.* This could be a good reference for the PSI-user countries. Countries using PSI services may want to build support for the creation of a valuation database into their PSI contract.

- *International databanks, already existing or being developed, in particular by information technology companies that specialize in establishing data warehouses on world prices.* Diligent use of Internet sites can provide valuable data that could provide useful valuation-related information.[13] Customs can even make available to the importing community the references to the sites they consult, as in Pakistan. Developed countries that operate databanks for valuation purposes could assist developing ones by providing information from their databases.

- *Increased use of electronic data interchange suggests that there exists technology to obtain valuation information.*[14] Use of this procedure would provide internationally recognized and standard product descriptions. It is tied to prices at a given stage in the distribution cycle. This approach could also detect counterfeit products (using the barcode of the original product but made by unlicensed producers, and thus cheaper) that could rightfully be valued at the price of the original product. Uganda has initiated some research on this topic. This approach, based on the use of bar codes and electronic chips that use radio frequency identification (RFID) technology to keep track of items and automatically discriminate between various types of information through a wireless exchange of data between the built-in memory and the Reader (also called IC tags), deserves

---

12. These issues were discussed at a symposium held at the WCO in April 2003; the report is on the WCO Web site www.wcoomd.org.

13. Customs in Pakistan makes available to the public a list of "Price Related Links" that give Web sites that customs consults to obtain information on import values. See www.cbr.gov.pk/newcu/portals.htm. The same Web site provides weekly updates on *Assessed Values Evidences* by detailed Harmonized System classification. Another source for price data is www.pricesaroundasia.com where subscribers can obtain price searches. Obviously these sources must be used cautiously.

14. The WCO Customs Data Model that defines a customs data set for electronic transmission includes information on valuation.

further experimentation and the lessons learned would need to be disseminated.

### Exchanging Information with Exporting Countries' Customs Administrations

At the Doha Ministerial Conference a proposal was submitted for a multilateral solution within the framework of the ACV that would enable customs administrations of importing countries to seek and obtain information on export values contained in exporters' declarations, in doubtful cases.[15] A previous attempt to commit WCO members to assisting each other in the areas of prevention, investigation, and repression[16] has not been successful to date as only 28 members ratified the provisions relating to valuation fraud. Most of industrialized countries have not done so. The Doha proposal intended to match the ACV obligation with a binding obligation on member countries to render assistance to verify customs value in doubtful cases.

The Doha Ministerial Conference agreed that customs administrations may seek assistance from the customs administrations of an exporting member on the value of the goods concerned, and that the exporting member shall offer cooperation and assistance, consistent with domestic laws and procedures, including furnishing information on the export value of the goods concerned. As a result of these discussions, the WTO Committee on Customs Valuation and the WCO Technical Committee on Customs Valuation were mandated to identify and assess practical measures to address the concerns expressed by several developing countries regarding the accuracy of the declared value, including the exchange of information and guidelines for the use of a valuation database.[17]

It is clear from discussions at the WTO Committee on Customs Valuation as well as from debates at the WCO Policy Commission that there are major difficulties with implementing the exchange of valuation information. In December 2002, the WCO Policy Committee Meeting examined how assistance in valuation exchange could be used as a short-term

strategy to supplement a customs modernization effort. Representatives of developing countries' customs administrations strongly endorsed the mutual assistance approach for valuation issues. However, customs representatives from industrialized countries were not supportive of this approach outside of criminal investigations or where important national revenue implications were involved. They asserted that they are not allowed to provide such data, that the burden of doing so would be excessive, and that the value of the data they could provide would be of no great assistance anyway.

A number of industrial countries noted that their domestic legislation (confidentiality laws, secrecy laws) prevents their customs authorities from routinely providing such information or that the legislation contains outright prohibitions for such information to be provided outside of criminal cases. This information is usually under the purview of other agencies that often refuse to share it.

They also noted their concern that an avalanche of requests would place an undue burden on customs to provide the information to the importing country. Some customs administrations may not have the necessary resources to meet such demands. To counter such fears the WCO prepared, in 2002, a Draft Guide to the Exchange of Customs Valuation Information to seek a way forward on the problems identified with the exchange of valuation information. The guide provides a checklist for valuation verification actions to be taken by an importing customs administration before requesting information from the exporting one. The steps are demanding and would ensure that such requests would neither be frivolous nor substitute for diligent customs work in the country requesting such information. The guide was adopted by the Technical Committee on Customs Valuation in early 2003. The guide was also submitted to the WTO Committee on Customs Valuation as a practical measure to address the valuation concerns of developing countries.

The value data at the disposal of the exporting country are also not reliable and not subject to the same level of scrutiny as in the importing country. Some countries keep export value information only for statistical purposes and not on the transaction-by-transaction basis required for the purpose of the mutual assistance request that would allow cross-matching the data. Also, the information would not

---

15. The proposal was submitted by India and supported by several developing countries.

16. WCO 1977.

17. Ministerial Conference, Fourth Session, November 14, 2001: Decisions on Implementation-related Issues and Concerns, and Ministerial Declaration. See WTO 2002.

be helpful in cases of collusion between importer and exporter. The fact that the declared export value does not match the declared import value would not necessarily suggest fraud unless the exporting country authorities verify the information. Representatives of industrial countries argue that this would result in shifting the burden of investigation to the exporting country, something they cannot agree with. To counter their position, some have argued that the fiscal authorities carefully verify most exporter values when VAT credits and refunds are involved. Better coordination between customs and VAT refund authorities could lead to more reliable data.

In conclusion and for the reasons mentioned above, most industrial countries stated that they would comply with requests for mutual assistance with respect to valuation issues on a case-by-case basis, mainly in the context of bilateral assistance agreements. Prospects for establishing a workable multilateral system of exchange of information on declared export values that could be used for ACV-based customs valuation in importing countries therefore do not look very promising in the immediate future.[18] More promising are the agreements made between members that operate under customs unions or economic unions. These agreements could build on established mutual trust and procedures, and could be inspired by the WCO Model Bilateral Agreement on Mutual Assistance. The assistance received by the Botswana Department of Customs and Excise in valuation matters from its neighbors is such an example.

### Minimum Values and Reference Prices

Many developing countries use minimum values to cope with import valuation problems in cases of fraud-sensitive goods and border traffic regulation. In those cases, invoices are either not available or reliable, and post-clearance verification is impractical. Some countries also use such procedures to circumvent collusion between customs officers and

importers, while other countries use this mechanism to protect national production.

ACV provisions allow the use of minimum values on a limited and temporary basis. Would the trading world be better off if greater latitude was allowed for a wider use of administered minimum values or reference price systems, rather than implementation of a transaction-based value system, which it cannot do properly? Some observers reply positively—certainly for standardized imports (raw material, vehicles, and so forth) that rely on world prices that are readily available or on widely used price lists (used cars, for example). The option of making such lists available to the trading community could be considered, but this would require high levels of transparency in establishing these lists as there is the danger that traders will try to influence the lists for protective purposes. Such lists would have to be periodically reviewed with full disclosure of how the data were collected. An interagency group could be involved in the preparation of the lists, and an independent contract group could be charged with its maintenance. (See Finger and Schuler 1999.) This initiative merits further discussion in international forums.

### Technical Assistance

Substantial TA has been provided to prepare developing countries for the introduction of the ACV, especially by the WTO and WCO. During 1998–2001, the WTO held a total of 47 missions in developing countries for this purpose. From 1996 to 2001 the WCO conducted 50 valuation missions in developing countries. These missions have been helpful in providing customs officers and senior managers with a good understanding of the ACV system and its implementation requirements. However, while a good understanding is a necessary condition for ACV implementation, customs valuation work is only as good as the overall quality of the customs administration. As such, training customs officers in ACV provisions will have limited results if customs is not fully computerized, if adequate valuation data are not available, if laws and regulations remain complex and uncoordinated, if discretionary decisionmaking by officers remains the rule and not the exception, and if problems of integrity persist. Unless an enabling environment is created in which valuation training can be put to good use, much of the TA effort will be lost.

---

18. The WCO Council adopted a new International Convention on Mutual Administrative Assistance in Customs Matters in June 2003. It includes the provision that stipulates assistance in providing information for the assessment of import or export duties and taxes. As this convention is yet to be ratified, it would be premature to see how it could actually address the concerns of the developing countries.

Much could be gained if institutions that provide TA were to better coordinate their efforts. But there is no escaping the fact that it is the responsibility of the TA beneficiary countries to orient TA toward overall modernization of customs services as a precondition for effective ACV implementation. Political commitment to this endeavor is absolutely necessary and will require donors to be involved in the modernization process. In the meantime, TA should focus on the development of value databases, specialist training, risk analysis and management, valuation-specific training, and post-clearance review and audit.

## Preshipment Inspection Companies and Other Related Services Programs

Preshipment inspection (PSI) companies have been providing services in the customs area since the mid-1970s. These services were initially performed for central banks, to help them address the issue of capital flight resulting from overinvoicing of imports. With increased liberalization of capital flows, the focus of PSI services has gradually shifted toward revenue issues. Currently the main objectives of PSI programs in the customs area are to control overinvoicing and underinvoicing of imports; to provide governments with accurate information on importers' import transactions and tax liabilities; and, in some cases, to control misappropriation of donor funds provided for import support.

At present, some 40 countries, many of them among the least developed countries, use PSI services (annex 8.D and table 8.D.1). The International Federation of Inspection Agencies (IFIA), a worldwide association of inspection companies, promotes internationally accepted standards and methods, and provides documentation and qualifications of companies and personnel. The WTO Agreement on Preshipment Inspection, negotiated under the Uruguay Round, recognizes the need of developing countries to have recourse to PSI for as long as necessary to verify quality, quantity, or price of imported goods. Mindful that such a program must be carried out without giving rise to unnecessary delays or unequal treatment, the agreement establishes rights and obligations of both user

members and exporter members to ensure that the principles and obligations of GATT 1994 apply to the activities of PSI entities. It also provides for the speedy, effective, and equitable resolution of disputes between exporters and PSI entities that arise under the agreement.[19]

Box 8.1 describes Peru's use of a PSI company for its import verification program.

PSI intervention for customs purposes has been a controversial issue. Proponents argue that PSI intervention deters fraud in international transactions and reduces opportunities for malpractice and corruption in customs administrations. In their view, the cost is justified because of the positive impact on revenue collection and the reduced distortions in trade transactions. Critics contend that

- inspection of shipments at export is a burden on exporters and importers, creating delays and additional costs
- there is no guarantee that goods imported are the same as goods inspected, as changes can occur following inspection because of practical problems related to complete sealing of all inspected shipments
- the requirement for exporters to entrust sensitive information about their transactions to PSI companies is an intrusion into commercial confidentiality
- the scarce foreign exchange spent on PSI could be better used to finance customs reforms. Governments should compare the costs of hiring a PSI company to how customs could improve its operations if given this amount of additional resources
- inspection results are erratic and untrustworthy.

Still other critics argue that PSI agents abroad are no more above integrity problems than local customs officers and that PSI companies often use undue influence and financial incentives to obtain

---

19. This concerns matters in carrying out PSI, inspection standards, transparency in procedures, protection of confidentiality in business information, maximum times for carrying out PSI operations, price verification, methodology, and appeals procedure. The agreement also stipulates obligations for exporting countries relating to nondiscrimination, publicity of laws and regulations, and provision of TA to user members.

---

**BOX 8.1    Peru: Import Verification Program**

In the context of Peru's 1990 customs reform, an Import Verification Program (IVP) was initiated that required importers to obtain a certificate of inspection issued by an authorized PSI company before the goods were to be shipped from the country of exportation. This measure was aimed at assisting customs in the verification of import shipments for purposes of duty assessment and collection. Even though the Peruvian Customs has strengthened its valuation capacity, the PSI contract has been annually renewed. (See Goorman 2004.) Customs considers this arrangement to be satisfactory despite periodic challenges.

*Core Provisions.* The IVP required that the PSI company certify the nature, quality, and value of the goods in accordance with national legislation and physically seal the cargo container after inspection. Originally customs was required to assess duties using the data specified in the inspection certificate; but since accepting the obligation of the ACV in 2000, customs has used the PSI information as an indicator of risk and importers are no longer required to use the PSI value in their declaration. Customs can use this indication in conjunction with its risk management system or valuation database for further investigation or post-clearance control. Before releasing the goods, customs verifies that the nature and the quality of the goods correspond to what is declared in the inspection certificate and that the tariff classification is correct. If there is a discrepancy between the data in the inspection certificate and the findings of the verification, customs permits release of the goods and submits the case, duly substantiated, to the National Valuation Department within 48 hours. The discrepancy will be decided by the National

Valuation Department and can be appealed to the Customs Court, and then to the Fiscal Tribunal (entirely independent of customs), which will decide the final outcome.

The services of four PSI companies were initially retained (in 1996 one was dropped). They were required to present a training program to customs personnel and to assist in the creation of the value database, as well as to provide customs with monthly statistics to permit the monitoring, control, and evaluation of the company's activities and performance.

*Inspection Fees, Importers Choice, and Imports Exempted from the Program.* Since 1999 in Peru, the inspection fee for all goods has been 0.5 percent of the value of inspected shipments, with a minimum US$ 250 per inspection. The fees are paid by the importer directly to the PSI companies. Importers are free to choose any of the approved companies to inspect their import transactions. Customs must inform importers of their obligations to adhere to the provisions of the IVP. Exemptions from the program include imports with a value of less than US$5,000 (a recent measure requires inspection for goods sensitive to fraud when the value exceeds US$2,000), goods imported under the temporary admission regime, donations under certain conditions, embassy imports, and postal shipments without commercial value. About 80 percent to 85 percent of imports are subject to inspection. According to data from the PSI companies, in only 0.17 percent of the total import inspections undertaken did customs state irregularities in quantity, quality, or value.

*Source:* Goorman 2004.

---

contracts.[20] Hiring PSI companies is often characterized as counterproductive to customs reform, if PSI services are used to substitute for efforts to improve customs services.[21] Based on these arguments and experiences, many knowledgeable observers point out that under certain circum-

stances, including the cases where government services have been devastated by conflicts and no expertise is available, the use of PSI services for a short time is an advantage for some developing countries.

### Traditional PSI Programs

Under traditional PSI programs, the company inspects the goods in the exporting country before they are shipped to the importing country; checks their quality, quantity, price, and tariff classification; and, in some programs, computes the duties and taxes due. The company issues a verification report, which is provided to the importer and included in the

---

20. A notorious case was the PSI contract granted by Pakistan in the early 1990s that led to a management overhaul of the PSI company involved.

21. See Low (1995). Low explains what PSI is, how it works, how it can benefit user countries, its drawbacks and pitfalls, and under what conditions it can benefit user countries. The paper contains various case studies and recommendations regarding the design, implementation, and monitoring of PSI programs.

customs declaration at import. The importer can rely on the report or decline to do so in the process of customs valuation and calculation of duty payment. Use of PSI certificates varies greatly among countries. When determining the final customs value, where justified, customs can also disregard the PSI report on price.

PSI programs typically cover all imports except for low value shipments (the threshold is US$5,000, but may be as low as US$2,000), and some other categories such as duty-exempted goods, imports for defense, diplomatic supplies, and personal effects. PSI arrangements often contain provisions for customs officers' training and for assistance in the construction of a valuation database. The PSI cost depends on the range of services being provided and might be borne by governments or importers. It falls in the range of 0.6 percent to 1 percent of the value of the inspected shipments, and is usually borne by importers.

Under the BDV-based valuation system, PSI price verification was aimed at verifying that the invoice price corresponded to an open market price in line with the valuation norm. Customs at that time often used the prices recommended by the PSI companies to determine the customs value. Under the ACV, customs cannot automatically determine dutiable value on the basis of prices recommended by a PSI company. PSI price verification concentrates on comparing the invoiced price with the price of identical or similar goods being offered for export from the same country of exportation at or about the same time. When such prices are not available, PSI companies draw on information from prices charged to different export markets (third-country export prices). However, as all WCO countries are committed to implementing the ACV, which prohibits the use of third-country export prices for customs valuation, such PSI information can only be used as test values or advisory opinions in checking the truth or accuracy of the importer's declared value.[22] When the PSI-verified price differs from the importer declared price, it may provide customs with "reasons to doubt the accuracy of the declared value." This may be used as a risk indicator to question the applicability of the transaction value method of valuation and, following the procedures spelled out in the ACV, in dealing with cases of underinvoicing. Price information from the PSI company, moreover, can be used as a reference to complement import histories for establishing and updating the country's valuation database. The whole process provides customs with information that normally would not be readily available to their countries as long as they do not have a well-established valuation practice. The use of PSI services in Peru is reviewed in box 4.1.

### Evaluation of Effectiveness of Traditional PSI Services

Most PSI services were introduced to assist customs organizations in improving revenue collection and streamlining the processing of foreign trade operations (Anson, Cadot, and Olarreaga 2003).[23] This support would provide the time needed for a government to strengthen its customs administration. However, PSI services have largely been used without measurable improvements in customs administration. This has frequently resulted in automatic renewal of PSI contracts. This should not be seen as a failure of the PSI program itself, which had a limited and mainly short-term objective that did not include building customs capacity. It should be seen, however, as a failure of the government to implement the necessary reform to take over the valuation function with confidence. The usefulness, efficiency, and effectiveness of PSI services need to be judged against results in revenue collection, trade facilitation, and their collateral impact on customs administration. However, the evaluation of PSI programs remains unclear.

22. When the WTO PSI Agreement was negotiated, all PSI user countries were using the BDV system, which does not preclude use of third-country export prices in determining customs value. To accommodate this situation, negotiators added a footnote to the PSI Agreement, clarifying that PSI-using countries are to be bound by the obligations imposed by the ACV when using opinions or prices given by PSI companies for determining customs value. See Rege 2002.

23. The paper proposes a new econometric approach to evaluate the impact of PSI services on revenue collection and fraud. It shows that theoretically PSI intervention has an ambivalent effect on customs fraud, and that for the cases reviewed the findings were not consistent. Yang (2003) presents evidence that if PSI is introduced as an isolated initiative, smugglers will find ways to reduce their duty burden, either by splitting up shipments to stay below the threshold set for PSI inspection or importing through export processing zones, where leakage controls may be loose.

Obviously, the costs at which these results are achieved are not immaterial to the analysis.

**Revenue Impact** The revenue impact of PSI interventions is difficult to measure because the introduction of PSI often coincided with the lowering of trade taxes and other aspects of trade liberalization. Separating the effects on revenues from each of these factors is nearly impossible, even though PSI companies provide detailed statistics indicating the impact that could have resulted from acting on the information provided. Also, the possible deterrent effect of the existence of PSI is not measurable, but could be substantial. The impacts on fiscal revenues as a result of PSI programs have been mixed, and in many countries disappointing. One reason could be the fact that PSI information has at times not been systematically used in the process of determining import values. Customs officers have also expressed doubts about the informational value of some PSI data. In many countries there is a lack of serious monitoring and follow-up of information provided by PSI companies, and no after-the-fact reconciliation is undertaken.

**Trade Facilitation** It is not clear how far PSI services facilitate trade in terms of reduced clearance times and more streamlined customs processing of import shipments. Much of the evidence in this respect is anecdotal. There have been claims of delays caused in the country of exportation, duplication of controls, and errors caused by the PSI companies; but there have also been reports of speedier clearances and less hassles with corrupt customs officers.

Detailed measurements on PSI trade facilitation have only been made in a few cases. A World Bank paper reported that the PSI program introduced in Indonesia in 1985 led to a significant reduction in the clearance time for containers. After the beginning of the program, the percentage of containers that cleared customs in less than four days rose from 13 percent to 63 percent. Similar results were obtained under the Philippines PSI program. In both Indonesia and the Philippines, the PSI program was only part of a wider trade facilitation program. Some of the program's success was due to the sealing of full container loads by PSI companies at the point of embarkation and the requirement that customs let these shipments proceed to their final destination without inspection, except in a restricted number of cases.

**Impact on Customs Administration** The use of PSI services can demoralize customs personnel, and cause them to not cooperate with PSI companies. This may be related to the fact that most PSI contracts are entered into by the Ministry of Finance without the full support of customs. PSI may also negatively affect customs modernization efforts as work undertaken by PSI companies reduces the pressure to reform and to gain the needed experience in valuation. This may also result in some customs administrations tending to neglect valuation work. Although training provided by these companies under some arrangements has been helpful, it is not a substitute for the hands-on experience and responsibility that the officers would develop in valuation work in the absence of PSI companies. Experience has shown that PSI companies are usually not good at training and at the transfer of technology.

**Impact on Traders' Behavior** There is no clear indication so far that the repeated increases of import values brought about by customs' relying on PSI interventions has significantly changed the proclivity of some importers to try to underinvoice their imports. While some importers appear to learn by doing and less frequently undervalue their imports, the practice in some countries of not penalizing traders for it, does not give importers an incentive to declare the full transaction value of their imports.

**Conditions to be Examined When Considering Recourse to PSI Services** Experience in some countries shows that reliance on PSI services could be useful, if carefully integrated in a customs modernization program, or if the inability of customs to assume the valuation function is compensated for. PSI can play a role in ensuring proper duty assessment and collection during the first years of customs reform while capacity is being built. Based on broad experience with PSI services, the following capture some conditions to be examined when considering recourse to PSI services or when evaluating such programs:

- Contract only with PSI companies that have a good reputation. IFIA provides a Code of Conduct for the PSI companies.

- Select PSI service providers, and renew their contracts, through transparent competitive bidding procedures.[24]
- Contract with a single PSI company for a period of only a few years and, if it is so decided, renew the contract under competitive conditions. Avoid split contracts, because multiple companies are more complex to supervise, contracting costs tend to be more expensive, and the individual companies are less carefully supervised by their respective headquarters for whom they represent smaller profit opportunities. Also, split contracts may cause importers to adjust their import pattern so as to benefit from the most helpful inspection services providers. Better to keep to a single contractor for a fixed time period and adhere to competitive bidding for the renewal of the contract.
- Have PSI contracts be fully endorsed by customs, not imposed on customs by the Ministry of Finance or the central bank.
- Link the PSI contracts with a customs modernization project that clearly delineates the respective responsibilities of customs and the PSI company.
- Make the PSI contract explicit: services to be rendered (price, classification, duties paid, special import regimes); time limit without automatic extensions; list of goods to be inspected with exceptions detailed; assistance to customs in setting up a valuation database; clear performance criteria to allow the government to verify PSI performance, with penalties for failing to adhere to the criteria; commitments to train customs staff and to transfer technology; required reports

including the number of inspections, irregularities addressed, adjustments to value made, and resulting additional assessments; and complaints received.
- Record the PSI inspection reports in the customs declaration and record them in the automated customs management system. Reconcile the findings of PSI inspection reports with customs declarations and values retained for the calculation of duties and taxes. This process should explain the reasons for deviations detected.
- Apply the penalties provided in the law for offenses of undervaluation so as to enhance importers' compliance.
- Specify an arbitration or appeals procedure to provide importers with an avenue to contest PSI assessments.
- Create a steering committee (located outside customs, but with customs participation) to oversee PSI activities. Periodic reports should be made available to civil society.
- Possibly articulate an exit strategy to ensure a smooth transition of the functions that were performed by the PSI service to customs. Following exit, PSI companies could be retained to assist in dealing with fraud-sensitive goods, or in other cases where valuation poses particular problems.
- Introduce a publicity campaign to inform traders and the public about PSI systems.

### New Trends in the Provision of Customs Valuation Services

Along with the migration of many developing countries from the BDV system to the ACV system, the private sector that used to offer PSI services started seeking ways to move away from the traditional PSI schemes. The new direction includes more selective programs that rely on selective checking, risk analysis, and post-clearance audits. To what extent these new services will be successful remains to be seen. The trend is for private sector service providers to focus on the following issues:

- Development of risk assessment tools to assist customs in implementing a selective approach to verification so as to focus on the riskier foreign trade transactions, a key element to faster clearance of goods. (See annex 1.D for a description.)

24. Bidding documents should detail services to be procured, request price proposals, instruct the bidder to spell out its prior qualifying experience to undertake the task, and specify the exit strategy. The evaluation criteria and weights to be assigned should be made available beforehand to bidders. An evaluation committee should be established with representatives from concerned government agencies and with private sector representatives involved in trade. Its composition should be made public prior to issuing the bidding documents. Companies should be prohibited from contacting individual committee members from the time of publication of the tender to announcement of the results. The committee should communicate the results of the technical and financial evaluation to all bidders, and it should be published in the local press. If the tender document calls for the committee to submit a recommendation to a higher authority, the recommendation should be made public before the final decision.

- Specification that the services provided will decline over time and that the company will assist customs to take over at an agreed on pace. The recent PSI contract in Madagascar specifies such provisions and will constitute a test for this new approach (see box 8.2).
- Valuation verification service and development of valuation databases. The purpose is to provide customs with information that will allow it to challenge import values and to further carry out valuation in full compliance with ACV rules. The building and updating of a database on import values are an important part of this process. Such information is essential to applying alternate methods of valuation when reasonable doubt is being raised with regard to the transaction value of the goods being imported.
- Support for post-clearance audits where the PSI company, upon the request of the customs department, provides intelligence information regarding shipments selected for audit after the goods have cleared customs. Mexico initiated such a service in 2003.
- Assistance to customs in support services, including information technology.

There has been limited experience with these more selective programs, so the jury is still out. They are likely to be less expensive than traditional PSI services because they are more limited in scope and focus better on risky imports. To adhere to the contract terms, these programs will require the effective transfer of skills and technology. Their success will also depend on capacity building in customs, particularly in the areas of gathering price information and creating valuation databases, the implementation of the ACV, implementing selectivity in applying the control mechanisms available, and developing post-clearance audit capacity. Close monitoring of these new services is needed to evaluate their effect on customs modernization.

---

**BOX 8.2   PSI Contract in Madagascar Introduces Targeted and Evolving Verification Services**

In early 2003 the Republic of Madagascar entered into a four year PSI contract with Société Générale de Surveillance (SGS). This contract provides for a gradual transfer of capacity to manage the inspection, valuation, and classification functions to the customs authorities. This transfer is made possible through the extensive use of risk management techniques and tools.

*Inspection.* During the first six months of the program, SGS will inspect 100 percent of goods (with a value exceeding US$3,000) destined to Madagascar, prior to their shipment. This share is to be reduced to an average of 45 percent during the second year and to 10 percent in the third and final year of the contract. This reduction process will be monitored closely by customs and SGS to ensure that the program's effectiveness remains unaffected. SGS will assist the authorities in setting up a "second inspection" program of a small percentage of shipments at arrival to maximize the results of inspections conducted by customs, an inspection that will be transferred over time to a special audit unit of the Ministry of Finance.

*Valuation.* During the first two years of the contract all transactions above US$3,000 will be subjected to this validation process. During year three, the share of transactions validated will be reduced to 65 per cent to 70 percent and then to 30 percent in year four with transaction values identified by customs to be validated by SGS. SGS will provide a valuation reference system to guide customs' own valuation assessment. Customs staffs will be trained in postclearance controls.

*Tariff Classification.* From 100 percent of imports over US$3,000 in the first year, the share of transactions subjected to customs classification inspection will rapidly decrease in years two and three, to eventually reach 40 percent. During the last year of the contract tariff classification will be wholly the responsibility of customs.

The program includes immediate implementation of a risk management system, extensive training, and close cooperation between the PSI company and the authorities. To maximize the effectiveness of the program and to ensure systematic feedback of information, the authorities will reconcile the SGS information with that used in their assessments prior to final clearance of goods. This should minimize the risk of the PSI option not being used.

*Source:* Communication from the Customs Department of Madagascar.

### *International Value Databases*

In recent years a number of information technology companies have specialized in developing data warehouses on world prices and systems to label and track internationally traded goods. The programs could provide price information to buyers and sellers worldwide via online access to databases. Prices are obtained and updated through an international network of representatives and agents. The suppliers can update the specifications and prices of their products online. The data provided could be used in a manner consistent with WTO valuation rules. The cost at which information could be made available to customs is not clear.

Another initiative, based on barcodes designed for tracking goods in international trade, provides an attractive option. While not specifically designed for customs valuation purposes, this approach could provide customs officials with valuable price information if price information was added to the typical product-specific data. This approach was tested in one country and provided customs with relevant price information for 80 percent of consumer goods. Experiments are continuing, based on data provided by a retail sales outfit from a neighboring country. Further testing and research are needed to find out how readily available these databases are, and at what cost; assess how this method can assist customs officers in reaching conclusions regarding the existence or not of the "reasonable doubt" required by the ACV to reject the price; and determine how this would compare with the newer PSI services. As noted, the use of IC tags in this respect could also be explored.

## Operational Conclusions

Developing countries originally objected to introducing the ACV because it complicates efforts to address underinvoicing issues in a commercial environment that is very different from the commercial environment existing in industrialized countries. Developing countries face the problem of the informal sector and the lack of compliance even with larger known traders. At the Uruguay Round, a decision was appended to the ACV that provides for shifting the burden of proof to the importer when serious doubts exist regarding the accuracy of the declared value. While this decision

provides developing countries with a tool to deal with underinvoicing, the procedure is complicated and leaves the ACV ill-adapted to the countries' needs. The countries lack ownership of the ACV system. Moreover, implementation of the ACV requires price information that they do not have and that is costly to obtain. Finally, a transaction value system can only be introduced effectively in a well-organized and trained administration that is largely computerized and where information flows are smooth and adequate. This is not the case with many developing countries and causes concerns about possible revenue loss in implementing the ACV.

There are a number of measures that could contribute to proper implementation of the ACV:

- Governments should realize that piecemeal TA for customs valuation without comprehensive customs modernization programs is likely to disappoint. It would be illusory to expect good valuation practices in an administratively and technically ill-equipped customs department. Reforms should encompass the streamlining of operational procedures; the introduction of a modern customs control strategy based on selective checking, risk management, and post-clearance audit; professionalizing of the service through appropriate personnel development and management policies, better salaries, and sustained training; and the introduction of modern forms of organization based on greater autonomy coupled with accountability and transparency.
- A greater part of TA should be redirected toward comprehensive customs modernization projects. Valuation-specific TA needs to be concentrated on the development of valuation databases, risk analysis and management systems, and post-clearance review and audit.
- The valuation function should be strengthened by setting up an appropriate legal framework; establishing valuation control procedures based on selective checking, risk analysis and management, and post-clearance audit; establishing central and regional valuation offices; and specialized training.
- A valuation database should be established and constantly updated.

- Advance rulings on valuation should be introduced whenever possible, so as to speed up the clearance process and give importers assurance of the tariff and tax burden.
- Hiring of PSI companies may be useful to assist customs in certain circumstances. The objective is to facilitate valuation work during the initial reform stages as capacity is being built up to carry out the valuation function. However, if and when PSI services are used, care needs to be exercised to make good use of these services to complement a sustainable customs modernization. Otherwise, governments should reconsider recourse to such services.
- When using private sector services, countries should take full advantage of the recent programs that concentrate on selective price verification, the building up of valuation databases, the development of risk management systems, and other important services. These appear better focused on the crucial needs of ACV implementation than older programs, and are less costly.

## Annex 8.A Decision Regarding Cases Where Customs Administrations Have Reasons to Doubt the Truth Or Accuracy of the Declared Value

Ministers invite the Committee on Customs Valuation established under the Agreement on Implementation of Article VII of GATT 1994 (*viz.* Agreement on Customs Valuation) to take the following decision:

*The Committee on Customs Valuation*

*Reaffirming* that the transaction value is the primary basis of valuation under the Agreement on Implementation of Article VII of GATT 1994 (hereinafter referred to as the 'Agreement');

*Recognizing* that the customs administration may have to address cases where it has reason to doubt the truth or accuracy of the particulars or of documents produced by traders in support of a declared value;

*Emphasizing* that in so doing the customs administration should not prejudice the legitimate commercial interests of traders;

*Taking into account* Article 17 of the Agreement, paragraph 6 of Annex III to the Agreement, and the relevant decisions of the Technical Committee on Customs Valuation;

*Decides* as follows:

When a declaration has been presented and where the customs administration has reason to doubt the truth or accuracy of the particulars or of documents produced in support of this declaration, the customs administration may ask the importer to provide further explanation, including providing documents or other evidence, that the declared value represents the total amount actually paid or payable for the imported goods, adjusted in accordance with the provisions of Article 8. If, after receiving further information, or in the absence of a response, the customs administration still has reasonable doubts as to the truth or accuracy of the declared value, it may, bearing in mind the provisions of Article 11, be deemed that the customs value of the imported goods cannot be determined under the provisions of Article 1. Before making a final decision, the customs administration shall communicate to the importer, if requested, its grounds for doubting the truth or accuracy of the particulars or documents produced and the importer shall be given a reasonable opportunity to respond. When a final decision is made, the customs administration shall communicate to the importer in writing its decision and the grounds thereof.

It is entirely appropriate in applying the Agreement for one Member to assist another Member on mutually agreed terms.

*Source:* WTO 1994.

## Annex 8.B Agreement on Customs Valuation: Implementation Requirements

Implementation of the ACV requires the establishment of a legislative and regulatory framework, a mechanism for judicial review, administrative procedures, organizational structure, and training.

### *Legislation and Regulations*

The provisions of the ACV need to be incorporated in national law. While legislative practice in the country may dictate the actual form, the valuation legislation should be comprehensive, covering the ACV and its interpretative notes, as well as a number of specific provisions, including the following:

*Exchange rate.* How and when the exchange rate for conversion of values expressed in foreign currency shall be published, and whether the rate at the time of exportation or at the time of importation needs to be considered.

*Right of appeal.* The agreement requires that members provide for the right of the importer to appeal, in relation to the determination of customs value, and provide for final appeal to the judiciary. A fair and independent review mechanism needs to be established within the customs administration in the first instance, with further right to an appeals tribunal (if available) or to the judicial authority in the second or third instance.

*Release of goods before final determination of value.* The legislation must allow the importer to withdraw goods from customs control in situations in which final determination of the customs value is delayed, provided the importer posts a guarantee to cover the duty liability that may result from the review.

*Transportation and insurance costs.* National legislation needs to determine whether these costs are to be included in, or excluded from, the dutiable value (CIF or FOB basis of valuation).

*Reasons to doubt.* Nothing in the ACV shall be construed as restricting or calling into question the rights of customs administrations to satisfy themselves as to the truth or accuracy of any statement, document, or declaration presented for customs valuation purposes.

### Valuation Procedures and Control

The complexity of the valuation norm and its application to actual transactions makes it necessary for customs to judiciously organize the valuation function in terms of policies, procedures, and organizational setup. Customs valuation does not operate in isolation of the overall clearance and control system, but is a core element of it. The quality of customs valuation depends on the quality of the customs administration overall, and the degree to which it uses information technology applications and implements modern control strategies.

Valuation procedures as complex as the ACV require, as a minimum, the following:

*Value declaration self-assessment.* The importer needs to be made responsible for determining the value in accordance with the ACV. The importer must declare the essential elements affecting the dutiable value in a value declaration form, to be presented or lodged electronically with the import declaration.

*Limited and selective checking at time of clearance (local office).* Checking at the time of clearance for most imports should be limited to determining the acceptability and validity of the declaration, and on the basis of available information, identifying whether additional action is required, such as physical inspection or submission of the matter to the regional or central valuation office.[25] In computerized systems, selection for inspection or other action will normally be made by the systems on the basis of a risk management program. Shipments should not be retained because of value disputes, but cleared with reservation as to the value and under security for additional duties that may be at stake.

*Selective post-clearance release verification and audit (regional office).* As a general principle, valuation control should concentrate on post-clearance verification and audit. The present days' volume of trade and the complexity of customs valuation make effective valuation at the point of importation impossible. Post-clearance checks should be carried out by the regional office, or in some countries, the central valuation office. The selection of declarations for post-clearance verification or audit should be based on information from the risk management system. Action may consist of documentary verification, or may include a physical inspection, or consist of accounts-based checking at the importer's premises to examine in detail the conditions of the transaction.

*Value information system and database.* Information and data are needed for the following:

- to enable customs to detect cases of underinvoicing or overinvoicing

---

25. Valuation does not require physical inspection in most cases. However, inspection may be needed to ensure correct identification of the type, brand name, model, serial number, and other characteristics of the goods, so as to allow for correct identification when a verification or audit is done later.

- to allow comparison of values for application of ACV Articles 2 (identical goods) and 3 (similar goods)
- to develop and update a risk analysis and management system
- to enable the central and regional offices to respond to queries from the clearance offices.

The primary source of information for the value database is the price obtained from reliable, scrutinized, recent import declarations. This information needs to be supplemented with data from price lists, catalogues, market research, and various other sources. The information from the database should not be taken at face value, but used for guidance in examining transactions. Taking the data from the value database strictly would be inconsistent with the ACV and unacceptable as a valuation system.

### Organizational Setup and Training

Effective organization for valuation requires the establishment of a central valuation office, complemented with regional and local offices as needed based on the size of the country and the overall organization of the customs department. The central valuation office, unit, or division at headquarters is responsible for valuation policy, developing procedures, supervising the correct and uniform implementation by regional and local offices, ensuring adequate human resources and their training, monitoring international developments concerning valuation, serving as the importer's final internal appeal stage on disputed value decisions, and maintaining relationships with relevant institutions (WCO, for example). Local and regional offices have an operational role as described in the section on "Valuation Procedures and Control." The central office should develop the value database and the risk management system. The complexity of the ACV and the control strategy (post-clearance audit) require valuation specialists trained in value legislation and procedures and auditing of company accounts.[26]

---

26. For more detailed information, see WCO (1996).

## Annex 8.C Implementation Issues Related to WTO Bodies Under the Doha Ministerial Decision on Implementation-Related Issues and Concerns

*Paragraph 8.3: Agreement on Implementation of Article VII of GATT 1994 (Customs Valuation)*

Ministerial Decision:
The Ministerial Conference decides as follows:

8.3 Underlines the importance of strengthening cooperation between the customs administrations of Members in the prevention of customs fraud. In this regard, it is agreed that, further to the 1994 Ministerial Decision Regarding Cases Where Customs Administrations Have Reasons to Doubt the Truth or Accuracy of the Declared Value, when the customs administration of an importing Member has reasonable grounds to doubt the truth or accuracy of the declared value, it may seek assistance from the customs administration of an exporting Member on the value of the good concerned. In such cases, the exporting Member shall offer cooperation and assistance, consistent with its domestic laws and procedures, including furnishing information on the export value of the good concerned. Any information provided in this context shall be treated in accordance with Article 10 of the Customs Valuation Agreement. Furthermore, recognizing the legitimate concerns expressed by the customs administrations of several importing Members on the accuracy of the declared value, the Committee on Customs Valuation is directed to identify and assess practical means to address such concerns, including the exchange of information on export values and to report to the General Council by the end of 2002 at the latest.

Consideration by the Customs Valuation Committee:

This issue was considered by the Customs Valuation Committee, which reported to the General Council in December 2002 (G/VAL/50), *inter alia,* that the Committee would require technical input and advice to further evaluate all submissions and views, which it had requested from the Technical Committee on Customs Valuation (TCCV), and that the TCCV was to conclude its examination and report to the Committee by 15 May 2003 in order that the Committee might consider the technical inputs and advice provided. The Committee requested the General Council to take note of the progress to date, to allow it to continue to work under the existing mandate, and to establish an appropriate time for reporting on the matter.

Consideration by the General Council in December 2002:

The General Council considered the Committee's report in December 2002 (WT/GC/M/77). Following the discussion on the report, the General Council took note of the report and of the progress to date and authorized the Committee to continue its work under the existing mandate and to report back to the General Council once its work had been completed.

Follow up:

The TCCV submitted its response to the Committee on 15 May 2003 (G/VAL/54), which was dis-

cussed at the Committee's meeting on 23 May. The Committee agreed that its incoming Chairman would consult informally on how further work should proceed and, in the meantime, suspended its consideration of this item. The Chairman is consulting with delegations and will report to the Committee on the outcome of the consultations, at which time the Committee will decide on how to complete its mandate, including reporting to the General Council.

*Source:* WTO document WT/MIN(01)/17 of November 20, 2001, WTO document WT/GC/M/77 of February 13, 2003, Committee on Customs Valuation Documents G/VAL/50 of December 11, 2002 and G/VAL/54 of May 16 2003.

## Annex 8.D PSI Programs Operated by Members of the IFIA PSI Committee

**TABLE 8.D.1   PSI Programs Operated by Members of the IFIA PSI Committee (as of January 21, 2004)**

| Country | Type | IFIA PSI Members Under Contract[a] | Basis of Contract Split |
|---------|------|-----------------------------------|-------------------------|
| Angola | Customs | BIVAC | – |
| Bangladesh | Customs | BIVAC, BSI-Inspectorate, Intertek | Geographical |
| Benin | Customs | BIVAC | – |
| Burkina Faso | Customs | SGS | – |
| Burundi | Forex/Customs | SGS, Baltic Control | Importers' choice |
| Cambodia | Customs | SGS | – |
| Cameroon | Customs | SGS | – |
| Central African Rep. | Customs | BIVAC | – |
| Chad | Customs | BIVAC | – |
| Comoros | Customs | COTECNA | – |
| Congo | Customs | BIVAC | – |
| Côte D'Ivoire | Customs | BIVAC, COTECNA | Customs regime[b] |
| Dem. Rep. of Congo | Forex/Customs | SGS | – |
| Ecuador | Customs | BIVAC, COTECNA, Intertek, SGS | Importers' choice |
| Ethiopia | Forex/Customs | SGS | – |
| Ghana[c] | Customs | BIVAC, COTECNA & others[d] | Air & land freight/sea freight. |
| Guinea | Customs | SGS | – |
| India[e] | Quality/quantity | BIVAC, BSI-INSPECTORATE, SGS & others[c] | Importers' choice |
| Indonesia[f] | Quality/quantity/ classification | Open to any surveyor licensed to operate in country of supply[c] | Importers'/exporters' choice |
| Indonesia[g] | Quality/quantity/ classification | SGS | – |
| Iran, Islamic Rep. of[h] | Quality/quantity | BIVAC, COTECNA, BSI-INSPECTORATE, Intertek, OMIC, SGS and others[c] | Importers' choice |

**TABLE 8.D.1**    (*Continued*)

| Country | Type | IFIA PSI Members Under Contract[a] | Basis of Contract Split |
|---|---|---|---|
| Iran, Islamic Rep. of | Customs | BIVAC, BSI-INSPECTORATE, OMIC, SGS, Intertek | – |
| Kenya | Customs | COTECNA, BIVAC | Geographical |
| Liberia | Customs | BIVAC | – |
| Madagascar | Customs | SGS | – |
| Malawi | Forex/Customs | Intertek | – |
| Mauritania | Customs | SGS | – |
| Mali | Forex/Customs | Cotecna | – |
| Mexico[i] | Customs | BIVAC, Intertek, SGS | Importers' choice |
| Mozambique | Customs | Intertek | – |
| Niger | Customs | COTECNA | – |
| Nigeria | Forex/Customs | COTECNA, Intertek, SGS | Geographical |
| Peru | Customs | BIVAC, COTECNA, SGS | Importers' choice |
| Rwanda | Customs | Intertek | – |
| Senegal | Customs | COTECNA | – |
| Sierra Leone | Customs | BIVAC | – |
| Tanzania | Customs | COTECNA | – |
| Togo | Customs | COTECNA | – |
| Uzbekistan | Forex/Customs | Control Union Intl., Intertek, OMIC, SGS | Importers'/exporters' choice |
| Venezuela, R. B. de | Customs | BIVAC, COTECNA, Intertek, SGS | Importers' choice |
| Zanzibar[j] | Forex | SGS | – |

*Source:* International Federation of Inspection Agencies (IFIA) 2004 www.ifia-ac.org/.

BIVAC = Bureau of Inspection, Valuation, Assessment and Control.

BSI = British Standard Institute.

OMIC = Overseas Merchandise Inspection Corporation.

SGS = Societe Generale de Surveillance.

Forex = Foreign Exchange.

– = no split.

a. Nonmembers of the IFIA PSI Committee are also operating in Iran and India.

b. BIVAC for goods entered into direct consumption; COTECNA for goods entered for customs suspense regimes.

c. PSI consists of valuation and classification by BIVAC or COTECNA. Physical inspection is carried out on arrival in Ghana by local companies that are joint ventures with BIVAC and COTECNA, respectively.

d. Others = Nonmembers of the IFIA PSI Committee also operating for Ghana, India, Indonesia, and Iran. Verification by BIVAC for goods entered into direct consumption; COTECNA for goods entered for customs suspense regimes.

e. Only covers quality and quantity of importers' contractual specifications.

f. Only covers waste and used equipment.

g. Only covers nitrocellulose, steel, and textiles.

h. Voluntary program at importers' discretion (for trade facilitation); may be undertaken simultaneously with the quality–quantity program.

i. Only covers goods of certain categories and origins published in Article 10 of the "Agreement on Automatic imported Advice"; are subject to PSI if their unit value is below estimated prices published by the government.

j. Only covers certain imports at the discretion of the government.

## Annex 8.E Checklist for Customs Valuations

- Is the valuation legislation fully in line with the WTO ACV?
- Has sufficient training been given to both customs and importers, or their agents (brokers), to make them fully understand and properly implement the ACV?
- Are value checks at the time of importation limited and selective, and is selection based on a risk analysis and management system?
- Is the valuation practice consistent with the requirements of the ACV, in particular:

  - Does customs apply the transaction value of the imported goods as the primary method of valuation, and if the transaction value cannot be accepted, does it apply the subsequent valuation methods in strict hierarchical order?
  - If customs has reasonable doubt about the declared value and deems that the transaction value method cannot be used, does it properly consult with the importer and give the importer the opportunity to respond to customs' decision?
  - Does the importer have a right to appeal the decision of customs on the customs value, with first appeal to a higher administrative authority or an independent body, and final appeal to a judicial authority?

- If the determination of the value cannot be made at the time of importation, is a mechanism in place to release the goods provisionally, and solve the valuation questions after release?
- Is there a central valuation office at customs headquarters, responsible for developing procedures, supervising the correct and uniform implementation of the ACV, ensuring adequate training, and developing or maintaining a central valuation database?
- Does customs have adequate numbers of staff specially trained in customs valuation and auditing of company accounts?
- Does customs use a computerized database that is updated continuously and in a timely manner?
- When using PSI services, are these services monitored against established criteria?
- Are the penalties for undervaluation adequate, are they realistic (neither too high, nor so low that there is no deterrent), and are they being effectively applied?

## Further Reading

Finger, Michael J., and Philip Schuler. 1999. "Implementation of Uruguay Round Commitments: The Development Challenge." Policy Research Working Paper No. 2215. Washington, D.C.: The World Bank.

International Trade Center, and Commonwealth Secretariat. 2001. "Frequently Asked Questions on Customs Valuation." Geneva.

Low, Patrick. 1995. "Pre-Shipment Inspection Services." World Bank Discussion Paper No. 278. Washington, D.C.: The World Bank.

Rege, Vinod. 2002. "Customs Valuation and Customs Reform." In Bernard Hoekman, Aaditya Mattoo, and Philip English, eds. *Development, Trade, and the WTO: A Handbook.* Washington, D.C.: The World Bank.

WCO (World Customs Organization). 1996. "Brief Guide to the Customs Valuation Code." Brussels: WCO.

———. 1997. *Compendium: Customs Valuation,* with Amending Supplements. Brussels: WCO.

———. Various Years. Legal Texts on Customs Valuation. See WCO Web site at www.WCOOMD.org/.

World Trade Organization. Various years. Customs Valuation Agreement, technical information, discussion papers, minutes of meetings, working documents, decisions and recommendations, and other work of the Committee on Customs Valuation. See WTO Web site at http://www.wto.org/.

———. 1993. *Agreement on Pre-Shipment Inspection.* Geneva. www.wto.org/english/docs_e/legal_e/21-psi.pdf

## References

The word *processed* describes informally reproduced works that may not commonly be available through libraries.

Anson, José, Olivier Cadot, and Marcelo Olarreaga. 2003. "Tariff Evasion and Customs Corruption. Does Pre-Shipment Inspection Help?" Policy Research Working Paper No. 3156. Washington, D.C.: The World Bank.

Customs Cooperation Council. 1985. *Customs Valuation, Economic Considerations.* Document 31906E. Brussels.

Finger, Michael J., and Philip Schuler. 1999. "Implementation of Uruguay Round Commitments: The Development Challenge." Policy Research Working Paper No. 2215. Washington, D.C.: The World Bank.

Goorman, Adrien. 2004. "Peru." In Luc De Wulf and José B. Sokol, eds. *Customs Modernization Initiatives.* Washington, D.C.: The World Bank.

Low, Patrick. 1995. "Pre-Shipment Inspection Services." World Bank Discussion Paper No. 278. Washington, D.C.: The World Bank.

Rege, Vinod. 2002. "Customs Valuation and Customs Reform." In Bernard Hoekman, Aaditya Mattoo, and Philip English, eds., *Development, Trade, and the WTO: A Handbook.* Washington, D.C.: The World Bank.

WCO (World Customs Organization). 1977. *The International Convention on Mutual Administrative Assistance for the Prevention, Investigation and Repression of Customs Offences.* Signed in Nairobi on June 9, 1977.

www.wcoomd.org/ie/EN/Recommendations/naireng.pdf.

———. 1996. *Brief Guide to the Customs Valuation Agreement.* Brussels.

WTO (World Trade Organization). 1990. GATT Document MTN.GNG/NG8/W/73. Geneva.

———. 1993. *Agreement on Pre-Shipment Inspection.* Geneva. www.wto.org/english/docs_e/legal_e/21-psi.pdf

———. 1994. Agreement on Customs Valuation. Decision 6.1. Geneva.

———. 2001. "Implementation-Related Issues and Concerns." WTO Document WT/MIN(01)/17. November 20.

———. 2002. Compilation of Discussions in Various WTO Bodies on Implementation-Related Issues Concerning Customs Valuation—Background Note by the Secretariat. Document G/VAL/W/97 of March 26, 2002. Geneva.

Yang, Dean. 2003. "How Easily Do Lawbreakers Adapt to Increased Enforcement? Philippine Smugglers' Responses to a Common Customs Reform." University of Michigan. Processed.

# 9

# RULES OF ORIGIN, TRADE, AND CUSTOMS

*Paul Brenton and Hiroshi Imagawa*

This chapter has benefited from the comments and suggestions
of Antoni Estevadeordal, Moshe Hirsch, Holm Kappler, Kunio
Mikuriya, Mark Pearson, and Kati Suominen, to whom the
authors are most grateful. This paper reflects the views of the
authors and should not in any way be attributed to the organizations with which they are or have been affiliated.

Determining the country of origin or "nationality"
of imported products is a requirement for applying
basic trade policy measures such as tariffs, quantitative restrictions, antidumping and countervailing
duties, and safeguard measures as well as for

requirements relating to origin marking, public procurement, and for statistical purposes. Such objectives are met through the application of basic or nonpreferential rules of origin. Countries that offer zero or reduced duty access to imports from certain trade partners will apply another and often different set of preferential rules of origin to determine the eligibility of products to receive preferential access. The justification for preferential rules of origin is to prevent trade deflection, or simple transshipment, whereby products from nonpreferred countries are redirected through a free trade partner to avoid the payment of customs duties. Hence the role of preferential rules of origin is to ensure that only goods originating in participating countries enjoy preferences. Therefore, preferential rules of origin are integral parts of preferential trade agreements such as bilateral and regional free trade agreements and the nonreciprocal preferences that industrial countries offer to developing countries.

The nature of rules of origin and their application can have profound implications for trade flows and for the work of customs. Rules of origin can be designed in such a way as to restrict trade and therefore can and have been used as trade policy instruments. The proliferation of free trade agreements with accompanying preferential rules of origin is increasing the burdens on customs in many countries with consequent implications for trade facilitation. Perhaps surprisingly, given their potential to influence trade flows, rules of origin is one area of trade policy that has been subject to very little discipline during the almost 50 years of the multilateral rules–based system governed by the General Agreement on Tariffs and Trade (GATT) and more recently the World Trade Organization (WTO). It is also worth noting that during this period the determination of the country of origin of products has become more difficult as technological change, declining transport costs, and the process of globalization have led to the splitting up of production chains and the distribution of different elements in the production of a good to different locations. The issue becomes which one or more of these stages of production define the country of origin of the good.

This chapter seeks to summarize the key issues relating to both preferential and nonpreferential rules of origin and to highlight the economic impact that rules of origin can have. It concentrates on the implications of rules of origin for customs, drawing on a recent survey of customs administrations throughout the world. The main conclusion is that the specification and implementation of rules of origin can have significant effects both on traders and on the work of customs. Complex rules of origin that differ across countries and agreements can be a significant constraint on trade and a substantial burden on customs and on the improvement of trade facilitation. The nature of the rules of origin can act to undermine the stated intentions of preferential trade agreements.

The first section of this chapter explains what is meant by origin. The second section examines methods for determining substantial transformation. The third section discusses the current situation with regard to nonpreferential rules of origin, where a concerted attempt (yet to bear fruit) has been made to harmonize the rules regarding wholly obtained products and substantial transformation. The fourth section elaborates on the definition of preferential rules of origin for which, to date, there has been no attempt to achieve harmonization and for which there are no real and effective multilateral disciplines. The fifth section looks at the rules of origin in existing free trade and preferential trade agreements. The sixth section reviews the economic implications of rules of origin. The seventh section discusses the links between the rules of origin and the use of trade preferences. The eighth section analyzes the use of the rules of origin as a tool of economic development. The ninth section deals with the costs of administering preferential rules of origin by customs. The tenth section looks at the Doha Round and the rules of origin. The final section provides some operational conclusions.

## Defining Origin

When a product is produced in a single stage or is *wholly obtained* in one country the origin of the product is relatively easy to establish. This applies mainly to natural products and goods made entirely from them and hence products that do not contain imported parts or materials. Proof that the product was produced or obtained in the preferential trade partner is normally sufficient. For all other cases in which two or more countries have taken part in the production of the good, the rules of origin define the methods by which it can be determined in which country the particular product has undergone *sufficient* working or processing or has been subject to a *substantial* transformation (in general these terms can be used interchangeably). A substantial transformation is one that conveys to the product its essential character.

## Methods for Determining Substantial Transformation

Unfortunately, there is no simple and standard rule of origin that can be identified as determining the nationality of a product. The International Convention on the Simplification and Harmonization of Customs Procedures (the Revised Kyoto Convention) defines (in Annex D1 to the convention) the three main techniques for the determination of origin: change of tariff classification, value-added, and specific manufacturing process.

### Change of Tariff Classification

Origin is granted if the exported product falls into a different part of the tariff classification to any imported inputs that are used in its production. This tariff-shift method forms the basis of the efforts by the World Customs Organization (WCO) to harmonize nonpreferential rules of origin. Application of this approach has been enabled by the widespread adoption of the Harmonized System (HS) whereby the majority of countries throughout the world (more than 190) are now classifying goods according to the same harmonized categories. There is, however, the issue of the level of the classification at which change is required. Typically it is specified that the change should take place at the heading level (that is, at the four-digit level of the HS).[1] The following are examples of simple HS headings:

- beer made from malt (HS 2203)
- umbrellas and sun umbrellas (HS 6601).

The following is an example of a more sophisticated heading:

Machinery, plant or laboratory equipment, whether or not electrically heated (excluding furnaces, ovens and other equipment of heading 8514), for the treatment of materials by a process involving a change of temperature such as heating, cooking, roasting, distilling, rectifying, sterilizing, pasteurizing, steaming, drying, evaporating, vaporizing, condensing or cooling, other than machinery or plant of a kind used for domestic purposes; instantaneous or storage water heaters, non-electric (HS 8419).

However, the HS was not designed specifically as a vehicle for conferring country of origin; its purpose is to provide a unified commodity classification for defining tariff schedules and for the collection of statistics. Thus, in particular cases it can be argued that change of tariff heading will not identify substantial transformation, while in other cases substantial transformation can occur without change of tariff heading. As a result, schemes using the change of tariff heading criterion usually provide for a wide range of exceptions so that other criteria must be satisfied to confer origin.

The change of tariff classification can provide both a positive test of origin, by stating the tariff classification of imported inputs that can be used in the production of the exported good (for example, those in a different heading), and a negative test by stating cases where change of tariff classification will not confer origin. For example, in the North American Free Trade Agreement (NAFTA) the rule of origin for Tomato Ketchup, which is defined at the subheading or six-digit level of the HS, states that a change to Ketchup (HS 210320) from imported inputs of any chapter will confer origin except subheading 200290 (Tomato Paste). In other words, any ketchup made from imported fresh tomatoes will confer origin but ketchup made from tomato paste imported from outside the area will not qualify for preferential treatment even though the basic change of tariff classification requirement has been satisfied.[2] In European Union (EU) preferential rules of origin, bread, biscuits and pastry products (HS 1905) can be made from any imported products except those of chapter 11, which includes flour, the basic input to these products.

---

1. The Harmonized System comprises 96 chapters (two-digit level), 1,241 headings (four-digit level), and around 5,000 subheadings (six-digit level).

2. The apparent reason for this rule in NAFTA is to protect producers of tomato paste in Mexico from competition from producers in Chile. See Palmeter (1997).

The World Trade Organization (WTO) Agreement on Rules of Origin (the Origin Agreement or ARO) stipulates that preferential and nonpreferential rules of origin should be based on a positive standard. However, it allows the use of negative standards (a definition of what does not confer origin) if they "clarify a positive standard." The latter is sufficiently vague as to have had very little impact so that EU and NAFTA rules of origin, for example, are rife with negative standards.

Thus, while in principle the change of tariff classification can provide for a simple uniform method of determining origin, in practice instead of a general rule there are often many individual rules. Nevertheless, the change of tariff classification rule, once defined, is clear, unambiguous, and easy for traders to learn. It is relatively straightforward to implement. In terms of documentary requirements it requires that traders keep records that show the tariff classification of the final product and all the imported inputs. This may be undemanding if the exporter directly imports the inputs but may be more difficult if they are purchased from intermediaries in the domestic market.

### Value-Added

When the value-added in a particular country exceeds a specified percentage, the goods are defined as originating in that country. This criterion can be defined in two ways, either as the minimum percentage of the value of the product that must be added in the country of origin or as the maximum percentage of imported inputs in total inputs or in the value of the product.

As in the case of change of tariff classification, the value-added rule has the advantage of being clear, simple, and unambiguous in its definition. However, in actual application the value-added rule can become complex and uncertain. First, there is the issue of the valuation of materials, which may be based upon ex-works, FOB, CIF, or into-factory prices. Each method of valuation will give a different, here ascending, value of nonoriginating materials. Second, the application of this method can be costly for firms who will require sophisticated accounting systems and the ability to resolve often complex accounting questions. Finally, under the value-added method origin is

sensitive to changes in the factors determining production cost differentials across countries, such as exchange rates, wages, and commodity prices. For example, operations that confer origin in one location may not do so in another because of differences in wage costs. An operation that confers origin today may not do so tomorrow if exchange rates change.

### Specific Manufacturing Process

This criterion delineates for each product or product group certain manufacturing or processing operations that define origin (positive test), or manufacturing or processing procedures that do not confer origin (negative test). The formulation of these rules can require the use of certain originating inputs or prohibit the use of certain nonoriginating inputs. For example, EU rules of origin for clothing products stipulate "manufacture from yarn," while the rule for tube or pipe fittings of stainless steel stipulates "turning, drilling, reaming, threading, deburring and sandblasting of forged blanks."[3]

The main advantage of specific manufacturing process rules is that once defined they are clear and unambiguous so that from the outset producers are able to clearly identify whether their product is originating or not. However, there are also a number of drawbacks with this system, including obsolescence following changes in technology and the documentary requirements, such as an up-to-date inventory of production processes, which may be burdensome and difficult to comply with.

Table 9.A.1 in annex 9.A summarizes the main advantages and disadvantages of these different methods of determining sufficient processing or substantial transformation. No one rule dominates others as a mechanism for formally identifying the nationality of all products. Each has its advantages and disadvantages. However, it is clear that different rules of origin can lead to different determinations of origin. For example, in the case of nonpreferential rules of origin, the United States changed its rules for textile and clothing

---

3. The rule for this product also requires that the total value of the forged blanks should not exceed 35 percent of the ex-works price of the product.

products in 1996 in a way that changed the origin of products previously deemed as being of European origin as originating in Asian countries and hence subject to quantitative restrictions under the Agreement on Textiles and Clothing. These changes also required that products such as silk scarves previously labeled "made in Italy" had to be relabeled "made in Pakistan," with implications for the purchasing decisions of consumers who take the country of origin indicated on such labels as an indicator of quality (Dehousse, Ghemar, and Vincent 2002).

In the late 1980s, the EU changed its nonpreferential rules of origin for photocopiers to ensure that the operations carried out in the United States by a subsidiary of a Japanese company did not confer origin to the U.S. The products concerned were deemed to be originating in Japan and subject to antidumping duties (Hirsch 2002). Under preferential schemes, producers who are eligible for preferential access to different markets under different schemes with different rules of origin may find that their product qualifies under some schemes but not others. For example, a company in a developing country may find that its product qualifies for preferential access to the EU market under the EU's General System of Preferences (GSP) scheme but that the exact same product does not satisfy the rules of origin of the U.S. GSP scheme.

While it is difficult to derive specific recommendations with regard to the best approach to the design of rules of origin, certain general propositions can be made which apply to both preferential and nonpreferential rules of origin:

- Rules of origin should be simple but precise, transparent, predictable, and stable. Rules of origin should avoid or minimize scope for interpretation and administrative discretion.
- Rules of origin should be designed to have the least trade distorting impact and should not become a disguised nontariff barrier to trade. Protectionist lobbying should not compromise the specification of the rules of origin.
- As much as possible the rules should be consistent across products and across agreements. The greater the inconsistencies, the greater the complexity of the system of rules of origin both for companies and for officials administering the various trade schemes.

## Status of the Harmonization Work Program for Nonpreferential Rules of Origin

Harmonization of rules of origin has long been a dream of customs and trade officials. Under the General Agreement on Tariffs and Trade (GATT, established 1947) the contracting parties to the GATT were free to determine their own rules of origin. Nevertheless, records show that the GATT first considered the harmonization of rules of origin in 1951. Two years later, in 1953, following a recommendation from the International Chamber of Commerce for the adoption of a common definition of nationality of manufactured goods, a GATT working party was established on the "Nationality of Imported Goods" and examined both the definition of origin and proof of origin.

Despite the fact that these early GATT attempts were not successful, the WCO took a significant step forward through the establishment of the International Convention on the Simplification and Harmonization of Customs Procedures (the Revised Kyoto Convention) that came into force in 1974. Annexes D.1 to D.3 to the convention deal with rules of origin, including administrative matters. Although not many members have ratified these annexes,[4] the annexes have been influential because they set out the first international standards or models in the field of origin. For instance, a number of existing preferential and nonpreferential rules of origin, including those of non-contracting parties to the Revised Kyoto Convention, have adopted similar or almost identical definitions of wholly obtained goods as those set out in Annex D.1. But with regard to manufactured goods, that annex does not provide a single set of standard rules of origin concerning the criteria for identifying a substantial transformation. Instead, it explains the most commonly used criteria—change in tariff classification, value-added, and specific manufacturing or processing operations—and suggests recommended practices with regard to their use. Nevertheless, each

---

4. There are 31 annexes to the Revised Kyoto Convention. Contracting parties to the convention do not have to accept all the annexes, but they are required to notify the Secretary General of the WCO that they accept one or more annexes. Out of the 63 current contracting parties to the convention, 26 members have accepted Annex D.1, 25 have accepted Annex D.2, and 8 have accepted Annex D.3). A particular annex enters into force when at least five members ratify or accede to that annex.

administration has remained free to choose any one or combination of those criteria and to specify those criteria how they wish.

With regard to the change of tariff classification rule, the underlying technical constraint to harmonization in the past was the absence of a common internationally agreed on tool for classifying products. Different countries could classify the same good in different ways. A major breakthrough came in 1988 with the entry into force of the Harmonized System so that all major trading nations now use the same classification system for coding products for customs and for statistical purposes.[5] However, because of the trade policy implications (antidumping measures, for example), attempts to harmonize rules of origin only occurred following inclusion of the issue on the negotiating agenda of a large-scale multilateral trade negotiation, the Uruguay Round of GATT negotiations.

### The Uruguay Round and the Agreement on Rules of Origin

During the June 1989 Uruguay Round meetings, Japan proposed to negotiate the harmonization of preferential and nonpreferential rules of origin, as well as a mechanism for notification, consultation, and dispute settlement. This was motivated, among other things, by a series of trade disputes during the 1980s between Japan and other East Asian countries, on the one hand, and their major trading partners, on the other. Some of these trade disputes stemmed from the application of rules of origin in conjunction with antidumping proceedings. While the United States endorsed the idea to include this issue on the Uruguay Round agenda, the European Community and the European Free Trade Association (EFTA) countries were initially reluctant. They considered the issue better suited to the more technical WCO and believed that the discussion should not address the rules of origin used under preferential arrangements (Croome 1995).

In February 1990, agreement was reached that the negotiating group should define policy principles (for example, nondiscrimination, transparency,

predictability) to govern the application of rules of origin. Another compromise agreement was reached prior to the Brussels Ministerial Meeting in December 1990 that the harmonized rules of origin should cover nonpreferential trade only. A nonbinding common declaration with regard to preferential rules of origin was agreed to at this meeting. This contained a number of general exhortations to members to make their preferential rules clear, to base them on a positive standard, to publish them in accordance with GATT rules, and to assert that changes should not be applied retroactively and that judicial review should be available.

The outcome of these negotiations was compiled as an Agreement on Rules of Origin annexed to the Marrakesh Agreement Establishing the World Trade Organization, which entered into force in January 1995. The Origin Agreement mandated the Technical Committee on Rules of Origin (TCRO) under the auspices of the WCO and the Committee on Rules of Origin (CRO) under the WTO to undertake a Harmonization Work Program (HWP) for nonpreferential rules of origin, to be completed within a three-year period. Under the Origin Agreement, members are obliged to adhere to the following disciplines after the implementation of the results of the HWP (Article 3: Disciplines after the Transition Period):

- Rules of origin are applied equally for all purposes (for example, application of most favored nation [MFN] treatment, antidumping and countervailing duties, safeguard measures, origin marking requirements, any discriminatory quantitative restrictions or tariff quotas, government procurement, trade statistics).
- Rules of origin determine origin of goods either by definition of wholly obtained goods or the substantial transformation criteria.
- Rules of origin observe national treatment and MFN requirements.
- Rules of origin must be administered in a consistent, uniform, impartial, and reasonable manner.
- Laws, regulations, judicial decisions, and administrative rulings of general application relating to rules of origin must be published.
- Origin assessments must be provided, upon request, within 150 days (and be valid for three years).

---

5. The HS is used by over 190 countries and customs or economic unions (including 112 contracting parties to the HS Convention), representing about 98 percent of world trade (as of the time of writing).

- Changes in rules of origin are not to be applied retroactively.
- Any administrative action regarding the determination of origin is subject to possible review.
- Confidentiality of information must be observed.

### The Harmonization Work Program and the Draft Harmonized Nonpreferential Rules of Origin

Imagawa and Vermulst, in *Rules of Origin in a Globalized World: A Work in Progress* (2003) studied the issue of the HWP and rules of origin, and this forms the basis of the following discussion.

From its inaugural session in February 1995, the TCRO undertook technical work, developing definitions of wholly obtained goods and minimal operations or processes and elaborating upon substantial transformation criteria. At the same time, the Geneva-based CRO has carried out the policy work, including endorsing the results of the TCRO's technical review. It took nearly four years (and 20 formal and informal sessions) for the TCRO to complete its technical review. A key feature of this process was discussion of the rules on a product-by-product basis, as dictated by the Origin Agreement.[6] The work of the TCRO was submitted to the CRO in May 1999. The TCRO agreed to product-specific rules for over 500 of 1,241 headings; 486 issues[7] were referred to the CRO. The CRO has continued the HWP based on the results of the TCRO's technical review and has substantially narrowed the number of outstanding issues.[8] In September 2002, 94 core policy issues were referred to the WTO General Council and negotiations at the ambassadorial level still continue.[9] The

General Council has mainly argued about the so-called "implications issue" as to whether the harmonized nonpreferential rules of origin (HRO) should be applied on a mandatory basis to other WTO instruments, in particular antidumping and countervailing duty proceedings.[10] Despite all its efforts, the WTO has not been able to complete the HWP; the deadline has been exceeded several times.

What are the underlying factors that have hindered the completion of the HWP? The process of harmonization has required the standardization of definitions, rules, and practices that differ across countries and regions. This has required a consensus-building approach that has been time consuming because the issues were highly technical and the work involved was extremely voluminous and labor intensive; the disparity among delegations with regard to technical arguments on certain crucial product-specific and other issues was deeply rooted in national industrial and trade policy, so members had to be ready to change the national policy in question if they accepted an alternative position. The Origin Agreement itself (Article 9.2c) required that the harmonization work of the TCRO be "conducted on a product sector basis, as represented by various chapters or sections of the HS nomenclature." This reflects the view of those who believe that such an approach is necessary to achieve nonpreferential origin rules that are "objective, understandable and predictable," the objectives defined in the Origin Agreement. However, it appears that when negotiations are conducted on a product-by-product basis it is inevitable that specific domestic interest groups will become involved, ensuring that different countries adopt different and often entrenched positions.

It is important to note that most of the core problems relating to product-specific rules that are still to be resolved relate to products of particular relevance in the exports of developing countries. Of the 94 remaining key product-specific issues, 69 (or 75 percent) are concerned with agricultural products (45) and textiles and clothing (24) (WTO

---

6. The Origin Agreement denies the possibility of a conceptual definition of substantial transformation in terms of a simple rule, based, it seems, on the assumption that such a rule would lack precision and would be difficult to implement. Instead, the TCRO is mandated to "consider" use of change of tariff subheading or heading on a product basis (Art. 9.2(c)(ii)), although the supplementary use of other methods is provided for.

7. The scope of an issue varies from one split (sub) heading to several HS chapters. Consequently, the fact that 486 issues exist does not mean that there are unresolved product-specific rules for 486 headings.

8. By the end of 2002, 349 issues out of 486 had been resolved by the CRO (WTO 2002c).

9. The CRO was to complete its work by year end 2001. The deadline was initially extended to July 2003 for 94 core policy issues and December 2003 for the remaining technical work. These deadlines were extended to July 2004 and December 2004, respectively.

---

10. According to the WTO Secretariat, strong support has emerged among delegations for the notion that "whenever there is a mandatory legal requirement in the determination of origin in the WTO Agreement other than the Agreement on Rules of Origin, the harmonized rules of origin must be used" (see WCO 2003).

2002c). These are products that are subject to the highest levels of protection in industrialized countries. Only 10 percent of the outstanding issues concern engineering products, which dominate the exports of the industrialized countries.

The draft HRO consists of Definitions, General Rules, and two appendixes. When the HWP is completed, the results will be annexed to the Origin Agreement as an integral part thereof (Article 9.4). Definitions and General Rules are general provisions governing the entire HRO. Appendix 1 sets out two rules and definitions for wholly obtained goods, which evolved from the current Kyoto definitions. It consists of two parts: goods wholly obtained in one country and products taken from outside the country (such as from the high seas). It is the latter group that is still under discussion in the WTO. Appendix 2 consists of product-specific rules of origin for goods that are not wholly obtained (there is a sequential application of these two appendixes with Appendix 1 having precedence over Appendix 2). Seven rules, which are to be applied for the purposes of Appendix 2 only, have been proposed and largely agreed on. Rule 3 is the core (Determination of Origin) and sets out a series of provisions to be applied in sequence.

In these rules product-specific requirements are set out for each HS heading or subheading. Two types of rules are specified, primary and residual rules. Primary rules, in the form of change-in-tariff-classification, value-added, or specific-process rules, or a combination of these rules, are applied first (there is a sequential application between the primary and residual rules). There is no precedence among these different primary rules, that is, the primary rules are considered to be equal. Regardless of the placement of the rules, that is, at the chapter, heading, or subheading level of the HS, there is no hierarchy among them. The residual rules determine the country of origin of a good that fails to meet the primary rule, such as a change of heading rule. It is worth noting that while preferential rules of origin lead to either a "yes" (qualified) or "no" (not qualified) answer, under the HRO a decision defining the country of origin must ultimately be made; there will be no good for which the country of origin cannot be determined. Residual rules do have a hierarchical structure, with those defined for specific products at the chapter level taking precedence over the general residual rules.

### Implementing the HRO: Implications

The benefits of harmonized rules of origin to the globalized world economy cannot be overstated. The application of a single set of rules of origin for the various nonpreferential purposes would save time and cost to traders and customs officers all over the world. It would add to the certainty and predictability of trade by ensuring consistency of origin determination across countries and across time. Harmonized nonpreferential rules of origin would also help to avoid potential trade disputes arising from uncertainties in the determination of the country of origin with regard to antidumping and countervailing duties, safeguard measures, origin marking requirements, quantitative restrictions or tariff rate quotas, and government procurement decisions.

The WTO Secretariat has been notified that, as of the time of writing, 41 WTO members do not use nonpreferential rules of origin in their customs and trading systems.[11] When the HRO are established as an integral part of the ARO, these members will be expected to reform their legislative and administrative systems as follows:

**Legislative Matters**
- For those countries that do not have nonpreferential rules of origin, there will be a need to adopt and implement the HRO.
- For those countries that have one or more nonpreferential rules of origin, those rules will have to be aligned to the HRO and implemented.
- Because the TCRO preferred not to harmonize the procedural matters of the HRO, each country will need to establish or modify its national rules to implement the HRO according to domestic legislative or administrative procedures.

**Organizational Structure**
- For those countries that do not have central and regional units responsible for the HRO, a proper organizational structure to implement the HRO will become necessary.

---

11. These members are: Bolivia; Brazil; Brunei Darussalam; Burundi; Chad; Chile; Costa Rica; Cyprus; Dominica; Dominican Republic; El Salvador; Fiji; Guatemala; Haiti; Honduras; Iceland; India; Indonesia; Jamaica; Kenya; Macao, China; Malaysia; Maldives; Malta; Mauritius; Mongolia; Namibia; Nicaragua; Oman; Pakistan; Panama; Papua New Guinea; Paraguay; Philippines; Singapore; Suriname; Thailand; Trinidad and Tobago; Uganda; United Arab Emirates; and Uruguay (WTO 2002b).

## Capacity Building and Dissemination of Information

- For those countries that do not have nonpreferential rules of origin, extensive training and orientation programs for customs officials, trade officials, and traders must be planned and conducted in time for the implementation of the HRO. Therefore, international organizations, such as the WCO, and donor countries might wish to take this need into account in their planning activities.

- For those countries that have one or more nonpreferential rules of origin, the changes between present and future rules need to be communicated to customs officials, trade officials, and traders.

### The Harmonization of Nonpreferential Rules of Origin: Conclusions

After nearly a decade of negotiations, an increasingly defined shape of the HRO has emerged. The HRO are guided by the clear principles laid down in the ARO. From the technical point of view, it has been observed that members cannot pursue absolute consistency between product-specific rules of origin as long as the results of the HWP are the fruit of compromise. However, such a fact does not undermine the benefit of having harmonized nonpreferential rules of origin. Transparency and consistency in origin determination cannot be ensured without a clear standard. Nevertheless, the existence of a far-from-perfect standard is better than the absence of any standard whatsoever, as shown by the benefits of introducing the HS, which has led to the benefits of a "common language" for purposes of classification. Thus, whatever the applicable rules of origin are, once harmonized, those rules are the same both in the exporting and in the importing country. In a highly interconnected world there can be substantial benefits from having a single set of rules applied in all WTO member countries.

A further advantage of harmonized nonpreferential rules of origin would be that they would provide a benchmark by which to assess rules of origin applied on preferential trade flows. Countries seeking rules of origin that deviate from the nonpreferential rules could be asked by partners to explicitly justify why the nonpreferential rules of origin are

insufficient. It is in this context that the chapter now proceeds to a more detailed discussion of the preferential rules of origin and their impact on trade and customs.

## The Definition of Preferential Rules of Origin

Preferential rules of origin define the conditions that a product must satisfy to be deemed as originating in a country that is eligible for preferential access to a partner's market and has not simply been transshipped from a nonqualifying country or been subject to only minimal processing. In practice, the greater the level of work that is required by the rules of origin, the more difficult it is to satisfy those rules and the more restrictive those rules are in constraining market access relative to what is required simply to prevent trade deflection. This is particularly true for small less-diversified developing economies. Thus, the higher the amount of domestic value-added required by a value-added rule, the more difficult it will be to comply with, because there will be less scope for the use of imported parts and materials. A rule of origin that prevents the use of imported flour in the production of pastry products such as biscuits, for example, will be excessively restrictive for countries that do not have a competitive milling industry.

Preferential rules of origin often differ from nonpreferential rules. In the main it is the requirements relating to specific processing that vary and are usually more demanding in preferential trade agreements. However, there are also cases, some of them initially rather surprising, where rules relating to what would appear to be wholly obtained products are more restrictive in preferential trade agreements. (See box 9.1 for such an example.)

### Methods for Determining Sufficient Processing

With regard to requirements relating to sufficient processing, change of tariff classification is used in the vast majority of current preferential trade agreements and is featured in both EU agreements and NAFTA. WTO research shows that of 87 free trade agreements (FTAs) and other preferential trade agreements investigated, 83 used change of tariff classification in the determination of origin (WTO 2002a). Most agreements specify that the

---

**BOX 9.1    Example of Restrictive Rules of Origin: The Case of EU Imports of Fish**

On the face of it, determining the origin of fish, fresh or chilled, would appear to be straightforward with origin being conferred to the country whose trawler caught the fish; there is, after all, no apparent import content in the fish. However, in practice the determination of origin for fish caught outside territorial waters but within the exclusive economic zone of a country can be complex. To receive preferential access to the EU under the GSP, all of the following conditions must be satisfied:

- The vessel must be registered in the beneficiary country or in the EU.
- The vessel must sail under the flag of the beneficiary country or of a member state of the EU.
- The vessel must be at least 60 percent owned by nationals of the beneficiary country or the EU or by companies with a head office in either the beneficiary country or an EU state of which the chairman and a majority of the board members are nationals.
- The master and the officers must be nationals of the beneficiary country or an EU member and at least 75 percent of the crew must be nationals of the beneficiary country or the EU.

Under the EU's Cotonou Agreement, which gives preferential access to the EU market to countries in Africa, the Caribbean, and the Pacific (ACP), the rules of origin for fish are slightly different and a little more liberal than those for GSP countries:

- The vessel must be registered in the EU or any ACP state.
- The vessel must sail under the flag of any ACP country or the EU.
- The vessel must be at least 50 percent owned by nationals of any ACP or EU state, and the chairman and the majority of the board members must be nationals of any of those countries.
- Under certain conditions the EU will accept vessels chartered or leased by the ACP state under the Cotonou Agreement.
- Under Cotonou, 50 percent of the crew, the master, and officers must be nationals of any ACP state or the EU.

So identifying the nationality of a fish can be a complex task.

*Source:* Official Journal of the European Communities 2000.

---

change should take place at the heading level (that is at the four-digit level), although in many agreements, especially those involving the EU and in NAFTA, the tariff shift requirement varies across different products. For example, other research shows that in NAFTA, while around 40 percent of tariff lines require change of tariff heading, for most tariff lines (54 percent) it is change of chapter (two-digit level) that is required (Estevadeordal and Suominen 2003). The requirement of change of chapter is more restrictive than change of heading. For a small number of products in NAFTA it is only change of subheading that is required.

While change of tariff heading is used in the majority of preferential trade agreements, it is seldom the only method applied. It is also important to note that in some agreements, for example, those involving the EU, change of tariff classification is applied to some products while the other methods (value-added rules and specific technical processes) will be applied to other products. In the NAFTA rules of origin, all rules tend to require at least

change of tariff classification, but the level at which change is required varies across products. This typically leads to considerable complications for customs officials in the determination of origin in preferential agreements. In contrast, many of the agreements involving developing countries tend to provide general rules of origin and eschew the detailed product-by-product approach adopted by the EU and NAFTA. Further, in EU agreements and in NAFTA for certain products, rules will be stipulated that require satisfaction of more than one method to confer origin. This is clearly more restrictive than a requirement to satisfy a single method. For example, in NAFTA rules of origin, the requirement for passenger motor vehicles (HS 870321) is a change to subheading 8703.21 from any other heading, provided there is a regional value content of not less than 50 percent under the net cost method.

In some agreements for certain products, two or more methods will be stipulated and satisfaction of any one of the methods will be sufficient to confer origin. For example, in the EU rules of origin, the requirements for wooden office furniture (HS 940330) are

- Manufacture in which all the material used is classified within a heading other than that of the product, or
- Manufacture in which the value of all the materials used does not exceed 40 percent of the ex-works price of the product.

Providing alternative means of satisfying origin requirements is more liberal and will facilitate trade under preferential trade agreements.

With regard to the value-added requirements, the WTO concludes that on average a threshold on domestic content of between 40 and 60 percent is the norm, with the average import requirement being between 60 and 40 percent (WTO 2002a). In the EU agreements there are various thresholds on import content ranging from 30 to 50 percent. In NAFTA there is a domestic content requirement of either 50 or 60 percent according to the method used to value the product. A value-added requirement of 50 percent can be very demanding in the globalized world of today in which production has become split across, often many, countries. A further feature of globalization is that in a range of products such as clothing products, computers, and telecommunications equipment, much of the value-added lies in the intermediate products. High value-added requirements, therefore, become particularly difficult for developing countries to satisfy because it is the final labor-intensive stage that they host. In this way restrictive rules of origin act to constrain specialization at the country level.

In general, these percentage value rules are rarely applied as the sole test of origin and are typically applied with the change of tariff classification. Exceptions are Australia New Zealand Closer Economic Relations Trade Agreement (ANZCERTA), South Pacific Regional Trade and Economic Co-operation Agreement (SPARTECA), and AFTA, which have percentage requirements without any additional need for change of tariff heading, although all three agreements do require that the last process of manufacture be undertaken in the exporting country.

As noted, under the value-added method origin is sensitive to changes in factors such as exchange rates, wages, and commodity prices. This means that the value-added method will tend to penalize

low labor cost locations, which will find it more difficult to add the necessary value relative to higher cost locations, and is likely to cause particular problems of compliance for companies in developing countries that lack the sophisticated accounting systems necessary under this method.

Rules based on specific manufacturing processes are widely used (in 74 of the 83 preferential trade agreements analyzed by the WTO [2002a], often in conjunction with change of tariff classification or the value-added criterion or both, and are a particular feature of the rules applied to the textiles and clothing sectors.

Two examples of rules of origin and their implications for conferring origin follow:

- A producer imports cotton fabric (HS5208), which is then dyed, cut, and made up into cotton shirts (HS6105). The value of the imported materials amounts to 65 percent of the value of the shirts. In this case the product would be originating under the change of tariff heading rule. The product would not be originating under a value-added rule requiring an import content of no more than 60 percent (or a domestic content of more than 40 percent). A specific manufacturing process requirement, that the product be manufactured from yarn (the production stage before fabric), would mean that the product would not be originating.[12]
- A doll (HS9502) is made from imported plastics and imported ready-made garments and footwear. The value of the imported materials amounts to 50 percent of the value of the doll. In this case the doll would be originating under a value-added rule requiring an import content of no more than 60 percent but would not be originating under the change of tariff heading because garments and accessories for dolls are normally classified under the same tariff heading as dolls.

Most preferential trade agreements also specify a range of operations that are deemed to be insufficient working or processing to confer origin. Typically these include simple packaging operations,

---

12. This yarn-forward rule is common in EU agreements for all clothing products. The United States typically applies an even stricter process rule that the clothing be made from fibers, meaning that both spinning into yarn and weaving into fabric as well as the making up into clothing are required in the exporting country to confer origin on the product.

such as bottling, placing in boxes, bags, and cases, and simple fixing on cards and boards; simple mixing of products and simple assembly of parts; and operations to ensure the preservation of products during transport and storage. These requirements act to ensure that these basic operations do not confer origin even if the basic rule of origin, such as change of tariff heading, has been satisfied.

### Additional Features of Preferential Rules of Origin

There are several other typical features of the rules of origin of preferential trade schemes that can influence whether origin is conferred on a product and hence determine the impact of the scheme on trade flows. These are cumulation, tolerance rules, and absorption. The treatment of duty drawback and of outward processing outside the free trade or preferential trade partners can also be important.

**Cumulation**   The basic rules of origin define the processing that has to be done in the individual beneficiary or partner to confer origin. Cumulation is an instrument allowing producers to import materials from a specific country or regional group of countries without undermining the origin of the final product. In effect, the imported materials from the identified countries are treated as being of domestic origin of the country requesting preferential access. There are three types of cumulation— bilateral, diagonal (or partial), and full.

The most basic form of cumulation is *bilateral cumulation,* which applies to materials provided by either of two partners of a preferential trade agreement. In this case, originating inputs—that is, materials—that have been produced in accordance with the relevant rules of origin, imported from the partner, qualify as originating materials when used in a country's exports to that partner. For example, under the EU's GSP scheme, the rule of origin for cotton shirts states that origin is conferred to a beneficiary country if the shirt is manufactured from yarn. That is, nonoriginating yarn may be imported but the weaving into fabric and the cutting and the making up into a shirt must take place in the beneficiary. The EU's GSP scheme allows for bilateral cumulation so that fabric that originates in the EU—that is, fabric that has been produced in accordance with the rule of·origin for fabric (in the case of the EU scheme, it has been produced from

the stage of fibers)—can be treated as originating in the beneficiary country. Thus, originating fabrics can be imported from the EU and used in the production of shirts, which will qualify for preferential access to the EU. However, the EU is often not the least-cost supplier of inputs, so the benefits of this type of cumulation can be limited. If the extra cost of using EU-sourced inputs rather than the lowest cost inputs from elsewhere exceeds the available benefit from preferential access, then cumulation will have no effect and there will be no improvement in market access.

Next, there can be *diagonal cumulation* on a regional basis so that qualifying materials from anywhere in the specified region can be used without undermining preferential access. In other words, parts and materials from anywhere in the region that qualify as originating can be used in the manufacture of a final product that can then be exported with preferences to the partner country market. Diagonal cumulation is widely used in EU agreements but is not applied by NAFTA. In Europe, a pan-European system of rules of origin with diagonal cumulation has been developed that governs EU free trade agreements with the EFTA countries and countries in Central and Eastern Europe. Diagonal cumulation is allowed under the EU's GSP scheme but within a limited set of regional groups that have pursued their own regional trade agreements. For example, under the EU's GSP scheme, diagonal cumulation can take place within four regional groupings: Association of Southeast Asian Nations (ASEAN), Central American Common Market (CACM), the Andean Community, and South Asian Association for Regional Cooperation (SAARC). Diagonal cumulation allows *originating* materials from regional partners to be further processed in another country in the group and treated as if the materials were originating in the country where the processing is undertaken.[13] However, this flexibility in sourcing is constrained by the further requirement that the value added in the final stage of production exceed

---

13. For both bilateral and regional cumulation there can be an additional requirement that the processing carried out be more than "insufficient working or processing." This is typical in EU agreements but not those of other countries, and requires that more than packing, mixing, cleaning, preserving, and simple assembly of parts take place.

the highest customs value of any of the inputs used from countries in the regional grouping. Thus, for example, with diagonal cumulation shirt producers in Cambodia can use fabrics from Indonesia (providing they are originating, that is, produced from the stage of fibers) and still receive duty-free access to the EU, but the value-added in Cambodia must exceed the value of the imported fabric from Indonesia. Similarly, producers in Nepal can import originating fabric from India and still qualify for preferential access to the EU if the value added in Nepal is sufficient.

However, UNCTAD and The Commonwealth Secretariat (2001) show how the value-added requirement mentioned above can render regional cumulation of little value. For example, value-added in the making up of clothing in Bangladesh ranges from 25 to 35 percent of the value of the product so that the import content of the fabric from India is around 65 to 75 percent. In this case the value-added requirement placed on regional cumulation is not met and origin of the made-up clothing is not conferred on Bangladesh but on India. Regional cumulation still allows clothing produced in Bangladesh from Indian fabrics preferential access to the EU but not at the zero rate (for which Bangladesh is eligible) but at the rate for which India is eligible, which is a 20 percent reduction from the MFN rate. Thus, instead of the zero duty, which is in principle available to Bangladesh under the Everything but Arms (EBA) initiative, a tariff of over 9 percent would be levied on these exports from Bangladesh to the EU.

Finally, there can be *full cumulation* whereby any processing activities carried out in any participating country in a regional group can be counted as qualifying content regardless of whether the processing is sufficient to confer originating status to the materials themselves. In certain GSP schemes, cumulation is permitted across all developing country beneficiaries. Full cumulation allows for more fragmentation of production processes among the members of the regional group and so stimulates increased economic linkages and trade within the region. Under full cumulation it may be easier for more developed, higher labor cost countries to outsource labor intensive low-tech production stages to less developed, lower wage partners while maintaining the preferential status of the goods produced in low-cost locations. Diagonal

cumulation, by requiring more stages of production or higher value-added to be undertaken in the lower cost country, may make it more difficult for the products produced by outsourcing to qualify for preferential access. However, the documentary requirements of full cumulation can be more onerous than those required under diagonal cumulation. Detailed information from suppliers of inputs may be required under full cumulation while the certificates of origin, which accompany imported materials, may suffice to show conformity under diagonal cumulation. For this reason it is desirable that traders be offered the opportunity to use either diagonal or full cumulation.

Under full cumulation, all the processing carried out in participating countries is assessed in deciding whether there has been substantial transformation. Hence, full cumulation provides for deeper integration among participating countries. Full cumulation is rare and is currently applied in the EU agreements with the EFTA countries; in the EU agreements with Algeria, Morocco, and Tunisia; and under the Cotonou Agreements between the EU and the ACP countries. It is also available in the GSP schemes of Japan and the United States; among countries within specified groupings; and on a global basis among all developing country beneficiaries in the schemes of Australia, Canada, and New Zealand; as well as in ANZCERTA and SPARTECA.

For example, a clothing product made in one country from fabric produced in a regional partner, which in turn was made from nonoriginating yarn, would be eligible for duty-free access to the EU under full cumulation but not under diagonal cumulation because the fabric would not be deemed originating (the rule of origin for the fabric requires manufacture from fibers).

A second example follows: Country A provides parts (say chassis for bicycles) to country B, which are then processed (painted and prepared) and sent to country C for final assembly using other locally produced parts (tires and seat) before being exported to country D. Countries B, C, and D participate in the same FTA; country A is not a member. The value of the final product (bicycle) exported from country C to country D comprises 25 percent of parts from country A, 25 percent of value-added in country B, and 50 percent of parts and value-added in country C. The value of parts from country A comprises 50 percent of the value of the intermediate product exported from country B to country C. If there were a 40 percent maximum import content for all products, the bicycle exported from country C to D would qualify for preferential access under full cumulation (only the 25 percent of parts from country A is nonoriginating). However, it would not qualify under diagonal cumulation (the value of nonoriginating materials in the product exported by country B exceeds 40 percent). This intermediate product would not be treated as originating, and the total of nonoriginating materials in the final product is now calculated as 50 percent of the final price of the bicycle (the value from both countries A and B).

**Tolerance or De Minimis**  Tolerance or *de minimis* rules allow a certain percentage of nonoriginating materials to be used without affecting the origin of the final product. Thus, the tolerance rule can act to make it easier for products with nonoriginating inputs to qualify for preferences under the change of tariff heading and specific manufacturing process rules. This provision does not affect the value-added rules. The tolerance rule does not act to lower the limitation on the value of imported materials. The nonoriginating materials will always be counted in import value content calculations.

Under NAFTA, nonoriginating materials can be used even if the rule on sufficient processing is not fulfilled, provided their value does not exceed 7 percent of the value of the final product. Under the EU's GSP scheme, the threshold is 10 percent, but under the Cotonou Agreement between the EU and the ACP countries the tolerance rule allows 15 percent of nonoriginating materials that would otherwise not be accepted to be used. For example, in the case of the doll given above in which the use of dolls clothing accessories denied origin to the final product under the change of heading rule (because the accessories are classified under the same heading), origin would have been conferred under the EU GSP if the value of the dolls' clothing and accessories was less than 10 percent of the value of the doll.

Thus, the tolerance rule can act to make it easier for products with nonoriginating inputs to qualify for preferences under the change of tariff heading and specific manufacturing process rules. However, the tolerance rules applied to the textiles and clothing sector were often different and generally less favorable than the general rules on tolerance. In many cases the rule is applied in terms of the maximum weight rather than value of nonoriginating materials that are tolerated, and in cases where the value threshold is maintained it is set at a lower level than in the general rule.

**Absorption (or Roll-Up) Principle**  The absorption principle provides that parts or materials that have acquired originating status by satisfying the relevant rules of origin for that product can be treated as being of domestic origin in any further processing and transformation. This is of particular relevance to the value-added test. For example, in the production of a particular part, origin is conferred because imported materials constitute 20 percent of the final price of the part and are less than the maximum 30 percent import content rule of origin. This part will then be treated as 100 percent originating when incorporated into a final product. The 20 percent import content of the part is not taken into account when assessing the import content of the final product. The converse of this is that if the part does not satisfy the relevant rule of origin, it is deemed to be 100 percent nonoriginating (so-called "roll-down"). Ideally, if the part or materials do not satisfy the relevant rule of origin, the portion of value added domestically should still be counted in the determination of the origin of the final product.

**Duty Drawback**  Provisions relating to duty drawback can lead to the repayment of duties on nonoriginating inputs used in the production of a final product exported to a free trade or preferential trade partner. Some agreements contain explicit no-drawback rules that will affect decisions relating to the sourcing of inputs by firms exporting within the trade area and will switch the previous incentives for the use of imported inputs from nonparticipating countries toward the use of originating inputs from participating ones. Increasingly important are rules concerning *territoriality* and the treatment of outward processing by companies located within the free trade area to locations outside it. These rules determine whether processing outside the area undermines the originating status of the final product exported from one partner to another.

## Rules of Origin in Existing Free Trade and Preferential Trade Agreements

Table 9.B.1 in annex 9.B provides a simplified look at the key features of the rules of origin applied in a number of regional and bilateral trade schemes. The table contrasts the nature of the rules applied as well as the use of cumulation mechanisms, tolerance rules, and absorption.

Table 9.B.1 shows that all three methods of determining origin are employed in agreements involving the EU and NAFTA. A key feature of the EU and NAFTA models of rules of origin is that the rules are specified at a detailed level on a product-by-product basis. The recent Japan–Singapore agreement also follows this approach. The U.S.–Singapore FTA has rules of origin that are similar to those of NAFTA, which means that product-specific and sometimes complex rules are used. The annexes specifying these rules of origin can be massive. In the U.S.–Singapore agreement there are over 240 pages of product-specific rules of origin. Box 9.2 provides a further

---

**BOX 9.2    More Restrictive Rules of Origin: The Case of Clothing Under NAFTA Rules**

The following example is for men's or boys' overcoats made of wool (HS620111).

"A change to subheading 620111 from any other chapter, except from heading 5106 through 5113, 5204 through 5212, 5307 through 5308 or 5310 through 5311, Chapter 54 or heading 5508 through 5516, 5801 through 5802 or 6001 through 6006, provided that:

The good is both cut and sewn or otherwise assembled in the territory of one or more of the Parties."

The basic rule of origin stipulates change of chapter but then provides a list of headings and chapters from which inputs cannot be used. Thus, in effect the overcoat must be manufactured from the stage of wool fibers forward, because neither imported woolen yarn (HS5106–5110) nor imported woolen fabric (HS5111–5113) can be used. However, the rule also states that imported cotton thread (HS5204) and imported thread of man-made fibers (HS54) cannot be used to sew the coat together. This rule in itself is restrictive; however, the rule for this product is further complicated by requirements relating to the visible lining:

"Except for fabrics classified in 54082210, 54082311, 54082321, and 54082410, the fabrics identified in the following sub-headings and headings, when used as visible lining material in certain men's and women's suits, suit-type jackets, skirts, overcoats, car coats, anoraks, windbreakers, and similar articles, must be formed from yarn and finished in the territory of a party: 5111 through 5112, 520831 through 520859, 520931 through 520959, 521031 through 521059, 521131 through 521159, 521213 through 521215, 521223 through 521225, 540742 through 540744, 540752 through 540754, 540761, 540772 through 540774, 540782 through 540784, 540792 through 540794, 540822 through 540824 (excluding tariff item 540822aa, 540823aa or 540824aa), 540832 through 540834, 551219, 551229, 551299, 551321 through 551349, 551421 through 551599, 551612 through 551614, 551622 through 551624, 551632 through 551634, 551642 through 551644, 551692 through 551694, 600110, 600192, 600531 through 600544 or 600610 through 600644."

This stipulates that the visible lining used must be produced from yarn and finished in either party. This rule may well have been introduced to constrain the impact of the tolerance rule that would normally allow 7 percent of the weight of the article to be of nonoriginating materials. In overcoats and suits the lining is probably less than 7 percent of the total weight.

Finally, it is interesting to note that the rules of origin also provide a number of very specific exemptions to the rules of origin for materials that are in short supply or not produced in the United States, reflecting firm-specific lobbying to overcome the restrictiveness of these rules of origin when the original NAFTA rules of origin were defined. The most specific example is where apparel is deemed to be originating if assembled from imported inputs of

"Fabrics of subheading 511111 or 511119, if hand-woven, with a loom width of less than 76 cm, woven in the United Kingdom in accordance with the rules and regulations of the Harris Tweed Association, Ltd., and so certified by the Association;. . ."

So, the job of business and of the relevant officials to check consistency with such rules are clearly not simple ones.

*Source:* U.S. International Trade Commission 2004.

example of complex and restrictive rules from the NAFTA rules of origin for clothing products.

This detailed product-specific approach to rules of origin of the EU and NAFTA can be contrasted with most of the agreements involving developing countries, such as AFTA, Common Market for Eastern and Southern Africa (COMESA), and Mercado Comun del Sur (MERCOSUR), where general rules are typically specified and there are no, or very few, product-specific rules of origin. This suggests that domestic industry did not play a significant role in the specification of these rules. Some agreements, such as AFTA, rely solely on the value-added method. The COMESA rules of origin require satisfaction of a value criterion (either the CIF value of imports must not exceed 60 percent of the value of all materials used, or domestic value-added should be at least 35 percent of the ex-factory cost of the goods)[14] or a change of tariff heading.[15]

What are the merits of these different approaches to the specification of preferential rules of origin? Specifying detailed product-by-product rules can lead to precise rules that leave little scope for interpretation. Indeed, some argue that a product-by-product approach based upon input from domestic producers is the best way to deal with the specification of rules of origin. However, as the examples in this chapter show, product-specific rules can become complex and restrictive, reflecting that a product-by-product approach offers opportunities for sectoral interests to influence the specification of rules of origin in a way that is not directly related to their function of identifying the nationality of products and of preventing trade deflection. The more complex and the more technical the rules become, the greater the scope for the participation of domestic industries in setting restrictive rules of origin (Hoekman 1993). Indeed "the formulation of product-specific rules of origin is, by its nature, very much out of the practical control of generalists, which is to say government officials at the policy level, and very much in the practical control of specialists, which is to say the

representatives of concerned industries" (Palmeter 1997, p. 353). Other interests, such as consumers of the relevant product, are effectively excluded from discussion concerning the rules of origin. Those who lobby hardest for trade policy interventions are not altruistic and their objectives with regard to rules of origin are likely to be to restrict competition from imports and to expand their own exports within a free trade area at the expense of third-country suppliers. Such objectives can be more effectively pursued when policy is determined in an environment that lacks transparency and openness, as can easily occur when rules of origin are determined in a product-by-product manner.

From a trade policy perspective, the restrictiveness of a value-added rule, in terms of its impact on trade, is clearer and more apparent than the change of tariff classification and specific manufacturing process rules. It is relatively straightforward to compare alternative proposals concerning a value-added rule. The extent of protection engendered by complex and technical rules of origin that differ across products is much more difficult to detect. This asymmetry of information is one reason those groups seeking protection will push for complex rules of origin and why the change of tariff classification and specific manufacturing process rules may be more susceptible to capture by protectionist domestic interest groups (Hirsch 2002).

Thus, it is apparent that adopting a product-by-product approach to rules of origin will tend to lead to rules that are more restrictive than is necessary to prevent trade deflection—that is, protectionist rules of origin—and can lead to an overly complex system that is difficult to implement by traders and adds considerably to the burden of customs.

However, it appears that more general rules of origin can lead to greater scope for interpretation, as noted by Izam (2003), for example, with regard to the rules of origin in the Latin American Integration Association. In Asia there are some suggestions of underutilization of AFTA preferences reflecting uncertainties concerning the rules of origin. It appears that the rules of origin may be subject to different interpretations in different ASEAN countries leading to inconsistent application of the rules throughout the region.[16] Nevertheless, this suggests

---

14. The COMESA agreement also specifies that a range of goods deemed to be of particular importance to economic development need only satisfy a 25 percent domestic value-added criterion.

15. At the present time, however, the change of tariff heading provision is not being implemented.

16. Pricewaterhouse Coopers (2002).

the need for more effective coordination between customs and other relevant authorities in different partners to clarify existing rules and regulations rather than formulating more restrictive rules of origin. It is also important that alternative rules be considered so that producers are allowed some flexibility in proving origin. Hence, providing producers with the option of satisfying either a value-added rule or a change of tariff classification rule is likely to be trade facilitating.

In table 9.B.1 the column showing the use of the value-added methods highlights the variation in the permitted amount of nonoriginating import content across the different agreements. In the Canada–Chile agreement, for example, products are typically subject to a change of tariff classification (the level of change required varies by product) and a domestic value-added requirement that varies between 25 and 60 percent (according to the product and the method of valuation used). In the U.S.–Chile agreement, where the rules are similar to those of NAFTA but not identical for all products, the required domestic content is between 35 and 55 percent. Under the Canada–Chile agreement, for example, plastic products (HS39) must satisfy requirements of change of tariff heading and between 50 percent and 60 percent of domestic value-added (depending on the method of valuation). Under the U.S.–Chile agreement most plastic products need only satisfy the requirement of change of subheading to be originating. To be originating under the U.S.–Chile agreement nonelectrical engineering products (HS84) must satisfy a change of subheading and a domestic value content of between 35 and 45 percent (according to method of valuation), while under the Canada–Chile agreement such products need satisfy change of subheading but only a 25 to 35 percent content requirement (depending on valuation method). Thus, certain products produced in Chile that are granted duty-free access to Canada may not receive such treatment in the United States due to the more liberal rules of origin applied in the Canada–Chile agreement for those products, while other products may satisfy U.S. rules of origin requirements but not those of Canada.

Table 9.B.1 also shows that all the agreements contain provisions regarding cumulation but also that there is considerable variation in the nature of cumulation. For example, the EU allows for diago-

nal cumulation in the Pan-European Area of Cumulation encompassing EFTA, Central and Eastern European and Balkan countries, while there is full cumulation among the African and Caribbean countries under the Cotonou Agreement. Similarly, for tolerance rules, which are widely applied in agreements that are not based on the sole use of the value-added method, there are considerable differences across agreements—even those involving the same country. Under the EU–Mexico Free Trade Agreement, nonoriginating materials of up to 10 percent of the value of the final product can be used, while under the agreement between the EU and South Africa the level of tolerance is set at 15 percent. Different rules of tolerance are often established for certain sectors, especially textiles and clothing.[17] Table 9.B.1 also shows the widespread use of the absorption principle.

Thus, this simple and brief look at the nature of the rules of origin applied in a number of existing free and preferential trade agreements highlights that the methods of defining origin and provisions relating to cumulation, tolerance, and absorption are widely applied. However, there is little commonality across agreements in the precise nature of the rules that are adopted. In general, recent agreements involving the EU and the United States are based upon detailed, often complex, product-specific rules of origin. The restrictiveness of these rules would appear to vary across sectors. For example, the rules for clothing products requiring production from yarn can be particularly difficult to satisfy for small less-developed economies. As such, the impact of these agreements will not be uniform across sectors.

## The Economic Implications of Rules of Origin

The specification and implementation of rules of origin can be a major determinant of the impact of free trade and preferential trade agreements. In practice, rules of origin are controversial because the available evidence, discussed in the next

---

17. Nevertheless, the tolerance rule may be important because in NAFTA there are chapter-specific rules for clothing products relating to the originating status of "visible linings" that appear to be motivated to limit the impact of the tolerance rule. See box 9.2 for details.

section, suggests that the use of preferences tends to be substantially less than full. That is, a substantial proportion of actual exports that are eligible for preferences do not enter the partner's market with zero or reduced duties but actually pay the MFN tariff.

Compliance with rules of origin can affect the sourcing and investment decisions of companies.[18] If the optimal input mix for a firm involves the use of imported inputs that are proscribed by the rules of origin of a free trade agreement in which the country participates, the rules of origin will reduce the value of the available preferences. The firm will have to shift from the lowest to a higher cost source of inputs in the domestic economy that will reduce the benefits of exporting under a lower tariff. In the extreme, if the cost difference exceeds the size of the tariff preference, the firm will prefer to source internationally and to pay the MFN tariff. The ability to cumulate inputs from a partner under bilateral, diagonal, or full cumulation will tend, in increasing order, to open the possibilities for identifying low cost sources of inputs that do not compromise the qualifying nature of the final product. Nevertheless, if the lowest cost supplier is not a member of the area of cumulation, the benefits of the preferential scheme will always be less than indicated by the size of the preferential tariff.

Rules of origin can also distort the relative prospects of similar firms within a country. For example, a clothing producer in, say, Moldova may have established an efficient manufacturing process on the basis of importing fabrics from Turkey. A less efficient producer who uses imported EU fabrics may be able to expand production on the basis of preferential access to the EU market under the GSP (with bilateral cumulation). The more efficient firm may not be able to expand because its product does not qualify for preferences due to the use of nonqualifying fabrics, and there may be substantial costs in changing suppliers of fabrics.

These problems will be exacerbated in sectors where economies of scale are important. A producer that supplies both preferential and nonpreferential trade partners, or faces different rules of origin in different preferential partners, will have to produce with a different input mix for different markets if the producer is to receive preferential access. This may undermine the benefits from lower average costs that would arise if total production were to be based on a single set of material inputs and a single production process.

Rules of origin may be an important factor determining the investment decisions of multinational firms. Such firms often rely on imported inputs from broad international networks that are vital to support the firm-specific advantages they possess, such as a technological advantage in the production of certain inputs. More generally, if the nature and application of a given set of rules of origin increases a degree of uncertainty concerning the extent to which preferential access will actually be provided, the level of investment will be less than if such uncertainty were reduced.

## Rules of Origin and the Utilization of Trade Preferences

Difficulties that may arise in satisfying the rules of origin and the costs of proving conformity with those rules are suggested by the relatively low utilization rates that are observed in preferential trade schemes.[19] Sapir (1998) showed that 79 percent of EU dutiable imports from GSP beneficiaries in 1994 qualified for preferential access to the EU market, yet only 38 percent actually entered the EU market with a duty less than the MFN rate. The reasons for this difference were the effects of rules of origin and tariff quotas for particular products, which set limits on the amount of imports that can receive beneficial access to the EU market. It also reflects the treatment of textiles and clothing products, which accounted for over 70 percent of EU imports from

---

18. Economists have generally given little attention to rules of origin within the voluminous literature on free trade areas. The key initial contributions on rules of origin are Krueger (1997) and Krishna and Krueger (1995), who demonstrate how rules of origin can act as "hidden protectionism" and induce a switch in demand in free trade partners from low-cost external inputs to higher-cost partner inputs to ensure that final products actually receive duty-free access. Falvey and Reed (1998) show how rules of origin can be used to protect a domestic industry from unwanted competition based from a partner, even in conditions where trade deflection is unlikely.

---

19. For many years UNCTAD has been highlighting the relatively low levels of utilization of preferences granted by developed countries to developing countries. For a recent discussion of utilization rates of GSP schemes and rules of origin, see Inama (2002).

countries covered by the GSP but where the utilization rate (the ratio of imports receiving preferences to eligible imports) was only 31 percent. In 2001 the utilization rate for least developed countries (LDCs) stood at 47 percent. It is important to stress that the utilization rate of preferences measures the proportion of exports to the EU that are recorded *at the border* as requesting preferences, so the low level of utilization cannot reflect the inability of the recipients to meet other requirements to access the EU market, such as health and safety or sanitary requirements or deficiencies in their infrastructure, as is sometimes suggested. Lack of infrastructure might explain why there is a very muted response from trade to preferences but cannot explain why at the border some products that are eligible for preferences do not request them.

It is worth noting here that the coverage rate of the EU scheme is comprehensive; over 99 percent of imports from developing countries of products that are subject to duties in the EU are eligible for preferences. The striking feature of the EU scheme is the low utilization of these preferences. The U.S. GSP scheme in contrast has a much higher utilization rate (over 76 percent in 1998 and as high as 96 percent for LDCs in 2001), but is much less comprehensive in terms of coverage (only about half of dutiable imports from developing countries are eligible for preferences). This is because textiles and clothing products are essentially excluded from the U.S. GSP scheme. They are included in the EU scheme, but only a small proportion of imports covered actually receive any preferences. However, an important feature of the U.S. scheme is that there are preferences on mineral fuels for LDCs, whereas in the EU there are zero duties on imports of oil. UNCTAD reports that when mineral products are excluded, the utilization rate for LDCs falls below 50 percent. Also important is that under the U.S. scheme the preferences are 100 percent, that is, products granted preferential access pay no duty. Under the EU GSP scheme there is a range of "sensitive products" for which preferences for nonLDCs are partial. Under the current scheme there is a reduction of 3.5 percentage points, although for textiles and clothing the reduction is only 20 percent of the MFN rate. Hence, the low utilization rate of the EU may reflect that the costs of satisfying the origin rules, or of proving conformity with them, or both, exceed the

margin of preferences. In 2001 around 70 percent of exports to Canada from the LDCs that were eligible for preferences actually benefited from preferential access.[20]

Under the EU's EBA Agreement for the LDCs, which offers duty-free access for all products, almost all of Cambodia's exports to the EU are eligible for zero duty preferences, yet in 2001 only 36 percent of those exports obtained duty-free access. Brenton (2003) shows that this lack of use of preferences meant that on average Cambodia's exports to the EU paid a tariff equivalent to 7.7 percent of the value of total exports. Again, the main suspect for this underutilization of trade preferences is the rules of origin, particularly because Cambodia specializes in the production of clothing products for which EU rules of origin are very restrictive, requiring production from yarn.

Brenton and Manchin (2003) show that a large amount of EU imports of clothing products from Eastern European countries made from EU-produced fabrics still enter the EU market under an alternative customs regime—outward processing—even though there is no fiscal incentive to do so because EU tariffs have been removed under free trade agreements. This probably reflects the costs and uncertainties in proving origin that would be necessary under the normal preferential customs procedures.

In recent developments the United States has introduced the African Growth and Opportunity Act (AGOA), extending the number of products eligible for duty-free access to the United States under the GSP. These products include clothing. However, AGOA eligibility does not automatically imply that those countries are entitled to the provisions on clothing. Countries must first be approved based upon the implementation of what are deemed to be effective enforcement mechanisms. Under the GSP there is a standard value-added requirement of 35 percent with cumulation permitted between (certain) members of regional groups, including the Andean Community, ASEAN, Southern African Development Community (SADC), Caribbean Community (CARICOM), and the West African Monetary Union. AGOA extends the GSP rules by allowing

20. The data in this paragraph come from UNCTAD and the Commonwealth Secretariat 2001 and UNCTAD 2003.

for full cumulation between any Sub-Saharan countries and also for bilateral cumulation with the United States, with inputs from the latter limited to 15 percent of the value-added. However, the rules of origin for clothing are different (textile products remain effectively excluded from preferences).

The rules of origin for clothing stipulate the making up or assembly in one or more beneficiary countries but require the use of fabrics made and cut in the United States from yarns and thread formed in the United States. Fabrics made in beneficiary countries from yarns formed in those countries or the United States can be used, provided that imports of the finished products into the United States do not exceed a current limit of 4.2 percent of total United States imports of clothing, rising to 7 percent over the period to 2008.[21] Finally, there is a special provision that allows the use of fabric from any country, again subject to approval, quantitative limits, and initially for only least developed Sub-Saharan African countries but now granted to certain higher income countries such as Namibia and Kenya. However, this provision is only available until the end of September 2007. This provision provides for liberal rules of origin.

Mattoo, Roy, and Subramanian (2002) show how the basic AGOA rules of origin for clothing severely constrain the benefits of AGOA and that the general use of more liberal rules could increase the gains to beneficiary countries by as much as a factor of five. Further, recent trends in U.S. imports from AGOA beneficiaries strongly suggest that restrictive rules of origin can severely constrain trade. Between 1999 and 2002, U.S. imports of clothing from those countries that have been able to source fabrics from any country increased by 92 percent. U.S. imports of clothing from those countries that have been eligible for the preferences for clothing but have faced the more restrictive rules of origin (essentially Mauritius and South Africa) have increased by only 23 percent.

Systematic empirical analysis linking restrictive rules of origin directly to trade outcomes is currently limited. Estevadeordal and Miller (2002) show how in the transition from the U.S.–Canada FTA to NAFTA, rules of origin for certain sectors,

such as textiles, became more restrictive and that as a result the use of the available preferences declined. Estevadeordal and Suominen (2004) introduce a synthetic measure of the restrictiveness of rules of origin into a standard gravity model of bilateral trade flows. Their econometric analysis leads them to conclude that restrictive product-specific rules of origin undermine overall trade between partners and that provisions such as cumulation and *de minimis* rules, which act to increase the flexibility of application of a given set of processing requirements, serve to boost intraregional trade. Applying this approach at the sectoral level finds support for the hypothesis that the restrictiveness of rules of origin for final goods stimulates trade in intermediate products between preferential partners. Cadot and others (2002), using a similar measure of the restrictiveness of NAFTA rules of origin, find that for sectors where tariff cuts are larger than average, the rules of origin are more restrictive and the utilization rate of preferences by Mexican exporters lower than average. They conclude that rules of origin are the prime culprit for the very modest impact of NAFTA on Mexican exports identified by other researchers.

## Rules of Origin and Economic Development

Can and should rules of origin be used as tools to stimulate economic development within a regional grouping? The Draft Ministerial Text for the Cancún meeting of the WTO members as part of the Doha Development Round of trade negotiations proposes, under provisions for special and differential treatment, that "developing and least-developed country Members shall have the right to adopt preferential rules of origin designed to achieve trade policy objectives relating to their rapid economic development, particularly through generating regional trade." Strict rules of origin are viewed by some as a mechanism for encouraging the development of integrated production structures within developing countries to maximize the impact on employment and to ensure that not just low value-added activities are undertaken in the developing countries.

There are problems with this view. First, such rules discriminate against small countries where

---

21. It does not appear as if this quota is, or is likely to be, binding.

the possibilities for local sourcing are limited or nonexistent. Because most developing countries are small countries, they are particularly disadvantaged by restrictive rules of origin relative to larger countries. Second, there is no evidence that strict rules of origin over the past 30 years have done anything to stimulate the development of integrated production structures in developing countries. In fact, such arguments have become redundant in light of technological changes and global trade liberalization that have led to the fragmentation of production processes and the development of global networks of sourcing. Globalization and the splitting up of the production chain does not allow the luxury of being able to establish integrated production structures within countries. Strict rules of origin act to constrain the ability of firms to integrate into these global and regional production networks and in effect act to dampen the location of any value-added activities. In the modern world, flexibility in the sourcing of inputs is a key element in international competitiveness. Thus, it is quite feasible that restrictive rules of origin, rather than stimulating economic development, will raise costs of production by constraining access to cheap inputs and undermine the ability of local firms to compete in overseas markets.

Flatters (2002) and Flatters and Kirk (2003) document the evolution of the rules of origin in SADC, and highlight these points. They show that the adoption of restrictive rules of origin is more likely to constrain than to stimulate regional economic development. This example provides a salutary lesson of how sectoral interests and misperceptions of the role and impact of rules of origin can act to undermine regional trade agreements.

SADC initially agreed to simple, general, and consistent rules of origin similar to those of neighboring and overlapping COMESA. The initial rules required a change of tariff heading, a minimum of 35 percent of value-added within the region, or a maximum import content of 60 percent of the value of total inputs. Simple packaging and so forth were defined to be insufficient to confer origin. However, these rules were subsequently revised and are now characterized by more restrictive sector- and product-specific rules with the change of tariff heading requirement being supplanted by detailed technical process

requirements and with much higher domestic value-added and lower permitted import contents. The rules became much more similar to those of the EU and of NAFTA, reflecting in part the influence of the recently negotiated EU–South Africa agreement and the rules of origin governing EU preferences to ACP countries: "The EU–South Africa rules were often invoked by special interests in South Africa as models for SADC. Such claims were too often accepted at face value and not recognized as self-interested pleading for protection by already heavily protected domestic producers. There were few questions about the appropriateness of the underlying economic model (whatever it might be) for SADC" (Flatters and Kirk 2003, p. 7).

Flatters (2002) also points out that in the SADC case it has also been argued that customs administrations in the region are weak and this makes it likely that low-cost products from Asia could enter through porous borders and then claim tariff preferences when exported to another member state. It is then suggested that restrictive rules of origin are required to prevent this from happening. However, there is no reason to expect that weak customs administrations should be better able to enforce strict rules of origin than less restrictive rules. In fact, in many cases the rules of origin become so strict that no producers in the region can satisfy them so that no discretion from customs is required—preferences are not granted. This, of course, means that the preferential trade agreement has no impact. A better approach is to adopt economically sensible rules of origin and a program to improve administrative capacities in customs. Clearly designed safeguard measures can also be adopted to deal with surges of imports entering via partner countries.

To conclude, rules of origin are an inefficient tool in achieving development objectives. Better policies are available. Rules of origin should be used as a mechanism for preventing trade deflection. Restrictive rules of origin that go beyond this function and that seek to force use of local content are more likely to be counterproductive by undermining the competitiveness of downstream industries (Flatters 2001). If the objective is to stimulate regional trade, this is best achieved by adopting simple, clear, consistent, and predictable rules of origin that avoid administrative discretion and onerous burdens on customs and that minimize the costs to businesses in complying with them.

## Customs and the Costs of Administering Preferential Rules of Origin

Customs is typically responsible for implementing the system of rules of origin. Customs usually has the responsibility to check the certificate of origin; customs can also be involved in the issuing of origin certificates for local exporters. Rules of origin, while an essential element of free trade agreements, add considerable complexity to the trading system for traders, customs officials, and trade policy officials. For companies there is not only the issue of complying with the rules on sufficient processing but also the cost of obtaining the certificate of origin, including any delays that arise in obtaining the certificate. The costs of proving origin involve satisfying a number of administrative procedures to provide the documentation that is required and the costs of maintaining systems that accurately account for imported inputs from different sources to prove consistency with the rules. The ability to prove origin may well require the use of, what are for small companies in developing and transition economies, sophisticated and expensive accounting procedures. Without such procedures it is difficult for companies to show precisely the geographical breakdown of the inputs they have used.

There is limited information on these costs but the available studies suggest that the costs of providing the appropriate documentation to prove origin can be around 2 to 3 percent or more of the value of the export shipment for companies in developed countries.[22] The costs of proving origin may be even higher, and possibly prohibitive, in countries where customs mechanisms are poorly developed. Thus, even if producers can satisfy the rules of origin by meeting the technical requirements, they may not request preferential access because the costs of proving origin are high relative to the duty reduction that is available.

The costs of complying with the certification requirements of rules of origin will tend to vary across different agreements depending upon the precise requirements that are specified. With regard to issuing and inspecting the preferential certificate of origin, EU agreements, MERCOSUR, AFTA, and Japan–Singapore all mandate that certificates must be verified and endorsed by a recognized official body, such as customs or the Ministry of Trade. In certain cases private entities can be involved provided they are approved and monitored by the government. In contrast, agreements involving the United States provide for self-certification by the exporter. The authorities of the exporting country are not involved and are not responsible for the accuracy of the information provided in the certificates. In principal this should reduce the administrative burden of complying with the rules of origin. Further, under NAFTA a certificate of origin is valid for multiple shipments of identical goods within a one-year period, while in most other agreements a separate certificate of origin is required for each shipment. EU agreements, however, do allow for exporters whom the authorities approve and who make regular shipments to make an invoice declaration of origin.

Under NAFTA, both the importer and exporter are required to keep relevant records. Both exporter and importer must keep the certificate of origin and the supporting documentation for five years. If customs wishes to make inquiries concerning a particular shipment or shipments under NAFTA, they are directed to the exporter of the product. In cases where the exporter cannot substantiate a claim for preferential access, the importer becomes liable for the duty. In cases in which fraud is suspected, liability extends to both exporters and importers, whereas prior to NAFTA importers bore all financial and legal liability for compliance with customs rules. Under EU agreements it is the importer who is legally liable for any penalties for tax evasion should it be subsequently found that a product was not eligible for preferential access.[23] Under the EU's GSP, the EU also holds the government of the exporting country responsible for

---

22. See Cadot and others (2002) and Herin (1986). The Herin study also found that the costs for EFTA producers of proving origin led to one-quarter of EFTA exports to the EU paying the applied MFN duties.

23. Because it is the importer who bears the risk regarding the accuracy of the certificate of origin, the preferential tariff may not be claimed. A recent study suggests that this is an important concern of EU importers (Cerrex 2002).

administrative cooperation, with suspension and removal of GSP preferences the ultimate sanction for inadequate cooperation. The EU insists that government bodies issue the certificates of origin because it "considers that a certificate of origin is a blank check, which will be drawn on the EC budget" (European Commission 2003).

An important feature of most preferential trade schemes is the requirement of direct consignment or direct transport. This stipulates that goods for which preferences are requested must be shipped directly to the destination market and that if they are in transit through another country, documentary evidence may be requested to show that the goods remained under the supervision of the customs authorities of the country of transit, did not enter the domestic market there, and did not undergo operations other than unloading and reloading. In practice it may be very difficult to obtain the necessary documentation from foreign customs.

To understand better the implications for customs of rules of origin, especially preferential rules of origin, the WCO and the World Bank recently instituted a postal survey of customs agencies. Questionnaires were sent to all 161 members of the WCO, with 63 completed questionnaires being returned, a response rate of 39 percent. The majority of responses (43) came from developing countries. Responses were received from countries of all continents. The questionnaire sought information on the role of customs in issuing and checking certificates of origin and requested the views of customs officials on their experiences of administering rules of origin. The following summarizes the main conclusions drawn from these responses from customs administrations.

### Checking the Authenticity and Validity of Certificates of Origin

Table 9.1 shows the proportion of respondents confirming the involvement of their customs authorities in issuing certificates of origin for products exported from their customs territory, in checking the validity and authenticity of certificates of origin on products exported, in checking the accuracy of such certificates, and in responding to requests from other customs authorities for information regarding such certificates of origin.

About two-thirds of the customs administrations that responded confirmed that their administrations were responsible for issuing certificates of origin to exporters under at least one trade scheme. The vast majority of customs administrations are involved in checking the validity and authenticity of certificates of origin for exports and in confirming the accuracy of the country indicated as the origin of the product. Those administrations not involved are typically those in which the certificate of origin is based upon self-certification. Finally, a further task for customs in administering preferential rules of origin is in responding to requests for information on origin matters from other customs administrations, again reflecting the involvement of public authorities in matters relating to origin documentation in most preferential trade schemes. This information confirms that in most countries customs plays a key role in administering systems of rules of origin on exports as well as imports. Customs clearance for exports from many countries is influenced by the need for the customs authorities to check preferential origin information. An important exception arises in schemes that allow for self-certification by exporters.

**TABLE 9.1  Involvement of Customs in Issuing, Checking, and Providing Information on Preferential Certificates of Origin for Exporters**

| Customs Role | Proportion of Responses (percent) |
|---|---|
| Issues certificates of origin to exporters | 66 |
| Checks the validity and authenticity of the certificate of origin for export | 88 |
| Checks the accuracy of the indication of origin for export | 90 |
| Provides origin information to requesting administrations | 91 |

*Source:* World Customs Organization and World Bank Survey of Customs Directorates 2003.

Difficulties arise for businesses and for customs when the same product has different countries of origin depending upon the market, and the rules of origin of the market, for which it is destined. For example, at present clothing companies in certain African countries can obtain duty-free access to the U.S. market under AGOA (with liberal rules of origin), but exactly the same product will be denied duty-free access to the EU under the EBA Agreement (because of the requirement that the product be manufactured from yarn under the EU rules of origin). A company in Singapore could find that its product can enter ASEAN markets duty free, by satisfying the maximum import content requirement of 60 percent, but does not satisfy the origin rules of the Singapore–Japan agreement. This considerably complicates production and investment decisions. It also increases the burden on customs in clearing exports because shipments from the same establishment of the same product but to different markets will need to be individually assessed.

### Labor Requirements to Deal with Preferential Rules of Origin

Table 9.2 shows that 52 percent of those customs officials who responded accepted that the clearance of exports for preferential access overseas requires more manpower and that almost three-quarters of respondents believe that clearance of preferential imports requires more manpower to deal with issues arising from the preferential rules of origin. One element of this is likely to be that in most trade agreements proof of origin is required for every single shipment. Of the respondents to the survey, 88 percent reported that proof of origin must be presented for each and every shipment. Thus, even identical shipments made at different times still require individual certificates of origin, which may then be checked by customs for validity, authenticity, and accuracy.

These responses support the argument that the requirements generated by rules of origin under preferential trade agreements have important implications for customs and for trade facilitation. Preferential trade agreements increase the burden on customs. This burden will be greater the more complicated the rules of origin and the more manpower resources that are required to check conformity with those rules of origin. It is interesting to note that 42 percent of all respondents and more than half (55 percent) of administrations in developing countries could foresee additional preferential rules of origin coming into operation within the next 12 months. This reflects the proliferating number of free trade agreements. It also, however, implies a trend toward an increasing burden on customs and, given the above finding, additional resources will be required to effectively implement these new agreements if trade facilitation is not to be compromised.

### Overlapping Rules of Origin From Multiple FTAs

Most countries are party to more than one preferential trade agreement. In certain cases the same countries are partners in different trade agreements. For example, the developing countries in Sub-Saharan Africa can now export to the EU and receive preferential access under the Cotonou Agreement or under EBA, which is a part of the GSP. These two schemes have rules of origin that differ in certain key respects. There is full cumulation between ACP countries under the Cotonou rules of origin but only bilateral cumulation with the EU is possible under the GSP rules of origin. As noted earlier, the *de minimis* or tolerance levels differ between the two schemes. (See Brenton 2003 for more details.) In Southern Africa, countries such as Namibia and Swaziland are members of both SADC and COMESA, which have different rules of

**TABLE 9.2 Resource Implications of Rules of Origin in Preferential Trade Agreements**

| | Responses Agreeing, "Customs Clearance for Goods Under Preferential Schemes Need More Manpower to Deal With Preferential Rules of Origin Requirements" (percent) |
|---|---|
| For exports | 52 |
| For imports | 73 |

*Source:* World Customs Organization and World Bank Survey of Customs Directorates 2003.

**FIGURE 9.1    Regional Trade Agreements in Eastern and Southern Africa**

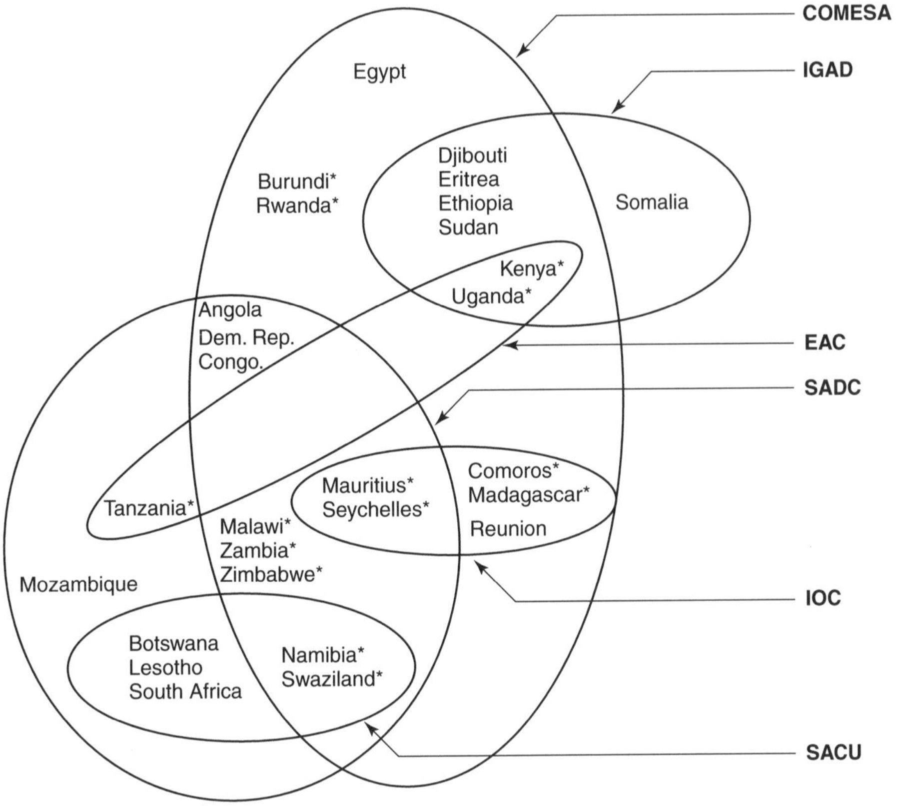

| | |
|---|---|
| **COMESA** | Common Market for Eastern and Southern Africa |
| **EAC** | East African Cooperation |
| **IGAD** | Intergovernmental Authority on Development |
| **IOC** | Indian Ocean Commission |
| **SACU** | Southern African Customs Union |
| **SADC** | Southern African Development Community |
| **\*RIFF** | Regional Integration Facilitation Forum |

*Source:* World Bank staff.

origin. Indeed, as Figure 9.1 shows, the issue of membership in multiple trade agreements and overlapping rules of origin is a major feature of regional trade agreements in Africa.

Table 9.3 shows the views of respondents to the questionnaire on whether such overlapping rules of origin cause particular difficulties for customs. Almost half the respondents said that in their experience overlapping rules of origin were a problem. Of respondents in Africa, two-thirds agreed that problems arose from the presence of overlapping rules of origin. This suggests that there would be gains from some coordination of rules of origin across regional trade agreements with common members. Further, it suggests that a movement toward simple and clear rules of origin in preferential trade agreements would help minimize the problems caused by overlapping rules of origin.

### Implementation Difficulties of the Value-Added Criterion

More than 75 percent of the respondents reported that, of the different methods of conferring origin, the value-added criterion was particularly difficult to implement. This is a striking result but one that is understandable given the heavy demands on data and calculations made by value-added rules. Value-added rules lack predictability because changes in factors outside the firm, such as exchange rates, can lead to different determinations of origin. This is important because, as shown in table 9.B.1, the vast majority of trade agreements use the value-added

**TABLE 9.3  Overlapping Trade Agreements Cause Problems for Customs**

| | Proportion of Respondents Agreeing That in Their Experience "Overlapping Rules of Origin for FTAs Cause Problems" (percent) |
|---|---|
| All respondents | 48 |
| Respondents in Sub-Saharan Africa | 67 |

*Source:* World Customs Organization and World Bank Survey of Customs Directorates 2003.

criterion for at least some product codes. However, the restrictiveness of value-added rules is more apparent than for other methods, which tend to be more prone to capture by domestic protectionist interests. Nevertheless, trade within regional or preferential agreements could be facilitated by a review of value-added rules with a view to simplifying their implementation, for example, through agreement on standard formulas to be used in calculation, and perhaps by providing for alternative means of conferring origin, such as through change of tariff classification.

These responses from customs administrations confirm what may be obvious to some, but is clearly worth stating, that implementing preferential trade agreements increases the burden on customs. Limited resources and weak administrative capacity in many developing countries mean that there are inevitable repercussions for trade facilitation arising from these trade agreements. At the very least, when designing trade agreements the participants should bear in mind the implications for customs and that if such agreements are to be effective in stimulating trade, issues of administrative capacity in customs need to be considered. Complicated systems of rules of origin increase the complexity of customs procedures and the burden upon origin certifying institutions. In a period in which increasing emphasis has been placed upon trade facilitation and the improvement of efficiency in customs and other trade-related institutions, the difficulties that preferential rules of origin create for firms and the relevant authorities in developing countries is an important consideration.

In general, clear, straightforward, transparent, and predictable rules of origin that require little or no administrative discretion will add less of a burden to customs than complex rules. In this regard, if the objective is to stimulate trade, the use of general rather than product-specific rules appears to be most appropriate for preferential rules of origin applied by and applied to developing countries. Less complicated rules of origin encourage trade between regional partners by reducing the transactions costs of undertaking such trade relative to more complex and restrictive rules of origin.

**The Doha Round and Rules of Origin**

Rules of origin are not directly mentioned in the ministerial text that launched the Doha Development Round, although ministers have called for completion of the HWP for nonpreferential rules of origin. As noted, there has been some discussion of rules of origin in the context of special and differential treatment in using preferential rules of origin to achieve development objectives through generating regional trade. As discussed earlier, rules of origin are unlikely to be appropriate measures for attaining such objectives and their use could well be counterproductive. Although rules of origin are not explicitly on the agenda in the Doha negotiations, it is clear that the outcome of these negotiations could have important implications for rules of origin and at the same time that the rules of origin that countries have adopted will have important implications for the impact of any agreement.

For example, progress in clarifying the application of antidumping measures and the effective liberalization of all remaining quotas on textiles and clothing products, as mandated under the Uruguay Round Agreement on Textiles and Clothing, could facilitate progress in the harmonization of nonpreferential rules of origin because these trade policy instruments have been at the heart of disputes concerning the determination of nonpreferential origin. Preferential rules of origin have important implications for the impact of any MFN tariff cuts that are agreed on between preferential partners. As tariffs are cut, margins of preference decline and the potential threat of trade deflection diminishes. Given the additional administrative costs of proving preferential origin, it is likely that rules of origin for products with a margin of preference of less than 3 percent are unnecessary, because in their absence there will be no trade deflection.

Restrictive rules of origin constrain the ability of developing countries to benefit from preferences. This is important in the context of ongoing discussions over special and differential treatment for developing countries and concerns regarding the erosion of the preferences currently granted to such countries by rich, industrialized countries. On the one hand, this becomes all the more important as margins of preference decline. On the other, where restrictive rules of origin prevent the full use of preferences, the impact of MFN tariff reductions on preference-receiving countries is ambiguous. Countries with low levels of preference utilization could gain because the benefits of MFN tariff reduction could exceed any losses due to preference erosion. For example, it was noted earlier that only 36 percent of Cambodia's exports to the EU are actually granted the zero duty access for which they are eligible. This implies that MFN tariff reductions will benefit 64 percent of current exports while preference erosion will have an impact on only just over one-third of Cambodia's exports to the EU.

Either way, it is clear that the liberalization of industrialized country rules of origin under the GSP, particularly those governing imports of textiles and clothing and food products, would have important beneficial impacts for developing countries such as Cambodia. More liberal rules of origin would help mitigate the impact of MFN tariff reductions on those products currently receiving preferences and help developing countries fully utilize the preferences that are available to them. The analysis included in this chapter would suggest a simple and clear set of rules of origin that are common across preference-granting countries.

## Key Operational Conclusions

The nature of rules of origin will typically reflect the purpose that is set for them, the transparency of the process by which they are determined, and the composition of the group involved in that process.

Within preferential trade areas, complex and restrictive rules of origin act to dampen the increase in competition for final producers within a country from suppliers in partner countries and stimulate intra-area exports of intermediate products by diverting demand away from third-country suppliers. Such rules typically emerge when the process by which they are determined lacks transparency and openness and does not have widespread participation and in particular is dominated by input from domestic industry. If the purpose set for preferential rules of origin is simply to prevent trade deflection, a simple and more liberal set of rules of origin implemented through general rather than product-specific rules would be the result. In the current globalized world market such rules are more likely to stimulate trade and investment in the region by providing producers as much flexibility as possible in sourcing their inputs without compromising the ability to prevent transshipment of goods from third countries that are not members of the agreement.

What is important is that the purpose set for the rules of origin is clearly specified and is consistent with the objectives that have been set for the particular trade agreement or policy. If the objective is to foster trade and development, this is best achieved through simple and liberal rules of origin rather than using rules of origin as opaque measures of trade protection. In this way the rules of origin are a key trade policy issue and their determination should be open and transparent with participation from all affected groups. The rules of origin are a major factor determining whether preferential trade agreements work in achieving their objectives. The analysis of this chapter leads to the following broad conclusions:

- Restrictive rules of origin constrain international specialization and discriminate against small low-income countries where the possibilities for local sourcing are limited. Simple, consistent, and predictable rules of origin are more likely to foster the growth of trade and development. Rules of origin that vary across products and agreements add considerably to the complexity and costs of participating in and administering trade agreements. The burden of such costs falls particularly heavily upon small and medium-sized firms and upon firms in

## Annex 9.A Summary of the Different Approaches to Determining Origin

| Rule | Advantages | Disadvantages | Key Issues |
|------|------------|---------------|------------|
| Change of tariff classification in the Harmonized System | Consistency with nonpreferential rules of origin.<br>Once defined, the rule is clear, unambiguous, and easy to learn.<br>Relatively straightforward to implement. | Harmonized System not designed for conferring origin; as a result there are often many individual product-specific rules, which can be influenced by domestic industries.<br>Documentary requirements may be difficult to comply with.<br>Conflicts over the classification of goods can introduce uncertainty over market access. | Level of classification at which change required—the higher the level, the more restrictive.<br>Can be positive (which imported inputs can be used) or negative (defining cases where change of classification will not confer origin) test[a]—negative test more restrictive. |
| Value-added | Clear, simple to specify, and unambiguous.<br>Allows for general rather than product-specific rules. | Complex to apply—requires firms to have sophisticated accounting systems.<br>Uncertainty due to sensitivity to changes in exchange rates, wages, commodity prices, and so forth. | The level of value-added required to confer origin.<br>The valuation method for imported materials—methods that assign a higher value (for example, CIF) will be more restrictive on the use of imported inputs. |
| Specific manufacturing process | Once defined, clear and unambiguous.<br>Provides for certainty if rules can be complied with. | Documentary requirements can be burdensome and difficult to comply with.<br>Leads to product-specific rules.<br>Domestic industries can influence the specification of the rules.<br>Can quickly become obsolete due to technological progress and therefore require frequent modification. | The formulation of the specific processes required—the more procedures required, the more restrictive.<br>Should test be negative (processes or inputs that cannot be used) or positive (what can be used)? Negative test more restrictive. |

a. A positive determination of origin typically takes the form of "change from any other heading," as opposed to a negative determination of origin, such as "change from any other heading except for the headings of chapter XX." It is worth noting that change of tariff classification, particularly with a negative determination of origin, can be specified to have an effect identical to that of a specific manufacturing process. See box 9.2 for an example.
*Source:* Authors.

**Annex 9.B  Rules of Origin in Existing Free Trade and Preferential Trade Agreements**

| | Change of Tariff Classification (principal, secondary level) | Value-Added | | Specific Manufacturing Process | Cumulation | Tolerance (percent) | Absorption |
|---|---|---|---|---|---|---|---|
| | | Domestic or Import Content (percent) | Implied Import Content (percent) | | | | |
| **Agreements Involving the EU** | | | | | | | |
| EU  Pan Euro | Yes (4,2) | Yes—Import (50 to 30) | 50 to 30 | Yes | Bilateral, diagonal | Yes 10[b] | Yes |
| EU  GSP | Yes (4,2) | Yes—Import (50 to 30) | 50 to 30 | Yes | Bilateral, diagonal[a] | Yes 10[b] | Yes |
| EU  Cotonou | Yes (4,2) | Yes—Import (50 to 30) | 50 to 30 | Yes | Full | Yes 15[b] | Yes |
| EU–Chile | Yes (4,2) | Yes—Import (50 to 30) | 50 to 30 | Yes | Bilateral | Yes 10 | Yes |
| EU–Mexico | Yes (4,2) | Yes—Import (50 to 30) | 50 to 30 | Yes | Bilateral | Yes 10 | Yes |
| EU–South Africa | Yes (4,2) | Yes—Import (50 to 30) | 50 to 30 | Yes | Bilateral, diagonal (ACP), full (SACU) | Yes 15[b] | Yes |
| **Agreements in the Americas and with the United States** | | | | | | | |
| NAFTA | Yes (2,4,6) | Yes—Domestic (60 to 50) | 50 to 40 | Yes | Bilateral | Yes 7[b] | Yes[e] |
| Canada–Chile | Yes | Yes—Domestic (60 to 25) | 75 to 40 | Yes | Bilateral | Yes 9 | Yes |
| U.S.–Israel | | Yes—Domestic (35) | 65 | | Bilateral[c] | NA | Yes |
| **Agreements in Asia and Pacific and with Asian countries** | | | | | | | |
| AFTA | | Yes—Import (60)[d] | 60 | | Diagonal | NA | Yes |
| ANZCERTA | Yes (4) | Yes—Domestic (50)[d] | 50 | | Full | NA | Yes |
| Singapore–Japan | | Yes—Domestic (60) | 40 | Yes | Full | Yes | Yes |
| Singapore–New Zealand (ANZSCEP) | | Yes—Domestic (40)[d] | 60 | | Bilateral | NA | No |
| Singapore–U.S. | Yes (2,4,6) | Yes—Domestic (55 to 35) | 65 to 45 | Yes | Bilateral | Yes 10[b] | No |
| **Agreements Among Developing Countries** | | | | | | | |
| CACM | Yes (4) | | | | Bilateral | No | No |
| CARICOM | Yes (4) | Yes—Import (60), Domestic (35) | | | Bilateral | No | No |
| COMESA | Yes (4) | Yes—Domestic (60) | 60 | | Full | No | Yes[e] |
| MERCOSUR | Yes (4) | | 40 | | Bilateral | No | Yes[e] |

NA = Not applicable; ACP = Africa, the Caribbean and the Pacific; AFTA = Asian Free Trade Association; ANZCERTA = Australia New Zealand Closer Economic Relations Trade Agreement; ANZSCEP = Agreement between New Zealand and Singapore on a Closer Economic Partnership; ASEAN = Association of Southeast Asian Nations; CACM = Central American Common Market; CARICOM = Caribbean Community; COMESA = Common Market for Eastern and Southern Africa; GSP = General System of Preferences; MERCOSUR = Mercado Comun del Sur; NAFTA = North American Free Trade Agreement; SAARC = South Asian Association for Regional Cooperation; SACU = Southern African Customs Union; *Note:* In the column "Change of Tariff Classification" the numbers in brackets give the digit level at which change may be required.; a. Within Andean, ASEAN, CACM, SAARC only and subject to a 50 percent value-added requirement in the country of export. b. Alternative rules for textiles and clothing products, often in terms of weight rather than value. Sectoral exemptions are common. For example, the EU–South Africa agreement excludes certain meat products, fish, and alcoholic beverages and tobacco from the general tolerance rule. Under NAFTA, tolerance does not cover dairy products, citrus fruits and juices, and certain machinery, such as air conditioners, among others.; c. Up to a maximum of 15 percent of the value of the product, with the additional requirement that the last stage of manufacture be performed in the exporting country, excluding automotive products.; d. With the additional requirement that the last stage of manufacture be performed in the exporting country.; e. Excluding automotive products; *Sources:* WTO 2002a, Estevadeordal and Suominen 2003, and individual agreements.

low-income countries. Complex systems of rules of origin add to the burdens of customs and may compromise progress on trade facilitation.

- Cumulation mechanisms are important. Full cumulation provides for deeper integration and allows for more advanced countries to outsource labor-intensive production stages to low-wage partners. Full cumulation allows low-income countries the greatest flexibility in sourcing inputs. Nevertheless, the sometimes-onerous documentary requirements and administrative difficulties that can be associated with full cumulation suggest that diagonal cumulation should also be permitted.

- The value-added criterion appears to be particularly difficult to implement from the perspective of customs. Agreement on a standard formula for calculation would be particularly helpful. Providing traders with alternative means of proving origin could be an important way of increasing flexibility in trade agreements.

- Harmonization of nonpreferential rules of origin, and consolidation, if not harmonization, of preferential rules would bring substantial gains in terms of increasing the predictability of conditions under which companies trade and in reducing the burden on customs in administering both the multilateral and preferential trade agreements.

The analysis leads to the following recommendations:

- Specifying generally applicable rules of origin, with a limited number of clearly defined and justified exceptions, is appropriate if the objective is to stimulate integration and minimize the burdens on firms and customs in complying with and administering the rules. Unnecessary use of a detailed product-by-product approach to rules of origin is likely to lead to complex and restrictive rules of origin and to constrain integration.

- Producers should be provided with flexibility in meeting origin rules, for example, by specifying that *either* a change of tariff requirement[24] *or* a value-added rule can be satisfied.

- When change of tariff classification is used, the level of the classification at which change is

required should, as much as possible, be common across products. Change at the heading level seems most appropriate as a principal rule.

- Preferences granted by Organisation for Economic Co-operation and Development countries would be more effective in stimulating exports from developing countries if they were governed by less restrictive rules of origin. Ideally, rules of origin for these schemes should be common. The WTO provides an appropriate forum by which to achieve this objective. Producers in developing countries should be able to gain preferential access to all industrialized country markets if their product satisfies a single origin test.

- Restrictive rules of origin should not be used as tools for achieving economic development objectives, as they are likely to be counterproductive. The potential benefits of trade agreements among developing countries can be substantially undermined if those agreements contain restrictive rules of origin.

- Bilateral agreements between a member of an existing regional trade agreement and a third country should provide for an alternative approach to allow for the benefits of both diagonal and full cumulation with the other members of that regional group.

## Further Reading

Flatters, F., and R. Kirk. 2003. "Rules of Origin as Tools of Development? Some Lessons from SADC." Presented at Institut National de la Recherche Agronomique Conference on Rules of Origin. Paris. May. www.inra.fr/Internet/Departements/ESR/UR/lea/actualites/ROO2003/articles/flatters.pdf.

Garay, S., Luis Jorge, and Rafael Cornejo . 2002. "Rules of Origin and Trade Preferences." In Bernard Hoekman, Philip English, and Aaditya Mattoo, eds. *Development, Trade, and the WTO, a Handbook*. Washington, D.C.: The World Bank.

Harilal, K., and P. Beena. 2003. "The WTO Agreement on Rules of Origin: Implications for South Asia." Working Paper 353. Trivendrum, India: Centre for Development Studies. http://www.cds.edu/download_files/353.pdf

Hirsch, M. 2002. "International Trade Law, Political Economy and Rules of Origin: A Plea for a Reform of the WTO Regime on Rules of Origin." *Journal of World Trade* 36(2): 171–88.

## References

The word *processed* describes informally reproduced works that may not commonly be available through libraries.

Brenton, P. 2003. "Integrating the Least Developed Countries into the World Trading System: The Current Impact of EU

---

24. Or, to a very limited extent, specific manufacturing processes or operations.

Preferences Under Everything But Arms." *Journal of World Trade* 37(3): 623–46.

Brenton, P., and Manchin, M. 2003. "Making EU Trade Agreements Work: The Role of Rules of Origin." *The World Economy* 26(5): 755–69.

Cadot, O., J. de Melo, A. Estevadeordal, A. Suwa-Eisenmann, and B. Tumurchudur. 2002. "Assessing the Effect of NAFTA's Rules of Origin." Research Unit Working Paper 0306. Laboratoire d'Economie Appliquée, Institut National de la Recherche Agronomique—France.

Cerrex. 2002. "The Usage of the EU Trade Preferences (GSP and Lome)." Study prepared for DFID. London. Processed.

Croome, J. 1995. *Reshaping the World Trading System—A History of the Uruguay Round*. Geneva: World Trade Organization.

Dehousse, F., K. Ghemar, and P. Vincent. 2002. "The EU-US Dispute Concerning the New American Rules of Origin for Textile Products." *Journal of World Trade* 36(1): 67–84.

Estevadeordal, A., and E. Miller. 2002. "Rules of Origin and the Pattern of Trade Between US and Canada." Washington, D.C.: Inter-American Development Bank.

Estevadeordal, A., and K. Suominen. 2003. "Rules of Origin in FTAs in Europe and the Americas: Issues and Implications for the EU-MERCOSUR Inter-Regional Association Agreement." In G. Valladao and R. Bouzas, eds., *Market Access for Goods and Services in the EU-Mercosur Negotiations*. Paris: Chaire Mercosur de Sciences Po.

———. 2004. "Rules of Origin: A World Map and Trade Effects." In A. Estevadeordal, O. Cadot, A. Suwa-Eisenmann, and T. Verdier, eds. *The Origin of Goods: Rules of Origin in Preferential Trade Agreements*. Inter-American Development Bank and Centre for Economic Policy Research. Forthcoming.

European Commission. 2003. *The European Community's Rules of Origin for the Generalised System of Preferences: A Guide for Traders*. Brussels. http://europa.eu.int/comm/taxation_customs/customs/origin/gsp/index_en.htm.

Falvey, R. and G. Reed. 1998. "Economic Effects of Rules of Origin." *Weltwirtschaftliches Archiv* 134: 209–229.

Flatters, F. 2001. "The SADC Trade Protocol: Which Way Ahead?" *Southern African Update* 10: 1–4.

———. 2002. "SADC Rules of Origin: Undermining Regional Free Trade." Paper presented at the Trade and Industrial Policy Secretariat Forum. Johannesburg. September.

Flatters, F., and R. Kirk. 2003. "Rules of Origin as Tools of Development? Some Lessons from SADC." Presented at Institut National de la Recherche Agronomique Conference on Rules of Origin. Paris. May.

Herin, J. 1986. *Rules of Origin and Differences Between Tariff Levels in EFTA and in the EC*. Geneva: EFTA Secretariat.

Hirsch, M. 2002. "International Trade Law, Political Economy and Rules of Origin: A Plea for a Reform of the WTO Regime on Rules of Origin." *Journal of World Trade* 36(2): 171–88.

Hoekman, B. 1993. "Rules of Origin for Goods and Services: Conceptual and Economic Considerations." *Journal of World Trade* 27(4): 81–99.

Imagawa, H. and E. Vermulst. 2003. *Rules of Origin in a Globalized World: A Work in Progress*. New York: Kluwer. Forthcoming.

Inama, S. 2002. "Market Access for LDCs: Issues to be Addressed." *Journal of World Trade* 36(1): 85–116.

Izam, M. 2003. "Rules of Origin and Trade Facilitation in Preferential Trade Agreements in Latin America." Paper presented at International Forum on Trade Facilitation. Geneva. May 14–15. http://www.unece.org/trade/forums/forum03/presentations/ventura_en.pdf.

Krishna, K., and A. Krueger. 1995. "Implementing Free Trade Areas: Rules of Origin and Hidden Protection." NBER Working Paper 4983. Cambridge, Mass.: National Bureau of Economic Research.

Krueger, A. 1997. "Free Trade Agreements Versus Customs Unions." *Journal of Development Economics* 54(1): 169–187.

Mattoo, A., D. Roy, and A. Subramanian. 2002. "The Africa Growth and Opportunity Act and its Rules of Origin: Generosity Undermined?" *The World Economy* 26(6): 829–51.

Official Journal of the European Communities. 2000. L317. Volume 43. December 15. http://europa.eu.int/eur-lex/en/archive/2000/l_31720001215en.html.

Palmeter D. 1997. "Rules of Origin in Regional Trade Agreements." In P. Demaret, J. F. Bellis, and G. Garcia Jimenez, eds. *Regionalism and Multilateralism after the Uruguay Round: Convergence, Divergence, and Interaction*. Brussels: European Interuniversity Press.

Pricewaterhouse Coopers. 2002. "Strengthening the AFTA Rules of Origin." Presentation to the 10th Meeting of the ASEAN Directors-General of Customs, Singapore.

Sapir, A. 1998. "The Political Economy of EC Regionalism." *European Economic Review* 42(3-5): 717–732.

UNCTAD (United Nations Conference on Trade and Development). 2003. "Main Recent Initiatives in Favour of Least Developed Countries in the Area of Preferential Market Access: Preliminary Impact Assessment." Note for the 50th Session of the Trade and Development Board. October 6–17. Document TD/B/50/5. Geneva: UNCTAD Secretariat.

UNCTAD and the Commonwealth Secretariat. 2001. "Duty and Quota Free Market Access for LDCs: An Analysis of Quad Initiatives." London and Geneva. http://www.unctad.org/en/docs/poditctabm7.en.pdf.

U.S. International Trade Commission. 2004. "Harmonized Tariff Schedule of the United States. General Notes." Washington, D.C. http://hotdocs.usitc.gov/tariff_chapters_current/0410gn.pdf.

World Customs Organization. 2003. "Report of the 21st Session of the Technical Committee on Rules of Origin." Document OC0085E2. February 24–25. Brussels.

WTO (World Trade Organization). 2002a. "Committee on Regional Trade Agreements — Rules of Origin Regimes in Regional Trade Agreements—Background Survey by the Secretariat." Document WT/REG/W/45. April 5. Geneva.

———. 2002b. "Committee on Rules of Origin—Eighth Annual Review of the Implementation and Operation of the Agreement on Rules of Origin—Note by the Secretariat." Document G/RO/55. December 3. Geneva.

———. 2002c. "Committee on Rules of Origin—Report by the Chairman of the Committee on Rules of Origin to the General Council." Document G/RO/52. July 15. Geneva.

# 10

# DUTY RELIEF AND EXEMPTION CONTROL

*Adrien Goorman*

## TABLE OF CONTENTS

## LIST OF BOXES

This chapter deals with two aspects of customs administration that are of considerable economic, fiscal, and administrative importance—administration and control of duty relief regimes for temporarily imported goods, and administration and control of all other duty exemptions.

Duty relief refers to the customs regimes under which goods are imported with suspension of duty payment pending their re-exportation. Such duty relief might be for temporary admission for inward processing, manufacturing under bond, export processing zones, temporary admission for re-exportation in the same state, customs warehousing, and transit. It also refers to the regime under which duties paid on importation are refunded when the goods are re-exported (drawback).[1]

Exemption control refers to the mechanisms used by customs to administer and monitor full or partial duty exemptions unrelated to exportation

---

Adrien Goorman is an independent customs administration consultant, former Deputy Division Chief, Tax Administration Division of the Fiscal Affairs Department of the International Monetary Fund. This chapter has benefited greatly from cooperation with the Inter-American Development Bank.

1. The duty relief regimes are often referred to as duty suspension regimes, economic regimes, or special customs regimes. There is no uniformity in the use of the terms "relief" and "exemption" among customs laws and practitioners. In the Revised Kyoto Convention the term "duty relief" refers to what is generally known as exemption, while each duty suspension regime is dealt with under its individual name—inward processing, drawback, free zones, customs warehousing, temporary admission, and so on.

---

**BOX 10.1    Duty Relief and Exemption Regimes**

Duty relief concerns the exemption from duties and taxes on temporary imported goods or, if duties and taxes were paid on their importation, the refund of these duties and taxes upon re-exportation.

*Goods imported for re-exportation after processing*
   Temporary admission for inward processing (TAP)
   Manufacturing under bond (MUB)
   Drawback
   Export processing zone (EPZ)
*Warehousing, temporary admission, and transit*
   Customs warehousing
   Temporary admission for exportation in the same state
   Transit

Exemption involves importation under full or partial waiver of import duties for reasons unrelated to exportation or re-exportation. These exemptions exist for a variety of government

policy objectives or result from international conventions and agreements.

*International conventions*
   Embassies and international organizations
*Government social and economic objectives*
   Government imports
   Fiscal incentives to investment
   Foreign financed projects
   Relief goods
   Charitable, religious, educational, cultural, and other social purposes
*Noncommercial imports*
   Migrant workers, persons settling or resettling in the country
   Baggage allowances
   Samples of no commercial value
   Inherited goods, gifts, trophies, medals, prizes, and so forth
   Other noncommercial imports.

*Source:* Author.

---

or re-exportation. The main exemption categories concern investment incentives; imports for the government, foreign-financed projects, and diplomatic representations; imports of relief goods; and imports for institutions with charitable, cultural, educational, or religious purposes.

Experience shows that many developing countries have difficulty properly administering and monitoring duty relief regimes and exemption regimes. This has resulted in abuse, fraud, and revenue leakage. In the absence of smoothly operating duty relief mechanisms, export manufacturers have to produce at higher cost than would be the case if they had full and easy access to production inputs at world prices. Therefore, their competitiveness in export markets is impaired.

The chapter gives an overview of the main duty relief and exemption regimes, and summarizes their economic rationale, as well as the main requirements for effective administration. The chapter also reviews the experiences relating to the implementation of various systems in a number of countries and provides guidelines for best practice. The first section reviews the regimes for duty relief for inward processing. The second section concentrates on duty relief for goods temporarily imported for reasons other than processing. The third section deals with economic and administra-

tive aspects of outright exemptions. The final section summarizes the operational conclusions and guidelines. Annex 10.A provides a checklist for duty relief and exemption control.

A systematic classification of the main duty relief and exemption regimes in operation around the world is presented in box 10.1.

## Duty Relief for Inward Processing

This section first reviews the economic rationale for duty relief for inward processing, identifies the main approaches to duty relief, discusses administrative issues relevant to all duty relief systems, then reviews administrative aspects of the main systems one by one.[2]

### Economic Rationale

Governments levy duties on the importation of goods to collect fiscal revenue or protect industrial activity. When the inputs are imported for the manufacture of export products, the duties paid on

---

2. The standards and guidelines of the Revised Kyoto Convention with respect to the duty relief regimes are included in the Convention as follows: temporary admission for inward processing, Specific Annex F.1 on Inward Processing, Specific Annex D.2 on Free Zones, and Specific Annex F.3 on drawback.

them increase the cost of production and, therefore, make it more difficult for the exporters to sell their products abroad. The objective of duty relief is to remove this tariff burden and to give exporters access to industrial inputs at world prices. This is done through exempting the inputs at the stage of importation, or refunding the duties paid at the time of importation, when the products in which the inputs are incorporated are exported. Customs laws make provisions for these regimes and establish regulations for their administration and control.

The economic justification for relieving export producers of the payment of duties on imported inputs rests on the destination principle of taxation, under which no indirect taxes should be levied on goods that are not destined for domestic consumption. Following this principle, there is no ground for levying import duties, for instance, on goods in international transit, or on materials and components imported for incorporation into manufactured products that are subsequently exported.[3] The failure to relieve export producers from import duties would effectively establish a tax on exports, increase their cost, and reduce the competitiveness of domestic manufacturers in export markets.

In line with the destination principle, the refund of duties paid on the importation of industrial inputs incorporated in export products is acceptable under, and fully compliant with, World Trade Organization (WTO) rules provided the refund does not exceed the actual amount of duties paid. A refund that exceeds that amount would be equivalent to an export subsidy and would violate the WTO rules on Export Subsidies and Countervailing Duties.

Clearly, providing duty relief is only a second best alternative to a free trade regime. Free trade eliminates the need for schemes to insulate exporters and obviates the administrative requirements that are often difficult to meet. Most countries do not have a free trade regime, however, and can relieve export products from the burden of import duties and taxes only through the implementation of one or more of the duty relief systems.

In today's highly competitive economic environment, exporters are compelled to attain a high degree of efficiency in production and to cut production and marketing costs to the minimum if they are to survive in export markets. Therefore, it is important that policymakers and customs managers make available to the export sector duty relief systems that provide full (100 percent) relief from the duty burden on industrial inputs. It is also important for policymakers and customs managers to create the conditions for effective administration of these regimes. For customs administrators whose responsibility it is to collect import duties according to the tariff schedule, the implementation of duty relief regimes clearly establishes a problem of customs control. Customs must establish mechanisms to ensure that claims for duty relief are legitimate and correctly executed.

### Prior Exemption versus Drawback

There are two basic approaches to providing duty relief for inward processing: (a) exempting goods from the payment of the duties at the time they are imported, conditional upon their re-exportation after processing (often referred to as temporary admission); and (b) drawback, which is the payment of duties on the imported goods, with refund of the duties upon re-exportation of the goods after processing. Prior exemption exists in different forms, including temporary admission for inward processing (TAP), manufacturing under bond (MUB), passbook system, variations on or combinations of these forms, and export processing zones (EPZs).

While prior exemption systems and drawback have the same objective, there are differences in the way they operate, in the benefits they provide to the manufacturer, and in the control measures customs may want to put in place to protect revenue. One system may be better suited to a particular exporter than another. In general, exporters prefer prior exemption to drawback, but prior exemption carries greater revenue risk for the government because of the possibility of diversion of the imported goods, or the products made from them, to the local market without duty payment. Drawback involves less risk to revenue, but one disadvantage is that the manufacturer must pay the duties and taxes first and then wait (often for a considerable period

---

3. Some countries charge a transit fee, which may have the character of, for instance, a service charge for using the national road system.

of time) before the refund is made, which reduces the company's working capital. Delays and uncertainties about repayments under the drawback system may also act as a disincentive to exporters, and may lead them to factor the delays and uncertainties into their cost and price calculations, thereby reducing their competitiveness abroad.

It is in the interest of the export sector that all manufacturers (from the large enterprise exporting the bulk of its production to the occasional export processor) have access to one or more schemes that fit the type of business and provide full relief at minimum administrative and operational cost. Therefore, the best policy is to make both prior exemptions, in one or more of its forms, and drawback available. If there is economic justification for establishing free zones, EPZs should be made available. However, EPZs are established on the basis of a broader set of objectives and conditions, and involve a much bigger undertaking than other prior exemption regimes and drawback. They may not be an appropriate solution in many cases.

The availability in the domestic market of substitute goods—materials that are identical in description, quality, and technical characteristics to the imported materials—should not be a determining factor in whether to give export manufacturers access to duty relief systems. Even though the use of imported materials may limit the development of domestic backward linkages, duty relief remains consistent with the policy objective of giving export manufacturers access to production inputs at world prices.

### Administration: From Physical Control to Audits

Traditionally, customs procedures to administer, control, and enforce duty relief schemes, as with other aspects of customs control, have relied heavily on physical control. Physical control allows customs to monitor the movement of imported materials into the manufacturer's warehouse, the use of the materials in producing goods for export, the quantities produced, and the removal of finished goods from the factory for exportation. Physical controls are burdensome to both customs and manufacturers, and economically inefficient compared to accounts-based controls.

Over the last few decades the worldwide liberalization of trade, combined with rapid technological

developments, has led to a rapid expansion of international trade and to cutthroat competition in export markets. Trends in trade and industry, including the need for rapid delivery of goods, just-in-time inventory, and the use of technology, have forced many customs administrations, in both industrialized and developing countries, to adopt modern customs control strategies. Such strategies are based on risk assessment and management, selective checking, post-importation audit, and extensive use of information technology. They concentrate more on overall assessment of the traders' level of compliance than on verification of individual transactions. For companies judged to represent a low risk, customs reduces its level of regulatory scrutiny and relies more on the company's self-assessment of customs compliance. Thus, low-risk traders can operate under less onerous reporting and procedural arrangements, which largely facilitates their import and export business. Experience shows that such strategies not only substantially facilitate trade, but are also far more effective in protecting revenue than the old systems.

The ability to implement modern customs control strategies differs from country to country. Among the factors that influence that ability are the degree to which traders keep records and accounts, which is essential for accounts-based control to be meaningful; the overall degree of modernization of the trading sector, which may determine the extent to which customs can interact electronically with traders in connection with their foreign trade operations; the level of trade liberalization (tariff level, openness of the economy), which may cause the trading sector to be more or less tax-compliant; and the degree to which human, financial, and physical resources are made available to the customs department, which will help determine its ability to respond to the needs of the modern economy. Depending on these factors, some countries may have to rely on a higher level of physical control than others, until such time as the customs department has built up sufficient capacity to rely mainly on accounts-based controls, and the trade regime and trading environment are conducive to such an approach.

Regardless of their degree of modernization, customs administrations should adhere to the international standards and guidelines for administration of the duty relief systems included in the Revised

Kyoto Convention. These standards and guidelines are taken into account in the discussion, proposals, and guidelines that follow. No attempt is made to cover all the provisions of the Revised Kyoto Convention. Rather, the discussion concentrates on principles and practical measures for the design and effective implementation of the duty relief regimes, and the experience of some countries in this arena.

### Temporary Admission for Inward Processing

TAP is the regime under which materials can be imported, conditionally relieved from payment of import duties and taxes, on the basis that they are intended for manufacturing, processing, or repair, and subsequent exportation. The products resulting from the processing under certain conditions may also be obtained from materials other than those imported for inward processing. (See Equivalence and Prior Equivalence below.) The TAP regime also covers contract or "job" processing, whereby the foreign customer remains the owner of the imported goods. TAP is being implemented in many developed countries and in a number of developing countries.

**Issues** Effective implementation of TAP requires a well-developed customs administration. Manufacturers exporting a given minimum percentage of their production on a regular basis can request advance authorization for operating under the TAP regime. They may have to post a bond to secure the customs duties and are required to keep prescribed books and accounts to document the materials imported and the final products made of them. The rate of yield (ratio of imported materials used in one unit of output) needs to be determined and agreed on between the manufacturer and the customs administration, and updated when manufacturing processes or tariff rates change. A control mechanism needs to be set up by customs, in cooperation with the producer, to periodically verify the percentage of total production exported and the percentage sold in the local market, and to determine the amount of suspended duties and taxes to be cleared (for the goods exported) and the amount of duties and taxes to be paid (for the goods sold in the local market). This requires detailed accounting and careful verification by officers skilled in auditing manufacturers' accounts.

As the system is administratively demanding, it normally is not a practical solution for manufacturers that export only a small part of their production, or export only occasionally. Such manufacturers should have access to a simpler system of temporary admission or a smoothly operating system of drawback.

**Operational and Administrative Requirements and Procedures** The main requirements for effective operation and administration of the TAP regime include the following:

- *Authorization.* Manufacturers wanting to import under TAP need to register for the system at customs. Authorization from customs is needed for follow-up and control purposes. Upon the first application under the TAP regime, customs may visit the plant to check that records and systems are adequate for customs purposes and to find out more about the import and export trade.
- *Security.* The manufacturer will have to establish security for the duty in the form of a bond to secure duty payment in case of abuse or fraud. The bond can be waived for established and solvent companies that pose no revenue risk.
- *Rate of yield.* The ratio of imported materials used in one unit of output needs to be determined and agreed on between the manufacturer and the customs administration, and updated periodically and each time that manufacturing processes or tariff rates are changed.
- *Importation.* The manufacturer may import the goods to be processed directly or buy them from another TAP-authorized trader. On importing directly, the manufacturer declares the goods for the TAP regime and the goods are released to the importer with suspension of the duties and taxes. When buying from another TAP-authorized trader, the manufacturer needs to provide its TAP registration number to the supplier, and the manufacturer takes over the responsibility for the suspended duties and taxes from the supplier.
- *Exportation and discharge of responsibility.* The manufacturer clears its responsibility for the unpaid duties and taxes mainly through exportation of the processed goods. Exportation

includes direct exportation, sales to duty-free shops, sales by duty-free shops, sales to persons entitled to diplomatic privileges, and use as stores for bunkers on ships traveling to destinations abroad. Furthermore, the responsibility for the unpaid duties can also be cleared by putting the goods in a customs warehouse or an EPZ, transferring the goods to another temporary importation regime, selling the goods to another TAP trader, and any other export-equivalent procedures provided for in the national customs legislation.

- *Diversion of goods to local market.* Diversion of goods to free circulation beyond the authorized quantity results in payment of the suspended duties. Interest may be charged for the late payment. Byproducts, scrap, and waste from the processing are normally subject to payment of duty unless they are exported (national legislation may differ).
- *Periodic returns.* The manufacturer files periodic returns to the duty relief unit at customs showing the goods imported under the TAP regime or purchased from other TAP traders, and the destination of the goods after processing. There are two principal ways of accounting and controlling. One method is the matching of export documents with specific import documents. This is a traditional and complicated method, which should be avoided. The other method is to make a single, global declaration for the total quantity of materials imported during a given period and the total quantity of final goods delivered for export and to the local market in the same period. Global declaration is the only method that allows for effective implementation of the system, and is the recommended method.
- *Prescribed books and records.* The manufacturer needs to maintain records and accounts of raw materials imported and duties and taxes suspended; materials stored; materials used in production; final goods produced; quantities exported; quantities sold in the local market; and byproducts, scrap, and waste resulting from the process. The records must enable customs to monitor the goods under temporary admission.
- *Customs duty relief unit.* Customs monitors and controls the TAP system through a special unit, which may be called the Inward Processing unit or Duty Relief unit, for example. The unit reviews applications, gives authorizations for the TAP regime, reviews input–output ratios (rates of yield), and monitors the performance of the manufacturer on the basis of periodic returns, periodic visits, and audits of its accounts. Additional units at the customs offices in the main industrial centers may need to be established to monitor and audit the manufacturing companies approved under the system in these centers. Staff involved with the TAP should be adequately trained, particularly with respect to auditing.
- *Computerization.* The TAP control system should be computerized to allow for accurate follow-up on temporarily imported materials and the exported goods made from them; monitoring of the manufacturer's duty suspension account; and calculating and updating rates of yield as a basis for calculating the use of materials in finished products. (Examples of computerized support for duty relief administration are included in boxes 10.2 and 10.3.)

The requirements can be simplified for (a) traders importing only occasionally for export processing, for instance when the total value of imports for processing in a calendar year does not exceed a given amount, or the goods are imported for repair; and (b) operations that do not change the tariff classification of the goods, such as simple operations to ensure preservation, or improve presentation and marketability, or prepare the goods for distribution or sale.

In such cases, no prior registration for the system would be needed, but authorization would be given for each importation at the customs office. The authorization form would identify the imported goods, the process, the processed products, the rate of yield, and the re-exportation time limit.

**Equivalence and Prior Equivalence** The products resulting from manufacturing or processing, called compensating products, need not be obtained solely from goods admitted for inward processing, because it may be necessary for the manufacturer to substitute goods of national origin or that were previously imported with payment of

**BOX 10.2   The Reform of Duty Relief Regimes in Morocco**

Inward processing is an indispensable aspect of the Moroccan economy. In 2002, duty relief regimes accounted for over 50 percent of foreign trade transactions. About 82 percent of the duty relief was under the TAP regime.

For many years the management of the duty relief regimes was disorganized and opaque, until it became totally unmanageable. In 1996 more than 70,000 accounts, some established as far back as 1985, were waiting to be regularized. These delays were due to complicated, bureaucratic, and rigorous procedures involving excessive paperwork and meticulous recording and accounting. All import and export shipments were examined and many samples were drawn. Traders suffered large operational delays, and substantial funds were tied up in government accounts through delayed refund of security deposits.

A decision was made to implement two measures: complete reform of the procedures, and the regularization of the delays. The TAP regime was revised in close cooperation with the industrial sector. The procedural reform introduced less rigorous and less cumbersome requirements and allowed for more operational flexibility, including the acceptability of different types of guarantee, allowances in calculating the rate of yield, and the option to sell part of the production in the local market with duty payment but without interest. By 2003, over 90 percent of the accounts were regularized, thanks to the use of an automated mechanism for identifying anomalies and fraudulent activities, and the development of a procedure for identifying fictitious companies. A study of industrial sectors and research in the field led to the sanctioning of fictitious and fraudulent accounts.

In addition to these two measures, special efforts were made to improve service to the trading sector, including the reduction of clearance times to less than one hour, and the design of automated programs for the duty relief regimes. This gives operators online information about progress in the processing of their declarations, their customs account situation, and their guarantee situation, as well as providing a virtual window through which they can execute their clearance operations.

In recent years, Moroccan customs management has concentrated on motivating personnel and stimulating innovation. Results are already visible, for instance in the introduction of a personalized management system for the duty relief operations. This system responds to the needs of both trade facilitation and revenue control, and is fully integrated with the enterprises' methods of management. Already about 30 enterprises make use of this arrangement. Study and research for other improvements are ongoing.

*Source:* Steenlandt and De Wulf 2004.

---

duties and taxes. Such substitute goods need to be equivalent to the goods imported for inward processing that they replace.

Equivalence is the procedure that allows the manufacturer to use substitute goods in place of TAP goods, as long as the substitute goods are in free circulation in the customs territory and can be considered equivalent to the TAP goods. To be equivalent, the substitute goods must be of the same kind, technical specification, and commercial quality as the TAP goods. They must be mutually interchangeable.

Prior export equivalence allows the exportation of products made from equivalent goods to take place before the TAP goods are imported. Several countries allow for duty-free importation of materials of the same kind, technical specification, and quality as local materials that were incorporated in goods produced by TAP-approved manufacturers for export.[4]

**Illustration of Successful TAP Reform**   As inward processing is an important activity in the Moroccan economy, the duty relief regimes are an indispensable aspect of the strategy to attract investors.

---

4. Such systems are available, for instance, in Brazil, Chile, and the EU. This facility can be useful to the export manufacturer in several ways: The manufacturer can respond to urgent export orders when insufficient TAP goods are in stock. When it is difficult to apportion imports in advance to TAP and free circulation, the manufacturer can import all goods to free circulation initially and when it has exports, it can import TAP-equivalent goods to replace the goods used from the duty-paid stock. When the manufacturer has underestimated its TAP needs, it can supply export markets with products made from free circulation materials, and then import TAP-equivalent goods to replenish the duty-paid stock.

---

### BOX 10.3    Fiji's Duty Suspension Scheme

Fiji's DSS was developed to facilitate and encourage exportation by giving exporters access to manufacturing inputs at world prices.

The DSS is managed by a private sector–run organization—The Exporters Club—on behalf of Fiji Islands Revenue and Customs Authority.

Members must be in the business of importing materials for transformation into products for export. The Exporters Club assesses the qualifications of applicants, recommends a list of materials to be imported and subsequently used in the production of exports, calculates advance credits and Entitlement Proportion (EP) ratios, and advises customs when all requirements are met.

The exporter receives credits for every dollar of exports achieved under the system. It can use these credits to import approved materials duty free. The credit is based on the EP, that is, the proportion of imported goods required to produce one unit of the export product. As long as the company operates within its EP ratio, it can continue to import approved goods duty free. The EP is calculated initially when companies enter the scheme, using the company's import and export history and an audited set of accounts. For the first export operation, companies can be provided with advance credits that would enable them to import for two months using the credits.

Specially developed software has been created for customs as an attachment to the ASYCUDA system. The software enables the Exporters Club to manage the day-to-day operations of the program and customs to audit arrangements with individual members. Members have access to their own data, but cannot access the details of other members.

The Exporters Club is a nonprofit organization owned by eight peak industry groups involved in promoting exports. A board manages the Club, representing the owners and the Customs Service. In addition to the abovementioned responsibilities, the Club monitors the performance of each club member. This is done by a computerized system that calculates the amount of credits earned and automatically reduces these credits when products are imported. To cover the cost of operations, the Club charges an application and assessment fee, an annual subscription fee, and an activity fee.

*Source:* T. O'Connor, Director General of Customs, Fiji Islands Revenue and Customs Authority. Note prepared for this chapter (June 2003).

---

Box 10.2 summarizes the problems that had built up over the years in the management of the relief systems and the kind of reforms undertaken by the government to solve these problems and establish far more efficient management of the TAP regime.

**Variations on the TAP Procedure**    *Fiji's duty suspension scheme.* The Fiji duty suspension scheme (DSS), introduced in 2002, is an inward processing system that aims at the full relief of the import tariff and tax burden on export products. The system has some unique features of design, management, and operation. Since its inception, Fiji's DSS has been successful in achieving the stated objectives. It is managed by a private sector organization, known as The Exporters Club, on behalf of the Fiji Islands Revenue and Customs Authority. The system has a hybrid character with features of both the TAP and drawback mechanisms. For more detail, see the summary description in box 10.3.

*Passbook.* The passbook system is a mechanism for providing duty relief under the conditional exemption system, which has been used in a number of Asian countries including India, Bangladesh, and Nepal. It operates using a ledger (the passbook) through which both the trader and customs keep track of the quantity and value of materials imported and the processed goods exported.[5] The ledger also keeps the trader's security account. For a description of how it operates in Nepal, see box 10.4.

*Manufacturing under bond.* The customs regulations of many countries incorporate provisions for manufacturing under bond (MUB) to provide duty relief to export manufacturers. The system is in operation in numerous countries including Bangladesh, Canada, India, Nepal, Tanzania, and the United States. This system is similar to TAP.

---

5. The passbook system in Bangladesh is difficult to monitor, as exports and imports are recorded in different passbooks if they are effected through different customs houses. Also, the description of the imports does not follow the Harmonized System classification, complicating the task of audits. A Bank project is financing the automation of the Warehouse and Bond system. Once implemented, this will gradually replace the passbook system.

## BOX 10.4 The Passbook System in Nepal

Following years of disappointment with the failures of a drawback system, Nepal introduced the passbook system in 2001. Under this system, export manufacturers are relieved from the duty burden on materials imported for processing or transformation into products to be exported or sold in the local market for foreign currency. The system is available only for operations that add at least 20 percent of value to the imported goods. The rate of yield, that is, the quantity of imported materials used in the production of one unit of export product, needs to be approved by the Technical Committee of the Department of Industry. The exportation or sale needs to happen within 12 months following importation.

On importation, the quantity, value, and duties and taxes suspended are recorded in the passbook. Security in the form of a cash deposit is required to cover duties and taxes suspended, and credit for the deposit is given in the passbook. On proof of exportation of the processed goods, the deposit corresponding to quantity of inputs incorporated in the exported goods is released. For regular importers–exporters, the released amount is not refunded but used as a deposit for subsequent imports of materials. Excess amounts of deposit not used within one month are refunded. Failure to export within 12 months after importation of the materials results in payment of the duties and a 10 percent penalty. The Department of Customs specifies the customs offices through which the trader can import the materials and export the processed goods under the system. Any particular company can import only through one given customs office. Such restrictions have created problems for some traders, but overall, the system has performed well. Traders have been generally more satisfied with the passbook system than with the drawback system.

*Source:* Author.

Like TAP, it allows manufacturers to import raw materials without duty payment. On exportation of the manufactured products, the duties on the corresponding amount of raw materials are cleared. The MUB system is especially useful for the assembly of goods made entirely from imported dutiable components, or goods using a high content of imported dutiable inputs. In these cases, the savings in financing costs relating to duty payments can be substantial.

Considering that the primary objective of authorizing MUB is to promote exports, rather than to postpone the payment of customs duty on the imported materials and components, there is no advantage in allowing manufacture under bond if most of the production is sold in the local market. However, it may be necessary for the manufacturer to sell parts of the goods produced in the domestic market.[6] The government must decide the minimum percentage of production required to be exported.

Many developing countries have had difficulty monitoring that all imported inputs are actually used in the manufacture of export goods and not diverted to other industrial uses, and that all finished products are actually exported. Furthermore, the legal and administrative requirements imposed on MUB users often are excessive and costly. In some cases, the license for operating the bonded warehouse needs to be renewed every year. The user can access the raw materials only when customs opens the warehouse, and procedures involve too much paperwork and bureaucratic hassle.

The operational and administrative requirements and procedures for the MUB regime are broadly similar to those discussed under the TAP regime. Traditionally, MUB programs have relied more heavily on strict physical controls than the TAP regime, but here, too, physical control is gradually being replaced by accounts-based control. In most developing countries, physical controls are still heavily relied on.

Such controls may involve supervision of the transfer of the imported materials from the docks to the bonded warehouse; joint control by customs and the manufacturer of access to the warehouse; control over access to the raw materials, finished

---

6. This would be the case, for instance, when some of the production does not come up to the quality required on the international market, but there may be a local demand for such products; or when the company is not able to sell its entire production in export markets and finds it uneconomical to restrict production to the quantity it can sell abroad; or when an export order is cancelled; or, finally, when the product manufactured in bond is in strong demand in the domestic market and would have to be imported if the bonded factory is not allowed to sell to the local market.

goods, and any intermediate materials including wastes stored in the warehouse; and physical supervision of the exportation or other means of disposal of the finished products and other goods arising from processing under bond.

Control can be exercised through simpler procedures similar to the TAP procedures that, while protecting the interest of revenue, also facilitate trade. In brief, this would involve a security to protect revenue; a formula expressing the rate of yield; prescribed accounts of production operations, that is, raw materials received and used and final products manufactured and exported; accounts-based customs verification; and periodic unscheduled visits to the factory to ensure that accounts are correctly kept.

Computerizing MUB control can greatly improve the quality of control and the efficiency of the whole operation at savings for both the manufacturer and the customs administration. Computerization allows for such functions as the electronic tracking of goods moving into and out of the bonded warehouse; calculating and updating rates of yield, and on that basis calculating the utilization of materials in finished products; and producing accurate accounts of imported materials, goods produced, and goods exported.

The facility operating in Bangladesh provides a good example of the revenue risk involved in the duty relief systems and how the risk can be addressed by establishing computerized customs control (see box 10.5).

---

### BOX 10.5    The Bangladesh Special Bonded Warehouse Facility

In Bangladesh, the Ready Made Garments (RMG) sector is significant and relies heavily on the use of the special bonded warehouse (SBW) facility. Raw materials used in the production of RMG products are imported duty-free into SBW, manufactured into finished articles of clothing, and exported. There are some 3,400 SBWs, located mainly in Dhaka and in the Chittagong port area. Another, approximately 700, backward linkage or supply industries operate a different kind of warehouse and supply inputs, such as packing, thread, embroidery, and labels to the RMG export trade. These supplies are treated as exports.

The Commissioner of Customs, following the approval of the facility and the posting of a bond that must cover the duty liability on the goods warehoused, issues licenses to the SBW. The bonder is issued passbooks, one for the bond operator, and one for customs at the port of import–export for recording goods both imported into and exported out of the bonded warehouse. A bonder can import raw materials duty-free up to 75 percent of the value of the total export. At the time of import the bonder submits a utilization declaration (UD) issued by the Bangladesh Garments Manufacturing and Export Association, along with other import documents. The quantities imported are recorded in the bonder's and customs' passbooks, which act as a record of stock going into the SBW. Thereafter, the bonder accepts delivery of the raw materials for transfer to the warehouse. After completion of the manufacture of finished products, the bonder presents all documents for export together with the UD for a second time,

and the necessary export entry is made in the passbooks. It is the bonder's responsibility to match import accounts with export accounts in the passbook.

The system is not foolproof and there are reports of significant revenue loss due to illegal diversion of finished products to the local market. A recent investigation of a single fraud case revealed that a bonder had falsified export documents and the entries in the passbook, leading to a loss in customs revenue of US$3.2 million.

A key component of the customs modernization project that started in 1999 is to address the loss of revenue created by the operation of the SBW facilities. The main initiatives include centralized management of the SBW facilities, relicensing of the SBW operators (which reduced the number of licenses by 20 percent), and the electronic tracking of the goods using the ASYCUDA++ computer system. This enables customs to retrieve accurate accounts of total imports and exports of any individual SBW operator and to reconcile the movement of goods into and out of a bonded warehouse, reducing its reliance on the passbook system. In the future, this reconciliation is expected to benefit from a new software program that takes the ASYCUDA++ import and export data and uses the UD formula for calculating the utilization of raw materials to finished articles, thus automatically tracking the goods flow and highlighting potential inconsistencies.

*Source:* Thomas, January 2003. Note prepared for this chapter. World Bank staff.

*Drawback*

Drawback is the refund of import duties and taxes paid on imported materials that are used in the manufacture of goods that are then exported.[7] Drawback is not an export subsidy and is compliant with WTO rules insofar as the refund does not exceed the amount of duties and taxes paid on importation of the materials.[8]

**Issues** Drawback is in operation in many countries, usually along with one or more systems that are based on temporary admission. While the principle of drawback is the same everywhere, there are substantial differences among countries in the scope of drawback allowed, and in the administrative rules and procedures by which the system operates and is implemented. In some countries drawback seems to be considered as a privilege or a benefit to the export manufacturer, rather than the refund of what should not have been charged in the first place. This is reflected in the kind of problems experienced with drawback schemes in various countries, which may include some of the following:

- The categories of goods that qualify for drawback are restricted to encourage the use of domestically produced equivalents of the imported goods. This handicaps the competitiveness of the exporter.
- The exporter is not given full relief of the duty burden because not all import-related taxes are included in the system, or refunds are made only up to a given percentage of what was paid. An example of restricted access to drawback is the Indian drawback scheme, which covers only those products included in an exhaustive list and

permits refund only for the central government duties and not of the state taxes and duties levied on the inputs.

- Processing or service fees reduce the drawback at times. For instance, Tanzania used to charge a processing fee of 4 percent of the refund.
- Bureaucratic requirements, ill-conceived procedures, or inefficient customs administration (or all three) result in undue costs to the exporter through delays in the payment of the refund, service charges, or other direct or indirect administrative costs.
- Payment delays often are excessive, or payment simply is not made, a problem occurring particularly in countries where refunds are to be made out of a special annual budget line for drawback. When payments are finally made, inflation may have substantially reduced the value of the drawback payments, thus increasing the exporter's already high cost of financing the duties, and reducing its working capital. For instance, before Tanzania reformed its system a few years ago, substantial arrears in drawback refunds had accumulated due to both an inadequate budget for drawback and excessive documentary requirements. Similar problems prevail in Nepal, India, and several African countries.[9]
- Excessive documentary requirements also contribute to delays in refunds, and add costs to the exporter (and customs). Some countries require the drawback claim to be supported not only by the export entry and invoice, but also by the bill of lading, the landing certificate, proof of export proceeds, and import entries concerning the inputs for which the duties were paid. Apart from the fact that most of these documents should play no role in the routine processing of drawback claims, they are a major source of delay because it may take the exporter months after exportation before being able to produce some of them.

---

7. Some countries use the term "drawback" for the refund of duties paid for any goods imported and subsequently exported without undergoing processing. The appropriate customs terminology for such refunds is simply "refund."

8. Some countries have applied a flat drawback rate per category of products. In this case, the refund will normally not equal the amount of duties paid on the imported inputs, because technical input/output coefficients, prices of inputs, and duty rates vary for each specification of export product. If the amount is too low, the exporter does not receive full relief of the duty element in the export products. If it is too high, the drawback contains an element of subsidy and does not comply with WTO rules. Kenya, Bolivia, and Colombia used to apply a flat duty drawback rate. In Bolivia, a flat rate of 10 percent of the export value was in place until about 1990. The drawback system has been reformed since then.

9. Tax Notes International reports that the Nepalese government's delays in duty drawback hurt the country's export industry. Business opportunities have been lost as a result of the failure of the Revenue Committee to refund the duties. The government allocated only NPR 200 million (about US$ 2.8 million) for duty drawback, despite estimates that the total duty refundable at the end of the year would exceed NPR 1 billion (about US$ 14 million) (Tax Notes International 2001a, p. 76; 2001b, p. 168).

The absence of a well-designed drawback system, or the inability of the customs administration to properly implement one, is frustrating and discouraging for exporters and may make duty and tax evasion more tempting. The following summarizes principles and guidelines for the design and administration of an effective drawback system.

**Determination of Drawback Rates**  The determination of drawback rates involves the following:

- The setting of drawback rates should be the responsibility of a high-level committee, which should normally consist of industry, trade, customs, inland revenue, and possibly other government departments.
- Drawback rates should be based on calculations of the duties on imported inputs incorporated in one unit of output. The amount to be refunded should equal the sum of inputs times their tariffs, for a given unit of exports. A certain amount of aggregation may be possible in setting drawback rates. For final goods that convert inputs according to a standard formula, product rates or fixed rates can be set. When input–output ratios vary, individual rates are more appropriate.

Under the fixed rate system the refund is calculated according to a set schedule for each exported good based on input–output coefficients. This provides ease of administration because it uses automatic rates of drawback not related to the specific performance of the manufacturer. However, it requires the frequent updating of the input–output coefficients. Korea and Taiwan use this system and publish updated drawback schedules every six months.

Under the individual rate system the drawback is based on the manufacturer's performance, verified by audit of the books and records of the enterprise. This system relies more heavily on self-assessment, because the manufacturer is responsible for establishing rates of yield or conversion ratios to claim drawback. It is the responsibility of the administration to verify the yields or conversion rates through audits. This approach is fair to all manufacturers because it relates specifically to the performance of an individual company and is not based on an industry average. Most industrial countries use this system.

**Guiding Principles for Drawback Design**  The following principles should be followed in designing a drawback system.

- Duty relief should be complete (100 percent of all duties and taxes paid) and rapid. It should cover all export products that incorporate imported inputs, as well as all raw materials and intermediate goods used for the production of final exports, including imported packaging. Refunds should not exceed the duties actually paid, ensuring consistency with WTO rules.
- The system should be simple, easily understood by manufacturers, and easily administered by customs. It should operate at minimal cost to the exporter. This implies that the exporter is not charged any special service fee for obtaining drawback; the refund is immediate or within a few days after exportation; and the documentary requirements are minimal, while protecting revenue from abuse and fraud.
- The export declaration should be taken as sufficient proof of exportation, and no other documentation should routinely be required. Drawback should not depend on proof of exchange receipts, but on the simple fact of exportation. If questions of underinvoicing or other fraudulent practices need to be addressed, this should not be done through the drawback system, but through other appropriate control methods.
- The scheme should include both direct and indirect exporters, that is, the refund should reflect all duties and taxes paid on the imported materials that have been incorporated into the export product, whether paid by the exporter, or by other traders from whom the materials were purchased.[10]
- Exporters should be accountable for revenue losses resulting from failure to inform the customs drawback unit of changes in the factors underlying the drawback rate.
- Customs should publicize and maintain performance standards in administering drawback and, in particular, commit itself to paying drawback within a set number of days following the receipt of the drawback claim.

---

10. This is done for instance, in Korea, Chile, and Colombia, but it is not the case in many countries.

**Operational Guidelines** The main operational guidelines for a drawback system follow:

- The drawback system should be the subject of a regulation that would set out the principles and the main legal, administrative, and procedural requirements. Customs should provide further useful information to drawback users through information leaflets or seminars.

- Claiming drawback and paying the amount of drawback should require only a simple procedure with minimal documentary requirements. The claim can be made on the same form as the export declaration or on a separate form. Payment should not be delayed until all controls are finalized. Once customs has certified the exportation of the goods on the basis of the export entry, the drawback should be paid, with verification of the validity of the claim afterward. In situations where delays are unavoidable because, for example, the drawback rate has yet to be determined for a product at the time it is exported, a provisional payment should be made, perhaps 80 percent of the amount claimed by the exporter, subject to the necessary adjustment when the rate is determined.

- The drawback can be paid in cash, check, electronic fund transfer, or in the form of a credit certificate or voucher, which could be used for paying duties on the next import consignment. If the voucher is not sufficient to pay the duties and taxes on the next import, the difference is paid in cash. The advantage of the voucher system is that it is simple to operate, not disruptive to government accounts, and less conducive to corruption. (Such a system is in operation in Brazil.) If payment is made in cash, the budget for paying drawback should be set high enough to satisfy all drawback claims, and procedures should be streamlined to avoid lengthy delays.

- The option to claim drawback and receive payment periodically should be made available for exporters that have a large number of drawback claims on a regular basis. This simplifies the work for both the exporter and customs.

- Control of the amount of drawback should be made after exportation through periodic audit of the books and records of the manufacturer. There may be benefit in periodically coordinat-

ing audit for drawback with audit for value-added taxes (VAT).

- A dedicated technical unit at customs headquarters needs to be established to monitor and audit the manufacturing companies approved under the system and audit drawback claims. A selected number of staff need to be trained in the audit for drawback.

- The drawback formula should be periodically reviewed to take into account changes in the factors underlying the drawback rate (changes in input–output ratios, import prices, and duty and tax rates).

- Drawback control should be automated through a module or program especially developed for managing the drawback system, using the existing customs computerized system (for instance, similar to the Fiji solution for TAP management—see box 10.2).

### *Export Processing Zones*

EPZs are geographical enclaves established outside the country's customs territory to encourage manufacturing for export and to provide services to foreign enterprises.[11] The objectives for establishing EPZs in general are to promote exports of nontraditional manufactured goods, strengthen the competitiveness of exporters, attract investors, diversify the economy, create employment, transfer technology, and achieve development and growth.[12]

**Issues** In EPZs, enterprises can import raw materials and components without payment of import duties and taxes. In addition, they enjoy several other advantages, which may include exemption from sales taxes, excise duties, and profit taxes; exemption from industrial regulations applied elsewhere in the country; benefits relating to labor regulations, foreign exchange, and others; and

---

11. Export processing zones have been given a variety of names including Free Trade Zone, Duty Free Zone, Tax Free Zone, and Free Export Zone.

12. Historically, free zones were originally established to facilitate entrepot trade focusing on commercial, warehousing, and repacking operations, and not for export manufacturing. Present day examples of such free zones are the Miami free trade zone, which acts as a distribution center for European and Asian companies exporting into South America and the Caribbean, and the free zone of Colon in Panama, which is concerned almost exclusively with entrepot trade.

provision of infrastructure. These benefits are subject to the condition that the manufactured products are exported, and that all the imported inputs are either used in the zone or are re-exported. In some countries, sale to the local market of a part of the output is allowed.[13]

In recent years, with the shift of emphasis from import substitution to export-oriented industries, many developing countries have been attracted to establishing EPZs, and their use has proliferated. However, experience has shown that only in a limited number of cases has the establishment of EPZs been successful in promoting exports.[14] Many of these zones have proved to be poor investments as a result of unwise location, high investment costs, inadequate management, or, more profoundly, because the economic policy environment within the country was not conducive to efficient production for export.[15]

EPZs are usually restricted to a designated industrial estate; but in some cases, and recently more so, factories outside the restricted area have been approved as single factory zones.[16] Leakage of EPZ goods to the domestic market without duty payment has been frequently reported by developing countries. This has been the case especially where the EPZs are not well separated geographically from the regular customs zone, and where several single factory zones exist, making it difficult for customs to organize control over what enters and exits each of these zones. Unless the EPZ enterprises keep

books and accounts properly and are mostly tax compliant, and customs has the capability to rely mainly on accounts-based controls, diversion of EPZ goods to the domestic market is bound to be a problem, with revenue loss as a result.

**Customs Administration of Export Processing Zones**    For application of the customs law, EPZs are located outside the customs territory, although they are physically located within the national boundaries and are part of the national economy. EPZs, therefore, require customs to arrange for two types of customs control.

First, with respect to the movement of goods from the EPZ to the local market and vice versa, the EPZ has to be dealt with like a foreign country. Customs posts need to be established on the roads from the zone to the rest of the country to ensure that the relevant customs laws are properly enforced. Imports from the EPZ into the local market, if allowed, need to be dealt with like imports from abroad. Deliveries of goods from the domestic market to the EPZ need to be dealt with like exports. Customs surveillance needs to be established, to prevent incidents where goods imported or manufactured in the EPZ enter the local market fraudulently. Insofar as the EPZ is a geographically enclosed area, all this should not establish major difficulties for customs, because this is all part and parcel of normal customs operations. However, the situation is different when the EPZ is not well separated geographically from the regular customs area, and especially when it comes to single factory zones. As mentioned above, single factory zones are difficult to police.

Second, with respect to imports into and exports out of the EPZ, customs documentation is required for control and statistical purposes. One of the main characteristics and conditions for smooth operation of the typical EPZ is streamlined administration. This includes streamlined customs documentation requirements for imported raw materials and capital goods and exported final products. In countries where customs administration is not up to modern standards, the customs documentary requirements in connection with EPZ trade may interfere with its smooth operation. To solve that problem, a separate administrative branch has often been created to mediate between EPZ firms and the government, with the purpose to reduce zone firms' administrative costs and to prevent unnecessary

---

13. For instance, in Mauritius, Israel, Syria, and the United States.

14. Mauritius is probably the best example of a successful EPZ. Other successful cases are the Republic of Korea, Taiwan, Malaysia, and the Dominican Republic.

15. For an analysis of the role of EPZs in promoting manufactured exports see, for instance, Madani 1999. Madani concludes that EPZs have limited applications and that general liberalization of a country's economy is a better policy choice. See also Warr (1989). Warr concludes that the experience of East and Southeast Asia confirms that the role of EPZs in promoting manufactured exports is at best minor, and that the most effective means of promoting exports is to ensure that the economic policy environment within the country is conducive to efficient production for export.

16. This is the case in Fiji, Korea, Mauritius, Mexico, Senegal, and the United States. In Senegal, the single factory regime was introduced in 1991, but due to a wave of applications, approvals were suspended in 1992, and the regime became fully effective only in 1993. The government explained the suspension and delays by the difficulties of customs control and, more specifically, by the tax losses that would be incurred if existing enterprises were approved under the EPZ system. By 1995, eight single factory zones were operating.

delays in their operations. However, as pointed out by Warr (1989), the degree to which these bodies are empowered to act on behalf of the government varies, but other departments can resent interference with their "normal" functions and become uncooperative with the zone bodies. The experience with the arrangements in Jordan's Aqaba export processing zone illustrates some of the difficulties that, for instance, the creation of a separate customs agency for the zone can create. (See box 10.6.) Instead, the recommended arrangement is to give responsibility for customs functions relating to the EPZ operations to an autonomous or semi-autonomous division under the umbrella of the national customs service.

**Other Administrative Issues and Guidelines**  If sales in the local market are provided for in the

regime, they should be limited to wholesale transactions. It would be impossible for customs to effectively control retail transactions.

If there is no adequate customs capability for auditing manufacturer's accounts, single factories located outside the EPZ enclave should not be granted EPZ status. However, such factories could possibly qualify for the MUB regime.

### Conclusions and Guidelines for Duty Relief for Inward Processing

From both a tax policy and administrative point of view, the first best practice for providing exporter manufacturers access to industrial inputs at world prices is to have a zero tariff. In the presence of tariffs, the best system is the one that relieves export manufacturers from duty payment, fully and at the

---

### BOX 10.6   Customs Administration of the Aqaba Export Processing Zone

The government of Jordan established the Aqaba Special Economic Zone at the Red Sea port of Aqaba in January 2001 to enhance economic capability in the Kingdom by attracting different economic activities and investments thereto. The zone began operations under the administration of the Aqaba Special Economic Zone Authority (ASEZA). The zone has clear borders of its own, and to that extent is a territory that has been separated from the national territory of Jordan. ASEZA is empowered to make its own laws to apply within the zone, and is specifically granted authority relating to customs procedures. As a result, there are two separate customs authorities operating in ASEZA: the National Jordanian Customs, which retains responsibility for administering the Customs Law of Jordan to the extent that it applies in the zone, and the customs agency within ASEZA, which is responsible for administering ASEZA's customs regulations.

The two agencies have very different cultures. The National Customs is a long-established organization with a focus on ensuring that Jordan's borders are properly protected. It has a control-based approach to the clearance of goods, transport, and people. Its staff consists largely of long-serving uniformed officers with a traditional view of customs processing. The ASEZA is new, and is staffed largely by young talented graduates who are committed to the development of the zone, and are impatient with process. They are keen to see the traditional transactions-based approach of the National

Customs replaced with a more contemporary post-transaction, audit-based approach.

The existence of two customs agencies was difficult to manage. It is also not consistent with the Revised Kyoto Convention, and the resulting practices do not deliver the simplified procedures promoted by the Convention.

Specific difficulties include the following:

- Zone operators have to deal with two agencies with separate headquarters and facilities.
- While both have access to ASYCUDA, the two agencies' systems do not communicate, and there is a failure to share information.
- Different procedures apply, depending on which agency is involved in the transaction.

As a consequence of these difficulties, there are the following concerns:

- Legitimate traders are not receiving the appropriate level of service necessary to attract investment to the zone; there is duplicate documentation, and no "one-stop-shop."
- Fraudulent traders are exploiting the perceived lack of controls and there is a heightened risk of revenue leakage through inadequate management of goods moving in and out of the zone to and from national territory.

In view of these difficulties the Jordanian authorities are considering integrating some of the functions of the two organizations.

*Source:* Harrison, Mark. 2003. Note prepared for this chapter.

least cost. Thus, the best options are systems that do not require payment or advance payment of import duties on the inputs, and that involve no, or only minimal, paperwork and no more than the routine formalities as applied to all imports.

However, in real life, some administrative cost is unavoidable. Customs administrations are always faced with the possibility that not all importers and exporters are fully tax compliant. Therefore, safeguards against abuse and evasion are needed. In designing systems, procedures, and safeguards for the implementation of duty relief systems, countries can take into account the standards and guidelines stipulated in the Revised Kyoto Convention, and incorporate these in the country's laws, regulations, and administrative procedures, in line with specific country circumstances.

The recommended practice for any particular country depends on both tariff level and structure, and administrative capacity. For countries with an efficient and modern administration, in particular for countries with the capability of accounts-based control, the temporary admission for inward processing under any of its forms (TAP, MUB, and EPZ if economically appropriate) should be available to reliable companies. Drawback should also be available, especially where the government fears too much revenue risk in relation to temporary admission regimes, as well as for all cases in which, for one reason or another, the duties have been paid on importation of the materials when their use in import processing was not anticipated.

Countries with only limited control capabilities may have to rely mainly on drawback, but TAP facilities should be provided to companies that are in good standing with respect to their fiscal obligations. Duty relief should be provided in all cases in which the interest of revenue can be reasonably well protected, while making all efforts to facilitate trade operations. The customs administration's accounts-based control capabilities should be fully developed and temporary admission for inward processing gradually should become the main method for duty relief.

## Warehousing, Temporary Admission, and Transit

This section reviews the customs regimes under which goods are imported with suspension of duty payment for reasons other than inward processing.

This includes customs warehousing, temporary admission for re-exportation in the same state, and transit.[17]

### Customs Warehousing

Customs warehousing is the procedure under which the importer stores the imported goods in a warehouse under customs control, without payment of import duties and taxes, until the goods are taken into home use, or until the goods are re-exported, in which case no duties are payable. The customs warehousing procedure is available in virtually every country.

**Issues** This regime provides valuable facilities to the trading sector; but if it is not administered properly, there may be costs that are too heavy to the owner of the goods, or the government, or both. This is especially so where customs still relies heavily on physical controls.

The establishment of proper control over customs warehouses to prevent evasion and revenue loss through leakage of warehoused goods to the market without duty payment, has at times gone beyond the capability of some customs administrations. This results from a multiplicity of warehouses, inadequate documentary follow-up, poor procedures, and generally weak administration. For instance, faced with rampant abuse and evasion and resulting revenue losses, as well as the inability of its customs administration to establish needed controls, Tanzania saw no better solution than closing down virtually all customs warehouses during 1997–98.[18]

**Economic Rationale** Customs warehousing facilitates import trade. When imports are intended for home consumption, the procedure allows the importer to delay payment of duties and taxes until the importer actually clears the goods for home use. When the importer decides not to clear the

---

17. The standards and guidelines of the Revised Kyoto Convention with respect to the duty relief regimes are included in the Convention as follows: customs warehousing: Specific Annex D.1; temporary admission: Specific Annex G.1; transit: Specific Annex E.1. Customs warehousing is often referred to as bonded warehousing.

18. The bonded warehousing regime was made available again shortly thereafter, but the number of warehouses was drastically reduced and the control system improved.

goods for home consumption but to re-export them, perhaps because market conditions have changed, the importer obviates the need to pay the duties. The goods can also be given another customs destination, such as TAP. Bonded warehouses are also used to store goods that are domestically produced under TAP or MUB, or that are subject to excise duties. Such storage clears the duty liability on these goods from the time they are warehoused, provided actual exportation follows. For drawback products, storage in the customs warehouse triggers the refund.

Another advantage for the importer or owner of the goods is that certain operations are allowed during storage, including inspecting and sampling of the goods, packing and repacking, and other operations aimed at improving the marketability of the goods.

**Requirements for Effective and Efficient Administration**    The customs department must be satisfied that the goods can be stored in the warehouse without serious risk of loss due to theft, diversion, and other problems, and that the agency operating the warehouse takes responsibility for the safe custody of the goods. Customs must also be certain that the procedure for transferring the goods from the customs warehouse for exportation (which cancels the exporter's liability to pay duty on the goods) or for clearing them for home consumption by paying duty is adequate. The administrative requirements may differ substantially according to the risk of fraudulent removal or substitution of goods. In general, requirements may include the following:

- customs approval of the warehouse—among other things, the warehouse needs to have reasonable structural security and safe access
- double-locking of the warehouse (warehouse keeper and customs)
- permanent or intermittent supervision
- unannounced spot checks
- keeping of stock accounts
- periodic inventory
- financial security, although this may be waived if there is no special revenue risk and if customs control can be adequately exercised.

Traditionally, warehouse control has relied heavily on physical control, typically involving the sta-

tioning of customs officers at licensed premises. The officers exercise control over warehoused goods; supervise a range of commercial activities, including the movement of all goods entering or leaving the warehouse, and the stuffing and unstuffing of containers; and authorized operations such as sorting, packaging, and conditioning. The control system often includes a requirement that customs locks the warehouse in the evening and reopens it the following morning. In addition, without the physical presence of customs staff, no commercial activities are allowed to be carried out. The warehouse operators are charged for the cost of customs supervision, including officers' salaries, overtime, and the provision of appropriate on-site accommodation and equipment.

Many countries, both Organisation for Economic Co-operation and Development (OECD) and developing countries, have moved from physical control arrangements (closed bond arrangements) to documentary and accounts-based systems for customs warehouse control (open bond arrangements), thereby improving the efficiency of warehouse operations and reducing the cost of both regulation and compliance. For example, the practice of physically controlling bonded warehouses was terminated in Australia in the late 1960s, and in the United States in the early 1980s. Following the introduction of its new approach to warehouse compliance, the U.S. Customs Service announced

> The Customs Regulations were amended in 1982 . . . to replace physical supervision by Customs with the audit-inspection supervision method. Through this change, Customs reduced reimbursable costs to proprietors from $8 million to $2 million annually, and allowed much more flexibility in warehouse operations. . . At the same time, the change saved taxpayers almost $2 million annually in customs costs and reduced the number of customs officers needed to supervise warehouses from about 300 to about 50. (U.S. Customs Service 1996, p. 2-1).

Following Hong Kong's lead, Thailand introduced an open bond arrangement in 2002. (See box 10.7.)

### Temporary Admission

Temporary admission is the customs procedure that provides for full or partial relief from import

---

### BOX 10.7   Thailand's Move to Open Bond Arrangements

Thailand's customs warehousing system is moving from a closed to an open bond system. Thailand's Customs Act No. 18 of 2000 provides for the legal instrument to establish bonded warehouses. Within the parameters of the law, the Customs Department has flexibility in administering the law. Following a government decision that required all government agencies to streamline their services, the Customs Privileges Bureau has focused on improving the customs control of bonded warehouses. The closed bond arrangements, which Thailand has traditionally applied to the management of bonded warehouse compliance, was characterized by real-time physical control, with the compliance assessment focus being directed toward individual transactions rather than the broader concept of a warehouse operator's systems, procedures,

and controls. The open bond arrangements to which the Customs Department is moving rely on computer-based controls to replace the physical presence of officers at the premises. This includes a warehouse inventory control system that can be connected to the Customs Department in real time, and the electronic monitoring of incoming and outgoing warehouse goods. The arrangement is reflective of a risk-based approach to compliance management, due to the greater reliance on warehouse operators' self-assessment of their compliance, verified through post-transaction customs compliance audits of the relevant systems and procedures to determine the integrity of such systems.

*Source:* Ue-srivong, Chintana. 2003. Note prepared for this chapter.

---

duties and taxes on goods imported for a specific purpose, on the condition that they are to be re-exported in the same state. As a rule, the procedure allows for total conditional relief. In certain cases the relief may only be partial. Temporary admission is a widely used procedure.

**Issues**   Temporary admission is a relatively simple customs procedure. The risk to government revenue of allowing the temporary entry of foreign goods without payment of duties and taxes can be managed through proper use of documents and financial security for the revenue involved. Nevertheless, in a number of less advanced customs administrations temporary admission has been abused. This happens most frequently with vehicles of experts and other personnel visiting the country for the duration of project implementation or for other temporary assignments.

**Economic Rationale**   There are various economic and social reasons for allowing goods to be imported temporarily without payment of duty and taxes. The main categories of such imports include goods for display or use at exhibitions, fairs, meetings, and similar events; professional equipment of persons visiting the territory to carry out specific tasks; commercial samples; containers used in international transport of goods; travelers' personal effects; and vehicles in international traf-

fic. International trade and economic and social activities would be hindered if duties and taxes were to be paid on importation and then refunded on re-exportation. Apart from increasing the cost of the activity, it would also complicate customs administration.

**Requirements for Effective and Efficient Administration**   The conditions and administrative requirements include the following:

- Temporary admission is granted based on the intent to re-export the goods.
- A declaration for temporary admission needs to be lodged for importation. However, no declaration should be required when there is no doubt about the subsequent re-exportation of the goods, regardless of their value (containers, for example).
- The goods must be identifiable. Customs must be able to ensure that the re-exported goods are the same as those presented at temporary importation. Customs may take identification measures if commercial means of identification are not sufficient.
- Security is required for the duties and taxes that would become due if the temporary admission conditions are not complied with. The security may be furnished by an international guaranteeing chain, as is the case under the ATA

(Admission Temporaire-Temporary Admission) system.

- A time limit for re-exportation needs to be set; it should be adequate for the purpose of the temporary admission, should not encourage abuse, and should be easy to monitor.
- The re-export declaration should refer to the initial temporary admission document. Security should be released provided customs is satisfied that the re-exported goods are the same as those initially imported and that all conditions have been met.

As with the other customs regimes, follow-up on goods admitted under the temporary admission regime can be largely facilitated and improved when customs control is computerized. This is particularly so when re-exportation of the temporary admission goods takes place through one or more offices other than the office of importation.

### Transit

Because chapter 11 is devoted to customs transit, the comments here are limited to identifying transit as one of the duty suspension regimes, highlighting its revenue risk, and summarizing some of the main requirements for effective customs control.

Customs transit is the procedure under which goods are transported under customs control from one customs office to another. When the whole movement is within the same customs territory, this is referred to as national transit or removal under bond. When the customs offices are in more than one customs territory, it is international transit. Customs transit procedures are designed to facilitate the movement of goods crossing the territory of one or more countries, without jeopardizing customs revenue, which is threatened by the diversion of goods to the local market.[19]

The transit regime has often been used as a means for fraudulent importation in both industrialized and developing countries. Substantial revenue may be lost when transit goods are diverted to the local market fraudulently. The administrative

measures needed for the effective control of transit shipments are straightforward and simple. Nevertheless, few developing countries have succeeded in establishing an adequate control system, due to problems of infrastructure at the border offices, inadequate systems for securing the suspended duties and taxes, poor means of communication, and generally weak administration.

The measures needed for customs control over transit include, among others, restricting the licensing of transporters for transit to solvent, reputable transporters that are in good standing relative to their tax obligations; strictly monitoring transit shipments through proper documentation; establishing security measures to insure the suspended duties and taxes; establishing an efficient system of information exchange between the customs office of entry and the customs office of exit; and taking rapid action if transit shipments are not presented at the office of exit in the time set for completing the transit.

## Exemptions

Exemptions are exceptions made to the application of the ordinary customs tariff.[20] They can take the form of a full or partial waiver of duties and taxes that would ordinarily be payable on imports. Unlike duty relief regimes, exemptions are unrelated to exportation or re-exportation. They apply to goods imported for home consumption by certain eligible categories of importers, and on condition that the goods are used for specified purposes.[21]

Some exemptions are stipulated in the international conventions to which the country adheres. Others are established at the discretion of the government for a variety of social and economic purposes. Still others concern imports of a mainly noncommercial nature, also called traditional exemptions. For a more detailed classification, see box 10.1.

19. To facilitate international transit of goods, standard procedures have been established in bilateral and multilateral agreements. The main international conventions in this regard are the Convention on the International Transit of Goods (1971) and the Convention on International Transportation by Road (1975), usually referred to as the TIR convention.

20. The standards and guidelines of the Revised Kyoto Convention with respect to exemptions are included in Specific Annex B.3.

21. Exemptions are sometimes confused with zero tariff rates. However, zero tariff rates are of general application to all importers, while exemptions only apply to selected importers or categories of importers, to which the government gives preferential treatment for a variety of reasons.

*Issues*

Exemptions are used to a greater or smaller extent by most, if not all, countries that have a nonzero tariff. Even if it is government policy to make no exceptions to the application of the tariff, the government would still grant some exemptions, such as those stipulated in international agreements—those in the Vienna Convention on Diplomatic Immunities, for example. Exemptions are pervasive in many developing countries, due to these countries' large inflows of foreign aid that come in the form of development projects and relief goods; misguided policies with respect to investment incentives; pressures for exemption from numerous entities involved in educational, charitable, and a variety of other social projects; and often, an ill-designed tariff regime. In many countries the value of exempt imports amounts to over 30 percent of all imports, and in some cases to over half of all imports.

*Economic Rationale*

Good economic justifications for exemptions are rare. Most of the time exemptions have been incorrectly used as instruments for achieving policy objectives. Apart from causing substantial revenue loss for the government, exemptions create several distortions and costs that include destroying the transparency of the import tariff, creating an uneven playing field for foreign trade operators and domestic industry, distorting producer and consumer choices, and complicating customs administration.

*Economic or Administrative Issues by Category*

The economic and administrative implications and issues for the main categories of exemption can be summarized as follows.

**Diplomatic Imports**  This category comprises exemptions stipulated by the Vienna conventions on diplomatic and consular relations. Exemptions under this category usually make up only a small part of all exempt shipments in a country. However, several countries have experienced abuse of these exemptions, particularly in the quantities of imported goods for which exemption is claimed that apparently go beyond the needs of the embassy or mission. Instances of claiming exemption for commercial shipments have also been reported. For customs, enforcement is difficult as customs has only limited authority to inspect diplomatic shipments, and investigating suspected abuse may be politically sensitive.

**Government Imports**  Historically, many countries have exempted government imports from import duties and taxes. In recent years several countries have eliminated these exemptions because they found that the disadvantages outweigh the benefits. It is often argued that there is no budgetary benefit to the government collecting duties on its own imports because this would amount to a zero sum operation. This argument ignores the fact that exempted government imports can be, and often are, diverted to nongovernment use, thus creating a route for avoiding the duties that are lawfully due on such imports. In addition, there are administrative costs for customs to verify that the goods imported under exemption by the public sector are actually used for the stated purposes. Apart from the budgetary and administrative costs, exemption of government imports distorts the prices applicable to the private and public sector and can distort decisionmaking, for instance, on the appropriate prices to charge for the output of public enterprises such as electricity. Furthermore, exemptions for the government understate the true cost of government expenditure, as they are not scrutinized through the budgetary approval process and, therefore, hide the real cost of government operations. Thus, for the sake of transparency and good administration, government imports should not be exempt.

**Investment Incentives**  Many countries offer tax incentives, including import duty and indirect import tax concessions, to attract new investments and encourage economic development. The question of whether tax incentives are a factor in business investment decisions has been researched and debated extensively in economic literature, and there is a virtually unanimous consensus that these fiscal benefits are not crucial, because other considerations commonly weigh more heavily in investors' decisionmaking. (See Zee, Stotsky, and Ley [2002] for a more complete discussion of these issues.) Exemptions are vulnerable to abuse through leakage of the exempt goods to the private-sector gray market, rather than being used in the most useful investments. Exemptions also give rise to unfair competition relative to businesses that do not benefit from such incentives. From an administrative point of view, these exemptions require customs to devote a substantial amount of its scarce resources to exemption monitoring and control activities, resources that could otherwise be assigned to more productive uses. Developing countries, therefore, would be well advised to abolish these exemptions in combination with a rationalization of import tariffs. A simple and transparent import tariff with zero or low rates on investment and capital goods is likely to be a more powerful tool for attracting investors than the prevalence of exemptions.

**Foreign Financed Projects**    Lenders and donors generally do not finance duties on the goods they import for use on specific projects, because funds are intended to be used only on those specific projects and not to be contributed to government revenue by way of import duties. Experience in many countries shows that these exemptions lead to abuse and problems of control. First, the quantities of materials and items needed for the projects are not always properly determined. Even when they are, it is difficult to control the quantities imported and the actual destination of the goods. Second, the exemption is at times extended to consumer goods for personnel employed in the project. In both cases, exempt items can easily be diverted to uses not envisaged by the exemption. To protect themselves against such abuses and the resulting revenue losses, a number of countries no longer exempt such imports, but implement a system whereby the duties and taxes are paid through Treasury vouchers. See the section entitled Establishing Effective Administrative Systems and Procedures.

**Relief Goods**    Many developing countries are dependent on foreign aid and the delivery of that aid through nongovernmental organizations (NGOs). Food, medicines, and other items imported under foreign aid programs are generally given duty-exempt status on condition that they are distributed at no cost to the needy. However, control over the free distribution is difficult. Whatever control is established often turns out to be inade-

quate. In many cases imported relief goods, especially foodstuffs and pharmaceuticals, are diverted from their intended destination and end up being sold in the market. This is done sometimes by unscrupulous organizations disguised as NGOs that abuse their exempt status to import goods for uses not related to the exempt justification. Yet another problem is that, in most cases, customs is not involved in the verification of the credentials of the NGO, or consulted in the agreement between the NGO and the Ministry of Planning, Supply, Cooperation, or whatever other entity is responsible for relief imports. Most of the time, customs appears only at the implementation stage and not at the point where the request is examined and the conditions are established. The abovementioned problems can be avoided by following the guidelines in Establishing Effective Administrative Systems and Procedures below.

**Imports for Charitable, Religious, Cultural, Educational, and Similar Social Purposes**    In many countries the customs law and other laws provide exemptions for goods needed for the operation of organizations or institutions with charitable, religious, cultural, educational, or similar social objectives. Often the Minister of Finance or Customs is burdened with numerous, sometimes illegitimate, requests from schools, churches, cultural, or similar organizations for exempt importation of equipment, motor vehicles, and miscellaneous consumer goods. These exemptions are difficult to control and are often abused through diversion of the exempt goods from the exempt purpose. Economically there is no justification for these exemptions, and they are equivalent to hidden subsidies. They should be eliminated and support or relief for those organizations, if deemed necessary, should be provided in the form of budgetary expenditure, subject to the usual public scrutiny through the budgetary approval process.

**Noncommercial Imports**    Exemptions under this category are generally based on tradition or international practice. They are frequently abused. For instance, migrant workers, persons settling or resettling in the country, and travelers often attempt to bring in more goods than they are legally entitled to under the exemption allowances. Usually these are exemptions of minor importance and can be administered fairly well, provided customs establishes clear and simple rules and procedures and informs the public of them.

### Rationalizing the Exemption System

Exemptions are difficult to justify economically, have high administrative costs, and tend to be abused. They should be reduced to a minimum and effectively administered to avoid abuse. No other exemptions should be maintained other than those required by international agreements and conventions, and those for noncommercial imports that have been exempt traditionally (for example, travelers' and migrants' goods).

The administrative resources and effort needed to administer exemptions places a heavy burden on customs administrations and distracts them from concentrating on more productive control, revenue collection, and enforcement activities. Moreover, customs' ability to monitor exemptions effectively is largely impaired when numerous exemption cases have to be processed.

If the government cannot fully restrict exemptions as recommended above, it should remain on guard against their proliferation. Major causes of proliferation are (a) the numerous exemptions, as sectors, companies, and individuals that are not exempt feel at a disadvantage compared to their exempt competitors and pressure the authorities to obtain similar preferential treatment; and (b) the discretionary power granted to the Ministry of Finance, and often to other ministries, to grant exemptions. Unless the conditions and limits of the exemptions are clearly specified in the law, it may be hard for the minister to withstand the pressures for exemption that are exerted by certain importers. To reduce the pressure for, and avoid proliferation of exemptions the following measures should be in place:

- All exemptions should be provided for in the law and the conditions for exemption should be spelled out in specific terms, including who qualifies for exemption, what goods are eligible for exemption, and under what conditions. This would eliminate all discretionary exemptions issued by high officials and organizations.
- Proposals and requests for exemption under the investment incentives provisions and foreign financed projects, made by the investment board or ministerial agencies, should be submitted to the Minister of Finance for approval. They should include a list containing the description (and HS code), quantity, and value of the goods to be imported and a calculation of the revenue cost of the exemption.

### Establishing Effective Administrative Systems and Procedures

For effective administration and control of exemptions the following guidelines should be kept in mind.

- *Rules.* The rules should clearly stipulate the processes to be observed in requesting and authorizing an exemption and in importing the exempt shipments, including documentary requirements, time frames, limits on value and quantity, controls at the time of importation, end use conditions, and punitive measures in cases of abuse or evasion.
- *Request and authorization.* The rules should contain complete information about the goods to be imported for the execution of the project (investment project, foreign financed project, relief goods, imports by institutions with charitable objectives, and the like). Thus, a list should be appended to the request, showing the correct description of the goods, as well as identification by HS code, quantities, and value.
- *Controls at time of importation.* This includes verification of the eligibility for exemption, and determining that the type, quantity, and value of the goods are as specified in the exemption authorization. Methods must be established to monitor exempt imports that consist of more than one shipment and that are cleared through more than one customs office. Computerization can largely facilitate this function, as the Moroccan system example shows (see box 10.8).
- *Checking end use.* Customs needs to determine that the exempt goods are actually being used for the intended purposes. This should be done through a combination of periodic verification of the accounts of the enterprise or institution receiving the exemption or, where appropriate, through periodic unannounced visits to the

---

**BOX 10.8    Computer Application for Management of Investment Project Exemptions**

The Customs and Indirect Tax Administration of Morocco recently introduced a computer application for the management of the list of goods that are permitted for importation under exempt status in the context of investment agreements between the government and private sector companies.

These agreements stipulate the exemption of import duties and taxes and value-added tax for all materials, tools, and equipment needed for execution of the projects, and are valid for a period of 36 months. These goods are specified in a list attached to the agreement.

The computer application, which can be accessed via the intranet of the customs offices responsible for processing the project imports, allows for continuous online monitoring of the imports, computerized management of the list of exempt goods, and easy and automatic detection of cases of excess over the authorized quantities. It allows the clearance offices to capture the import data directly, to detect and regularize online the imports that are in excess of the authorized quantities or values, and to control the deadlines for the execution of the projects.

*Source:* Steenlandt, Marcel. 2003. Note prepared for this chapter.

---

plant to physically check whether the end-use conditions are being met.

- *Exemption monitoring and control unit.* Customs should establish a monitoring and control unit with responsibility for overseeing all administrative matters concerning exemptions. The unit should scrutinize exemption requests; monitor quantities imported by embassies, exempt enterprises, and institutions; carry out post-importation visits to the enterprises or institutions; and monitor trends, revenue cost, and other indicators by category of exemptions. It should collect the data on exempt imports and compile statistics showing the revenue forgone, and prepare pertinent reports for the minister.

- *Reimbursement instead of immediate exemption.* An exemption control system based on payment of duties and taxes at the time of importation, and reimbursement of the duties and taxes after post-importation verification that all conditions for the exemption are fulfilled, was introduced in Mali in 1998 and has been successfully implemented since then (see box 10.9).

- *Treasury voucher system.* This exemption control mechanism has been introduced in a number of countries to monitor exempt imports under NGO and other foreign financed projects, and to avoid the diversion of exempt goods to the local market without the required duty payment. Under the system, duties and taxes on project imports are to be paid on importation, but payment is made by way of Treasury credit checks or vouchers issued by the government. Donors and financing agencies are required to make their project tenders tax-inclusive. This requires careful identification of the type and quantity of goods to be imported, and a detailed assessment of duties and taxes to be covered under the government budget for that project. A tax credit is then provided to the donor or financing agency in the relevant amount, in the form of credit checks. The credit checks are used for the payment of duties and taxes on the importation of goods covered under the project. The monitoring system is automatic and works as follows: If the bidder overestimates the amount of taxes, the bidder will probably not get the contract. Conversely, if the bidder underestimates the amount of taxes and wins the contract, the bidder will then be responsible for the difference between the actual and the underestimated taxes, because credit checks will only be issued up to the approved credit amount. This system does not require quantities to be monitored. In practice, implementation results have been mixed. The system has proven to work well and to reduce abuse and revenue loss in some African countries (Mali and Mozambique, for example), but has not been successful in some other countries (Benin and Côte d'Ivoire). While the system is technically sound, failure has been due mainly to such factors as private sector

---

**BOX 10.9    Reimbursement of Taxes and Customs Duties on Imported Petroleum Products in Mali**

Mali successfully implemented a reform of the reimbursement of tax and customs duty exemptions in 1998, doubling customs revenues from the importation of petroleum products. Duties on petroleum products were an important source of fiscal revenue. These products were imported by a small number of companies (around 12), making the management of the program feasible.

Three principles of the new procedure were set forth:

- Full payment of all taxes and duties at the customs barrier on the import of petroleum products.
- The establishment of a system to quickly reimburse paid customs duties and taxes to the beneficiaries of exemptions from duties upon justification of their right. At the time, these beneficiaries included, among others, diplomatic and consular representatives (Vienna Convention), projects financed with foreign resources (including World Bank projects), and conventions resulting from the Mining Code.
- The affirmed separation of functions between (a) the Customs Offices in charge of assessing the duties and taxes and (b) the Treasury Office in charge of reimbursement.

This new procedure occurs in four steps:

1. At the beginning of each year, the beneficiaries of these rights file, at the Societe Generale de Surveillance (SGS) office, the document attesting to their right to exemption accompanied by a monthly consumption schedule

for petroleum products. After registration of this file, the SGS conveys it to the Ministry of Finance for certification. Once certified, the SGS enters the rights of the beneficiary into its information system. The whole registration process takes less than a week.

2. The beneficiaries of the exemptions buy the products, paying all taxes at customs. The receipts are accounted for as customs revenues and are entered as state budget revenues.

3. Reimbursement by the Treasury, of the duties and taxes paid, occurs on a monthly basis in two steps:
   - the issuance of a secure "reimbursement coupon" by SGS in the name of the beneficiary.
   - the transfer of the amount owed by the Treasury to the beneficiary's account, on the basis of the reimbursement coupon and a copy of the invoice. Cash payment is prohibited. This Treasury expenditure is charged to an expense account to be adjusted.

4. Each month the Treasury conveys to the Budget Department a summary of the reimbursement coupons paid by payment authorization for this expense. On sight of the authorization, the Treasury adjusts its accounting situation, definitively entering the expense as a budgetary expenditure.

*Source:* Finateu, Emilie. 2003. Note prepared for this chapter.

---

opposition to rigorous control and the lack of strong support by higher authorities. In some countries where it was introduced at the insistence of international organizations, it was not implemented in a convincing way. On balance, provided there is a real will from the high authorities to make the system work, it is the only effective method to eliminate or greatly reduce abuse and revenue loss through these types of exemptions.

- *Embassy imports.* For countries experiencing abuse of exemptions under the cover of diplomatic privileges, the most appropriate action probably is to take the issue up with the diplomatic mission using the proper channel, which

is normally the Ministry of Foreign Affairs. Customs should always request a listing of embassy staff that benefits from diplomatic status. Many countries agree with the diplomatic missions on annual quotas for the goods most sensitive to abuse, that is, alcoholic beverages and tobacco products. The use of annual import quotas for fuel is also standard in many countries.

## Operational Conclusions and Guidelines

The above review leads to the following recommendations and guidelines for customs administration.

## Duty Relief

In designing duty relief policy and administration the following guidelines should be kept in mind:

- There are valid fiscal, trade, and economic reasons for customs laws around the world to make provision for the duty relief regimes discussed in this chapter. Therefore, policymakers should design, and customs administrations should implement and administer, these regimes in a secure and cost-effective way for both the user of the regimes and the government. Customs management must understand that such systems are not subsidies to the exporters, only remedies to allow the user of the regimes (export manufacturer, warehouse operator, transit enterprise, sales prospector) to operate outside the tariff system and to do so at minimal cost to the business. In the presence of tariffs, the competitiveness of the export sector and the country's appeal to foreign investors may depend on the availability of efficiently operating duty relief systems. The government must ensure that it is safeguarded against loss of revenue due to abuse, and that these regimes operate efficiently.
- Customs administrations should adhere to the international standards and guidelines for the administration of the duty relief systems, as included in the Revised Kyoto Convention.
- The choice between prior exemption (temporary admission systems) and drawback depends mainly on the capacity and degree of modernization of the customs administration. Export manufacturers clearly have a preference for temporary admission as compared to duty drawback, especially when tariffs are high, when inflation erodes the duty refunds, and when interest rates to obtain working capital are high. However, governments in most developing countries require customs administrations to focus primarily on revenue collection rather than trade facilitation and, therefore, tend to prefer drawback to temporary admission systems. For countries with an efficient, modern administration, particularly those with accounts-based control capability, TAP under any of its forms should be the primary method for duty relief. In addition, drawback should be available for cases in which the use of the imported materials in inward processing was not anticipated. Coun-

tries with only limited control capabilities may have to rely mainly on drawback, but TAP systems should be available to companies that are in good standing with respect to their fiscal obligations and that pose little or no risk to revenue. As the customs administration refines its accounts-based control capabilities, TAP should become the primary method.
- The capacity of the customs administration should be taken into account in choosing between alternative ways of providing duty relief. In particular, no facilities should be granted that go beyond the customs administration's control capability. For instance, single factory zones located outside the geographically separated EPZ area should not be established if customs has no adequate accounts-based control capability. Similarly, exemptions should not be granted if customs cannot effectively monitor them.
- Customs managers should take all possible measures to ensure that compliance with the administrative requirements and procedures under duty relief regimes entails no more than minimal costs for the users. For instance, payment of duty drawback should be prompt and the necessary checking should be done later. Wherever possible, closed bond systems of customs warehouse control should be replaced by open bond systems, thus eliminating the need to pay for the costs of customs surveillance of the premises.

## Exemption

There are good economic and administrative reasons for restricting duty exemptions and for maintaining only those required by international conventions (such as diplomatic immunities) and those for noncommercial goods (for example, travelers and migrants). Until the redundant exemptions are eliminated, customs administrations should devote adequate technological and manpower resources to organizing and implementing the necessary control and monitoring systems.

## Other Conclusions

The following conclusions and guidelines are applicable to the administration of duty relief and exemption regimes alike.

- Customs should move from physical controls to selective and periodic compliance checking through post-importation accounts-based audits. Effective use of information technology can substantially contribute to such controls while facilitating trade. This should be complemented by a consistently enforced penalty system to deter abuse and fraud.
- Maximum use of computer applications should be made to enable and strengthen duty relief and exemption control. Functions and activities that should be computerized include the following: tracking of goods imported for inward processing; customs warehouse inventory management; exchange of information and data between customs offices of entry and exit for goods under temporary admission and in transit; and the control of quantities and values of exempt imports under projects involving multiple shipments or different customs offices.
- For all duty relief and exemption regimes, clear, simple, and easy-to-understand rules should be established and made known to foreign trade operators, manufacturers, and, as needed, to the public in general. Information notes should explain conditions, requirements, processes, and procedural steps, and how and where to obtain additional information.
- Organizationally, customs administrations should establish an adequately staffed special unit for management of the duty relief and exemption systems. This unit should oversee all duty relief and exemption control activities at customs, including developing efficient procedures; developing operational instruction manuals; checking the eligibility of importers for the special regimes they claim; monitoring the legality and correct implementation of large duty relief and exemption projects (foreign financed, NGO, and investment incentives projects); assessing the credentials of importers, manufacturers, and exporters for the TAP, MUB, drawback, and transit regimes; and compiling statistics showing trends in, and revenue costs of, exemptions.

### Annex 10.A Checklist for Duty Relief and Exemption Control

For reviewers of duty relief and exemption control systems the following checklist should be useful.

- Do exporters have access to industrial inputs at world prices through one or more duty relief systems—TAP, drawback, or EPZ (or any combination)?
- Is the TAP system based on the initial determination of input–output ratios and are these ratios periodically reviewed?
- Is TAP control based on periodic global returns showing the goods imported under TAP or purchased from other TAP traders, and the destination given to the goods after processing (exportation or sale in the local market)?
- Does the drawback system operate through the initial determination of the drawback rate based on input–output relationships and are the drawback rates reviewed periodically to take into account changes in the factors underlying the rate, such as type or mix of inputs, or changed input costs?
- Is the process for claiming drawback simple and with no requirements other than proof of export?
- Is drawback paid immediately, or within no more than a few weeks after exportation, while verification is performed periodically in the exporter's books and accounts?
- Does customs commit itself to paying drawback within a set short time frame?
- Are exporters held accountable for revenue losses resulting from their failure to signal changes in the factors underlying the input–output ratios or drawback rates?
- Are drawback rates set by a committee that includes representatives from customs, inland revenue, industry, and trade departments of the government?
- Are exporters and the public well informed about the available duty relief systems and how they operate, and are these systems well understood?
- Has customs organized a dedicated technical unit to monitor and audit manufacturing companies operating under the TAP (or one of its variants) or drawback systems?
- Are TAP (or its variants) and drawback control computerized?
- For occasional export processors (manufacturers exporting only a limited amount of their production, or simple operations), are simplified TAP procedures in place or do they have access to drawback?

## Further Reading

Alter, Rolf G. 1990. "Export Processing Zones for Growth and Development: The Mauritian Example." IMF Working Paper No. 90/122. Washington, D.C.

Corfmat, François, and Adrien Goorman. 2003. "Customs Duty Relief and Exemptions." In Michael Keen, ed. *Changing Customs: Challenges and Strategies for the Reform of Customs Administration.* Washington, D.C.: IMF.

International Trade Center UNCTAD/GATT. 1979. *Duty Drawback on Exports.* Geneva.

Madani, Dorsati. 1999. "A Review of the Role and Impact of Export Processing Zones." World Bank Working Paper 2238. Washington, D.C.

Warr, Peter. 1989. "The Potential for Export Processing Zones: Lessons from East Asia." *Pacific Economic Bulletin* 8(1): 18–26.

World Customs Organization. 1999. *International Convention on the Simplification and Harmonization of Customs Procedures (as amended).* Brussels.

## References

Madani, Dorsati. 1999. *A Review of the Role and Impact of Export Processing Zones.* World Bank Working Paper No. 2238. Washington, D.C.

Steenlandt, Marcel, and Luc De Wulf. 2004. "Morocco." In Luc De Wulf and José B. Sokol, eds. *Customs Modernization Initiatives: Case Studies.* Washington, D.C.: The World Bank.

Tax Notes International. 2001a. January 1.

Tax Notes International. 2001b. January 8.

U.S. Customs Service. 1996. "Bonded Warehouse Manual for Proprietors, Importers, Customs Officers." Washington, D.C.: Department of the Treasury.

Warr. P. 1989. "The Potential for Export Processing Zones: Lessons from East Asia." *Pacific Economic Bulletin* 8(1): 18–26.

Zee, Howell H., Janet G. Stotsky, and Eduardo Ley. 2002. "Tax Incentives for Business Investment: A Primer for Policy Makers in Developing Countries." *World Development* 30(9): 1497–1516.

# 11

# TRANSIT AND THE SPECIAL CASE OF LANDLOCKED COUNTRIES

*Jean François Arvis*

Customs transit refers to customs procedures under which goods are transported through countries from one customs office to the other without paying import duties, domestic consumption taxes, or other charges normally due on imports. These procedures are intended to protect the revenues of the country of transit, and to avoid the circumstance that goods intended for transit are leaked to the domestic market. Transit procedures should be simple so as not to generate excessive delays and costs. A poor transit system constitutes a major obstacle to trade. Many international organizations and transport facilitation forums have identified dysfunctional transit procedures as a major cost-increasing factor for landlocked developing countries.

Based on material prepared by ECORYS N.V. and supported by a grant from the government of the Netherlands.

Transit most frequently refers to road transportation to and from landlocked countries. However, it is useful to make a distinction between national transit and international transit. International transit refers to crossing national borders. National transit occurs when goods are transferred within national borders, from the first point of entry in the country to a location where customs procedures are undertaken (for example, dry ports or inland container depots). The two types of transit can be combined; in fact, this is a standard situation in many landlocked developing countries. Imported goods arriving at national borders from transit countries are most often shipped under national transit to the main economic centers. The basic customs mechanisms are similar in both cases; however, implementation is easier for the national transit link.

Most transit takes place between landlocked countries and countries with access to the sea. In some instances, transit is simply from one country to the destination country, and borders are crossed only once. In other instances the transit shipment crosses several borders, as is the case when a shipment goes from the Netherlands to Russia, and crosses Germany and Poland. In other cases the cargo originates and ends up in the same territory, but transits through a second country. For example, commodities destined for the northeastern part of India that originate from other parts of India transit Bangladesh, as all alternative Indian routes are much longer.[1] When available, transit by rail offers a number of advantages, including simpler customs transit mechanisms. Rail transit is widely used in central Asia and is being rejuvenated in West Africa.

This chapter focuses on international transit. The first section reviews the general principles of transit while the second section details a typical transit operation. The third section reviews existing major transit arrangements based on the Transport International Routier (TIR). The fourth section presents various institutions set up to facilitate transit, such as bilateral and regional agreements. The final section provides some operational conclusions.

### The Case of Landlocked Developing Countries

Customs transit is only one part of a wider transaction range that includes many other participants

and procedures—cross-border vehicle regulations, visas for truck drivers, insurance, police controls, infrastructure quality, quality of available transport services, and the organization of the private trucking sector. Even if transit procedures are made effective and efficient, full trade facilitation will require that these issues be dealt with, too.

The interdependence of these issues is well illustrated by the Action Plan issued by the International Ministerial Conference of Landlocked and Transit Developing Countries (August 2003) that notes, "An integrated approach to trade and transport sector development is needed that takes into account social and economic aspects, as well as fiscal policy, as well as regulatory, procedural and institutional considerations" (UN 2003 p. 4). These concerns will be returned to in the Implementation Issues section of this chapter. However, the customs component is the principal bottleneck of transit and is a source of major inefficiencies that affect many activities.

### Costs of Transit Operations

The high logistics costs and the many developmental problems faced by the landlocked countries of the world can be attributed to their geographical fate. The importance of the transit facilitation agenda to these countries and to the countries of transit stem from these circumstances.[2] Indeed, out of 31 landlocked developing countries, 16 are classified as highly indebted poor countries (HIPC), while 20 out of the 50 least developed countries worldwide are landlocked.[3] Research conducted by the World Bank and other organizations[4] concludes that in typical landlocked countries, transport costs are 50 percent higher than in a typical coastal country, while the volume of trade is 60 percent lower. Furthermore, a substantial part of the cost may be attributed to border crossing. It is

---

1. Lakshmanan (2001).

2. Faye and others (2004).

3. The 31 landlocked countries are distributed as follows: Europe—FYR Macedonia, Moldova; Asia/Caucasus—Afghanistan, Armenia, Azerbaijan, Bhutan, Kazakhstan, Kyrgyz Republic, Lao PDR, Mongolia, Nepal, Tajikistan, Turkmenistan, Uzbekistan; Africa—Botswana, Burkina Faso, Burundi, Central African Republic, Chad, Ethiopia, Lesotho, Malawi, Mali, Niger, Rwanda, Swaziland, Uganda, Zambia, Zimbabwe; South America—Bolivia, Paraguay.

4. Limao and Venables (1999), Amjadi and Yeats (1995).

**TABLE 11.1  Transportation Costs from Main World Markets for Coastal and Landlocked Countries in Africa**
(in US$ by TEU)

| Destination Country | Origin | | |
| --- | --- | --- | --- |
| | Northern Europe | Japan | North America |
| Senegal | $1,610 | $4,100 | n.a. |
| Mali via Senegal | $2,380  +48% | $4,870  +19% | n.a. |
| Ghana | $1,815 | $3,025 | $2,460 |
| Burkina Faso via Ghana | $2,615  +44% | $3,835  +27% | $3,260  +32% |
| Cameroon | $1,520 | n.a. | n.a. |
| Central African Republic via Cameroon | $2,560  +68% | n.a. | n.a. |
| Tanzania | $1,380 | $1,350 | $2,000 |
| Rwanda via Tanzania | $3,880  +181% | $3,850  +185% | $4,500  +125% |
| Burundi via Tanzania | $4,530  +228% | $4,500  +233% | $5,150  +157% |
| Zambia via Tanzania | $3,250  +135% | $3,220  +138% | $3,870  +93% |

n.a.= not available.

TEU = twenty-foot equivalent unit.

*Note:* Percentage refers to the increase in transportation costs for the landlocked country compared to its coastal country of transit.

*Source:* UNCTAD 2003.

estimated that the total cost of crossing a border in Africa is the same as the cost of inland transportation of over 1,000 miles (1,600 km) or the cost of 7,000 miles of sea transport (11,000 km). This places landlocked countries at a great disadvantage. In comparison, the cost of crossing a border in Western Europe is equivalent to only 100 miles of inland transportation.

Table 11.1 compares the costs of importing a container into a few landlocked developing countries with the costs of importing the same container into the neighboring transit country. In many cases the costs for landlocked developing countries are significantly higher.

The differences in absolute transportation costs between countries, as well as the increase in transportation costs induced by borders, reflect direct transportation and legitimate fees. However, these costs are increased substantially by cumbersome customs transit procedures—excessive deposits, mandatory convoys, and gratuities to customs staff and police—without which these transit operations cannot be undertaken.

Transit operations often involve long delays that substantially add to the transportation cost. For instance, a recent trade audit for Chad estimated

that, the trip from the sea gateway takes as long as a month, due in large part to procedural delays.[5] These induced costs include the financial charges related to the guarantees, the cost of transport equipment held up by these transit procedures, as well as the requirement to maintain high inventories. Poorly functioning transit operations also increase the vulnerability of transported goods to theft.[6]

Transit procedures in landlocked countries affect exports and imports differently.[7] The transit costs are somewhat less for exports than for imports. Exports frequently leave the country without paying any duties, so countries are less worried about

5. These can include customs documentation processing; immigration, insurance, and transit bond procedures; security inspections and weigh stations; phytosanitary and traffic checks. A World Bank study conducted in July 2000 examined delays at selected Southern African border posts. Results showed that, for example, delays at Machipanda (Mozambique–Zimbabwe) amounted to 24 hours, 36 hours at Beit-Bridge (South Africa–Zimbabwe), 36 hours at Victoria Falls (Zimbabwe–Zambia) and 24 hours at Kazungula (Botswana–South Africa).

6. Although not easy to quantify, it is estimated that within the Southern African Development Community (SADC) region, border delays cost between US$48 million and US$60 million per year in business revenues forgone (IntraAfrica Ltd. 2001).

7. Amjadi and Yeats (1995).

revenue loss, thus making complex controls unnecessary. Also, exporters are fewer than importers and are better equipped to deal with transit logistics. Therefore, for the most part, customs transit is an import concern.

## The Principles of Customs Transit Regimes

Transit regulation aims to facilitate the transport of goods through a customs territory without payment of duty and taxes in the countries of departure and transit. This is in accordance with the destination principle of taxation, which states that indirect taxes should only be levied in the country of consumption. Transit legislation should be provided in the Customs Code. In the absence of such codification, transit can be regulated by a binding agreement between customs and the different parties affected by the transit operation. The core provisions for customs transit have been around for centuries (box 11.1). They include the following:

- sealing of the shipment at the point where the transit operation is initiated
- providing financial security to customs in the country of transit, which will guarantee the

payment of duties if the goods do not leave the country of transit
- using an efficient information system that allows certification that the transit goods have effectively left the country of departure so that the security can be released.

Over the years, transit provisions have been codified by a number of international conventions, the most important being the General Agreement on Tariffs and Trade (GATT) agreements on transit, the World Customs Organization (WCO) Revised Kyoto Convention, and the 1982 Geneva Convention on the harmonization of frontier control of goods. Annex E, Section 1 of the Revised Kyoto Convention is about transit and focuses in detail on applicable customs formalities and seals, the essence of which is reflected in the section of this chapter titled "Description of a Typical Transit Operation". Table 11.2 summarizes the key principles derived from these international instruments. The actual customs transit regimes across countries vary widely. In many countries and regions the basic transit arrangements, such as guarantees, are poorly implemented and greatly penalize landlocked countries. In other countries and regions, national transit provisions have evolved into harmonized and

---

### BOX 11.1    The Genesis of Transit Procedures in the Middle Ages

Today's transit principles and procedures can be tracked back to the trading revolution that took place in preindustrial Europe in the 12th and 13th centuries. Seals, carnets, and guarantee systems were designed at that time in major trading centers. Compared to other regions of the world, Western Europe was fragmented politically, with a multiplicity of tolls and charges. The development of inland transportation between major cities stimulated creative solutions by the merchants and the rulers.

In 12th century southwestern France, the local guilds from Bordeaux were worried that grain might be exported from the city—where it was needed—to other inland districts. There was, therefore, an export duty, which was differentiated according to the relations with the various "jurandes" of the region. The highest duty was retained until the arrival note was returned to the customs of departure with the signature of the customs of arrival. The carrier kept two copies, one of which was used to justify the legal

right to carry the goods and to establish their origin. Customs brigades could inspect these notes along the way. Rapidly, merchants asked for an "acquis à caution" (the expression is still used) system, whereby merchants would purchase an underwritten guarantee instead of depositing the duty.

In the Duchy of Milan in Northern Italy, a national transit system was available in the 14th century to facilitate the movement of imports inside the territory. Customs officers sealed shipments of goods at the main inland gateway of the duchy. Carnets were issued and could be produced at checkpoints during the journey. At the final destination, Milan or another city, seals were broken and duties paid. Local officers of the central office in Milan sent the information about shipments at the beginning and at the end of transit.

*Source:* Adapted from Favier 1971.

**TABLE 11.2  General Provisions Applicable to Customs Transit as Codified by International Conventions**

| Category | Provisions |
|---|---|
| General | • Freedom of transit<br>• Normally no technical standards control<br>• No distinction based on flag or origin ownership<br>• No unnecessary delays or restrictions. |
| Customs diligences in transit | • Limitation of inspection (especially if covered by an international transit regime such as TIR)<br>• Exemption from customs duties<br>• Normally no escort of goods or itinerary<br>• No duty on accidentally lost merchandise<br>• No unnecessary delays or restrictions. |
| Health and safety | In addition, when an international transit regime such as TIR is active<br>• The TIR regime applies to multimodal transport when some part of the journey is by road<br>• Flat rate bonds are used for transit goods<br>• No sanitary, veterinary, or phytosanitary inspections for goods in transit if no contamination risk. |
| Security offered by the carrier | • Declarant to choose the form of security in the framework offered by the legislation<br>• Customs should accept a general security from declarants who regularly declare goods in transit in their territory<br>• On completion of the transit operation, discharge of the security without delay. |

*Source:* UN/CEFACT and UNCTAD 2002.

regionally integrated transit regimes. The best working example is the TIR, detailed in the Major International Transit Procedures section.

Article V of the GATT provides the freedom of transit and determines that "[t]here shall be freedom of transit through the territory of each Contracting Party, via the routes most convenient for international transit, for traffic in transit to or from the territory of other Contracting Parties." Further, it affirms that ". . . except in cases of failure to comply with applicable Customs laws and regulations, such traffic coming from or going to the territory of other contracting parties shall not be subject to any unnecessary delays or restrictions and shall be exempt from Customs duties and from all transit duties or other charges imposed in respect of transit, except charges for transportation or those commensurate with administrative expenses entailed by transit or with the cost of services" (Grosdidier 2004, p. 16).

The 1982 Geneva Convention covers transit facilitation and recognizes the importance of transit for the economic development of countries. It promotes joint customs processing through the simplification

of customs procedures and the harmonization of border controls. It also draws heavily on the European experience. Article 10 applies to goods in transit: "contracting parties are bound to provide simple and speedy treatment of goods in transit, especially for those traveling under an international transit procedure" (Grosdidier 2004, p. 24). Parties should also facilitate, at the utmost, the transit of goods by containers and other vessels that provide adequate security. Articles 4 to 9 posit the harmonization of control and procedures. Contracting parties are bound to provide staff and facilities that are compatible with the traffic requirement (Article 5), organize joint border processing to ease controls (Article 7), and harmonize documentation (Article 9).

## Description of a Typical Transit Operation

Transit procedures should permit the movement of goods from the point of entry, into the customs territory of the transit country, and finally to the country of destination, without the payment of import duties,

---

**BOX 11.2    General Requirements with Respect to Seals**

"The seals and fastening shall:

a) be strong and durable;
b) be capable of being affixed easily and quickly;
c) be capable of being readily checked and identified;
d) not permit removal or undoing without breaking or tampering without leaving traces;

e) not permit use of more than once, except seals intended for multiple use (e.g. electronic seals);
f) be made as difficult as possible to copy or counterfeit."

*Source:* Revised Kyoto Convention, Annex E1. www.wcoomd.org.

---

taxes, and other charges due on importation, and without being subject to other import regulations, such as health and safety inspections, applicable in the transit country. In the absence of streamlined operations, the transit procedures can be daunting, as suggested in table 11.3.

### Three Key Elements of a Transit Operation

Seals, guarantees, and efficient flow of documentation are the underpinnings of transit.

*Seals.* There should be a physically secure mechanism so that goods present at the start of the transit operation will leave the transit country in the same quantity, form, and status. The best and easiest way to guarantee this is for customs to seal the truck[8] to ensure that goods cannot be removed from or added to the loading space of the truck without breaking this seal or leaving visible marks on the loading space of the truck. Seals and trucks approved for use in the transit operation must, therefore, conform to well-specified criteria that guarantee their effective operation and security. New transport seals are under study and prototypes are already in use. One of these seals includes a microchip that is activated when broken. When activated, these chips transmit a signal, picked up via a satellite network, and send information to the organization or principal of the sealed container, including information on the location of the container. Although the prices of such automated seals are relatively high now, it is expected that prices will decrease in the coming years. The requirements for seals in the Revised Kyoto Convention are presented in box 11.2.

*Guarantees.* Customs must be given a guarantee to cover the payments of import duties, taxes, and

other charges due on importation in the transit country, to cover cases where goods do not leave the country when using the transit procedure. This guarantee is used to recover the duties and taxes due if the transport forwarder does not pay the customs invoice for these duties and taxes when requested (if goods cannot be proven to have left the country of transit as specified in the transit regulation).

*Documentation flow.* To control the start and completion of a transit procedure, a monitoring system for the flows should be operational. This system could be based on paper documentation that is shipped between the customs post at the exit of the country, after validation of the transit transaction, and the customs post that controls the origin of the transit shipment. Increasingly the transmission of these documents is done electronically. When the copies of the documents match, the transit operation is completed and the guarantee released. When they do not match, the transit procedure is not completed satisfactorily. The payment of the import duties, taxes, and other charges are due, and are increased by a stipulated fine.

### Principal and Guarantor

The *principal* is the owner of the goods, or his representative, such as the carrier, which is most often the case. The principal initiates the transit procedure and is responsible for following the transit procedures—providing guarantees and the necessary documentation. Companies that want to act as a principal (or agent) making use of the transit procedure must be registered; must obtain a guarantee to cover the transit operations; must use a transit customs document and bill of lading; must present the goods and declaration at the customs offices of departure, transit, and destination; and must be responsible for sealing the transit vehicle.

---

8. For illustrative purposes trucks are focused on; however, the same applies for other modes of transport, such as wagons, barges, and so forth. In practice, the procedures may be simplified for trains.

**TABLE 11.3    Transit Procedures without Facilitative Measures**

| | Documentation | Charges | Comments |
|---|---|---|---|
| Sea transport | | Sea freight | |
| Unloading in port | Bill of lading | Port charges | |
| Inspection and clearance by customs | Invoice to determine value, classification, and weight that permit the calculation of the duties to be guaranteed<br>Transit declaration | Guarantee (deposit) | Deposit equal to part or total amount of duties, taxes, and other charges due on importation in country of departure |
| Loading of vehicle | | | Seals applied |
| Formation of a convoy | | Convoy charges | Noncompliant with generally agreed principles, may lead to inappropriate practices |
| Road transport in transit country | | Road transport charges | |
| Controls en route | | | Noncompliant with generally agreed principles. Transit often is impeded by a number of road checks (police and customs) involving payments of gratuities |
| Customs inspection upon exit from first country | Copy of transit document | | Seals are checked. If the transit operation can be cleared, a copy of the transit document is sent to the central customs office and then the guarantee can be discharged |
| Border inspections (vehicle) | | | Driver's license and insurance of vehicle checked. If invalid, change of operator needed |
| Transfer to other truck | | Transfer charges | Noncompliant with generally agreed principles. Cargo can be damaged, lost, or stolen |
| Customs inspection upon entry in the destination country | Transit declaration (Beginning of a national transit link) | Guarantee (deposit) | Deposit equal to part or total amount of duties, taxes, and other charges due on importation in second country |
| Other inspections upon entry into second country | All documents | | Security, health checks, involving several stops. Control of seals |
| Arrival at destination | All | Costs of damage or loss | Seals broken; duties paid; guarantee discharged |

*Source:* Author.

A *guarantor* is a private or legal person who undertakes to pay jointly and separately with the debtor (in most cases, the principal) the amount of duties and taxes that will become due when a transit document is not discharged properly. A guarantor may be an individual or firm or other body that is eligible to contract as a legal third person. Normally it is a bank or insurance company. Guarantors must be authorized by customs, which usually publishes a list of financial institutions that are authorized to act as guarantors.

### Guarantees

The guarantees acceptable by customs are defined by the regulations of the transit country. Within the open options of financial securities, the choice is the exclusive responsibility of the principal. A guarantee can be provided by a bank (in the form of a bond) or as a form of insurance by a guarantor that can be reinsured internationally by well-known and reliable insurance companies. Nonguarantee forms of security, such as deposits, may still be in place in some transit countries, although they are obviously not recommended. A principal may also be its own guarantor. This is a common practice for rail transport, and grants customs access to more direct recourse mechanisms.

There are two categories of transit guarantee:

- An individual guarantee covers only a single transit operation effected by the principal concerned. It covers the full amount of duties, taxes, and other charges for which the goods are liable.
- A comprehensive guarantee covers several transit operations up to a given reference amount, which is set equal to the total amount of duties and other charges that may be incurred with respect to goods under the transit operations of the principal during a period of at least one week.

In general, the calculation of the guarantee is based on the highest rates of duties and other charges applicable to the goods, and depends on customs' classification of the goods. The amount covered by the comprehensive guarantee is 100 percent of the reference amount. If the principal complies with certain criteria of reliability, the amount of guarantee to be specified to the guarantors may be reduced by customs to 30 percent of the reference amount. In case of movement of high-risk goods, customs can be allowed to calculate the guarantee at a percentage that is related to the risk of nonclearance. International transit regimes such as the TIR allow for further savings.

Customs will only address its claim to the guarantor for the full amount if debtors do not meet their obligations. When goods are unlawfully removed from the transit procedure the debtor is deemed to be one of the following:

- the person who unlawfully removed the goods from the transit procedure
- any persons who participated in the unlawful removal of the goods or who were aware or should reasonably have been aware of the removal of the goods
- any persons who acquired or held the goods, and who were aware or should reasonably have been aware that they had been removed from the transit procedure
- the principal.

If the goods have not been unlawfully removed from the procedure, but one of the obligations or conditions of using the transit procedure are breached, the debtor is the person who breached the obligation or condition.

### Applicable Documents and Flows

A transit procedure requires a transport document, a bill of lading, and the transit customs document. The transit customs document can contain four copies:

- Copy 1 is validated by the customs office of entry in the country of transit and forwarded to the central customs office (CCO) of the country of transit. This will permit later reconciliation when the transit is completed, and will also serve statistical purposes. These documents can be transferred daily.
- Copy 2 accompanies the transit shipment to the customs office of exit from the country of transit. This copy will be retained by customs as the basis document for any succeeding customs destination—warehousing, importation in free

circulation, or inward processing—at which point the fiscal responsibility will be taken over by the consignee.

- Copy 3 also accompanies the shipment to the customs office of exit. This copy, after being completed (signed and stamped) by that customs office, is sent to the CCO. The CCO verifies the completion of the transit procedure by comparing Copy 1—which it kept at the start of the operation—and Copy 3. If Copy 3 is not received within a period of typically six weeks from the validation date of the document, the CCO will initiate an investigation.
- Copy 4 also accompanies the shipment to the customs office of exit. This copy, after being completed (signed and stamped) by that customs office, is returned to the principal or his agent and gives proof that the procedure has been completed, even before the CCO confirms clearance of the operation.

In a situation in which the transit operation is not completed satisfactorily, the taxes and duties calculated at the initiation of the transit operation would be due from the principal. If only one border is crossed, this becomes a simple matter—the principal owes the full amount of the taxes and duties already calculated at the outset. When more than one border has been crossed, a decision needs to be made as to which duties and taxes are due, that is, the duties and taxes applicable in the country of departure, the country or countries of transit, or the country of destination. To solve this issue, the transporters using the transit procedure are required to file a notification of border passing when they enter a new country of transit and when they enter the country of destination. When a transit operation is not completed within a specified time, the customs office of entry will ask every intended customs office at the borders of the countries of transit and destination whether they have received a notification of border passing for that specific transit procedure.

### Clearance of a Transit Procedure

The clearance of the procedure is formally based on the administrative confirmation by the CCO that it has received Copy 3 of the transit customs document. If this administrative procedure fails, the principal or agent should present Copy 4 of the transit document or be offered the possibility to deliver alternate proof to clear the regulation. Such a request from the CCO should be made within six weeks after the validation date of the document.

Principals or agents in possession of Copy 4 of the transit customs document who do not receive any request from the CCO within six weeks of the date of validation can consider the transit procedure complete and can close the files.

Principals or agents not in possession of Copy 4 of the customs transit document who receive a request for further investigation on the clearance by the CCO within six weeks can present alternate proof. Such proof should always include official stamps and signatures from the customs office of destination. One of the following might serve as alternate proof:

- a signed copy of Copy 2 of the customs transit document
- a signed copy of the documents of the customs procedure succeeding the transit regime (confirming that a customs debt is not related to the transit procedure).

Figure 11.1 depicts a Legitimate Transit Operation.

### Nonclearance of the Transit Procedure

If the CCO cannot formally clear the customs transit document, the nonclearance leads to a customs debt for the debtor. Although parties other than the principal can be debtors, the principal will always be jointly liable.

Where a debt arises due to nonclearance, the guarantor should be informed about such debt within a period of 12 months. If customs does not inform the guarantor within the set terms, customs can no longer collect a debt from the guarantor. Further, a debt can only be collected from the guarantor when the State collector has failed to collect the debt from the fiscal debtors.

According to international standards, any party subject to the payment of a debt, as stated in a formal decision by its authority, has the right to file

**FIGURE 11.1 Typical Transit Operation**

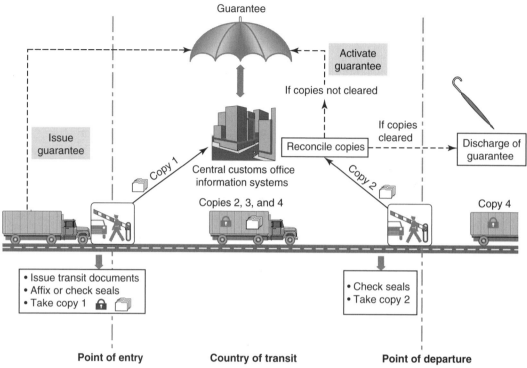

Source: Author.

that party's motivated objections to such formal decision. Reasons for objection might be alternate proof of clearance; incorrect determination of value, classification, or debt; designation of the debtor; and so forth. An objection can be filed within a certain period (in general, four to six weeks) after the authority has validated the formal decision.

The debt that arises from nonclearance of goods amounts to what would be the total of applicable duties if the products had been declared for free circulation in the country of departure. In addition, interest and fines may be due. The fines and interest are most often stipulated in the transit regulations. These relate only to the fiscal debt. If nonclearance is the result of criminal offenses, criminal legislation should specify a fine schedule. Interest becomes due on the debt from the date that nonclearance is established, or from 20 days after the date of validation of the transit customs document.

### Implementation Issues

International experience shows that many developing countries could not develop smooth transit regimes. There are several bottlenecks to overcome in implementing the previously described mechanisms.

*Availability of guarantees.* The availability of actual guarantees constitutes the bottleneck for customs transit in most developing countries. This difficulty may reflect the immaturity of the financial system in the country and the unwillingness of international financial institutions to guarantee transit transactions in particular countries. For customs, the calculation of the guarantee may be a problem when the value on which it is based cannot be determined properly. In developing countries, the carrier tends to provide undervalued invoices to limit the value of the guarantee (or deposits). Thus, the nondischarge of the security might not be an efficient deterrent of fraud.

*Quality of transport services.* The quality of transport services in the transit country can also be a major constraint. Large operators are more likely to provide guarantees for customs and may be eligible for comprehensive guarantees. The extreme case is that of railway companies, which are usually not subject to deposits or guarantees. Alternatively, as is often the case in Africa, some guarantee may be available but not at an accessible cost for the average operator. Also, the vehicle might not meet the customs requirement for a secure transit.[9] Hence, the need for convoys arises.

*Convoys.* Customs often suspects—as the result of experience—the presence of fraudulent practices in transit operations. In reaction, customs often resorts to the use of convoys that accompany the transit vehicle during the transit trip, accompanied by police and a customs official. Convoys cause delays as well as additional costs, borne by the principal, but do not fully eliminate all risk of fraud and corruption.

*Corruption.* Transit operations are vulnerable to fraud and extortion because they take place over an extended period of time, over long distances, and often with minimal supervision. One method to reduce corruption is to ensure that tamper-free seals are applied. It is also recommended that the transit operation be concluded at a level higher than the exit station, leading to the importance of creating the CCO and ensuring that it is well staffed and its operations periodically audited.

*Weak enforcement.* Independent of the corruption problem, enforcement in transit is not easy, as customs is not in a position to check consignments all over the territory. Conversely, other agencies involved in fighting national fraud are less concerned with transit. In most industrialized countries, fraud in transit is treated as smuggling and is subject to heavy penalties, including seizing of the truck and shipment, as well as fines that can amount to three times the value of the shipment.

*Lack of standard documentation.* Because a transit operation normally involves at least two countries, the use of standard customs forms will facilitate the overall operation. Standard forms will prevent having to use new customs forms upon entering a new country, which certainly adds to the complexity of the operation and causes delays at border crossing points. Using standard documentation will also

facilitate the use of information technology for information exchange.

### Computerization and Information Technologies

A number of developing countries have developed different Electronic Data Interchange (EDI) systems adapted to their needs. Within the variety of software employed, ASYCUDA (Automated System for Customs Data) has proved particularly popular (see chapter 13). Automation brings a number of positive changes for transit operations. Some applications are virtually all-inclusive. For instance, the European Union has developed a New Computerized Transit System (NCTS), which is fully computerized.

More directly applicable to developing economies, the UN Conference on Trade and Development (UNCTAD) has developed transit add-ons to the ASYCUDA. The MODTRS (transit) module handles transit documents in conjunction with other modules of the ASYCUDA++ functions. The module can be adapted to all types of transit and can, therefore, electronically handle the TIR carnet. Within customs in the transit country, the system electronically informs the exit post of the arrival of a shipment within a plausible time frame. When the exit post closes the transit information, the information is keyed in and the guarantee is automatically released.

In developing transit economies that have begun implementing EDI, it is likely that the transit operation will not be automated at first. Goods in transit will enter the country through the main gateway (port or airport), whose transit processes will likely be computerized according to priority. Most often, they will exit through a faraway border post where EDI has not yet been deployed. Yet, transit is likely to benefit from automation as it brings about a more efficient and centralized information system overall. For instance, even if the transit information is sent by traditional means to the CCO, the use of EDI already carries a lot of potential (this promise is exhibited by Ghana's expansion of its automated GCNet operations to the border post with Burkina Faso). ASYCUDA can be adapted to suit the specific needs of its different users, and it provides customs with a variety of functions that support its activities and increase its efficiency (box 11.3).

---

9. If the truck cannot be sealed by customs, customs may consider, as an alternate option, limiting transit traffic to specific transit corridors where each truck carries a special transit sign affixed to it or time limits are set for transporting the goods from the customs office of departure to the customs office where the goods will leave the transit country. Customs can then patrol these special transit corridors and concentrate inspections on trucks with the special transit signs.

---

### BOX 11.3    ASYCUDA Customs Operations in Zambia

Zambia has implemented the ASYCUDA transit module between Chirundu at the border with Zimbabwe and Lusaka, using the Wide Area Network (WAN). This transit system calculates the total duties and taxes as the guarantee amount, which is deducted from the bond as security. Once a transit document is processed and sent to the destination office, the record at the departure office remains outstanding and is acquitted only when all items have been fully cleared or have made an exit at the destination office. The availability of the WAN between the two ports and enhancements in ASYCUDA++ have, respectively, resulted in instantaneous data flow and efficiency in management of transits.

*Transit guarantees.* To carry out transit operations, a declarant needs to have a Transit Guarantee Account. Transit Guarantee Accounts have been set up on the accounting module of ASYCUDA (MODAAC) by customs for all licensed agents. For the account to operate, the maximum authorized guarantee should be specified. This is the amount from which the suspended duties and taxes will be deducted as bond to cover the movement of transit goods. Once this amount is exhausted, no further transits can be processed.

*Departure office—Chirundu.* Submissions of all entries to customs is done through Direct Trader Input (DTI). The bureau is situated within the customs premises and is managed by a private contractor. Chirundu is one of the major entry points, with a high volume of traffic. From inception, sufficient DTI terminals were available to cope with business volume. The declarations are sent to a specialized transit declaration desk, which generates a transit document (T1). When issuing the T1, the equivalent suspended duties and taxes (the bond) is deducted from the guarantee. With the WAN in place, the T1 is automatically transmitted through the ASYCUDA message manager module (Gateway) to both Chirundu and Lusaka. Finally, the release order is generated as proof that the consignment has been released after full compliance with the relevant transit requirements.

*Destination office—Lusaka.* The declarant reports to the transit counter at the customs office and files the copies of the documents issued by the departure office. The transit officer will access the list, T1, transmitted on the computer. The details on the computer are compared with the information on the hard copy of the T1. If the information is correct and consistent with the physical consignment, the T1 is validated and the status of the transit document is changed to validated. The bond is then credited back to the Transit Guarantee Account.

*Source:* UNCTAD 2003.

---

## Major International Transit Procedures: The Transport International Routier

The previous section describes a set of procedures specific to the country of transit. International transit procedures stipulate the harmonization of country-specific procedures and documentation, as well as an internationally accepted guarantee system. Hence, an international regime facilitates transit further, compared to a chain of national procedures. The Transport International Routier (TIR) is a best practice that sets the standard in this domain and is discussed in detail in this section.

### The TIR Convention: General Principles

The TIR Convention, based on the UN Customs Convention on the International Transport of Goods under Cover of TIR Carnets (1960), is not only one of the most successful international transport conventions, but also the only existing universal customs transit system. In this sense, it serves as a benchmark for any future effective regional transit frameworks and deserves a detailed examination.

The TIR Convention allows the temporary suspension of customs duties, excise duties, and value added taxes (VAT) payable on goods originating from or destined for a third country while under transport across the territory of a concrete customs zone. Such suspension remains in place until the goods either exit the customs territory concerned, are transferred to an alternative customs regime, or the duties and taxes are paid and the goods enter free circulation. The TIR specifies five main pillars:

- *Secure vehicles.* The goods are to be transported in containers or compartments of road vehicles constructed so that there is no access to the interior when secured by a customs seal, so that no goods can be removed or added during the transit procedure, and so that any tampering will be clearly visible.

- *International guarantee valid throughout the journey.* In the situation in which the transport operator cannot pay for the customs duties and taxes due, this system ensures that the customs duties and taxes at risk are covered by the national guaranteeing system of the operator.
- *National associations of transport operators.* National associations control access to the TIR procedures by transport operators and issue the appropriate documents and manage the national guarantee system.
- *TIR carnets.* This is the standard international customs document accepted and recognized by all members of the TIR Convention.
- *International and mutual recognition of customs control measures.* The countries of transit and destination accept control measures taken in the country of departure.

In essence, TIR operations can be carried out in participating countries by a truck operator member of a national association, with the network of national associations acting as guarantor.

The TIR system has been a success. The number of TIR carnets issued rose from 3,000 in 1952 to 2.7 million in 2001. The main reason for its success to date is that all parties involved (customs, other legal bodies, transport operators, and insurance companies) recognize that the system not only saves time but also money, due to its efficiency and reliability. The TIR Convention is simple, flexible, and cost reducing, and ensures the payment of customs duties and taxes that are a result of the international transport of goods. Furthermore, it is constantly being updated according to the latest developments, mainly concerning fraud and smuggling. The TIR is used mostly in European countries but is also used in transit operations in Central Asia, the Caucasus, the Maghreb, and in some parts of the Middle East.

### Insurance and Issuance of TIR Carnets

In countries using the TIR, the national guaranteeing association is recognized by the customs administration of the country. In most cases it is an association that represents the transporters. The association guarantees payment within that country of any duties and taxes that may become due in the event of any irregularity occurring in the course of the TIR transport operation. The amount payable is a maximum of US$50,000 for normal carnets and US$200,000 for tobacco and alcohol carnets. The national guaranteeing association is not a financial organization; therefore, its obligations are usually backed by insurance policies provided by the market. The International Road Transport Union (IRU) can help national guaranteeing associations find such services.

There are three types of carnets, each of which contains two sheets for each country of departure, transit, and destination:

- The regular TIR carnet.
- The multimodal TIR carnet, which was introduced in 1987, and specifically caters to the requirements of regional and intercontinental multimodal transport. This carnet contains an additional sheet identifying the persons who compose the transport chain.
- The tobacco/alcohol TIR carnet, which became an integral part of the TIR Convention in 1994.

The transporter should execute a contract with the national guarantee association, which would include the obligation to meet all requirements set in the TIR Convention; to return the used TIR carnet after completion of the TIR transport; and to pay any amount of duties, taxes, and other charges on first demand of the national guarantee association.

To ensure the security of the revenues, the TIR system is only applicable to containers or road vehicles with load compartments to which there is no interior access after a customs seal has secured it. If tampering does take place, it will be clearly visible.

### The Sequence of the Transit Operation Under TIR Cover

A TIR transport is an international transport operation. It is a transit operation of goods, across one or more borders, of which only a part of the transit has to be made by road. The transit operation itself involves the movement of goods from one country (country of departure) to another country (country of destination), through a third country (transit country). All countries involved should be active members of the TIR Convention.

The customs office in the country of departure administers the seals. Both the country of transit and the country of destination accept the control measures taken in this country. Thus, at customs offices en route (at border points between countries of departure and transit, and between countries of transit and destination), only the seals and containing body are inspected. The goods are not inspected unless irregularities are suspected. Such spot checks should be the exception. The customs office of the destination country removes the seals and controls the goods.

During this transit process, various steps can be discerned regarding the issuance of the carnet as well as the insurance situation. To illustrate the functioning of the system, an outline of a TIR transport from Rotterdam (the Netherlands) to Moscow (Russian Federation) follows. This procedure is also depicted in figure 11.2.

**Step 1. TIR Carnet Presented at the Customs Office of Departure** The truck driver should present the TIR carnet at the customs office of departure in Rotterdam. Before loading the goods, customs will check the TIR certificate (stating that the loading space of the truck fulfills the requirement of construction and can be sealed properly by customs) and customs will seal the loading space after loading has been completed. The customs office of departure will then validate the TIR carnet (put customs stamps on the manifest, and on each of the sheets for the countries that will be transited between the Netherlands and the Russian Federation, two copies for each of these countries). Customs removes one sheet of the TIR carnet and forwards this copy to the Dutch CCO. The rest of the TIR carnet is returned to the truck driver, who can leave Rotterdam en route to the exit customs office.

**Step 2. TIR Carnet Presented at the Customs Office of Exit of the Departure Country** The Netherlands is a Member State of the European Union (EU), which is a customs union, so no customs formalities need to be fulfilled at the internal border between the members. Therefore, the customs office of exit of the EU is, in this example, situated at the Polish–German border.

**FIGURE 11.2 The Sequence of the TIR Operations**

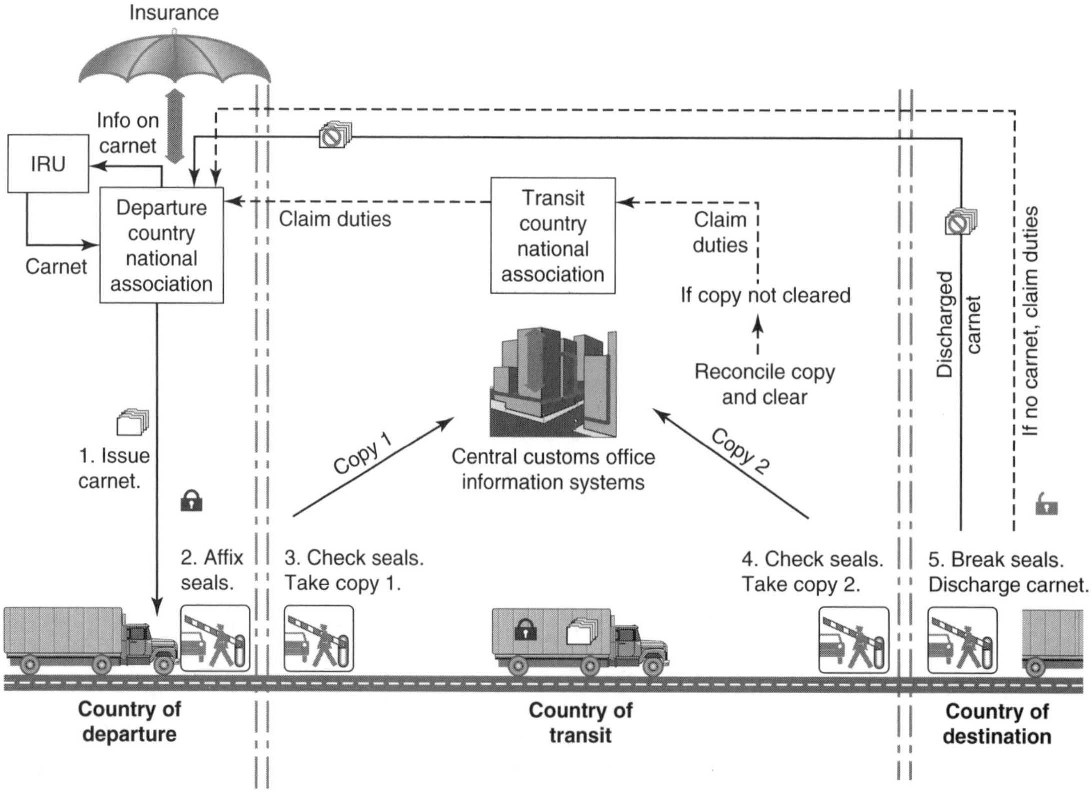

*Source:* Author.

The truck driver presents the TIR carnet at the German customs office of exit in Frankfurt (Odder), Federal Republic of Germany. German customs inspects the Dutch customs seals and whether the loading space of the truck is still intact. If no irregularities are found, German customs removes a copy from the TIR carnet and stamps the second copy in the TIR carnet. The TIR carnet is returned to the truck driver, who is allowed to leave the EU and drive to the Polish customs office at the same border. German customs forwards the copy it removed from the TIR carnet to the Dutch CCO.

Copies from the TIR carnet received from the customs offices of departure and exit are compared at the Dutch CCO. If no irregularities are determined, duties are not payable. However, if the second copy does not arrive at the CCO, goods are considered to have remained in the EU and the duties and taxes applicable in the EU become due. The principal of the TIR carnet (that is, the transporter) is obliged to pay these duties and taxes. If the principal is not willing to pay or cannot pay these duties and taxes on demand of customs, the national guaranteeing association must pay the demanded amounts.

**Step 3. TIR Carnet Presented at the Customs Office of Entry of the Transit Country** The truck driver presents the TIR carnet to the Polish customs office at the Polish–German border. Polish customs inspects the Dutch customs seals and whether the loading space of the truck is still intact. If no irregularities are found, Polish customs removes a copy from the TIR carnet and stamps the second copy in the TIR carnet. After completion, the TIR carnet is returned to the truck driver, who is allowed to leave the Polish customs office and drive to the Russian–Polish border. Polish customs forwards the copy it removed from the TIR carnet to the Polish CCO.

**Step 4. TIR Carnet Presented at the Customs Office of Exit of the Transit Country** The truck driver presents the TIR carnet at the Polish customs office of exit at the Russian–Polish border, and the procedure that took place at the German border is repeated.

Copies from the TIR carnet are received from the customs offices of departure and exit and are compared at the Polish CCO. If no irregularities are

found, duties are not payable. If Polish customs does not receive the documents or if irregularities are observed, the duties are payable. Polish customs can turn to the guaranteeing Polish national association for payment of the demanded amount. The Polish association will then recover this amount from its Dutch counterpart.

**Step 5. TIR Carnet Presented at the Customs Office of Entry in the Country of Destination** The truck driver presents himself or herself and the TIR carnet at the Russian customs office at the Russian–Polish border and performs the controls that were described for leaving the German exit border before sending the driver and the transit truck to Moscow. This part of the journey is identical to a national transit operation. Russian customs files the copy it removed from the TIR carnet to monitor the clearance.

**Step 6. TIR Carnet Presented at the Customs Office of the Country of Destination** The truck driver presents himself or herself along with the TIR carnet at the customs office in Moscow. Russian customs inspects the Dutch customs seals and whether the loading space of the truck is still intact. If no irregularities are found, Moscow customs removes a copy from the TIR carnet and stamps the second copy in the TIR carnet. After completion, the TIR carnet is returned to the truck driver. The TIR transport operation is now complete. Moscow customs forwards the copy it removed from the TIR carnet to the Russian customs office of entry.

The copy of the TIR carnet received from the Moscow customs office at the Russian customs office of entry is compared to the copy of that specific TIR carnet in the files of that customs office. If no irregularities are found, duties are not payable. However, if the second copy does not arrive at the Russian customs office of entry, goods are considered to be in free circulation in Russia and the Russian duties and taxes become due. The principal of the TIR carnet (the transporter) is obliged to pay these duties and taxes. If the principal is not willing to pay or cannot pay these duties and taxes on demand of Russian customs, the Russian national guaranteeing association must pay the demanded amounts. The Russian national guaranteeing association will recover this amount, via the Dutch national guaranteeing association, from the Dutch principal of the TIR carnet.

**Step 7. TIR Carnet Discharged by Customs of the Country of Destination**    After discharge, the principal or holder returns the TIR carnet to the Dutch National Guaranteeing Association. The Dutch National Guaranteeing Association returns the TIR carnet to the IRU for control and archiving.

### Advantages of the TIR System

The TIR system was devised to facilitate (under customs control) to the maximum extent possible, the international movement of goods. The system provides transit countries with adequate guarantees to cover customs duties and taxes at risk. TIR is a win–win arrangement between the public sector and the private sector. The counterpart of the simplification of procedures is the exercise of more responsibility by the private sector through the national associations.

For the transport industry the benefits include the following:

• Goods can move across international borders with minimum customs interference.
• The delays and costs of transit are reduced.
• The documents are simplified and standardized.
• There is no need to make customs guarantee deposits at transit borders.

Customs authorities enjoy benefits, too:

• Duties and taxes at risk during international transit movements are guaranteed up to US$50,000 (with a higher maximum for alcohol and tobacco).
• Only bona fide transport operators are permitted to use TIR carnets, thus increasing the reliability of the system.
• Disputes can be arbitrated through national associations (the one in the country of transit and the transporter's national association).

• The system facilitates customs control and documentation.
• Use of central clearance points allows more efficient use of customs personnel.

However, in 1992, the TIR system had been endangered by its eastward expansion, especially in the former Soviet Union, where massive fraud occurred. A guarantee system that can collapse in the final leg of the journey is not secure. Fortunately, Russian customs reacted to address the issue, aided by a proper tracking system backed by adequate investigation and enforcement mechanisms. As a response to this crisis, the IRU developed an electronic backup of the TIR carnets called SafeTIR that makes tracking easier (box 11.4).

Another reponse to this type of tracking problem is provided by the the Unique Consignment Reference Number (UCR) of WCO. The WCO has been working for several years on the implementation of the UCR. The UCR has a broader customs purpose than transit; however, it constitutes a consistent information system for tracking consignments. Therefore, it can provide a reliable tool for customs agencies willing to facilitate legitimate transit while keeping control of the movement of goods in transit. From the carrier perspective, the UCR has a number of potential benefits, beginning with the fact that a single UCR is created and used by the exporter irrespective of the number of transit countries (box 11.5).

Experience also shows that the TIR mechanisms remain difficult to implement in some countries for the same reasons that make a national-based system inefficient, such as the unavailability of an efficient guarantee system. If the private sector is not well organized, the national association may not be strong enough. Even when a credible association emerges, quite often it is not in a position to set up

---

### BOX 11.4    The SafeTIR

SafeTIR is a control system that aims at electronically confirming the termination of a TIR transport at the customs office of destination and validating the certification of the termination demonstarted by a customs stamp affixed to a TIR carnet. SafeTIR provides the status of the TIR carnet to customs and the TIR carnet issuing association with a confirmation, directly from the customs authorities, of the final or partial termination of the TIR carnet, mainly to enable comparison of this confirmation to the paper-based termination. The electronic confirmation should reach the guarantee chain without delay.

*Source:* IRU, available at www.iru.org.

---

**BOX 11.5    The Unique Consignment Reference Number**

UCR is a unique reference number that may be required at any point during the customs procedure. It should (a) be applied to all international goods moving under customs control, (b) be used only for tracking, audit, and reconciliation purposes, (c) be truly unique at the international level, and (d) be issued at the beginning of the trade process.

The objective of the UCR is to define a generic mechanism with sufficient flexibility to cope with the most common scenarios of international trade. UCR is making maximum use of existing supplier, customer, and transport references.

UCR is a 35-digit alphanumeric code bound to the consignment. The agreed on structure consists of the following:

- a first character for the year over a 10-year period
- two-digit country ISO code identifying the nationality of the supplier
- 32 characters used as the national identifying code of the supplier plus a transaction code created by the supplier.

*Source:* Guidelines on Application of Information and Communication Technology (Kyoto Convention, General Annex, Chapter 7, Appendix 9.)

---

the guarantee system due to the underdevelopment of the local financial infrastructure and the unwillingness of international insurance companies to provide a cover given their perception of political and commercial risk. In other instances, political tension between countries makes the mutual recognition of carnets elusive, as is too often the case in Central and Western Asia.

### *Attempts to Duplicate TIR Success Elsewhere*

Due to the enormous success of the TIR system, its concept has been the basis for attempts to establish bilateral and multilateral agreements between countries elsewhere, such as in Asia, Africa, and South America. However, none of these initiatives have been successful yet. A main reason for this has been the absence of a common regional guarantee system. The internationally agreed on and recognized guarantee system is one of the core elements of the TIR system, and in its absence TIR-like systems will not be successful. On occasions, even when such a system is included within a transit agreement, the failure to implement it fully jeopardizes the efficiency of the regional transit regime. For example, the Economic Community of West African States' (ECOWAS') 16 member states signed, in June 1982, a convention for the establishment of an ECOWAS Inter State Road Transit System commonly known as TRIE (Transit Routier Inter-États). Chambers of commerce are assuming the role of national associations. However, the TRIE has been largely ignored, and about 70 percent of

the transit procedures in the ECOWAS region still stem from bilateral accords and national regulations and practices. These are, for the most part, inward looking and protectionist rather than supportive of the free movement of goods (N'Guessan 2003). Practical implementation shortfalls are often at the root of the failure of regional or international transit agreements.[10]

### Transit Facilitation Institutions

Active cooperation between and among transit and landlocked countries can help ease trade barriers. Such regional and bilateral cooperation can promote an integrated approach to transit that goes beyond customs transit issues. Many agreements have a strong focus on the transit infrastructure, and also deal with visa, permit, and vehicle regulation issues. This section presents a selection of such agreements and their accompanying institutional arrangements, and highlights those factors that have contributed to their successes or shortfalls in supporting transit.

### *Bilateral Agreements*

Bilateral transit agreements are key building blocks of customs harmonization initiatives. In the absence of TIR-like conventions, bilateral agreements are

---

10. Regional TIR-like mechanisms are under consideration in Central Africa, Central Asia (under the leadership of the Asian Development Bank), and in Western Asia.

needed to make transit possible. They are also needed as a basis for regional agreements. In practice, bilateral agreements have strategic importance for developing landlocked economies.

The scope of bilateral agreements is usually practical and reflects a balance between the interests of the two countries, which are not always in accordance with general principles of customs transit (convoy practices , for example). It usually includes preferred route and freight sharing agreements, as well as the location of warehouses of the landlocked countries.[11] However, some core customs transit issues, such as guarantee procedures, are usually left out of the bilateral agreements.

Together the Indo-Nepal Treaty of Trade and the Treaty of Transit govern transit operations between the two countries. Both treaties, which are renewed every five years, go into great detail in outlining the specific procedures required for the transit of Nepalese imports and exports through India. The Transit Treaty includes specific points of entry and exit, a description of the 15 mutually agreed on transit routes to and from Calcutta and Haldia, a description of the warehouses and open spaces provided, and detailed guidelines on the simplified administrative procedures involved in the import or export of Nepalese goods via India. The Nepalese–Indian example includes a number of elements that can help facilitate transit operations between the two countries:

- a clear description of import and export procedures
- simplified customs administrative requirements and documentation (in this case, the Customs Transit Declaration)
- a reliable guarantee framework (backed by the government of Nepal)
- a clear distribution of responsibilities and duties among the different stakeholders
- customs support infrastructure (warehouses, the provision of dry ports)
- a description of the agreed on transit routes.

---

11. Efficient dry ports, such as Ngaounderé in Cameroon or Birgajn at the Indo–Nepalese border, are also part of this framework of bilateral facilitation.

### Regional Agreements

The last few decades witnessed a proliferation of regional agreements between or involving developing countries. A number of them have direct implications for customs transit:

- the already-mentioned Transit Routier Inter-Etats (TRIE) in the ECOWAS, the only example beyond TIR of an agreement dedicated only to transit
- the Association of Southeast Asian Nations (ASEAN) Framework Agreement on the Facilitation of Goods in Transit
- the Greater Mekong Subregion (GMS) Agreement for Facilitation of Cross-Border Transport of Goods and People
- Economic Cooperation Organization (ECO) Transit Framework Agreement—formed by Afghanistan, Azerbaijan, Iran, Kazakhstan, Kyrgyz Republic, Pakistan, Tajikistan, Turkey, Turkmenistan, and Uzbekistan
- Common Market for Eastern and Southern Africa (COMESA) agreement on single administrative document.

Except for the TRIE, these regional agreements tend to lay down broad goals and policy directions. Actual customs transit facilitation may be dependent on other existing agreements or procedures. A 2001 UNCTAD report points out "there has not been any shortage of measures and initiatives to improve facilitation of transit traffic. COMESA, EAC, . . . and SADC all have various measures that are in place to address transit facilitation. Unfortunately, the major problem has been poor implementation." (InfraAfrica Ltd. 2001, p. 45)

To achieve a significant impact on customs transit, regional agreements should address, directly or through related mechanisms, the following components:

- *Common customs documentation and procedures.* The use of common procedures and documents, such as carnets or Single Administrative Document (SAD), are now available in many regions or sub-regions.
- *Cooperation between authorities, or one-stop border posts.* Within Africa, a number of initiatives have been discussed over the years on

one-stop border posts. Unfortunately, these have not been translated into concrete effective measures.
- *Regional customs guarantee system.* So far, the guarantee system has proven to be the most elusive objective.

That regional agreements can work in the presence of political will is illustrated by the successful introduction of the COMESA Yellow Card or Third Party Regional Motor Vehicle Insurance Scheme. This scheme allows prepurchase of insurance, honored by all participants, in local currency at the point of origin. This means, for example, that a trucker traveling from Zimbabwe to Uganda who has to traverse Zambia, Tanzania, and Kenya does not need to stop at each border post to purchase insurance, but uses the Yellow Card to gain access and coverage. According to COMESA, the Yellow Card has, since its inception, generated revenue worth US$2 million, with only US$200,000 worth of claims processed. In theory, transit guarantee schemes are not that much more difficult to implement than this insurance scheme.

### Transit Corridors

In transit corridors all relevant stakeholders aim to work together to ensure efficient and secure transit along specific routes, to the benefit of landlocked and transit countries.

The potential strength of transit corridors lies primarily in the possibilities they offer in confronting the concerns and interests of all relevant stakeholders, public and private, who can focus on policies and initiatives to cater to specific routes and border crossings. Transit corridors thus offer the possibility of tackling transit in a holistic manner (institutional, administrative, and infrastructure), initiating and effecting changes that may otherwise be difficult to obtain at a wider national or regional level. In this sense, promoting specific transit documentation or introducing harmonized border crossing procedures for specific routes are more easily attainable objectives that, once in place, can be expanded to national levels. The quality of the governance structure of the corridor is of critical importance in achieving those objectives. Transit corridors benefit greatly from the involvement of private sector stakeholders.

An UNCTAD document, "Strategies for Landlocked and Transit Developing Countries," points out that "experience shows that most effective facilitation measures concentrate on trade and transport corridors linking inland origins/destinations in landlocked countries with entry/exit seaports in coastal countries" (UNCTAD 2003, p. 13). In practice, the experience with transit corridors has been somewhat mixed. Yet, there have been some encouraging initiatives and results that provide a basis for further developments in the field of transit. The following examples illustrate the potential benefits conveyed by transport corridors for customs transit.

*Walvis Bay Development Corridor.* The Walvis Bay Development Corridor (now Trans Kalahari) became operational in late 1999. The driving force behind the project was the Walvis Bay Corridor Group (WBCG), a public–private partnership. In November 2003 the Trans Kalahari Corridor Memorandum of Understanding was signed. It introduced a new single customs administrative document, which until then had been in use on a pilot basis. This new simplified approach provides a streamlined and effective tool for managing customs transit transactions throughout Namibia, Botswana, and South Africa and will replace the cumbersome set of procedures involving up to 10 national documents in each country transited.

*Northern Corridor.* This corridor provides a lifeline through Kenya to the landlocked economies of Uganda, Rwanda, Burundi, and the landlocked areas within the Democratic Republic of Congo. The corridor is governed by the Northern Corridor Transit Transport Coordination Authority, which aims to help harmonize and simplify the procedures involved in transporting goods within the region. Significant achievements accomplished so far include the following:

- Simplification of port clearance procedures.
- Documentary simplification, achieved through the creation of the Road Transit Customs Declaration (RTCD), which is meant to be the single administrative document attached to a shipment through the corridor. However, in practice the RTCD is often copied at the border onto another RTCD issued by the next country, an illustration of how difficult it may be to change old habits.

- The use of the COMESA Customs Declaration Document by Northern Corridor countries.
- Reduction by half of the transit time between Mombasa, Kenya, and Bujumbura, Burundi, from over 30 days to about 15 days. Some unnecessary border formalities along the corridor have been removed.

*TRACECA.* TRACECA is an EU-initiated program, launched in 1993, to develop a transport corridor on a west-east axis from Europe, across the Black Sea, through the Caucasus and the Caspian Sea to Central Asia (a modern Silk Road). It aims to harmonize the legislative base in the transport and transit sectors of its member states[12] and places a great emphasis on infrastructure development and improvement. During its 10-year existence, TRACECA has implemented 53 projects and channeled over US$120 million in infrastructure investment and technical assistance.

A key tool in the execution of this project was a border audit whereby the transit procedures at 70 designated TRACECA border crossing points (in all 14 countries) were observed and recorded into a database. This comprehensive set of data has been the basis upon which subsequent recommendations on harmonized procedures at border crossings have been put forward.

### The Program of Trade and Transport Facilitation in Southeast Europe

The Trade and Transport Facilitation in Southeast Europe (TTFSE) regional program, supported by the World Bank, the EU, and bilateral partners, was set up in 1998 upon the request of the region's countries and the Southeast European Cooperative Initiative. Its aim is to create a framework that will help to reduce transport costs, fight corruption, and help customs administrations gradually align their procedures with EU standards. The countries included in this program are Albania, Bosnia and Herzegovina, Bulgaria, Croatia, Romania, Serbia, and the landlocked Moldova and Federal Yugoslav Republic of Macedonia. Since most of the trade flows are bound to or from the EU and the majority of the

countries involved fall within the TIR system, it is already built on a strong transit base.

The design and implementation of the TTFSE was based on a participatory methodology to ensure a sense of ownership among the various stakeholders involved—national agencies, customs officials, and transport operators. The TTFSE program builds on a number of regional mechanisms:

- a high-level Regional Steering Committee convening all countries twice a year to facilitate cooperation and experience sharing
- a regional Web site presenting all requirements and procedures of border agencies
- public–private working groups interacting quarterly
- regional conventional and distance-learning programs to harmonize the quality of transport service providers
- paired local project teams gathering all border agencies at pilot border crossing points with interactions across the border
- indicators that monitor border crossing times.

This customs modernization initiative has been implemented at a number of selected border crossing points and inland clearance terminals with a considerable degree of success. The program's progress report for 2002 highlights the significant reduction in waiting time, the establishment of a transparent and public customs performance monitoring system (see box 11.6), and the visibly improved dialogue among customs administrations within the region.

The success of this program so far can be attributed to reliable funding from the World Bank and various other donors, strong commitment by the national governments involved, direct participation of all stakeholders, extensive use of information technology, the introduction of human resources programs, and the emphasis on close and meticulous monitoring to fine-tune and identify changing needs and priority areas.

Two key ingredients of the success of TTFSE as a transit facilitation initiative have been the development of joint border facilities and the monitoring of indicators. TTFSE has a harmonized set of indicators (box 11.6). Joint processing allows all customs and noncustoms (veterinary, phytosanitary) procedures to be carried out in a single stop in a common border processing zone.

---

12. Armenia, Azerbaijan, Bulgaria, Georgia, Kazakhstan, Kyrgyz Republic, Moldova, Mongolia, Romania, Tajikistan, Turkmenistan, Turkey, Uzbekistan, and Ukraine.

---

**BOX 11.6　TTFSE Indicators**

Agreed to by all participating countries, the set of indicators has allowed both general performance and the real time impact of the different pilot site initiatives to be monitored. To improve the efficiency and relevance of this initiative, the program has tried to institutionalize the collection procedures at each of the pilot sites, relying on local computer applications or simple measurement techniques to obtain most of the key figures automatically. An important feature of transit-related indicators is that the design of the indicators and the data collection involve both public agencies and the private sector (trucking industry). Transit related indicators include the following:

- Trucks cleared in less than 15 minutes
- Irregularities per number of examinations
- Truck examinations
- Average border exit time
- Average border entry time
- Surveyed occurrences of corruption.

*Source:* TTFSE report 2002 at www.ttfse.org.

---

## Operational Conclusions

Customs transit is, in a sense, straightforward as it is built on proven principles: secure the cargo, provide a guarantee mechanism, and use a centralized flow of documentation. Customs transit is vulnerable to poor institutional frameworks. Transit operations are extended in space and time and are, therefore, exposed to inefficient bureaucracy and to corrupt practices. The guarantee system needs a minimum degree of sophistication of the local financial infrastructure, which is not always available in developing countries. Transit cannot work without a certain amount of trust between customs and the private sector, which means cultivating a mature and organized private sector.

While transit facilitation is a bottleneck to the development of a number of developing countries, this is precisely where the reforms face the most daunting challenges. In many countries inadequate practices or procedures, such as convoys, are deeply entrenched. Here are some important operational conclusions.

Customs transit is only one part of a wider range of policy issues that involves many other participants and procedures, including cross-border vehicle regulations, visas for truck drivers, insurance, and police controls. The quality of infrastructure is also a major concern for many landlocked countries. Even if customs transit procedures are made effective and efficient, full trade facilitation will require that these other issues be dealt with. Some measures can be taken at the national level while others require some form of regional cooperation.

The existence of an efficient guarantee system, which is adhered to by customs authorities and proves not too cumbersome for exporters–importers and transport operators, is a prerequisite for transit operations. The TIR and its network of national guaranteeing associations propose the best current reference system. So far there is no convincing example of a fully functioning guarantee system available to transporters in developing countries. In part, this is because financial institutions have not been in a position to propose products similar to the TIR insurance in the development context. A working guarantee system is also dependent upon customs enforcement and information systems.

Transit is dependent upon customs information systems within the country of transit. Customs should be able to efficiently track the transit flows in and out of the country. Information processing and automation, particularly the implementation of e-transit modules in information technology systems, will ultimately facilitate transit.

Customs modernization programs should encompass transit. The following components are crucial for a transit module:

- harmonization of procedures at the regional level, for example, single documents
- development of enforcement capabilities beyond the border to enhance the credibility of customs transit provisions
- consideration of the feasibility of joint border processing
- monitoring of indicators of transit performance, as in TTFSE.

Transit facilitation institutions such as corridor agreements promote active cooperation between and among transit and landlocked countries, and are a pivotal element in helping reduce or remove physical, administrative, and institutional barriers to trade. Transit agreements are important in forming and shaping such cooperation, either at the bilateral, subregional, or regional level. In practice, such agreements promote an integrated approach to transit that goes far beyond customs transit, and tackles issues such as infrastructure, visas, permits, and insurance.

Public–private cooperation will bring decisive contributions to transit cooperation. It is recommended that appropriate frameworks, such as National Trade and Transport Facilitation Committees, be set up and be strengthened (UNECE 2000). Regular exchange of information between public agencies and stakeholders will help to identify where the shortfalls lie in border crossing procedures. Furthermore, basic transit provisions, including guarantees, work considerably better with a mature and organized transport sector. Reforms in this sector go far beyond customs reform. Public policies must foster the emergence of modern operators, and phase out transit activities by obsolete equipment and informal operators, with whom efficient transit provisions are virtually impossible.

## Further Reading

Global Facilitation Partnership. www.gfptt.org.

Grosdidier de Matons, Jean. 2004. "Facilitation of Transport and Trade in Sub-Saharan Africa: A Review of Legal Instruments." SSATP Working Paper No. 73. Washington, D.C.: The World Bank.

International Road Transport Union. www.iru.org.

UN/CEFACT (United Nations Centre for Trade Facilitation and Electronic Business) and UNCTAD (United Nations Conference on Trade and Development). 2002. "Compendium of Trade Facilitation Recommendations." ECE/TRADE/279. February.

UNCTAD. 2003. "Strategies for Landlocked and Transit Developing Countries to Plan and Implement Sustainable Trade and Transport Facilitation Initiatives." Issue Note by the Secretary General of UNCTAD. Document UNCTAD/SDTE/TLB/ 2003/2. July 23.

## References

Amjadi, A., and A. Yeats. 1995. "Have Transport Costs Contributed to the Relative Decline of Sub-Saharan African Exports?" World Bank Policy Research Paper 1559. Washington, D.C.: The World Bank.

Favier, Jean. 1971. *Finances et Fiscalité au Bas Moyen Age.* Paris: SEDES.

Faye, Michael, John McArthur, Jeffrey Sachs, and Thomas Snow. 2004. "The Challenges Facing Landlocked Developing Countries." *Journal of Human Development.* 5(1): 31–68.

Grosdidier de Matons, Jean. 2004. "Facilitation of Transport and Trade in Sub-Saharan Africa: A Review of Legal Instruments." SSATP Working Paper No. 73. Washington, D.C.: The World Bank.

InfraAfrica Ltd. 2001. "Review of Progress in the Development of Transit Transport Systems in Eastern and Southern Africa." Prepared for the Fifth Meeting of Governmental Experts from Land-locked and Transit Developing Countries and Representatives of Donor Countries and Financial and Development Institutions. Document UNCTAD/LDC/115. New York. July 31–August 3.

Lakshmanan, T. R. 2001. *Integration of Transport and Trade Facilitation: Selected Regional Case Studies.* Washington, D.C.: The World Bank.

Limao, N., and A. Venables. 1999. "Infrastructure Geographical Disadvantage and Costs." World Bank Policy Research Working Paper No. 2257. Washington, D.C.: The World Bank.

N'Guessan N'Guessan. 2003. *La problématique de la gestion intégrée des corridors en Afrique subsaharienne.* The World Bank and SSATP. Document d'analyse SSATP No. 3F. Washington, D.C. May.

UN (United Nations). 2003. "Almaty Programme of Action: Addressing the Special Needs of Landlocked Developing Countries within a New Global Framework for Transit Transport Cooperation for Landlocked and Transit Developing Countries." Adopted by the International Ministerial Conference of Landlocked and Transit Developing Countries and Donor Countries and International Financial and Development Institutions on Transit Transport Cooperation in Almaty on August 28–29, 2003. www.un.org/special-rep/ohrlls/imc/ Almaty%20Programme% 20of%20Action.pdf.

UN/CEFACT (United Nations Centre for Trade Facilitation and Electronic Business) and UNCTAD (United Nations Conference on Trade and Development). 2002. "Compendium of Trade Facilitation Recommendations." ECE/TRADE/279. February.

UNCTAD (United Nations Conference on Trade and Development). 2003. "Strategies for Landlocked and Transit Developing Countries to Plan and Implement Sustainable Trade and Transport Facilitation Initiatives." Issue Note by the Secretary General of UNCTAD. Document UNCTAD/SDTE/TLB/ 2003/2. July 23.

UNECE (United Nations Economic Commission for Europe). 2000. "Creating an Efficient Environment for Trade and Transport—Guidelines to Recommendation No. 4, National Trade Facilitation Bodies." Document ECE/TRADE/256. Geneva.

# 12

# THE ROLE OF CUSTOMS
# IN CARGO SECURITY

*Luc De Wulf and Omer Matityahu*

This chapter is intended to assist customs administrations in dealing with the security challenges faced by international transport and shipping service providers. The guidance and concepts provided here are geared toward helping governments in the development of national security policies and strategies, including preparing a needs assessment and implementing the strategy within the context of an overall risk management approach.

The emergence of international terrorism has caused the issue of security to become one of the major challenges facing customs administrations. In the past, many customs administrations performed most of their preventive operations as goods arrived at seaports, airports, and land borders based upon an entry declaration made at the time of importation. Improving security in the supply chain, however, requires that this traditional method of operating must change. For it to do so, customs now needs to gather information and assess risk in advance of arrival, so that effective action can be taken, preferably before a ship embarks or an aircraft takes off, or at the latest, at the time of its arrival. The information needed for these security processes comes from several sources, but a crucial element is the advance information available from the businesses exporting or transporting the goods. Customs' skill in assessing the information through analytical processes, deployment of resources, and effective communication and decisionmaking, therefore, has become even more important than in the past.

Security is of great importance to governments, but so is facilitating legitimate trade. If applied correctly, security can enhance facilitation by building business confidence, increasing predictability and trade flow, and, as a consequence, improving

Omer Matityahu is a consultant for ICTS Global Security B.V., whose contribution was financed by a grant from the government of the Netherlands. The contribution of Will Robinson of the World Customs Organization is gratefully acknowledged.

inward investment. The information required by customs can also be enhanced by customs–trade cooperation.

Protecting society in an effective and efficient manner requires the international trade supply chain to become the focus of attention in its entirety, rather than simply when goods are entering, leaving, or transiting a country. This changing environment requires an "all of government" approach. Governments would thus have the opportunity to use customs as a key resource in border security by using customs' experience with managing risks and its knowledge of international trade as important elements in addressing issues of national security. Customs' roles in security and facilitation complement those contributions made by other competent agencies as part of an integrated response. Cooperation and communication between customs and the lead agencies for terrorism; immigration; and policing maritime, aviation, and land transport; and intelligence operations are vital. In this manner, customs can contribute toward the wider security agenda as outlined in the United Nations Security Council Resolutions, particularly 1373 (passed in 2001) and 1456 (passed in 2003), which call for an integrated response to fighting terrorism. Customs' role is therefore changing rapidly.

Developing and implementing security standards across international borders is likely to present a formidable challenge, but doing so is essential to safeguard the integrity of the international supply chain. Efforts to develop international standards are underway on several fronts, but much still remains to be done to standardize these norms and implement them effectively. Due to the number and diversity of nations and stakeholders involved in the international supply chain, achieving consensus on these and other standards could be difficult and time consuming.

This chapter examines some of the operational and management considerations that will be of interest to those establishing or reviewing customs' security arrangements. The first section presents initiatives relating to the areas of border security. The second section analyzes the management implications of the heightened concern for customs security risks. The final section focuses on operational practices for customs in light of these renewed concerns.

## Initiatives to Improve Cargo Security

International trade involves many partners and processes that together constitute a logistics chain. Each link in that chain is to some extent subject to security risks. These risks are not new and have historically concerned many professional organizations. The protection of society has always been one of customs' main missions. However, with the events of September 11, 2001, security has attracted renewed focus from governments. Existing initiatives to strengthen security have been revisited and new ones have emerged. Both international and bilateral initiatives have been reviewed and strengthened. This section briefly reviews these initiatives and details what these mean in the context of customs' operations.

### World Customs Organization

The WCO's activities in the area of security are undertaken in close cooperation with the specialized international organizations that focus on specific transport modes, such as the International Maritime Organization (IMO), the International Civil Aviation Organization (ICAO), and the International Air Transport Association (IATA). In light of its mandate to enhance the effectiveness and efficiency of customs administrations, the WCO aims at building trade facilitation–appropriate security initiatives, so that world trade is not unduly affected or hindered by enhanced security measures.[1]

In June 2002, the WCO Council approved a resolution on security and facilitation of the international trade supply chain. This resolution led directly to the formation of an international Task Force on Security and Facilitation of the International Trade Supply Chain, comprising customs administrations, other international organizations, and international trade and transport organizations. The task force has produced a comprehensive package of guidelines and other measures that would enable customs administrations to implement and apply modern risk-based control procedures. The security and facilitation concepts developed by the task force involve the submission of advance electronic information at the earliest

---

1. This section is based on information from the WCO Web site www.wcoomd.org.

moment in the supply chain cycle, so that customs administrations can perform risk assessment processes well in advance of shipment. This approach allows customs' security role to be performed at or before export, while goods are in transit, or at or before importation. The information itself is provided by the most appropriate private sector entities involved in the supply chain, that is, the electronic information message is composed of information from exporters, importers, and service providers such as carriers. The procedures are contained in the Advance Cargo Information Guidelines, which form a central part of a comprehensive package of measures. The WCO has developed other instruments to fulfill its security mandate:

- a list of essential data elements required to identify high-risk consignments
- a new multilateral Convention for Customs Administrations, which will provide a mechanism for customs administrations to share relevant information on a bilateral, regional, or multilateral basis
- guidelines for businesses operating in the international trade supply chain that describe the measures and procedures that should be adopted by private sector operators
- guidelines concerning the purchase and operation of container scanning equipment
- a databank of modern technological devices.

The implementation of the guidelines is being managed through an international action plan and by a high-level strategic group of Directors General who provide strategic advice on the further development of security and facilitation methodologies and standards. The WCO relies on voluntary compliance of its members, because it does not have an enforcement mandate.

### Sea Cargo: Organization and Initiatives

World trade is dependent on maritime transport and great strides have been made in recent years to render this system as open and frictionless as possible to spur greater economic growth. However, the factors that have allowed maritime transport to contribute to economic prosperity also potentially increase its security risks. The risks range from the possibility of physical breaches in the integrity of shipments and vessels to documentary fraud and illicit money-raising activities by terrorist groups.

**International Initiatives**  Both international organizations and national governments have undertaken initiatives to enhance sea cargo security.

*International Maritime Organization.* The International Maritime Organization[2] (IMO) is a specialized organization within the United Nations established to develop international maritime standards, promote safety in shipping, and prevent marine pollution from ships. However, after September 11 the IMO amended its International Convention for the Safety of Life at Sea (SOLAS) and established an International Ship and Port Facility Security (ISPS) Code in December 2002. ISPS requires ships on international voyages and the port facilities that serve them to conduct a security assessment (for details, see annex 12.A), develop a security plan, appoint security officers, perform training and drills, and take appropriate preventive measures against security incidents. It is a comprehensive, mandatory security regime for international shipping and port operators (at this time, only the security assessments are mandatory), intended to enable better monitoring of freight flows to combat smuggling, and to respond to a threat of terrorist attacks. The International Labor Organization (ILO), also a United Nations agency, determines the requirements to be included in identification documents for seafarers. Since February 2002, ILO and IMO have been working on the issuance of seafarer documents, which would involve checking the background of crewmembers onboard ships transporting cargoes that are destined for the United States. In addition, the ILO may consider standards for port worker identification documentation. Noncompliance with ISPS requirements can result in loss of revenue and the potential for increased liability in the event of a security incident.

Contracting parties to the ISPS Code are to bring their national legislation in line with the code, ensure its enforcement, undertake security

---

2. For details on the IMO, see www.imo.org/home.asp. Further information can be obtained from The Subcommittee on Coast Guard and Maritime Transportation Hearing on Interim Final Regulations on Port Security at www.house.gov/transportation/cgmt/07-22-03/07-22-03memo.html.

assessments, prepare security plans, and notify the IMO of progress made with respect to these assessments and plans. The code also requires the national authorities to notify the IMO administration and its contracting governments of the control measures instituted for a vessel calling at a noncompliant port facility. Finally, IMO measures will also contain a strong port state control mechanism that authorizes taking control of vessels that have called on foreign ports that are not in compliance with SOLAS and the ISPS Code.

The ISPS Code became mandatory on July 1, 2004. This implies that by that date the prescribed security measures will need to be implemented for ports and ships to be certified. The government would issue the security certifications; but the local administrations that register ships may grant authorization to a private company to act as a Recognized Security Organization (RSO) to approve ship security plans, audit ship security systems, and, where appropriate, issue the certificates on behalf of the local administration. At this point the requirements for RSOs have not yet been agreed upon. The IMO intends to provide for ISPS certification under strict conditions following a careful inspection. Under the ISPS rules, the principal responsibilities of contracting governments are to determine and set security levels, and communicate information regarding security levels to ships flying their flag, to their port facilities, and to foreign vessels in or about to enter their ports.

Noncompliant ships or ports can be decertified, pending corrective action. If this occurs, such vessels will not be allowed to operate or such ports will operate subject to international penalties. This would have negative economic consequences for ships and ports that fail to meet the requirements of the ISPS Code. The most likely scenario for a noncertified ship entering a certified port is that it will be subjected to thorough and time-consuming inspections once it enters a country's territorial waters.

Enhancing the safety of maritime cargo transport will not come cheaply. An Organisation for Economic Co-operation and Development (OECD) study published in July 2003 (OECD 2003) estimated that the initial cost to ship operators for ISPS Code compliance would be at least US$1,279 million, with subsequent annual expenditures of US$730 million. This is equivalent to

about US$30,000 in initial costs and US$17,000 in annual expenditure per vessel (based on an estimate that 43,291 vessels were trading internationally in 2000). For international seaports the costs were estimated at US$963 million and US$509 million for initial and annual costs, respectively. For the United States, the average cost per seaport was estimated at US$4.26 million in initial costs and US$2.25 million in annual expenditures.

See box 12.1 for an example of how the ISPS Code is being implemented at the Panama Canal.

*United Nations Economic Commission for Europe.* The UNECE is currently reviewing its relevant instruments in the areas of trade and transport.[3] A useful basis for UNECE work in this area may be the Supply Chain Model and possibly the International Trade Transaction Model, both developed by UN/CEFACT (United Nations Centre for Trade Facilitation and Electronic Business). UNECE is currently updating both of these models.

**The United States' Initiatives** Since September 11, 2001, there has been growing concern that terrorist weapons could be smuggled in some of the millions of maritime containers arriving annually at United States seaports. Based on international legislation, the United States enacted the U.S. Maritime Transportation Security Act (MTSA) of 2002 to establish parallel domestic requirements for U.S. facilities and vessels. While many of the requirements in the MTSA directly align with ISPS requirements, it includes domestic vessels and facilities. There are several U.S. government initiatives related to cargo security. The U.S. Bureau of Customs and Border Protection (CBP) initiatives consist of the Customs-Trade Partnership Against Terrorism (C-TPAT), the 24-Hour Advance Manifest Rule, and the Container Security Initiative (CSI) to screen containers that pose a potential risk for terrorism at overseas ports. The U.S. Coast Guard initiative is the 96-Hour Notification of Arrival.

*CBP Initiative—Customs-Trade Partnership Against Terrorism.* In November 2001, the concept of C-TPAT[4] was introduced to the trade community as a cooperative initiative with the private sector,

---

3. See www.unece.org/trade/welcome.htm.

4. See CBP Web site at www.cbp.gov/xp/cgov/import/commercial_enforcement/ctpat/.

## BOX 12.1    Maritime Security Initiative at Panama Canal Waters

The SOLAS amendments and the ISPS Code of the IMO contain comprehensive measures that provide the option of requesting vessels to provide preliminary information regarding crew, passengers, origin, and destination of cargo. This information can be used by the Port Security Officer to perform risk assessments, but would need to be available before the vessel arrives in the port.

By virtue of its new framework, the Panama Canal Authority (ACP) is responsible for ensuring the most efficient use of its resources and for providing an optimum level of service and security to its clients. The ACP has deemed it necessary to develop an adequate information system to improve the information that is needed for security verifications and transit operations. Such a system will make possible the electronic reception of preliminary information, its proper analysis, and risk level assessments. The current process is time and resource consuming for ACP clients, particularly for Masters and Captains of vessels, and involves manually filling out the required forms to ensure a secure, safe, and efficient transit through the Panama Canal. It is also prone to human error, leading to costly delays resulting from incorrect or untimely data.

On September 2, 2003, ACP awarded its Automated Data Collection System Project (ADCS) to CrimsonLogic Pte Ltd. The ADCS consists of the following elements:

*Electronic Data Collection System (EDCS).* The EDCS allows international carriers and local Panamanian carrier agents to submit Ship Due and Transit Booking requests to ACP via the Internet through the World Wide Web, EDI, or XML, 96 hours prior to arrival in Panama Canal waters. It also facilitates the electronic submission of passenger and crew lists, admeasurer data sheets, and other necessary documents to ACP for advance processing. The advance document submission enables ACP to carry out risk assessment on the arriving vessels and their cargoes.

*Mobile Data Collection System (MDCS).* MDCS is an internal operating system that allows ACP's Canal Boarding and Security Officers to conduct inspections aboard the vessels passing through Canal waters and ensures heightened general security within ACP's jurisdiction. The data are collected and stored in real time using pen-based wireless mobile systems. In the next phase of the project, the MDCS will be linked to a data warehouse where a Risk Assessment Analysis tool, linked to federal agencies such as customs, national security agencies, and the Coast Guard, will provide real-time information on all vessels passing through Panama Canal waters. The advance information would be beneficial for customs and other federal agencies to more effectively monitor and facilitate the flow of cargo and to detect high-risk shipments for security, contraband, and other enforcement reasons.

The ADCS project is expected to generate the following benefits: (a) accurate and timely collection of security data and maritime operations information to help optimize vessel schedules and enhance security in the Canal; (b) improved and more accurate data validation; (c) efficient electronic information interchange between ACP and its clients; (d) improved user-friendly access through the use of the Web-based interface by ACP and its clients, including customs administrations all over the world; (e) overall reduction in operation costs and improvement in the competitiveness of the organization; (f) reduced form processing time and overall improvements in productivity; and (g) enhanced information and system security, ensuring that hackers or saboteurs do not interrupt ACP's operations.

*Source:* CrimsonLogic.

with the objective of fortifying the supply chain and deterring terrorists and the implements of terror from being introduced into the international commercial environment. As of February 24, 2004, 5,730 companies had enlisted in C-TPAT. Through C-TPAT, CBP and the trade community cooperate in designing a new approach to supply chain security to strengthen the borders against terrorism while continuing to facilitate the legitimate flow of compliant cargo and conveyances. Companies fill out a questionnaire, pulling together internal information about a company's security-related assets and procedures. C-TPAT continues to actively conduct visits to its member companies to confirm that their supply chain security measures contained in their security profiles are reliable, accurate, and effective. CBP is also working with its members to develop and implement the CBP Smart Box initiative. Sealing standards and techniques, coupled with a Container Security Device (CSD), are designed to detect evidence of tampering during the transit process and to enhance container security and the integrity of containerized cargo. C-TPAT aids companies in optimizing their internal and external management of assets and functions while at the same time enhancing security. When administered together, enhanced security practices and procedures, and improved supply chain performance, mitigate the risk of loss, damage, and theft, and reduce the likelihood of introduction of potentially dangerous elements into the global supply chain.

*CBP Initiative—24-Hour Advance Manifest Rule.* Advance information is the key component of CBP's strategy to protect legitimate trade from terrorists. The "24-hour rule" for advance manifest information was put into effect on February 2, 2003 (ref B-CBP). It instructs carriers in possession of containers to be loaded on board a U.S.-bound vessel to make a declaration to CBP at least 24 hours before the cargo is loaded at a foreign port. This declaration includes information pertaining to the shipper and consignee, as well as a precise description of the container's contents. Vague descriptions such as "said to contain," "FAK" (Freight of All Kinds), and "General Merchandise" are not accepted. Upon inspecting the manifest, CBP will make a decision to load the container or send a "DO NOT LOAD" message to the carrier or Non-Vessel Operating Common Carrier (NVOCC) before the container's scheduled load time. If a carrier loads a container for which a "DO NOT LOAD" message has been sent, the vessel will not be allowed to unload at the U.S. port until the information is amended. At this point, the clock for the 24-hour requirement starts again. The rule was effectively implemented in cooperation and in partnership with the trade and transportation industry.[5]

*CSI Initiative—Container Security Initiative.* Launched in January 2002, the CSI involves bilateral arrangements between the United States and foreign countries to reduce the risk of global containerized cargoes being exploited by terror-

ists.[6] The CSI moves the focus of container inspection to the port of lading for early detection of any potential threat. It aims to establish security criteria to identify any container that poses a potential risk for terrorism, prescreen those containers identified as posing a risk before they arrive at U.S. ports, use technology to quickly prescreen those containers, and develop and use smart and secure containers. The CSI deploys U.S. officials to the host country to work in conjunction with local officials. This is a reciprocal program, and several countries have stationed their personnel in U.S. ports as well. The objective of the CSI is to work with the host country to identify and screen cargo to detect potential risks for terrorism at the earliest possible opportunity. The first phase of CSI is focused on implementing the program at the top 20 foreign ports, which ship approximately two-thirds of the volume of containers to the United States.[7] So far, the benefits for goods in containers passing through CSI ports and destined for the United States are not clearly spelled out, nor are the disadvantages for goods moving through other channels. The CBP intends to expand the program to additional ports based on volume, location, and strategic concerns.

*U. S. Coast Guard Initiative—96-Hour Notification of Arrival.* Issued on February 28, 2002, the 96-Hour Notification of Arrival initiative requires 96-hour advance notification of vessel arrival at U.S. ports (Pluta 2001). This requirement includes the submission of cargo manifests, itinerary, and thorough information about the crew, including ports where they boarded and possible aliases that crew members are known to employ. The submission of crew details and cargo manifests is time-consuming and may require investment on the part of carriers and

---

5. See CBP Web site at www.cbp.gov/xp/cgov/import/carriers/24hour_rule/.

6. See CBP Web site at www.cbp.gov/xp/cgov/enforcement/international_activities/csi.

7. As of mid-January 2004, eight European Union (EU) countries had signed bilateral agreements with the United States. The container traffic from these ports to the U.S. covers approximately 85 percent of all maritime container traffic from the EU to the U.S. The European Community has launched infringement procedures against those Member States that have signed declarations of principle with the U.S. CBP. It is concerned that these measures will have negative effects on trade flows and will lead to competition between EU ports. It argues for an expansion of the 1997 EC–US Agreement to cover these aspects (www.europa.eu.int). For an update on the ports included in the CSI, see the Web site of the U.S. CBP, www.cbp.gov.

freight forwarders to improve their information technology systems to ensure the timely and accurate electronic submission of data.

**The European Union** At the end of July 2003, the European Commission (EC) presented to the European Parliament and the European Council a series of measures to address security issues. Part of this package was in response to U.S. security initiatives in the customs area. These measures bring together the basic concepts underlying the new security management model for the EU's external borders, such as a harmonized risk assessment system. The EC proposed a number of measures to tighten security of goods crossing international borders. These include requiring traders to provide customs authorities with information on goods prior to importing goods to or exporting goods from the EU, providing reliable traders with trade facilitation measures, and introducing a mechanism for setting uniform community risk-selection criteria for controls, supported by computerized systems. A technical working group is to be set up to further develop these measures (European Commission 2004).

### Air Cargo: Organizations and Initiatives

The world has in the past spent billions of dollars on security initiatives to protect the aviation industry as well as countries' freedom of movement and progress in spite of terrorism. Many countries and industrial organizations have already enacted or followed up with air cargo security laws, rules, or guidelines. These laws have affected the way that airports, airlines, and shippers worldwide must interact if they are to use, or be part of, the aviation community. Strengthening international standards, agreements, and common commitment is the logical next step to protect air travel and transport against terrorism. The main initiatives and organizations that strive to improve air cargo security worldwide, and with whom customs administrations need to enter into strategic alliances, are briefly described here.

### The International Civil Aviation Organization

The ICAO is a specialist agency of the United Nations that was created in 1944 with a mission "to ensure that International Aviation may be developed in a safe and orderly manner." Until the events

of September 11, 2001, the ICAO security model was regarded as adequate and sufficient to ensure the safety of passengers, aircraft, and goods. Contracting states are obliged to adjust their national legislation to bring it in line with the ICAO Conventions.

The Council of ICAO approved in June of 2002, in principle, an ICAO Aviation Security Plan of Action for strengthening aviation security. A central element of this Plan of Action is regular, mandatory, systematic, and harmonized audits to enable evaluation of aviation security systems in place in all of the 188 member states of ICAO, and to identify and correct deficiencies in the implementation of ICAO security-related standards. These audits should include aircraft security checks, background checks of any individuals requiring unescorted access to a security restricted area, and screening ability to detect weapons, explosives, or other dangerous devices which may be used to commit an act of unlawful interference. Security arrangements and measures should be extended to all civil aviation, whether international or domestic travel, and should cover all areas relating to access to the aircraft for staff as well as passengers and cargo handlers. Contracting states should share with other contracting states any threat information that applies to the aviation security interests of those States, as far as is practicable. They should also empower the appropriate authority to manage the national civil aviation security program.[8]

### The International Air Transport Association

The IATA is the world trade association of scheduled international airlines.[9] Airline members now total more than 260, under the flags of over 150 independent nations, and carry more than 95 percent of the world's scheduled international air traffic. The IATA has a Security Advisory Committee, which makes recommendations to airlines with regard to the security of all international aviation. These recommendations pertain to the security precautions that should prevail in all areas of the airport, including parking areas and boarding areas for passengers. Most airlines conform to these standards but adjust their implementation to

---

8. See the ICAO Web site at www.icao.int, and the Institute for Security Issues Web site at www.iss.co.za.

9. See the IATA Web site at www.iata.org.

local circumstances. IATA has established the Cargo Security Task Force (CSTF) to define the airline industry's position on cargo security and to ensure that all members implement cargo security measures properly. It deals with issues as they are put forward by member airlines. The CSTF coordinates its actions with the IATA Security Committee on issues relating to lobbying international organizations and national regulatory bodies, and promotes the implementation of unified cargo security standards worldwide. In that capacity it works with customs, airline members, freight forwarders, shippers, and government authorities to improve standards in shipment documentation and the automated tracking of cargo. Working closely with IATA CSTF is the Global Aviation Security Action Group,[10] which is an industry group that coordinates the global aviation industry's input to achieve an effective worldwide security system and ensure public confidence in civil aviation.

**European Civil Aviation Conference** The European Civil Aviation Conference (ECAC), based in Paris, was established to promote the coordination, better utilization, and orderly development of air transport within Europe, as well as to consider any special problems. Its most recent directive (December 16, 2002), issued by the European Parliament and the European Council, aims to establish and implement common basic standards on aviation security measures to prevent acts of unlawful interference against civil aviation; provide a basis for a common interpretation of the related provisions, called those of the Chicago Convention;[11] and set up appropriate compliance monitoring mechanisms.

---

10. Its members are: IATA, regional airline associations, International Air Carriers Association, Airports Council International, the International Federation of Airline Pilots Associations, International Transport Workers Federation, Airbus, plus participation and input from Boeing, ICAO, and INTERPOL as observers.

11. Annex 17 to the ICAO Chicago Convention (a convention held by ICAO in response to hijacking and terror threats that increased prior to it), the document on security with its mandatory standards came into being on March 26, 1974. It is the regulatory benchmark against which States are able to quantify their contractual commitments to international civil aviation. From it should evolve compliant legislation, a national program, and airport and airline programs.

**U.S. Transportation Security Administration Initiatives** The U.S. Transportation Security Administration (TSA) issued an Air Cargo Strategic Plan, which will set in motion a course of action to significantly expand current security policies, procedures, and systems for the protection of both cargo and passenger-carrying aircraft, and all air cargo operations (TSA 2003). TSA has tailored the air cargo security program to manage various security risks in a cost-effective manner. It is based on the TSA's goal of securing the air cargo supply chain, including cargo, conveyances, and aircraft, through the implementation of a layered solution. This system includes the screening of all cargo shipments to determine their level of relative risk, working with U.S. industry and federal partners to ensure that 100 percent of items that are determined to be of elevated risk are inspected, developing and ensuring that new information and technology solutions are deployed, and implementing operational and regulatory programs that support enhanced security measures.

TSA has established the Aviation Security Advisory Committee (ASAC), as a standing committee composed of federal and private sector organizations (U.S. Department of Homeland Security 2003). The ASAC was created in 1989 in the wake of the crash of Pan Am 103 over Lockerbie, Scotland. Its members include groups representing victims and survivors of terrorist acts, corporate shippers, freight forwarders, aircraft owners, airports, state aviation officials, aircraft manufacturers, and representatives of passenger and cargo airline management and labor. In May 2003, ASAC formulated recommendations to enhance air cargo security. These recommendations focused on strengthening the known shipper programs, enhancing regulations of indirect air carriers, and strengthening security for all cargo aircraft. TSA will use these recommendations to develop a strategic plan.

**The United Kingdom—Known Shipper and Cargo Screening** The United Kingdom is a leader in "known shipper" programs, having enacted laws and implemented programs for vetting shippers in the 1990s (Sander 2003). Operation Safe Commerce and the TSA known shipper programs are investigating, testing, and developing new technologies and alternative strategies for cargo and container security screening, which for the moment is usually conducted in facilities other than those of baggage security screening at most airports around the world. A future design strategy might be to consolidate baggage and cargo security screening at the same location.

A known shipper regime currently exists only for U.K. airfreight and requires that the shipper register its organization with the relevant authorities (U.K. or EU) on an official database of "known shippers." This information can then be sent electronically to port and customs authorities to alert them of the shipper's or the consignment's integrity. To achieve known shipper status, a company prepares a Shipper Security Plan (SSP), which demonstrates to customs and to the security forces that appropriate security measures are in place, covering premises and day-to-day operations, that secure and prevent infiltration by terrorists and their materials. Premises and security practices are checked periodically to ensure that SSP's are still appropriate and are being observed by the shipper.

### Land Border Security

Controlling cargo at land borders poses a different challenge for any country wishing to improve it. By nature, a border control point does not always constitute a bottleneck, unlike airports and seaports, which are characterized as mandatory transit points for all regulated international shipping. Because most countries lack "hermetically sealed" land borders, smuggling of goods that can present security threats can take a variety of routes. Also, land border control depends largely on local laws and regulations, making it difficult to set international standards for border control. For this reason, this chapter focuses on air and sea cargo control. Countries may use the security concepts and tools in this chapter and adapt them to meet their border control needs.

## Management Implications for Customs

Such major changes to the operating environment of international trade require customs to review its structure and operations to respond to the twin challenges of security and facilitation. Many administrations have started to adjust their technical operations, but there may be a need to consider

reforms of a much broader nature. These reforms are spelled out in the following sections.

### Strategic and Operational Planning

Strategic and operational planning should take account of the changing environment, including with respect to security threats. The fight against terrorism is a "whole of government" undertaking, and customs should assist in defining its role and specific responsibilities within this integrated approach. Customs should strive to establish targets and performance criteria for each of these tasks. In the process, customs should maintain communication arrangements with other key stakeholders in the public and private sectors.

To be in a position to implement these new responsibilities, customs should ensure that the necessary legislative and procedural frameworks are in place. Customs also needs to identify the resources required to implement these new assignments—human resources, technical infrastructure, and processes—and ensure that these resources are available where needed.

### Organizational Structure

Customs needs to consider how well its current structures match up to the new operating environment and the enhanced security requirements of that new operating environment, without unduly hindering international trade. Ideally, this question should be considered within the context of the issues addressed during the strategic and operational planning phases. Each customs administration has a different range of responsibilities and a different configuration and relationship with other national agencies. As such, the new demands placed upon customs with regard to security and facilitation and other national, regional, and international requirements may suggest some organizational restructuring. To become effective in managing security risks, for example, customs will need to perform risk-based management and assessment processes in the early stages of shipment, before ships or aircraft leave or arrive. It will also need to handle large quantities of data and enhance its analytical capabilities. There should be an ongoing migration from the current control processes, which are performed at the time of the transaction, to working intelligently by using data that becomes available in advance of the arrival of cargo. Some countries, such as Canada and the United States, have decided that a more drastic reorganization of customs is required to enhance the close cooperation necessary to address the security concerns of the day. The United States has created a Department of Homeland Security that has absorbed customs.

### Legislative Framework

Because customs administrations will be required to significantly alter their operating procedures to manage risks in advance of shipment, there may be a consequent need for governments to review and amend their national legislative framework to provide an adequate legal base. An existing legislative base for the sharing of information, and international or bilateral agreements on security and facilitation may have to be adjusted.

### Access to Information

Because the new customs controls will be based on information relating to goods and people associated with the supply chain, access to "real time" information from commercial operators and risk-based information from within customs and other government agencies becomes an important issue. Customs administrations should review their sources of information, data-handling capabilities, and legal protection provisions as part of a wider objective to develop policies and strategies for access to commercial and governmental information to aid risk management processes.

### Risk Management, Redeployment of Resources, and New Procedures

Modern customs practices and operations need to fully reflect the principles of risk management. So far, risk management has largely been used to deal with existing customs' priorities, such as the detection of violations of legislation pertaining to valuation, origin, and so forth. Now that security has become a major policy objective of customs, risk management principles need to be applied to meet this new concern.

In the context of security, risk analysis is required as early as possible in the supply chain, at the time of loading of the container, or before export, and before importation. In the future, risk assessment processes will be based on real-time information, supplied by those business entities that have ownership of the data, and sent via electronic means to customs at import or export. All of these procedures will occur before the departure or arrival of the vessel so that security concerns can be fully addressed and the vulnerabilities of the cargo supply chain taken into account. Electronic advance cargo information has therefore become a key factor in managing security risks. Each of the companies contracted to facilitate the handling and movement of cargo through its supply chain needs to be included in the risk analysis. The security preparedness of each of these companies has an impact on the level of risk associated with the overall chain. This includes the companies involved in loading the container at the overseas warehouse, the truck company that transports the cargo to the warehouse of the port terminal, terminal operators, the carrier, and the ports where the carrier stops en route to its final destination.

Risk management can operate in any organization, can use manual or automated applications, and can be used for either strategic or tactical purposes. While the overall risk management principles remain the same for all customs agencies, each administration will need to develop and refine its individual risk management regime to meet national and departmental objectives. Such an approach has the potential to improve effectiveness and efficiency and can significantly help build the ability to deploy resources toward the greatest areas of risk. Customs management should recognize that implementing effective security-oriented risk management implies a significant level of management attention. While the overall personnel levels may remain the same, many of the core activities of those staff members working within central policy divisions, as well as in regional and local offices, will be affected. There will also be implications for front-line control and enforcement units, intelligence capabilities, and the supporting infrastructure, including legal, information technology, and training services.

There are multiple risks to be considered, including targeting of the carrier by terrorists, using the carrier to transport weapons of mass destruction, or using it as a weapon to launch an attack on the destination country. Carriers can also be used to disrupt the infrastructure of a country. The risks to the destination country include the use of cargo to smuggle people or weapons or both, and the use of cargo to transport conventional, nuclear, chemical, or biological weapons into the country. The risk to the port itself is the potential loss of life or damage to property. In all cases, a terrorist incident creates the possibility of trade disruption and high security costs.

The fact that customs administrations will be performing many risk-based functions in advance of shipment means that adjustments in customs systems and procedures will be required. Enhanced intelligence, dissemination of security related information, and decisionmaking processes will also require consideration. Procedures to deal with security risks need to address issues of detection (screening, analysis, and focus on high risk) and deterrence (significantly reducing the terrorists' chances of success, and inducing them to invest greater efforts to achieve success). There is an advantage to developing a modular risk-based approach in that some or all elements may be applied according to needs and available resources. These elements include, visual and physical cargo inspection, document and manifest inspection, access control checkpoint, shipper and carrier control, security personnel, integrity, and technical capacity. Examples of new procedures are contained in table 12.1.

### Cooperation with Other Than National Customs Partners

Transport security requires the cooperation of all partners in the trade logistics network.

**Business Partnership** Security has always been high on the list of traders' concerns, because traders have a commercial interest in secure trade practices. Customs can greatly benefit from a close relationship with the trading community. A large share of trade is conducted among multinational enterprises, which have tight logistics chains and systematic approaches to ensuring the security of those chains. The information provided through advance notification can be used to enhance both security and trade facilitation. Representatives of the international and local Chambers of Commerce and of

the International Express Carriers Association are prime candidates for involvement in an ongoing dialogue.

**National and International Cooperative Arrangements** Customs is not the only agency responsible for security; therefore, an efficient government-wide approach to security will involve many agencies. A review of the cooperative arrangements between customs and other relevant agencies, at the national and international level, should be part of the overall strategy.

**Intergovernmental and Internal Communication** The renewed concerns of security in trade have given rise to the emergence of international agreements and bilateral security initiatives. The situation changes rapidly and the implementation of regulations and practices also vary. Customs will need to stay abreast of these changes and open formal and informal lines of communication with the relevant international agencies and trading partner countries that develop such security initiatives.

## Technical Means to Assist Security Checks

Security enforcement can draw on a number of techniques that operate together and reinforce one another. This section focuses on how best to incorporate the available security technology to improve cargo security (WCO 2003, U.S. GAO 2002b). The aim is to allow maximum system performance while ensuring the smooth flow of cargo.

Effective security arrangements for goods and passengers require that a central control point (CCP) be established to enforce mandatory passage for all containers en route to and from the ship or plane and to ensure that all ships and planes undergo the prescribed security checks. The CCP is placed at the entrance to the seaport, pier, or airport to match the data to information that was received in advance.[12]

A number of technologies have been identified for cargo inspection. These techniques vary in terms of their intrusiveness and their levels of

---

12. The process for receiving this data from the shippers must be established beforehand.

**TABLE 12.1    Selected Operational Practices to Enhance Cargo Security**

| Practice | Comments |
|---|---|
| Develop an industry-wide, computer-assisted cargo profiling system that can be integrated into air and sea carriers' and freight forwarders' reservation and operating systems. | • Develop a known shipper database.<br>• Make the database available to participating air carriers and freight forwarders.<br>• Define whether participation is voluntary. |
| Improve the oversight of and enforcement pertaining to air and sea carriers and freight forwarders. | • Allocate personnel for cargo inspectors. |
| Use identification card systems to verify individuals authorized to enter cargo-handling facilities. | • Require checks for individuals entering certain areas of seaports and airports.<br>• Determine requirements for identity checks at cargo facilities that are located off seaport or airport property according to the security plans of the individual facilities.<br>• The use of technology such as smart cards can make this process more efficient and reliable. |
| Conduct background checks on all individuals who convey and handle sea or air cargo and who have access to cargo areas and documentation. | • Require background checks for certain airport workers.<br>• Individual employers, in accordance with their security plans, determine requirements for background checks on other individuals who convey and handle air cargo. |
| Collect and disseminate information concerning cargo security, including threat-related information, to sea and air carriers, forwarders, and government agencies. | • Disseminate general threat information to the industry in security directives and information circulars. |
| Establish written policies and procedures and training programs for the employees of companies that convey and handle cargo. | • Require sea and air carriers that transport passengers to have security programs. |
| Employ a sufficient number of qualified security officers at cargo facilities to provide physical security. | • The use of security officers at cargo facilities is determined by the individual facilities in accordance with their security plans. |
| Use physical barriers (walls, fences) to guard against unauthorized access to cargo areas. | • The use of physical barriers at cargo facilities is determined by the individual facilities in accordance with their security plans. |

*Source:* U.S. GAO 2002b.

technical sophistication. They can be categorized as manual and low-tech equipment, intrusive detection technology (seals), and higher technology equipment (radiation detection pagers, and X-ray and gamma ray scanners). Each technology has its security-enhancing benefits as well as its potential drawbacks. Table 12.2 describes these technologies and the potential costs, benefits, and drawbacks associated with each. Some of the technologies are then discussed in greater detail. These technologies can be used for both air and sea cargo.

### Manual and Low-Technology Approaches

The most important tool of any inspector is a sharp eye. To augment this tool in manual inspections, fiber-optic scopes, hydraulic jacks, wet and dry vacuums, torches, magnesium arc cutters, chainsaws, drills, electronic stethoscopes, and many other common and specialized tools are used. It is unlikely that these tools differ greatly across the international arena.

Canines have been identified as one of the most effective tools to screen cargo, and their use has

**TABLE 12.2 Technical Means to Assist Security Checks**

| Type of Technology | Description | Costs, Benefits, Drawbacks |
|---|---|---|
| Technology to screen objects for threat | Technologies capable of detecting explosives and WMD, including radioactive, chemical, and biological agents. These include<br>• Gamma ray<br>• Pulsed fast neutron analysis<br>• Thermal neutron activation<br>• X-ray, including bulk EDS<br>• Radiation detection<br>• Trace detection<br>• Vapor detection<br>• Canine use | **Cost:** Ranges from under US$50,000 per unit for trace or vapor detection and canine use to over US$10 million per unit for pulsed fast neutron analysis and certain X-ray equipment.<br>**Benefit:** Can indicate potential presence of threat objects without opening packages and containers; canines are considered the best means to screen air cargo because they have the fewest drawbacks.<br>**Drawback:** Some technologies (pulsed fast neutron analysis, thermal neutron activation) can take an hour or more per object to screen; some technologies (pulsed fast neutron analysis, bulk EDS) are very costly; some technologies (X-ray, gamma ray) do not identify specific threat; some technologies (X-ray, gamma ray) cannot distinguish different materials in high-density cargo; some technologies (bulk EDS, pulsed fast neutron analysis) require building modifications to accommodate the equipment; all technologies have difficulty identifying biological threats. |
| Seals and other intrusion detection technology | Technology that can be used to determine whether a container or conveyance has been tampered with by visual inspection, or that emits an alarm, or notifies a central control station. Includes tamper-evident tape that shows "void" when tampered with, tamper-evident seals and locking devices, and electronic seals that emit a radio signal when they have been tampered with. | **Cost:** Ranges from under US$1 per unit for tamper-evident tape to US$2,500 per unit for electronic seals.<br>**Benefit:** Easy and inexpensive way to verify tampering with a container or other conveyance.<br>**Drawback:** All types of seals are known to be vulnerable to tampering, given the appropriate tools, time, and opportunity. There is no worldwide standard for radio frequency. |
| Blast-hardened containers (air cargo only) | Technology to harden cargo containers to control the damage caused by an explosion by confining it to the container. | **Cost:** At least US$15,000 per unit.<br>**Benefit:** Designed to protect aircraft from catastrophic structural damage or critical system failure caused by an in-flight explosion.<br>**Drawback:** Containers are expensive and heavy, which results in increased fuel costs. |
| Access control and authentication | Technologies to identify and authenticate individuals or vehicles allowed into a restricted area, or to authenticate a driver or individual loading goods. This technology includes picture badges, biometrics, and "smart cards." | **Cost:** About US$100 per unit for card reader devices; cards are a few cents each.<br>**Benefit:** Ensures that only authorized persons are handling cargo; creates a record of access to controlled areas.<br>**Drawback:** Does not protect cargo shipments from access by persons who are authorized to access cargo and cargo-handling areas. |
| Tracking systems | Technology such as global positioning systems and bar codes that can be placed on cargo and used to identify freight being shipped or to track the shipment. | **Cost:** Ranges from about US$.50 per unit for bar coding to about US$3,000 per unit for some radio frequency tags.<br>**Benefit:** Tracks the cargo throughout transport.<br>**Drawback:** Does not protect cargo shipments from tampering; technology only tracks the location of cargo. |
| CCTV | Video camera to monitor and store video images. CCTV can be used to record the loading of a container onto the ship or aircraft and the container can be inspected by viewing the archived video. | **Cost:** Ranges from about US$50 to about US$1,000 per camera; cost of additional components (switching and recording devices) vary greatly.<br>**Benefit:** Improves cargo surveillance by reducing time and costs.<br>**Drawback:** Video screens require continuous monitoring; does not protect cargo shipments from tampering. |

CCTV = closed-circuit television   EDS = explosive detection systems   WMD = weapons of mass destruction
*Source:* U.S. GAO 2002b.

increased significantly in recent years. In addition to screening cargo, canine teams are used at seaports and airports to respond to suspicious events such as bomb threats. According to the TSA, security experts, and industry officials, canine teams have proven successful at detecting explosives and are the most promising method for screening cargo (U.S. GAO 2002a).

### Intrusion-Detection Technology

Several technologies, including electronic seals and tamper-evident tape, could be used to help determine whether cargo has been tampered with during its chain of custody from the point at which a package is sealed by a known shipper to its placement on a ship or aircraft. An electronic seal (also known as a radio seal), for example, is a radio frequency device that transmits shipment information as it passes reader devices and indicates whether a container has been compromised.

Once security staff members are alerted to a possible problem, they can physically inspect the cargo. Seals range in cost from less than $1 per unit for tamper-evident tape to $2,500 per unit for electronic seals. Within the shipping industry, it is recognized that first generation seals can easily be tampered with, either by entering the cargo area without breaking the seal or by removing and replacing the seal. Now there are more advanced seals on the market that report motion and report any suspicious tampering exercise imposed on the container. In any event, seals should be used in conjunction with other security procedures as part of a comprehensive security plan. Industry officials have expressed concern about the use of electronic seals on aircraft because of the potential to interfere with avionics.

### Modern Technology in the Service of Security

The high technology category includes radiation detection pagers, trace explosives detection devices, X-ray scanners, and gamma-ray scanners.

Radiation detection pagers are specialist devices used to detect the presence of radioactive material that may present a potential health hazard and may be used in the production of weapons that depend on this material. Rogue nations or terrorist groups are prime suspects for buying such material from illicit traders. Radiation detection pagers are small, self-contained gamma radiation detectors that alert the wearer to the proximity of radioactive materials. Such devices, developed particularly for the use of government agencies and emergency responders, are approximately the size of common messaging pagers. Radiation pagers are several hundred times more sensitive than commercially available Geiger-Muller tube-type detectors, which are of similar size. Using such pagers, the authorities were able to detect in March 2001, radioactive material shipped through Uzbekistan en route to Pakistan. Future developments could include the installation of radiation detection devices on quay cranes, gantry cranes, and other container-handling devices.

Trace explosives detection devices and bulk explosives detection systems, which are currently used to screen passenger baggage for explosive material, can also be used to screen cargo containers.

### Container Scanning Equipment

Container scanning equipment can increase the number of consignments that receive customs attention without causing undue delay, and can identify illicit goods. The equipment requires a large capital outlay, however, and the process of introducing it, from conception through operation, affects the entire control and intelligence sectors and requires changes to the infrastructure and procedures of customs. To justify the outlay, and to ensure maximum return for the investment, it is necessary to ensure that scanning equipment is used effectively and that it is fully integrated into the risk assessment regime. The experience of customs administrations that currently use it suggests that planning for the equipment's introduction should precede the purchase of the equipment.

The acquisition of scanning equipment should be based on sound cost-benefit analysis. Costs include the capital, maintenance, and operational costs, while the benefits expected from the use of the scanner will depend on the specific objective for its introduction. Potential returns will, however, vary depending on the volume of traffic, its nature, and the assessed risk. For example, if the principal purpose is to control revenue, the overall value of traffic, the level of duty rates, and the projected level of misdeclaration are necessary components of the analysis. If drug interdiction is the major concern, the level of traffic from source countries is relevant. Benefits will obviously be a function of how effectively and efficiently the equipment detects irregularities. This will depend on the rate of container inspection, which is likely to be faster than with manual inspection; the integration of the use of the scanner with the availability of well-trained and experienced image analyzers; and the adequacy of the infrastructure for the equipment. Perhaps as important as those issues is the need to ensure that the risk assessment infrastructure is in place before introducing the equipment. Inherent within this is a requirement for pre-arrival data to permit the risk assessment procedures to take place in time to advise necessary parties that a given container has been selected for scanning. Good risk assessment practices require that a percentage of containers be selected at random, as a control sample to assist performance measurement of the risk assessment system.

**Selection of the Appropriate System** The purpose of container scanning equipment is to allow inspection of what is inside a container without opening the container; a process often called "non-intrusive examination." There are a number of ways to achieve this objective, although most systems are based on either X-ray or gamma ray technology. Whatever the energy source, it is governed both by the laws of physics and by economics. Higher penetration of the contents of a container gives a better quality of image but requires more energy, which is more expensive; requires more operational space; provides less mobility; and must have higher levels of protective shielding. Lower levels of penetration have a corresponding decrease in image quality and cost, but also have lower requirements for space and shielding, and provide greater mobility. Whichever type of system is selected, effective overall operation, from a technical point of view, is dependent on all of the parts of the system being effective. This includes the emission unit, the detection line, the linked computer system, and the image interpretation software.

While both X-ray and gamma ray technologies are available in fixed, relocatable, and mobile systems, there are differences between the two, which pertain largely to space and flexibility of use, as well as to infrastructure requirements. Fixed units require a purpose building with high walls, safety doors for entrance and exit, facilities for computer equipment and image interpretation, as well as sufficient space to accommodate the traffic flow. Vehicles must have adequate access to the facility. Observers note that this may require 5,000–8,000 square meters. Most fixed units are X-ray units. Mobile and relocatable units provide greater flexibility, and can be used to surprise traders that adjust their traffic pattern to avoid scanners. These units tend to be less powerful and would depend on a good energy source (X-ray). These disadvantages could be a limiting factor; however, less fixed infrastructure would be required because units can be moved to where the traffic flow is.

To determine the most appropriate system for any administration, it is necessary to consider its principal intended purpose. Revenue evasion suggests quantity differences between the goods and the declaration. The better the image quality, the more likely any such difference would be identified. Some goods, such as raw materials, fruit, and vegetables, and frozen foods, are denser than others and would require the higher penetration rates of X-rays. For drugs concealed in the fabric of a container, a system with a backscatter facility (in which the rays do not penetrate into the cargo but are scattered back from the walls) is beneficial, although it will have limited use apart from this. If prevention of human smuggling is a priority, lower penetration rates are preferable so as to avoid hurting people. Some systems are designed to be highly specific. For example, using a system that identifies the presence of Potassium K40, a chemical component of cigarettes, can target cigarette smuggling.

**X-Ray Inspection Systems** X-ray based inspection systems are the most common form of noninvasive inspection technology currently in use. The power source for X-ray systems is electrical, so the power can be turned on and off. It also means that in a site where the electricity supply is not certain, it is essential to have a back-up generator. X-rays detect differences in material densities to produce an image of the vehicle or container contents. Contraband detection is actually performed by the system operator who visually inspects the X-ray images for anomalies, sometimes with the help of sophisticated software.

When cargo and contraband are of similar densities, contraband detection is difficult. For example, the density of a plantain appears exactly the same as that of cocaine molded and painted to resemble a plantain when both are put through an X-ray machine. Density differences are projected across the entire width of the container; if a container is tightly packed, detection of contraband may be difficult, as the X-ray image will also be cluttered and visually complex. In addition, due to the projection methods, contraband could be hidden in the shadow of a highly dense item of cargo. However, the use of multiple X-ray beams can eliminate most of the shadow effects. Due to the nature of X-ray methods, specific materials cannot be identified; but it is possible with gamma ray systems to detect specific materials like drugs and explosives.

It generally takes X-ray systems only a few minutes to scan a standard 40-foot container, while some of the more advanced systems take only several seconds. However, total inspection cycle times may range from 7 to 15 minutes or longer, due to image analysis (which could result in scanning less than 100 containers per day).

**Gamma Ray Inspection Systems**    Gamma ray inspection systems directly apply gamma rays, or fast-pulsed neutrons to generate gamma rays, that produce images of the container's contents, three-dimensional mappings of content location, as well as other important information. Gamma rays are produced from natural isotopes such as Cesium-137 or Cobalt-60. These are radioactive sources and the energy emission is continuous. Because of this, the isotopes must be kept in a shielded cabinet at all times. Over time, the radioactive isotope's emission decreases, and would need to be tested for effectiveness. A gamma ray unit is much smaller than an X-ray unit, giving it a higher degree of mobility. This feature means that gamma ray units are far more likely to be mobile than fixed.

Claiming many benefits over X-ray technology, gamma ray systems may be a key step toward more efficient container inspection. Gamma ray systems can scan standard 40-foot containers in a few seconds and result in a total inspection time of less than a minute. The average inspection throughput of gamma ray systems is more than 10 times greater than the fastest X-ray system.

Gamma ray systems can cost 3 to 20 times less than X-ray systems in terms of initial capital investment, four to five times less in terms of installation, and when considering other benefits, gamma ray systems can yield a cost per inspection that is 50 times less than that of conventional X-ray systems. A downside is that gamma ray images are more difficult to interpret and would thus require better trained image analyzers.

**Cost of the Scanning Equipment**    Fixed units operate with the highest energy levels and are the most expensive. X-ray units tend to have higher penetration levels than gamma ray units and are consequently more expensive. Costs include the following:

- *Capital costs.* Fixed costs include both the purchase of the equipment and the installation of fixed equipment. Often new land needs to be purchased and access roads and parking facilities need to be built.
- *Maintenance costs.* In light of the safety issues involved in operating the scanners, adequate safety requires periodic inspections of the equipment to ensure proper functioning.
- *Operating costs.* Containers need to be selected, released, and moved to the scanner and images need to be made and interpreted. Staff members need to be trained.

**Other Operational Considerations for the Use of Scanners**    The introduction of scanning equipment will have a significant effect on the customs control staff. They should be fully briefed on the new procedures, and their justified health considerations should be addressed early on. Similarly, staff responsible for risk assessment should be brought on board at the early stages of the process to ensure that they have adjusted their procedures to the new technology.

Much is to be gained from involving the trading community in the early stages of preparations. They will need to be informed about the new procedures, and assured that these procedures will not cause excessive clearance delays.

Port authorities should be made aware of the need to facilitate the movement of containers. Port authorities may be concerned about the additional cost that new procedures would bring to port users, and whether this will affect the competitive position of the port.

The use of scanners will interest other government agencies such as immigration, border police, and the nuclear agency. They should be kept abreast of developments.

## Operational Conclusions

Despite additional security-related costs in all of the areas discussed in this chapter, the enhancement of cargo security in air and sea transport and shipping should ultimately benefit the countries implementing the measures described here. In an environment with greater security risks, such precautionary measures should facilitate the flow of trade worldwide, particularly to countries that have strict security measures in place. Thus, it should prevent costly delays at the ports of destination and shorten the time to resume shipping operations in the event of a large-scale incident.

Yet, the renewed attention to security issues is only a few years old and the many initiatives that have emerged still need to be confirmed and translated into detailed operational guidelines and instructions. The impact on trade is still somewhat uncertain. While it is desired that these new security measures contribute to trade facilitation, some observers are not fully convinced. Some, particularly from the developing world, wonder how security screenings that are certified by importing countries in some exporting countries but not in others, will affect the competitiveness of these latter ports and of the goods that pass through them. Some observers compare this situation with nontariff barriers, certainly as long as the advantages and disadvantages of complying with these security regulations and guidelines are not clarified to traders (Raven 2004).

The use of new technologies such as scanners holds promise for assisting customs in achieving its main objectives. Promoters of this equipment have at times simplified the process and inflated the expected advantages for customs. Hence, customs needs to exercise due diligence in deciding whether to acquire the new technology and what technology to acquire. It is clear that the use of this technology does not provide a magic solution. Effective use of new technology will depend on several factors. Foremost, it requires that the use of the equipment take place in an environment of active risk management. It also depends on good cooperation between customs and the port and

terminal authorities, as well as the availability of infrastructure and management to ensure a smooth flow of containers to the scanning unit. Staff must be trained and funding for maintenance and operation needs to be provided on time. Monitoring of the results against clear performance indicators is also important. Neglect of any one of these requirements will seriously detract from the results achieved and impede rather than facilitate trade.

As with other elements of good customs operations, success will depend largely on the commitment of port and customs leadership, the adherence of the staff to the impending changes in procedures, the cooperation of the commercial community (mostly exporters and shippers), and the ability to tighten relationships with them. Ports should establish supervision and control mechanisms for the security operation related to the port and customs, including the training and qualification of customs and port security personnel.

## Annex 12.A Port Risk Assessment

The company or government agency operating the port facility (the port operator) is responsible for setting security policies for the facility. Customs staff will need to be intimately familiar with these policies, and adjust their own operational policies. At a minimum, those policies must conform to international and domestic requirements. Yet, they should also reflect the port operator's objectives in maintaining safety and security on board its vessels, wherever they operate. This security concern will, by necessity, not be absolute because due consideration will need to be given to the delays it will impose on trade transactions.

An effective port security system integrates information gathering, quality control procedures, personnel, and equipment, and enhances the ability to respond to incidents appropriately and in a timely manner. Port Risk Assessment (PRA) must carefully consider the various possibilities and variants of security risks, including damage to facilities, transport equipment, or cargo, and the use of transport vehicles to smuggle persons or weapons, including nuclear material.[13]

---

13. See International Maritime Organization ISPS code Web site at www.imo.org/Newsroom/mainframe.asp?topic_id=583&doc_id=2689#code.

*Methodology for Port Risk Assessment*

The process of conducting a PRA should involve all who are responsible in any way for maintaining security at the port, as well as law enforcement and military staff of the facility's locale. The PRA should address the particulars of the port facility; the types of ships, cargo, and passengers it serves; the locations from which cargo or passengers are accepted; and the likelihood of various security-related scenarios and possible responses to those scenarios.

The information should be collected and processed to produce a list of vulnerabilities to be used in the risk analysis. Today, new technological products provide automated tools to perform security assessments.

*Elements of the Integrated Security System*

The integrated security system is made up of various elements.

**Information and Intelligence**  To learn about potential threats and discern changes and developments in a timely manner, information must be collected on a continuous basis and incorporated into current security principles, to ensure that the system remains effective and appropriate. An important starting point would be a historical analysis of terrorist planning, organization, weapons, and tactics. Careful analysis should yield reasonable, logical, and defensible assumptions regarding possible capabilities. The information should be collected routinely through several different channels, including through local and international media sources, an incident database, national and international publications and research centers, international security initiatives, and cooperation with local and international security agencies. The information collected must be processed and analyzed, and the risk analysis and preventive measures updated accordingly.

**Personnel**  Personnel is the most important and most sensitive element, due to the potential for human exposure to acts of malicious intent, and must be handled accordingly. Customs staff should be included in these personnel action programs. Such programs should cover recruitment, training, and inspections.

Recruitment of the most suitable candidate for each function is vital to the success of the entire operation, because security systems are too vulnerable to allow even the smallest breach. Initial staff training provides awareness, motivation, and knowledge, and might well be combined with real-life simulations to provide the experience of dealing with potentially dangerous situations and to ensure the prevention of errors, shock, or panic in an actual emergency situation. Personnel and system inspections and drills should serve to ensure that the highest possible level of professionalism is maintained. All personnel employed at a facility involved in the security process, whether directly or indirectly—including temporary employees who have access to sensitive areas—must be carefully screened. A sampling of these employees should be interviewed in the PRA.

**Technical Means**  The most suitable equipment to be used at a particular facility must be determined, taking into account the equipment type, quantity required, and location. When selecting the required equipment, the needs of the facility, the costs, and the dependability of the equipment must be taken into consideration. An analysis should be performed to examine the equipment in relation to all aspects of the integrated security system, including maintenance and operating costs, benefits, as well as advantages and disadvantages. The selected equipment must have a direct impact when properly implemented. Such measures ensure a high level of security, and must always be supported by operational procedures, training, and intelligence.

**Procedures**  A set of routine and emergency procedures covering the duties of security personnel, management, emergency service personnel, and crews must be formulated. These procedures should also outline the chain of command and the responsibilities of all involved parties, under both routine and emergency conditions. Each procedure will include definitions, methods (operational measures and requirements), and responsibilities. The procedures should be prepared and approved by the local authority, communicated to all relevant entities, and updated periodically based on changing needs.

**Control, Audit, and Drill**  Control and audit mechanisms must be established to continually monitor the attentiveness, alertness, and effectiveness of the security system. The mechanisms will take into account the types of operations of the port facility, personnel changes at the port facility, the types of ships served by the port facility, and other relevant circumstances and regulatory guidelines. The results of these activities (simulations, surprise visits, and so forth) should be recorded and analyzed to establish a cycle of continuous feedback and improvement.

## Further Reading

International Maritime Organization. http://www.imo.org/home.asp.

The Subcommittee on Coast Guard and Maritime Transportation Hearing on Interim Final Regulations on Port Security. www.house.gov/transportation/cgmt/.

U.S. Coast Guard. www.uscg.mil.

U.S. Customs and Border Protection (CBP). http://www.cbp.gov.

U.S. Department of Homeland Security. www.dhs.gov.

U.S. General Accounting Office. 2002. *Container Security: Current Efforts to Detect Nuclear Materials, New Initiatives, and Challenges.* Statement of JayEtta Z. Hecker before the Subcommittee on National Security, Veteran's Affairs, and International Relations, House Committee on Government Reform. Document GAO-03-297T. November 18, 2002.

U.S. Transportation Security Administration (TSA). www.tsa.gov.

## References

European Commission. 2004. "Commission proposes to strengthen security in European ports." Brussels. europa.eu.int/.

European Union. 2002. *Regulation (EC) No. 2320/2002 of the European Parliament and of the Council of 16 December 2002 establishing common rules in the field of civil aviation security (Text with EEA relevance)—Interinstitutional declaration. Official Journal L 355 of March 12, 2002.* EU: Brussels.

International Civil Aviation Organization. 1944. *Convention on International Civil Aviation.* Chicago. December 7.

OECD (Organisation for Economic Co-operation and Development). 2003. "Security in Maritime Transport: Risk Factors and Economic Impact." Directorate for Science, Technology and Industry, Maritime Transport Committee. Paris.

Pluta, Paul J. 2001. "Temporary Requirements for Notification of Arrival in U.S. Ports." USCG News Media Advisory. United States Coast Guard. *Federal Register,* Volume 66, Number 193, Docket USCG-2001-10689, RIN 2115-AG24. October 4. Washington, D.C.

Raven, John. 2004. "Security's Effect on Trade." *Journal of Commerce.* January 19–25, p. 38.

Sander, Charles. 2003. "Initiatives in Aviation Procedure." *Journal of International Security.* 13(11/12): 377.

TSA (Transportation Security Administration). 2003. "Air Cargo Strategic Plan." TSA Press Release, November 17. U.S. Department of Homeland Security. Washington, D.C.

U.S. Department of Homeland Security. 2003. "New Recommendations to Contribute to Improved Security in Air Cargo." Press Office. October 1. www.airportnet.org/depts/securitypolicy/DHScargoPR.pdf.

U.S. GAO (General Accounting Office). 2002a. *Aviation Security: Vulnerabilities and Potential Improvements for the Air Cargo System.* Report to Congressional Requesters. Document GAO-03-344. December 2002.

U.S. GAO (General Accounting Office). 2002b. *Container Security: Current Efforts to Detect Nuclear Materials, New Initiatives, and Challenges.* Statement of JayEtta Z. Hecker before the Subcommittee on National Security, Veteran's Affairs, and International Relations, House Committee on Government Reform. Document GAO-03-297T. November 18, 2002.

WCO. 2003. "Container Scanning Equipment: Guidelines to Members on Administrative Considerations of Purchase and Operation." Secretariat Note. Brussels.

# 13

# THE ROLE OF INFORMATION TECHNOLOGY IN CUSTOMS MODERNIZATION

*Luc De Wulf and Gerard McLinden*

## TABLE OF CONTENTS

## LIST OF TABLES

## LIST OF FIGURES

## LIST OF BOXES

Customs administrations today face a variety of political and administrative pressures and challenges. These include fluctuating workloads with static or declining resources, greater business expectations, and continuing pressures to meet often-conflicting government revenue, trade facilitation, social protection, and national security objectives. Moreover, customs administrations are increasingly required to integrate their systems and procedures with the sophisticated global logistics networks used by international trade and transport operators. To cope with these pressures and challenges, the international customs community looks to the applied use of information technology (IT) as a catalyst for improving organizational and operational efficiency and effectiveness. As a result, many modernization programs in the customs sector over the last decade have incorporated significant computerization components. Many customs administrations today use varying degrees of automation to support core customs functions such as goods declaration processing, revenue assessment, revenue collection, risk management, and management reporting.

The contributions of consultants Tony Mort and Alan Hall and of David Kloeden and Patricio Castro of the International Monetary Fund are recognized with gratitude.

This chapter is not designed as a technical guide for IT specialists, nor as a business process re-engineering guide. Rather, it summarizes the benefits of applied use of information and communications technologies (ICT) in the customs sector, and the important role ICT can play in the wider process of customs modernization and reform. The chapter discusses the advantages and disadvantages of nationally built ICT solutions and briefly presents the various off-the-shelf solutions that are presently on the market. It draws on some important lessons learned by a range of organizations, donors, consultants, and customs professionals, and emphasizes key issues to be considered when developing appropriate computerization strategies for the customs administrations of developing economies.

The first section highlights the importance of the use of ICT for effective and efficient customs operations. The second section focuses on the various components of a computerized customs management system. The third section presents the key points of a strategy for computerization of customs. The fourth section briefly describes the advantages and disadvantages of adopting national versus off-the-shelf customs management systems, and summarizes the major third-party products that are available. The final section contains operational conclusions. Where possible, case studies have been incorporated to illustrate points made.

## The Role of Information and Communications Technology in Customs Modernization

While it is evident that IT is assuming an increasingly important role in modern customs administration, the priorities, expectations, experience, capabilities, and resources of individual customs administrations vary considerably. Beginning in the early 1970s, customs administrations of many developed economies began to recognize the significant advantages of using technology-based solutions to improve their operational efficiency. They designed and developed their own customs computer systems, tailored to meet national needs. Over the years such systems have been enhanced, simplified, and in some respects standardized in line with international best practices. They were adjusted over time to capitalize on changes in information and communications technologies. As a result, such countries have computer systems that reflect modern customs management practices such as self assessment, clearance on minimum information, deferred payment of revenues, an intelligence-led and targeted risk management approach to clearance of international consignments, and sophisticated post-clearance audit regimes.

The historical experience with ICT of many developing and emerging economies has been quite different and not without significant difficulty and, in some cases, high financial cost. Lacking the necessary financial and human resources and access to a well-established domestic IT market, customs administrations of many developing countries have been slow to take advantage of the full potential offered by the appropriate application of modern technological advances. Fortunately, this situation has changed over recent decades, partly as a result of the commercial availability of customs-specific computer systems, and the international donor community that has stepped up support to strengthen customs administrations. Yet, the technological infrastructure and support available in many developing countries lags far behind that which is available in more developed economies, and increasingly, behind the technology-intensive business practices of many international traders. Moreover, when automated systems are introduced, they are often not used to their full potential. At times, the Customs Code requires the submission of paper documents for cargo clearance purposes, thereby duplicating information often provided to customs electronically. More frequently though, customs staff and management have been reluctant to implement the processing simplification required by the new IT systems or to adjust workflow and staff assignments accordingly. At times the ICT was introduced without first streamlining, standardizing, and simplifying existing manual processes and procedures. In such cases it is hardly surprising that the implementation fails to meet business expectations. Experience clearly shows that the basic principle should be to first standardize, consolidate, modernize, and simplify processes and procedures before computerization. In the absence of such simplification, the inefficient manual system may at best be replaced by an inefficient computerized system, with no gain to anybody.

Designing new, simplified practices and processes inspired by international best practices that have proven to reduce the compliance cost to the commercial community may require changes in government policy, in the legislative base, in the application of human resources management policies and procedures, and in the way customs policies and procedures are applied. Given the possible implications of these changes, much benefit can be gained from securing political support for the reform and full support from the government and senior management of the customs administration.

Customs often administers the value added tax (VAT) or similar consumption taxes. Hence, effective VAT administration at the border should be designed along with effective customs management practices. Customs initiatives, such as *de minimis* values for declaration, deferred payment of revenues, clearance on minimum information, periodic goods declarations, tariff-free policies and duty-free imports, and so on have to be carefully reviewed and integrated with any new VAT legislation. It should be clear, therefore, that the IT system should be designed to support a systems-based approach to total revenue administration at borders.

The automation efforts for customs processes must be cognizant of at least two key features of modern customs practices:

- *Modern customs processes must be simple and transparent but cannot be simplistic.* This does not, however, prevent complex systems from emerging, as customs needs to cope with a wide range of special issues, many of which pose considerable danger to revenue and other policy objectives. For instance, some goods, imported under suspense regimes on the grounds that they are not intended for home consumption, may be fraudulently diverted to the domestic market. This will require that special safeguards be provided.
- *Modern customs processes are migrating from physical to post-clearance control, with substantial reliance on self-assessment by taxpayers.* It is increasingly recognized that the key to effective revenue administration is voluntary compliance by the taxpayer, and that the key to voluntary

compliance is self-assessment. In the customs context, this means less emphasis on extensive physical inspection at the point of entry as traders (or their agents) declare the revenues payable—but with effective control exercised after goods have been cleared for free circulation. Post-clearance control will involve audit and other checks focused on addressing transactions in which the risk of incorrect declaration is greatest. Clearly, this will require reliance on an intelligence-led and targeted risk management approach that isolates high risk consignments, or consignments of special interest. Appropriately designed computer modules can help greatly.

### The Need to Integrate ICT in Customs with an Overall Modernization Program

In recognition of the pivotal role computerization plays in modern customs administration, many customs reform programs have placed a high priority on the selection and implementation of appropriate and effective technological solutions. Indeed, donors have often allocated large percentages of project funds to the upgrading or replacement of such computer systems. In recent years, however, there has been a growing acknowledgement of the problems and limitations of fully technologically-dominant modernization strategies and of the need to integrate technology into a wider and more comprehensive capacity-building effort across the entire organization.

A recent International Monetary Fund (IMF) publication (Corfmat and Castro 2003, pp. 119–120) addresses this issue and notes that "international experience has demonstrated that customs administrations often find it difficult to implement . . . complementary components of the modernization effort [and that it is not difficult to find examples] where inappropriate introduction and use of computer systems have exacerbated existing problems. In both developed and developing countries a disturbing pattern has been observed in which investment in computer systems in customs departments has grown steadily, while the average time needed for the release of cargo still exceeds several days, with no clear improvement in assessments and detection of frauds."

The stage at which each administration is currently situated greatly influences both the IT solutions that might be appropriate and the range of complementary reforms necessary to achieve sustainable improvements in overall corporate effectiveness. The three-stage typology presented by Appels and Struye de Swielande (1998) is instructive in this respect.

In *stage one,* customs administrations concentrate on the physical control of goods, relying heavily on high levels of physical examination and on the submission and inspection of paper-based documentation. Where computerization is employed, it is usually only for processing goods declarations and performing revenue assessments. Furthermore, the use of such systems is typically applied after the goods have arrived in the country of import. In many cases, such systems merely replicate existing manual processes and procedures. Customs officials typically perform data entry functions after submission of paper-based documentation, which is time consuming and can result in high error rates. Limited attention is often paid to research and analysis of the trader population, and risk management–based targeting of suspect consignments is often limited or nonexistent. The focus is on maximizing revenue yield and little attention is usually paid to developing trade facilitation initiatives. Quite a few customs administrations in developing and transition economies appear to be stage one countries.

In *stage two,* customs work emphasizes the collection and analysis of information, with decisions on admissibility, revenue assessment, and intervention made on a risk management basis. Such approaches require significantly more sophisticated IT infrastructure, both within customs and within the wider trading community. Direct input of declarations by importers or customs brokers is often a feature of such systems, and there may also be a limited amount of electronic information exchanged with other government agencies. Customs clearance of international consignments is typically provided in a timely manner; the use of resource-intensive physical inspections is often reduced, and concentrated on trade transactions that represent the highest revenue risk. Such an approach is typically designed to strike a balance between physical control and trade facilitation. This description characterizes the current situation in most developed and middle-income countries.

In *stage three,* customs administrations rely heavily on information and accounting systems, and on following the processes that constitute a trader's total activities. All information is exchanged electronically, decisions on treatment of consignments are made on a risk management basis, and the compliance record of traders becomes a key consideration. The focus is on informed compliance, intervention by exception, and rationalization of service delivery (for example, the single window concept). Customs resources are moved from resource-intensive, low-value activities at the time of arrival of the consignments, to low-resource, high-value prearrival clearance and post event, systems-based audit activities. All customs administrations in developed economies are now working toward achieving these methods of operation.

Each stage in this evolutionary model requires increased use of IT combined with the adoption of modern administrative systems and procedures. However, while many countries have broadly followed this evolutionary process, progression from one stage to the next is neither necessarily linear nor predetermined. The experience of many developed economies is that the need to redevelop or improve the functionality of computer systems typically followed, or occurred simultaneously with, the adoption of new and more effective strategies and working methods, such as those described in stages two and three above. The key lesson here is that automation must proceed as part of an overall modernization strategy for the institution, and must be accompanied by a range of complementary reforms in all aspects of customs administration. However, it is clear from many country examples that IT can act as a catalyst for the simplification of customs procedures for no other reason than that a good customs management system does not permit the continuation of idiosyncratic and overly bureaucratic work procedures. This catalytic role of ICT can at times precede the modernization of many other aspects of customs, as was the case in Bangladesh and Ghana (see box 13.4), and can achieve good results, if customs is ready to reflect the new discipline in its work procedures. Even in these circumstances, issues of sustainability need to be addressed head-on, and may contribute to the realization that non-ICT aspects of customs need to be dealt with to make the most of the possibilities offered by ICT. It should be clear that the use of IT is not a panacea, nor should it be seen as an end in itself.

The appropriate technological infrastructure for a given customs administration will depend on a number of factors, many of which are outside the direct control of the customs administration itself. The World Economic Forum's *Global Information Technology Report 2003–2004* provides a comprehensive analysis of the ICT readiness of individual countries and regions (Dutta, Lanvin, and Paua 2004). It takes account of the environment, readiness, and usage of information and telecommunications technologies. The research suggests that a certain threshold needs to be reached before there can be effective usage of, and consequent impact from, ICT. For customs administrations the implications of this research are particularly relevant. They do not necessarily need to employ the very latest and most sophisticated technological solutions available, but rather the ones that are most appropriate for their own operating environment, resource base, telecommunications infrastructure, and realistic development ambitions. In other words, the solutions should be coordinated, relevant, appropriate, and achievable to meet national needs, given local conditions and resources. They should be affordable and sustainable in the long-term, taking into account resource obligations, resource availability, political and administrative will, and long-term system support, maintenance, and flexibility. Clearly, there is no "one size fits all" approach for implementing IT in customs.

### *Summing Up: Benefits of Computerization in Customs*

Well-implemented computer systems linked to complementary improvements in customs practices will result in the following:

- enhanced customs control over international consignments
- improved control of exemptions, concessions, and duty suspension regimes
- reduced cargo clearance times for the discharge of customs formalities
- closer cooperation and rationalization of activities with other border control agencies

- uniform application of customs and other border-related legislation
- increased transparency and predictability for the business sector
- reduced opportunity for inappropriate exercise of officer discretion
- enhanced management information
- more efficient revenue collection and accounting
- more accurate and timely trade statistics
- more effective deployment of human and technical resources
- more accurate information for risk management and post-clearance audit purposes.

These benefits are further enhanced when it is decided to leverage the pivotal role that a customs administration plays in the entire international trade cycle, to create an electronically connected trade community wherein all stakeholders are members. Conceptualizing and implementing such a national approach to trade community development does not come spontaneously and requires a clear vision and political commitment that goes well beyond customs. However, successful implementation is possible,[1] either as national systems or as local seaport or airport community systems, through significant cooperative efforts from all concerned over many years.

## Key Customs Computer Applications

Many customs functions lend themselves to the application of technological solutions. The following areas are typically covered by customs-specific computer systems:

- inventory control of international cargoes
- processing of goods declarations for release of international cargoes
- tariff and documentation control
- determination and evaluation of customs value
- control of goods in transit, entering warehousing regimes, or imported under temporary admission

---

1. Such as in Chile, Singapore, Mauritius, the United States, Great Britain, Ireland, France, New Zealand, and Australia. Work is actively underway to introduce such systems in developing countries such as Ghana, Saudi Arabia, and Senegal.

- management and discharge of inward processing or drawback regimes
- risk management (risk profiles, risk analysis, intelligence analysis)
- broker applications
- management information systems
- customs enforcement
- revenue accounting
- production and maintenance of trade statistics and statistical analysis for identification of unusual trading patterns worthy of closer analysis.

Table 13.1 provides an overview of the customs processes and the ICT support that is normally built into a customs management system. It summarizes the entry and exit points for the cargo, the public and private sector stakeholders involved, the controls required, the strategies typically employed, and the IT elements involved. Table 13.1 illustrates the complexity of the task and the interdependence of the various elements necessary to establish effective ICT support for a modern customs administration. Such systems result in faster processing of goods declarations, targeting of controls to specific traders, improved revenue collection and control, data exchange, improved accuracy of data and accounts, improved management information, and up-to-date statistics. All these, in turn, play a key role in supporting post-release control activities.

Figure 13.1 illustrates the concept of modern customs risk management practices in relation to the processing of international trade transactions. It shows the functions and processes that a modern computerized customs management system supports.

The typical goods declaration and processing environment as represented on the left of figure 13.1 acts like a conveyor belt. Documentation for individual consignments are lodged with customs and processed on a transaction-by-transaction basis. This is a repetitive, time-consuming, and mechanical process. It also tends to be excessively control oriented if, as is the case for the majority of international trade transactions in mature countries, traders tend to be in compliance with established customs requirements. To facilitate trade and more accurately target deliberate revenue leakage, advanced ICT systems can support customs administrations in the move toward an operational method based on risk

management principles. Under such a system, higher risk consignments are identified through back-office customs activities relying on intelligence-led, risk management–based analysis of historical customs data. High-risk cargo is targeted and extracted from the normal processing path through use of an effective selectivity mechanism. Such consignments may then be subjected to full customs scrutiny including extensive documentary or physical examination (or both). Nonselected consignments are typically released with minimal scrutiny, as being of little interest to customs.

This targeted approach to cargo processing represents the frontline activity of modern customs administrations. It is extensively supported by, and reliant on, an effective feedback mechanism being in place to channel the results of post-release controls and systems-based audit strategies back into the risk management mechanisms so that profiles can be updated and risks continuously reassessed.

The post-release control and audit regime represents the safety net for the entire facilitation approach. It acknowledges that many aspects of customs interest, such as valuation verification, fiscal evasion, smuggling, and customs fraud, cannot be detected through examination of individual customs declarations. To uncover such indiscretions it is often necessary for customs to examine a trader's entire international trading patterns, including the movements of foreign currency. This can only be achieved through systems-based auditing of the entirety of the trader's international trade transactions.

In addition to these computerized customs management systems that assist in the clearance of cargo, the customs administration, like many other large organizations, also uses computer systems and other technological advances to more effectively and efficiently manage the organization as a whole. This includes the use of technologies in support of functions including the following:

- human resources management—payroll, career development, personnel placement, vacancy tracking, disciplinary processes, and effective use of resources
- management information and executive support systems
- asset and estate management
- fleet management

**TABLE 13.1    Customs Parameters and Information Technology Building Blocks**

| Entry and Exit Points | Entities Controlled or Affected | Controls Required | Strategies | IT Elements |
|---|---|---|---|---|
| —Seaport<br>—Airport<br>—Border or free zone<br>—Inland controlled area<br>—Post office | —Shipping and airline companies and agents<br>—Post office<br>—Transport companies and agents<br>—Port managers<br>—Airport managers<br>—Free zone managers<br>—Importers<br>—Exporters<br>—Customs brokers<br>—Freight forwarders<br>—Warehouses<br>—Other regulatory agencies (Immigration; Agriculture; Health; Cultural Heritage; Police; Central Bank)<br>—Banks<br>—Ship or airline crew<br>—Drivers<br>—Passengers<br>—Entity employees | *Physical*<br>—Secure entry and exit<br>—Secure movement<br>—Secure storage<br>—Inspection<br>—Seizure<br><br>*Information*<br>—Summary data (manifest)<br>—Clearance data (bill of entry)<br>—Verification data (inspection, additional info., audit)<br><br>*Authorities to deal with goods*<br>—To land (goods and mode)<br>—To move<br>—To store or unpack or break bulk<br>—To treat or transform<br>—To dispose | *Information*<br>—Planned and targeted distribution of information on legal require-ments, policies, procedures, incentives, facilities, and sanctions<br><br>*Facilitation tools*<br>—Gathering and mobilizing knowledge<br>—Single regulatory window clearance for transport mode, goods, and passengers<br>—Prerelease of cargo and passengers<br>—Client accreditation<br>—Periodic declarations<br>—Advanced customs declarations<br>—Electronic processing, payment, and clearance<br><br>*Control tools*<br>—Advanced cargo and passenger information<br>—International customs cooperation<br>—Effective threat assessment (intelligence service)<br>—Risk management and profiling<br>—Post-clearance audit<br>—Mobile inspection and audit teams | *Conveyance registers*<br>—Ships<br>—Aircraft<br>—Land transport<br>*Report (inward and outward)*<br>—Ship's manifest<br>—Aircraft manifest<br>—Load list<br>—Consolidations (including couriers)<br>—Passenger manifest<br>—Crew list<br>—Stores list<br>*Licenses and permissions*<br>By customs<br>—Store<br>—Move<br>—Pack and unpack<br>—Consolidate and deconsolidate<br>—Dispose<br>By other parties<br>—Reference data<br>—Licenses<br>—Permits<br>Declaration regimes<br>—Importation for home use<br>—Exportation<br>—Warehousing<br>—Transit<br>—Transshipment<br>—Carriage of goods coastwise<br>—Inward processing<br>—Outward processing<br>—Drawback<br>—Processing of goods for home use<br>—Temporary admission<br>*Goods declaration data*<br>—In accordance with WCO Data Model and including data fields necessary for all agency regulatory requirements<br>*Results of physical (by inspection) and documentary (audit) verifications*<br>—Automated, online, real-time input of results in standardized formats<br>—Categories<br>—Variations<br>—Treatment (consequences)<br>*Intelligence profiles*<br>—Information that has been analyzed, classified, and converted into profiles for targeting |

*Source:* Hall, Alan. 2003. Prepared for this chapter.

**FIGURE 13.1    Modern Customs Declaration Processing Environment**

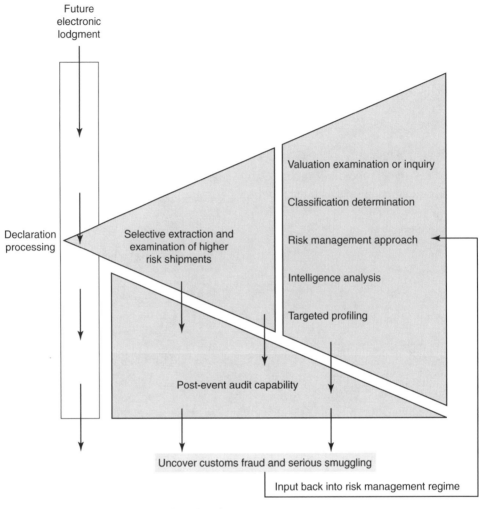

*Source:* Mort, Tony. 2003. Prepared for this chapter.

- inventory management of consumable assets and general logistics support for stores and supplies
- management and disposal of seizures
- operational planning and resource allocation to achieve tactical objectives
- intelligence collection, analysis, and dissemination to frontline staff
- audit planning and control, both internal and external
- physical examination of cargoes and persons, for example, X-ray installations, body scanners, chemical analysis, and so forth
- technical support to customs laboratories
- library management systems
- technological tools and systems in support of personnel development and instruction delivery
- general office automation tools.

These applications are not directly related to customs clearance, and before considering their introduction the administration should review its computerization strategy to decide whether to integrate these noncore functions into its computerized clearance system. In many instances it is likely that developing separate ICT solutions for these noncore functions may be the best approach.

## Developing a Computerization Strategy for Customs

Computerization is not an end in itself, only a means that should lead to better customs operation. Computerization of customs processes is likely to bring about the full advantage of process improvements only if complemented by associated changes to legislation, a review of organizational structures and human resources management policies, revised cargo clearance policies, and enhanced operational procedures. Failure to incorporate these associated institutional reforms will prevent computerization from fully achieving its role as a catalyst for change, to make customs operations both more effective and efficient. Note, however, that a careful introduction of appropriate ICT solutions, even unaccompanied by the full range of customs modernization features mentioned here, can at times lead to the simplification of clearance procedures, the acceleration of the clearance process itself, and the promotion of revenue mobilization.

The planning process must clearly identify the capabilities and functions that IT will support in meeting the immediate tactical needs and strategic goals of the customs service and those of its other stakeholders.

The process can be thought of as consisting of five stages:[2]

- becoming aware of a need for change in the use of ICT in customs
- setting up a steering committee that will oversee and manage the change
- planning—strategic, project, and business continuity
- development planning that goes from detailed investigation and analysis of the current system to implementation
- post implementation.

### Awareness of the Need for Change

Nearly all customs administrations realize that effective and efficient clearance of goods is a priority and have over the years come to rely in varying degrees on ICT. However, the technology has changed drastically over the last few years and the demands of the trading community for more efficient and transparent customs services also have become more vocal. Examples of such technological changes are the increased facility and cost efficiency of using the World Wide Web, Direct Trader Input (DTI), Electronic Data Interchange (EDI), and electronic payments. The Revised Kyoto

Convention urges customs to adopt advanced ICT, and the World Customs Organization (WCO) has periodically organized ICT fairs at which vendors present their wares and that constitute a forum for customs officials of various countries to exchange experiences. Also, much of the need to change ICT systems comes from the aging of the legacy systems and the difficulty of maintaining them. In some instances hardware platforms are no longer supported by their vendors and maintenance has become an extremely difficult and costly affair.

### Reliance on a Steering Committee

It may take a steering committee to organize ICT reform. The steering committee's task is to initiate, guide, and review any computer project within customs. This committee should have representatives from the management of the various departments that will be affected by the intended change. The Director General or Commissioner of Customs should chair this committee, as it will deal with core issues of customs control, revenues, and trade facilitation—the three key objectives of the organization. Also, the Ministry of Finance should be a member of this committee as the preparation and implementation of the ICT solution will be costly, and because the sustainability of the ICT solution will require annual funding for upkeep and upgrading. At times, it may be advisable to have a technical expert or external consultant on the committee to advise the other members of the technical issues. The steering committee will need to consider, at various stages in the process, what consultancy services to call upon to assist it in determining a good strategy and in working out the details of the chosen ICT solution.

### Planning

Good planning, at both the strategic and project levels, is crucial to the success of any IT program.

**Strategic Planning**    The long-term computerization plan for the administration will be the result of a strategic planning process. Such planning must include the following steps:

- Determine the objectives and commitments of customs—what are its strategic and tactical

---

2. This section is inspired by the WCO Revised Kyoto Convention, General Annex Guidelines, Chapter 7 Application of Information Technology and Communication Technology, available at www.wcoomd.com.

objectives in the areas of safety, trade facilitation, revenue mobilization, and so forth?

- Obtain a good understanding of the current state of the administration, operations, and systems and technology infrastructure of customs.
- Assess how ready the organization, its staff, and the trading community are to change the present way of doing customs business. Can the organization change? Does it have the required staff or can it acquire such expertise where it is missing?
- Define the target state scenario. This will provide a realistic and actionable transition objective for modernization based on current capacities, tactical readiness, and critical transition requirements as defined by the key stakeholders and decision makers.
- Apply a gap analysis that will compare the target state and the current state so as to arrive at the Customs ICT Modernization Strategic Plan. The plan is a set of specific project recommendations, the details of which will be worked out in the project stage of the planning process.

**Project Planning**    The Customs Modernization Plan consists of a number of projects, each of which will require individual planning and control. These projects may include detailed descriptions of the present processes, and may investigate whether to go with an off-the-shelf solution or a national solution, look into the human resources aspects of the greater reliance on ICT, investigate how the new system will be implemented without disrupting the ongoing clearance processes, study how customs' business will be affected if the ICT system were to fail temporarily and how the impact of such failures can be minimized. Funding and project leaders need to be assigned. Project leaders should receive a budget and timetable and clear direction as to who will be held responsible for what aspect of the project. Progress reports must be provided to the steering committee, which should provide continuous guidance, clarify sequencing and dependencies, and decide on the start of the development stage.

### System Development Process

Depending on the solutions chosen by the steering committee, the system development process stage will require a detailed review of the existing procedures, so as to instruct the detailed design of the new system. This will be the work of a systems analyst and should result in the preparation of a User System Specification that describes the main features of the new system and how it will affect management and staff. If the steering committee decides to acquire an off-the-shelf solution, the User System Specification will closely reflect that of the provider and will detail how customs will adapt or modify and add on to the processes proposed, and how this will affect processes, staff, and management. If a made-to-order solution is agreed upon by the steering committee, the next step will be to develop a specific system design. This specifies the computer and manual processing requirements, the inputs to the system, the outputs of the system, the computer files used to store information, and the segmentation of the processes into program design. Programming of the new procedures follows next. Care must be taken to fully document the exercise. A User Manual (for the customs officers that will operate the system), an Operations Manual (for the IT department staff), and the changeover instructions to ensure a smooth transition from the old to the new system should also be readied.

**Procurement and Installation of Hardware, Software, and Communications Equipment**    Equipment and software procurement is normally undertaken in parallel with the system development process. The type of hardware to be procured needs to be tailored to the specific computing requirements of the solution chosen. Proper procurement rules should be followed to ensure that customs gets value for its money. The World Bank has procurement guidelines that need to be followed when the project relies on Bank funding (World Bank 2004). The Bank frequently updates these guidelines. Box 13.1 describes the procurement process for Turkey's ICT project in customs, which complied with World Bank procurement guidelines. These guidelines should still be kept in mind even if procurement uses alternative internal or external financing, as these guidelines provide best practice to obtain value for money. The installation also needs to be carefully planned, as it involves site preparation, staff training at the ICT center, and communications planning, including the installation of data circuits, modems, and other communication infrastructure. The system will only be functional once fully tested in an operational environment.

**Implementation of the New ICT System**    Once all the ICT and complementary preparations are ready and the system has been satisfactorily tested, it is time to abandon the older processes and adopt the new ones. There are various options for implementing this transition to the new system. One option is to run the new system in parallel with the old system, and compare the results. However, this implies that the staff is running two systems at the same time, which may be taxing. This is likely to be an option only for customs services that deal with a relatively small number of declarations per day, or can be done on a pilot basis at a site with few declarations per day. The generalized transition then takes place when the eventual problems with the new system are ironed out. If testing was done in a comprehensive manner this should not take too long. The second option is to roll out the new system in a pilot site. The pilot site can be a smaller site, with less risk of disruption and good back-up procedures. Airports are often used as pilot sites, as trade there is more streamlined and less varied than at major seaports and land border crossings. Trade documentation is often also of higher quality. With this option, the resource-intensive training of customs staff, traders, and brokers can be phased out over time. Success in the pilot site then is followed by gradual rollout to the other sites. The third option is to organize the transition from the old to the new system for a given day. In this case, solid testing and good preparation of a contingency plan for major problems, or even breakdown, will pay off handsomely.

### Post-Implementation Evaluation

Any good project cycle includes a thorough post-implementation evaluation, to verify that the initial objectives of the project were attained and whether the cost estimates were realized. Obviously this evaluation will only be completely valid if the project preparation phase clearly spelled out the expected costs and benefits in terms of revenue mobilization, integrity, trade facilitation, and security. Customs staff and management as well as users should be associated with this evaluation. Their observations may serve to modify certain aspects of the new processes.

## Systems Options

When considering the introduction of computerization in any organization, there is always the basic question of developing the system in-house, outsourcing development to a third party, or acquiring an existing system from the market. Each option has its advantages and disadvantages, depending on the local business environment and the technological environment in which the organization operates. Also, there is the question of whether the system will be solely a customs management system or will have broader ambitions, such as electronically connecting all members of the trading community.

As noted earlier, computerization is not an objective in itself. It only makes sense if it serves as a tool to support implementation of modern customs management practices. To do this, the technology should fully take into account the practical realities of the local environment, resources, and capabilities. In particular it should be attuned to the size and scope of the customs function and the organizational capabilities to deliver and support. The solution must be coordinated, relevant, appropriate, affordable, and sustainable. There is no "one size fits all" solution. This section discusses the advantages and disadvantages of national IT systems, the off-the-shelf solutions, and the "beyond customs" systems. Given the rapid developments in the IT arena, this section provides only broad guidelines and suggests that any decision on IT solutions carefully consider all the options available. The section also recommends that customs officials visit with neighboring customs organizations to learn from their experiences in the selection and implementation of the most appropriate system.

Occasionally the decision to automate customs processes is made by the government within the context of a wider information and communications strategy for the public sector. This may narrow the options available to customs, yet it opens the way for substantial synergy and crossfertilization. This will be particularly important if the objective of the government's ICT strategy is to connect the various members of the trading community electronically.

### Developing an In-House IT System

Developing an in-house system, whether through use of existing resources or through an outsourcing

## BOX 13.1    IT System Procurement and Costs: Case Study—Turkey

A major customs IT modernization project can be a complex, multiyear, and costly exercise. First, a choice needs to be made either to adopt and customize a package to local requirements or to try bespoke development. In addition to the question of applications software, many more decisions are needed, including choices of database, operating system, hardware, networking, training, transitional arrangements for system deployment, and follow-on support. Turkey's experience is useful in terms of its complexity, timeframe, and compliance with World Bank procurement requirements, which can be extrapolated to other sources of funding or national circumstances. Although several years and much effort were expended in Turkey, the results were impressive and have been sustained.

*Software selection.* Given the poor results from prior attempts to develop their own systems, Turkish customs decided upon a package. Two options were available in the mid-1990s, and the authorities chose SOFIX over ASYCUDA, primarily because the source code that allowed for subsequent enhancement of the software was provided. The application, its customization (including translation to Turkish), transfer of "know-how," plus hardware, facilities, and support for pilot implementation were provided at a cost of US$6 million under a contract with a consortium of French customs and the French IT firm, Bull S.A. Support and funding were provided by the French government, but with subsequent system rollout dependent on World Bank financing, and technical assistance from the IMF.

*System deployment.* Plans required SOFIX to be deployed to 50 sites spread across Turkey, of which six sites had heavy transaction volumes, 12 were medium-volume sites, and the rest had more moderate traffic. Concurrent with preparations to pilot implementation of SOFIX at the busy Istanbul airport site, a two-year procurement process was undertaken to ensure that the most capable, and best value-for-money vendor was chosen to deploy SOFIX under a turnkey contract that covered a multiplicity of extra services and goods. The original selection of SOFIX was conditional upon open competition in the award of the deployment contract, which was expected to cost around US$40 million.

*Prequalification of deployment bidders.* A prequalification exercise was undertaken to limit bidders to those firms who could demonstrate the wherewithal and experience to successfully complete such a contract. Six out of seven applicants were prequalified following a yearlong process that ideally should have been completed in half the time. All but one of the applicants were multinational IT firms, with the exception being a Turkish conglomerate (and eventual winner) that was the agent for a United States hardware manufacturer.

The deployment contract required 50 customs sites to be equipped with hardware and facilities, construction of a national network linking all the sites, plus a new national center, with a sophisticated data warehouse. The successfully piloted SOFIX system had to be ported to the UNIX platforms offered by the bidder, and the contractor had to complete a massive training exercise covering thousands of customs officials and traders. Of the US$40 million budgeted, the following breakdown of costs was anticipated: 55 percent for hardware, 20 percent for services, 13 percent for training and implementation, and 12 percent for additional system and application software.

*Two-phase bidding process.* In phase one, bids were made against the clearly defined requirements, but without prices. Of the six qualified bidders, four submitted bids; one bid was made jointly by two qualified firms, and one bidder dropped out. All bids were judged acceptable, so all bidders were given a chance to rectify deficiencies that were identified to ensure full compliance at phase two.

In phase two, updated and corrected technical proposals were submitted, including full costings. Bids were subjected to a thorough technical evaluation and scoring that resulted in the award of a contract for around US$28 million, a substantial saving over anticipated costs. The contract required delivery of all goods and services over 30 months in five batches, with several implementation teams operating concurrently around Turkey in conjunction with a massive training and change management exercise. Given the complexity of monitoring the prime vendor's performance against the contract terms, a separate contract was awarded to an independent third party to verify compliance of the prime contract and to ensure systems, facilities, and hardware were fully integrated, and all services and goods were to the required standards.

*Source:* David Kloeden, Note prepared for this study.

arrangement, has certain advantages—such systems can more easily meet specific needs of the individual customs administration, future modifications can be prioritized and controlled internally, and customs has full control over the computer software. Some countries initiated their own ICT systems early on, at a time when the most readily available system at that time (ASYCUDA) was still not the powerful system it is at present, and did not satisfy the country-specific ambitions and requirements of the time. For instance, Morocco, where managing the temporary admission system was important as early as the early 1980s, chose to develop its own ICT system gradually, fully taking concerns regarding temporary admission into account. When that system became increasingly obsolete, the solution was to build on to the existing system rather than go for an outside solution, which, in the minds of the policymakers would have involved changes they were not ready to make. Developing an in-house system has the additional advantage that it may strengthen the local expertise that can be drawn upon later to support the long-term sustainability of the system. Whether local ICT capacity will be built up depends greatly on the quality of the local staff that can be attracted to the project and how it is integrated into the external teams that are often called in to develop the ICT system.[3] In the case of Morocco, the local customs staff is fully integrated into the foreign consultant team, holding good promise for the ability of customs to maintain and further develop the system once it is handed over to them. (See box 13.2.) In some other countries, the national customs organization has not been able to attract expert IT staff (largely because of its inability to provide attractive and competitive compensation packages) and has to rely on local ICT consultants. Obviously, as their experience is outside customs and tends to rest in individual expertise, this approach does not provide the same assurance for the future availability of these resources to maintain and upgrade the system once the project is completed. Also, ICT staff in

customs have frequently been attracted by lucrative career prospects outside customs, depriving customs of the in-house expertise. In Uruguay, the ICT system (LUCIA) was built from the ground up through a joint effort between customs and a local software firm. Uruguay customs relied heavily on the support of staff from Peruvian customs, which had implemented an in-house system in the early 1990s. The project used the functional specifications of the Peruvian system, adapted to the needs of Uruguay and to the local and regional norms and regulations, as the starting point for defining the system requirements. The system was gradually implemented (during 1998–99) throughout the country for all customs operations and is operated jointly by customs and the Broker's Association. Maintenance and support is outsourced. Uruguay customs is pleased with the system, and relies heavily on it to support its control strategy. The user community is also satisfied with the system, which they refer to as reliable and easy to use. The Senegal case study (box 13.5) also contains some interesting features of building a national solution to computerized customs management, particularly as it has ambitions of connecting to other members of the trading community.

Experience has also shown that customs managers at times underestimate the complexity of programming the various modules of the integrated customs processes and overestimate their capacity either to adapt an off-the-shelf system to their own needs or to create a new system that reflects the national preferences. It has often not been easy for customs technical experts to communicate these complexities to the ICT experts, causing implementation delays and cost overruns. Also, if these operational requirements are not well specified and internalized in the customs management system at the outset, it becomes difficult to retrofit them.

Designing national systems tends to be expensive and substantial cost overruns are frequent. Customs managers should carefully review the advantages and disadvantages of trying to "reinvent the wheel." Given the number of negative case studies to date in developing in-house systems, there is much to be gained from carefully studying the generic software products currently on the market, and to review in a flexible and critical manner how to acquire the specific functionality not present in those products. After wide consultation with

---

3. In the case of Russia, given the extensive professional investment within customs, the customs administration chose to develop and maintain many of their computer systems in-house. This is acknowledged in the current Bank-funded initiative for customs reform, while at the same time various other elements of their reform program are testing the market through consultancy support for specialist assistance in key areas.

## BOX 13.2 Morocco Case Study

In the 1970s, Morocco implemented computer support for the management of special import regimes—it was not much more than mechanized accounting support. In 1992, customs rolled out an in-house system that improved customs clearance, but fell short of meeting all of customs' business needs and was not responsive to the rapidly changing needs of its users. Some key customs activities were only partially computerized, and others were not covered at all.

In the mid-1990s, customs became increasingly aware of the shortcomings of SADOC (the computerized support system for customs clearance) and undertook an in-depth assessment of SADOC, and reviewed the future requirements and the design of operational models reflecting the new customs environment. This led to the 1999 Customs Computerization Master Plan that proposed to (a) consolidate the SADOC system to ensure continuity of computer support for customs clearances, (b) totally overhaul SADOC to bring it in line with the requirements of a modern customs organization and the latest technologies, including an advanced electronic commerce–based environment, and (c) build a data warehouse that would support management decisions as well as risk analysis.

Morocco investigated options of changing over to an off-the-shelf system, namely ASYCUDA, and eventually chose to build on the SADOC system. This decision largely stemmed from three issues: customs' desire for strong modules to manage temporary admissions and payments in dispute, which they viewed as not fully developed in the ASYCUDA system; their belief that ASYCUDA was not sufficiently tested in large countries with a complex set of trade procedures and regimes; and Morocco's reluctance to enter into a dependency relationship with the UN Conference on Trade and Development (UNCTAD) regarding operational support and maintenance of the software. The government wanted to develop the computer skills within Morocco, at the customs department as well as at local consulting firms. The fact that the in-house system was a national IT solution convinced some to favor it.

The Master Plan called for transitional implementation, including a five-year migration to an open standard operating environment (UNIX) that combined robustness, transparency, and amenability to upgrades. The responsibility for consolidating the existing systems to ensure better customs services in the transitional period was given to customs. To do this, customs strengthened its own computer management and development capacity by retraining its computer programmers and recruiting several computer scientists. Emphasis was placed on ensuring the new systems would be responsive to the needs of its customers and improving the quality of system support, with revised procedures, standardized operations, and documentation of changes.

The development and implementation of a totally new customs management system involved the following:

• the preparation of a detailed description of the various functions of the new system and an estimate of the development and implementation costs
• the preparation of a detailed study of the new IT system, taking recommendations of users into account
• project preparation that involved a detailed study of system requirements for the new computer network system, front-end hardware and software for customs brokers and importers, as well as system requirements at the customs clearance locations and headquarters, and the development of all functional modules of the new system and the test platform
• detailing the implementation requirements, including process changes and staff training
• gradual rollout, with modules launched one at a time over the total territory of the country.

Staff and clients were exposed to intensive training before the rollout of each stage to ensure smooth adoption. This rollout process also permitted full and thorough testing of the system in all its application environments.

The financing of the preparatory studies as well as the required investments were fully borne by the investment budget of customs through the Ministry of Finance, in contrast to many other computerization initiatives by customs administrations that rely heavily on outside financing sources and technical assistance.

*Source:* Steenlandt and De Wulf 2004.

practitioners in the field, the authors find that there is a presumption in favor of off-the-shelf solutions.

### Adopting an Off-the-Shelf Solution

There are a number of existing and emerging customs management computer systems available today on the market. All have a core of similar modules that permit customs to manage its customs clearance operations using computer and communications-supported modules. Not all of these solutions have the same modules and some of them have been more widely tested in the market than others. It is not the intention here to list the functionality of each available system and compare them to each other. The products on the market evolve rapidly and current details can be found on the respective Web sites for each product. This list is also not intended to be exhaustive as new products are emerging on a regular basis. The Bank retains its neutrality with regard to these products, in line with its established procurement rules.

Note that many of the off-the-shelf packages do not provide all the necessary modules a country might want to use, or provide modules that are not as well defined and articulated as particular country objectives and circumstances warrant. This should not necessarily lead to rejection of these off-the-shelf solutions in favor of a national solution because most off-the-shelf solutions are designed with the capacity to interface with specialized add-on modules that can be custom tailored to adequately respond to national objectives. Examples of such add-on modules are the selectivity modules that are presently made available by a number of preshipment inspection (PSI) companies. Another example is derived from the implementation of ASYCUDA in Bangladesh, where an external contractor was recruited to prepare four country-specific advanced modules: risk analysis, management information system, bonds and warehouses, and drawback system. What can be learned from the Bangladesh exercise, financed by a Bank credit, is that the preparation of these modules needs to be carefully dovetailed with the main customs management system itself and that to be fully operational, these add-ons require the same attention to staff training, infrastructure changes, and modification of workflow and staff assignments as the main computerized customs management system.

**ASYCUDA**  The UNCTAD ASYCUDA (Automated System for Customs Data) Program[4] was developed in the early 1980s to automate the operations of customs administrations. It is presently installed in 84 countries. The program was developed to support customs administrations in their objective of trade facilitation and efficiency of customs clearance control. The program is provided at no cost, which means that countries do not pay for the software development costs. Countries do pay, however, for the system implementation that is undertaken by the UNCTAD Technical Assistance project. The implementation comprises general support activities, training, documentation, and development of specific support on a cost recovery (nonprofit) basis. In line with agreements between the UN and the international donor (UNDP or the European Commission, for example) and the UN guidelines in this matter, UNCTAD is limited to a markup of 7–13 percent over cost.[5] This markup can be partially used by the ASYCUDA Program to finance further development. UNCTAD has developed three versions of ASYCUDA so far and is currently rolling out ASYCUDAWorld.

- *ASYCUDA Version 1 (1981–84).* ASYCUDA Version 1 operated on early personal computers (PCs). Created at the invitation of the Economic Community of West African States (ECOWAS) Secretariat, its main achievement was to assist in the preparation of trade balances and other related trade statistics. Implemented in three countries, it demonstrated that computerized customs clearance systems could be developed on low-cost computers.
- *ASYCUDA Version 2 (1985–95).* ASYCUDA Version 2 took advantage of the availability of new programming languages and new operating systems for PCs. This version introduced Local Area Network computing in hundreds of customs offices, allowing for a comprehensive integration of functionalities. Initially running on the only multitasking operating system (PROLOGUE) available on the market, ASYCUDA Version 2 was, over the years, overhauled by the UNIX operating system, opening the way to

---

4. See the ASYCUDA Web site at www.asycuda.org/.

5. This markup is modest compared with development expenses in commercial software ventures.

high transaction volumes and, consequently, ASYCUDA implementations in large customs offices. UNCTAD does not develop its functionality anymore. It was introduced in 40 countries and still operates in 15 countries that have not yet migrated to ASYCUDA++.

- *ASYCUDA++ (1992–present).* ASYCUDA++ is based on real client-server architecture, takes advantage of the power of object-oriented programming languages and uses the potential of relational database systems such as Oracle and Informix. From a technical standpoint, ASYCUDA++ is an advanced customs information system that integrates a number of modern and robust technologies.[6] ASYCUDA++ built on the full suite of customs modules provided in ASYCUDA Version 2, and added more customs functionality, particularly in the areas of Direct Trader Input, risk management, and transit monitoring. ASYCUDA++ client computers feature a text-based, multiwindow user interface. The most common operating systems on ASYCUDA++ client computers are MS/Windows 9x and MS/Windows XP. The ASYCUDA Program has incorporated the complementary use of another generation of technological tools and the emergence of the widely used Internet environment. A first outcome of this work is that the current version of ASYCUDA++ allows customs brokers to submit declarations through the Internet. The ASYCUDA++ EU Version is currently operational in four European countries that became members of the EU in May 2004—Estonia, Latvia, Lithuania, and Slovakia.

- *ASYCUDAWorld.* ASYCUDAWorld is UNCTAD's solution for e-customs. The development of this system began in 1999 and a first roll out (in Moldova) was undertaken in early 2004. It allows customs administrations and traders to handle most of their transactions—from cargo manifests and transit documents to customs declarations—via the Internet. Its platform is based on a sophisticated technical architecture that does away with the need to maintain permanent connection with a national server—something that is especially important for countries with unreliable

telecommunications. Where telecommunications are more reliable, the traditional World Wide Web approach can be used. ASYCUDAWorld can work with all major database management systems (including Oracle, Sybase, DB2, Informix, SQL Server) and most operating systems (Linux, Solaris, HP-UX, AIX, and MS/ Windows). The platform's use of XML (extensible mark-up language) allows the exchange of any document inside and outside the system, between customs administrations and traders and between customs administrations in different countries. It is "Java-native," meaning that it was designed as an open standard to be used with Java and that countries can thus modify and extend the system without requesting assistance from UNCTAD. It implements the concept of "e-documents" that, once plugged into the ASYCUDAWorld platform, reflect in the IT world the paper documents used currently and implement the required business processes. ASYCUDAWorld is being developed to coexist with and operate in the environment of ASYCUDA++. Each beneficiary country can decide when to implement ASYCUDAWorld according to its technical decision and available financial resources.

**Trade Information Management System**    Trade Information Management System[7] (TIMS) is a product of Crown Agents. It is a software package aimed at supporting and sustaining the efficient day-to-day operation of a modern customs department and consists of a full declaration system as well as stand-alone or integrated support modules. The Declaration system includes the usual modules, such as manifest handling and acquittal, data entry, tariff management, receipt and validation of Single Administrative Documents, accounting, and trade and revenue reporting. The stand-alone or integrated modules include intelligence handling systems, risk management, price referencing support in accordance with GATT regulations, transit control, exemptions management, and management information. The system is modular in design. It can be installed gradually, or some modules can be used in combination with other customs management systems. The system can be

---

6. UNIX servers, Windows 9x/2000/XP clients, Internet Protocol, and so on.

7. See the Crown Agents Web site at www.crownagents.com/.

implemented in environments with limited or advanced levels of communications capability and can grow to maximize the benefits as more sophisticated technology becomes available. The full TIMS has been installed in Mozambique and Angola, in conjunction with the management contract that Crown Agents has with customs in these two countries. Partial rollout has been undertaken in, among other countries, Bulgaria and Kosovo.

All TIMS functions are structured using local and central (or regional) modules with EDI facilities allowing the transfer of data. Where it is possible to take advantage of a wide area network, TIMS can be implemented in the distributed mode as a result of its modern two-tier database architecture. TIMS was developed using an open system technology. The underlying database is ORACLE. TIMS is available on any UNIX or Microsoft Windows 2000 or XP platform.

**SOFI and SOFIX**    The Solutions Françaises Informatiques (SOFI) system was developed by French customs and became operational in 1974. Designed to run in a mainframe environment, it was first rolled out at the airports of Paris and was gradually extended to all Custom Houses in France. The original system went through several upgrades and redesigns, and is still in operation today.

Several attempts were made at creating an export version, and systems based on the SOFI concept but still under proprietary mainframe operating systems were successfully rolled out in Egypt and Côte d'Ivoire in the early 1980s. With the arrival of the open systems concept and the consolidation of the UNIX operating system, in the early 1990s French customs decided to support the development of SOFIX (SOFI under UNIX), both as a replacement for SOFI for their own use, and to offer the system to other countries. The development was undertaken through a joint venture with several French hardware and software companies. The idea was to offer the system as an open code product, with a small kernel around which different modules covering the main customs functions were organized. One of the premises of this approach was that the system could easily be adjusted to local requirements.

In the end, SOFIX was never implemented at French customs. Attempts to roll it out in Gabon and New Caledonia were abandoned as well due to

various reasons. In Turkey, however, the local adaptation of SOFIX was undertaken with success (box 13.3) and is still operational. Another version of SOFIX was adapted to the requirements of Argentina, where it was rolled out in 1993, and was subsequently adapted for implementation in Paraguay in 1995. Up-to-date versions are still in use in both countries. A simplified version was also implemented in 1999 in French Polynesia (Tahiti) and is still operational.

SOFIX implementation is no longer directly supported by French customs. However, a consultancy firm (Solutions Informatiques Françaises [SIF], one of the original partners in the joint venture) continues to support SOFIX and its derivatives in Argentina, Paraguay, and French Polynesia and is actively interested in applying its expertise in other countries.[8]

SIF is currently rolling out a new Web-based version of SOFIX, called SOFIWEB. SOFIWEB is functionally equivalent to the current version of SOFIX, and benefits from the use of J2EE technology and object-oriented development and implementation tools.

**TATIS**    TATIS[9] provides IT-enabled customs solutions to customs administrations globally. These solutions are marketed, delivered, and supported by TATIS' business partners, Hewlett-Packard, Pricewaterhouse Coopers, and Société Générale de Surveillance, in combination or individually. The scope of the product range extends from automated declaration processing through to management of suspense regimes, such as transit, and is completed by compliance and enforcement solutions with risk and valuation systems as well as inspection and workflow management. These solutions include guarantee management, covering risk management, claims administration, financial clearing, insurance and guarantee placement for duty suspense regimes; and extend beyond customs to include financial institutions, operators, and traders. These applications can function independently or as an integrated suite.

The solutions are along the lines of the Revised Kyoto Convention and are consistent with the

---

8. See the SIF Web site at www.sifamerica.com/html/inicio.asp.

9. See the TATIS Web site at www.tatis.com/solutions/index.html.

## BOX 13.3 Customs ICT Deployment Case Study: Turkey

In January 1996, Turkey entered into a Customs Union with the EU and worked as early as 1993 on the modernization of its customs organization. The World Bank supported this initiative with a Public Financial Management Project loan of US$62 million (US$48 million for customs). Between 1996 and 1999, IMF technical assistance advisors worked with Turkish customs to implement modern, up-to-date customs legislation, simplify and automate customs procedures, introduce greater reliance on post-release controls and reduce inspection rates and release times, provide good service to the trade community, and delegate increased responsibilities to regional and local offices.

*ICT Strategy.* A multifaceted approach was necessary to tackle the many reform challenges, although often the momentum was focused on ICT. Previously, ICT support was relatively insignificant, limited to trade statistics generation and minor usage of an in-house developed legacy clearance system. To save time and cost, and to minimize implementation risks, customization of a package was chosen rather than bespoke development of a new system. Eighteen months of intensive work was needed to customize a software package to the new streamlined operational procedures and to translate the user interface to Turkish, including a transfer of know-how to Turkish customs staff so that they could subsequently maintain and enhance the application source code that was provided.

*SOFIX/BILGE.* The package chosen was SOFIX, a derivative of the French customs administration SOFI system. In Turkish it was called BILGE. The software was provided by a consortium of French customs and Bull S.A., with an initial contract covering the provision of the software source code, its customization, hardware, and implementation support at a pilot site. It was successfully launched in a pilot operation at Istanbul Airport—one of the busiest customs facilities in Turkey—in the summer of 1998. BILGE was installed in a distributed configuration at 59 customs offices throughout Turkey between 2000 and 2002 following an international tender and contract award to Koç, a large Turkish firm. In addition to installing a LAN and application/database servers at each site, a Wide Area Network (WAN) redundantly linked all localities with a center at customs headquarters in Ankara where a national data warehouse was established to produce trade statistics and management information. The contractor successfully trained thousands of customs staff and traders, as the system was simultaneously rolled out across the country.

BILGE is a client/server application based on an Oracle database that supports a full range of customs operations, including integrated tariff, accounting, import and export clearance, inspection selectivity, transit and other temporary admission regimes, and trade statistics. Traders were initially required to input manifest and declaration data in kiosks provided at each customs office, but are now encouraged to submit transactions electronically through EDI or a secure Web site.

*Modernization Results.* Today, customs operations in Turkey are vastly different from 1996, mostly as a result of effective automation. Some improvements achieved include the following:

- Ninety-nine percent of all transactions are processed by BILGE and statistics are a by-product. Previously, all transactions were processed manually and subsequently input for statistics generation.
- Only 25.5 percent of imports and 9.6 percent of exports are subject to pre-release controls, instead of 100 percent of all consignments being inspected, as had been done previously. Additionally, pre-approved importers (356 as of May 2002) are now entitled to immediate release of consignments subject to post-release controls.
- Seventy-five percent of imports are now cleared within 24 hours, and 83 percent within 48 hours.
- Customs was the first implementation of EDI in Turkey, and now 42 percent of all customs transactions are submitted electronically (EDI or via the Web site).
- By 2001, staff numbers were reduced by 10 percent, 73 offices with little or no operational activity were closed, and the numbers and locations of regional offices were rationalized. A new customs law that complies with EU standards came into effect in February 2000.

*Source:* David Kloeden, Note prepared for this study.

WCO Agreement on Customs Valuation. The focus is on both revenue protection and trade facilitation. The solution can be extended on a regional and global networking basis by incorporating features for customs unions and trade security. The technology platforms used are Web-enabled, incorporate mobile technologies, and are geared toward openness and flexibility. The software applications themselves are modular and are designed to integrate with existing customs systems.

TATIS is currently engaged, through its business partners, in the systems procurement process of a number of customs administrations.

**MicroClear**    MicroClear is offered as a state of the art, fully integrated, functionally rich system that delivers secure and efficient processing of all customs-related documentation through a Web-based network.[10] It is offered by Inspection and Control Services (ICS) and developed using .NET technology that is authenticated and supported by Microsoft. Current or previous releases of Micro-Clear—partially or the full solution—are working in China, Dubai, Kuwait, the United States, the Russian Federation, the United Kingdom, and India. In its promotional literature MicroClear notes that its .NET architecture provides for flexible solutions required to meet the enforcement of varying laws, highly secured Web-based solutions, easy customization, fully integrated solutions, maximum scalability, connectivity to external systems, and easy integration with existing systems. The system can easily translate paper-based documentation to electronic protocols and standards in accordance with WCO conventions.

MicroClear provides for a back-office tool that is used to configure the system to introduce new business rules or duty calculation formulas, change existing logic, change the business pipeline system process flow, define workflow, and build new e-forms or pages. These modifications require minimum coding. MicroClear considers this a main advantage, as it reduces future dependence on vendor support. The license to use and modify the source code is provided with the system with a view to permitting future support of the system from domestic sources. The system is built on a platform that supports nonalphanumeric characters.

**PC Trade**    New Zealand's Statistics Department's PC Trade software was initially designed to produce national trade statistics, relying on ASYCUDA-generated import data. Providing a basic front-end goods declaration processing and duty assessment module has further enhanced PC Trade. The system works on stand-alone PCs, but can be networked using Novell or Windows 95 Networking. It is also a full statistical analysis package. It is widely used in island states of the Pacific such as Tonga, French Polynesia, Vanuatu, and Guam.

**ALICE**    The European Commission is currently developing, as part of its Customs and Fiscal Assistance Office program, a customs management system that is compatible with the integrated tariff of the European Community. Called ALICE it is based on the newest technology (.Net framework), and uses Oracle as its database management platform. ALICE is scheduled to provide export, import, and transit modules and to include all regular modules that make up a full customs management processing instrument. At present, ALICE is under construction and testing with scheduled rollout at the end of 2004 in Bosnia and Herzegovina. If this development is successful it is possible that ALICE will become the system of choice for future EU accession partner countries.

**Danish Customs Administration Solution**    The Danish customs administration developed a simple goods declaration processing system in conjunction with Bull S.A. This product is now being marketed by Bull S.A. and is already incorporated as a key element in a comprehensive computerization project being developed by the Cyprus customs administration. This project includes many innovative solutions and will be totally Internet enabled when implemented.

*Information Technology "Beyond Customs"*

A new trend in the use of ICT to promote trade facilitation is to create an electronically connected trade community that includes all trade partners. Such a community is made up of, among others, customs, banks, shippers, ports and airports, brokers, regulatory agencies, statistics departments, and motor vehicle registration. Such a system is fully operational in Singapore and Mauritius. Based on this

---

10. See the ICS Web site at www.icsinspections.com/.

model and using the same technology, Ghana is in the process of implementing its Tradenet. Tunisia and Senegal are also committed to implementing a customs management system with the ambition of constituting the core of an electronic trade network.

The Singapore TradeNet links multiple parties involved in external trade—including 34 government controlling units—to a single point of transaction for most trade-related transactions, such as customs clearance and payment of duties and taxes, processing of export and import permits and certificates of origin, and collection of trade statistics. One of the first steps was to review the prevailing and required trade documentation and to propose to reduce these multiple trade documents into one single online form to serve nearly all trade documentation needs in the country. CrimsonLogic[11] was entrusted to own and operate the TradeNet system, with the Singapore Trade Development Bureau, the port and civil aviation authorities, and the international airport as stakeholders. IBM developed an EDI system to allow computer-to-computer exchange of intercompany business documents between connected members of the Singapore trading community. One document was to be submitted by the trader, and had to contain all the information required for that import or export by any party involved in any way in that transaction. The system was rolled out gradually in 1989 and by 1991, 95 percent of all air and ship transport was transacted through Tradenet. The progress of the project benefited greatly from the fact that many of the members of the trading community had already acquired substantial computer knowledge and relied on sophisticated computer equipment in their operations.

Other countries that desire to leverage e-government and e-commerce initiatives can adopt a customs solution that provides a single portal through which traders and officials involved in the transaction can submit and access all information associated with processing the consignments. Such a portal can interface with a variety of existing customs management tools. In Ghana, the EDI portal has been combined with the customs management system of Mauritius (See box 13.4). In Senegal, Orbus 2000 has the same ambition of

electronically connecting all trade-related institutions (box 13.5).

### Guidelines for Selecting an Appropriate ICT System for Customs

The evaluation of the appropriate IT solution is not an easy task, certainly now that so many alternatives are offered on the market, and the option of building a national solution is always present. The selection process could be done in two stages. First, the various possibilities can be scored against each other, so that only a few solutions are retained for further investigation. At the second stage, the procurement process can spell out more detailed requirements and let possible providers, and even the national solution proponents, declare their preparedness to bid—technically first and financially second. These two phases can work in succession, with the first stage delivering a short list to be used in the second. This approach is now briefly described.

**Prequalification: Scoring the Different Possible Solutions**    The prequalification stage requires a systematic evaluation of the various solutions and their suitability for a particular country. This evaluation would take place on the basis of a review of the product descriptions, and seeing the systems in operation, where possible, in situations similar to those in the country in question. The evaluation may want to score the various solutions (on a scale from 1 to 100), and combine the component scores into an overall score. These scores can then be compared across vendors and possibly against an "ideal ICT solution" that would follow all WCO guidelines and adopt the most modern hardware platforms. The providers with the highest scores would then constitute the short list to be contacted for further discussion and the second phase. The task of developing such a solutions assessment could be contracted out to a computer consultancy firm.

The components to be scored for each provider may include the following:

- *Provider strategy.* The evaluation could include the provider's vision and principles, the type of solutions and services it provides, its track record on capacity building and assistance, its experience and expertise, the company's stability and financial base, and its installed base.

---

11. Called Singapore Trade Services until 2002.

## BOX 13.4   Ghana Gateway Project Case Study

The trade liberalization measures of the 1990s had for several years not delivered the hoped-for new foreign direct investment or export expansion in Ghana, and several studies suggested that for this to happen structural reforms were required. To launch these reforms, a dynamic export promotion strategy was developed. Its main operational features were that (a) Crimson-Logic, the Singapore firm that managed the Singapore TradeNet system would provide the software for the electronic commerce–based community system, which would become the core of the Ghana TradeNet community; (b) Ghana would adopt the customs management system that was designed for Mauritius and that was successfully interfacing with the Mauritius electronic commerce trade community; and (c) a new company would be created to implement both TradeNet and the Ghana Customs Management System (GCMS) at customs. This company was to be given a Build Operate and Transfer (BOT) contract. In return for its equity contribution and adherence to the service contract, it would receive annual payments for services rendered and would transfer equity in the company to the government of Ghana after 10 years.

The Ghana Community Network (GCNet) was created as a joint venture company with foreign shareholders (Societe Generale de Surveillance with 60 percent, customs with 20 percent, the Ghana Shipping Council with 10 percent, and two local banks, each with 5 percent). In November 2000, GCNet was incorporated with equity of US$5 million. It operates under a service contract with the Ministry of Trade and Industry. This contract lasts until 2010. It instructs GCNet to install the electronic commerce–based system and a new customs management system.

GCNet adopted a hands-on approach during this whole process, and provided assistance to customs through local staff training and installation of the information technology.

*Community Networks.* A start has been made to connect various members of the trading community. The following members are already connected:

• the shipping lines that provide electronic manifests to GCNet, which are then transferred to Ghana Ports and Harbors Authority
• Ghana Shipping Council, which obtains all information regarding the movement of ships and airplanes
• customs, which obtains customs goods declarations electronically
• banks, which inform customs electronically of payments made
• the statistical office, which is connected to receive from customs all relevant trade statistics—the statistical office has not yet taken advantage of this connection
• Ministry of Finance, which is connected and can download all trade information as well as all transactions of taxpayers identified by personal identification number.

*Lessons Learned.* Private–public sector partnerships along the lines of the BOT format can work. GCNet anchored the reforms and assured continuity and focus on the reform objectives during a period of political transition.

Drawing on IT can yield quick results. It took three-and-a-half years to roll out GCNet and GCMS in ports that account for more than 90 percent of all Ghana's trade. Clearance times and revenue performance far exceeded expectations. The overall costs were reasonable.

Change of customs operations can be speeded up by hands-on technical support. Whereas customs had struggled for years to upgrade its information system or to make the best use of it, the reforms required an outside push and hands-on implementation support to force the process simplification through for the adoption of advanced computerization processes.

Top-level support helped to launch and sustain the project.

Customs has actively participated with the rollout of the ICT technology, but will now actively pursue its own modernization process in nearly all areas but ICT and related processes. This modernization process will give the overall project a better chance of being sustainable over time. Also, a modern customs might be in a position to take over from GCNet when the service contract expires.

*Source:* De Wulf 2004.

## BOX 13.5 Senegal Case Study

Senegal is preparing a suite of products to make maximum use of IT to facilitate trade through initiatives collectively called GAINDE 2000. These products consist of an electronic commerce–based environment to accept and disseminate trade transaction data to all members of the trading community; an advanced customs management system; and an electronic payment system.

### ORBUS 2000

ORBUS is intended to become a real preclearance system. It is designed to accept the electronic declarations of traders (using Internet connections) containing all information requested by the various regulatory agencies; transmit this information to all pertinent agencies to provide electronic clearances; and transmit all this data to the customs management system. Members of the trading community to be connected include customs, banks, monetary authorities, regulatory agencies and agencies responsible for quality control, the federation of insurance companies, Directory of Foreign Trade in the Ministry of Commerce, Metrology Department, the PSI company, Treasury, and others. Its design was inspired by the system operating in Singapore. Using resources of a World Bank project, the "Direction de l'Informatique de l'Etat" under the Presidency of the State financed the installation of the necessary communications and transmission equipment for all connected government agencies. The ORBUS 2000 module is managed by GIE GAINDE 2000, a company created to ensure the proper installation and implementation of the electronic commerce environment and the new customs processes.

The technical architecture set up for the ORBUS system is built on a data infrastructure using the latest information technologies with the view to guaranteeing data accessibility, reliability of communications, system availability, data integrity, and security. System testing started in early 2004. Effective and efficient rollout of the full ORBUS 2000 with its various capabilities requires that all members of the trading community activate their connectivity and adjust their own operating procedures to issue clearances electronically; and the technique (front-end and operating system at ORBUS 2000) must prove itself to be robust and easily accessible by all involved. National rollout will require a major public relations and education campaign.

### TRADE X/ GAINDE

In the late 1980s the Technology Division of the Ministry of Finance designed and operated a customs management system. One objective of choosing a national solution was to improve the country's national IT skills. The system was introduced in 1990 and periodically upgraded. Transferred to customs in 1998, the system was outmoded and expensive to maintain. Hence, TRADE X was designed as a replacement. The logic for continuing an in-house solution stemmed from a legacy attitude, and, in part, from a deliberate pursuit of the development of national ITC capacities as well as to gain acceptance for its adoption by customs staff and the private sector. The private sector was intensively consulted as the modules and their various aspects were being designed. Local consulting firms were twinned with customs experts to design the new TRADE X system and are expected to provide ongoing maintenance services. The TRADE X system is based on the most up-to-date technology and incorporates a series of new functionalities. It interfaces with ORBUS 2000, has an advanced risk assessment module, a valuation database, and cargo processing facilities, and anticipates electronic payments. It will also interface with the simulator that permits traders to simulate clearance costs and find out what clearance regulations apply, and with a data warehouse.

TRADE X contains all the functions available in most off-the-shelf modern customs management systems and is in full conformity with the WCO guidelines on computerization. The system was rolled out on a pilot basis for imports to selected locations in October 2003. Further rollout is expected during 2004. Customs is now considering adjusting its organizational structure, originally designed around manual customs processes, to fully leverage the enhanced use of modern customs management tools.

### SEPAY—Electronic Payment System

A working group, bringing together staff from customs, Treasury, and the banking sector, designed a system to permit customs brokers to pay duties and taxes electronically. Rollout is expected during the second half of 2004.

*Source:* Ibrahima Diane, General Manager of GIE GAINDE 2000. Personal communication.

- *Functional architecture.* How complete is the suite offered? How do the functions offered compare with the specific needs of the country? How easy would it be to add on more specialized modules?
- *Application architecture.* What is the complexity, scalability, performance, security, and volatility of the system architecture?
- *Software infrastructure.* What is the software basis for the user interface, the application server, data management, software integration, and security?
- *Technology infrastructure.* What platforms are proposed for the hardware, application server, data communications, system management, and security?
- *Implementation and deployment.* How will implementation details—project management, design, development and delivery, change management, training and implementation, operations and support—be carried out?
- *Deployment resources.* What are the bidder's plans for resource management, technical support, capacity building, governance, and planning?
- *Deployment and delivery costs.* What are the costs for software development and delivery, technological infrastructure, implementation and deployment, support and training? What are the options for operational funding, and system lifecycle costs?

**The Process of Selecting the Provider** At this point a choice must be made between the various national solutions and off-the-shelf solutions, or simply among the latter if only off-the-shelf solutions are being considered. Including a national solution in the process should be a straightforward exercise when the solution is proposed by a third party, but may be more challenging when the proposal emanates from within customs. While difficult, a partisan decision in favor of customs' proposal without adequate evaluation should be avoided.

Three broad determinants can be used to evaluate proposals, assign a score, and select a winner: (a) compliance with the terms and conditions of the tender (other terminology may be used, such as bidding documents, request for proposal, request for bids, and so forth); (b) technical compliance against specified criteria using a weight-based scoring mechanism; and (c) value for money—which balances the other components, subject to satisfaction of minimum standards against cost.

*Terms and conditions of the tender.* The bidding document must provide detailed specifications. The document should reflect a balance between providing too broad and general specifications, which would qualify all possible providers, and providing specifications that are too narrow so that no provider can bid, or only one. Specifications should cover a broad range of issues including functional requirements, technical requirements, project and implementation requirements, support requirements, security requirements, capacity and performance requirements, and contractual requirements. The bidder's prior track record is particularly relevant, with consideration given to successful outcomes with other clients under similar circumstances. Vendor claims should be verified. The quality of prior results is more important than the quantity. A small number of very successful contracts may be preferable to a large number of mediocre outcomes. Additionally, in the rapidly evolving technology world, new participants in the market should not necessarily be disregarded because of a limited track record. However, the issue that will determine the new entrants' potential is their understanding of modern customs administration and how technology can be best applied to the business rather than knowledge of technology with an intention to learn about customs operations on the job.

*Evaluation against technical requirements.* An application's functionality should be the main driver of the decision. The functions should be tailored to local circumstances and the extent to which modernization and reform have progressed (or will progress). Some functions will be core to any system, and some may be desirable. Functionality determination is a task for customs administrators (that is, the users) rather than technologists. The functions need to be prioritized and weighted according to importance. Table 13.1 provides a list of the desired functions. A scoring model is needed to uniformly compare bids against technical requirements. The actual score weighting needs to be determined carefully, but functional requirements should predominate in the decision. By way of example, a model could assign a 40 percent weight to functional requirements (further subdivided for each function), 25 percent to project and implementation requirements (including vendor experience), 13 percent to technical requirements, 10 percent to vendor support, 5 percent for security features, 5 percent for contractual issues, and 2 percent for local capacity building.

*Financial evaluation.* The financial conditions of only those proposals that have met a minimum technical standard should be considered. Anything under the threshold should be eliminated, or depending on the procurement rules, given a chance to be brought up to standard provided all bidders have similar opportunities. The weighting between cost and scoring is important, as more emphasis on cost will favor the lowest cost solution even if it is not technically the best (and maybe even the worst). In considering costs, all proposals that meet the technical conditions must be considered equally. Therefore, all similar costs must be included and properly quantified (including costs borne by the purchaser), and possibly including lifetime costs of the project.

Costs vary widely from one project to the next. Obviously, the size of the country and complexity of the desired functions will affect costs. For a particular country the hardware costs for customs as well as the front-end costs for traders are not likely to vary too much from one solution to the next, as they are more or less dictated by the available technology platforms of the day. Also, implementation costs that include training of staff and the trader community also will not differ much from one solution to the next. Hence, costs will tend to vary according to the level of design, programming, and modification that will be involved. The degree of reliance on local contractors will also affect costs substantially, as will built-in markups.

National solutions tend to be expensive because they require that the functions of the system be designed and programmed in detail. These design and programming costs tend to be heavy. In Morocco, for instance, of a total project cost of about US$10 million, US$6.5 million went to development.

One of the great attractions of the off-the-shelf solutions is that the development costs can be shared with others. At one extreme is ASYCUDA, which provides the ASYCUDA program at no cost, permitting the adopting countries a proverbial free ride on the massive investment undertaken by UNCTAD in the process of readying ASYCUDA for implementation. Despite this free aspect of the ASYCUDA solution, the implementation still requires substantial resources for hardware, facilities, and communications. In Lebanon, for instance, installing ASYCUDA++ in the late 1990s had a total price tag of about US$5 million. In Bolivia, software maintenance costs are embedded into the operational budget of the National Bureau of Customs. Total development costs for the overall project (the local project team plus the UNCTAD team that assisted in transferring ASYCUDA), ran to about US$3.85 million. Hardware, communications, and infrastructure improvements for the 5 large and 19 medium and small offices throughout the country added another US$3.1 million to total costs. The Philippines Tax Computerization project—using ASYCUDA—with the Bureau of Customs project came to US$28 million.

Other off-the-shelf solutions need be adjusted to local requirements and circumstances, and that does not come free either. For instance, SOFIX's installation in Turkey required considerable modification and rewriting (see box 13.3). This was also the case for the installation of SOFIX in Argentina. The TIMS solution is often bundled with a management contract, as was the case in Mozambique and Angola, and its implementation costs are consolidated with the other interventions of Crown Agents in these countries. In Ghana, the Crimson-Logic portal was bundled with the Customs Management System of Mauritius; the overall cost of the project was about US$5 million in equity for GCNet plus about US$2.5 in loans taken out by GCNet, which included the acquisition of the software, the modifications for the Ghanaian context, the purchase of the equipment and infrastructure, as well as extensive training of staff and traders. In Bolivia, the National Bureau of Customs has developed a number of satellite systems around ASYCUDA++ to support post-release review and data warehousing functions, and has plans for additional satellites to improve risk-assessment and data-mining capabilities.

As noted earlier in this chapter, the costs of implementing ITC at customs is only part of the life cycle cost of these systems. All too often these maintenance and upgrading costs are underestimated and not adequately included in the life cycle costs. As a result, many systems are implemented without adequate financial support. The investment required after a few years is then usually larger than what would have been required if proper ongoing financial support had been available.

## Operational Conclusions

Information and communications technology can substantially contribute to making customs operations both more effective and more efficient. This fact has been known to many customs administrations for more than two decades. However, the possibilities of ICT change constantly. The newest technologies provide for more friendly user interfaces by allowing electronic submission of data and electronic payments, better support for the management of exemptions and suspense regimes, and have made great progress in risk assessment and selectivity modules. There is no doubt that the use of ICT has substantially contributed to safeguarding the revenue mobilization function of customs and to speeding up the clearance processes. Every customs service must attempt to implement the most advanced ICT appropriate for its particular circumstances. Hence, managing ICT must be a key function in customs administration.

Implementing ICT is not an objective in itself. It should be tailored to assist customs in attaining its objectives. Therefore, any ICT strategy should be pragmatic and realistic. It should be attuned to the real needs of the country and the customs administration and to the capacities of customs staff to make the best use of the new possibilities offered. Clearly, there is no "one size fits all" solution.

Designing the appropriate ICT solution is only part of the ICT strategy and can be dealt with by experts, consultants, and technicians. More important and more difficult than designing the system is to effectively implement the system. To do so, customs needs to adjust work processes, train staff and traders, and at times adjust the organizational structure. All too often customs underutilizes the ICT system—paid for so dearly—by failing to make the accompanying changes.

Policymakers should review the pros and cons of designing a national ICT solution. The authors suggest that most countries would do well to carefully investigate the various off-the-shelf solutions now available because unique systems tend to be expensive and often not as well designed as those on the market. Many of the off-the-shelf solutions incorporate the most advanced technologies and give the assurance that the functions of the different modules have been fully tested and the programs are stable and robust.

Selecting a computerized customs management system is a complex affair and proper safeguards should be adopted to obtain value for money. The chapter suggests how to tackle this process by systematically reviewing the technical and financial implications of the various options.

Customs needs to pay adequate attention to full funding of its ICT systems. ICT is expensive to install and to maintain, certainly in light of the rapid progress of technological change. Software programs and hardware platforms need to be upgraded to adjust to these technological advances. Hence, funding needs to be assured not only for the installation but also for the maintenance and upgrading of the software and the hardware. All too often the ICT budget is starved once foreign financing is depleted. This does little harm to the ICT in the short-run, and may lead to complacency. Yet, before long this will lead to costly ICT breakdowns and the need to overhaul the system at costs that are much higher than if regular upgrading and maintenance had been undertaken.

## Further Reading

Corfmat, François, and Patricio Castro. 2003. "Computerization of Customs Procedures." In Michael Keen, ed. *Changing Customs: Challenges and Strategies for the Reform of Customs Administration.* Washington, D.C.: International Monetary Fund.

Lane, Michael. 1998. *Customs Modernization and the International Trade Superhighway.* Westport, Conn.: Quorum Books.

World Customs Organization. *Guidelines to the Revised Kyoto Convention.* Chapter 7. Brussels. www.wcoomd.org.

## References

Appels, T., and H. Struye de Swielande. 1998. "Rolling Back the Frontiers: The Customs Clearance Revolution." *The International Journal of Logistics Management* 9(1): 111–18.

Corfmat, Francois, and Patricio Castro. 2003. "Computerization of Customs Procedures." In Michael Keen, ed. *Changing Customs: Challenges and Strategies for the Reform of Customs Administration.* Washington, D.C.: International Monetary Fund.

De Wulf, Luc. 2004. "Ghana." In Luc De Wulf and José B. Sokol, eds. *Customs Modernization Initiatives: Case Studies.* Washington, D.C.: World Bank.

Dutta, Soumitra, Bruno Lanvin, and Fiona Paua, eds. 2004. *Global Information Technology Report 2003–2004.* New York: Oxford University Press. www.weforum.org/site/homepublic.nsf/Content/Global+Competitiveness+Programme%5C Global+Information+Technology+Report.

Steenland, Marcel, and Luc De Wulf. "Morocco." In Luc De Wulf and José B. Sokol, eds. *Customs Modernization Initiatives: Case Studies.* Washington D.C.: World Bank.

World Bank. 2004. "Procurement Guidelines." Washington, D.C. http://siteresources.worldbank.org/INTPROCUREMENT/Resources/Procurement-May-2004.pdf.

# INDEX

*Boxes, figures, notes, and tables are indicated by b, f, n, and t respectively.*